A LIFE OF THOMAS CHATTERTON

From Skelton's " Etchings of the Antiquities of Bristol " (*Pl. xi*).

ST. MARY REDCLIFF. NORTH PORCH.

Frontispiece.

A LIFE OF THOMAS CHATTERTON

BY

E. H. W. MEYERSTEIN

"I do not know what 'poetical' is: is it honest in deed and word? is it a true thing?"—*As You Like It.*

NEW YORK / RUSSELL & RUSSELL

FIRST PUBLISHED IN 1930
REISSUED, 1972, BY RUSSELL & RUSSELL
A DIVISION OF ATHENEUM PUBLISHERS, INC.
L. C. CATALOG CARD NO: 70-173551
PRINTED IN THE UNITED STATES OF AMERICA

THIS IMPERFECT ESSAY
IS DEDICATED
TO ITS SUBJECT
IN HUMBLE CONSCIOUSNESS
THAT I HAVE NOT BEEN UNJUST
TO THE MEMORY OF
AN
ENGLISH POET

ACKNOWLEDGMENTS

FIRST, to the dead. To Sir Ernest Clarke I owe a debt which is inadequately stated by the few references to his *New Lights on Chatterton* (1916); for it was he who told me of the Chattertoniana in the Bristol Library. Also I must thank my late chief, Mr. J. P. Gilson, Keeper of MSS., British Museum, for encouragement, and advice as to the disposition of material; in almost the last talk I had with him, this year, he dwelt on the necessity, apropos of the de Bergham pedigree, of running down Chatterton's sources of information. No one has helped me quite so much as these two men.

Of the living, in this city, Mr. Arthur Ellis, Superintendent of the reading-room, British Museum, has continuously hastened my researches by practical suggestions. Mr. Walter Bell, F.S.A., my predecessor in these chambers, I was glad to consult about London coffee-houses. In Chatterton's city many names should be mentioned: among them the Vicar and Vestry of St. Mary Redcliff (in particular Mr. Mortimer and Mr. Sefton Clarke); the Archdeacon of Bristol, for most kindly verifying references by the Temple Church register; Mr. Ward, Treasurer of the Society of Merchant Venturers, for permission to inspect the Colston Hospital Admission Books; Dr. Bolton, Director of the Museum and Art Gallery, and Mr. Acland Taylor, City-librarian, for permission to examine and publish material. Mr. James Ross, deputy-librarian, made, *inter alia*, valuable suggestions as to two Chattertonian localities. Nor must I forget the kindness of Miss Parry, of the Reference Library, whose knowledge of all things Bristolian is as deep as it is unobtrusive (assistance rendered for over seven years), and Miss Dunman, of the Museum, in lightening my labour with the Redcliff deeds. Mr. A. H. Russell, secretary of the Chatterton Society, must be thanked for the loan of George Cumberland's

MS. ; Mr. Wells, editor of the *Bristol Times and Mirror*, for replying to queries concerning *Felix Farley's Journal* ; and Mr. B. R. Davis, for the use of his copy of Bryant's *Observations*.

The index is the work of Miss I. Oxley and Capt. S. H. Atherley.

Finally, thanks are due to the authorities of the Bodleian Library, with regard to MS. Eng. poet., e. 6, to Sir William Rose Smith for allowing me to examine the " Yeloue Rolle " and the " Songe to Ælla," to Mr. Herbert Chitty, Keeper of Archives, Winchester College, for readily verifying sundry references by the College register, and to the printers and proof-readers at the Burleigh Press, established on a Chattertonian site, " St. Bartholomeweis Priorie." Other acknowledgments are mentioned in the work itself.

3 GRAY'S INN PLACE.
October 23rd, 1929.

CONTENTS

CONTENTS

INTRODUCTION

THE idea of superseding extant works on Chatterton has been farthest from my thoughts ; rather have I sought to supplement them, by

(1) an attempt to appraise the Rowley Poems as English Poetry,

(2) an attempt to see the poet as part of his environment, mainly through the medium of contemporary evidence.

Most of what I have to say on the first point will be found in Chapter XI ; all that need be premised here is that very little work has been done on Chatterton's antiques since Thomas Warton's time. Always excepting the pertinent remarks in Professor Saintsbury's *History of English Prosody* (1906-1910), Professor Ker's notice in *The Cambridge History of English Literature* (Vol. X, ch. x, 1913), Buxton Forman's critique (1874) of Skeat's edition, and the important essay by Theodore Watts Dunton in the third volume of T. H. Ward's *The English Poets* (1880), they have been neglected, for even Skeat cannot be said to have handled them as literature. Even Professor Elton, in his admirable *Survey of English Literature* (1928), is deaf to all in *Ælla* except the lyrical appeal. An essay by the Hon. Roden Noel (1886) should perhaps be mentioned, Helene Richter's study of the subject (Vienna, 1900), and Mr. Maurice Hare's introduction to the Clarendon Press *Rowley* (1911). As for Chatterton's biographers, they have always been far more interested in him than in his poetry.

The second point I must elaborate, that the reader may know how he stands with me from the start. Until a little over two years ago I had purposely refrained from reading nineteenth century accounts of the poet, and was wholly satisfied with foraging in eighteenth century and earlier books and manuscripts for details that would bring him and his work nearer to my mind ; thus I reached the reactionary position, which later and wider reading has hardly affected, that his age's vision of him, as a personality, was on the whole correct : it is fairly expressed in a biographical dictionary of 1784 :

"This unfortunate person, though certainly a most extraordinary genius, seems yet to have been a most ungracious composition. He was violent and impetuous to a strange degree. From the first of the above-cited letters to his sister [May 30, 1770] he appears to have had a portion of ill-humour and spleen more than enough for a youth of 17."

It was only with the dawn of a sentimental era—Dix's *Life* appeared in 1837—that the acrimonious prodigy, who rushed into the presence of his Maker, became the helpless, starving, boy poet, who stoically resigned his life before his eighteenth birthday ; though there were materials for the latter view early enough. Even if truth lie between the extremes, I think it must incline to the former, though that has not the sanction of Sir Daniel Wilson, whose biography (1869) must remain the standard one.

A year after Chatterton's death the first book of James Beattie's *The Minstrel, or the Progress of Genius*, was published, containing this stanza :

And yet poor Edwin was no vulgar boy,
Deep thought oft seem'd to fix his infant eye.
Dainties he heeded not, nor gaude, nor toy,
Save one short pipe of rudest minstrelsy :
Silent when glad, affectionate, though shy ;
And now his look was most demurely sad ;
And now he laugh'd aloud, yet none knew why.
The neighbours star'd and sigh'd, yet bless'd the lad :
Some deem'd him wondrous wise, and some believ'd him mad !*

This, already applied to Chatterton by Sir Herbert Croft in 1780,† has coloured well-nigh every full-dress life of him save the first, Dr. Gregory's (1789) ; it was reinforced by a tribute of

* *Cf.* And some her frantic deem'd, and some her deem'd a wit.—*The Castle of Indolence*, Canto I.

† *Love and Madness*, ed. 1780, p. 193. (The references throughout are to the first edition.)

Vicesimus Knox (*Essays*, ed. 5, no. 144), part of which was held up to ridicule by Hazlitt in his seventh lecture on the English poets :

> "Unfortunate boy! . . . In the gloomy moments of despondency I fear thou hast uttered impious and blasphemous thoughts, which none can defend, and which neither thy youth nor thy fiery spirit nor thy situation, can excuse. But let thy more rigid censors reflect that thou wast literally and strictly but a boy."

However accurate that portrait might be of the *child* Chatterton, of the product of Colston's Hospital, a man in aims before his time, and a poet among poetaster schoolmates and apprentices, it is misleading.

Such a life, for instance, as C. E. Russell's (1908), and to some extent J. H. Ingram's two books (1910, 1916)—Ingram's second book, *Chatterton and His Poetry* (in a series edited by W. H. Hudson) is a fair short exposition of the subject—are little else than free fantasias on the "poor boy" motif. The author of the French memoir (1839), and Mr. Hare, stand almost alone among post-Gregorians in escaping from it, though, oddly enough, Croft himself, sentimental as he was, dared to doubt that the cause of the suicide was "real indigence."* This commiserating attitude has even played a part in marring Skeat's two-volume text of 1871, where Chatterton's findings in old dictionaries, and his coinages, are subjected to the treatment of a schoolboy's exercise : and indeed every book or essay on him which apologizes for the death, and dwells on the promise rather than the performance, is in a lineal descent from "Edwin" and Dr. Knox.

I have ventured, where practicable, on the substitution of "poet" for "boy," in no sentimental sense, but because, personal conviction apart, Chatterton has been accepted as an English poet by such judges of the matter as Wordsworth, Coleridge, Keats, Shelley, and Rossetti. Poetry is not record-breaking ; there is nothing more remarkable in a poet producing a masterpiece before his sixteenth than on his eighty-fifth birthday; and though it is cause for regret that he did not

* *Ibid.* pp. 196, 197.

subject his antiques to what Coleridge called "the poetical filter" (*Table Talk*, October 23, 1833) or to the treatment advocated in the case of Chaucer (*ibid.*, March 15, 1834), Rowley needs no allowances, except that

> you must love him ere to you
> He will seem worthy of your love.

For Chatterton is *Rowley*, and, so far as literature is concerned, nothing else, not even the *African Eclogues*. Whether he was or was not a stupendous prodigy, or merely a victim of "accelerated mentality" (to use a modern Bristolian's phrase), what he would have achieved had he lived on,* whether he was an insipid or a tiresome person, whether his suicide was premeditated or impulsive, or the direct outcome of bodily rather than mental anguish, or his eighteenth-century satire better or worse than Churchill's, all this is beside the mark; it is as "the true day-spring of modern romantic poetry" that he enjoys any real posthumous existence, and, if I am accused of saying too little about this aspect of him, I agree cordially with the accuser. I trust, however, the reader will be satisfied that, as evidence goes, *The Unknown Knyght*, a prosodic landmark in our poetry, was composed before March 6, 1768 (Ch. VIII).

At the same time, if an honest attempt be made to see him as he lived, the vision is hardly a pleasing one. Very early the discipline of Colston's, enforced self-education, solitude, and lack of encouragement, conspired to produce a cross-grained habit of mind with but few restful intervals—was he not always writing?—as well as a contempt for the solid, but less gifted, youths by whom he was surrounded, not to speak of Barrett, George Catcott, and the local clergy. Bristol, alike in literature and town-planning, was in the first throes of a change, and it was part of his misfortune to precede Coleridge and Southey by a quarter of a century. At their epoch (I am not forgetting Lovell's satire) the reproach of commercialism

* This question is often asked; I have not attempted to answer it; but few readers of Chatterton can fail to perceive that the sense of drama was very strong in him. *Otho* and *King Stephen* do not impress one with the idea that Keats was a born dramatist; it is otherwise with *Ælla* and *Goddwyn*.

was, to some extent, removed from the city, and he might have found an audience for verses other than satirical. As things were, his rash temper, and its reflex, disingenuous secrecy, were bred and swollen by the pettiness of that environment ; and his collaborator in the history of Bristol, when he affirmed that the poet changed his climate, not his spirit, by migrating to London, wrote neither more nor less than the strict truth.

For this reason I have dwelt more on eighteenth century Bristol—for it is a Bristol life, all but four months—than is customary, in the belief that Chatterton's ruling passion, thirst for fame, is so unmistakable that the background, in this portrait, is as important as the features. For instance, the suicide of Peter Smith in August, 1769, has a bearing on the tragedy of Brooke Street one year later, yet the significant piece dealing with that subject (maybe because it is hardly poetry) is passed over in all the " lives " with a bare mention ; nor, I think, has adequate stress been laid on the fact that the poet was *only one* of a " juvenile club," which wrote for the journals and magazines, and stood out from its members merely as a splenetic and ambitious person, with the " one excellence of railing well," who had accidentally discovered some ancient poems.

Frankly, I am not in the least concerned to destroy the picture of the romantic child whose day-dreams were peopled by fifteenth century familiars. That is no sentimental accretion, but a truth. It was revealed to William Smith (Peter's brother), all unable as he was to interpret it ; but the intense dreariness, the fiery egotism, the abstracted and bitter melancholy, finding most relief in imitative satire, when the garb of the imaginary monk was thrown by, this is the Thomas Chatterton whom Bristol saw, knew, and remembered, a being whom we are permitted to recapture : the other is inherent in the Rowley cycle, it scarcely has an existence outside ; and any effort to revivify it, unless by a sort of spiritual intuition, must result in lame or shadowy reconstruction, the *ana* of a George Cumberland. Whoever has troubled to study the pedigree which was devised for Henry Burgum, the pewterer, must have perceived the difficulty of extricating the strands of fancy, playfulness, sheer hoaxing, and disinterested vision in the character the poet chose to present to his contemporaries, apart from that of an omniscient, unmanageable, provincial Don Juan, a warning to apprentices—

> Who pens a stanza, when he should engross.

I am reactionary too, perhaps, in refusing to expatiate on his domestic affections. Well before the close of his century it was observed that too much had been made of the box of presents from London. I find more illumination in the free tone pervading the letters to his mother and sister. It can hardly have been a rigid household; and as for nothing being "too good" for them, on which the "nested home-loves" motif has largely been built, Chatterton's family was but one aspect of his pride; *he* was serving it, and, as is proved by the wills of his sister and niece, he fulfilled his vaunt.

Of the poet's practice of dating his pieces I have availed myself more boldly than previous writers, as also of the Rev. Michael Lort's MS. memoranda preserved in the Bristol Library (11063, 11457). This painstaking and unobtrusive antiquary (1725-1790), whose "cool curiosity" in sifting human beings is mentioned by Horace Walpole,* paid several visits to Bristol within eight years of Chatterton's death—the first as early as the autumn of 1771—with the sole object of ascertaining the truth about him and Rowley. You will not find his name in lives of the poet, but the notes signed "O" in Dr. Gregory's are his.† He had made up his mind as early as 1773 that Chatterton was the author of Rowley, and on May 11 of that year wrote to Lord Hardwicke (Add. MS. 35350, f. 45) inclosing an account of his researches. He was, in fact, the first scholar of intelligence to investigate the matter; James Beattie wrote to John Carr, headmaster of Hertford Grammar School (June 13, 1782):

> "I first heard of Rowley from Dr. Lort, as I was passing through Cambridge in the year 1771. None of the poems were then published;

* Letter to William Cole, March 13, 1780.

† Nichols, *L. I.*, VII, pp. 553, 556. "I could wish my name was not introduced but to authorize some important facts" is Lort's view of his function. 11457.

but he showed me a few in writing. I immediately pronounced them modern. 'There it is now,' said he in his jocular way, 'we reject your Ossian, and you will not admit our Rowley.'"*

Into the quarto volume, too, where George Catcott copied his Rowleian correspondence, together with his own naive replies (5342, also in this rich library) I have delved, I fear, deeply enough.

At the risk of appearing tedious I have gone, with some painfulness, into three episodes:—1. The poet's rejection by Walpole, as there is still a suspicion abroad—or was in 1910, when *The True Chatterton* was published—that the blame rests on the dilettante; if this problem is not solved, I hope it is now, at least, stated accurately (Ch. XII).† 2. The suicide; here, I believe, all available evidence is, for the first time, fairly marshalled (Ch. XVIII). 3. The thirty-three years between the suicide and Southey and Cottle's edition of the *Works*, a period which can hardly be neglected, since it marks the passing of *Rowley* from the antiquaries to the poets (Ch. XIX).

It may seem strange that I have said so little on the subject of literary imposture, but poetry is the theme; and, quotations only excepted, I have avoided the word "forger" as the word "boy." Psalmanazar, Bertram, W. H. Ireland (a profound admirer of Chatterton), and the author of poems attributed to Clotilde de Surville, do not strike me as in point; Macpherson *does*, and, of course, Walpole. That Chatterton was short-sighted enough to put forward original work under the name of a supposititious fifteenth-century poet, and to bolster up that folly by a few parchments fabricated mainly for a couple of his fellow townsmen, is a biographical, not a poetical datum; it

* I found this letter quoted in an autograph catalogue of Messrs. Maggs, some years ago.

† The reader who cares only for truth in literary matters may come to the conclusion that not Horace Walpole but Samuel Johnson was Chatterton's real enemy among his famous contemporaries. Walpole, whatever he said about his morals, never denied his genius, but praised it on all occasions. Johnson, after the two sentences of astonishment recorded by Boswell, seems to have doubted that Chatterton wrote Rowley unaided, scoffed at the powers of a "vulgar, uneducated stripling," and certainly abstained from admitting him among his poets. The motive, political bias, may be doubtful; the fact remains.

shows merely that he could not wholly forgo his century's influences, and that he was apt to confuse publicity with fame, a weakness shared by older persons in other centuries. Besides, the deception to which he stooped, has been practised by mature and acknowledged genius.

" Je pourrais vous rappeler encore," writes Hector Berlioz (1803-1869) in his *Mémoires,** "à propos des préventions Françaises contre moi, l'histoire du chœur des bergers, de *l' Enfance du Christ,* exécuté dans deux concerts sous le nom de Pierre Ducré, maître de chapelle imaginaire du dixhuitième (i.e. dix-septième, ' 1679 ') siècle. Que d'éloges pour cette *simple mélodie* ! Combien de gens ont dit ' Ce n'est pas Berlioz qui ferait une pareille chose ! ' " The Romantic composer, who was a spectator of Alfred de Vigny's drama *Chatterton* in 1835,† has told the story of the *Chœur des Bergers,* which dates from his forty-fifth year, at length in *Les Grotesques de la Musique* (1859), where the phrase " faire le Chatterton " is actually used.

On this score the words of Rowley's first editor are to the purpose : " It is more natural to suppose, that his first essays in forgery were for his own private amusement ; the suggestions of an active irregular mind, eking out the scanty supplies of knowledge, which came within its reach, by invention. In the pursuit of ambition, it has been said, a man never goes so far, as when he knows not whither he is going ; and I suspect that the same may be said of forgery."‡

Lastly, Sir Sidney Lee has thus decided the question : " The Rowley Poems were the fruit of an artistic sense which had not yet submitted to the control of a fully developed moral consciousness."§

These three quotations, if considered in relation to the success, in their time, of *Ossian* and *The Castle of Otranto,* should, I venture to think, excuse me from a diatribe on the " forgery " motif.

* Ed. 1870, p. 463.
† Lauvrière, *Alfred de Vigny,* p. 189.
‡ Tyrwhitt, *Vindication,* p. 142.
§ Chatterton's Rowley Poems. Methuen's Standard Library, *Intr.* p. xi.

Something should be added as to the use made of John Dix's (George Spencer Phillips, *c.* 1800-1865) biography. That work, as is well known, is the stumbling-block to Chatterton's would-be historian, for Dix proved himself not only uncritical but dishonest.* Statements derived therefrom are qualified by his name. Except in the last chapter, where they are unavoidable, there can be hardly more than six mentions of his name in the book; they have been reduced by the discovery of the MS. of George Cumberland's appendix to Dix, in Cumberland's handwriting, *circa* 1828, which transfers the burden of proof from fraud to credulity. Statements derived from this source are qualified likewise.

Paraphrase is the enemy of exactitude; I trust it will not be imputed to me as a vast fault that I have allowed the words of others, sometimes faultily transcribed, to appear at least as often as mine. In a task of this sort, too, it is hard to avoid a controversial, without assuming a dogmatic, tone; and it is possible to steer a middle course and be wearisome. The footnotes are inadequate, doubtless, but I have tried to repress them. I dare not hope that the book is objective, accurate, or exhaustive, though it was prompted by a desire for truth, and a passion for English Poetry. It may appear that I have professed a loyalty to my subject, which is somewhat to seek. According to Keats, "the good man base detraction bars" from Chatterton's "fair name, and waters it with tears"; but Poetry is a Spirit, and neither truth nor detraction can wither it.

July 15, 1929.

* The reader who thinks this language too strong is referred to Walter Thornbury's article, "John Dix," in *N. and Q.*, Apr. 13, 1872.

A LIFE OF THOMAS CHATTERTON

Chapter I

NAME, PARENTAGE, BIRTH

The name Chatterton, or Chadderton, though possibly derivable from a personal name connected with Ceadda, is more likely local in origin, the first element being a British name identical with the Welsh *cader*, a hill fort (Irish *cathir*). Thus the variation between *t* and *d* in the earlier forms may be accounted for, and the same element may enter into the Yorkshire Catterton (Cadretune, Cadertune). It is borne by two places in Lancashire, Chadderton in Oldham Chapelry and Chatterton in Bury. Both are hilly; in the former an elevation of five hundred feet is reached, at Chadderton Heights, while the latter stands east of the Irwell on a steep projecting ridge. Not far from Chadderton is Hanging Chadder (Hanging, says my authority, means steep), which is at an altitude of seven hundred feet; this fact alone would seem to preclude the personal derivation of the surname.*

The earliest document bearing it which I have seen is a quitclaim by Ricardus de Chaterton " de com Lancastrie " at Chesterfield, Derbyshire, 1403 (Wolley Charter VIII, 48) in the British Museum; but the registers of the Cathedral Church of Manchester† are full of the christenings, weddings, and burials of Chattertons. From 1573 to 1616 there are 33 entries under Chadderton (Chaddertonn, Chaderton), and 53 under Chatterton (Chattertone, Chattertonn); in ten of the latter the christian name is Thomas. From 1616 to 1653 under Chadderton (Chaderton, Chatherton, Chatterton) there are 56 entries.

* Ekwall, *The Place-names of Lancashire* (Chetham Society's Publications) pp. 50, 53, 54. 64.

† Publ. Cambridge 1908, L.P.R.S. *Indices*.

It is allowable to guess that the poet's remote forebears migrated from the North Country, for the journey was not impracticable by sea, to Bristol, at any rate, in the Middle Ages; and it should be added, perhaps, that the town and gorge of Cheddar cannot explain the existence of Chattertons in the West of England, both etymology (Cetdre, Cedre) and lists of Somersetshire wills being adverse to such a conjecture. The name does not appear in calendars of wills proved in the consistory courts of Bristol (1572-1792), Gloucester (1541-1800), Exeter (1559-1799), or in the Great Orphan Books of Bristol (1379-1674). The marriage of one John Chatterton occurs in the register of Urchfont (Wiltshire) in 1574, true; but Lancashire would seem to be the home of the Chattertons.*

Mary Newton, the poet's sister, writing to Robert Southey, said that her father in 1750 discovered by some writings which he found among the parchments taken from Redcliff Church that "persons of the name of Chadderton" were sextons of St. Mary Redcliff parish a hundred and twenty years before, and that his father had affirmed the family had held that office "time out of mind."† An earlier note by Michael Lort states that the poet's mother told Dean Milles that, among these

* With regard to the distribution of the name, in England, the following may assist:

1497. Chaderton (Edw.) late Sheriff, co. Suss. Add. Ch. 30992.
1499. Chaderton (Edm.) clerk, Chancellor to Queen Elizabeth; Southwell, co. Nott. 38 Horne.
1553. Chatterton (Will.) "grome of the chamber," at funeral of Edw. VI. *Archaeologia*, XII, 380.
1558. Chaterton (John) land late held by in Sevenoaks, co. Kent. Harl. 78, F. 2.
1569. Chaderton (Rob.) gent. Middle [Inner (P.A.)] Temple, London. 3 Lyon.
1581. Chaterton (Rob.) Citizine of London and fishmonger, St. Peter's, Cornehill, Gracious Streete in London; Derby. 6 Tirwhite.
1592. Chatterton (Rob.) Lewisham, co. Kent. 72 Harrington.
1607. Chatterton (John) Gent., Market Harborough, co. Leic. 4 Huddlestone.
1608. Chadderton (Will.) Bp. of Lincoln. 47 Windebanck.
1620. Chadderton (Cath.) widow of above, Halliwell, co. Hunt. 102 Soame.

† Oct. 17, 1802. *Works* III, 525: but to Lort's enquiry of the vicar of Redcliff, through Daniel Debat, "How many of and for how long have any of the family of the Chattertons been sextons of Ratcliffe Church?" the answer was returned "one only, who died about 30 years ago." 11457.

parchments, her husband had found his own name in a lease, spelt Chadderton.*

In the register, which starts in 1559, of St. Mary Redcliff, Bristol, I have found no earlier reference to the family than the baptism of Mary "daughter to Tymothy Chaterton and Patience his wife" on Dec. 3, 1643. Keeping to this register for the moment, on Aug. 29, 1680, I find that William Chatterton and Mary Bernett were married "per banns"; on Dec. 14, 1690, William "son to William Chatterton" was baptized; on Aug. 19, 1713, is the entry of the poet's father's baptism, "Thos. son of Wm Chatterton" (he was born on Aug. 8, 1713†), and on Jan. 30, 172⅔ the burial of "William Chatterton aged about 30 years." On Sept. 29, 1727, William Chatterton, possibly Mary Bernett's husband, was buried, "aged near 80 years"; but which, if either, William Chatterton was the poet's grandfather I would not venture to conclude.

A correspondent in the *Gentleman's Magazine* for Feb. 1791 stated that in 1783 he copied the following epitaph from a stone fixed up against the south wall of the church; he did not remember seeing any other stones to Chattertons at the time:

Here lieth
WILLIAM CHATTERTON,
Sexton of this Parish;
and BRIDGET his wife.
He } died { 1726.
She } { 1747.
Mors Janua Vitae.

The register, however, affords no confirmation here.

The parish Account Books are not poor in details of the occupations of the Chattertons. They appear to have been freemasons (workers in freestone), and to have done odd jobs on and about the church, which Leland called "by far the fairest of all churches,"‡ from 1661 onwards. Under the year

* 11457.

† Mary Newton to Dr. Glynn, Feb. 20, 1790; copy in G. Catcott's Letter-book, p. 480.

‡ Redcliffe longe pulcherina omnium ecclesia. *It.* ed. L. T. Smith, Vol. 5, p. 88.

1662, among disbursements made during the preceding year, is the entry, first quoted by George Pryce in his *Memorials of the Canynges* (1854, p. 276):

"Aug: 22th. To Thomas Chatterton freemason
for worke donn as p[er] note 04 10 07"

For May 7, 1662, there is the entry "To Chatterton for a paire of gloves to pull the weedes out of the leads and tower 00 00 05." There are also payments for work done "att the conduit 00 11 00," and "more to Chatterton for worke att the pipe 00 05 00."

Under 1663, for Feb. 3, 166⅔, I find "then also paid to Chatterton the mason for worke donn by him as per note 01 13 00"; under 1664, for March 5, the then large sum of £4/18/9 "on the church for stone," 6/7 on May 26 for marking the churchyard bounds, and (May 13) £1 / 10 to "Chatterton & his sonn for 20 dayes work about the churchyard walls"; under 1665 payments of 5/ and 7/6 to Chatterton "for him and his sonn" at the pipehead; and in 1666, as noted by Pryce, 2/6 to Chatterton "for a daies work att Redcliff Steppes," also 10/ "for worke donne about the vault."*

In 1676 "Chattertons two sons" are paid 13/8 for cleansing the pipehead and for candles; their names seem to have been William and John.† On March 2, 168⅘, 8/2 is paid to "William Shatterton the Freemason for worke done about the church"; and, during 1690, William Chatterton receives 12/ for a week's work about the church windows and vault, and, less than two months later, £1 / 4 for several days' work on the church. Among other payments to this name are 1/ for carrying away dirt under the churchyard wall, 3/ for attending in taking distress (both in 1693), 15/2 "for work done to the Tower Stepps" (1701), "for lighting ye lampes" £1 / 13, and £1 / 10 (in 1716 and 1717 respectively), 1/ for mending the church gate and conduit in the former year, and £1 for "new doing

* Latimer (*Annals of Bristol in the Seventeenth Century*, p. 348) quotes the Chamberlain's accounts for May, 1668: "Paid Thomas Chatterton, mason, for work done about Redcliff horse-pool [in the moat, near Redcliff Gate] £5 5*s*. 8*d*."

† *Ibid.* William was occasionally employed by the Corporation.

the diall" in the latter, and £2 for "doing the cross," also in 1717. In 1719 William Chatterton is paid his year's salary £6 / 2 / 7, and, for the last quarter of 1722, "Widow Chatterton" £1 / 9 / 4.

These entries can be supplemented by the Burgess Roll of the City of Bristol,*

"1680. John Chatterton Freemason is admitted unto ye Liberties of this Citty for y^t^ he was ye apprentice of his Father, Thomas Chatterton, and hath taken the oath of allegiance, and paid fee 4/6."

In 1713 "William Chatterton, Junr Freemason," is admitted as son of William Chatterton, and in 1729 "John Chatterton, weaver" as apprentice to Richard Noble (Apr. 14).

Turning to another source, the Redcliff Vestry Minute Book, I find, under 21 March 172⅔, "At a meeting of the Vestry ordered that the widow Chatterton shall continue her office of sexton till Easter next and that then Edward Morris shall and is hereby nominated to succeed the said widow Chatterton as sexton during pleasure."†

In the same book, on "25 March 1725," there is the appointment of John Chatterton as sexton, whom Dr. Gregory, no doubt on Lort's information, whose note runs "the last was uncle to T. Chatterton sen.,"‡ called the last of the name to bear that office. He is entered as "weaver" of St. Mary Redcliff in a Bristol Poll Book of 1734, but in the British Museum copy a contemporary hand has added "Sexton" and "Recd a Loafe Evry 14 days."

Some difficulty attaches to the date of this man's death; but on the score of the Vestry Book entry under 9 July 1747, "Widow Chatterton 4/ a week during the pleasure of the Vestry, and that Mr Perrott do pay Mrs Chatterton two guineas for her service since the decease of her late husband," it seems natural to identify him with the John Chatterton, whose burial, at the age of 46, occurs in the Redcliff register for March

* Glos. Notes and Queries. Vol. III. p. 12.

† A female sexton was not uncommon n the eighteenth century; see the account and picture of Hester Hammerton, of Kingston, Surrey (d. 1746) in Kirby's *Wonderful Museum* (1813), Vol. IV. p. 311.

‡ 11457.

27, 1747. In the *Bristol Weekly Intelligencer*, however, for June 27, 1752, appears "An Epitaph on a Departed Sexton, lately interr'd in Redcliff Church-yard, Bristol," as follows:

Near this Place,
In a cold Bed of an other's making
Lies JOHN CHATTERTON:
Who was Death's Chamberlaine here
For *Twenty* Years;
And after having provided Lodgings
For various passing Travellers,
Lay down himself
A.D. 1752. Of his sojourning 48.

When living, JOHN, pursuant to his Trade,
Many good Beds for weary Pilgrims made,
May the same kindness now their Host receive,
Dead JOHN will lie among them—*By their Leave.*

Dean Milles and Dr. Gregory put the death in 1748.* No stone thus inscribed is now known to exist in Redcliff churchyard. It is not inconceivable that we may have here a composition by "T. Chatterton sen." schoolmaster, the poet's father, who in 1743 had received from its subject some of the ancient charters from the muniment room or "Treasury" of the church "to cover his boys' copy-books"†; in any case it is the first appearance of a member of the Chatterton family in any quasi-literary connection.

Enough perhaps has been said to show that the Chattertons, if humble folk, earned good wages, and had grown to some extent into the fabric of the church which they served. They may be presumed to have lived in Redcliff parish or hard by. In a deed of sale, dated Aug. 8, 1678, one Thomas Chatterton is mentioned as occupying one of three tenements called The Three Trouts in St. Thomas Street, bounded on the one side by the lane leading from that street to Redcliff Street called Ivy Lane.‡ According to Pryce,§ John Chatterton the sexton

* "John C. sexton from 1725 to 1748." Lort, 11063, f. 413.

† *Ibid.*

‡ Bristol Council House title-deed 00947 (8); verified *ex inf.* Miss E. E. Williams.

§ *Op. cit.* pp. 278, 333.

and his predecessors (as well as, by a hazardous inference, the widowed mother of the poet) paid a yearly rent of 6/8 to the parish for a house on Redcliff Hill, situated at the back of what were, in 1854, the premises of Isaac Selfe, chemist. By the aid of directories (for the houses on Redcliff Hill have been re-numbered) Mr. James Ross, Bristol's Deputy City Librarian, has proved that the dwelling in question is a four-roomed one at the back of No. 42, which is still a chemist's; but a confirmation of Pryce's statement as to the rent and occupation remains to be gleaned from the Redcliff church books, one at least of which has gone astray.

Of their education, except in the case of Thomas Chatterton, the poet's father, evidence is not forthcoming. He, when not quite nine and a half, on Jan. 21, 172⅔, according to the school record book, entered Colston's Hospital, as a nominee of the founder's heirs, and left on Sept. 5, 1729, to be bound to Captain Edm. Saunders, a freeholder of the parish of St. Mary Redcliff, who, on Oct. 31, 1738, granted to James Gibb the vicar, and others, for £72/10, a messuage in Pile Street for the purposes of the School (founded in 1733) for forty boys from the parishes of Redcliff and St. Thomas, of which his apprentice became the master.* This Thomas Chatterton was, according to his daughter, for seven years an assistant at "an academy in Chipping Sodbury" (a market-town on the road from Bristol to Cirencester), residing with the master, the Rev. Mr. Shellard, and inscribed himself as "de Chip Sodbury" in a book which she gave to Dr. Glynn in 1790 as containing a specimen of her father's handwriting. In 1738 he succeeded William Wallice, appointed in 1733 master of the School; and in 1739 the School was new built, on the site of the messuage granted for that purpose in 1738.† He is described as "Writing Master, St Mary Redcliff" in a Bristol Poll Book for 1739. In 1775 the master's salary at this, "The Redcliff and St. Thomas Charity School," was £30 a year "for instructing the boys and finding them pens ink and paper."‡

* Manchee, *Bristol Charities*, Vol. II, p. 51.

† Pile Street School Record Book, St. Mary Redcliff Archives, and Manchee, *ib.*, p. 52.

‡ *An Account of the Hospitals . . . in Bristol*, p. 34.

The most important fact ascertained about his tastes is his musical abilities. One of the few records in Bristol Cathedral which survived the Riots of 1831 is a note that "in Jan. 1746 Thomas Chatterton was nominated appointed and sworn a singing man" (i.e. a lay clerk) "of this cathedral, which appointment he held until his death Aug. 1752," together with a bill in his clear, unadorned script—he had been employed in London in engrossing deeds for the attorneys, Dean Milles says*—for £1/10/6½, an "account" of the music written in the books belonging to the Cathedral, from Jan. 9, 1748, to June 9, 1750, with additional paper, the charge being 2½d. a side in the choir books and 2d. in the organ book.

The Bristol Museum possesses a seventeenth century MS. commonplace book (containing *inter alia* Sir Henry Wotton's famous lines on Elizabeth of Bohemia), on the blank leaves of which he has transcribed the tenor part of "Tallis's Benedictus, end of Mr. [Charles] King's Evening Service, and Dr. [Benjamin] Rogers in A." A catch for three voices, printed in the *European Magazine* for March, 1792, and given to the editors of the 1803 edition of his son's works by Edward Williams, the Welsh Bard, attests his powers of composition, and has been sung at Bristol in recent years with some effect. "The Pineapple," which he celebrates, was a tavern kept by one Golden, a bookbinder, where a convivial club met weekly. On his deathbed, according to one of Lort's notes,† he showed Dr. Woodward (1721-1785, who practised in Trinity Street,‡ and employed him to copy music) an anthem he had composed, and desired it might be performed at his funeral.

Of his antiquarian pursuits William Barrett, himself hardly an antiquary, gives this proof. Not far from Cadbury Camp three urns of Roman coins were dug up, several hundreds of which were given to Sir John Smith, of Ashton Court, by the elder Chatterton, and Sir John Hugh Smith, Bt., the then (1789) owner was a living witness of Chatterton the father's speaking about them and saying they were found near Ken-

* *Poems . . . by Thomas Rowley* (1782) p. 6.

† 11457.

‡ G. Munro Smith, *A History of the Bristol Royal Infirmary*, p. 81. We shall meet Dr. Woodward again in Chapter XIX.

moor.* There are still some Roman coins at Ashton, with no note to say whence they came ; but Barrett was the family doctor, and can, in the opinion of the present (1929) owner, be trusted in this particular.

He had about 150 books of his own, which were sold at his death to a Mr. Long ; and, Seyer says in his MS. collections for the History of Bristol, frequently borrowed books from Mr. Broughton, the Vicar of Redcliff.†

There remains, if we exclude late gossip,‡ his belief in magic Edward Gardner, one of the very few persons to whom the poet revealed the husk of his own mystery, stated in 1802 that his father was the very intimate acquaintance of "old Mr. Chatterton," and was Mrs. Newton's godfather by proxy ; they frequently lent books to one another, and the schoolmaster was "deeply read in Cornelius Agrippa.§" His copy of Agrippa (did it contain Robert Turner's translation of the spurious fourth book of the *De Occulta Philosophia* ?‖) found its way, as we shall see, into his son's possession. Allied to this credulity is his entering the age of the moon into Laurence Clarke's *History of the Holy Bible* (where also he recorded his marriage) after the births of his first two children, with their horoscopes in view, it may be.

On March 13, $174\frac{8}{9}$, according to the Redcliff register, "Mary daughter of Thomas Chatterton Schoolmaster" was baptized, and the above-mentioned family document bears this out, adding that she was born on Feb. 14, $174\frac{8}{9}$; the name is there spelt Chadderdon, but in this instance only. Her godparents were George Pew of Temple parish, John Pipping of Maryport

* *History of Bristol*, p. 19 (n.)

† Mathias, *Essay*, p. 18 ; B. 4533, f. 119.

‡ *Viz.*: that his mouth was so wide that he could put his clenched fist into it, that he was brutal, would often pass the whole night roaring out catches with his pot companions, or writing music for "old Mr. Wells, the musician," and neglected his wife, whom he married "solely for a housekeeper." The earliest date for these *ana* is 1808 (George Cumberland). The statement sometimes quoted from *Love and Madness* (p. 148) that he used to walk by the riverside talking to himself and flourishing his arms about refers to the poet, not his father, as the context shows.

§ *Works*, III., p. 523.

‖ This manual of infernal evocation is frequently found bound up with J.F.'s translation of the genuine work (London, 1651). See p. 68, *inf.*

(" haberdasher " and " baker," respectively in a Poll Book of 1759), Jane Moses, and Jane Arden.

Next in order of time comes the note of his marriage in Chipping Sodbury register under 1749*: "April 25th. Thomas Chatterton of ye Parish of St. Mary Redcliff Bristol and Sarah Young of Stapleton." It should be mentioned that the record of this event in Clarke's *History of the Holy Bible* has been scratched through in old ink, but is quite legible; it gives the year as 1748, and the day as Monday; April 25 fell on a Tuesday in 1749.

The contracting parties were respectively thirty-five years old and well under eighteen. Nothing is known of Sarah Chatterton before her marriage to the Pile Street Schoolmaster, and little enough afterwards; it may be inferred, perhaps, that hers was a colourless personality. She cannot, anyhow, be classed among the remarkable mothers of famous men.

The date of her birth, 16 Dec., 1731, is ascertained from George Catcott's letter to Dr. Glynne† announcing her death, and from the family tombstone; it is not to be found in the register at Stapleton (the birthplace of Hannah More, later her benefactress, two and a half miles out of Bristol), the births and christenings, to the year 1737, there being " register'd according to y[e] knowledge and intelligence of their parents." The singing man survived his wedding by something over three years.

Whatever might be her subsequent fortune, Mrs. Chatterton started married life at Bristol in a compact house of four rooms, which was added behind and at right angles to the school as a dwelling for the master, in that year (1749), as a contemporary tablet over the porch attests, by the gift of Giles Malpas, a

* Ingram (*The True Chatterton*, p. 24) says " owing to the defective state of the register of that period, the date is not certain." That is not so. I have seen it. See also Phillimore, *Glouc. Par. Registers*, Vol. XI., p. 129, and W. George, *New Facts relating to the Chatterton Family*, 1883. The writer says (p. 12): " Can it be conceived that five weeks *after* her baptism in Redcliff Church her parents were married at Sodbury, and that this delayed wedding occurred in the very town in which fourteen [? seven] years of her father's life had been passed ? " I can conceive it, and so, I imagine, can most persons at all conversant with the century.

† Jan. 10, 1792. *Letter Book*, p. 491.

From a Sketch in the Bristol Museum.

CHATTERTON'S BIRTHPLACE.

face p. 11

successful pinmaker. Here, on Dec. 12, 1750, a son was born to the couple, and christened Giles Malpas on New Year's Day, $175\frac{0}{1}$; the Redcliff register notes his burial on April 17. A little more than a year later, on Aug. 9, 1752, the register notes the burial of "John Chatterton, aged 39 years." There can be little doubt that "John" is the clerk's error for "Thomas," for not only does the age agree with the date of the schoolmaster's birth, but his daughter, in a letter to Dr. Glynn, already referred to, states that her father died on Aug. 7, 1752, and so does the poet, in his "Will" (1770). There may, of course, be some confusion with John Chatterton, the sexton, but I hardly think two deaths can have been entered as one.

His opportunities considered, Thomas Chatterton, senior, appears a person remarkable enough, and his early death the first of those misfortunes which have rendered his second son at least as notable as have that son's native powers.

By "an indulgence granted her for some time after her husband's death"* the widow was not ousted at once, and on "November the 20 in 1752 on a Monday night between 6 and 7 o'clock"† a posthumous child, an English poet, was born, in the northernly upper room (it is supposed) of the Pile Street master's house. Like his dead brother he was christened on New Year's Day, the officiant being the Rev. Mr. Giles.‡ No godfathers or godmothers are mentioned in the family record of this birth. The baptismal entry, in the register of St. Mary Redcliff, under 1753, runs:

"Jany 1. Thomas son of Thomas Chatterton deceased and Sarah his wife."

* Milles, p. 7. According to the School record book, the new master was Edmund Chard (from 1752 to 1757); he was succeeded by Stephen Love (to 1778).

† Ebenezer Sibly gives the hour as 6 p.m. See Appendix B., Chatterton's Horoscope.

‡ Gregory (p. 3) says by the vicar "the Rev. Mr. Gibbs" [Gibb] but the then vicar was the Rev. Thomas Broughton, appointed in 1744.

A Catch for Three Voices

The Words and Music by MR. CHATTERTON (Father to THOMAS CHATTERTON the Poet) one of the Choristers of Bristol Cathedral

1
Since now we are met and re-solv'd to be jol-ly, and
2
Then pass it a-bout, my brave Boys nev-er fear; there's
3
While Zea-lots and Fools with their Factions do grap-ple, they
drink our Good Li-qour to drown Me-lan-cho-ly,
1
Meat, Drink, and Clothes in Good Ale and strong Beer.
2
taste not those joys that are at the Pine-ap-ple.
3

Chapter II

ENVIRONMENT

The Bristol, into which the poet was born, and in which all but four months of his brief life was passed, though a changing city, with no monasteries, and its castle destroyed, was not only second to none in the kingdom but London, for civic pomp and commerce, having eclipsed the rival Norwich, but in most outward respects more nearly resembled its mediæval than its modern self.

It was still entered by gates and surrounded by walls, fragments of which can even now be seen close to St. John's Church, where is the brass of the true Thomas Rouley, *mercator*. Avon and Froom were common sewers, the washing-places were as William of Worcester had described them in his *Itinerary*; lanes and alleys smelt aloud. The twisted streets were laid out for packhorses, not pedestrians, that is to say paved with rough stones laid with serrations or ridges to help the animals to climb. Though iron-bound carts were suffered to enter the city (in Camden's and as late as Pepys's time they had been forbidden for fear of injuring the goutes, or sinks, arched under the ground), all heavy goods were drawn on sledges, called "geehoes"; and this practice killed a good many horses.* Even at the end of the eighteenth century the "bar-

* "It will be necessary to inform the reader before we proceed further, that in Bristol it is morally impossible to walk straight through a street; the drays which are used there oblige the passenger to travel in this direction:

This inconvenience may indeed be remedied when you are acquainted with the place, and, by the principles of mathematics, know how to accompany the horses."

One Hour after Marriage, *Town and Country Magazine*, Supplement, 1770; and cf. *The Pickwick Papers*, ch. xxxviii, second paragraph.

barous custom" of the sledges was notorious, limbs of men and cattle being endangered by packages overhanging the edge, as they jolted down the narrow lanes where "pride and luxury with meanness meets," and pigs and goats wandered with impunity. Heaps of mortar, brick, tanners' bark, dirt and ashes stood outside the churches. There were no footpaths, the channels for carrying off water in the middle of the causeways were choked with mud, and between the bases of many of the houses there was under twenty feet breadth.*

According to the calculations of John Browning of Barton Hill, published in the Royal Society's Transactions for 1753, the population was then 43,692, of which about 36,500 lived within the city, and 7,200 in the suburbs. "The streets," Pope wrote to Martha Blount in 1739, "are as crowded as London; but the best image I can give you of it is, it is as if Wapping and Southwark were ten times as big, or all their people ran into London."† The blunted spire of St. Mary Redcliff was obscured by the glass houses, "twenty odd pyramids smoking over the town"; but there were fields hard by, and Temple Meads was meads still. Queen Square, which supplanted College Green in point of fashion, was the sole quarter which could compare, for formal elegance, with the thirteen mile distant beauties of Bath.

"Since the year 1758," says Matthews's *Bristol Guide* for 1794, "the increase of houses has been without intermission." Barrett reckons that about 2,000 additional houses were built between 1735 and 1788.‡ Except where building was in progress—and *wholesale* demolition did not really start much before 1766—the houses were of timber and plaster (thatch being forbidden in 1703), often of great height, with overhanging storeys, as remain yet on one side of Maryleport Street.

* Ye channels, wandering through the spacious street,
In hollow murmurs roll the dirt along;
With inundations wet the sabled feet,
Whilst gouts, responsive, join th' elegiac song.
February.

† *Works*, ed. Elwin and Courthorpe, Vol. IX, pp. 325-329. Pope was seemingly unaware of St. Mary Redcliff: "there is a Cathedral, very neat, and nineteen parish churches."

‡ *History of Bristol*, p. 100.

The shops had penthouses or bulks, which projected low, and no windows; they were like shambles, and there were only occasionally lattices of chequered willow or laths. Apart from the congestion without, there was, not only during the Saturday markets, great noise, for articles were made in the shops. The dithyrambic poets whom Plato ridiculed* would have found many banausic sounds worthy their imitation; smiths, coopers, braziers, joiners, soapboilers, tallow-chandlers, dyers, and the workers of looms and lathes, laboured in full view behind their emblematic signs, which must have given the streets almost a heraldic appearance. The whole business of this polity was trade:

> Every idea of a city mind
> Is to commercial incidents confin'd.†

"The very parsons of Bristol," says a writer of 1724,‡ "talk of nothing but trade and how to turn the penny"; in addition to the industries mentioned there was shipbuilding, the manufacture of sugar, cotton, brass, pipes for smoking, pins, imitation Delft, and chocolate (as early as 1728); and Bristol milk, "which is Spanish sherry," was famous.

The people were early risers, for St. Nicholas tolled curfew at nine every night, and the streets were so ill-lighted—public lamps being extinguished at that hour—and the watchmen so drunk or somnolent, that walking even in the city by the pair (three was a reckless extravagance) of tallow candles in the shops was hazardous.§ Not only robbers were to be feared; late hours were propitious for the wreaking of private vengeance. In 1764 (June 30) *Felix Farley's Journal* reports the case of two persons, one of whom had his face blacked or covered with crape, attacking a woman in the Back Lane near Old Market because she spread a report of the other starving a manservant

* *Rep.* 396, A, B.

† *Kew Gardens.*

‡ *A Journey through England, ap.* Latimer, *Bristol in the Eighteenth Century*, p. 6.

§ "Lamps here, few as they are, are mere superfluities, as it is well known we may walk the streets in the darkest nights by the light of each other's noses, without endangering either the head or shins; but neither of our present magistrates can quite see through a mill stone."
"A Bristolian" in *T. & C. Mag.*, Feb., 1771.

to death who died in the house while she lived with him; and there is a legend (told, it is true, to the credulous George Cumberland) that the poet was waylaid on the Drawbridge shortly before he left for London, by someone who threatened to "spoil his writing arm." Street fights were frequent and sanguinary; in 1762* the butchers in the market and the Glamorganshire militia men had a "fray" in Nicholas Street; one butcher was mortally wounded, and the rioters went unpunished. Nor was this to be wondered at when pugilism was the Bristolian's pet sport. In a boxing match of 1756† the challenger had "one eye beaten out, eight ribs broke, his brisket sunk in, his omoplates in four quarters, and his under jaw-bone in three pieces; it is said he is since dead," while his opponent had "his nose struck level with his face, his collar-bone broke, and his left ear torn off." If the bloodthirsty tone of *Battle of Hastings* be derived from Drayton and Pope's Homer, that of *The Consuliad* is local and contemporary. In Wine Street, as well as a pump, stood pillory and whipping-post, and the city boasted five cock-pits, not to speak of the fashionable Ostrich Inn on Durdham Downs, besides its bowling greens. The panoply of Bristol's satiric muse was the bludgeon, not the rapier; and, later in the century, Jemmy Thistlethwaite, the blackmailing poetaster, used to walk about with the butt ends of two pistols peeping from his pockets.‡

Illiteracy joined hands with display. A citizen's will was an imposing matter (when the mourning-ring fashion was in its decline, there was a Bristolian bequest of 91 to gentlemen and 67 to ladies),§ but rarely was there a legacy of a book, except it were a Prayer Book or Bible. Wealthy citizens could not write their names on leases. The heiress of a Bristol alderman, Lady Dinely, wrote to a female friend in 1741, in the first flash of bereavement—her husband had been murdered: "Itt have all mostt ben my Deth for I am frit outt of my wits," but she required a mourning dress "in the very pink of ye

* *F.F.J.*, Oct. 30.

† *F.F.J.*, Feb. 14.

‡ R. Smith's *Chattertoniana*.

§ Chatterton's mock bequest of *one*, on condition that the legatee pays for it himself, is a sardonic gibe at this practice.

mode . . . & everything as be Long to a Widw." Funerals were extravagant, and at night; and in the printed reports of weddings the bride's wherewithal was thrown in with her charms, as "agreeable young lady with a handsome fortune," and, more often than not, in round figures. In his cynical comment on Esther Saunders's letter, "the Lady is not handsome but a great Fortune," the poet was only emulating the newspaper announcements of his time.

In the matter of costume the city was "crazy to excess," and the tradesman indistinguishable from the lord, with his "new mazareen blue coat lined with white" and "silk camblet coat lined with green silk,"* gold button-holes and buttons, large powdered wig, cocked hat laced with gold, lace sleeve ruffles, scarlet cloak and muff for winter. The reader of *Felix Farley's Bristol Journal* for the period 1763-1769 is surprised by the modernity of the drapery advertisements of "Harris opposite the drawbridge on St. Augustine's Back," "Avis Steevens and Co. at the sign of the Golden Fan and Lace in High Street," and "Atkins and Lyne's at the Turk's Head in Broad Street," and the frequency of their consignments of scarfs, ribbons, and "strip'd and flower'd silk gauzes" from London. Raffishness spread to all ranks; Southey, whose father was a draper in Wine Street, heard persons who remembered Chatterton say that he was at one time a great coxcomb in his dress†; and, fourteen years after the tragedy of Brooke Street, the newspaper aforesaid laments that, whereas the apprentices and attorneys' clerks were accustomed to dress in a plain suit of clothes and worsted stockings, now gold-laced waistcoats, ruffled shirts, and silk stockings are become the ordinary wear of almost every shop boy in the city.‡

Whatever trade might be on week-days, Sunday was observed with Puritanical rigour, though, as far back as 1699, some of the wealthier Quakers had coaches in which to go to chapel. In 1753 two barbers were placed in the stocks in Temple Street

* Stolen contents of a watchmaker's bureau in Orchard Street. *F.F.J.*, Jan. 20, 1753. The clergy wore winter muffs, three-quarter hats, cauliflower wigs, and walked the streets in their cassocks.

† Letter to John Britton, Nov. 4, 1810, in Bristol Museum.

‡ *F.F.J.*, Nov. 20, 1784.

for "shaving on the Lord's day," and, a fortnight later, two more were in the stocks at the Back for the same offence.* In that year (Nov. 25) Whitefield opened his Tabernacle, and "bargain and sale for remission of sins"† started in Penn Street. In the same year the Assembly Room in Prince's Street, perhaps that which "boasted one gorgeous lamp of copper gilt" was erected. Mention of the theatre will come more fitly later in the story; pleasure still "had a hut at Jacob's Well."

An ominous feature of the middle of the century was the strikes. There was one of the journeymen tailors in May, 1755, and again in April, 1762, which John Latimer calls the first recorded lock-out,‡ when they demanded a reduction in hours of labour, then fourteen a day, less an hour for dinner. The same occurred at Bath; the men desired their hours to be only from six in the morning to seven in the evening, "which is usual throughout the kingdom." In 1753 the Kingswood colliers rioted,§ and in 1766 the carpenters wanted twelve shillings a week.

There were three newspapers; *Felix Farley's Bristol Journal*, which started independently on March 28, 1752, was one; carried on from May 5, 1753, by his widow and son, it was published every Saturday in Small Street, and is the direct ancestor of the present *Bristol Times and Mirror*. Civic pomp has been mentioned as a mediæval feature of the city, and whoever has read the account in Seyer's *History*‖ of the procession on the proclamation of Queen Anne must have realized that the poet did not have to go back even a century for specimens of the pageantry which he used to such effect in *Bristowe Tragedy* and *On the dedication of our Ladie's Church*. Nay more, to celebrate the Coronation of George III and his consort in 1761, the Smiths' Company, preceded by a man in armour,

* *F.F.J.*, Oct. 20, Nov. 3, 1753.

† *Journal* 6th.

‡ *Bristol in the Eighteenth Century*, p. 351. This bare acknowledgment does not, of course, cover the extent of my debt to Latimer's great work.

§ Chatterton has described a Kingswood collier, "a troop of thousands swarming on his back" in his single fragmentary effort in Somersetshire dialect, *A Burlesque Cantata*, 1770.

‖ Vol. II., p. 548.

marched through Bristol ; but, of " the different Companies which preceded the mayor and displayed several curiosities of their trade," the exhibition of the woolcombers and printers pleased most. " On a stage, cover'd with bayse, ornamented with gilt and green laurel, and drawn by four horses abreast with two postilions " the printers " ingeniously " composed and printed an ode, which was distributed to the populace. " To this," the newspaper declares, " they were very attentive, few having seen the nature of that noble mystery, as it was never exhibited in so public a manner before in England."* Following the Companies came the boys of Queen Elizabeth's Hospital with their hair powdered ; and the ceremony wound up with the roasting of an ox whole at Temple Meads. Chatterton was on the verge of nine and in his second year at Colston's ; and the event, whether witnessed or heard of, was bound to leave its mark on any candidate for fame, however young. Of another sort was the reception of the news of peace with France and Spain two years later, when the mob paraded with a jackboot and hanged and burnt an effigy in a plaid.†

The hundreds of ships with their masts as thick as they could stand by one another, which Pope found " the oddest and most surprising sight imaginable," played little part, I fancy, in the first imaginings of one who would not take a step to the sea whilst he could continue on land ; but the Guinea slaves were felt for later, no doubt, and the actual sight of them on the quays, as much as the example of William Collins, may have gone far to make the *African Eclogues*.

A *picture* of Bristol in the poet's time is not here attempted; such indeed would be far beyond the scope of one short chapter. A very few facets of the city life have been chosen to serve as a biographical fingerpost, and to suggest a cause for the lack of repose, not wholly due to the prick of fame, in the poems which he acknowledged. True peace was in St. Mary Redcliff alone ; but of that not yet. A quotation from *Magna Britannia*‡

* *F.F.J.*, Sept. 26, 1761.

† No politician can dispute
My knowledge of the Earl of Bute.
Fables for the Court.

‡ Vol. IV, pp. 744, 5.

fairly summarizes these straggling data : "It is very populous; but the people give themselves up to trade so entirely, that nothing of the gaiety and politeness of Bath is to be seen here ; all are in a hurry, running up and down with cloudy looks, and busy faces, loading, carrying and unloading goods and merchandises of all sorts, from place to place ; for the trade of many nations is drawn hither by the industry and opulency of the people. This makes them remarkably insolent to strangers, as well as ungrateful to benefactors, both naturally arising from being bred, and become rich by trade, as (to use their own phrase) to care for nobody, but whom they may gain by ; but yet this ill-bred temper hath produced one good effect, which our laws have not been able to do, and that is the utter extirpation of beggars."

This, printed in 1727, is as applicable to the Bristol of Thomas Chatterton, as to the Bristol which the ingrate Richard Savage denounced almost with his last breath nine years before her poet's birth:

Boast thy base Tolsey, and thy turn-spit dogs,
Thy Halliers horses and thy human hogs ;
Upstarts and mushrooms, proud, relentless hearts ;
Thou blank of sciences ! thou dearth of arts ! *

* *London and Bristol delineated,* publ. 1744.

CHAPTER III

INFANCY

INTO some such a pandemonium or mercenary beehive, then, at the dawning of 1753, with Protestant rites over an early fifteenth-century font, built of the same stone as the church, was this dreamer introduced; and from it—to repeat—till late April, 1770, so far as is known, he was not absent a single night, or farther than he could walk in half a Sunday: there he was to learn that to create beauty is not enough, it must somehow be imposed on a world alien and unwilling. Almost the first sounds he heard must have been St. Mary's bells,* and his first sight, outside the home, the sacred building, with its massive steps and balustrades, whose vista was encroached on by tightly wedged houses, gabled many of them, and the Newgate-like Redcliff Gate, rebuilt not a quarter of a century before his birth.

The child was slow, the mother young, poor, not of her husband's mental calibre, and daughtered; latterly at any rate a grandmother† (her mother-in-law, it has been presumed

* Where eight harmonious musick-Engines hang,
That strike soniferous peals in tuneful clang,
Attractive pulls in quick vibrations fling
Revolving bells and nimble changes ring.
W. Goldwin, *Description of Bristol,* revised by I. Smart. 3rd. Ed. 1751, p. 32.

These bells, new cast in 1762, are remembered in *Happiness* (1769), where "young Yeatman . . . rings bob-majors by Leibnitzian rules." William Yeatman was churchwarden in 1765. *Redcliff Vestry Book.* Cf. also Rowley's *Memoirs*: "his wife did come out, and made a dinn to speake by a figure would have oversounded the bells of our Ladie of the Cliffe."

† "An old female relation" (*Love and Madness*, p. 148), to which Warton (*Enquiry*, p. 107) adds, "who undoubtedly thought him mad."

on no evidence) completed the household. Mrs. Chatterton became a seamstress and taught a few children, girls, to sew. Dates are obscure here, and we have to rely, with one important exception, mainly on the poet's sister's letter to Herbert Croft,* a letter, be it noted, written at a distance of nearly twenty-six years from her brother's birth. He did not know many letters at four, she says, " and always objected to read in a small book. He learnt the Alphabet from an old Folio musick book of father's my mother was then tearing up for wast paper, the capitals at the beginning of the verses." She omits to say that he was sent to the Pile Street School and thrown back on his mother's hands as a dullard, " incapable of improvement," by Mr. Love,† which detail Dr. Gregory (p. 4) reports on the authority of Jacob Bryant, adding, on that of Dean Milles, that the old folio was a French MS. (Milles says " on vellum "). Dr. Gregory gives the mother's own words : " *he fell in love* with the illuminated capitals." If the schoolmaster antiquary's volume were indeed of such a nature, one can gauge his widow's intelligence, even at that time, by the domestic act of vandalism, which is hardly on a par with using ancient deeds to cover Bibles and copy-books. Later, the little boy was taught to read from a black letter Testament : thus early was a love for antiquity, part of the paternal inheritance, stimulated by pure accident.

But the guiding star was fame ; here we are on surer ground, the testimony being not only explicit, but dated. Mrs. Newton, whose spelling at times, if Croft has transcribed her fairly, emphasizes the loss of a father, speaks of her brother's " thurst for prehemince," and his presiding over his playmates as their master and they his hired servants before he was five years old‡ ; and now let a familiar anecdote appear in a new form, as

* Sept. 22, 1778. *L. and M.*, pp. 143-147.

† Love, Stephen, Schoolmaster, 3 Guinea Street. (*Bristol Directory*, 1775). Stephen Love, March 18, 1778. (Redcliff Register, Burials).

‡ Cf. Thomas Cary's tribute :—

Ere vital utterance could scarce transpire,
His infant lips evinc'd a manly soul.

Elegy, T. and C.M., Oct., 1770.

taken down by Michael Lort in October, 1784, among "anecdotes of Chatterton from his sister"* :

"When he was five years old, he with the rest of his family had a present made him of a Delft cup with some figures or other upon it, by a relation of theirs who made that kind of ware.† Chatterton's cup had a lyon rampant ; he desir'd however to have an angel with a trumpet 'to *blow his name about*,' as he said. I saw the cup which his relation made in compliance with his request, and there is at the bottom of the outside of it T.C. 1757, and the angel and trumpet on the side."

She told Lort also that he was six before he could read, and after that time took much to reading ; the rest of her statements to him, as dealing, doubtless, with a later period, may be left for the present. Here, too, the words of Croft, in his parallel between Chatterton and Milton, may fitly be quoted : "C. became his own teacher, and his own schoolmaster, before other children are subjects for instruction."

As it seems certain that the child was sent to the Pile Street School, though how soon he was removed thence is doubtful—Bryant (p. 519) says in November, 1757—some further details of that establishment, from *An Account of the Hospitals . . . in Bristol* (1775) may be acceptable. The boys were admitted from six and a half—note the difficulty—to twelve, and remained till fourteen. They were presented by the foundation with leathern breeches, a pair of shoes and a pair of stockings yearly, and every two years with blue coats, caps, and red stockings. They attended morning prayers in school and evening prayers in St. Mary Redcliff daily ; so that an acquaintance with the interior of that church was forced on the young Chatterton apart from his family's connection therewith.

One cannot but lament the passing of the patch of green, with its two trees, which till 1924 separated the school building from Pile Street, in spite of the careful re-erection of the small

* 11457. See also *European Magazine*, Apr., 1792. A poem on this subject, called "Chatterton," will be found in *An Asylum for Fugitive Pieces*, ed. 1798. Vol. IV., p. 235. The anecdote's first appearance is in *The Public Advertiser*, June 8, 1772.

† Probably William Chatterton, described in Poll Books of 1754 and 1774 as a potter ; he was apprenticed to Richard Frank on Nov. 14, 1741. W. J. Pountney, *Old Bristol Potteries*, p. 202.

pedimented front in order to bring it into line with the Redcliff Men's Club.

Mrs. Newton, writing to the author of *Love and Madness*, recollected nothing remarkable till he went into " the school " (Colston's Hospital), in his eighth year, " except his promising my mother and me a deal of finery when he grew up as a reward for her care " ; for the little girl had assisted her mother in teaching him. That promise was kept.

From a water-colour painting in the Bristol Museum.

COLSTON'S HOSPITAL, BRISTOL. ENTRANCE.

From a water-colour painting in the Bristol Museum.

COLSTON'S HOSPITAL, BRISTOL. INNER COURTYARD.

face p. 25

Chapter IV

COLSTON'S

Dr. Gregory, whose *Life*, short, barren, unsympathetic, and disliked of Southey as it was, instinct tells me to prefer, on the whole, to Sir Daniel Wilson's, remarks (p. 81) that there are three great eras in Chatterton's existence, " his admission into Colston's School, his being put apprentice to Mr. Lambert, and his expedition to London." The meagre chronicle has been carried up to August 3, 1760, on which day, according to the record books of Bristol's Blue Coat School, the Redcliff boy became an inmate of the Great House on St. Augustine's Back (the Colston Hall now stands on the site), built by Sir John Young, who had entertained Queen Elizabeth there in 1574. It had sheltered the consorts of James I and Charles I, been owned by Sir Ferdinando Gorges—a surname the poet did not forget—in 1642, and was bought for £1,300 by the merchant prince, Edward Colston, a Bristolian and governor of Christ's Hospital, London, in 1707, to house the hundred scholars of his 1708 foundation. The yearly expenditure was £1,318 15s. 6d.; and it was opened in July, 1710.* Here, be it noted, had once stood a Carmelite Priory, known at the time of the Dissolution as White Friars, and praised by Leland,† of which, according to Barrett,‡ several very ancient arches were still extant twenty-nine years after Chatterton's admission to the school.

* *An Account of Hospitals* (1775), H. J. Larcombe, *Progress of Education in Bristol*, (MS. 1924); T. Garrard, *Edward Colston* (1852); H. J. Wilkins, *Edward Colston* (1920) and J. Latimer, *History of the Society of Merchant Venturers* (1903) are the authorities used in this chapter, other than those mentioned.

† " iiii houses of freres, of the wiche the White Freres place ys very fair."
It. ed. L. T. Smith, Vol. III, p. 101.

‡ *History of Bristol*, p. 413.

The event must have been welcome to his mother ; there was one mouth less to feed ; her son was where his father had been educated, and they would see him at home at least once a week. The nomination was supplied by the Rev. John Gardiner, vicar of Henbury " at the request of " the Rev. Thomas Harris, master of Redcliff Grammar School. In a list of admissions written by the " nominor " in a copy of *Copies of Mr. Colston's Settlements* the name is said to be spelt Chadderton,* but in the school record books (I have seen two) it is as we know it.

And here let the reader pause to consider. There are ten more years left, of which six years and eleven months, all but a day or two, are schooling, and barren but for a few early poems, and a thimbleful of testimony, including the Thistlethwaite anecdote, the date of which is debatable. Yet, to a large extent, that schooling must have made the poet react to his environment as latterly he did, though we know scarcely anything definite about the processes of his mind between his becoming a Blue Coat Boy and his letter to Baker of March 6, 1768, when he had been just on eight months in Lambert's office. All we can say positively is that during the Colston's Hospital period he was quietly acquiring knowledge on his own account.

The wrong school had, doubtless of necessity, been chosen. Beyond Redcliff, as for the young Sordello,

was for him
No other world ; but this appeared his own
To wander through at pleasure and alone.

The dreamful, contemplative, studious child, whose free hours—and the popular mind cannot be mistaken here—had been passed in and round St. Mary's, with or without the sexton, *reading*,† now in a reverie beside the mailed and shielded figure of the Knight Templar, or the two monuments to William

* *Glos. Notes and Queries*, I. p. 357, and Wilson, p. 28 *n.*

† Mary Newton told W. H. Ireland, whom I believe on this point, that her brother would sit for hours, reading, by Canynges' tomb, and often climbed " the towers of the church," where he would read ; the date, of course, may be later than this time, but I hardly think so. *Confessions* (1805), p. 15.

Canynges, the church's traditional enlarger and beautifier,* five times mayor of Bristol, now within the gloomy, hexagonal, *domus thesauraria* above the north porch, with its cirque of coffers, and litter of parchment deeds, or by that porch itself before the carvings of kings that filled its crumbling niches,† or, it may be, in the primrosed, daisied and celandined "meads" that then lay on either side of "this maystrie of a human hand," the park or airing ground for the poor children of Redcliff, St. Thomas, and Temple parishes, was now immured‡ in no monkish cloister, but a training prison for a hundred future apprentices, tradesmen in embryo, near the heart of the noisy city, with its shipping in full view.

At the free Grammar School in Christmas Street, Latin was taught, and there were two thirty pounds a year fellowships at St. John's College, Oxford, for "qualified boys," besides five exhibitions; the pupils there declaimed in Vergilian hexameters and English verse. The reader may be referred to the headmaster, the Rev. Alexander Catcott's, preface to the Exercises performed at a Visitation in 1737; he suggests that boys should be sent to the Grammar School, as soon as they can read, though but five or six: "I have frequently known boys detained *four* or *five* years, in learning what might be known in as many months, and then they are sent to the Grammar School, at ten, or twelve years old." The first half of this sentence is applicable to Colston's Hospital in 1760. *There* nothing was *taught* but writing and accounts, and the headmaster's qualifications were that he "must be a member of the Church of England, of a sober life and conversation, not under the age of five and twenty years, one that can write a good

* That modern research (see *Calendar of Deeds collected by G. W. Braikenridge* ed. F. M. Bickley, Deed 267, p. 94) tends to show that the second William Canynges was nothing of the sort, and benefited St. Mary's only to the extent of £340 to maintain two chaplains and a clerk, does not affect the case. Common fame, *teste* John Halfpenny's engraving of the church (1746), spoke far otherwise. Chatterton knew of this, latterly anyhow, for a copy hung in Henry Kator, the sugar-baker's, parlour.—Tyrwhitt, *Vindication*, p. 212; Dix, *Life*, p. 46, *n*.

† Cum ymaginibus regum operatis subtiliter in opere de frestone.
William of Worcester. *It.* p. 272, *ed.* 1778.

‡ Jacob Bryant's verb, *Observations*, p. 550.

hand and understands the grounds of arithmetic."* Scarcely anything in the whole life of Chatterton is more significant than this, that a commercial education was forced on him before he was eight.

The routine of this, the largest Bristol school of the time, was that of a reformatory. Rule XXI ran: "That poor Boys rise before Six in the Morning, and having dressed themselves, to attend Prayers in the School-Room, or some other convenient place in the House; and after reading some Portion of Scripture, and singing of Psalms, their Breakfast be given them, and then enter into the School by Seven of the Clock, and from thence precisely at Eleven in Order to go to Dinner, and return thither at One of the Clock, and continue there 'till Five only; on *Thursdays* they may study but 'till Three, and *Saturdays* in the Afternoon, they are to be catechised, and also *Sundays* after Evening Prayer; and after reading of a Chapter, singing of a Psalm and Prayers, they are to be in Bed by Eight of the Clock, and that either the Master or one of his Assistants, attend at their Meals and Times of Devotion to prevent Disorder."† These "Orders" were placed in some convenient place in the school, and read publicly at least four times a year in the presence of the visitors (Rule XX).

The intentions of the founder, "a charitable gentleman,"‡ were admirable; he had thriven by trade, and wished to create a nation of Colstons. He lived and died a bachelor (1636-1721); "Every helpless widow is my wife," was his usual reply when urged to marry, "and distressed orphans my children." This school was merely one of his benefactions. Nothing if not High Tory, he could not bear Dissent. Expulsion was the lot of any boy whose parents should prevail on him to attend a meeting, and appeal was even allowed against the trustees,

* *Copies of Mr. Colston's Settlements*, p. 57.

† *Colston's Settlements*; cf. Gregory, p. 7 and *Bristoliensis* (i.e. George Catcott) in *Gentleman's Magazine*, Sept., 1778:—"The school-hours are, in mornings, from 7 till 12; afternoons, from 1 till 5 in the summer: in the winter, from 8 till 12, mornings; afternoons from 1 till 4. Bed-time, all the year, 8 in the evening. Allowed to be *out* of school Saturdays and Saints-days, *only*, in the afternoon from 1 till 7 o'clock; *never* on Sunday, that whole day being passed in public and private religious exercises."

‡ Chatterton's "Will" (1770), his one reference to Colston.

the Society of Merchant Venturers, if any of *them* should be found to be smuggling in Nonconformist doctrine. The Church of England catechism, reading, writing, and arithmetic, these were to stand for ever as the be all and end all of his alumni, many of whom were even named after him, half their number being elected by his "heirs," twelve nominors, and half by Merchants' Hall, such as were akin to Edward Colston, or of the name of Colston, always preferred.

A master, at a yearly salary of £100, with 2½ per cent. on the sum which might be spent for sickness and other expenses, conducted this institution with two ushers*; and there was a clergyman, who was paid ten pounds, which he enjoyed for life, to instruct the school in the Catechism. Every boy—his keep cost £10 a year—was "bound" at the end of his time, seven years, to a master who had to be Church of England, a premium of £10 being paid out of the founder's bequest at the drawing of his indentures; if a place were not found for him, the schoolmaster had to maintain him a year at his own expense. In plain terms the boys were farmed to the schoolmaster at a fixed yearly sum. Drapers, smiths, mariners, braziers, carpenters, cordwainers, upholders, merchants, hoopers, glaziers, shipwrights, saddlers, potters, brushmakers, ropemakers, perukemakers, staymakers, organbuilders, grocers, and tobacconists were recruited therefrom; esquires and attornies but rarely.

A mooning, omnivorous, fatherless urchin of seven and three-quarters, dismissed his first school as dull, and thereafter taught by a widow mother and a sister not four years older than he, eager moreover to have his name blown about, is not likely to have found himself at home in such a gathering immediately. Chatterton was this; but had he been what some of his apologists have represented him, he would not have waited till he was nearly seventeen and three-quarters before killing himself.

The school had passed through a bad period, and was advancing to a worse, the present headmaster, Mr. Millbourn, assures me, and the minutes of the Merchant Society, for the

* Both *An Account of Hospitals* (1775) and Barrett (1789) say two ushers.

latter part of that century, bear him out. Mr. Samuel Gardner, headmaster during the elder Chatterton's pupillage, had still two more years to run; his comment on accession (March 25, 1718) in the Record Book (p. 1) stamps him as a reformer, in intention at least:

> Then I came into Edward Colston's Esq
> Hospitall as master of the same at wch
> time I found most of the Boys in a
> most deplorable Condition wth the Itch.

In 1757 a boy was "expelled for a leprosy"; in March, 1762, William Rogers, admitted that January, "died with his friends"; and on Sept. 29 Mr. Gardner resigned, after forty-four years' service, William Haynes, who was headmaster during the rest of the poet's time, being elected in his room. He, as undermaster, Dr. Gregory was informed,* conceived a strong and affectionate attachment for him. Hardly a discerning one, however; for in 1781, when transcribing the extract relating to Thomas Chatterton (Junior) from the school register for George Catcott to send to the Rowleian Jacob Bryant, Mr. Haynes said "he was a lad of quick conception, but that he had several contemporaries, whose parts were at least equal to his, and 3 or 4 of them having a poetical turn, he had been inform'd they used frequently to send little detached pieces of Poetry to each other, but he does not recollect ever to have seen them"; adding that in his opinion Chatterton was by no means capable of composing the poems attributed to Rowley.†

But this is to anticipate; with an exception, which will be mentioned at the end of the next chapter, only one of the youths whose names come into this "strange history," appears in the Colston record books. He is Thomas Cary of St. Philip's parish, a nominee of Merchants' Hall (admitted March 11, 1760, bound to Henry Cruger, merchant, later M.P. for Bristol, on Sept. 30, 1766) and, though, like his headmaster, but with less excuse, and being avowedly "witness to the progress of his

* *Life*, p. 19.

† Catcott to Bryant, July 4, 1781. *Letter Book;* and cf. Bryant, *Observations*, p. 560. Thomas Warton's comment is: "the teacher of arithmetic could not discern the future poet." *Enquiry*, p. 106.

genius "* a confirmed Rowleian, ought always to be remembered as the writer of the artless and affecting *Elegy*, the first tribute to the poet's memory, which appeared in the *Town and Country Magazine* for Oct. 1770.† Fine poetry it may not be; but "heroic mental fire," and more than one other phrase, bring the subject to mind, if crudely, in the absence of a portrait. According to Mathias‡ Cary was called Chatterton's second self, and he is probably the schoolmate "that had been his bedfellow," with whom, Mrs. Newton says in her letter to Croft, he corresponded soon after his apprenticeship; that friend "was I believe bound to a merchant at New York." She says he read a letter at home that he wrote to his friend, a collection of all the hard words in the English language, "and requested him to answer it." As we shall see, a similar letter was written to another friend, William Smith. At the Great House two of the elder, or three of the younger, boys slept in each bed—they did not sleep singly till 1837; and, since they had to spend nearly half their time in bed (as Ingram truly remarks), a congenial mate was perhaps more of a solace than at a boarding school to-day. Chatterton wrote more than once from London to the other T.C. with the "empty pericranium," and Cary seems to have been chosen for the job of Bristol factotum in the generalissimo's absence.§

The boys fed in messes of eight, and each mess had a gallon of beer every day at breakfast, dinner and supper; beer, it will be remembered, not only wine, was drunk at Ælla's wedding feast. The beer was brewed on the premises by the master at a trifling cost; the brewery was turned into a bathroom in 1837. Latimer comments that, even under these conditions, the master's profit, after defraying the annual tailor's and shoemaker's bills, must have been inconsiderable. The Society, recognizing this fact, were accustomed to appoint

* Letter to G. Catcott, *Works*, III, p. 482.

† See Appendix E. He is stated to be the author of the dramatic piece, *The Squire in his Chariot* (London, 1775). 11457.

‡ *Essay* (1783), p. 23.

§ "Let Mr. Cary copy the letters on the other side, and give them to the persons for whom they are designed, if not too much labour for him."
To his mother, May 6, 1770.

him as their beadle. His time being thus largely absorbed in the collection of rents and the supervision of repairs to property, not only in Bristol but on the extensive Charity estates in various parts of Somerset, his scholastic duties must have been somewhat perfunctorily discharged.* Thus, perhaps, we can understand *Apostate Will* having escaped Mr. Haynes's attention.

To return to the diet: for breakfast 2 loaves, each of 12 oz., beer, broth, or watergruel, or 2 loaves and ½ lb. of butter. For dinner, 4 loaves a day with meat and vegetables, or other substitutes, according to schedule. Here is a week of "dinners":

Sunday.	4 lbs. beef.
Monday.	12 oz. butter; the loaves to be hot.
Tuesday.	4 lbs. beef.
Wednesday.	8 oz. butter and 1 quart of raw pease boiled.
Thursday.	45 lbs. mutton boiled and divided equally among the 100 boys.
Friday.	As on Wednesday.
Saturday.	Milk Pottage.

For supper, Sunday, 4 loaves and 40 lbs. of mutton to be roasted and divided equally; other evenings 4 loaves and 1 lb. of cheese per mess.† Thus it appears that animal food was served only three days a week.

"I am a great eater of beef," says Sir Andrew Aguecheek, "and I believe that does harm to my wit." The school bill of fare, we may be sure, did not irk *one* of the hundred very grievously, for Croft assures us: "Chatterton when a boy, hardly ever touched meat, and drank only water: when a child he would often refuse to take anything but bread and water, even if it did happen that his mother had a hot meal,' because

* In his will (May 26, 1720) Colston complains that for want of such inspection and care [by the members of the Merchants' Society] the said boys have been so neglected by the Schoolmaster that when they were examined it was found that they had made so little improvement in their writing and cyphering, by the absence of their master from his school, that they were not fitly qualified to be put out apprentice, as likewise he had not given them sufficient allowance of provisions for their comfortable subsistence.

Copies of Mr. Colston's Settlements, p. 75.

† *Proc. of Merchants' Soc.*, Feb. 1718. MS., *ap.* Larcombe, *op. cit.*

he had a work in hand, and he must not make himself more stupid than God had made him.' "*

The only recreation seems to have been "stamping about the court in pairs." Bristol Cathedral was attended for services, and it is not surprising that the poem entitled by the 1803 editors *Sunday* (1769), from the day of its composition, hardly ranks among the more devotional of its author's avowed pieces.

> If (but 'tis seldom) no fair female face
> Attracts my notice by some glowing grace,
> Around the monuments I cast my eyes,
> And see absurdities and nonsense rise.
> Here rueful-visag'd angels seem to tell
> With weeping eyes, a soul is gone to hell;
> There a child's head supported by duck's wings,
> With toothless mouth a hallelujah sings:

is a legacy from the Cathedral rather than St. Mary's. The sentiment here, incidentally, is mediæval; compare Gower's *Confessio Amantis*:

> In cherches and in menstres eke
> Thei gon the wommen forto seke,
> And wher that such on goth aboute,
> Tofore the faireste of the route,
> Where as thei sitten alle arewe,
> Ther wol he most his bodi schewe.

Chatterton had almost certainly not read this passage (V, 7055-7088), which illustrates his mental affinity with the early English poets. A caveat should, however, be entered that he was "remarkably indifferent to females," according to his sister, all through his school days.

In 1762 the Dean and Chapter undertook to select their six choristers from Colston's Hospital and, as vacancies occurred, to promote such of them to singing men as should "behave well and make good proficiency in music." Had the poet been possessed of a voice, it is at least possible that, as his father's son, an opening might have been found for him; but there is silence

* *L. and M.*, p. 239.

on this matter. Apart from the evidence of his verse practice he is known to have been musical.*

At the beginning of the previous year, as a result of complaints from Colston's nominees as to the conduct of the headmaster, the Merchants' Society ordered that a rule be fixed up in the school requiring boys who had a complaint against the master to make it known to the Master of the Society.† In April of the same year (1761) complaints of "immodest correction" were declared by the boys concerned to be without foundation. In July the nominees stated that the headmaster had made use of an expression "tending to overthrow their authority," and insisted on his "making a concession" to them; this was apparently made. Here possibly Chatterton realized for the first time the blessings of a popular government.

At all events the departure of Mr. Gardner in Sept. 1762 must have been a signal for great rejoicings, and I cannot forbear identifying him with the mysterious and unknown "upper-master, Mr. Warner," with whom, according to Dr. Gregory, Chatterton "was no great favourite" at a time when Mr. Haynes was "under-master," which answers very well to the poet's first two years at the Great House.‡ George Cumberland, on the authority of Richard Phillips's son, Stephen Chatterton Phillips, a Colston boy from 1794 to 1800, has a tale of Chatterton writing scurrilous verses on the master (who caught him finishing the last line, and corrected him) at the instance of,

* *L. and M.*, p. 148. "C a great lover of music." Lort's note, 11457.

† School Register, Jan. 1761. Rule XVIII ran thus:—"The Parents shall submit their Children to the Rules of the House, and Discipline of the School, when guilty of any Fault, without coming to complain; but that no Injury may be done to them by their Master, it will be necessary that the Hall appoint a Committee of some of their Members to visit them Monthly, or at least once every Quarter, who shall enquire into their Behaviour, and also how they are treated by their Master, as to Provisions, *&c.*, who shall take a daily Note of such Faults as they are guilty of, and at the Visitation acquaint the Committee of them; and if they find that after due Admonition hath been given them, they remain incorrigible, then their Crimes shall be represented to a General Court of the Hall; and if they are heinous, and often repeated, they shall have Power, by the Majority of their Voices, to displace them, and to take from them their School Cloaths.

‡ *Life*, pp. 17, 18. Lort, who provided Gregory with material, has a note (11457) "Mr. Haines the schoolmaster C was a favourite ungrateful to Mr. Warner the headmaster wrote an anonymous letter reflecting on him." *Vide inf.* Ch. VII. Davis (*Life*, 1806, p. 12) says the poet secretly despised "Mr. Warner" for his want of literature and taste.

and for, a boy called Bess, nicknamed Crazy Bess. One William Best of St. Philip was admitted on April 10, 1759 (Merchants' Hall) and bound to a haberdasher on Dec. 10, 1765. There were also members of the school during the poet's time named James Patience and John Slumber, who possibly did not require nicknames.

The boy who died with his friends has been noticed. In Sept. 1765 two died "in the house"; and there was an epidemic of fever, and forty-five boys were afflicted. The minutes of the Merchant Society mention an allowance of £287 to the headmaster for expenditure during this period. The King's Evil was also a great trouble during the century.

I do not find that any boy was expelled during Chatterton's pupillage, though one at least was taken out by his friends; a boy had to run away—"elope" was the earlier term—thrice before he was "displaced," and this was so at Christ's Hospital in Coleridge's and Lamb's time: but in all, between 1762 and 1800, according to Mr. Larcombe's calculations, more than fifty were expelled. William Haynes did not retire from the headmastership till 1784.* In 1774 two boys who had entered the school in 1768 were displaced for elopement and misdemeanour, and theft and misdemeanour respectively; in 1778 four were flogged "with a degree of severity and put the wooden collar on two of them"; in 1779 one was displaced for "running away, throwing his school clothes over the wall, and for theft"; and in 1781 Dan Morgan was "expelled," presumably in his last year, for "a conspiracy to stab the usher." The worst time, however, was 1785-6, when thirteen were expelled. In 1785, on the occasion of a visit by members of the Merchants' Society, the headmaster complained of the gross conduct of fourteen boys; five of them had conspired to cut off the usher's hair at night, and had cut up their coats and made them into trousers; nearly all had run away more than once. Of these, eleven were whipped in the presence of the Committee, including one who called himself "Young Turpin," kept separate from the other boys, and given a bread and water dietary; eight were expelled, and six flogged "with much seriousness": the crime is

* *Minutes of Merchants' Soc.*, Sept. 1762, Jan., 1784. *ap.* Larcombe, *op. cit.*

designated "sedition" in the Admission Book. Four years earlier (April, 1781) a Colston boy who stole a penknife and went off in the coat and waistcoat of the master had been lodged in the Bridewell, and threatened with the alternative of a public prosecution, or a whipping by the city beadle followed by sending to sea. If the reader complains that the period is overstepped here, it is humbly submitted that a volcano contains lava long before it is in eruption.

The uniform of the Hospital was a blue robe, with an orange-colour lining, a band, and a blue bonnet, with orange-colour stockings; each boy had a number, wore a brass badge* bearing the founder's crest, a dolphin; and he "had the tonsure."† In that last bare fact, I believe, lies the genesis of Thomas Rowley, the monk.

* No silver badges before 1776; these were the gift of John Purrier, an old boy (1743-1751), *ex inf.* W. Pethybridge, at the school on St. Augustine's Back, 1853-1860.

† He told me, that he saw Chatterton, the very day that he came from Coulston's, with the tonsure on his head, and in the habit of the place.
Capel's testimony, *ap.* Bryant, *Observations*, p. 523.

Bryant writes to G. Catcott (June 25, 1781), "You seem not to have known or seen him till after the opening of the new Bridge which was a good deal above a year after he had left Colston's and his Hair in that space must have been grown." *Letter Book*, p. 211.

The tonsure is shown in Nicholas Pocock's fancy sketch of the child Chatterton being conducted by Genius to her altar, with St. Mary Redcliff in the background (1784).

Chapter V

EARLY VERSES

THUS far perhaps, though his picture about the " work in hand " is disquieting, we may agree with Mrs. Newton that there is nothing remarkable about her brother, the promise of the finery when he grew up being a still unrealized vaunt ; and that his first years at " the school " passed without notice is explained by the conditions of that school, where his intimates were few, and they " solid lads," while outside it, so far as she was aware, he knew only the next neighbour's sons. Apart from a reference to his veracity at Colston's and to the fact that " nothing would move him so much as being bely'd," her testimony for the whole period, from his admission in 1760 to his being bound apprentice to the attorney in 1767, is comprised in these words :—

" About his 10th year he began (with the trifle my mother allowed him for pocket money) to hire books from the circulating liberay and we were informd by the usher made rapid progress in arithmatick. Between his 11th and 12th year he wrote a caterlogue of the books he had read to the number of 70. History and divinity were the chief subjects, his school mates informd us he retired to read at the hours allotted for play. At 12 years old he was confirm'd by the Bishop,* he made very senciable serious remarks on the awfullness of the ceremony and his own feelings and convictions during it. Soon after this in the week he was door-keeper he made some verses on the last day, I think about 18 lines, paraphrased the 9 chapter of Job and not long after some chapters in Isaiah. He had been gloomy from the time he began to learn, but we remark'd he was

* " aet 12, 1764, confirmed by Bishop." Lort, 11457.

more chearfull after he began to write poetry. Some saterical peicis we saw soon after."*

Whether we accept her and Lort's date for his confirmation by "Tom" Newton, the bishop he was thereafter to abhor, or with William Tyson, a Bristol antiquary (Appendix B to Dix's *Life*) put it two years earlier, the following sixteen lines, which appeared, unsigned, almost at the foot of the last column in *Felix Farley's Journal*, in the seventh week after his tenth birthday (Jan. 8, 1763), presumably the verses on the Last Day, have a claim to be considered his first poetical production; they have passed unquestioned since Tyson ascribed them to him in 1837:

On the last EPIPHANY, *or* CHRIST *coming to* JUDGMENT

BEHOLD! just coming from above,
The Judge, with Majesty and Love?
The Sky divides, and rolls away,
T' admit him thro' the Realms of Day!
The Sun astonish'd, hides its Face,
The Moon and Stars, with Wonder gaze,
At JESU's bright superior Rays!
Dread Light'nings flash, and Thunders roar,
And shake the Earth, and briny Shore;
The Trumpet sounds at Heaven's Command,
And pierceth thro' the Sea and Land;
The Dead in each now hear the Voice,
The Sinners fear and Saints rejoice:
For now the aweful Hour is come,
When ev'ry Tenant of the Tomb,
Must rise, and take his everlasting Doom.

There are three points to be noted; the dramatic visual quality, characteristic of this poet's verse at all periods (is it not in the finest stanza of the *Mynstrelles Songe*: "See! the whyte moone sheenes onne hie"?), and here apparent in the first line; the child's accuracy in mentioning the lightnings before the thunders; and the decasyllabic close, in which—fancy perhaps!—one seems to see already a groping towards

* *L and M.*, p. 144. I do not know if Croft altered Mrs. Newton's spelling, but in no autograph letter of her's that I have seen is it so illiterate as in this *pièce justicative* of Sept. 22, 1778. The others were supervised, perhaps.

that alexandrine which Spenser was to show him. It is not contended that the lines are extraordinary. "Choice" Pomfret has an ode with a similar title, and did Chatterton know that Thomas Randolph wrote the History of the Incarnation in verse when he was nine or ten years old? There was a book that could tell him so, Cibber's *Lives of the Poets* (1753), from which, as Lort demonstrated, he certainly drew at a later period.

The romantically inclined reader may like to picture a freezing little blue-coat boy, great-coatless and gloveless, poetizing for a whole winter's week in an erect posture close to dolphin-crested gateposts on St. Augustine's Back, with a Bible in his chilblained hands; for not till 1798, by the Will of William Vaughan, at the Great House from 1747 to 1754, was a bequest of greatcoats and gloves made to the doorkeepers, who I take it, stood, like the Christ's Hospital boys used to do at Newgate Street, in full view of every passer-by.

A Hymn for Christmas Day, seven stanzas which the editors of the *Works*, following Croft, stated to have been written "at about eleven," contains a simile, and is more sophisticated:

> Almighty Framer of the Skies!
> O let our pure devotion rise,
>   Like Incense in thy Sight!
> Wrapt in impenetrable Shade
> The Texture of our souls were made
>   Till thy Command gave light.

It is signed *X.Y.* but not found in *Felix Farley*; here apparently we have Chatterton's first pseudonym. The use of singular noun with plural verb, and contrariwise, was one which he favoured almost to the last.

We have now come to the satirical pieces. "His sister having made him a present of a pocket-book as a New Year's Gift, he returned it to her at the end of the year filled with writing, chiefly poetry." So Dr. Gregory,* to whom Lort adds, "When I was in Bristol in Aug. 1777 she showed me the remains of this pocket book containing about half a dozen

* p. 12.

leaves, on which were written two satirical poems, one on a follower of Mr. Wesley, the other on a schoolfellow."* The latter, printed first in the *Works*, and bracketed in date with the *Hymn*, is (I have not touched the punctuation):

SLY DICK

Sharp was the frost, the wind was high
And sparkling Stars bedeckt the Sky,
Sly Dick in arts of cunning skill'd,
Whose Rapine all his pockets fill'd,
Had laid him down to take his rest
And soothe with sleep his anxious breast.
'Twas thus a dark infernal sprite
A native of the blackest Night,
Portending mischief to devise
Upon Sly Dick he cast his eyes;
Then strait descends the infernal sprite,
And in his chamber does alight:
In visions he before him stands,
And his attention he commands.
Thus spake the sprite—hearken my friend
And to my counsels now attend.
Within the Garret's spacious dome
There lies a well stor'd wealthy room,
Well stor'd with cloth and stockings too,
Which I suppose will do for you,
First from the cloth take thou a purse.
For thee it will not be the worse,
A noble purse rewards thy pains.
A purse to hold thy filching gains;
Then for the stockings let them reeve
And not a scrap behind thee leave,
Five bundles for a penny sell
And pence to thee will come pell mell;
See it be done with speed and care
Thus spake the sprite and sank in air.

When in the morn with thoughts erect
Sly Dick did on his dream reflect,
Why faith, thinks he, 'tis something too,
It might—perhaps—it might—be true,

* 11063, f. 425. Possibly copied into the pocket-book later. Another note, "2 satires, one on a methodist, the other on a schoolfellow who had been guilty of theft," gives the book's date, 1766, and the date appended to *Apostate Will* tends to confirm this.

I'll go and see—away he hies,
And to the Garret quick he flies,
Enters the room, cuts up the clothes
And after that reeves up the hose ;
Then of the cloth he purses made,
Purses to hold his filching trade.

The rest is wanting. If, as would appear almost inevitable, seeing that the hundred boys never slept out (unless " Sly Dick " had left the school and were already " bound "), this effort be regarded as referring to some Colston boy who made free with the school bluecoats and orange-colour stockings laid up by the Headmaster in an attic of the Great House, it is the sole direct allusion to his school days Chatterton has left us ; quite clearly, too, it betrays that conversational style which he always managed with a glib gusto, and it contains a dialect word " reeve " ("to wrinkle, *Somers.*" Wright*) foreshadowing his love of local or obsolete terms. One may be forgiven, perhaps, for reading something more into the piece, and seeing, already dimly present to the writer's mind, the Muniment Room of St. Mary Redcliff, and the spirit telling him to make some use of the parchments in the unlocked coffers there. The model for the lines, as one scholar at least has perceived,† is Gay's fable of *The Miser and Plutus*, which begins

The wind was high, the window shakes,
With sudden start the Miser wakes

a poem whose influence can be traced in " Rowley's " *The Gouler's Requiem* "

For thee, O gould, I dyd the lawe ycrase ;
For thee I gotten or bie wiles or breme‡ ;
Ynn thee I all mie joie and good dyd place.

for Gay's miser exclaims :

Gold banish'd honour from the mind,
And only left the name behind ;
Gold sow'd the world with ev'ry ill ;
Gold taught the murd'rer's sword to kill : &c.

* Or for " reave," to snatch or lift *up*. *Obs.* N.E.D.
† Richter, *Thomas Chatterton*, p. 12. ‡ Violence.

and indeed Van der Gucht's engraving of the man kneeling by the chest in the vaulted chamber with small windows, which appears in most eighteenth-century editions of the *Fables*, a book widely read, bears sufficient resemblance to the Redcliff "Treasury" (as the room over the north porch was then called) to have started dreams in a young and impressionable brain.

The influence of *The Miser and Plutus* on the anonymous *The Churchwarden and the Apparition* (*Felix Farley*, Jan. 7, 1764) is downright and palpable:

> The door now creaks,—the window shakes,
> With sudden fear he starts and wakes.

These thirty lines are a description of the appearance of Conscience to one "J - E," identified as Joseph Thomas, churchwarden of St. Mary Redcliff, who was attacked by the Bristol rhymesters* for carting the clay from the graves for his own purposes as a bricklayer, and had now removed the Cross which William of Worcester had praised three centuries before† —the High Cross had been removed from College Green in 1763, because it "interrupted gentlemen and ladies from walking eight or ten abreast"; they are surely by the author of *Sly Dick*. The opening couplet

> The night was cold, the wind was high,
> And stars bespangled all the sky,

the "had laid him down" (l. 3) and

> Whatever part you take, we know
> 'Tis only interest makes it so.
> And tho' with sacred zeal you burn,
> Religion's only for your turn

are too much like Chatterton's "railing" to be the work of his usher. In other words I side with Tyson, its discoverer,

* *F.F.J.*, Dec. 17, 31, 1763, Jan. 7, 1764.

† Crux pulcherrima artificiose operata est in medio dicti cimiterii. p. 271. The Redcliff Minute Book (Apr. 8, 1763) says the churchwarden must apply to Bishop's Court for licence to take down and remove the cross in the churchyard, to lay the churchyard more level, and lower the tombstones.

From Chatterton's Works, 1803.

THE "TREASURY," ST. MARY REDCLIFF.

From Gay's "Fables," 1727.

"THE MISER AND PLUTUS."

face p. 42

Wilson, Skeat (who first noted the plagiarism from Gay), Ingram, and the editions, as against Latimer,* though willing to give Phillips, or some other, the prose letter of " Fullford the gravedigger " in the same issue of the newspaper, albeit confessing that the writer of the next poem to be considered was quite equal to that squib, at this time.

And here is the poem, as Croft transcribed it from what he took to be the " first and perhaps only copy " in the " old pocket-book in his mother's possession . . . aimed at somebody, who had formerly been a methodist, and was lately promoted (to the dignity perhaps of opening a pew or a grave . . .) in the established church "†: the Muse of Colston's stands in full panoply ; the lesson of *The Vicar of Bray* has been learnt.‡

APOSTATE WILL, by T.C.

In days of old, when Wesley's pow'r,
Gather'd new strength by every hour ;
Apostate Will just sunk in trade,
Resolv'd his bargain should be made ;
Then strait to Wesley he repairs,
And puts on grave and solemn airs,

* *Bristol in the Eighteenth Century*, p. 353. The name Fullford does not necessarily connect the prose piece with the author of *Bristowe Tragedy* :— *Redcliff Register*, 30 June, 1783, " John Fullford, the Gravedigger." (Burials.)

† *L. and M.*, p. 147, 8. George Catcott thought it was Chatterton's first effort, and certainly written at Colston's ; it was signed Thos. Chatterton, and dated 14 April, 1764. Letter to Bryant, July 4, 1781.

‡ There is local poetic inspiration for *Apostate Will*. See the " Fable " entitled " The Vicar of Bray in Somersetshire : or, the Batt's disappointment," written in 1754, in Emanuel Collins's *Miscellanies* (Bristol, E. Farley, 1762, p. 129) which begins :

In times of old, as Poets sing
The beasts had made their lion king,

and ends

The like, may such vile miscreants do
Who trim, and change their sides like you.

The lines in the middle

But tho' I can't describe you that,
I'll shew the maxims of the BATT . . .
For thus thought he, if I am taken,
By changing sides, I save my bacon.
So to the eagle first he flew,
With—" King of birds ! my heart's with you," &c.

have influenced *The Churchwarden and the Apparition* also :—

On this side now, and now on that
The very emblem of the batt.

William Batt, rector of Wraxall from 1750 to 1767, published a sermon " Union and loyalty recommended " at Bristol in 1754 ; he might with propriety be said to " keep the place " ten years later.

Then thus the pious man address'd,
Good Sir, I think your doctrine best,
Your servant will a Wesley be,
Therefore the principles teach me.
The preacher then instructions gave,
How he in this world shall behave,
He hears, assents, and gives a nod
Says every word's the word of God.
Then lifting his dissembling eyes,
How blessed is the sect he cries,
Nor Bingham, Young, nor Stillingfleet
Shall make me from this sect retreat.
He then his circumstance declar'd,
How hardly with him matters far'd,
Begg'd him next meeting for to make
A small collection for his sake;
The preacher said, do not repine,
The whole collection shall be thine.
With looks demure and cringing bows,
About his business strait he goes;
His outward acts were grave and prim,
The Methodist appear'd in him;
But, be his outward what it will,
His heart was an Apostate's still;
He'd oft profess an hallow'd flame,
And every where preach'd Wesley's name;
He was a preacher and what not,
As long as money could be got;
He'd oft profess with holy fire,
The labourer's worthy of his hire.

It happen'd once upon a time,
When all his works were in their prime,
A noble place appear'd in view,
Then—to the Methodists, adieu;
A Methodist no more he'll be,
The Protestants serve best for *he*;
Then to the curate strait he ran,
And thus address'd the rev'rend man
I was a Methodist, 'tis true,
With penitence I turn to you;
O that it were your bounteous will
That I the vacant place might fill!
With justice I'd myself acquit,
Do every thing that's right and fit

The curate straitway gave consent—
To take the place he quickly went.
Accordingly he took the place,
And keeps it with dissembled grace.
April 14th, 1764.

Croft surely is justified in hinting that in Cowley's *Poetical Blossoms* and Pope's *Ode on Solitude* we are apt to suspect a parent, friend, or tutor of "an amiable dishonesty," which is not the case here. The enthusiasts of precocity can clap their hands, for *life* has been observed, apparently at just under eleven and five months; "it has a degree of humour," says Warton,* "and an ease of versification, which are astonishing in such a child." It is indeed far superior to *The Methodist* (Jan. 1770), and, some may think, easily the best of Chatterton's satirical poems. In the subsequent ones there is almost always the note of acrimony, or personal spleen. English Satire, while its aim is "the amendment of vices by correction,"† is indifferent to its objects:

They got a villain, and we lost a fool

is an example; a fact is stated, and the stater of it appears to take no side. In *Apostate Will*, without raising his voice above a pleasant conversational tone, Chatterton has achieved the requisite impartiality. Later, under Churchill's influence, he was to become strident, and to lay about him; as a result satirical balance departed from his verse. The poem is one of the few things we have in English to compare with *Holy Willie's Prayer*; note the exquisite division into two parts, "In days of old"—"It happen'd once"; only a born creative artist has quite that power.

But, whatever its poetic value, it tells us what interests the poet. Apostasy was a fixed idea. "Rowley" wrote, or promised to write, *The Entyrlude of the Apostate*, from the "Entroductyon" to which "thie pryde will be abeste" and four whole lines are quoted in the glossary to *The Parlyamente of Sprytes*; the subject George Catcott, who, like ourselves,

* *Enquiry*, p. 105.
† Preface to *Absalom and Achitophel*.

knew of this fragment only, reports to have been the conversion of a Christian to Judaism.* At the very outset of his "Will" (April 14, 1770) Chatterton, apropos of his knowledge that "a great genius can affect every thing," speaks of representing an enthusiastic Methodist in certain poems which he had intended to impose "upon the infatuated world as a reality." Not a fortnight later, on the eve of his journey to London, he mentions turning Methodist preacher, if disappointed in his literary projects† ; and within a very short time of his death, according to a note of Lort, he tells Cross the apothecary in Brooke Street, with whom "he loved talking about religion and to argue against Christianity," that he means "to turn Mahometan."‡ *Apostate Will* is a key to much that is strange in the short life of this chameleonlike being.

There is no difficulty about the acquisition of Bingham, Young, Stillingfleet, or indeed of any books. The Rev. Daniel Debat, rector of Christ Church, Bristol, from 1764 to 1785, informed Lort that Chatterton belonged to Fisher's circulating library in St. James' parish, where he was "a subscriber for a considerable time," and his mother, to encourage him, sometimes made the quarterly payment.§ The first circulating library in Bristol, that of Thomas Sendall, at the "Lock's Head" in Wine Street, was started in 1728, according to Latimer, and boasted two hundred volumes latterly. It will be convenient to deal with the question of Chatterton and the bookshops here, though the Great House period may be outstripped, for Catcott says he did not subscribe to Green's Library till he left school. The Rowleian Milles however has—"before he left that school" (the Pile Street School!) "he grew fond of reading, and borrowed from Mr. Long" (who had bought his father's books), "Mr. Shircliff, and particularly from Mr. Green, who had the largest collection of any bookseller in Bristol, and to whom he was obliged for Speght's Chaucer."‖

* *Monthly Review*, May, 1777. Catcott writes to Dr. Glynn, Nov. 6, 1789, "I could never procure a sight of it, nor did Mr. Barrett ever see any more of it than he has introduced in his history." *Letter Book*, p. 466.

† Thistlethwaite's testimony, *ap.* Milles, p. 459.

‡ 11457. He is the "De Bat" of *The Exhibition*, l. 164.

§ Letter, July 6, 1778; 11457.

‖ p. 5.

An advertisement in *Felix Farley* (Jan. 30, 1768) runs: "Samuel Green, bookseller, from his circulating library on St. Michael's Hill begs leave to acquaint his friends and the public that he is removed into Wine Street the corner of Dolphin Lane." His books could be read by the year, quarter, month, or single volume, and he sold stationery. Possibly the small quarto copybooks into which *English Eclogues* and the pedigree of the de Berghams were entered came from Mr. Green. A note of Samuel Seyer* states that he had many old books including, at one time, a Wiclif's Testament in MS. and a French illuminated general history. The lines *To Mrs. Haywood* ("Let Sappho's name be heard no more"), first printed in *The Literary Magnet* for March, 1826, were inscribed in an odd volume of one of her novels formerly belonging to this circulating library, which passed from Chatterton to the libraries of W. S. Landor (in 1815) and the Earl of Limerick, where it was in 1842.† Catcott's words are: "After he left school, he subscribed to Green's circulating library. Mrs. Green who is a very intelligent Person inform'd me, he was very fond of reading black letter print particularly old Poetry; but does not recollect his having any Dictionaries. The Book which most attracted his notice was an old Edition of Chaucer, with a copious glossary, printed (I think) in Queen Elizabeth's reign,‡ I forget the editor's name, and also the Date. I bought it about seven years ago for 12/- and sold it at the same price to my very good and worthy friend Dr. Glynn, when he was last in Bristol."§

W. H. Ireland, who had no special cause for lying on this point, mentions in his *Confessions* (p. 17) that, being in Bristol after the discovery of the Shakespeare imposture, he called on a bookseller in a bye street who informed him that Chatterton used to frequent his shop after school hours, and "not having

* 4533, p. 119, Bristol Library.

† C. B. Willcox, letter to R. Smith, 25 Sept., 1841, in the latter's *Chattertoniana*, Bristol Museum; Braikenridge, *Redcliffe*, Vol. XXIV, Part II, p. 283, Bristol Library.

‡ The Elizabethan editions of Speght's Chaucer are of 1598 and 1602.

§ To Bryant, July 4, 1781. *Letter Book*, p. 214. Bryant (*Obs.* p. 534) says this copy of Speght had notes in Chatterton's handwriting; Milles (p. 17) that he transcribed the glossary.

money sufficient to make purchases, but his family being well known, he was permitted to take from the shelves any volume he chose to select: that he did not confine himself to any particular head, but perused promiscuously works on religion, history, biography, poetry, heraldry, and, in short the most abstruse treatises on every subject"; also that he made transcripts, but was uncommunicative, merely bowing as he entered and left the shop.

John Evans, printer, in his *Chronological Outline of the History of Bristol* (1824, p. 284) has this: "It has not before found a place in print, that Chatterton's favourite book-shop was that of Mr. Goodall, in Tower-lane, afterward Joseph Lansdown's, nearly opposite to Cider-house Passage. Here (as Mr. Goodall informed the writer) our youthful poet passed many hours in a day, buying such books as came within his means, and sitting to read those which he either did not wish to possess or could not afford to purchase. His reveries were seldom distracted by the presence of other customers. He was particularly attached to one book, on Saxon manners and customs, which remained in the shop after news arrived from London of his death, but was at last missed without the help of a customer." A mere guess is hazarded that the book in question was some edition of Verstegan's* *A Restitution of Decayed Intelligence, in Antiquities*, which contains pictures of the Saxon Idols, in a chapter headed "The old manner of living of our Saxon Ancestors, &c," and a glossary "of our most ancient English words." In the 1655 edition the names "Bertha" and "Aella" appear on the same page (110), which is odd, as they are not connected, except in Rowley.

As for the supposition of Chatterton having had access to the City Library in King Street, it was negatived twelve years after his death; the retired librarian's letter to George Catcott, who put the enquiry, is evidence of the mercantile taste of the poet's environment.

Sir, "Falmouth. Apr. 29, 1782.

In Answer to your applying to me to know if Mr. Warton's Assertion is true, that Chatterton used to be often at the Library, and that he was introduced to it by the Revd. Mr. Catcott your

* i.e. Richard Rowlands (*fl.* 1565–1620); see *D.N.B.*

Brother, I can only answer that I do not recollect, that your Brother or any other Person used to frequent the Library, whilst I liv'd in that House. I do not recollect Chatterton having visited it at all; perhaps it might be in Mr. Trevenna's Time.

Yr hum[l] Serv[t],

BEN[N] DONNE.

P.S. Harry [i.e., Mr. Donne's son] is desir'd to take a Copy of the above, if Mr. Catcott offers to take it away, as perhaps he may print it in the Dispute."*

Thus Mr. Benjamin Donne (librarian, 1765-1776). Mr. Trevenna was next applied to, who stated that during the whole time of his residence (1762-1764) he recollected only one gentleman, and he an entire stranger, visiting the place. He added that it was impossible Chatterton could be there, "his being then at Mr. Colston's, and very seldom permitted to go abroad."

The second city to London boasted plenty of accessible literature, however true it might be that "scarcely twenty in the town can read"; and one who spoke no language but his own had, while he was at Colston's, at any rate, no *need* to go elsewhere than St. Michael's Hill for pabulum.†

But the school, albeit commercial, was not wholly insensible to poetry. Though he had the opportunity of escaping sometimes from his fellows, and did not bring books into the house—one of Seyer's notes runs, "He never appeared to read at Mr. Haynes's; but was in all points like the other Boys"‡—he had the guidance of Thomas Phillips, a Gloucestershire lad from Fairford, who was admitted Dec. 14, 1758, and apprenticed to the headmaster on April 20, 1765; that is to say, for not quite five years he was a senior boy in the school with Chatterton, and usher for just over two. Phillips died at Fairford on Nov. 1, 1769; a letter to Michael Clayfield from one T. Stephenson is extant, announcing his death, and proves that he had dramatic aspirations besides the "taste for history and poetry" which Thistlethwaite claims for him: "He departed this morning ab[t] one o'clock. His brother David has

* Enclosed in G. Catcott's letter to Bryant, May 8, 1782. *Letter Book*, p. 227. "Mr. Warton's assertion" is in the *Enquiry* (p. 111).

† The Bristol Museum possesses a copy of Robert Dodsley's *The Oeconomy of Human Life* (Dublin, 1765) with Chatterton's autograph in three places, and the date "Novr. 3rd 1766," just before his fourteenth birthday.

‡ 4533, f. 117.

paid him a visit, and whether thro' his instigation (or Tommy's own desire) I am not well assur'd, but he has committed to the flames the three first acts of that fine well work'd up play."*

He is known to us, however, by Chatterton's *Elegy*, of which three versions exist, where he is hailed as "great master of the boundless lyre." The only piece of his I have been able to rescue, an acrostic, signed "P," and authenticated by the couplet of a correspondent who guessed it in the next issue of *Felix Farley*,† should, perhaps, be quoted:

A REBUS

What the vain World incessantly pursues;
A Foot which Bards in Composition use;
What guards our Properties from fraudful Men;
What ought to guide the grave Historian's Pen;
A Fruit in Spain to great Perfection grown;
An horizontal Point to few unknown.
Th' Initials with Precision join'd will name
A British Poet; whose immortal Fame,
Long as the Sons of Men shall bear in Mind
What by one's loss another has regain'd
Yes, ev'n till Time's remotest Sand's expir'd
Shall live; by all respected and admir'd!‡

This, at least, is evidence of the imaginative pursuits in which the more brilliant of the solid lads engaged, and from which Chatterton held aloof to such an extent that one acquaintance§ would not believe that he "attempted the composition of a single couplet" between the latter ends of 1763 and 1766. But that the younger boy's grief at the pupil-teacher's death was sincere can hardly be doubted; few in, or emancipated from, the Great House during the eighteenth century can have known what an iambus was.

* 11457.

† *F.F.J.*, Nov. 5, 1765.

Answer to the Rebus in your last.
O dire disgrace to MILTON's deathless Lays!
When piddling Ph-ll-ps undertakes to praise.
AMARYLLIS.

‡ *F.F.J.* Oct. 29, 1768.

§ James Thistlethwaite, who writes "The poetical attempts of Phillips had excited a kind of literary emulation amongst the elder classes of the scholars . . . and Phillips still, to the mortification of his opponents, came off victorious and unhurt."

Letter, 4 Apr. 1781, *ap.* Milles.

Chapter VI

THE BLANK YEARS

Apostate Will, then, is dated Apr. 14, 1764; the next date to a poem of Chatterton's is March 6, 1768, when he is writing love verses for his friend in Carolina, Baker, to send to Eleanor Hoyland in Bristol. There is, however, an exception, which is important, and teasing.

An acquaintance, but not a schoolfellow,* James Thistlethwaite, about fourteen months older than Chatterton, "going down Horse Street, near the school, one day, during the summer of 1764", met Chatterton, who told him that he had some old MSS. which had been found in a chest in Redcliff Church, and had lent some or one of them to Phillips, with whom Thistlethwaite had contracted an intimacy the summer before; in fact Phillips had, he says, introduced him to Chatterton. A day or two later, meeting Phillips, he repeated what Chatterton had told him, and Phillips produced a MS. on parchment which appeared to have been closely pared round the margin. The words were entire, the writing yellow and pale, and the lines written as prose without punctuation. Phillips had "traced and gone over" several of the lines with a pen, and neither of the youths could make it out properly: the name Rowley was not mentioned. Though avowedly "having little or no taste for such studies," Thistlethwaite was confident it was none other than the pastoral eclogue *Elinoure and Juga*, the only one of the antique poems printed in the author's lifetime, which appeared in the *Town and Country Magazine* for May, 1769 (from which it was reprinted), under the signature

* Lort has a note: "Thistlethwaite was put out by the parish." 11457.

D.B., having been sent to the editor by Chatterton, as he admitted to George Catcott.*

That is the incident. Thistlethwaite was apprenticed to a stationer in 1765, and says that he did not see the poet again till the end of 1767 or beginning of 1768. He is the " jealous poet " of this story, and the object of his letter to Dean Milles (Apr. 4, 1781), where he details his acquaintance with the rival satirist of Bristol, is to insist that Chatterton could not have written Rowley; hence the earlier Rowley can be made to appear, the better Thistlethwaite's turn is served; and, both Phillips and Chatterton being dead, and Bristol Rowleian to a man almost, he was fairly immune from contradiction.

There is no mystery to us now at any point except the alleged date, 1764. The description of the parchment corresponds well enough with the extant " originals " fabricated by Chatterton, and in that of the *Songe to Ælla* the lines are written as prose.† With regard to the identification of the MS. with *Elinoure and Juga*, it should be mentioned that, while the " original " of that poem is to seek, there is a MS. on quarto paper (once in the possession of Bishop Percy) which was clearly not made from the version in the *Town and Country*, being less antiquated and containing at least two important variants‡; in this portions of lines have been left blank and filled in by another hand; and it is, I venture to think, the earliest available text for the poem, though I cannot convince myself that any of the handwriting, unless it be an early form I have not met, is Chatterton's, as the late Sir Ernest Clarke affirmed it to be " on the authority of a modern Bristol expert,"§ or that one of the corrections and the endorsement is Barrett's.

* " I don't recollect I ever saw the MS. : Chatterton told me 'twas Rowley's, and that he inserted it." Catcott's answer (Apr. 25) to Tyrwhitt's queries of Apr. 4, 1776. *Letter Book*, p. 129.

† See facsimile in Sir Ernest Clarke's *New Lights on Chatterton*, 1916. The poetry may have been written as prose to make the " original " approximate in appearance to a charter from the " Treasury."

‡ L. 17. " Bewette," corrected in another hand " Be wette," as in *T. and C.M.*

L. 23. The Minstrel Dame good cheere & Morrice playe.
The minstrelle daunce, good cheere, and morryce place.
T. and C.M.

Tyrwhitt corrected " place to " plaie " (1777).

§ *Op. cit.* p. 19.

It should be added that " D.B. May '69 " has been written in a small hand at the foot of page 3. This by the way ; the real trouble is that all remaining testimony insists that Chatterton did not speak of the parchments till he had left school—Cary says " shortly after," W. B. Smith " about the time when he first went to Lambert's "—and the composition of an eclogue in the same metre as the poem of Milton's seventeenth year, *On the death of a fair Infant,* and in the vocabulary of Kersey and Bailey, before he was twelve, and before the publication of Percy's *Reliques* (though *Fingal* and *Temora* were abroad), is a piece of alarming, if not incredible, precocity. Still he who could write *Apostate Will* in 1764 was perhaps equal to the production of the other in the same year. Further consideration of the problem can be postponed till Rowley is dealt with seriatim.

But, whatever be the date of *Elinoure and Juga,* there can be few who will not at this juncture echo the words of Michael Lort : " That honesty is the best policy can scarce be more strongly exemplified than from the conduct and fate of Chatterton. Had he not had aimed at these impositions upon all mankind—for it does not appear that he made any person privy to them—but had exhibited his compositions as imitations of ancient bards, and appeared in his own proper character ; there is no doubt but that he would have met with that patronage which might in time have produced something very extraordinary."* Chatterton did, as we shall see, in three cases, make an attempt to tell the truth about his antique verse, and he avowed his (though not " Rowley's ") imitations of Ossian ; but the bent of his mind, a certain puerile love of mystery and sensation remaining till the end, was always to give the various sections of the world what he thought each wanted *at the time*; and to wait for fame till he did not require it was sport not good enough. His pride, on which so much stress has been laid, was, as Sir Walter Scott saw,† a consciousness of superior endowments, and there is no saying but what he would have been still content to remain as the *discoverer* of Rowley, even had Rowley gone well, while achieving personal success in a

* Letter to Horace Walpole, July 20, 1778. Add. MS. 12527. f.35.
† *Edinburgh Review,* Vol. IV. Apr., 1804.

journalistic, perhaps even a political, sphere. In other words his model, as an impostor, was not so much Horace Walpole as James Macpherson; and, immediate notoriety as well as lasting fame being his objective, it is difficult to see how he could have behaved as the Rev. Michael Lort prescribed eight years after the tragic event.

The mischief was that he could not, like Blake, five years his junior, be content to escape the century altogether.* Imposture, historical and literary, was a passport to having one's name blown about; and, when Rowley refers to Richard of Cirencester,† Romance is blown to the winds. His first year at Colston's coincided with the publication of *Fragments of Poetry translated from the Gaelic and Erse Languages*; a subscription was instantly raised to enable the farmer's son to travel, as Rowley did for Canynge, in search of more fragments of antiquity, and *Fingal*, an epic in six books (1762), and *Temora*, in eight books (1763), were the results. By 1764 Macpherson was famous, rich, and secretary to the Governor of Pensacola in Florida. His honest anonymous beginning, *The Highlander* (1758), a poem in six cantos, was forgotten; it had never been remembered; Ossian was the cry,

> Ossian, sublimest, simplest bard of all,
> Whom English infidels Macpherson call.‡

Well might the Bristolian exclaim, in *Kew Gardens*,

> Alas! I was not born beyond the Tweed.

On Nov. 24, 1764, *Felix Farley* printed an "Extract from the songs of Selma," a rhymed Ossianic piece, "translated from the Erse," the immediate source of which has so far baffled me; it may not have been taken from a publication, but it would be hazardous to connect it with Chatterton; though it derives from Macpherson's prose piece of that name which attracted the author of *Werther*.§ It starts:

* Even Blake was bound; but for Ossian—to say nothing of Swedenborg—we might have had more lyrical masterpieces and fewer prophecies.

† Letter to Wm. Canynge, *Works*, III, p. 326, and cf. Wilson, p. 154.

‡ Churchill, *Prophecy of Famine*.

§ See O. Elton, *Survey of English Literature*, 1730-1780, II, p. 101.

'Tis night; and on the hill of Storms
  Alone doth Colma stray,
While round her shriek fantastic forms
  Of Ghosts that hate the Day.

and closes

To raise the Song did I in Concert join;
Mixing the sounds of Ullin's Harp with mine.

Bristol, at any rate, had an ear for Ossianics.

Almost the next literary event was an imposition, *The Castle of Otranto* (Dec., 1764, 2nd Ed. 1765) "a story, translated by William Marshal, Gent., from the original Italian of Onuphrio Muralto." Here the author, "a canon of the church of St. Nicholas at Otranto," had declared himself, in the face of applause; and Chatterton, while not imitating the work, took, beyond doubt, good stock of the ancient MS. supposedly "printed at Naples in the black letter, in the year 1529," and of Horace Walpole, who incidentally visited Bristol from Bath in 1766, and described it as "the dirtiest great shop I ever saw, with so foul a river, that, had I seen the least appearance of cleanliness, I should have concluded they washed all their linen in it, as they do at Paris." Like Pope, Walpole found the Cathedral "very neat," admired the newly-built Church of St. Nicholas as being "neat and truly Gothic," and had no word for St. Mary Redcliff, unless it be "a charming old church at the other end of the town."*

The satirist, Charles Churchill,

who blazed
The comet of a season†

had died in 1764, on a visit to his friend John Wilkes at Boulogne; and *Felix Farley*, which had printed long extracts from *The Conference*, *The Author*, *The Candidate*, *The Farewell*, *Gotham*, and *Independence*,‡ on their appearance, contains, during the winter months of that year, a fair tribute of epicedes,

* Letter to George Montagu, Oct. 22, 1766.
† Lord Byron, *Churchill's Grave* (1816).
‡ *F.F.J.*, Dec. 3, 17, 1763; May 19, June 23, Aug. 18, Oct. 6, 1764.

more than one of which might well be our poet at his worst; and one most certainly, a monody (Dec. 1) is signed S. SH—RS, later one of his butts.* In 1765 a little book of "Genuine Memoirs" was published, at half a crown bound, parts of which, if it came his way—a reasonable expectation surely—may not have been without effect on the widow's son of Redcliff Hill†: "Mr. Charles Churchill was born near Westminster Abbey in the house where Mrs. Churchill, our poet's mother, now lives (p. 45). . . . At the accustomary age our poet was sent to a reading-school, where he behaved in much the same manner as children of his years generally do; displaying no characteristical marks of genius superior to his fellows, or acting different in any respect from them. At the age of six, however, . . . the temper of young Churchill might be seen; it was plainly apparent that his sensibility was very quick; his fortitude of mind very great," etc., etc. (p. 46).

The same year saw the first appearance of what might almost be called the efficient poetical cause of Rowley, the three duodecimo volumes of Percy's *Reliques of Ancient English Poetry*. In order to realize its full effect on the mind of the young Bristol poet, a copy should be examined; it is, in its modest way, one of the most charmingly printed English books of the century. The title bears a vignette of a harp and pages of manuscript lying against a tree, almost devoid of leafage, between a ruined Gothic window and a broken group of pillars abutting on a chancel arch; overgrown stones, fragments of the church, lie around, and beneath is the motto DURAT OPUS VATUM. The frontispiece, opposite, represents a harper playing to a group (which includes an armoured knight resting with one hand on his mantled shield) under trees, at some distance from a horseman and a city, towered and walled; above, in clouds, are putti, apparently engaged in throwing blossoms from a bowl, and uplifting a ribbon inscribed with the Horatian NON OMNIS MORIAR; and, at the foot, below "S. Wale del."

* All monosyllables a line appears?
Is it not very often so in Shears?

The Defence (Dec. 25, 1769).

† The earliest evidence for this change of address is Chatterton's first letter to James Dodsley, Dec. 21, 1768. See p. 7 *supr*.

and " C. Grignion Sculp,," these lines of Rowe, lifted from the title-page of the three volume *A Collection of Old Ballads*, which had suited the robuster taste of the '20's :

> These venerable antient Song-enditers
> Soar'd many a pitch above our modern writers :
> With rough majestic force they mov'd the heart,
> And strength and nature made amends for Art.

Moreover, each " book " is headed by a vignette, and each volume closed by one,* after the glossary ; recent poems like *Jemmy Dawson*, and recent antiques like *The Witch of Wokey*, are introduced ; and such readers as have " no relish for pure antiquity " can find included a more modern copy of, e.g. *The Boy and the Mantle*. This publication was, in short, a model to anyone who wished to produce antique verse, and appeal to his century at one and the same time.

On Apr. 27, 1765, *Felix Farley* printed Tickell's *Lucy and Colin*, " an Elegiac Ballad from Mr. Percy's ingenious Collection " ; this is one of the poems which Chatterton imitated :

> And at her window, shrieking thrice,
> The Raven flap'd his Wing.
>
> Harke ! the ravenne flappes hys wynge,
> *Ælla*, l. 864.
>
> She spoke, she dy'd ; her corse was borne,
> The bridegroom blithe to meet ;
>
> I die ; I comme ; mie truelove waytes.
> Thos the damselle spake and dyed.
> *ib.* ll. 901, 2.

The *Reliques* went into a second edition in 1767, the year of

* I have small doubt that the engraving to *The Friar of Orders Gray*, a piece whose influence is plain in the title of *The Freere of Orderys Whyte* and body of " O ! Synge untoe mie roundelaie " (the sixth stanza of the latter especially), with its two monastic figures, tree, religious house, and thrown down cloak and hood, suggested, in part, the lines

> Beneathe an holme, faste by a pathwaie side,
> Which dide unto Seyncte Godwine's covent lede,

in *An Excelente Balade of Charitie*. It will be found on the last page of Vol. I of the *Reliques*.

his apprenticeship. There is no evidence that he read Hurd's *Letters on Chivalry and Romance* (1762), a work which one is apt to-day to bracket, as an awakening force, with Percy's four *Essays*.

So much for the chief literary influences agog during his schooldays, minor ones will be mentioned as occasion arises; the political aura, to which Churchill gives the clue, must not be omitted. This aspect of Chatterton's career has been exploited once and for all with such brilliance and vivacity by Masson* that to attempt the feat again savours of impertinence. Suffice it then that in 1763, the year of the disgraceful peace, Wilkes had become the national idol and synonym of Liberty, thanks to the events which followed the publication of No. 45 of the *North Briton*. Arrested, discharged, and expelled from his seat in the Lower House (1764), he had escaped the sentence of the Court of Queen's Bench, only by flight to France; his life in this country recommenced early in 1768. Of more importance to Bristol, perhaps, was the resistance of the American Colonists to the Home Government, starting with the Stamp Tax of 1764-5, which had been exchanged for a duty on paper, glass, painters' colours, and tea in 1767. Both menaces to the Court Party were to reach a fair height in the course of the next three years.

Few who have pondered on Chatterton can imagine that he invented the Rowley romance at a stroke; rather it was a steady welling up, a slow infiltration, during the seven years at the Great House; though the actual *writing down* may have been and, to some extent, undeniably was, sudden, much later, a matter of days, weeks, and months, hastened and rendered more impetuous by necessity and demand. He loved antiquity; his hours of freedom were passed among books, in St. Mary's, and who can tell how many more of the old Bristol churches? Each night he slept on the site of a Carmelite House, and, it may be, of its very dormitory. "Heere," writes Thomas Rowley, of his deceased friend and patron William Canynge, "dyd beginne the Kyndnesse of oure Lyves, oure Myndes

* *Chatterton, a Biography* (1899), first published in 1856 as a book.

and Kyndes were alycke, and wee were alwaie togyder"*—one lonely bud of schoolboy sentiment—possibly accidental—in the whole range of his labours! Yes; the Bluecoat poet, with his tonsure, might well fancy himself a monk, the only true monk in spirit of those hundred future tradesmen, the "White Friars" of their time; and, lying awake beside his sleeping bedfellow, visualize in his place the recumbent priestly effigy of Canynges, by which he had mused but a little while earlier on his native hill.

Mere theorizing, doubtless, though there are some data! But how shall the question be answered when and why the name Thomas Rowley suggested itself? As to time one has no help at all. Chatterton's instinct, at some moment or other, was to graft on to William Canynges, the traditional enlarger of Redcliff Church, a friend or dependant who should sing his praises and those of the church. The christian name was his own; the surname may not have been found for years; but when he first mentioned it to Barrett (so Barrett told Samuel Seyer†) he constantly called his poet Ronley, and it was "after showing some papers to Mr. B. that he learned to call him Rowley." This piece of affected ignorance—we shall meet it again when we come to *Bristowe Tragedy*—goes to show that Chatterton had in mind the brass in St. John's Church of Thomas Rouley, bailiff in 1466-7, when William Canynge was mayor, and sheriff in 1475-6; *n* and *u* being difficult to distinguish in Gothic script. The entry in Ricart's *Maire of Bristowe is Kalendar*,‡ where Willelmus Canynges is set down as mayor and Thomas Rowley as bailiff in one and the same line, could hardly have been known to him before he met Barrett. Still he may conceivably have seen a transcript of the Kalendar, for Seyer implies that the Vicar of Redcliff had

* *Works*, III, p. 314. The sentence before is "In MCCCCXVIII he emprooved his Leore, togyder with myselfe, undderre the garde of the Whyte Fryarres."

† B.4533, f. 121. It is "Rowlie" on the title-page of "Antiquities. Book 3rd," but Thomas Eagles (1746-1812) who knew the poet, wrote to John Britton (Dec. 21, 1811) "I can prove that when these poems first came into Chatterton's hands, he did not know the name of the poet, whom he erroneously called Ronly." See also *Remarks upon Mr. Warton's History of English Poetry* [1779] p. 9, where the spelling is "Ronlie."

‡ *Ed.* L. T. Smith (Camden Society), p. 44.

one (4533, f. 119), and states that Chatterton's father borrowed books from him Much of the poet's knowledge of Bristol antiquities may be explained on the supposition that his father had made notes and transcripts. There is a hint that "Rowley" was intended first as a priest of Redcliff, for "Canynge," in Chatterton's saga, invites him to "leave the paryshe of our Ladie"; and in a MS. in the poet's hand (of which more two chapters ahead) "St. John's" is written above an obliteration. Barrett, it may be added, when mentioning that Rowley was the name of a family that flourished at Bristol "for many years and at different periods," says that one Thomas Rowley was "chauntry priest at Redcliff"; and one may be perhaps allowed to supply his authority, since he states two lines above that it is recorded in Chatterton's handwriting that Rowley was chauntry priest of St. John's.* Sir Daniel Wilson's brilliant guess that the name might have repeatedly occurred in deeds from the Redcliff chests is actually confirmed by a lease of 1475 where Thomas Rowley, sheriff, is witness, and "the tenement of William Canynges gentleman" occurs†; to this further reference will be made, under Oct. 1, 1768. It is worth while observing, too, that St. John's Gate, which supports the church containing the brass of Thomas Rouley, *mercator et vicecomes* (d. 1478), and Margaret his wife (d. 1470), has influenced two drawings by the poet‡; as a lover of antiquity it would appeal to him as holding in its niches the supposed images of Belinus and Brennus, the latter the mythical founder of Bristol. At any rate there is small doubt that this gate was regarded, in his time, as one of the most venerable antiquities of the city.§

These points will be developed, not, it is hoped, merely repeated, later. Precision is impossible here; Chatterton could "soare 'bove trouthe of hystorie," and, it may be, fixed

* *History of Bristol*, p. 489.

† F. B. Bickley, *op. cit.* Deed 272, p. 96.

‡ 5766A ff. 33, 34. The brass was originally on the floor of the chancel it is now on the south wall (Hirst: *History of St. John's Church*, 1921, p. 31). For a pedigree of the real Thomas Rowley, see *Proceedings of the Archaeological Institute*, 1853, p. liii.

§ cf. A. Hooke, *Bristollia*, 1748, Dissertation, p. 51, which speaks of it as "standing there in William the Conqueror's time, if not long before." Tyrwhitt suggests that Chatterton obtained the names Bithrickus, Algar, and Ailward from this book. *Vindication*, p. 149, *n.*

on the married merchant for his "secular priest" with as light a heart as when he grafted on the chaplain, John Lavington (whose coffin was removed to St. Mary Redcliff from the neighbouring Chapel of the Holy Ghost, demolished some time during his schooldays),* a "cognamesakes," Laymyngetowne, who was a pirate and a freebooter.

Thus tentatively, sketchily even, have the forces at play during the six years and eleven months (all but two days) of his immurement been brought forward, and there is scarcely need to say more than that these things were in the air; the literary forgeries, hardly separable from the romantic revival, the trenchant satire of Churchill, with its irreligious, Wilkesian, antiministerial jingoism, and, in Bristol, demolitions—St. Nicholas Gate went in 1762 or thereabouts, the "lazy dean" Cutts Barton "sold the ancient cross for one church dinner" to Henry Hoare of Stourhead in 1764, and Pithay Gate went in or before the same year, followed in 1766 by Castle Gate and Lawford's Gate, and talk of further demolitions, for which an Act of Parliament had been passed in May, 1765. "We are here improving vastly in our externals," writes Cosmopolitus in the *Town and Country Magazine* for June, 1771, "which will render that crooked line that describes the manner of travelling in our streets, inserted in your Magazine for the benefit of strangers, totally unnecessary. Pulling down houses, churches, nay, whole streets, building others on more elegant plans, constructing, repaving, and beautifying, are surely indications of superior taste and elegance." That all these conspired to make Rowley as well as the acknowledged verse is sure, but to the making of the former it were a boldness to assign a *terminus a quo*. If it was *Elinoure and Juga* that Thistlethwaite saw in 1764, it may have been, as Mr. Maurice Hare notes,† a very different poem from what we now know by that name.

Chatterton, who, though cross-grained, was possessed of a strange loyalty—witness his abstention from introducing his

* Latimer (*Bristol in the Eighteenth Century*, p. 358) gives March, 1763 as the date; Catcott (Monthly Review, May, 1777) 1762: Barrett (*History of Bristol*, p. 596), 1766.

† *Chatterton's Rowley Poems*, Intr. p. ix. *n.*

master Lambert into his satires—has left no authentic dictum on his education ; but, a little while before his visit to London (so Lort had it from her in 1784), he said to his sister, "I wish I knew the classicals, I then could do anything" ; and, she saying that he knew enough already, he replied, "As it is, my name will live three hundred years."*

* But my objections may be reckon'd weak,
As nothing but my mother tongue I speak.
Epistle to the Rev. Mr. Catcott. (Dec., 1769).

"July, 1779. Mr. Barrett assured me that Chatterton knew no other language than his own." Lort, 11457.

CHAPTER VII

LAMBERT'S

ON July 1, 1767, lacking not quite five months of fifteen, Chatterton left Colston's Hospital, and was apprenticed the same day to Mr. John Lambert, " gentleman," attorney, and member of the Church of England, for seven years, "to be educated a scrivener," during which said time " . . . Taverns he shall not frequent, at Dice he shall not play, Fornication he shall not commit, Matrimony he shall not contract," his master to find him good and sufficient meat, drink, linen, woollen, lodging, and all other necessaries, washing and mending excepted. At the end of the term Mr. Lambert was to pay his apprentice four shillings and sixpence towards his freedom of Bristol with two suits of apparel, one for holidays and the other in lieu of his salary. The school authorities paid the fee of ten pounds. There are three signatories to the indentures, now in the Bristol Museum,* one John McArthur, Elton, the town clerk (" Sir Abraham Isaac Elton, Bart., Barrister at law," 1775 Directory†), and Thomas Chatterton himself, in as round and plain a hand as he could assume for the occasion ; were not the mayor and two sheriffs standing by ? Indeed, no one can examine his eighteenth century penmanship without recognizing that this son of a writing-master had learnt one excellent lesson at his father's old school. No aberration is visible *there !* Taut, level, precise, it holds an upright course across the page, slanting perhaps a little to the right, when hurried ; and, cramped, often enough, from the need of paper‡ ; but even the final stroke of " Die " in the letter

* Photographs in Ingram, *The True Chatterton*, pp. 51, 53.
† Town Clerk from 1753 to 1786, Barrett, *History of Bristol*, p. 116.
‡ e.g., in the MS. of *Resignation*, 5766 B. ff 72-76.

giving his "motives for the supposed rashness" is executed according to pattern. An endorsement, signed by his mother, undertakes that the "friends or relatives of the within apprentice" shall be responsible for his washing and mending; Mrs. Chatterton's autograph resembles the entry of her son's birth in Clarke's *History of the Holy Bible*. Thus opens the second era of this short life.

It was, all things considered, an excellent place, though wageless. The school had done its best by its alumnus. The last Colston boy to be bound to an attorney was Fr. Child (Feb. 4, 1764), and the next after Chatterton, Robert Bellerton of Fairford, not far short of six years later (Feb. 18, 1773). Though there were apparently no half-holidays on Saturdays and Saints' days, the ghastly régime of Sunday was a thing of the past, and the apprentice had leave to roam where he pleased between certain hours on that day. Croft, on the authority of Chatterton's mother and sister, says that his Sundays were generally spent in walking, alone, into the country round Bristol, "as far as the day would allow him to return before night," and that from these excursions he would bring back sketches of churches, or something which had struck him. The *Elegy written at Stanton Drew*, and Rowley's alleged birthplace, Norton Malreward, about a mile and a half from that "Druidic" monument, are indications of the line of his wanderings when Clifton "the village" and St. Vincent's Rock were not his objective. Probably all his Salvator-Rosa-like pictures of torn rocks, violent rivers, and "deep romantic chasms"—

> "As when the erthe torne by convulsyons dyre," &c.,

in *Battle of Hastings*, *Ælla*, and the *African Eclogues*, were derived from what he saw standing on the site of, or near, the present Clifton Observatory, a natural inference from the poem called *English Metamorphosis* and *Clifton* (ll. 15-22):

> Yon dusky rocks, that from the stream arise
> In rude rough grandeur, threat the distant skies,
> Seem as if Nature in a painful throe,
> With dire convulsions, lab'ring to and fro,

(To give the boiling waves a ready vent)
At one dread stroke the solid mountain rent.
The huge cleft rocks transmit to distant fame
The sacred gilding of a good saint's name.

It was there, in the " woods that wave o'er Avon's rocky steep " (gracious pillage from *The Progress of Poesy* !), that Coleridge pictured him at the close of the 1794 version of the *Monody*, the seagulls screaming over his head,

With wild unequal steps he pass'd along,
Oft pouring on the winds a broken song :
Anon upon some rough Rock's fearful brow
Would pause abrupt—and gaze upon the waves below.

The " Rock " here is certainly " this wonderful theatre, known by the name of St. Vincent's rock," for a prose description of which Manby's *Fugitive Sketches of the History and Natural Beauties of Clifton* (1802, p. 31) may be consulted.

The following note of Seyer can be interpreted in relation to these Sunday excursions : " He once lent G. Catcott *a history of Portbury* written by Rowley, as he said. At the end he had added something of his own. This MS. G.C. returned to him, and it was never heard of afterwards. The only fact which he recollects is a line toward the latter end in which speaking of Rowley as a topographer, *He was*, says he, *in short the very Pausanias of the Age*. This I had from G. Catcott."* There are still the remains of an Augustinian " monastic grange," now the village school, at Portbury, a lovely spot, especially rich in Roman earthworks ; at Norton Malreward, too, are traces of a Roman camp. These green knolls, relics of early British or Roman occupation, of which so many are left in the country round Bristol, have played their part in the imagery and atmosphere of his " tragycal Enterlude " :

Sheenynge abrode, alyche a hyll-fyre ynne the nyghte.

Gazing or resting on them he may even have realized, intui-

* B.4533, f.121. Lort quotes this, and says of the MS.: " He had drawn up what he called proofs of the existence of Rowley and the authenticity of his poems." 11457.

tively, the derivation of his own surname. He cannot have journeyed as far as " Watchet's shore " afoot, but he can have traversed the Roman road from Portbury to the sea at Portishead, and returned in time to sleep with Lambert's foot-boy. That he was up betimes is shown by his fondness for sunrise and morning dew; the comparison of the "mormrynge sounde" of Ælla's army to the " slowlie dynnynge of the croucheynge streme," and

> Thycke as the ante-flyes ynne a sommer's none,
> Seemynge as tho' theie stynge as persante too.

are effects imposed, not by books, but Nature herself.

The weekly office hours were from 8 a.m. to 8 p.m.,* with an hour for dinner, at Lambert's private house, some distance from the office (which was first either in Small Street or below St. John's Steps),† and two hours of liberty in the evening; he was expected to be with the servants by 10 p.m. His sister speaks of his regularity: "He boarded at Mr. Lamberts, but we saw him most evenings before 9 o'clock and would in general stay to the limits of his time which was 10 o'clock. He was seldom 2 evenings together without seeing us. . . . Mrs. Lambert informd me not 2 months before he left Bristol, he had never been once found out of the office in the stated hours as they frequently sent the footman and other servants there to see. Nor but once stayd out till 11 o'clock; then he had leave, as we entertained some friends at our house at Christmas."

Her most telling statement as to the apprenticeship is " He had little of his master's business to do. Sometimes not 2 hours in a day, which gave him an oppertunity to persue his genius." This is confirmed by Lort: " Lambert had no employment for him "—and by the poet himself in his third letter from London (May 14, 1770): " Tho', as an apprentice none had greater liberties, yet the thoughts of servitude killed me." Even now,

* Lort and Gregory: Dean Milles (p. 5) says 7 a.m.

† Ingram, following Palmer, says the former; Wilson, following Evans's *Chronological History of Bristol*, and John Taylor, the latter. Richard Smith says " Mr. Lambert did not remove to St. John's steps until after Chatterton left him " (*Bristol Past and Present*, III, 202). Capel's testimony *might* imply that he went straight from Colston's to 37 Corn Street.

it is not sufficiently recognized that the tragedy of the attorney's office was that Chatterton was underworked. "His apprenticeship," Chalmers wrote in 1810,* "seems to have been of the lower order, and his situation more resembling that of a servant than a pupil."

His employment, "while Mr. Lambert was from home, and no particular business interfered," lay in copying legal precedents. Lort and Gregory speak of a large folio book of 344 pages and another of 36, closely written by him.† The office contained nothing but law books, except an old edition of Camden's Britannia, "placed there as being too big for the shelves," which, as will be seen, was quite enough for the apprentice's private purpose.

In the sale of Lambert's effects, however, at 6 Rodney Place, Clifton, in Sept., 1809 (Lambert died at Bath worth £10,200 ten years later‡) *Baker's Chronicle*, *Chaucer's Works*, *Charters of Bristol* [1736] and *Willis's Cathedrals*, together with "sundry old account books," were included.

John Lambert, gentleman, at the time Chatterton made his acquaintance, was 28, bore arms gules, a chevron, had a mother and, less certainly, a wife living with him, and was later to come into an estate, Pen Park. His grandfather had been an American merchant, whose son Jonathan was in the same business. Lambert himself, now or later, had an income of £1,000 a year, and was one of fifty gentlemen who contributed £50 each to the new theatre in King Street, the foundation stone of which had been laid on Nov. 30, 1764, exactly a year and a half before the opening, May 30, 1766.§ He is described, later in life, as a kindhearted man, who read a great deal.

The master had no positive fault to find with the apprentice. Once, quite early in their intercourse, he had occasion to correct him with a blow or two, on "his old schoolmaster" receiving

* *Life*, in *Works of the English Poets*, Vol. XV, p. 368.

† "In the noting book are thirty-six notarial acts, besides many notices and letters transcribed in the ordinary book.

Willcox, *Life*, p. li. 1842.

‡ March 5, 1819. These details of John Lambert are derived from Arthur Paget's papers in the Bristol Museum, whose grandfather and father were Lambert's executors, and the former his residuary legatee.

§ Latimer, *Bristol in the Eighteenth Century*, pp. 364, 5.

an abusive anonymous letter, which was traced to Chatterton by the ill-disguised handwriting and the paper, which was of a sort used in the office. If the identification of Warner with Gardner is correct, the poet must have waited at least five years for his revenge on an elderly man. But this was a solitary incident; what Lambert did complain of was "a sullen gloomy temper which showed itself more particularly in the family and among the servants by his therewith declaring his intentions of making away with himself." This is Lort's note,* which Dr. Gregory abbreviates, omitting the last eleven words—they may not apply to the first period of the apprenticeship. Years afterwards, when he was tired of being badgered about Chatterton, "a sore subject" with him, Lambert told his friend Paget that he did not pay the least attention to his doings in those days; he thought him a sullen-tempered lad, merely the office drudge, who had very little legal copying to do; but once he found him sitting up very late at night attempting to raise spirits from the instructions of a book of magic, which with a few papers, hereafter to be mentioned, was left behind on his dismissal.† This judgment coheres with what Lambert, whom Croft did not see,‡ must have told Lort (whose notes are headed "Lambert's Testimony")—"Nor did Mr. L. take notice of his being employed in any other way during the office hours than in the [word ill-written] business of it either in reading

* 11457. "A sullen and gloomy temper which particularly displayed itself among the servants." Gregory, p. 35.

† This book Lambert gave to Arthur Paget's grandfather in 1797; the notes in it were not in young Chatterton's handwriting, except a few words at p. 88. See p. 9, *supr.*

cf. Ah! could I charm by negromantic spells
The soul of Phillips from the deathy tomb!

Elegy on Mr. Thomas Phillips (Oct. 30, 1769).
Columbia MS.

Tyro, for necromancy far renown'd,
A greater adept than Agrippa found.

The Consuliad (Jan. 4, 1770).

and Shelley's

While yet a boy I sought for ghosts, and sped
Through many a listening chamber, cave and ruin,
And starlight wood, with fearful steps pursuing
Hopes of high talk with the departed dead.

Hymn to Intellectual Beauty, Stanza V.

‡ *L and M.*, p. 128.

for his amusement or copying on old parchments or other writings."* The sending of the footman, mentioned by Mrs. Newton, points to the attorney being but seldom at his place of business; and Palmer, the jeweller's apprentice, actually says so, adding that Chatterton had little to do.

In setting this down the poet's objections to his servitude have been anticipated; it has been inferred from p. 25 of Dr. Gregory's *Life* that he disliked taking meals with the servants in the kitchen, and sleeping with the footboy; so also did Crabbe, born two years after him, who, in his second letter to Burke, speaking of the time when he was an apothecary's assistant (1768-1771) wrote "There was indeed no other distinction between the boy at the farm and myself, but that he was happy in being an annual servant, and I was bound by indentures."† Maybe the fact his sister gives us that he studied best toward the full of the moon and would often sit up all night and write by moonlight‡ increased the friction with Lambert's staff; we shall find him at this habit in Shoreditch.

But, on the most sympathetic view, one is driven to admit that Thomas Chatterton was a "difficult employee," as we should say now. The change from Colston's to Lambert's must have been as from Hell to Purgatory. If he was no richer, he was no poorer; he had solitude; he need only appear to be copying precedents when the footman looked in on him; and the grisly spectre of formal religion was away. He might have been sent to sea, or bound to some noisy trade where he would have had to sit or stand day after day beside other prentice lads. Yes, here we have the first unmistakable sign of the "pride" that was going far to ruin him, and—worse—

* Capel says, "One reason for this privacy in writing he thought might arise from the dislike Mr. Lambert showed to Chatterton's being employed in this manner." *ap.* Bryant, *Obs.* p. 524.

† *Correspondence of Sir T. Hanmer, ed.* Sir H. Bunbury, p. 385.

‡ O Inspirations rising in my scull,
A certain token that the moon's at full.
The Exhibition.

Croft (p. 238) quotes Phillips on Milton, "his vein never happily flowed but from the autumnal equinox to the vernal." *The Parlyamente of Sprytes* might be described as a poetical fantasia on St. Mary Redcliff by moonlight; it and Celmonde's speech beginning "The worlde ys darke wythe nyghte" are the *loci classici* for the moon, in Rowley.

in most of the work which he acknowledged, to come between Nature and his art. The servants and the footboy were an insult to his intelligence; he refused to bring them into his scheme. Alas, if one has the high privilege of being an English poet, the only *practical* salvation, in nine cases out of ten, is to believe that one is, in most other matters, little short of an idiot, and that the rest of the world is preternaturally sane. There are some that have learnt this lesson at fifteen. Here there was no real servitude; but he would not, rather than could not, see that; Rowley, ironically enough, has expressed the truth:

Thieselfe, a flowrette of a small accounte,
Wouldst harder felle the wynde, as hygher thee dydste mounte.

At a date that has not been ascertained Mr. Lambert moved his office to 37 Corn Street, opposite the Exchange; the site is now occupied by the Midland Bank.* These premises were in part occupied by Beckett, a bookseller, in part by Anthony Henderson, a jeweller, and the attorney had two rooms. Thomas Palmer, son of a bookseller in Wine Street (his testimony is in the Bristol Library MS. numbered 11457, and dates from his old age, 1836), with Thomas Tipton and Thomas Capel, were apprentices to this jeweller, and in the habit of spending much of their time—in the evenings apparently—with Chatterton in the office, consulting him on literary projects, and preparing contributions for magazines and Bristol newspapers; at other times he liked to be alone. He was never very communicative about his own affairs, but read portions of Rowley to them. Palmer's business was engraving coats of arms on plate, and making devices for jewellers; he gave the lawyer's apprentice instruction in painting coats of arms. If the nine escutcheons of Chatterton arms, now in the British Museum (5766 B. ff. 93-101) be the result of this instruction, the poet did not learn much. Still, he was certainly aware of the Lancashire Chattertons, and, it may well be, read this extract from Collins's *The Baronettage of England* (ed. 1720, p. 19) with

* The next house but one to Small Street, standing in 1870, when it was occupied by T. H. Weston, a bookseller. *Directories, ex inf.* J. Ross, Esq.

as much interest as Sir Walter Elliot found in *his* favourite volume :

"*Sir Richard Molineux*, Kt. who *I Henry IV* was found cousin and next Heir of *Thomas Chatterton* (m) of *Ellal, viz.* Son of *William Molineux* Kt. Son of *William*, Son of Joan, daughter of *Alice*, sister of *Laderina*, Mother to Alan, father of *Alan*, father of William, who was Father to (the aforesaid) *Thomas Chatterton.*

(m) off. post. Mort. 1 H. IV."

On p. 27 of this book the Molineux arms are given : "Azure, a cross Moline or. Crest, Out of a chapeau gules turn'd up Ermin a Peacock's tail in her pride proper. Supporters, two Lyons azure."

The first of Chatterton's imaginary coats, "CHATTERTON descended from Sire de Chasteautonne of the House of Rollo the first Duke of Normandy, and Eveligina of Ghente",* has on the verso a note by him "Elall Dreton and Sycoston principal seats of the Chattertons in Lancashire went to Sr R^d^ Molyneux Knight & Banneret on the demise of Sir Thomas Chatterton Kn & Banneret of Ellall 13th Hen. 4. Collins."

Another fictitious account of his ancestry, from "Johannes Sieur de Chateautonne 1034", with no reference to the Lancashire family, professing to be derived from a work on heraldry by "Craish," equally fictitious, is to be found in the MS. "Antiquities Book 3rd" at the Bristol Museum. It may be mentioned apropos of "Radcliffe de Chatterton of Chatterton, the heir general of many families," who occurs only in the de Bergham pedigree, where his daughter is stated to have been the wife of Edward Ashton of Chatterton "in com Lanc," that in the Manchester Cathedral register, under date 16 May, 1574, is the entry of the marriage of "Wm Radclif paroch de Ashton & M^r^gret Chatterton istius" ; so that the poet *may* not have been thinking of his family's connection with St. Mary Redcliff in this instance, though the Manchester register was unknown

* Lort has a note to the effect that Palmer sent Lord Dacre in Apr., 1773, a parchment given to him by Mrs. Chatterton which had arms and a genealogy, which she said was an attempt of her son's to prove that his family was brought to England by William the Conqueror. 11457. One is here reminded of de Quincey.

to him almost certainly. Joseph Cottle, who made enquiries at the Heralds' College, has this note on the passage: "There are two Lancashire families of the name of Chatterton, but neither of them is entitled to arms resembling in any respect that ascribed to 'Radcliff de Chatterton' (a most significant and appropriate name!) The first being Gules, a Cross Potent cross'd, or, and the second argent, a cheveron gules, between three tent hooks."*

To argue that Chatterton had a serious intention of representing himself as the descendant of a noble family of that name would be a mistake in diagnosis, though he is known to have said that the greatest oath by which a man could swear was by the honour of his ancestors†; for, aware as he was of the Lancashire Chattertons, what he, in at least five places, represents as his family's arms, viz.: "Or, a Fess Vert"‡ are quite different from theirs, being actually those of Vernon, Shipbrook (Co. Ches.), a family to which he makes no reference.§ His heraldic dedications, about which too much cannot be said (so integral a facet were they of his nature), were neither scientific, snobbish, nor would-be parvenu, but purely romantic and poetical. More than once, in the person of Rowley, he laughs at those who trace "famylies, ynstedde of wytte":

> Lette trades, and toune folck, lett syke thynges alone
> Ne fyghte for sable yn a fielde of aure.

and elsewhere‖—"One Cantyng eke endeevered to prove himself a descendant of Kyng Centwyn of the West Saxonnes 680 but he gatte himself onlie the Proverb of

> Who canne be porer than Canting
> Thoughe he will saie he came from a kynge

* *Works*, Vol. II, p. 457. † *Europ. Mag.* Apr. 1792.

‡ (*a*) In his "Will."
(*b*) In his letter to Mr. Stephens.
(*c*) In the de Bergham pedigree.
(*d*) In 5766B, f. 93, where they are blazoned.
(*e*) In A. Catcott's *Treatise on the Deluge*, p. 17. Bodl. MS. Eng. poet. e6.
In "Antiquities Book 3rd," the "Auntient Familie armes" are "a castle triple-towerd proper." (Chateautonne).

§ See, however, an anonymous article, "The origin of Surnames" in *Felix Farley*, Aug. 25, 1764.

‖ "Craish's Herauldry."

and as poore as Canting the son of a kynge." In his copy of Prior, now in the possession of Mr. Sydney Cockerell, there is an inkmark against the line in *Cupid and Ganymede*

A Prince's Son? A Black-guard Boy.

Yet who can doubt that the sight of "Thomas Chatterton" in Collins, and his jugglings with ordinaries, tinctures, and terms of blazon ministered to his peculiarly isolating type of pride? With the power of poetry and the lust of fame overwhelming in a flood his eager self-trained intellect, the vision of a Thomas Chatterton who should embody a thousand champions and legendary jousts came as a trumpet call now that the tonsure was fast disappearing from his head; he stood in the arena of the world, and the secular monk needed to be reinforced by the knight-at-arms. Rightly therefore, in his incomparable sonnet, does Rossetti speak of "noble Chatterton"; pity, though, that the eighteenth century Romantic could take no solace from the knowledge that the crest attributed to Chaucer by a later age was a tortoise passant proper.

Few poets have used heraldic nomenclature so deftly as he. The First Player's "Now is he total gules," and the famous "threw warm gules on Madeline's fair breast" (in a poem influenced by Chatterton) are the heraldic quotations best remarked by English scholars; but the line in the modernized *Romance of the Knight*, describing the yellow flag

Hanging regardant o'er its wat'ry bed.

though unobtrusive, is just and perfect.

Apart from the hoax (so called) on Burgum, and the quiz on Martha Catcott, he took a delight in working out fictitious pedigrees for his acquaintance; there is one for Baker, and another for Rumsey in the extracts from "Craish"; and Dix says Palmer told him that Chatterton said *his* name was derived from the early palmers or pilgrims to the Holy Land, and that his family's arms were three palm branches, and their crest a leopard or tiger with a palm branch in its mouth.*

* *Life*, p. 30.

A coat which he executed for George Catcott—the original is in the Bristol Library*—was actually embodied, though incorrectly, in the armorial book-plate of Richard Smith, the pewterer's nephew, as the arms of his maternal ancestors. Few can think that he was always laughing at his circle, little as it esteemed his true worth.

Thomas Capel, Palmer's fellow apprentice, though disgusted by " the young man's pride," and disliking his principles, told Jacob Bryant, the least absurd of the Rowleians, that he had seen Chatterton in Lambert's office copying manuscripts, which the poet declared were ancient writings ; " he was studying to understand the old language in which they were written." The originals lay in heaps and in great confusion, and " seemed rumpled and stained."† He said he did not believe there were two persons in Bristol who thought Chatterton wrote Rowley's poems ; for himself, he knew that he was incapable of writing them, adding that Chatterton one time was composing a play for some itinerant players—" the real author of Ælla would never have written for strollers." This sagacious youth, who spoke of a light in the poet's eyes when he was irritated or otherwise greatly affected (Bryant had heard the same from others who knew him), has left well-nigh the most vivid thumbnail sketch of him that we have, and all the better as coming from an unsympathetic witness :

> " There was generally a dreariness in his look, and a wildness ; attended with a visible contempt for others."‡

Is not this exactly mirrored in the last couplet of *Clifton* ?

> So treading back the steps I just now trod,
> Mournful and sad I seek my lone abode.

At the end of 1767 or beginning of the next year James Thistlethwaite, apprenticed to Grant, a stationer near St.

* B.5375.

† Confirmed by his sister's letter to Croft (*L. and M.*, p. 145). There can be no doubt that he brought ancient Bristol deeds from " The Treasury " into the office ; many of those in Mr. Bickley's *Calendar* answer to Capel's description.

‡ *Obs.* pp. 523-5.

Leonard's Gate, at the bottom of Corn Street,* called, on his own showing, at No. 37 for some books of Mr. Lambert's that required binding. There he found his acquaintance of 1764, from whose talk he collected that he "had been venturing in the fields of Parnassus," and had lately had pieces in prose and verse in the public prints. He then, with reference to the years 1768-9, wherein he frequently saw and conversed with Chatterton, proceeds to draw what is frankly intended as a picture of a dilettante brain, but can now, Chatterton's fame being satisfactorily established, be read as an admirable description of the poetic temper:

"One day he might be found busily employed in the study of Heraldry and English Antiquities, both of which are numbered amongst the most favourite of his pursuits; the next, discovered him deeply engaged, confounded, and perplexed, amidst the subtleties of metaphysical disquisition, or lost and bewildered in the abstruse labyrinth of mathematical researches; and these in an instant again neglected and thrown aside to make room for astronomy and music, of both of which sciences his knowledge was entirely confined to theory. Even physic was not without a charm to allure his imagination, and he would talk of Galen, Hippocrates, and Paracelsus, with all the confidence and familiarity of a modern empirick."†

B. R. Haydon wrote in much the same strain of his friend Keats: "One day he was full of an epic poem; the next day epic poems were splendid impositions on the world. Never for two days did he know his own intentions." The painter called this trait "lack of decision and fixity of aim." Keats, in the letter where he styled Chatterton "the purest writer in the English language," spoke of "my unsteady and vagarish disposition."‡ Chatterton's phrase in his "Will"

The Wild Expences of a Poet's Brain

is equally apposite.

In 1768 Thistlethwaite found him copying Rowley from the

* Palmer's testimony.

† Milles, p. 456.

‡ Sept. 22, 1819. cf. "He would have such flights and *vagaries*," Walmsley's niece's testimony, *ap.* Croft, p. 191, and see Colvin, *Life of Keats*, p. 369.

"originals." He mentions the "Deathe of Sir Charles Bawdin," which was more antiquated than Tyrwhitt's text, "the assistance he received from the glossary to Chaucer," and his once consulting a copy of Skinner's *Etymologicon* (the same probably as he returned to Barrett in a few days, as useless, most of the interpretations being in Latin); and assigns to this year the Ossianic pieces which subsequently appeared in the *Town and Country Magazine*, the authorship of which Chatterton freely admitted to his friends, as to his relative at Salisbury, Mr. Stephens. Thistlethwaite's argument is that the attorney's apprentice was so vain and greedy for praise, never writing any piece, however trifling, without communicating it indiscriminately to all his acquaintance, that, had he written Rowley, nothing could have prevented him from owning the fact. In other words he did not plumb the depths of his neighbour's vanity; the contempt for others was more firmly rooted than this "Juvenile Society," as it was called, troubled to conjecture.

Thomas Cary told George Catcott in Aug., 1776, that his school friend was "not equal to the works of Rowley."* There was no jealousy here; Cary had no taste for ancient poetry; Chatterton had made mention of such writings being in his possession shortly after his leaving school, when he could not be more than fifteen, that was all. William Bradford Smith (1747-1836), on whose supposed death the fatherless and brotherless friend wrote

> I loved him with a Brother's ardent love,
> Beyond the love which tenderest brothers bear

said: "He not only never offered to claim them as his own, but never so much as dropped any hint that way; never seemed as if he wanted people to suspect, much less believe, that they were of his composing. He had no occasion to be beholden to any other man's labour for a character, Sir; he was one of the most extraordinary geniuses I ever knew."† So completely was his circle blinded; "the most extraordinary

* Milles, p. 15, 16.
† Bryant, *Obs.*, p. 531.

genius" his friend Smith, who wrote verses to within a few hours of his death, "ever heard of," but not the author of Rowley, all whose pieces Smith could have got of him "with a word's asking."*

More will transpire about this circle of literary apprentices, who not only fancied themselves men, but were in certain respects more adult than fifteen- or sixteen-year-olds of our day, as the story advances; something must be said before the next chapter as to Chatterton's "regularity." This, as we have seen, is vouched for by his sister, writing in Sept., 1778; and Thistlethwaite, writing in April, 1781, emphatically says, "whilst he lived in Bristol he was not the debauched character represented." Both these statements were doubtless made in consequence of two sentences in J[ohn] B[roughton]'s preface to the *Miscellanies*, June 20, 1778, which is Redcliff testimony:

"He possessed all the vices and irregularities of youth, and his profligacy was, at least, as conspicuous as his abilities. Although he was of a profession which might be said to accelerate his pursuits in antiquities, yet so averse was he to that profession, that he could never overcome it."

Now Lort, whose transparent honesty, no less than the early date and persistence of his enquiries, absolves him of the suspicion of blackening Chatterton's character (supposably to please Horace Walpole), has left the following detached notes in MS,† which are here, for the first time, I believe, transcribed, without comment:

"Both Mrs. Newton's and Mr. Thistlethwayte's testimony in favour of C's moral character is to be received with grains of allowance for the [word I cannot read] of a sister and a friend.

"C's Bristol acquaintance of the most abandoned sort.

"Regularity of his attendance not true, he was sometimes about at nights and not in the best company.

"It is certain that much time was spent in the company of very disreputable young men.

"Profligacy equal to his abilities. Considering the magnitude of the latter I am inclined to think this is rather too hard a censure but surely not without good foundation."

* Milles, p. 14.

† 11457.

"During the time of his being under the care of his master," writes the anonymous author of *The Life of Paul Wells, Gent.*, 1749, "he was like most other attorney's clerks, a wild, gay young fellow, but yet at this time of day, no vicious inclinations appear'd in him that seem'd to forbode the fatal catastrophe that at length befell him."

That is one side of the picture—and Masson saw it—the Tom Chatterton who conformed to the eighteenth century standard of youth's vagaries; but who will not prefer the other, the Thomas Chatterton, short and stocky in his person, his eyes grey, but extremely vivid, his tone of voice very pleasing, and smile fascinating, when cheerful; but of a melancholy cast of mind, and when in that humour quite oppressed with the cheerfulness of others; of great temperance in eating and drinking, his diet chiefly fish and tarts, tea and water? So his sister described him to Lort in Oct., 1784, who ended his note, "Chatterton in his melanchollly fits woud pass by his most intimate acquaintance in the streets without taking notice of them." How different from the merchant's apprentice in Bristol's crowning fifteenth-century glory, the anonymous poem *The Childe of Bristowe*!:

Here at Bristow dwelleth on
is held right a juste trew man,
as y here now telle;
his prentys will y be vij yer,
his science truly for to lere
and w[t] hym will y dwelle.

CHAPTER VIII

GIRLS

MARCH 6, 1768, is the date of Chatterton's first extant letter, really two letters, addressed to one Baker, whose Christian name is unknown, not a Colston boy, who had gone to Charleston, South Carolina ; at this time the poet was writing love verses for him to send to one Eleanor Hoyland at Bristol, as if he, Baker, had written them. It is not known if Baker rewarded him for this service. Coleridge, during his short cavalry career as Silas Tomken Cumberbatch, it may be recalled, bribed a young man of the regiment to rub down his horse by writing for him " Love Stanzas " to send to his sweetheart.*

" March 6th, 1768.†

DEAR FRIEND,

I have received both your favours—The Muse alone must tell my joy.

O'erwhelmed with pleasure at the joyful news,
I strung the chorded shell, and woke the Muse.
Begin, O servant of the Sacred Nine !
And echo joy through ev'ry nervous line :
Bring down th' ethereal Choir to aid the Song ;
Let boundless raptures smoothly glide along.
My Baker's well !—Oh words of sweet delight !
Now ! now ! my Muse, soar up th' Olympic height.
What wond'rous numbers can the Goddess find,
To paint th' extatic raptures of my mind ?
I leave it to a Goddess more divine,
The beauteous Hoyland shall employ my line."

* Cottle, *Early Recollections*, II, 56.

† First printed in *A Supplement to the Miscellanies of Thomas Chatterton* (1784), p. 1.

*" DEAR FRIEND,

I must now close my poetical labours, my master being returned from London.† You write in a very entertaining stile; though I am afraid mine will be the contrary. Your celebrated Miss Rumsey is going to be married to Mr. Fowler, as he himself informs me. Pretty children! about to enter into the comfortable yoke of matrimony, to be at their own liberty: just apropos to the old law—but out of the frying pan into the fire! For a lover, heavens mend him; but for a husband! O excellent! What a female Machiaval this Miss Rumsey is! a very good Mistress of Nature to discover a *demon* in the habit of a parson‡; to find a spirit so well adapted to the humour of an English wife, that is, one who takes off his hat to every person he chances to meet, to shew his staring horns, and very politely stands at the door of his wife's chamber, whilst her gallant is entertaining her within. O mirabili! What will human nature degenerate into? Fowler aforesaid declares he makes a scruple of conscience of being too free with Miss Rumsey before marriage. There's a gallant for you! Why a girl with any thing of the woman would despise him for it. But no more of him. I am glad you approve of the ladies in Charles-Town; and am obliged to you for the compliment of including me in your happiness; my friendship is as firm as the white rock when the black waves roar around it, and the waters burst on its hoary top, when the driving wind ploughs the sable sea, and the rising waves aspire to the clouds, teeming§ with the rattling hail. So much for heroics. To speak in plain English; I am and ever will be, your unalterable friend. I did not give your love to Miss Rumsey, having not yet seen her in private, and in public she will not speak to me, because of her great love to Fowler; and on another occasion. I have been violently in love these three-and-twenty times since your departure; and not a few times came off victorious. I am obliged to you for your curiosity, and shall esteem it very much, not on account of itself, but as coming from you. The poems, &c., on Miss *Hoyland* I wish better, for her sake and yours. The TOURNAMENT I have only one canto of, which I send herewith; the remainder is entirely lost. I am with the greatest regret

* First published in *Works*, III, p. 413, "furnished by Mr. Catcott," and bearing the same date, March 6th, 1768.

† "And Mr. Capel thinks, that he never saw the young lad copying, but when his master was gone from home." Bryant, *Obs.*, p. 524.

‡ Note the Shakespearean cadence; cf.. Edmund's "An admirable evasion of whoremaster man, to lay his goatish disposition to the charge of a star!" *King Lear*, I. 2.

§ Skeat's correction, confirmed by Catcott's transcripts, of the 1803 editors' "turning."

going to subscribe myself, your faithful and constant friend, 'till death do us part.

THOMAS CHATTERTON.

Mr. Baker, Charles-Town, South Carolina."

It is impossible to say which, if not all, of the ten poems to Miss Hoyland were enclosed, nor does it much matter; they are purely formal, and the acrostic is as empassioned as the rest. One of them has enjambement—

To sing the sparkling eye, the portly grace,
The thousand beauties that adorn the face
Of my seraphic Maid; whose beauteous charms
Might court the world to rush at once to arms.

one a reminiscence of Marlowe:

Since short the busy scene of life will prove,
Let us, my Hoyland, learn to live and love.

One, beginning—" Count all the flow'rs that deck the meadow's side," is palpably imitated from a translation of Skelton's hexameters (Salve plus decies quam sunt momenta dierum) in the *Miscellanies** of Emanuel Collins, a Bristol rhymester who occupied the Duke of Marlborough public-house at Bedminster, where he celebrated irregular marriages. Chatterton pokes fun at him in *February*, a Puckish local allusion which it is easy to miss:

Attempt no number of the plaintive Gray,
Let me like midnight cats, or Collins sing.

("Gray," the reading of the MS. (5766B, f. 78), has hitherto been printed "Gay")—and elsewhere speaks of "What Collins,

* 1762. p. 51.

Count all the moments that make up the day. E. Collins. l. 1.
Count all the minutes since the world began, Chatterton, l. 11.
Count all the flowers that bedeck the field. E. Collins, l. 3.
Count all the flowers that deck the meadow's side. Chatterton, l. 1.
Then count the torments that the damn'd sustain. E. Collins, l. 8.
Count all the beauties that make up a belle. E. Collins, ll. 13, 14.
As many times I wish my patron well.
Count all the tyrants of the damn'd in hell, Chatterton, ll. 13, 14.
These are the beautous charms that make my nymph excell.

happy genius, titles verse"; but has a use for him again in a love poem written in his own person *To Miss C. on hearing her play on the harpsichord.** In another the satirist peeps out, and the precentor of Bristol Cathedral, the vicar of the Temple Church, his brother the pewterer, and a dissenting preacher, Lewis, whom the poet elsewhere calls a "pulpit-fop," come in for a lash or two. This I hardly think can have been included in the letter of March 6, as the acquaintance of George Catcott, the "wild-antique and sputtering brother" of the poem, was apparently not made till the October of that year. There is a song "Tell me, God of soft desires," and an *Ode,* the latter clearly influenced by quite another Collins, the author of the *Ode to Evening,* who may be said to share the honours with Churchill of being Chatterton's favourite eighteenth-century poet:

Amidst the wild and dreary dells
The distant echo-giving bells,
　　The bending mountain's head;
Whilst Ev'ning, moving thro' the sky
Over the object and the eye
　　Her pitchy robes doth spread.

According to a MS. note of G. Catcott (B. 6489) the acrostic on Sally Clarke was included with the Hoyland effusions.

But to return to the letter which accompanied these, or some of them; it tells us a few interesting facts:

* To Miss ER*SK*NE at Bristol: upon her surprising execution on the guitar:—

O had the greatly troubled king,
Felt but the musick of thy string!
Whose sounds the frantick can assuage,
Then *Saul* had heard away his rage.
You have revers'd the ungrateful dart
First cur'd, then struck HIM to the heart.

Miscellanies, p. 120.

Which Chatterton works up thus:—

Had Israel's monarch, when misfortune's dart
Pierc'd to its deepest core his heaving breast,
Heard but thy dulcet tones, his sorrowing heart
At such soft tones, had sooth'd itself to rest.
Yes, sweeter far than Jesse's son's thy strains,
Yet what avail if sorrow they disarm;
Love's sharper sting within the soul remains,
The melting movements wound us as they charm.

1. The pleasure the writer takes in assuming another character.
2. His observation of human nature, first evident in *Apostate Will,* here in the case of Miss Rumsey.
3. His awareness of the style of Ossian—" my friendship is as firm," &c.*
4 The approximate date of *The Unknown Knyght or The Tournament,* i.e. a *terminus ad quem* for what is prosodically the most remarkable of all Chatterton's poems; for we can thus say that the piece in which he made fullest use of equivalent substitution, the old but neglected principle which Coleridge speaks of as " new " in the preface to *Christabel,* was written before he was fifteen and four months old.

The importance of *The Unknown Knyght*† (which will be discussed in Chapter XI, and must be carefully distinguished from *The Tournament, an Interlude*), in this regard, was noted as far back as 1880,‡ but I am not aware that the full extent of our luck in being able to *date* it has yet been observed, for through the existence of this letter we can similarly say that *Battle of Hastings* (I) was composed before March 6, 1768. The only thing that could upset this view would be inaccuracy on the part of the 1803 editors in transcribing that date, as the actual document is not forthcoming; it was among the MSS. that Catcott sold to Cottle for seven guineas (Aug. 1, 1799).

The ground for this assertion is in George Catcott's letter book. There, in a transcript of his letter of Aug. 18, 1780, to Dean Milles, he says that Chatterton cut *The Tournament* out of a book containing the first part of *Battle of Hastings* and sent it with " some of his own poems " to Baker, who a few

* Cf. also *Genuine Memoirs of Mr. Charles Churchill,* p. 159. " Finding our poet proof against their artifices, or force; and that he stood like a rock, against which the furious winds bellow, and waves beat in vain."

† The Rowleians called it " The Mock Tournament:" by the irony of ignorance it was never claimed as Rowley's, maybe because Chatterton abstained from antiquating it too grossly, and it first appeared in *A Supplement to Chatterton's Miscellanies,* as " in imitation of our older poets "; it is there dated 1769, possibly the year in which Catcott received " Antiquities Book 3rd " from the poet.

‡ By Theodore Watts Dunton, in Ward's *The English Poets,* Vol. III, p. 401.

days before his death* at Charles Town gave it with some other papers to Abraham Lloyd, formerly a Bristol merchant, then (1780) in the Monmouthshire Militia. Mr. Dyer, an apothecary, sent Lloyd to Catcott; and Lloyd gave up the MS. of *The Tournament*, which was restored to the book as being Catcott's property.

It seems sufficiently clear, though Catcott is evasive—" I have replaced it in the same book as contains the *Battle of Hastings* and *Craishe's Heraldry* from whence Chatterton took it in (I think) 1769," he writes to Dean Milles, Aug. 3, 1779—that this, and possibly the " Ode to Lais," which is still missing from the book, were torn out *before* Chatterton gave or disposed of the book to Catcott; as indeed *The Unknown Knyght* must have been, if March 6, 1768, is the date of his letter to Baker, enclosing it. Catcott never says " I had *that* poem, and Chatterton took it from me." What he says is that he had the book to which it belonged.†

Now this book (given by Catcott to Thomas Eagles in Jan., 1782), which is entirely in the poet's handwriting, may be seen in the Bristol Museum. The title page is printed opposite :‡

There are 549 lines, without glossary, of *Battle of Hastings* (I) ending abruptly after " But Ethelbert by a mischance did miss " with " Beneath the Rybbes " and a date, "1034." The text differs slightly from the received version, and it may be observed that he probably made copies of all his more important pieces.§

Thus it would appear that before March 6, 1768, besides

* Catcott in a note (May, 1783) amends this statement, " They were given him (Lloyd) as upon further recollection he afterwards told Mrs. Dyer, when in South Carolina, a little before the commencement of the American war, by a friend of Mr. Baker's into whose hands they had fallen, after Mr. Baker's decease." B. 5374 f. 65.

† " I should have premis'd that Chatterton did not give it me as the production of Rowley, it was as I informed you before, written in the same book with the *Battle of Hastings*, where I have replaced it."

To Dean Milles, June 15, 1779.
Letter Book, p. 348.

‡ Dean Milles writes to Catcott, Aug. 30, 1780 : " It is a strange thing that Chatterton should pick up such a man as you describe Mr. Mackintosh to have been for the patron of his collectanea " ; but unfortunately Catcott, in his transcript of the letter (Aug. 18), to which this appears to be a reply, has not a word about Mackintosh : information is sorely wanted here.

§ A copy was even made of the 26 lines on Immortality, which he improvised in William Smith's presence.

John Evans, *A Chronological Outline of the History of Bristol.* p. 288.

ANTIQUITIES—BOOK 3rd.

TO ALEXANDER MACKINTOSH ESQUIRE

This Book is most humbly Dedicated
By his obedient Servant
THE EDITOR—

CONTENTS of this BOOK

* The Battle of Hastynges was fought on the 14th of Octr; *1066.*

N.B. The Ode to Lais is a Modern production——

The Unknown Knyght or The Tournament and *Battle of Hastings* (I, all but sixteen lines), two books of "antiquities" had been compiled by Chatterton, one of which contained works, or some account, of his creation Thomas Rowley. There is a mystery about the date of *Elinoure and Juga*; but, if we accept the date of the letter to Baker—and it is doubled, remember—there can be none here.

Note that he tells Baker the remainder of *The Tournament* is lost, whereas on the MS. title page he says he has two more "centos." These may have been in his head; but no one can have studied his personality attentively without perceiving that, for all his blustering John-Bull-like airs, he seldom acted openly. Except in despair he could not be frank; Colston's, a commercial environment, and his private reading had made an artful man of him well before his time. There are two dicta of Michael Lort which will constantly recur to the mind of any unbiassed lover of this poet :

> Attentive to the tastes of those he wished to impose on.
> His Bristol friends allow he was a sad lyar.

There is no intention of stressing these unduly at any point in his story, but let the reader consider the title page of "Antiquities Book 3rd," and mark the disingenuousness, especially with regard to the date of the Battle of Hastings. It may be argued that " tenth century " was an ignorant blunder, and Catcott or Barrett pointed that out ; then why not scratch it through ?

This is a digression, essential it is hoped, from the business of this chapter. *The Unknown Knyght* contains the surname of an inamorata, in a passage which, as Watts Dunton saw, has exactly the *Christabel* ring, " the ring that Scott only half caught and Byron missed altogether " :

> But when he threwe down his Asenglave,
> Next came in Syr Botelier bold and brave,
> The Dethe of manie a Saracen,
> Theie thought him a Devil from Hells Black pen :
> Ne thinking that anie of mortalle Menne,
> Could send so manie to the Grave—
> For his Life to John Rumsee he renderd his thanks,
> Descended from Godred the King of the Manks.

In " Craishes Herauldry," where there are arms for " Baker," he thus romances under " Name Rumsey " :

> " 1065 Donnal Sonne of Godred Kynge of Manne to escape the Furie of his Brother Fingal fled to England and lived in Rumsey Town mindyng to be shorne a Monck and going to a Minster but louynge a fayr Mayd of the Familie of Osburn afterwards Lords of Wyght he wedded her he bare a white sheelde Gutte de Sang a Crown Or peerced with a bloudie Sworde Pommel and Hylt or."

Godred (cf. the Ossianic piece *Godred Crovan*) came from "A Chronicle of the Kings of Man " in Camden's Britannia (ed.

1695, p. 1053), but Maria Rumsey was the daughter of a cooper in Redcliff Street.*

Mrs. Newton, after remarking that her brother was a lover of truth "from the earlyest dawn of reason," and the allusion to the master's depending "on his verasity on all occations," which they learnt from the usher, continues thus, plainly referring to the period of his apprenticeship:

"Till this time he was remarkably indifferent to females. One day he was remarking to me the tendency sever study had to sour the temper† and declared he had always seen all the sex with equal indifference but those that nature made dear, he thought of makeing an acquaintance with a girl in the neighbourhood supposeing it might soften the austerity of temper study had ocationd, he wrote a poem to her and they commenced corrisponding acquaintance." Later in this letter to Croft, referring to the period just before Chatterton's leaving Bristol, she says, "He wrote one letter to Sr Horace Warpool and except his corrispondence with Miss Rumsey, the girl I before mentiond, I know of no other. He would frequently walk the Colledge green with the young girls that statedly paraded there to shew their finery. But I realy believe he was no debauchee (tho some have reported it) the dear unhappy boy had faults enough I saw with concern he was proud and exceedingly impetious but that of venality"—she derived this word from Venus, "he could not be justly accused with." She goes on to speak of the good hours he kept, a passage already quoted. For what it is worth, note that Davis (*Life*, p. 100) speaks of "the unhappy women who patrole the College Green." He was writing in 1806.

Here it will be convenient, with a glance at the London era, to gather up what scraps are available for illustrating the character of Chatterton, the Bristol amorist; all the pieces fall within two and a half years.

In his collected works, excluding the poems written to Miss

* "Miss Rumsey, a cooper's daughter," in a list of "Persons whom he knew in his lifetime." G. Cumberland's MS. (1828). "Rumsey and Randal, Wine Coopers, 86 Redcliff Street." *Directory*, 1775.

† This is not laughable precocity, but, as will be seen, a desperate truth.

Hoyland for Baker, and an "Epitaph on an old maid," unnamed, perhaps intended for Martha Catcott, there are eleven to females, a fraction no doubt of a vast quantity, one of which *The Advice* (Jan. 1, 1770) is addressed to "Miss M. R. of Bristol," and another, the Stanton Drew *Elegy*, laments "Maria."

Jack Fowler, whom Miss Rumsey (of whose marriage I can find no trace in the Redcliff register) seems to have favoured, was one of the Juvenile Society,* the members of which lampooned one another in the public prints; and he contributed verse, no less than Chatterton and Thistlethwaite, sometimes, like the latter (but never the former), signing his name in full. He was always Chatterton's butt, and went on the stage, for we find him playing Alwin in *The Countess of Salisbury* at Ludlow in 1775.† One of Lort's notes runs "Fowler turned player, C. above it." "Heavy as Fowlerian song," "his muse with tatter'd fragments grac'd," "poor Pitholeon's feeble line" (the name is from the prologue to Pope's *Satires*) "poet-laureate of the stews," "empty thin and long as Fowler's back or head or song" are among the phrases Chatterton applies to him. He was certainly courting Miss Rumsey at the end of 1769, for he is included among the "fools or empty beaux" of *The Advice,* where the lady is told

Tis empty admiration all,
'Tis all that you require.

This piece appeared in the supplement to the *Town and Country Magazine* for that year.

* Lort has a note: "His acquaintance at B. Smith, Thistlethwayte, Cary, Fowler, Wm. Mais, called themselves the Juvenile Club, acted plays the drummer." In another list "a club of these geniuses" Lockstone (Asaphides) is added. 11457.

cf. Verses spoken at the Juvenile Society, Asaphides, Feb. 12, 1771. *Lady's Magazine*, Feb., 1771.

Prologue to the Drummer, spoken by Mr. William Mais. May 14, 1771. *Wheble's Lady's Magazine*, May, 1771.

"Dismally sad like Smith's poor wooden verse."—J. Thistlethwaite, *Elegy* (imitating Chatterton) *T. and C. M.*, Feb., 1771.

† 11063, f. 363. Card, "Mr. Fowler's Benefit" Oct. 27. *The Three Old Women Weather Wise* was the interlude, and *The Register Office* the farce, in which Fowler played a Scotsman and an Irishman.

In the *Court and City Magazine* for Feb., 1770 (which contains *Heccar and Gaira*) is a piece " The Discontented Swain," addressed to Miss P.R—y, Bristol, dated Jan. 10 and signed " F." This is almost certainly by Fowler; " Maria's eyes shall guide my steps no more," it runs; " Henceforth in learning will I spend my time," " Newton and Pope with strict attention read." Miss Polly Rumsey of Redcliff Street was being sung as " Maria " in two London periodicals.

In Chatterton's third letter to his mother from London (May 14, 1770), among a long passage about girls—" there are so many pretty milliners, &c. that I have almost forgot myself " —comes a message to Miss Rumsey that if she comes to London she would do well, as an old acquaintance, to send him her address: " London is not Bristol—we may patrole the town for a day, without raising one whisper, or nod of scandal: if she refuses, the curse of all antiquated virgins light on her; may she be refused, when she shall request." Sixteen days later he writes to his sister: " Humbly thanking Miss Rumsey, for her complimentary expression, I cannot think it satisfactory. Does she, or does she not, intend coming to London ? " On June 19, to the same, he says a drunken woman in the street " hobbled out the ever-famous song, in which poor Jack Fowler was to have been satyrized—' I put my hand into a bush: I prick'd my finger to the bone: I saw a ship sailing along; I thought the sweetest flowers to find.' "

At the end of the month, in a letter to Cary,* which appears " metamorphosed into high life," as " genuine copy of a letter from the Earl of C——d to the Hon. Mr. C—," in the *Town and Country* supplement for 1771 (one of many contributions held over by the editors) he says, " I was in love once myself, with whom, think ye ? with the famous Miss Rumsey [" Miss H-l-r," in the magazine]. Three days, three wondrous days, I wore my chain; and as Jack Fowler [" the tuneful laureat " in the magazine] would have added, to make a rhime, and on the fourth I *bursted* it in twain." He then advises his friend, who is in love with Polly Lutley [" the hon. Miss Henrietta B—ll," in the magazine] " when the wound is cicatrised " to " make love

* B. 11063. f. 113, a copy.

to all, and love none" ; and a copy of Hudibrastics follows, urging inconstancy in love : some of the lines are :

> What is this constancy at best,
> A solemn cov'ring for a jest ;
> A painted fool's cap for the wise ;
> A blind to hide a lover's eyes.
> The ladies have this gen'ral rule,
> The man that's constant is a fool ;
> And he that is to none a slave,
> Is little better than a knave.
> This is the sense of woman-kind
> Women but seldom speak the mind...
> But roving you will never fall,
> Be conquer'd by, and conquer all ;
> Be ever welcome to the tea,
> And find the rigid goddess free ;
> 'Till tir'd of rambling, rapture, love,
> You think of happiness above ;
> And, stepping from this glorious life,
> Seek out damnation in a wife.

Finally, on July 11, with the long promised box of presents, about six weeks before his death, he bids his sister remember him to Miss Rumsey, who is wedged between two other flames and three &cs.

But that is not the end of this particular story. In the *Town and Country* for March, 1772, you will find an article entitled "A Bristol Oddity," and signed "Another Oddity Hunter," an attack on one F-l-o, who is first accused of being a quixotic reader of romances, who prepared to hang himself for his Dulcinea, after arranging that his father should enter his room in the nick of time and cut him down. Then, posting to his mistress, he found himself only an object of laughter, and "the paroxysm of his passion being abated, he publickly exalted in his exaltation between heaven and earth, in so glorious a cause as love. 'O what a nobility, what a fortitude of soul have I discovered, in so heroically hanging myself for the lovely Miss R—m—y' was his continual boast." He is next ridiculed for wearing a sword after he had ceased to be a midshipman ("during our last negotiation with Spain"); for trying his luck in London as an actor, buoyed up by his vanity, and being "still obliged to stick to his shoes and strut the Roscius of an alehouse spouting club"; for being turned out of a house of ill-fame and "obliged to walk home in his birth-day suit"; and lastly, after a sample of his spoken sentiments on Bristol, his poetical Cacoethes scribendi is lashed—"I cannot, with any degree of propriety, term him a plagiarist, his duplicates being as just copies of their originals, as a coat with sleeves in the skirts, is of one cut of the usual form." In the "Appendix for 1772" the wretched man, signing himself "J. F-R, Bristol, July 10," indignantly protested against the unknown hand that had defamed him.

In view of this Appendix also containing "Stanzas addressed to Mr. J. F–r of Bristol, a successful Imitator of Sternhold and Hopkins, in humble imitation of his own Doggrel" signed "S.E."* and referring to the New Year's Day Ode signed "J. Fowler, Bristol" in the January number, it would be uncritical to assign the prose attack to Chatterton, though a contribution of his appeared in the *Town and Country* as late as 1783; all one can say is that he did not live to see his rival routed.

Before Miss Rumsey is left, the *Elegy, written at Stanton Drew* (Oct. 27, 1769) should be quoted; it is the only one of Chatterton's acknowledged poems that breathes an amorous passion, if an exception be made of some lines in the first *African Eclogue*. The M.R. of *The Advice* is certainly Maria Rumsey; the Maria of the *Elegy* may be, but improbably, another Maria, or a Maria Rumsey supposed dead (as I like to think, with Wordsworth's "Lucy" to guide me), or a Maria who was never born and never died. Thomas Phillips was lying on the point of death just at this time, as Chatterton knew, and in the Stanton Drew "Maria" he may well be conflating two persons for whom he cared. Anyhow he has achieved real beauty here; and since the poem is of importance as illustrating his love for ancient, primitive things, the fascination violent death always had for him, and his sense

* S.E. are the last letters of James Thistlethwaite, with whom Lort identifies that pseudonym (11063 f. 366); but the writer of "A Bristolian Oddity" must be someone else, because of the phrase "wedded as close as the heart of Jemmy Th-ss-l-th-te is to that meanest of all vices, lying." Perhaps the avenger was Cary.

of changing rhythms, it is here given entire with the readings of the Columbia (the only known) MS.

Joyless I hail the solemn gloom,
Joyless I view the pillars vast and rude,
Where erst the foot of superstition trod,
In smoking blood imbrued,
And rising from the tomb,
Mistaken homage to an unknown God.
Fancy whither dost thou stray,
Whither dost thou wing thy way,
Check the rising wild delight,
Ah ! what avails this awful sight
MARIA is no more !

Why, curst remembrance, wilt thou haunt my mind,
The blessings past are mis'ry now,
Upon her lovely brow
Her lovelier soul she wore,
Soft as the evening gale
When breathing perfumes thro' the rose-hedged vale,
She was my joy, my happiness refin'd.
All hail, ye solemn horrors of this scene,
The blasted oak, the dusky green.

Ye dreary altars by whose side
The druid priest in crimson dyed
The solemn dirges sung,
And drove the golden knife,
Into the palpitating seat of life.*
As rent with horrid shouts the distant valleys rung,
The bleeding body bends,
The glowing purple stream ascends,
Whilst the troubled spirit near
Hovers in the steamy air,†
Again the sacred dirge they sing,
Again the distant hill and coppic'd valley ring.‡

* His knife with deep incision sought the breast.
The Constabiliad (Oct. 30, 1769).

Where Albion slept beneath the fatal Tree,
And the Druid's golden knife
Rioted in human gore
In offerings of Human Life ?
Blake, *Jerusalem*.

† Hover through the fog and filthy air.
Macbeth, I. 1.

‡ The words shall to me answer, and my Eccho ring.
Spenser, *Epithalamion* (refrain).

Soul of my dear Maria haste,
Whilst my languid spirits waste,
When from this my prison free,
Catch my soul, it flies to thee;
Death had doubly arm'd his dart,
In piercing thine it pierc'd my heart.

The M, to whom the Shoreditch *Elegy* (May 20, 1770) in the May *Town and Country* is addressed, might be the same person; a MS. copy of it at Bristol is endorsed by Dean Milles "a poem by Chatterton on Maria."*

I dare the danger of the mould'ring wall,
  Nor heed the arch that totters o'er my head:
O! quickly may the friendly ruin fall,
  Release me of my love, and strike me dead.†

though it would be bold to refer the last line "Thy smile or censure seals my final fate" to "Does she, or does she not intend coming to London?"

Now for the other names in the catalogue; too much importance must not be attached to them in view of his promise to write to some hundreds, and his leaving the young ladies all the letters they have had from him, assuring them that they need be under no apprehensions from the appearance of his ghost, as he dies for none of them. In the piece called *Astrea Brokage* (Jan. 3, 1770), the supposed female correspondent describes him as "a young author, who has read more than Magliabechi, and wrote more love-letters than Ovid," who is continually invoking the Nine to describe her, but never pays a compliment to her person without a concomitant one to her understanding. These were the days of the *Essay on Woman*, and the poet's attitude seems to have been neither that of a buck nor a rake—which characters he carefully differentiates in *Journal 6th*, addressed to Baker (Sept. 30,

* 11457.

† Imitated by *Asaphides* in the *Lady's Magazine* for Dec., 1770.

Pensive I range beneath the tott'ring wall
Which eating time is mouldering fast away;
Oh! that the quivering ruin soon would fall,
And crush my body to its primal clay!

Lort has a note: "C. raised up poets and imitators and satirists." 11457.

1769), but that of a male coquette. In attack he was of the intrepid type, and seems to have profited by Thomas Carew's poem, "Boldness in Love," printed in Cibber's *Lives of the Poets* :

So shalt thou thrive in love, fond boy ;
If thy tears and sighs discover
Thy grief, thou never shalt enjoy
The just reward of a bold lover.

He writes to Baker (there are no stops in the MS.) :

Such Tremors never coward me
I'm flattring impudent & free
Unmov'd by frowns and lowring eyes
'Tis Smiles I only ask and Prize
And when the Smile is freely given
You're in the highway Road to Heaven.

The moral of *Colin Instructed* (1770) is

Others do more than sigh their tale
To black-eyed Biddy of the Dale.

There was Sally Clarke (two poems) ; Skeat thought she was the Miss C who played the harpsichord ; Polly Bush,* to whom he announces his African project ; one "Fanny of the Hill," where "Betsy" was substituted—Shenstone had written *Nancy of the Vale*—doubtless Redcliff Hill ; a Miss C——am, whom he informs, with the approach of Spring, 1770

This passion celestial by heav'n was designed
The only fixed means of improving the mind ;

Miss Love, on whose name he proposed to publish "a crambo Song" ; she may be the Miss "P L" of *The Complaint* (*Universal Magazine*, Nov., 1769). In the *New Song to Mr. G. Catcott* (1769) the Misses Turner, Harding,† Grimes, and Flavia "blasted and old" are mentioned, also Miss Cotton, who was handsome till she returned his letter :

* Bush, George, cooper, 2 Redcliff St. 1775 Directory, where there are seven Bushes.

† Of five Hardings, one is Harding & Co., distillers and vinegar makers, 101 Redcliff Street, and another Sarah Harding, 1 Redcliff paving on churchyard.

She's damnable ugly, my Vanity cried,
  You lie, says my Conscience, you lie ;
Resolving to follow the dictates of Pride,
  I drew her a hag to my eye.

Here the point is

I scorn'd like a monkey to dangle my chain.

Catcott has let us into the secret that her Christian name was Lydia, and that she was the recipient of the copy of verses beginning "To use a worn out simile"* ; and the Redcliff register supplements him by stating that (just a year and two months after Chatterton's death) on Oct. 24, 1771, Lydia Cotton of Redcliff parish married Nevill Bath of the parish of St. Thomas by licence ; the bridegroom is designated cutler and hardware man of 1 Redcliff Street in Sketchley's directory of 1775.

The letter home of May 14, 1770, gives more names ; Miss Sandford, Miss Broughton (possibly related to the Vicar of Redcliff), Miss Baker, Miss Porter, Miss Watkins, who made herself ridiculous by a letter that was never intended for her but another young lady in the neighbourhood of the same name,† Miss Sukey Webb, Miss Singer,‡ whom he left in a very bad way, "that is in a way to be married," and Miss Thatcher§, who may depend on it that if he is not in love with her he is in love with nobody else, the rival here being the "whining, sighing, dying, pulpit-fop Lewis."

Miss Cotton, he says, he had offended somehow ; he begs pardon ; whatever has happened happened without his consent, but he did not give her this assurance when in Bristol, lest it should seem like an attempt to avoid the anger of her *furious* brother. The frankness with which he discusses the female coterie, of whose transaction she demands a journal of his sister,

* B.5374, f. 57.

† Of eighteen Watkinses in the 1775 Directory, two, a currier and leather dresser, and a lemon and orange warehouseman, lived in Redcliff St.

‡ Singer, Elizabeth, corn and flower shop, 75 Redcliff Hill, the only person of that name in the Directory ; out of three Redcliff Webbs, one, William Webb, kept *The Jolly Brewers*, 106 Redcliff Street.

§ Of three Thatchers, one is a stocking maker in Redcliff St., and another a shoemaker on Redcliff Hill.

is interesting in view of the fact that we have only one side of his domestic correspondence. But there is no doubt that his attentions were promiscuous, and that he must have known a girl or two of whom he did not speak to his mother and sister. The " worn out simile " in his verses to Lydia Cotton, is to the bee, which

> Alike from scents which give distaste
> By Fancy as disgusting placed
> Repletes his useful thighs.

Here, like Edmund in *Lear*, or perhaps rather Churchill in *The Prophecy of Famine*, he avows his dedication to Nature :

> In natural religion free
> I to no other bow the knee
> Nature's the god I own.

but an eighteenth-century nature, not Rimbaud's

> A Toi, Nature ! je me rends,
> Et ma faim et toute ma soif ;
> Et s'il te plâit, nourris, abreuve.*

The verses end with the characteristic stanza

> This vanity, this impudence
> Is all the merit, all the sense
> Thro' which to fame I trod ;
> These (by the Trinity 'tis true)
> Procure me friends and notice too,
> And shall gain you, by God.

This puts one in mind of his saying that God had sent his creatures into the world with arms long enough to reach anything, if they could be at the trouble of extending them !† But a very young man who observes that everything may be acquired by diligence and abstinence, and despises the rest of the world, can only have a use for women as recreation, and indulge the same feeling concerning them as did Keats before he met Fanny Brawne ; since it is a redoubtable fact that no male

* *Patience* (*Les Illuminations*).
† *L. and M.*, p. 160,

creature, whatever his age or talents, can impose himself on the world as a poet, in his lifetime, at any rate, without paying some attention to the sex. Chatterton, whose whole ambition was literary fame, realized this. Marriage, during his apprenticeship, was out of the question, though at best it might be " a stagnant pool of life." He cultivated these girls largely, as we should say now, for purposes of publicity, starring himself as the intellectual Don Juan of Bristol (the Bristol that he knew) rather than as " a devil of a buck," like his creation, Bob Barter :

" You may see him in the morning, sitting under a shed on the key registering the weight of sugars, and in the evening shining at a ball. He overturns a basket of oysters, or beats a dog, with a better grace than any youthful votary of Bacchus, in that elegant city."*

He was not of that type, but he had a waspish satirical twist which served him in his environment as well as healthy eighteenth-century brutality. In *Kew Gardens* he writes of himself thus :

Is there a street within this spacious place†
That boasts the happiness of one fair face
Where conversation does not turn on you,
Blaming your wild amours, your morals too ?
Oaths, sacred and tremendous oaths you swear,
Oaths, which might shock a Luttrell's soul to hear ;
Those very oaths, as if a thing of joke,
Made to betray, intended to be broke ;
Whilst the too tender and believing maid
(Remember pretty Fanny) is betray'd.

Making every allowance for youthful exaggeration and the desire, always strong in him, to put himself wrong in people's eyes—*épater le bourgeois*, I say he was promiscuous ; possibly he grew more careless as he grew more embittered, but the

* *Astrea Brokage.*
† cf. Is there a man of an eternal vein
Who lulls the town in winter with his strain,
At Bath in summer chants the reigning lass,
And sweetly whistles, as the waters pass ?
Young, *Love of Fame*, Satire I.

proof lies in his handwriting. Two letters of females to him are extant; only one of them is dated; but Masson, who first quoted the undated one, assigns it to the same period, near the end of his time in Bristol. Both bear a cynical endorsement by the poet, and illustrate a cardinal point in his nature, that of giving people as good as, or worse than, they sent.

The British Museum document (5766 B. f. 92) is in a crude, coarse hand on a small piece of paper that has been folded. The allusion to the gingerbread is obscure, but may refer to Chatterton's liking for it; Masson ingeniously connects it with the tradition* of his distributing gingerbread on the steps of St. Mary Redcliff before leaving for London; we can say no more than that it is an anonymous note of insult in doggerel.

> "Sir,
> I send my Love to you and
> Tell you Thiss if you prove Constant I
> not miss but if you frown and torn a way
> I can make Cart of better Hay pray Excep
> of me Love Hartley an send me word Cartingley
> Tell me how maney ouncs of Gre'n Ginger
> Bread can show the Eaker [?] of Honiste
> My house is not bilt with Stavis I
> not be Coarted by Boys nor Navis
> I Haive a man an man shall Haive me
> if I whaint a fool I send for the
> if you are going to the D
> I wish you a good Gonery"

The endorsement is headed:

"The Letter Paraphras'd"

Masson calls this retort "rather jocular."† To my ear and mind it speaks an implacably angry and outraged pride; it is *in essence* less obscene than splenetic. Even so, two lines

> Go * * * * green sickness girls and wenches
> On Bulks, in Lanes on Tombs on Benches.

* Mrs. Stephens, *ap.* George Cumberland.

† *Chatterton* (ed. 1899) p. 96. The rest of the twenty lines are suppressed at the publishers' desire; I regret that the reader should be debarred from testing my judgment by the evidence, but I am told that the language is too outspoken to be printed.

are an echo of David Mallet's (d. 1765) *Tyburn*:

> Sons of Fleet-ditch, of bulks, of benches
> Where peer and porter meet their wenches.

The other document is in the Bristol Library; the writer, whose name does not occur in the poet's letters to his family, is a person of more refinement than the anonymous girl; lines have been ruled in pencil, and the paper sealed with red wax, though unaddressed. The name Saunders was not a rare one at Bristol in his days, and it has already occurred here apropos of his father and the Pile Street School; Sketchley's directory, among seven persons bearing it in 1775, includes Hester Saunders, distiller of 15 Peter Street, John Saunders, victualler of The Fox, Redcliff Street, and William Saunders, glazier, of 79 Redcliff Hill.

> "Sir
> to a Blage you I wright a few Lines to you
> But have not the weakness to be Believe
> all you say of me for you may say as
> [erasure] much to other young Ladys for all I now
> But I Can't go out of a Sunday with you
> for I ham a fraid we Shall be seen toge[ther]
> Sir if it agreeble to you I had Take a walk with
> you in the morning for I be [erasure] Beliue
> we shant be seen a bout 6 a Clock
> But we must wait with patient for
> there [erasure] is a Time for all Things 1770
> April 3
> ESTHER SAUNDERS"

Beneath the recipient has written in a small, neat hand:

> "There is a time for all things—Except Marriage my Dear
> And so your hbl Serv[t].
> T. CHATTERTON,
> April 9th."

The endorsement is longer:

> "This Affair began Mar. 19th 70
> & broke off April 9th 70—
> The Young Lady wants to be
> married and can't keep her own
> Secrets—

N.B. Having no great Stomach to the Amour for
divers good Causes and Considerations she
therefrom otherwise moving, and having
been forc'd into Correspondence by the Officiousness
of B. was very indifferent about it &
far from being chagrin[d] at dismission
Had also the pleasure of seeming to break
first—
☛ The Lady is not handsom but a great Fortune
† Miss W. a very pretty Girl now in Chace."*

The wild gay young attorney's clerk, to be sure, but not the author of Rowley!

NOTE ON THE JUVENILE SOCIETY

THE *locus classicus* (if that is not too big a term to apply to what has not been reprinted hitherto) for this facet of provincial life in eighteenth century England, so essential to the understanding of Chatterton's position, is an article headed "*A* Bristol *Spouting-Club*" in the *Town and Country Magazine* for June, 1771, and dated that month. It was probably composed later than his time, as "repaving" is referred to, but who wrote it is inessential.† Part of the opening paragraph has been quoted in regard to demolitions and improvements; the salient features of his prentice environment, i.e., the youth of its members, their spirit of literary emulation, jingoism, dramatic zest, and satirical tendencies come out clearly in the following consecutive extracts.

"Nor are we altogether without literary improvements, a fondness for which seems to be infused even in the lower classes of society: amongst other modern refinements, there is started up a set of geniuses, who call themselves spouters, and have formed a society which they term a *spouting club.* These young artisans meet in a hired room at a public house, near the Exchange, once every fortnight, very prudently reflecting that their finances would be wonderfully impoverished

* Printed in the *Bristol Guardian.* March 26, 1921. "B" might be Burgum, or Broughton (see p. 332).

† The article is signed "Cosmopolitus." The writer of "Cosmopolitus Detected" in the July number attributes it to Harry Croker's (Henry Cruger's) apprentice, as Thomas Cary was.

by a weekly three-penny disbursement, besides the deposit of two-pence for supporting the general fund, which is expended as occasion requires in scenery, habits, truncheons, swords, and other theatrical properties.

" These disciples of Melpomene chuse to keep their scheme as private as the nature of the undertaking will admit, as many of the principal performers are still in their non-age, and servants by covenant for a certain term; but like lads of spirit, detest controul, scorn the drudgery of dirty mechanics, and pant for fame in the more glorious fields of literature. Here they give full scope to their natural free-born sentiments, curse the inventors of subordination and servitude, lament that Britons should ever be restrained, and, like true sons of liberty (for they are all staunch patriots) rail at their masters for keeping them to their duty: these are the mighty potentates they fear, who, were they to get scent of their haunt, would doubtless apply to the corporation (who it seems are plaguy enemies to the muses) when our young heroes, perhaps, at the very moment they were immortalizing their names, by sacrificing their lives for the good of their country, or some other noble exertion of human nature, might be hurried off, by virtue of a justice's warrant, to a situation not quite so agreeable in the house of correction. Besides, the proprietor of the premises not having obtained the King's licence for the toleration of a theatre, would probably undergo some severe censures from these foes to the republic of letters.

" Here the apprentice, who trembles at the commanding voice of his master, being stripped of his timidity and his apron, transforms himself to the victorious general of an army. Here you may see a blacksmith dying at the feet of a sempstress, a taylor roaring in Bajazet, a turner in Sir John Brute, or, by a Garrick-like transition, starting in Richard or Hamlet—here a phantom,

—clear'd of his deadly white,
Rises a haberdasher to the sight;

a linen-draper's shop boy in vellum, a bookseller's in tinsel, whilst a young lady in the neighbourhood, the only daughter and heiress of a very eminent cobbler, squeaks in Mrs. Abigail. Here are basket-makers, barbers, distillers, carvers, carpenters, and butchers, who bid fair to be great ornaments to the stage and society, though but very indifferent tradesmen.

" In this group of dirty-faced wits, are three or four *authors* and *poets*, who have already composed, or at least transposed, more verses than Dryden or Pope ever wrote, and with much more elegance and fire, as these prodigies of erudition, their fellow members, very confidently assert. The effusions of their brains are eclogues, elegies, epigrams, epitaphs, odes and satires, with the last of which they keep their neighbours in awe ; for if a man by any transaction has rendered himself ridiculous, these wits immediately publish his folly in a lampoon, by setting his name at the top of a half-penny publication, called A new Copy of Verses, to the great diversion of themselves and the public. Some cavilling critics, indeed, charge our adventurers with many heinous crimes, such as plagiarism and parricides upon their mother tongue, &c., but these we may suppose are rather the offspring of envy, from the conviction of superior abilities, than the dictates of truth and justice."

A writer in the *Monthly Mirror* for Sept., 1809, who states that much of the Bristolian articles in the *Town and Country* for 1771 is Chatterton's and that he has forgotten the characters, except Cruger, that are mentioned there, goes on : " A gentleman I once knew told me that he was a school fellow of Chatterton, and said what an extraordinary boy he was, but continued he, *we* three, naming another person, carried all before us. I do not remember the surname of this gentleman, my acquaintance, but I recollect he was a merchant settled in our *then* North-American dominions. He had little appearance of a trafficker—he seemed more in his manner and conversation an elegant French wit ; yet he understood commerce well, I was told. He remarked that Chatterton himself and their friend, were all poor boys of Bristol." The person referred to may well have been Cary ; and James Thistlethwaite, who, Lort tells us, " was put out by the parish," would do for the third, well enough.

Among the Chatterton MSS. in the British Museum, at the back of " There was a Broder of Orderys Whyte " (5766B. f. 88), and characteristically surrounded by rough coats of arms, is a note in his hand:

The Czar	Mr Thomas
Alcibiades	Williams
Pitholeon	Fowler
Messalina	P.R.

It must be either the key of a satire, or the cast of a play, in either case a relic of his connection with the " Juveniles "; and " P.R." *may* stand for " Polly Rumsey."

CHAPTER IX

THE BRIDGE AND THE PARCHMENTS

THE thread of the story has been broken. When he wrote to Baker in March, 1768, though a few of his associates may have judged him a smart but intractable lad, Chatterton had not achieved any more notoriety in his native place than the insertion of poems or squibs in *Felix Farley* may have gained for him ; but by the end of that year his name was blown about to the extent of enquiries being made after him by two local *literati*. This fatal result, as it was to prove, was effected by an aptly timed pseudo-archaic piece of journalism in the columns of the paper which had printed his devotional effort of 1763.

His connection with that paper, we may be sure, had been fairly constant, though not everything he sent was printed. Lort has a note : " Mr. Cocking, printer of the Bristol Journal, says a boy used to bring him some things to print in his paper, but he considered him as the bringer only ; several being satirical on persons in Bristol he would not insert them." Though this may refer to a slightly later time, it is in point.*

On Feb. 6 (and also in *Boddely's Bath Journal* for Feb. 8) is an account of " Sir Oliver Wilkie's Election dinner 1561," thus introduced : " As the topic of conversation previous to a general election is that of expensive entertainments, the following, though not new, may not be unacceptable to your readers." The bill of the dinner, which is stupid enough, follows, and the contributor, "Z," says he found it in an old Herodotus. It was indeed not new, having appeared in the issue for July 4, 1761, signed " T.R.," when Chatterton was not yet nine ; thus he

* See note at end of chapter.

can be acquitted of it; it showed, however, that mock antiquity, if used to illustrate current events, was acceptable to the editor.

On Sept. 17 (*Bath Journal*, Sept. 19) under the signature "Probus" (which was used by Chatterton in his letter to the Lord Mayor, Beckford, *Political Register*, June, 1770) appears "A card to John Wilkes, Esq. on hearing the rampant Exaltation of a Club of Scotchmen on his receiving sentence last June," twenty lines of inflammatory hectoring, the first and last couplets running:

Such are the honours thy lov'd country pays,
So patriots suffer when curst faction sways.

Then in each Briton's breast thou'll stand approv'd,
Not Cæsar e'er by Rome so much belov'd.

But there was a topic nearer and dearer to the Bristolians than either of these, namely their bridge. They had one on the site of the present structure as far back as the twelfth century. The ancient bridge of 1247 (with the chapel to St Mary, which was described by William of Worcester, and destroyed, all but two arches, in 1649) had, by 1758, become too narrow and impracticable for the city's needs; and in 1760, after much dispute as to the method for raising the money, an Act of Parliament was obtained for building a new one. Thereafter followed, while a temporary structure was in use, two years' controversy and seventy-six meetings of the trustees about the designs—one party favouring a single arch, the other a new bridge on the old piers—with a rain of pamphlets and weekly newspaper skirmishings. Finally Mr. James Bridges's scheme for three arches on the old piers was adopted, and the foundation stone laid on March 28, 1764. By 1768 the approaches to the bridge had been cleared on both sides by the removal of the Shambles (the site of the present Bridge Street), old houses in Thomas Street and Redcliff Street, and the re-erection of St. Nicholas' Church, the city gate of St. Nicholas having gone, as we have seen, about 1762. On Michaelmas Day the retiring mayor, George Weare, crossed the new bridge in a coach, and the opening for the general public was in November.*

Here was an excellent opportunity for gauging the effect on the Bristol public of some of the antique prose and poetry Chatterton had by this time secretly composed (indeed George Catcott said that on their first acquaintance he mentioned by name almost all the poems which afterwards appeared in print†), and on Oct. 1, 1768, a fortnight after the bridge had been opened for foot traffic, there appeared in *Felix Farley's Bristol Journal*:

MR. PRINTER

> The following Description of the Mayor's first Passing over the Old Bridge, taken from an old Manuscript, may not at this time be unacceptable to the Generality of your Readers.
>
> Your's &c
>
> DUNHELMUS BRISTOLIENSIS

On Fridaie was the Time fixed for passing the new Brydge: Aboute the Time of the Tollynge the tenth Clock, Master Greggorie Dalbenye,‡ mounted on a Fergreyne Horse, enformed Master Maior all thynges were prepared; when two Beadils went fyrst streyng fresh Stre, next came a manne dressed up as follows...Hose of Goatskyn, Crinepart outwards, Doublet and Waistcoat also, over which a white Robe without sleeves, much like an Albe, but not so longe, reeching but to his Lends; a girdle of azure over his left Shoulder, rechde also to his Lends on the Ryght, and doubled back to his Left, bucklyng with a gouldin Buckel, dangled to his knee; thereby representing a Saxon Elderman. . . . In his Hande he bare a Shield, the Maystrie of Gille a Brogton,§ who paincted the same, representynge Saincte Werburgh crossynge the Ford. Then a mickle strong Manne, in Armour, carried a huge Anlace; after whom came six Claryons and six Minstrels, who sang the song of Saincte Warburgh; then came Master Maior, mounted on

* Barrett, *History of Bristol*, p. 95, sqq; Latimer, *Bristol in the Eighteenth Century*, p. 335, sqq. Emmanuel Collins (*Miscellanies*, 1762, p. 136) writes: "I believe there has been more noise made about building this single bridge at Bristol than there has been about erecting both in London."

† *Monthly Review*. May, 1777. This was one of the great Rowleian arguments for Chatterton not being the author of them.

‡ An old Bristol name; "Dominus Wilelmus Dawbeny miles," buried in choir of the Black Friars. *W. Worcester*, p. 234, (ed. 1778).

§ In *The Ryse of Peyncteynge*, sent in his first letter to Horace Walpole, Chatterton says Gille a Brogtonne, "depycted notable yn eau." The Vicar of Redcliff, Thomas Broughton, occurs to one.

a white Horse, dight with sable Trappyngs, wrought by the Nunnes of Saincte Kenna, with Gould and Silver; his Hayr brayded with Ribbons, and a Chaperon, with the auntient arms of Brystowe fastende on his Forehead. . . . Master Maior bare in his Hande a Gouldin Rodde, and a Congeon Squier bare in his Hande his Helmet, waulking by the syde of the Horse: then came the Eldermen and Cittie Broders mounted on sable Horses, dyght with white Trappyngs and Plumes, and scarlet Copes and Chapeous, having thereon sable Plumes; after them the Preestes and Freeres, Parysh, Mendicaunt and secular, some syngyng Saincte Warburgh's Song, others soundyng Clarions thereto, and others some Citrialles. . . . In thilk Manner reechyng the Brydge the Manne with the anlace stode on the fyrst Top of a Mound, yree[r]d in the midst of the Bridge; then want up the Manne with the Sheelde, after him the Minstrels and Clarions. And then the Preestes and Freeres, all in white Albs, makyng a most goodlie Shewe; the Maior and Eldermen standyng round, theie sang, with the sound of Clarions, the Song of Sancte Baldwyn; which beyng done, the Manne on the Top threwe with great Myght his Anlace into the See, and the Clarions sounded an auntiant Charge and Forloyn: Then theie sang againe the Song of Saincte Warburgh, and proceeded up Chrysts Hill, to the Cross, when a Latin sermon was preached by Ralph de Blundeville. And with sound of Clarion theie agayne went to the Brydge, and there dined, spendyng the rest of the Daie in Sportes and Plaies, the Freers of Saincte Augustine doeyng the Plaie of the Knyghtes of Bristowe, makynge a greate Fire at Night on Kynwulph Hyll.*

All the hard words in this piece are in John Kersey's *Dictionarium Anglo-Britannicum*, 1708, except *Fergreyne*, iron grey, apparently a coinage, and Kersey has "Fer-de-moulin," which would give the hint for such a compound. *Crine part*, the hairy side, is got from "*crined* (L. in *Heraldry*) having hairs"; *lends* "(O) the loins," *maystry* "(O) a masterpiece," *anlace* "(O) a falchion or sword, in shape resembling a Scithe," *chaperon* "(F) in *Heraldry*, a little Escutcheon fixed on the Fore-heads of the horses that draw the Hearse at a Funeral," *congeon* "(O) a dwarf," *chapeau* "(F) a hat," *citriale* "a cittern or guittar, *Chaucer*," *forloyn* "(O) a retreat," are Kersey's explanations, "O" standing for "old word." The piece was printed without a glossary. The style is perhaps not directly traceable to any one source, though the description of the Kenilworth minstrel of 1575 from Robert Laneham's letter,

* "Thomas de Blunderville, a prieste" appears in *An Account of William Canynge*, one of the first pieces handed to Catcott.

quoted in Percy's Essay (*Reliques*, Vol. I) shows certain points of resemblance.

What is presumably the original MS., with Barrett's side-notes, in the British Museum (5766B. f. 12) corresponds with the newspaper version, but has not the words " at this time " in the address to the Printer ; moreover, it is followed by the *Songe of Saincte Werburgh,* which fills up the rest of the sheet; the fourth and last verse runs :

> Now agayne with bremie* Force,
> Severn in his auntient Course,
> Rolls his rappyd streeme alonge,
> With a Sable,† swift and stronge
> Movynge manie a okie wode—
> We, the Menne of Brystowe towne,
> Have yreed this Brydge of Stone ;
> Wyshyng echone it maie last,
> Till the date of daies be past
> Standyng where the other stode.

This version is far less antiquated than that printed in Milles's edition, which contains the other song supposed to be sung on the occasion, that of " Sayncte Baldwynne "—Whann Norrurs‡ and hys menne of myghte, &c. If the poet wanted to see his verses in print, he was disappointed, for the prose account only was inserted.

The titles of these two songs show the completely reckless spirit in which he dealt with antiquity. As for St. Werburgh, there is no *male* saint of that name, as he probably knew, for St. Werburgh's Church stood (till 1878) in Corn Street at no great distance from Lambert's office. In *Turgot's account of Bristol* we are told " Thys Wareburga was baptyzed bye Saynte Warburgus, and had a Chyrche ybuilte to her by the Bristowans " ; and in *The Storie of William Canynge,* after Ælla," Next holie Wareburghus fylld mie mynde." Chatterton was seldom satisfied with any fact that he found, but, like his own saint,

* Breme, " (O) furiously," K.
† F. Sand. K. has " Sabliere, a Sand-Pit."
‡ " Norrurs" is a legacy from " the king of Norse " in *Hardyknute.*

Tho blest with what us men accounts as store
Saw something further and saw something more.
Sancte Warbur.

The attributes of this personage have been lifted from St. Christopher. The poet was, indeed—it cannot be said too often—not a cunning forger at all (he had no need to be in that century and that milieu) but an undisciplined Puckish Romanticist.

St. Baldwin, again, we may be sure, was not the saint of Laon, of whom he had probably never heard, but an eponymous saint for Baldwin Street, which, according to a Bristol librarian one century later, was named after Baldwin Earl of Flanders, whose daughter Matilda, wife of William the Conqueror, was possessed of Bristol."*

The pseudonym, of which the initials D.B. were henceforth frequently used by him, needs explanation. The "Durham man of Bristol" is meant for Turgot, who was a real person, prior of Durham and a historian.† Chatterton, who read of him in Camden's Britannia (ed. 1695, pp. 776, 783,) has foisted on him a discourse of Bristol in "Saxonnes Latyn" (of which Barrett has made copious use), as well as the "Ur-text" of *Battle of Hastings.* Rowley was to be Turgot's translator and emender‡ in the fifteenth century just as Chatterton was Rowley's in the eighteenth. Behind Turgot, mercifully, we cannot go in this labyrinth of make-believe. So much then for "Dunhelmus Bristoliensis," and we can thus the better understand Chatterton's lament to William Smith that he knew no Latin,§ else we might have even had the pseudo-Turgot in that tongue, as well as in what Skeat called Rowleyese.

A jolly enough piece of pageantry (and as good as any of the

* John Taylor, letter to Sir Daniel Wilson, 22 Feb, 1869, *penes me,* as Barrett would say.

† See D.N.B., article "Turgot." The actual signature I take to have been evolved from "Simeon Dunelmensis," which he could find writ large at the beginning of Leland's *Itinerary,* Vol. VII, ed. Hearne, containing Bristol matter, which he certainly used: and see Gibson's *Camden* (ed. 1695, p. 779, additions to Durham): "*Simeon Dunelmensis* indeed (or rather Abbot *Turgot*) tells us," &c.

‡ All this business of "emendals" and "additions" was doubtless suggested by Gibson's edition of Camden's Britannia.

§ Bryant, *Obs.*, p. 532.

prose Rowley pieces incidentally), the newspaper contribution at once attracted notice, and enquiries were made at the office in Small Street, just round the corner from Lambert's, for the owner of the pseudonym. The printer could give no information, but after much enquiry it was discovered that " the person who brought the copy " was a youth between fifteen and sixteen named Thomas Chatterton, a Redcliff youth descended from sextons of the church. He was threatened—" agreeably to his age and appearance " are Croft's words—as a child, but " returned nothing but haughtiness and a refusal to give any account." On the application of milder usage he first said, anxious, no doubt, not to have to produce any originals, that he was employed to transcribe certain ancient MSS. by a gentleman who had engaged him to write love verses (see his letter to Baker of March 6)* ; this answer not satisfying the questioners, he said the original of the contribution was found by his father,† with many other MSS. in a large chest in the upper room over the chapel on the north side of Redcliff Church. This, apparently, was vouchsafed after many promises had been held out to him. It is practically certain that George Catcott, who took him up three weeks or a month later, was the main party to this scrutiny ; the questioners, anyhow, were made thoroughly happy by the last admission.‡

Now the mischief has fairly started ; and, leaving all excuses for boyish love of mystery and deception aside, we may be sure that Chatterton lied in this matter chiefly because he wanted fame as soon as possible. If he had been honest and said in effect, " This is all my own work, and there is plenty more at my home on Redcliff Hill," or in Corn Street, or wherever he had stowed it, curiosity would have been stilled

* Gregory, *Life*, p. 30, from Lort, (Apr., 1772), 11063, whose words are " pretended he was employed by a gentleman to write verses in praise of a lady whom he courted and occasionally to transcribe some of these old poems." Writing to Walpole on July 20, 1778, Lort adds this comment : " This prevented their being much surprised at not seeing the originals, though at the pressing solicitations of Mr. Barrett, he did after some time produce one or two vellum leaves." Nichols, *L. I.*, VII, p. 539.

† He had *received* them from his father (!) are the terms of the statement as given by Catcott to Tyrwhitt. Preface, *Rowley* (1777), p. vii.

‡ Preface to Tyrwhitt's edition (1777), *L. and M.* pp. 129, 163. *Gentleman's Magazine*, Dec., 1838. (Richard Smith's letter).

at once, and he, probably, sent about his business, not to speak of a word in Lambert's ear, who already knew of the scurrilous letter to the schoolmaster. At the best it would have been years before he was patronized as a writer of antique verse, and at the worst telling the truth would have gone near to stamping him as an unsatisfactory scrivener's apprentice. Nor, in the circumstances, is it credible that telling the truth ever occurred to him, except here and there, as his pride suggested, for neither Bristol nor London had a use for " imitations of our old poets " except by well-known names, or possibly, by gentlemen who could afford to publish them; but the Bristol of 1768 *had* a use for old civic records, whether in prose or verse, for nothing resembling a history of the city had yet been written, save a collection of charters printed in 1736, and the inchoate *Bristollia* of Hooke (1748). The Red Book and Ricart had not been given to the world, and the labours of Leland and William of Worcester remained locked up in Hearne's learned edition, and the library of a Cambridge college respectively. As a poet, there was no place for him save in magazines and newspapers; as a discoverer of ancient Bristol relics an honourable one awaited him, in no wise derogating from his indentures, in an age far from critical, and a community where, to a very large extent, local vainglory did duty for intelligence.

But, over and above this, he was not a straight-forward person, and the alternative may not even have presented itself.* At least three books of "Antiquities " had been written, and his masterpiece *Ælla* no doubt conceived, since he speaks of copies of several ancient poems and an interlude being procurable, in his letter to Dodsley of Dec. 21, not three months after the publication of the " Bridge " article. In fact much

* " He was not, however, of an open or ingenuous disposition, and, consequently, would never give any satisfactory account of what he possessed: but only from time to time, as his necessities obliged him, produced some transcripts from these originals, and it was with great difficulty, and some expense, I procured what I have." George Catcott, in *Monthly Review*, May, 1777. *Rowley*, on the other hand, according to this illuminate, was far otherwise: " If, besides this, we consider that extreme modesty (so inseparable from great minds) with which he speaks of himself and what he calls his " unworthie Poems,' " &c., &c., &c. " all these things give us so high an idea of the goodness of his heart, that we cannot forbear loving the man, as much as we admire the poet."

work was ready; if Thistlethwaite be believed, at least one "original" had been fabricated long before; and the intention was probably to produce pieces from the hoard, according as the wind blew. But the quiet sensation produced by the Oct. 1 issue of *Felix Farley* forced Chatterton into the declaration of his position as discoverer of MS. treasure trove in his city, to which he unflinchingly adhered to the day of his death.

Now what was the truth about the MSS. in the chest? A very simple matter really. In the muniment room, or Treasury, over the north porch of St. Mary Redcliff were, and are, several coffers, one of which was known as "Mr. Canynges' Cofre"; this contained the writings and rents of estates left for particular purposes by that benefactor (the fifteenth century merchant) and was secured by six keys, two of which were entrusted to the minister and procurator of the church, two to the mayor, and one to each of the churchwardens. These being lost, about 1727, according to Dr. Gregory,* who gives this account, following Bryant, who had it from Henry Dampier, a notion prevailed that some title deeds were in the "cofre," and an order of the vestry was made that it should be opened under the inspection of an attorney, and the more important deeds removed to the south porch. Accordingly not only this but all the coffers were broken open, the deeds relating to the church removed, and the rest left "exposed as of no value."

There is this much confirmation of the statement extant to-day in the Redcliff Vestry Book, No. 1:

"26 April 1722

"At a meeting of the Vestry this day it was ordered that the Churchwarden Mr Jno Price shall cause the way from the stile at the North Corner of Mr Davises garden wall to be pitched and likewise alsoe that he cause the old writings in the Treasury be again examin'd clean'd and put by in a safe place free from dust."

* *Life*, p. 31, sqq. Cf. "Item, the morowe vpon All Sowlen day, the Maire is vsid to walk to Redclyff, and the Toune clerk with him; there to sytte in Audite vpon William Canynges ij chauntryes, and the vicorye and the propters [i.e. Proctors, Procurators] with them. And aftir the seide Audyte is fynesshid, the Toune clerk to entre thaccompte of the same in a boke there, callid Canynges liger, and there the Maire to receyve 1 noble, the toune clerk xxd., the swerdberer viijd., and the four Sergeauntez of the Maire xvi d."
Ricart's Kalendar, ed. L. T. Smith, p. 79.

This minute is signed by John Gibb, "minister," and nine others.

Now though there were other depredators, including one Morgan, a barber, whose "rotten papers" (as Thistlethwaite called them) came into Barrett's hands, and a woman who carried off a lapful to clean her kitchen furniture,* the master of the Pile Street school, it may be remembered, had to find his forty pupils pens, ink and paper; so what more natural, when the vicar, Mr. Gibb, not long before his death,† presented the twenty boys who read best with a Bible apiece, that Thomas Chatterton senior, who, as nephew of the sexton John Chatterton, had the run of the church, should make use of these parchments to cover the Bibles, in order to preserve the latter (note that early deeds, being generally small, would serve ill for this purpose), especially when before this time he is known to have filled a whole "maund basket" with them, aided by his boys, who are said to have pulled them about, and torn off the seals to play with them?‡ There is no mystery here; Catcott wrote to Dean Milles (May 28, 1777): "It was not the sexton but the Church-wardens who permitted old Chatterton to take the parchments, and indeed he or any other person might have taken them without their knowledge, for neither the chest or doors were at that time kept locked."

Thus a quantity of parchments found its way to the Pile Street School in a basket which was stowed in a cupboard in the schoolroom, and after the schoolmaster's death, Mrs. Chatterton, regarding them as her property, put them partly into a long deal box where her husband used to keep his clothes, and partly into a smaller square oak box, and took both to her lodgings, when she moved out, using the contents for "thread-papers, dolls, patterns," and the various purposes for which a poor woman with no antiquarian tastes whatever, who had

* Bryant (*Obs.* p. 514), who gives a vivid description of the litter in the Treasury, "in heaps, some quite loose, some tied up . . . rumpled, stained and torn" from a Mr. Shiercliffe, who saw it in 1749. See also Milles, p. 16. Tyrwhitt (*Vind.* p. 129) says 1765 was "nearly the time of Mr. Morgan's death."

† John Gibb was vicar till 1744.

‡ Nichols, *L. I.*, I. 145.

a home and a sewing school to look after, would naturally employ fifteenth century and earlier charters, if she did not, as is equally probable, suffer them to remain neglected and undisturbed.

It may be so, but Mrs. Chatterton told two different stories about them.

To Palmer, before he wrote to Lord Dacre in 1773, she said that John Chatterton sent her husband a basketful of old parchments from the chest to cover his boys' copies; he had mentioned his great want of covers, and his uncle said he would set him up. She remembered that several had seals of green wax with the impression of a bishop; her husband took pains to read them, made covers of some, destroyed others, and carefully locked up the remainder saying they were very valuable (without communicating any of the contents to her), and went to and from the tower carrying off everything he thought valuable, frequently lamenting that the chest had been kept open. To Lort, on Aug. 14, 1777, she said, some he used, others he threw away as rubbish, "for she does not remember he *set any store by them*." After his death they lay in a heap in a basket, with an old music book (maybe that from which the poet learnt the alphabet) which he had transcribed and she sold later.

Subsequently she told Dean Milles that she supposed her husband had read some of them, as he told her that he had found his own name in a lease spelt Chadderton.*

It may be pertinent to add, from the same source, Lort's description of the "Treasury" at this time, seven years after Chatterton's suicide:

"These chests were all open in August 1777, and in a corner of the room were swept together fragments of dirty parchment writings. Mrs. Macleave, who was then the sexton and showed me the room, is daughter of the person who succeeded Chatterton the great uncle of the poet.† When this elder Chatterton was sexton, the contents of the chests having become accessible to many people, the Churchwardens did about 1731 fix up wainscote presses in a room over the

* 11457.

† "The next Sexton was Perrot, from 1748 to May, 1756." Tyrwhitt, *Vind.*, p. 126.

south porch and removed all the writings thither that remained and which seemed to be of any value. What remained in the north porch, and which I saw there, were slips of dirty illegible parchment law writings and probably about Cannings time. . . . Dr. Goldsmith I am told, filled his pockets with such."

Goldsmith had been there six years before. It need not, perhaps, be added that " The Treasury " to-day presents no more than "a beggarly account of empty boxes."

There are two accounts of the parchments' discovery by the poet, and in both the date would appear to be about the time he was apprenticed. In William Smith's, Chatterton's eye was caught by one of them which had been converted into a thread paper, and he acquired them all, after interrogating his mother.* It is hard not to believe that this hint was afforded by the preface to *Hardyknute* in the *Reliques* (ed. 1, Vol. II, p. 88): " One Mrs. Wardlaw . . . pretended she had found this poem, written on shreds of paper, employed for what is called the bottoms of clues. A suspicion arose that it was her own composition. Some able judges asserted it to be modern. The lady did in a manner acknowledge it to be so."

In that given by Mrs. Chatterton to a friend of Dean Milles, he discovered them under the bed in the long deal box where they had remained " neglected and undisturbed " since the move, and declared " he had found a treasure, and was so glad nothing could be like it." He then removed them into the square oak box, and was perpetually rummaging and ransacking every corner in the house for parchments, and carrying away those he found " by pocketsfull " ; and one day happening to see Clarke's *History of the Bible* (to this day in uncovered boards) covered with one of these parchments, he swore a great oath, and, stripping the book, put the cover into his pocket, and carried it away ; at the same time stripping a common little Bible, but finding no writing on the cover, he replaced it very leisurely. Having been told by his mother where and how his father procured them, he went to the place and picked up four more, which Mrs. Chatterton believed Barrett possessed in 1782.†

* Bryant, *Obs.*, p. 529. † Milles, p. 7.

The fate of these parchments is not uninteresting, and may be pursued farther. Seyer has a note " Mr. Barrett took about twelve MSS. deeds, &c. out of the same place as Chatterton took his, the Redcliff chest, these were the last."* Barrett's collection of deeds, to the number of nearly two hundred, which included Morgan's collection, was acquired by Dr. Glynn, who, it is said, obtained others from Chatterton's mother and sister. Unable to read them, he transferred them to Thomas Kerrich, the Cambridge University Librarian (1748-1828), whose widow delivered them to George Cumberland, William Blake's friend, as a " respectable literary person at Bristol," to be preserved. Subsequently they passed to G. W. Braikenridge, and are now in the Bristol Museum. They are included in the " Calendar of Bristol Deeds described by F. B. Bickley," who says, " I think there is little doubt but that the bulk of these deeds belonged to the great Bristol merchant of the fifteenth century—William Canynges—and was accumulated as the title-deeds of the large property he held." The greater number refer to the transfer of messuages and shops in the parishes of St. Mary Redcliff, St. Thomas, and Holy Temple, and comprise not only (Deed 268) the document of 8 Edw. IV. which Bryant (p. 508) mentions as being in 1781 in Barrett's possession, where the chest "is particularly described and stiled, cista serata cum sex clavibus," but (Deed 272), a rumpled and grimed lease from Nicholas Pyttes, the vicar of St. Mary de Redclyf, and three churchwardens to Thomas Hexston, his wife, and son, of a garden on Redclyfhill between the lane leading to Redclyf and the garden of St. John's Hospital, extending from the churchyard of the said church to the tenement of William Canynges, gentleman, at a rental of eight shillings, William Brydde, mayor, and Thomas Rowley, sheriff, being the first two witnesses (Christmas, 1475). Both these documents bear endorsements in Barrett's hand. Moreover, five of these deeds

* 4533. f. 117. Milles (p. 182) and Barrett (p. 567) mention certain thirteenth century Indulgences to persons subscribing to the fabric of the church as being found by Barrett in Canynges' chest after it had been ransacked by others ; three of those specified appear in Mr. Bickley's *Calendar*, where they are numbered 14, 34, and 36. No. 14 has been treated with galls, as we know Barrett to have treated some of Chatterton's " originals."

Bristol Museum.

A DEED FROM THE "TREASURY," 1475.
(Slightly reduced.)

face p. 116.

relate to property in Temple Street, and two of the five (Deeds 187, 210) to shops in that street (1384, 1402).*

That is the whole story of the parchments, without one mention of *poetry* from beginning to end† ; and luckily, so far as Chatterton is concerned, it can be verified (*ex pede Herculem*) by a fragment of a deed (5766A f. 41 in Dr. Glynn's bequest to the British Museum) on the back of which he has pasted a piece of vellum with a rude pen and ink drawing of his own of " William Canynge," " Isabella hys wyfe," and two other faces. About a third of the charter has been cut away, but sufficient is left to show that it is a quitclaim from William Pennesford to Thomas Botiller (a surname occurring as Botelier, Botiler, Botyler, Butyler in deeds of 1333-1338 in Mr. Bickley's *Calendar*), burgess of Bristol, of four shops situated together in Templestrete, bounded on one side by the land lately of Thomas Barugh which John Whityng holds ; the witnesses being John Droys (mayor in 1410), William Frome, John Draper, Robert Coluyle, William Beneley, and the date 10 Hen. IV (1408-9). As it is the only genuine piece of fifteenth century handwriting among the whole of Chatterton's papers, the curious may like to have a transcript :

" . . . in domino Noveritis me remisisse relaxasse et omnino pro me heredibus et assignatis meis imperpetuum quietum . . . thome Botiller Burgensi ville Bristollie heredibus et assignatis suis imperpetuum. totum ius meum et . . . quatuor shopis cum

* *Ancient Notices relating to Bristol.* J. Dallaway, 1830 ; Bickley, *op. cit.* ; Kerrich's Will, P.C.C. Sutton, 366 ; Add. MS. 36512. f. 328.

† Except that Mrs. Chatterton told Palmer " her H and son placed great value on the parchments, saying it was poetry of one Rowley that was invaluable. She remembers her son having a box full of these parchments about a foot square ; after he went to London he sent for this box, but when she saw it opened a little before he left Bristol it was not near so full " (11457). It is after this that Lort adds " his Bristol friends allow he was a sad lyar."

The only instances known to me of old English poetry being written in the neighbourhood, as it were, of a charter, are : (1) a roll of Rickinghall Manor, in Suffolk, formerly belonging to the Abbey of Bury St. Edmunds. Attached thereto is a memorandum on a strip of vellum made by the clerk of the court in 1370, and this strip contains a previously written fragment of a mystery play, consisting of a French and an English version of a single stanza, both in the same form, but with three lines of the English missing ; the speaker is a royal personage. The late Mr. Gilson conjectured (*Times Lit. Supp.*, May 26, 1921) that it belongs to a Nativity Play, and that the speaker is Octavian. The MS. is now Add. Roll. 63481 in the British Museum. (2) The fragment of the secular play *Dux Moraud*, written on the margin of an assize roll of Norfolk and Suffolk, 1250–1300, MS. Bodl. Eng. Poet. f. 2.

pertinenciis pariter situatis in suburbio Bristollie in Templestrete exopposito . . . inhabitat ex parte una et terram nuper Thome Barugh quam Johannes Whityng modo tenet ex . . . Ita vero quod nec ego predictus Willelmus Pennesford et heredes mei nec aliquis alius per nos . . . tium nec in aliqua parte earundem decetero exigere vel vendicare poterimus set ab omni actione aliquid . . . Pennesford et heredes mei predicti quatuor shopas cum pertinenciis ut supradictum est prefato Willelmo . . . heredibus et assignatis suis warrantizabimus et defendemus imperpetuum Ita quod warrantia illa . . . aliquid inde petendum et non ad reddendum in valorem pro shopis predictis In cuius rei . . . hanne Droys Willelmo ffrome Johanne Draper Roberto Coluyle Willelmo Beneley et multis . . . ci quarti post conquestum decimo."

This charter seems first to have been noticed by Sir Frederic Madden, in *Archæologia* (XXVII, p. 115).*

In other words, the secret of the "cofre" was exactly as one would have expected† ; but note how this poet goes to work ! He takes Butler's surname, spelt Botelier, no doubt as he found it in a deed, tacks on his sweetheart's, "antiquates" the last two letters, knights the pair, and lo ! Syr Botelier Rumsie of *The Unknown Knyght.* He might, it may be said, have found John de Romeseye, who was mayor of Bristol in 1325-6, in an old deed (see Nos. 70-72 and 76 in Mr. Bickley's *Calendar*).

It should be added that one of the fabricated parchments (5766A, f. 34) is endorsed "Thos Chatterton 1748 Number Five," but it would be rash to affirm that the hand is that of the elder Chatterton; the endorsement of another (*ibid.* f. 4) "Priory Roll No. 1. T. Chatterton" is certainly the poet's hand.

To sum up, though there was useful matter for the historian of Bristol in those chests, we can rest assured that poetry was away; nor does the *content* of a single poem of Chatterton's bear the imprint of having been derived at first hand from a

* It did not escape Sir Daniel Wilson (p. 130), or Skeat (Vol. I. p. 376).

† "Mr. Barrett confirms this testimony with regard to Chatterton's bringing parchments with him ; which he took from the room over the porch, who also said that he had been there more than once ; but Mr. Barrett observes that these parchments contained deeds of land, &c., in Latin, and that Chatterton desired Mr. Barrett to read them to him as he neither understood the language nor character in which they were written." Milles, p. 7. For a similar chest full of documents in a room called The Treasury, over the north porch of Hawkhurst Church, see Hasted, *History of Kent*, (1790), III, p. 73.

fifteenth century English poetical MS. ; though, often enough, being a poet and a student of our older poets, he attains to the vision and movement of ancient song.

But this is to anticipate ; back to the Bridge !

The newspaper article having been traced to Chatterton, he appears to have been at pains to have ready the " old manuscript " from which it was " taken," and from motives which cannot now be fathomed he confided in a certain John Rudhall, then apprentice to an apothecary named Gresley. In Matthews's *Bristol Directory* of 1794, John Rudhall is described as " Printer of Felix Farley's Journal, Small Street," and a MS. note at p. 436 of a copy of Milles's *Rowley* in the British Museum says he became proprietor of that newspaper. In 1768 he may be presumed to have been a youth of about the poet's age and aware of his avowed compositions.* He afterwards gave two accounts of the matter, one orally to Croft, for the prospect of a gratuity of ten pounds to Chatterton's mother (March 30, 1781, according to Croft), and another which found its way into Dean Milles's edition. These may be read in parallel columns in Dr. Gregory's *Life*,† but Ingram is going too far when he casts suspicion on this witness merely because of the discrepancy ; for the chief point, the fabrication of a parchment, is asserted in both accounts.

In the Croft, the anti-Rowleian version, Rudhall confesses to assisting Chatterton in disguising several pieces of parchment with the appearance of age shortly before the article was printed. After they had made several experiments, the poet said, "This will do, now I will black *the* parchment," *which* parchment not being stated. Rudhall did not think he saw Chatterton black it, but was told by him afterwards that it was " what he had sent to the printer containing the Account."

In the Milles, the Rowleian, version, the lawyer's apprentice appears as a frequent caller on the apothecary's apprentice, and ten days or a fortnight after the account was printed told him he was the author of it ; but, it occurring to him that he

* On Nov. 10, 1781 George Catcott received a page of *The Revenge* from Rudhall. *R. Smith's MSS.*

† p. 179 sqq. Croft's letter to George Steevens, Feb. 5, 1782.

might be called upon to produce the original, he brought him one day a piece of parchment about the size of a half sheet of foolscap, on which Rudhall saw him write several words, if not lines, in a character he did not understand, which, he said, was totally unlike English (a very fair description of one of Chatterton's "originals"); this, he understood, represented the original from which the account was printed. The visit did not exceed three-quarters of an hour. When Chatterton had written on it, he held it over a candle, which changed the colour of the ink (Rudhall said), and made the parchment appear black and a little contracted. He never saw him make a similar attempt, nor to his knowledge was the parchment produced. He promised the poet not to reveal this secret, and only did so to Croft, in 1779, to benefit the widow. Like the rest of the Bristol youth this witness thought Chatterton incapable of writing Rowley, and indeed he never mentioned Rowley to Rudhall, but only "though very rarely," intimated that he was possessed of some valuable literary productions.*

It is odd that the account given to Dean Milles should be more destructive of the Rowleian position than the other, but the Rowleians usually provided the best arguments against themselves.

Fortunately there is another account of the fabrication of a document, which admits of no dispute whatever.

Edward Gardner (his father was Chatterton's father's crony), an observant person, who particularly recollected the philosophic gravity of the poet's countenance and the keen lightning of his eye,† saw him some three months previous to his journey to London—Gardner was a lad at the time—first rub a parchment in several places in streaks with yellow ochre (cf. Add. MS., 5766B, f. 30), then rub it several times on the ground, which

* On Apr. 3, 1782, Rudhall, "by means of Catcott," made a statement adhering to the Milles version, correcting it only by saying that some lines were written on the parchment when Chatterton brought it, and a small addition made to them in his (Rudhall's) presence. He excuses his imperfect remembrance by saying he was very young at the time, denies assisting Chatterton in disguising any other piece of parchment than that in question, and that Chatterton ever informed him that he sent that to the printer. The time was subsequent to the account in *Felix Farley*. 11457.

† *Miscellanies*, 1798. Vol. II. p. 143 sqq. Davis (p. 36) says Gardner used frequently to walk with the poet about the streets of Bristol.

was dirty, and afterwards crumple it in his hand; "That was the way to antiquate it," he said, adding finally that it would do pretty well, but he could do it better were he at home. The scene was a breeches-maker's shop in Maryleport Street over the elder Gardner's wine cellar, the next door, towards Peter Street, to Tanner's the barber, and three doors above the Swan Inn. "I mention the circumstance of the Breeches-maker's shop," says this witness, writing to the editors of the 1803 *Works*,* "to account for the parchment and ochre being so ready to hand. It seemed the mad start of a moment, done without consideration." To him Chatterton appeared wholly absorbed in antiquarian and heraldic researches, and fascinated with the brilliancy of literary fame; and told him, moreover, that it was very easy for a person who had studied antiquity, with the aid of a few books (Bailey's Dictionary was named) to copy the style of the ancient poets so exactly that not Mr. Walpole himself should be able to detect him.

It may be that the intention was to leave openings by which the truth might leak out, since the authorship of *Bristowe Tragedy* was admitted to Mrs Chatterton, and that of *Battle of Hastings* (1) to Barrett, as we shall see; but it is vain to look for a motive; a genius (age apart) does not always know why he does certain things.

Here a caveat! Chatterton's "originals" are not strictly forgeries, i.e. the hand is not an imitation of a pre-existing hand; though they are undeniably attempts to pass off something new as something old. All are childish bunglings, such as any very young person, if left alone, might accomplish with a bit of parchment, some glue, gum, or varnish, watered ink, and yellow chalk. As one looks at them in their sad array it is difficult to credit that they were ever seriously intended to deceive. The "heads of kings and popes," that William Smith speaks of, are little more than scrawls. The penmanship is that of no age or country, though, when legible, it can be made

* Vol. III, p. 522. "Tanner, John, barber and peruke-maker" occupies "30 Maryport-Street" in the 1775 Directory; the next door toward Peter Street would be 29 (occupant not named), the *Swan* being numbered 27, as now (1929). "Ford, Edward, leather dresser and breeches maker" occupies 25. New houses stand on these sites.

out as a huddled and rounded form of Chatterton's normal hand. The verdict of an eighteenth century expert, Thomas Butler, in a letter from Bishop Percy to Lord Dacre (Sept. 6, 1773)* may be restated without modification:

"We remarked some of the Letters to have been written in 4 or 5 different manners†; so that the Writer evidently went upon no principles, had previously formed to himself no Alphabet; had a very imperfect random guess at the old Alphabets, & was incapable of imitating any of them truly."

That Barrett, who had, by his own admission, genuine fifteenth century documents in his hands, could write in his *History* (p. 202) that the *Songe to Ælla* is "transcribed from an old parchment in the handwriting like that in use in Henry the 6th's time," points to something more than ignorance or blindness, *me judice*, since he read both it and them.

This, perhaps, should be enough to disprove the theory of the poet's attempting to imitate old hands, in support of which, however, a page from the MS. Accounts of Canynges' Chantries (1509-1534) has twice been facsimiled.‡ The handwriting here (and there is no *proof* that this church book was in the Chattertons' house), as in the copy of *Promptorium Parvulorum* (Pynson, 1499) in the Bristol Library—an attribution now given up—has at least a prima facie appearance of genuineness, and, I think, may be the work of a person or persons named Boner, whose names are scribbled elsewhere in the book. The only other reason for connecting it with *Chatterton* seems to be the name "Thomas" written underneath the alphabet. If this page be indeed his work, he never again produced an antique a hundredth part as convincing, to judge from the incontestable specimens in Add. MS. 5766A.

* Add MS. 32, 329, f. 72. First printed *entire* in *The Welsh Outlook*, June, 1929. ("Fresh Light on Chatterton," P. G. Thomas).

† Cf. Crabb Robinson's Diary for 1813 (probably referring to facsimile of *Canynges Feast*):—

"Dec. 30. Lamb was in a pleasant mood. Rickman produced one of Chatterton's forgeries. In one manuscript there were seventeen different kinds of *e*'s. "Oh!" said Lamb, "that must have been written by one of the 'mob of gentlemen who write with ease.'"

Ed. 1872. Vol. I. p. 222.

‡ In Pryce, *Memorials of the Canynges*, p. 298, and Ingram, *The True Chatterton*, p. 66.

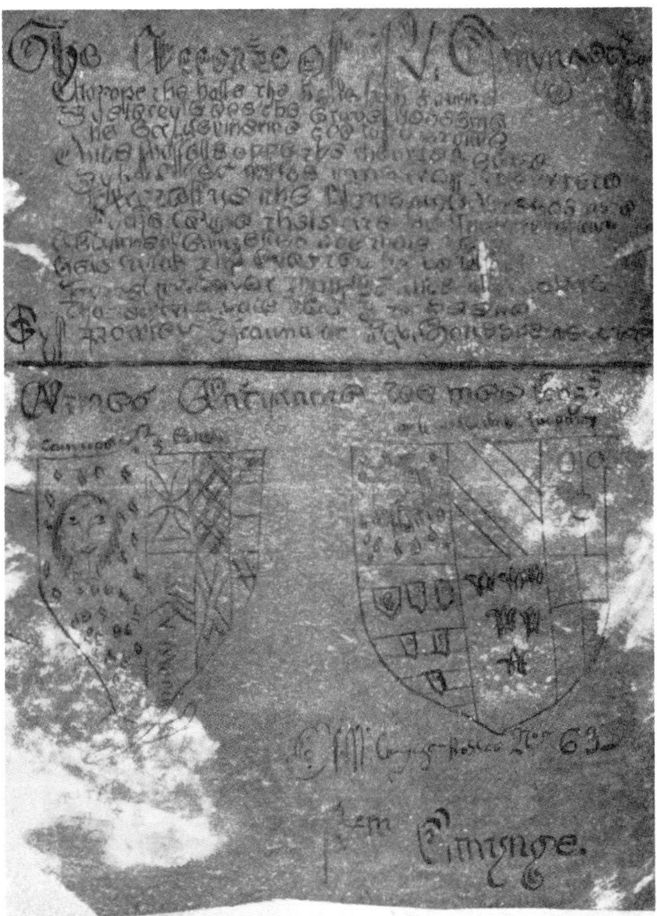

British Museum.

PARCHMENT FABRICATED BY CHATTERTON.

"The Account of W. Canynge's Feast."

(Actual size.)

face p. 122

"With regard to the Parchment itself," the editor of the *Reliques* continues, referring to the *Yellow Roll*, "it is evidently stained yellow on the back with oker, to look like old parchment. But the fraud is so unskilfully performed that you may see stains and besmearings on the other side, and if you rub the back with a wet white handkerchief, it will be stained with oker. He hath also contrived an Ink (than which nothing is more easy) that be very faint and yellow, which being washed with an infusion of galls,* would naturally become blacker."

The use of inverted commas, though a mark of ignorance, is perhaps hardly to the point; but it is strange that one who read poetry in the black letter, and used Kersey's dictionary, where all the words glossed are printed in that type, should, in his fabrications, have avoided a Gothic alphabet.

In the fanciful sketches of castles and churches, particularly one of a spire in "The Rolle of St. Bartholomewis Priorie" (5766C, f. 14), there is perhaps evidence that he could have learnt to draw; but he was generally content to take what he thought to be the quickest way. The partially antiquated figure, on paper (5766B, f. 118) of "Sire Gualeroyn Chatterton," holding a church in his hands, is traced from a full page woodcut in Weever's *Ancient Funerall Monuments* (1631, p. 846) representing a window in the now demolished Howard Chapel at East Winch. This book, which he mentions in his Essay on the Antiquity of Christmas Games, was lent to him by Barrett. according to a note of Lort dated "Bristol, July 79" (11457). No great time could have been spent in fashioning these indiscretions; and there are not more than half a dozen of his poems existing as "parchment originals,"† for neither Bristol nor Barrett wanted merely poetry.

A word more about John Rudhall. Soon after the parchment incident Chatterton broke with him, "improperly

* Barrett had treated the parchment with galls in order to read it.

† Viz.:
1. The first 34 lines of *The Storie of William Canynge*. 5766 a. f.3.
2. *The Accounte of W. Canynges Feast*. Ibid. f. 6.
3. *Epitaph on Robert Canynge*. Ibid. f. 7.
4. (a). *To John Lydgate*. (b). *Songe to Ælla*. (c). *John Lydgate's Answer*. } On one parchment, *penes* Sir W. Rose Smith.

The last was photographed for Sir Ernest Clarke's *New Lights on Chatterton* (1916).

resenting by a challenge some good advice which Mr. Ruddall had given him, in a point very essential to his temporal and eternal happiness."* George Catcott furnished Southey and Cottle with a note written to him, with an enclosure for a person who may perhaps be identified with the " Mr. Gaster " who is bidden, along with Rudhall and others, read the *Freeholder's Magazine* in one of the notes sent with his second letter from London. The date is not known. As a gloss on the enclosure it may be recalled that Goldsmith told Walpole at the Academy Banquet in 1771 that Chatterton " went by the appellation of the young villain."†

"TO MR. RUDHALL.

Sir, By copying this in your next epistle to Mr Baster, You will oblige, Yours &c. &c.

THOMAS CHATTERTON."

"TO MR BASTER.

Damn the Muses.—I abominate them and their works: they are the Nurses of Poverty and Insanity. Your smiling Roman Heroes were accounted such, as being always ready to sacrifice their lives for the good of their country. He who without a more sufficient reason than commonplace scurrility, can look with disgust on his native place, is a villain, and a villain not fit to live. I am obliged to you for supposing me such a villain.

I am,

Your very humble Servant,

THOMAS CHATTERTON."‡

The quarrel is perhaps illustrated by an item in the Sept. 30, 1769, issue of *Felix Farley*; whoever be the writer, he introduces us to the amenities of Georgian Bristol.

"A CARD.

Mr C . . . n presents his best compliments to his anonymous sympathetic *Friend*, and desires to return him Thanks, as grateful and unfeigned as his Friend's precaution and sage Advice are *excellent*. He is sorry any one who consults his interest in so affectionate and brotherly a manner should be unknown to him, especially

* Milles, p. 437.

† Walpole's Letter to Cole, March, 13, 1780.

‡ *Works*, III, p. 416. George Cumberland has a note "Baster, an American."

his new correspondent, who informs him he is a *Superior*! How agreeable an acquaintance with such a friend must be! He longs for the Discovery of his Vocation and earnestly entreats his good friend to unmask himself, as he would gladly cultivate an intimacy, retaliate the kindness, and render a Friendship reciprocally advantageous.*

Sept. 29, 1769."

It is into a period of friendship with superiors that we are now entering. But one last word on the Bridge first: Lort took a note in July, 1779, "Mr. B[arrett] told me y^t a person in Bristol assurd him he had seen C write the Acct of the Mayors passing over ye old Bridge & Mr Catcot says the same but neither of em coud tell me who y^t person was."†

NOTE ON SOME PIECES IN *FELIX FARLEY*, 1763-1768

"I LOOKED over a series of these journals before and after Oct., 1768, but I could not find anything that looked to me of C's insertion." So Michael Lort‡; and though, of Tyson's two findings, *The Churchwarden and the Apparition* (Jan 7, 1764) is assuredly Chatterton's, and *On the last Epiphany* (Jan. 8, 1763) generally accepted as his, albeit the acceptance has involved some juggling with the alleged date of his confirmation, the attribution of other pieces in this newspaper to him is attended with extreme hazard, and one is forced, reluctantly, to fall back on Lort's as the last word, in the lack of new sources of authentication. Eighteenth century Bristol was a large place, there is little in the way of signatures to guide the investigator, and no piece claims indisputable admittance on grounds of characteristic merit or the reverse. Neither is there a clean run of numbers from Jan. 8, 1763 to Aug. 24, 1770 in the Bristol Library, but I have been through what numbers there are cursorily. The following are in no sense results, but hypotheses, which remain to be tested. Unless otherwise stated, the pieces are unsigned.

* Friendship with equals only should be made. *Interest* (Oct. 27, 1769).
† 11457.
‡ 11457.

1763. Feb. 5. Dialogue between War and Peace. Very childish and charming. *Begins*: "Hark the Trumpet sounds afar." *Ends*: "Nor see again the light, nor view the azure Sky."

Oct. 1. Translation of Horace Odes IV, 7, signed "T.C." Almost certainly too polished for Chatterton at this time, whose versions from Watson's Horace only just antedate his journey to London.

1764. April 7. An Epistle from the Moon to the Earth. *Begins*: "Pray let me ask you, Madam Tellus." *Ends*: "Yours, Luna now, when married Phoebe," with explanatory notes about the eclipse.

May 26. An Exhibition of Polite Arts by Mr. Rams-Eye, 16 items. "(2) The Prophecy of Famine. (13) The pouring of Poison into the ear of a good and unsuspecting King.—A scene in *Hamlet*."

One would like to think that this is the first of Chatterton's "Exhibitions," but allusions to Churchill and Shakespeare are not enough.

June 2. A morning hymn. *Begins*: "Behold the Purple spangled Dawn." *Ends*: "In Praises to the Power Divine." The third line is "Drilling thro' the milky way." Drilling is used in a similar connection in *February*, "The bounding hail, or drilling rain descend."

Aug. 4. Epigram on the Majority and Minority.

"Thanks to my Sons! Britannia cries,
I'm happy by your joint Endeavour.
Mother, you'r humm'd, Argus replies,
You'll find them only Swiss for ever."

Ecnud Sutocs.

Cf. Hasmot Etchaorntt, signature of letter to W. B. Smith.

Aug. 11. This signature resolves itself into Dunce Scotus, and is appended to a prose "Anecdote taken from the original low Dutch."

Aug. 25. The origin of surnames. *Begins*: "Before the arrival of the *Normans* men were usually named from their condition and properties, as Godred, the *Saxon* word for good advice." *Ends*: "Thus if a man came from a village called *Vernon, Montague, Howard* or *Spencer* he transmitted to his posterity the surname of *Vernon, Montague, Howard* or *Spencer* to be put after the *Christian* names, so long as any of them should remain."

Oct. 27. A Dialogue between Reason and Fashion, Scene St. James' Park.

Begins: REASON: Madam, Good Morrow, it must be urgent Business that calls you abroad so early.

Ends: REASON (*alone*): Thou unsubstantial Chameleon farewell! . . . my faithful Votaries are often treated with Contempt and Ridicule.

DUNCE SCOTUS.

This is more like Chatterton than any of the preceding articles; e.g., the proper names, Meagre, Cringe, Lady Betty Various, Lord Rainbow, Sir Brass Outside, Miss Negligee, and—

FASHION: What an ignorant goth! Do you ever converse with the Beau Monde?

REASON: I am seldom absent from those that have any pretence to the Epithet of Great. Does your Fraternity ever think?

"Dunce Scotus" then vanishes from the columns of *Felix Farley*, and 1765 yields little or nothing.

1766 April 5. A Night piece on Death. *Begins*: "By the blue Taper's trembling Light." *Ends*: "And mingle with the blaze of Day."

Cf. the end of *The Revenge*, "And shines amidst the shining day." This piece is in the *Universal Magazine* for July, 1770.

Sept. 20. Custom, a Satire. *Begins*: "Mistaken World, considerate how few!" *Ends*: "Let each man act as Conscience shall direct."

1768. Oct. 22. The Particulars of a happy government. *Begins*: "Blest is that Government where greedy knaves." *Ends*: "And honest Men are counted downright Fools."

Dec. 10. The Cuckow Traveller, an original Fable. *Begins*: "Once says the Fable, a Cuckow,
Lords, knights and squires, the Tale's for you.
Ends: "For you, and all your rambling Pack,
Cuckows go out, Cuckows come back."

Based on Gay, "The Monkey who had seen the world."

Chapter X

BARRETT, GEORGE CATCOTT, AND BURGUM

THERE was one man in Bristol who must have read the issue of *Felix Farley* for Oct. 1, 1768, with unusual interest, a surgeon named William Barrett, a widower, with a son, rector of Higham, of whom he was very proud—Barrett *père* held the advowson of Higham—and four daughters, the youngest of whom, Sophia, he taught Latin and Greek. Nine years previously he had written to the Town Clerk communicating his design for a history of the city, and in the year following (Aug. 4, 1760) had applied to the mayor and aldermen for permission to examine records out of the Chamber with a view to obtaining new lights. At that time he was living in Wine Street, but later occupied a house (No. 41, in the 1775 Directory) on St. Augustine's Back, at the corner of Host, then Horse, Street, nearly opposite the Great House, with gardens that reached to the river.*

He was born at Notton, a hamlet in the parish of Lacock, Wiltshire, and was placed eleventh on the Election Roll of Winchester College in 1743, where he is described as "Gulielmus Barret de Lacock, comit. Wiltes Bapt: 6 Junii 1729."† The school "Long Roll," dated Sept. 1743, shows that a boy named "Barrett" was then a commoner in "5th Book, Middle Part," but his name does not occur on the Long Roll of the previous or

* A drawing of this house, by Henry Smith, attorney, brother of Richard Smith, junior, is reproduced in G. Munro Smith's *A History of the Bristol Royal Infirmary* (p. 260); to this work I am indebted for information about Barrett, also to the D.N.B., the Royal College of Surgeons, Braikenridge MSS. (Redcliff), *Bristol Times*, March 19, 1859, and to the Keeper of the College Archives, Winchester.

† The Lacock Register notes the baptism of William, son of Nicholas and Joan Barrot, under this date.

subsequent year. Richard Smith's Infirmary MSS. state that Barrett came as a boy to Bristol to learn his profession of apothecary. He was a pupil of "old Rosewell," barber-surgeon, who had a shop in All Saints' Lane, at the door of which was displayed a staff, a porringer, and a garter, the insignia of his trade. There his apprentice learnt to shave, bleed, and draw teeth. Old Rosewell died in April, 1752. The *Examination Book* of the Royal College of Surgeons records that "Willm Barrett" qualified on Feb. 19, 1755, as a surgeon's second mate, first rate, and that on April 1, 1756, "Wm. Barratt" qualified as Navy Surgeon, 5th rate. In 1755, according to Richard Smith, the future historian of Bristol was elected surgeon to St. Peter's Hospital, and in 1759 he was one of the unsuccessful candidates who competed for the post of surgeon to the Infirmary on the resignation of James Ford. About this time, at the age of thirty-one, he was painted by John Remsdyke, "a tall rawboned German, and excessively proud although a signpainter"* who painted many doctors, and often wore Barrett's cast-off clothing (or, as I have seen it stated, by one Daniel, a Bristol painter). An engraving of this portrait, made many years later by William Walker (1793-1867), shows a handsome, vain, self-indulgent face. The gossiping Richard Smith tells us that Barrett practised chiefly as a man-midwife, usually wore a waistcoat with large flap pockets, a coat with large open sleeves, breeches just reaching to the knee, slit in front, and small buttoned, that he sported two lamps at his door, kept a good table, and forgot his patients when "church-hunting."

In him we are confronted with a difficult personality, and it is due to John Ingram, the author of *The True Chatterton*, to state that he was the first to represent the surgeon-antiquary as less of a dupe than an accomplice and encourager of the poet in the production of spurious antiques; but the line of demarcation between uncritical acceptance and actual dishonesty is

* William Edkins's testimony *ap.* Munro, *op. cit.* p. 21. R. Smith says Remsdyke came into notice by a signboard of Bacchus astride a tun for a public house at the corner of Cart Lane, Temple Street. Chatterton asks for his address (May 6, 1770). In 1778 he and "Andrew van Rymsdyk" produced a book of plates of curiosities called *Museum Britannicum.*

hard indeed to draw in that century. Barrett's *laziness*, of which there is abundant evidence, may take us some part of the way.

There is discrepancy in the early testimony as to when Chatterton was first acquainted with Barrett. Catcott stated in the *Monthly Review* for May, 1777, that he introduced them, writing to Bryant on July 25, 1781, that Barrett " would perhaps never have known Chatterton if I had not first introduced him," and to Dean Milles (Apr. 8, 1779), " He was introduced to me before Mr. Barrett knew him."* Mary Newton's letter, referring to the period of her brother's commencing correspondence with Miss Rumsey, continues, " About this time the parchments belonging to my father that was left of covering his boys books, my brother carried to the office. He would often speak in great raptures of the undoubted success of his plan for future life. He was introduced to Mr. Barret, Mr. Catcott, his ambition increas'd dayly."† Croft, on the other hand, says, apropos of Chatterton's eyes striking fire, " Mr. Barrett adds, that he used often to send for him from the charity-school (which is close to his house), and differ from him in opinion, on purpose to make him earnest‡ ;" and Ingram suggests that " Lambert's office " should be read for " the charity-school " ; the bracketed words however, seem to forbid this. All through the Colston period Chatterton was reading in leisure hours ; a blue-coat boy with a book in his hand, or in a bookshop seeking out old volumes, is not unlikely to be noticed by a local antiquary, and we cannot disprove (odd as it is) Thistlethwaite's *Elinoure and Juga* story, which is assigned to 1764. It may be added that the head-master, William Haynes, was a friend of Barrett, and in 1789 a witness to the interlineations in his will,§ though that does not help this argument ; it is a fact, however, that Chatterton did not become necessary to Barrett till after Oct. 1, 1768. Davis (*Life*, p. 29) says that the *History* was at this time " suspended for the want of materials."

* *Letter-Book*, pp. 218, 342.
† *L. and M.*, p. 145.
‡ *ibid.*, p. 241.
§ P.C.C. Bishop, 58.

What comes out, I think, is that Barrett had asked his acquaintance to be on the alert for matter concerning old Bristol* ; all the city churches came within the scheme of his work, and he was doubtless acquainted with the Vicar of Temple Church, who was George Catcott's brother, and as the brothers lived together at the Vicarage, with George himself, who had no book under a hundred years old. At any rate, George Catcott was first on the scene after the "Bridge" article's appearance. Among Lort's notes is one to the effect that William Bradford Smith, Chatterton's friend, walking with his kinsman George Catcott in Redcliff Church in 1768, asked him if he had heard of old writings found there, and said Tom Chatterton had several. "Send him to me," said Catcott. Later "a boy with new cropped hair" appeared, "cap in hand," and produced some, which Catcott immediately put into Barrett's hands.† Chatterton did not own they came from Redcliff church till Catcott put it to him ; he said he had written love verses for a young gentleman who in return had given him these. Note the slightly different turn ; in Dr. Gregory's account he was transcribing them for this young gentleman (Baker).

In T. J. Mathias's *Essay* (1783, p. 23) Smith is reported as saying that it was through him "that Mr. Barret and Mr. Catcott became possessed of what they now have." Smith had mentioned *Bristowe Tragedy* and *Battle of Hastings* to Catcott ; and the next day after the talk in Redcliff Church, Chatterton called on Catcott, so the latter wrote to Dr. Glynn on Oct 23, 1788.

The order of the production of the first antiques is given in this letter‡ as follows :

(1.) A thin quarto copy book containing, in Chatterton's hand, Rowley's Memoirs of himself (first published in the

* "Such a discovery, therefore, as that of Chatterton could hardly escape the vigilance of Mr. Barrett's friends." Gregory, p. 39.

† 11457. In the *Gentleman's Magazine* for Aug., 1778, Catcott said Chatterton gave him the poems at the beginning of 1768, but Tyrwhitt elicited from him that it was about three weeks, or perhaps a month, after Oct. 1, 1768 (*ibid.*, Sept., 1778) ; writing to Dr. Glynn, Oct. 23, 1788, Catcott says "summer of 1768."

‡ *Letter-Book*, p. 458.

Town and Country Magazine, Nov., 1775), in which were included about thirty lines of *Battle of Hastings* (I), beginning " Where Thor's fam'd temple manie ages stood," a few stanzas from *Bristowe Tragedy*, the *Songe to Ælla*, and " some other little pieces," i.e , the two poems *On our Ladies Chyrche*.

(2.) " The next day" the *Epitaph on Robert Canynge*, " and one or two other small pieces."

(3.) " Soon after," two " originals," the *Songe to Ælla* and the *Yellow Roll*. The latter contains the names of other pieces, and is described by Sir Ernest Clarke as " a forgery to bolster up other forgeries."*

To these can be added (4.) the first 34 lines of *The Storie of William Canynge*, on a parchment, which, Dean Milles (p. 428) says, was the second piece of Rowley's composition produced to Barrett. " He gave Mr. Barrett the rest," Catcott goes on, " amounting to about twenty."

In an earlier account given by Catcott to Dean Milles (Sept. 21, 1778†) the " thin quarto book " (which has vanished, though there is a transcript of part of it by Catcott at the Bristol Museum among Richard Smith's MSS.), also appears as the first item in the list. This was immediately given to Barrett, and Chatterton introduced the next day. Here Catcott says the acquaintance began a few days—" Mr. Barrett thinks not a week "—after 1 Oct., 1768. Two or three days after, Chatterton brought all *Bristowe Tragedy*, where " Brandon " stood for " Bawdin," which Barrett corrected. More than once Chatterton said he had the original, which was more obsolete; Catcott frequently importuned him for this, but could not get it. Catcott continues thus : " After this, he generally visited us twice or thrice a week, and I never recollect his coming without bringing some of Rowley's Pieces either in Prose or Verse, and I perfectly well remember his mentioning the first part of the Battle of Hastings, as being then in his Possession ; and upon expressing a Desire of seeing it, he produced it, I think the Day following. The next thing I had of him was (to the best

* *New Lights*, p. 15.
† *Letter-Book*, p. 330.

of my Recollection) the Parliament of Sprytes, which I immediately took to Mr. Barrett, but he has not been generous enough to return it. A few Days after, he brought me the three Eclogues, & Fragment of the Tragedy of Godwynn, and shortly after *Turgot's History of Bristol* with Rowley's emendations, together with the Verses concerning *Johannes Lamyngtonn.*" *Ælla*, as we shall see, was the last antique of all to be handed to the pewterer.

There are two indications that the earliest " Rowleys " were not received open-mouthed. Lort has this note: " Not satisfied with the account he gave them of these MSS. they enquired after his connections, found out his mother, and by degrees got the history of their having been stolen out of Redcliff Church by the father, who, they found, had also destroyed most of the originals"; and also: "Mr. B seemed to doubt the authenticity of Rowley's life in Mr. Catcott's possession, particularly of his collecting drawings throughout England for Redcliffe Church and receiving £200 for em."* Catcott, too, always suspected this piece, "more than any other of the MSS.," because both he and Barrett " detected Chatterton in many falsities concerning it, and he was seldom consistent with himself in his answers on that subject "†; at least so he answered Tyrwhitt's queries of April 27, 1776; and on Jan. 1, 1778, writing to Dean Milles, he speaks of it as " cookd up (probably) by Chatterton's fertile genius."

It seems plain, however, in spite of the pewterer's inconsistencies and contradictions, that the Rowley cycle was evolved, and for the most part ready, before he and Barrett appeared on Chatterton's horizon. The thin quarto copy book contained samples of what Rowley could do; and, so far as the " ancient " poetry is concerned, little or none, we may be sure, was written to supply a demand.

Now begins the triumvirate, Barrett, George Catcott, and Chatterton; and, before a discussion of their common object, a glance at the second member will be profitable.

* 11063, ff. 389, 399. These memoranda were taken on Lort's first visit to Bristol, in March, 1771, and reduced to form in April, 1772.

† *Letter-Book*, p. 132.

George Symes Catcott was the second son of the Rev. Alexander Stopford Catcott of St. John's College, Oxford, who in 1722 was appointed master of Bristol Grammar School (his words at the Visitation have been quoted in Chapter IV), and in 1743 Rector of St. Stephen's; author in 1738 of a Latin treatise on the philosophy of John Hutchinson,* and a Hebraist, he died in 1749, leaving three sons and two daughters. The eldest son, the Rev. Alexander Catcott, vicar of the Temple Church, is important not least because he appears to have been the only man in Bristol at this time who thought Chatterton was the author of the Rowley Poems. Thomas, the youngest, "a mere accountant," in the employ of a copper company, lived till 1828 and does not enter into this history. Of the sisters, Augusta married in 1771 Richard Smith, surgeon (1745-1791), brother of Chatterton's friends, William and Peter Smith, the suicide, and father of the Richard Smith, third of that name, who made the collection of Bristoliana; Martha, the other, a spinster, kept house for her brother George, on his brother's death in June, 1779, when he quitted the Vicarage house (still standing) at the west entrance of the Church, and went to live at Temple Back. She has left on record a description of the poet as "a sad wag of a boy always upon some joke or other," which is borne out by a floral coat of arms which he designed for her, with "The Rose of Virginity" as legend.† This, her nephew tells us, was enclosed in a scolding letter, after she had taken him to task for some reason, by way of reprisal.

Now whether George or Thomas was the fool of the family is uncertain, but George, born Jan. 31, 1729, at Queen Elizabeth's Hospital, then the Grammar School, in Christmas Street, was clearly the oddity. His nephews, the brothers Richard and Henry Smith, have left an account of him (the MS. is numbered 5258 in the Bristol Library), which is here used, and trusted to the extent that the same degree of reliance is placed on his simplicity, as there illustrated, as on Chatterton's veracity, in Mrs. Newton's account.

* Author of *Moses' Principia* (1674-1737).

† In the Bristol Museum; see *Gentleman's Magazine*, Dec., 1838.

Nothing is known of his early life except that he is stated to have served his apprenticeship with a Mr. Cox in Thomas Street. In 1765* he went into partnership with Henry Burgum as a pewterer, and, according to the Smiths, brought £3,000 into the business; but, Burgum being a "musico-maniac," the business was left in the hands of "honest George," who delighted in actions heroic. On June 25, 1767, over a year before Bristol Bridge was open to the public, and the day after the last stone was set in the centre arch, he borrowed his partner's nag and, between 7 and 8 a.m., crossed it, riding over a few loose planks laid there on purpose, and paid the first toll, five guineas (given to the workmen for drink) simply to have the distinction of being the first person to cross the new bridge. Burgum, on witnessing the feat, is said to have exclaimed, "There go my horse and ass." "So exalted," writes *Another Hunter of Oddities*, "like Mordecai the Jew on the horse of Ahasuerus, he rode triumphantly over a few tottering planks, his horse being guided by one of the labourers, who acted the part of Haman in this grand scene." He may thus have read the Oct. 1, 1768, issue of *Felix Farley* with even keener interest than did William Barrett.

On Dec. 12, 1769, he was sufficiently brave, foolhardy, or self-advertising between 2 and 3 p.m. to scale the newly-built steeple of St. Nicholas Church, 205 feet, by the workmen's ladder,† to deposit in a cavity under the top stone, which he laid, two pieces of hard metal, pewter, five inches square, each bearing an inscription deeply engraved (written, I suspect, by his brother Alexander); they were fastened in with lead to ensure their diuturnity, and one of the inscriptions read:

> Summum hujusce turris Sancti Nicholai lapidem
> posuit mense Decembris 1769 Georgius Catcott
> phil-Architector Reverendi Alexandri Stopford Catcott filius.

But it was no *facilis descensus*, for the workmen, say his

* Writing to Dr. Glynn on Jan. 18, 1783, apropos of Burgum meeting his creditors, he says, "It will be eighteen years next March since our unfortunate connection first commenced." The Smiths give the date as "about 1770," which is absurd.

† "By a rope." *L. and M.*, p. 153.

nephews, removed the ladder, the bargain being for going up only.

These two performances are commemorated in an article in the *Town and Country* (June, 1771) ridiculing the brothers Sandy and George Catskin, where George is said to be "the man who in this city is the most ambitious of acquiring a name, in search of which, he has twice lately risked his neck." In the *Grand Imperial Magazine* for March, 1771, there is a caricature of him, armed with a spit, a pot-lid for shield, pair of tongs for sword, and iron pot for helmet, inscribed, "The celebrated Mr. George Catgut of B——l"; the letterpress explains that he is performing his favourite character of Alexander, in the kitchen; it is headed "George Catgut, the ambitious Knight of the Spit, a character," and signed "Ha! Ha! Ha!" Both articles may well be hackwork of Chatterton's, particularly the latter, which mentions the translations of "Sawney Macpherson," and falls foul of Catcott for declaring that "the late Mr. Holland" (Chatterton's favourite actor), "when compared with him (i.e. Catcott), was as coarse as a *dowlas*."*

He stammered, but recited with ease; later in life he was granted free admission to the theatre in King Street to the end of his days for reciting "Wolsey's Farewell," Mason's "Take holy earth," and Chatterton's *Bristowe Tragedy* to an audience which included Lord Charlemont and David Garrick†; and, on this occasion he also earned an annuity of £12 under Dr. Glynn's will, for obliging with that don's Seatonian prize poem on the Last Day, when begged to recite "something else." Not much simplicity here, in spite of his nickname "Great-heart"!

Like Chatterton, he was impetuous; "if the wish to do anything seized him he could not resist." Once in his shop, out of no ill-will, he spat in the eye of a customer who came for a pewter pot; and when pursued round the counter, over the Bridge, and into the High Street, and in imminent danger of a beating, exclaimed "I had a propensity." "Oh," said a member of the crowd, "if Mr. Catcott had a propensity and

* Dowlas, filthy dowlas. *I Hen.* IV, Act III, Sc. 3.
† Cf. also *Monthly Magazine*, May, 1799, p. 368.

could not help it, it was a mere accident, and he should not be beaten for it." He never ate animal food except roast beef, but not the " dry brown bits," which he skimmed off with a pocket knife ; carried with him sugar and cream (in a phial) and made his own toast in other people's houses. He had a large tumbler of punch after supper, which he mixed to the accompaniment of rolling up his garters ; saved all his old teeth, and wrote on the box containing them, " My teeth to be put in the coffin with me when I die." Of animals he was " dotingly fond," and held imaginary conversations with a turnspit dog when it was dead—" Here ! Paw ! Paw ! " " Here I am, Master, here I am ! "—and engraved him on the back of a brass toast tripod. He was deformed about the back and shoulders, generally wore dark brown or blue and, after June, 1779, in winter, a pair of his father's leggings with a long strip of iron up them, which had been an heirloom to " my brother the parson." His pet author was Charles I ; he collected books and prints on this subject, and on high days and holidays wore a cornelian ring with a representation of that monarch ; nineteen years after Chatterton's death he turned author himself to the extent of publishing a third edition of the *Pious meditations of Alderman Whitson,* founder of the Red Maids' School, an ancestor, and in 1792, an account of his descent in 1775 into Pen Park Hole, a cavern in Westbury, which, some years before, he had vainly endeavoured to get printed in the Royal Society's Transactions, through the medium of Dr. Jeremiah Milles. Such was " Rowley's midwife " in his life and habit.

In *Felix Farley* during December, 1769, appeared the following lines, headed :

A CHARACTER

Catcott is very fond of talk and fame ;
His wish a perpetuity of name,
Which to procure, a pewter altar's made,
To bear his name, and signify his trade,
In pomp burlesq'd the rising spire to head,
To tell futurity a pewterer's dead.
Incomparable Catcott, still pursue

From a water-colour painting in the Bristol Library.

GEORGE SYMES CATCOTT.

face p. 138

The seeming happiness thou hast in view ;
Unfinish'd chimnies, gaping spires complete,
Eternal fame on oval dishes beat ;
*Ride four-inch bridges, clouded turrets climb,
†And bravely die—to live in after-time.
Horrid idea ! if on rolls of fame
The twentieth century only find thy name.
Unnotic'd this in prose or tagging flower
He left his dinner to ascend the tower.
Then, what avails thy anxious spitting pain ?
Thy laugh-provoking labours are in vain.
On matrimonial pewter set thy hand ;
Hammer with ev'ry power thou canst command ;
Stamp thy whole self, original as 'tis,
To propagate thy whimsies, name and phiz—
Then, when the tottering spires or chimnies fall,
A Catcott shall remain admir'd by all.

These form part of the poem *Happiness* ; the first draft—it was extended—bears date Nov. 26, '69 (5766B, f. 59) and the sub-title " A Rhapsody." Catcott's story of them, according to Croft, is that, talking one day with Chatterton about happiness, Chatterton told him he had never yet thought on the subject, but that he would, and brought the lines next day, saying they contained his creed of happiness. Croft adds, " There can in this be no deceit ; for the pewterer produces the poem, and in the simplicity of his vanity, imagines it to contain a *panegyric* on himself."‡

Perhaps the twentieth century will forgive the horrid idea of so much space devoted to George Catcott (and he is not done with yet) in what is put forward as a life of Chatterton ; but he illustrates the thwarting environment of the poet so vividly that this course seemed inevitable.

Before 1768 was out the youth was in the toils. He had parted " *readily* and without reward "§ with *Bristowe Tragedy, The Epitaph on* (the supposititious) *Robert Canynge*, and other pieces to Catcott—it is not known if he was paid for the

* " To ride on a bay trotting-horse over four-inched bridges." *King Lear*, III, 4.

† " Fond pleasing thought, to live in after times." *The Rosciad.*

‡ *L. and M.*, p. 151. Chatterton and " Canynge " define happiness (" selynesse ") as content.

§ *Monthly Review*, May, 1777.

fabricated "originals," executed hastily, we may be sure—and was in the false position of making his way to esteem by fraud and not the genuine creations of his poetical self. He grew suspicious and reserved, said he had destroyed several "originals," and some MSS. which he produced were never seen again; the *History of Portbury* was one of these, a document elsewhere described as "proof of the existence of Rowley and the authenticity of his poems"*; some, like the *Interlude of the Apostate* never materialized beyond a fragment, and some, though mentioned, were not seen. The *Justice of Peace,* for instance, "which master Cannings advisd me secrett to keep, which I did" (Rowley's *Memoirs*), was frequently demanded by Catcott, who "never saw the MS., nor do I know that ever he was possessed of it."† He was not mercenary, though he wanted money for "books and learning and the Lord knows what," possibly dress; and, though disappointed, joked the matter off, as is shown by the still extant bill, which according to Croft was the only instance of his *asking* for a tangible reward.‡ It is written in red ink on paper stuck to a piece of parchment, 4 inches by 2½:

Mr Geo Catcott
to the Exors of T. Rowley, d.
To Pleasure rec^d in reading

his Historic Works	5 · 5
his Poetic Works	5 · 5
	10 . 10

There is no evidence of the payment of this sum.§ His sister gives both sides of the picture: "His spirits was rather uneven, sometimes so gloom'd that for many days together he would say very little and that by constraint. At other times

* 11457.

† Chatterton's note ran "Notwithstanding the most diligent search I could never meet with this." There is no reason to suppose that it was ever written.

‡ In Bristol Library, 5375. *L. and M.*, p. 208.

§ "I will not hesitate to assert (and I speak from no less authority than Chatterton himself) that he was disappointed in this expectation, and thought himself not sufficiently rewarded by his Bristol patrons." Thistlethwaite, *ap.* Milles, p. 458.

exceeding chearfull. When in spirits he would injoy his rising fame, confident of advancement he would promise my mother and me should be partakers of his success"

The Parlyamente of Sprytes, one of the finest of the poems, was handed to Catcott in the morning with the excited remark "I have sprung a mine," after an evening when the pewterer had left the poet in a state of complete despondency!*

But Barrett had no use for poems, unless they bore directly on his history; he wanted the entire collection of Rowley's MSS. Frequently, Seyer tells us, he told Chatterton how absurdly he acted in bringing him these piecemeal, and that, if he would bring the whole together with a fair account of them, he would run the risk of printing them and Chatterton should have the profits.† Very convenient for Barrett, for then Catcott would have been out of the concern, and he would have only had a minor, an apprentice, to deal with! As it fell out, there *was* friction between the surgeon and the pewterer, after the poet's death, but Barrett retained all that is in the volumes marked 5766, A. B. C. in the British Museum, which illustrate every side of Chatterton's literary activity, except the political letters and the non-Ossianic magazine contributions in eighteenth-century English.

One cannot resist the conclusion that Barrett is the real villain of the piece, an indolent and *poco curante* villain it is true; and, allowing full weight to Lort's "Though Barrett has been deceived himself, yet I verily believe he would use no unfair means to deceive others,"‡ one rests unshaken in the conviction that it is not Horace Walpole or the Magazine Editors, but Chatterton's pride and Barrett's cold, easy-going vanity, that engineer the catastrophe, and the surgeon's refusal to give the "physical character" (though, to be sure, the poet did not kill himself merely for the lack of that), and the results of the pride, that ring down the curtain in London. Without Barrett, the contribution to *Felix Farley* might have

* Gregory, p. 106.

† 4533, f. 121.

‡ Letter to Walpole, Aug. 4, 1789, Add. MS. 12527. These words refer directly to the publication of Chatterton's first two letters to Walpole in *The History of Bristol*, Walpole having repudiated them.

gone no farther than George Catcott, and its author, despite his temperament, have reached calm waters and the notice of a discerning patron at last. Barrett knew perfectly well what he was doing when, on being told that the first *Battle of Hastings* was Chatterton's, he accepted, *after a considerable interval*, the second and its continuation as Rowley's. How, after that, could he conscientiously tell Jacob Bryant repeatedly that he considered Chatterton's powers " by no means shining " ? Bryant calls him " a gentleman of reading and judgment, who was perfectly well acquainted with the extent of Chatterton's powers."* Indeed, this business of *Battle of Hastings* (I) stands in the clearest light possible :—

" He gave it," writes Catcott to Dean Milles on March 14, 1777, " Mr. Barrett and myself, as the composition of Rowlie, but finding we commended it, on account of the smoothness and regularity of the verse, and the many beautiful similies with which it abounded, he then said it was his own."†

The most one can say for him is that this admission did not *convert* him to a belief in the poet's genius. It is interesting to note how one jealous of Chatterton tried to explain away the truth : " It is easy to account for the answer given to Mr. Barrett, on his repeated sollicitations for the original, viz., *that he himself wrote that poem for a friend* ; thinking, perhaps, that if he parted with the original poem, he might not be properly rewarded for it."‡

At least Barrett cannot wholly be regarded as Chatterton's *dupe*. This is what Ingram contended,§ and I will develop his

* *Obs.*, p. 560.

† *Letter-Book*, p. 275. I cannot forbear quoting Sir Daniel Wilson's fine comment on this transaction : " Mr. Barrett was told in plainest terms that *The Battle of Hastings* was Chatterton's own work. But he treated the statement simply as an absurd lie : pressing the boy to produce the original fifteenth-century manuscript from which he persisted in taking for granted it had been copied. It was the same with the companions of the poet's own age. Ever and anon we find him trying their capacity to appreciate or comprehend his Rowleyan mystery ; and then, repelled by their stolid dullness, he retires once more to solitary communings with the creations of his own fancy." *Chatterton* (1869), p. 100. Wilson, of course, thought Barrett was completely duped. Two points are clear : (1) He thought that much of Rowley was ancient matter, and (2) he thought that Chatterton was a being out of the common.

‡ James Thistlethwaite, *ap.* Milles, p. 458.

§ *The True Chatterton*, Chapter VII.

argument along my own lines. It is not only stupidity but astuteness that lurks behind the statement in the Rev. Samuel Seyer's memoranda : " When Mr. Barrett first saw the poems he told Chatterton that they could not be of that age, for they were better than Chaucer's."* The cunning fool is the greatest enemy genius has to contend with. It is easy, I know, to strain the evidence against Barrett, and one has constantly to bear in mind that absolute honesty was, at that time, scarcely *demanded* of an antiquary. The fairest position to take up concerning him, and that most warranted certainly by his letters after Chatterton's death, is that he really thought there was a true basis in Rowley, but that Chatterton altered and "cooked up" what he found ; yet even when he discovered, from consulting archives at Wells, that a list of the Priors of St. Augustine's, which the poet had brought to him, as "original," was false in every name—he told Dr. Johnson this†—he still printed Rowley matter in his history, so loth was he to jettison his grand novelty. If I have been too severe in my treatment of him, let my remarks be tempered by this caveat.

There was an understanding, tacit, it may well be, between the pair. Chatterton provided antique accounts of certainly seventeen Bristol Churches, six spurious deeds, lives of " Rowley " and " Canynge," with their correspondence, not to speak of the " translation " of and " emendals " to " Turgot," plans of the castle and modifications of existing maps of the city. In return he had the run of Barrett's library, could and did, as his sister says, borrow many books on surgery, and received, as Lort says, at his own request, surgical instruction from Barrett, who tells us also that he often applied to Barrett to translate Latin passages for him, Barrett once having lent him a Latin grammar, which he soon returned, declaring it was too late Though the middle-aged man and the youth sat up over the latter's fabrications, " one assisting the other when at a loss "as Seyer puts it—as can still be seen from 5766 A, f. 25, where the decipherings on the paper to which a parchment has

* B. 4533, f. 121. The poet's reply, " Chaucer was a fool to Rowley " evinces *his* double nature, for Rowley confesses in his *Memoirs*, " I was never proud of my verses since I did read Master Chaucer."

† 11063, f. 421 ; *European Magazine*, April 1792.

been stuck are in the script of both—and words and sentences went unexplained till their next meeting, the former was aware that he had a remarkable creature in his house, and sounded him accordingly. His differing from him in opinion to make his eyes flash is not the action of a dupe, nor is his endeavouring to make him drink, the latter an inference from Seyer's note: "With all his profligacy Mr. Barrett could never make him drink: he spent the money he got upon gingerbread, &c., and was in his behaviour quite boyish"*—and confirmed by Chatterton's sole extant letter to Barrett.

He has my thanks sincere
For all the little knowledge I had here

was the poet's way of expressing his gratitude in his "Will"; and, in *The Exhibition*,

Barrett arose and with a thundering air
Stretched out his arm and dignified the chair.

Ingram conjectures that the surgeon is as likely as not to have suggested the subject of this scurrilous poem, but he is mistaken in denying Sir Daniel Wilson's identification of Barrett with "Pulvis"—it is "Bolus" in the first draft of *Happiness*, on the ground that he did not acquire the medical degree of doctor; none was necessary before the Apothecaries Act of 1815; and, as we have seen (Chapter I), Barrett attended the Long Ashton Smyths as their doctor. Some of the lines in this first draft are:

Bolus whose Knowledge lay in his Degrees
Is only happy when he's taking Fees;
First Son of Esculapius, his Brow
The spreading Smile was never known to plow
His Wig a Forrest of terrific Grace
†Catcott admires him for a Fossile Face.

The penultimate line in *Happiness* runs "Blest with a bushy wig and solemn grace," and recalls the description of the

* B. 4533, f. 121.
† The Rev. Alexander, of course, not George.

Oxford examiner in *Genuine Memoirs of Mr. Charles Churchill* (1765): " When Churchill after vast solemnity, and an awful preparation, designed to intimidate him, and lower his sense of his own qualifications, was led up to the examiner, whose solemn visage, rendered important by a bushy wig, bespoke credit from a superficial observer for vast wisdom, he began to think his father's description was a just one; and prepared to answer the extremely difficult questions he imagined would be put to him. . . . Our hero was so astonished and so irritated, at their thus treating him like an ideot, as he imagined it, that he could not but resent it. He accordingly satirized the person whose office it was to examine him" (pp. 69, 70).

Because Chatterton praises him in two places, that is no reason why he should not lash him in two more, for, by his own admission, in his " strong fits of satire " he spared neither friend nor foe, " and, not unlike Richard Savage, would ", as Lort puts it, " abuse his best benefactors."* " Here," writes *A Hunter of Bristolian Oddities,* " you may see a surgeon, by the inspiration of vanity, metamorphosed into a *wooden* antiquarian and writer of epitaphs, which would unimmortalize the poetical pen of Stephen Duck."†

Reserving his part in the Walpole business, let us examine two instances of the co-operation of Barrett with the lawyer's apprentice; the first has only come to light since Ingram wrote.

The plates for the *History of Bristol* were engraved in folio many years before the book was printed in quarto, and a volume belonging to Barrett, containing proof impressions of the original copperplates is the subject of a paper in the Transactions of the Bristol and Gloucestershire Archæological Society.‡ One of these proofs (facing p. 51 of the published *History*) had evidently been submitted to Chatterton, who added in black ink the High Cross and four Churches round it,

* 11063, f. 387.

† *T. and C.M.* Suppl., 1771. The reference is probably to the tablet to Barrett's wife (d. 1763) in Redcliff Church. See *History of Bristol*, p. 583. In a note on " a silver coin of Brightrick " (intended for the surgeon's eye) Chatterton speaks of " Mr. Barrett's incomparable MSS History of Bristol." 5766B. f. 42.

‡ Vol. XLIV, p. 79, by John E. Pritchard, F.S.A., who discovered the book in London.

the fourth being the mythical St. Andrew's, on the site of the present Dutch House, which puzzled succeeding Bristol antiquaries, though the shrewd Seyer, whose *Memoirs of Bristol* were published 1821-3, already suspected the authenticity of this plan. Chatterton first gave a spire to this church, and then struck it out, added the wall from St. Nicholas Gate to the upper end of the Shambles, and thence to New Gate, putting in the south section of the gateway, and writing at the foot :

"There is between ye outer Wall of the Castle & Godfreys Lodge a Chaple of the Lords of Gloster & being neither in the Precincts of the Castle & distant from any Liberty of the City owes Homage to neither standing near the long Wall of God's Lodge."

Mr. Pritchard's comment is : "I doubt if anyone can understand what was meant, and it is therefore further evidence of Chatterton's romantic mind." Still, I cannot agree that Barrett was *duped*, though he may well have *wished* to be deceived about the new matter which he was incorporating.

Chatterton's method was disingenuous, but a touchstone of disingenuousness in others. Catcott's note on *Bristowe Tragedy*, already cited, makes this plain. The poet who "found the argument and versified it,"* must have been perfectly aware that the subject of his piece was Sir Baldwin Fulford, yet he brought it as "The Execution of Sir C. Brandon," and Barrett altered the name. Seyer tells the story differently : "When he first mentioned the Bristowe Tragedy to Mr. Barrett, he told him that he had gotten the execution of *Sr C. Brandon. How ! Chatterton,* said Mr B., *that's impossible. Sr C. Brandon lived long after Rowley's time.* But Chatt : persisted in its being Rowley's writing and next time produced the Execution of *Sr C. Bawdin* for Mr. Barrett, who then first told him the right name."† In either case, if Barrett was deceived, he wished to be deceived.

The second instance is the familiar episode of the de Bergham

* Mrs. Newton to Cottle (Oct. 17, 1802). *Works,* III, p. 524.

† B. 4533, p. 119. Lort has a note, "C asked Barrett who Sir Tybalt Gorges and Sir Charles Baudin were." 11457.

arms and pedigree, which, thanks to Cottle mainly, has been viewed out of perspective hitherto as a boy's jape at a "presumptuous vulgar fellow," and has obscured the real merit of Burgum, who, for all his ostentation, was the only person in Chatterton's circle, except John Allen the organist, who had a feeling for true art.

Henry Burgum, born in 1739, was a self-made man; when young he pounded the mortar of old William Dyer, an apothecary who lived on Bristol Bridge.* In *Felix Farley* for July 28 and Aug. 18, 1764, he announces that he has removed from near the Bell in St. Thomas Street to the Corner of Thomas Street and Redcliff Street facing the new (i.e. the temporary) bridge, and describes himself as "Pewterer and Wormmaker." The partnership with Catcott started in the following March. The firm's first announcement is in *Felix Farley's Journal* of March 23, and during August of that year (1765) they advertised thus:

OVAL PEWTER DISHES
Best superfine HARD-METAL and newest
Fashion, are made and sold 25 per
Cent. under the old Price,
By BURGUM and CATCOTT,
Pewterers and Worm-Makers,
At their Warehouse the Corner of *Redcliff-street*, facing the New Bridge, *Bristol*.

On Dec. 7 the paper announced the marriage on "Saturday last, at St. Thomas's Church," of "Mr. Henry Burgum, an eminent pewterer, to Miss Betty Copner, who, besides a very handsome fortune, is rich in every requisite that makes the honourable state amiable." In 1767 Burgum was president of the Grateful Society, founded in 1759, one of the Bristolian clubs in memory of Edward Colston, but non-political in its

* Richard Smith's *Chattertoniana*.

object, "the placing out of poor Bristol boys to trades."* This was, perhaps, an honour—

> The man has credit and is great on 'Change.

He was also, William George says, Deputy Governor and Treasurer of the Corporation of the Poor.

In *Journal 6th* (Sept. 30, 1769) he is described as sending a complimentary ticket for a "turtle-a-la-stew" feast to a local rector.† Croft, commenting on Chatterton's observation that God had sent his creatures into the world with arms long enough to reach anything, if they would be at the trouble of extending them, says "This idea he could not but feel confirmed by what he knew of a Mr. Burgum (I think), Mr. Catcott's partner, who taught himself Latin and Greek"‡; but Croft may have mistaken the name.

In 1770 at least two things happened to Burgum; his portrait was painted by Thomas Beach (1738-1806), engraved many years later by Robert Graves (1798-1873), and he was impelled to insert the following notice in *Felix Farley* for March 17, not quite a month before Chatterton abused him in his "Will." As the man has never yet been allowed to speak for himself in a biography of the poet, the digression of an *ipse dixit* may perhaps be pardoned:

"*To the Public*

Whereas a villainous report hath been spread in this city and country adjacent that I had most inhumanly and cruelly treated one of my apprentices, by striking him with an Iron Bar, breaking his jaw bone and 2 *or* 3 *of his ribs; nay* some *have been so daring as to say he died of his wounds.*

Now I call upon, and ask, any and every person, who have been instrumental in propagating this Calumny, to ANSWER *me in the Bristol News Paper in their own Name this one plain question,* IS THE ABOVE REPORT, OR ANY PART OF IT TRUE.

All those who chuse to convince themselves to the contrary, are very

* See W. George's pamphlet, *The "Grateful Society"* (1879), and H. J. Wilkins, *Edward Colston*, p. 105.

† For allusions to turtle see Latimer, *Bristol in the Eighteenth Century*, pp. 323, 405, 517. The turtle soup of John Weeks, Matthew Mease's successor at the *Bush*, was famous.

‡ *L. and M.*, p. 161.

welcome to call at my house, and hear the true state of the case from the young man's own Mouth, or if calling at my house may be thought any way disagreeable, I will give the apprentice leave to wait on any one, at their own house, when and where they will have a fair opportunity to ask him such Questions as they please.

HENRY BURGUM.

[2] *Bristol-Bridge March* 13, 1770."

So much then in confirmation of the satirist's

But Burgum swears so loud, so indiscreet,
His thunders rattle thro' the list'ning street.

Though he may have had no connoisseurship in pictures and " bought a Bacon for a Strange," he knew what was good in music ; and, though he subscribed to quartets by Kotzwara, and concertos by Norris of Oxford, he worshipped Handel. Thomas Kerslake, the Bristol bookseller, in a letter to Sir Daniel Wilson,* says that he once bought a library in which were two chests containing concert sets of music for about twenty instruments with partitions for each volume ; one of the sets, he thought, was the *Messiah,* and the other "some of Haydn's pieces" ; each volume had the name " Henry Burgum" in gilt on the sides, and one set was " whole bound in red morocco." Now at the Red Lodge, in Park Row, is still to be seen a portrait (not that which was engraved, but by Jackson, I was told†) of Burgum in a flowered waistcoat and blue coat standing with his right hand on a red-bound volume lettered " Messiah."

His faith in Handel wafted him over his troubles. When the pewtering concern failed—and the Smiths accuse him of having robbed their uncle of the £3,000 he put into it—the " musico-maniac " fell on evil days. In 1775 he had published a narrative of facts relating to himself and James Thistlethwaite, who had grossly abused him in *The Consultation,* a satire against the Tories, dedicated to " Henry Burgum, Esquire, Lord of the Manor of Glastonbury, &c., &c.," and offered to suppress the poem for hush money. There he says he is settling himself in

* Oct. 9, 1868, *penes me*. See Wilson, p. 54.

† Ingram, p. 143, evidently referring to this painting, says by Simmons, following William George ; John Simmons, a native of Nailsea, died in 1780.

a new distillery in the parish of St. Philip and Jacob, Fear, Shoreland, Burgum & Co. (136 Redcliff Street). George Catcott called his creditors together in Sept., 1779, and on Jan. 18, 1783, wrote to the Rowleian Dr. Glynn, "My late partner is now made a bankrupt. . . . He has completely ruined himself, his wife and family, and by his haughty and artful behaviour, made all his best friends his greatest enemies. . . . As it is I shall lose upwards of £2,500 by his dishonesty and subtle evasions. In short I firmly believe (and am by no means singular in my opinion) that a more compleat or more artful villain than Henry Burgum Esqr scarcely exists, not excepting even Tom Warton himself."* In 1786 Burgum lost the use of his limbs through gout, and was lodged as an insolvent debtor in a London prison; rescued by his friends, he returned to Bristol and arranged for a performance of *Judas Maccabæus* (Sept. 1787) for which Bartolozzi executed the ticket of admission (5s.): the receipts just put him on his feet.† In April, 1788, *The Messiah* was performed for Burgum's benefit, and on June 5, 1789, the year of Barrett's *History of Bristol* and death, he died, aged fifty, suddenly at his home, on the Parade, St. James's Churchyard,‡ and was buried at Tickenham (where he had a country place, "Tickenham House") in the south aisle of the church, near the font, as "Henry Burgum of the city of Bristol, Pewterer," an inscription that can still be read.

Chatterton, who had an innate sense of justice, over and above his native spleen, exclaims indignantly at the Bristolian literati's scoffs at the man who, like himself, was self-educated, a man not more than thirty, by the way:

Burgum wants learning, see the letter'd throng
Banter his English in a Latin song.
Oxonian sages hesitate to speak
Their native language, but declaim in Greek.
If in his jests a discord should appear,
A dull lampoon is innocently clear.

* Glynn had written (Dec. 29, 1782) "Burgum and Warton—they were surely meant by nature to be of the same trade." Catcott liked to echo his learned correspondents.

† Latimer. *Bristol in the Eighteenth Century*, p. 480.

‡ *F. F. J.* June 6, 1789.

Ye classic dunces, self-sufficient fools,
If this the boasted justice of your schools?
Burgum has parts; parts which would set aside
The labour'd acquisitions of your pride.

And later, in the same *Epistle to the Rev. Mr. Catcott*:

Ye rigid Christians, formally severe,
Blind to his charities, his oaths you hear;
Observe his virtues: Calumny must own
A noble soul is in his actions shown;
Tho' dark this bright original you paint,
I'd rather be a Burgum than a saint.

It is odd that he never alludes specifically to his love of music, though himself a devotee of Handel.

The de Bergham pedigree, which, with the Walpole correspondence and the suicide, is an aspect of Chatterton's career on which the world in general likes to dwell, when it troubles about him at all, first made its printed appearance at the end of Vol. II of Southey and Cottle's edition of the *Works* (1803), ushered in by an essay of Cottle's, who rightly used the pedigree as a means to extinguish the last embers of the Rowleian Controversy and prove that Chatterton was the sole author of the poems attributed to Rowley*; and it may be mentioned in passing that not only as late as 1857 could a Rowleian be found, in the Rev. S. R. Maitland, D.D., F.R.S., F.S.A., but, even since Skeat's edition, in a West Country Anthology edited by Mr. Thomas Burke (1913), a modernization of the *Songe to Ælla* is designated "Traditional; a version by Chatterton"; so hard do fallacies die. Joseph Cottle's first version of the affair—for he afterwards, in *Malvern Hills* (4th Ed. 1829), quite unwarrantably dated it back to the Colston's period, throwing in an imaginary conversation between the bluecoat boy and the pewterer—is simply this. Chatterton was under some slight pecuniary obligation to Henry Burgum, and calling on him one day when he was about sixteen told him that he had his pedigree at home from the time of William the Conqueror, and informed him of the many distinguished families to which

* John Evans states that Cottle, when he began the task, was a Rowleian. *Chronological Outline*, p. 286.

he was allied. Burgum expressed a wish to see this pedigree, and a few days after was presented with it. That he gave the poet five shillings is a natural deduction from the " Will " :

> Gods ! what would Burgum give to get a name
> And snatch his blund'ring Dialect from Shame
> What would he give to hand his Mem'ry down,
> To times remotest Boundary—a Crown.*

That later he took the pedigree to the Heralds' College and there learnt that a de Bergham had never borne arms is in Cottle's second version, who adds that the officers of the College remembered the occasion and that Burgum, who brought it " merely to receive corroborative attestation," told them the pedigree was discovered for the most part in Redcliff Church.†

I am not the only heretic in this matter. Shortly before his death Sir Ernest Clarke expressed a doubt to me in talk whether Burgum was actually duped at all: " He may not have thought the pedigree *and* the arms on vellum worth more than a crown." As for the verification, it would be the first act of most sensible people ignorant of heraldry, in the circumstances.

The existence of the pedigree, together with Chatterton's undated letter to Ralph Bigland, Somerset Herald (1711-1784), giving " curious coats in and about Bristol "‡ was first made known to the learned world by a letter, Oct. 10, 1787, by J.D., probably the Rev. James Dallaway, to the *Gentleman's Magazine*; the presumption is that it was not in Burgum's possession at that time, and in 1789, according to Catcott, Thomas Eagles had both documents.§ The whereabouts of the letter is unknown, but Cottle obtained the two copy-books containing the pedigree (with *The Tournament* and *The Gouler's Requiem* written at the other end of the first), and the de Bergham arms,

* I am not sure what the next couplet means

> Would you ask more ? his swelling Face looks blue
> Futurity he rates at Two pounds Two

except it be that two guineas represent all that Chatterton had received from Burgum at the time of writing.

† *Malvern Hills*, p. 390.

‡ *Works*, III, p. 408. Seyer transcribed it from the original, undated, but with postmark of Jan. 31. B. 4533, f. 121.

§ *Letter-Book*, p. 461. See also Nichols, *L.I.*, Vol. VII, p. 565, " Chatterton's Knowledge of Heraldry."

blazoned on vellum, six inches by ten, from Mrs. Newton, and these are now in the Bristol Museum.* A word should be said about the motto to these arms, RYDE ON, which illustrates Chatterton's instinctive mediævalism, even in his most unscientific or caustic flights. On the seal of one John de Flory, dated 1300, which he could not have seen, is shown a hare mounted on a dog, and blowing a horn, and over it " Ride alonge."†

There is no need to go at length into the "Account of the family of the De Berghams from the Norman Conquest to this time," which starts with Simon de Seyncte Lys, alias Senliz, created Earl of Northampton by William I in 1075, and possessed of Burgham Castle in Northumberland; brings the de Berghams into the West Country through the extravagance of an Elizabethan William Burgham, whom the sparing queen compensated with the keepership of three forests in Gloucestershire after he had diminished his fortune by prodigality at a tournament on her accession; and ends, in the second copy-book, for which, according to Cottle, another crown was paid, with an ancestor who lived in the reign of Charles II and James II. It is a grotesque and studied mosaic, neatly written in black and red ink, from authorities real and feigned, garnished with marginal references to Leland, Camden, Battle Abbey Roll, Weever, Thoresby, Dugdale, Guillim, Stowe, Ashmole, Collins, &c., and of course, Rowley and Creeche (i.e. " Craishes Herauldry") not to speak of "oral deeds,"‡ and a plethora of heraldic footnotes, of which "azure three Hippotames naisant or " and " England depressed with a bend " are among the choicest. It is, indeed, the *locus classicus* for Chatterton's heraldic dedications, and a strange mingling of raillery and romance runs through the whole performance, reaching its height when, after a genuine diploma of the University of Oxford, lifted from Madox's *Formulare Anglicanum* (1702, p. 12), where the name "Johanno de Burgham" has been

* The last page of the second copy-book is defaced by specimens of Shakespearean forgery written there at Cottle's desire, by W. H. Ireland, Oct. 28, 1800.

† Charles Gatty, *Mary Davies and the Manor of Ebury*, Vol. I, p. 229.

‡ " Oral " is a contraction for " original." See *N. and Q.*, Oct. 27, 1855.

substituted for Roberto de Snytenfeld, and a "memoire" from the same book and page, giving the titles of early French romances,* a poem by John de Burgham, "wrote by him about 1320" is introduced "to give you an idea of the poetry of the age." This is *The Romaunte of the Cnyghte*†, which is written in very rude equivalenced octosyllables not unlike *The Unknown Knyght*:

Al downe in a Delle a merke dernie Delle
Wheere Coppys eke Thighe Trees ther bee
There dyd hee perchaunce Isee
A Damoselle askedde for ayde on her Kne
An Cnyghte uncourteous dydd bie her stonde
Hee hollyd herr faeste bie her honde
Discorteous Cnyghte I doe praie nowe thee telle
Whłest doeste thou bee So to thee Damselle.

This discourteous knight is surely an ancestor of "the tallest of the five" warriors who, according to her tale to Christabel, placed Geraldine underneath the oak. It is not suggested that Coleridge read it before 1797; descent in Poetry is spiritual. The little piece is accompanied by a free modernization by the real author, from which the line about the flag "regardant" has been quoted; here, *inter alia*, a comment on the action is inserted, in brackets:

Women and Cats, if you Compulsion use,
The pleasure which they die for, will refuse.

No better example of Chatterton's mental processes could be given than these two poems and their context.

But the point in mentioning the pedigree here is that the translation of every document actually cited in it (one of which, an alchemical patent, 24 Hen. VI, is to be found in Rymer's *Foedera*, Vol. XI, p. 128) is in William Barrett's clumsy sprawling hand, and fills a space left for the purpose.‡ That is to say,

* See *Archaeologia*, XXVII, 115.

† This poem was first printed on a single sheet, as one of the earliest productions of Chatterton, by James Dallaway, in 1788, and not reprinted till 1803.

‡ This is not only obvious, but vouched for by Cottle, from George Catcott's information, in a note written in the first copy-book.

Barrett must have been, if not party to the imposition from the very start, at least fully aware of what Chatterton was providing for the butt of Bristol's intelligentsia. Latimer asserts that all the books quoted were in Barrett's collection,* and we know this to be so in the case of Weever's *Funerall Monuments*, from which (p. 234), as Cottle saw, the epitaph of Sir William Molyneux was taken.

We have now done with Henry Burgum, at least he is not required till Sept., 1769; the local antiquaries and their trouvaille are our game, three very different characters: William Barrett, a vain, lazy, self-indulgent man of the world, eager to be thought well of in Bristol as its first historian and the discoverer of forgotten archives; George Catcott, an ignorant eccentric, who, partly for business reasons, desired his name to be always on the city's tongue in connection with some feat or other; and Thomas Chatterton, according to his own description, "a flighty youth as yet unlearnt to live," according to his discoverer's, "a young man of very uncommon abilities but bad principles." Yet, different as they were, they cherished one object in common, fame. The third alone was destined to win that, and in his posthumous blaze each of the others, according to his due, to be first exposed, and then remembered.

Meanwhile, before the storm gathers, Rowley be the theme.

* *Bristol in the Eighteenth Century*, p. 388. Barrett's library, by the codicil of his will (P.C.C. Bishop 58) was, with his cabinet of coins (whence, it may be, "Maystre Canynge's Cabynet"), divided between his daughters, Anna, Susan, and Sophia. Some relics of this library, stated to have been "some twenty years ago" in a Cardiganshire village, are named in an article, signed "Pauline Kingston James," in the *Bristol Times and Mirror* of Jan. 30, 1924. A first edition of Savage's *The Wanderer* is included, and it is said to have been rich in books of travel. Barrett's daughter, also an antiquary, according to this authority, said Chatterton was "a singularly stupid-looking boy, of dull and heavy countenance," though extremely youthful-looking. *She* did not even notice his eyes, apparently.

Chapter XI

THOMAS ROWLEY

" It was owing to his pride, which has been construed into veracity, that he so inflexibly persisted to the last, that these poems were by Rowley. To this secret of his bosom he had vowed eternal fidelity, and there is a degree of heroism in his obstinacy."

Thomas Warton, *Enquiry* (1782), p. 109.

I. THE IDEA

The conception of himself as a monk may have occurred to Chatterton while he was a Colston boy, " with the tonsure on his head," and boarded actually on the site of a Carmelite House ; but even if Thistlethwaite wrote the truth to Dean Milles, and *Elinoure and Juga* was produced on a parchment in 1764, there is no mention of Rowley *then,* and the earliest appearance of the name in Chatterton's handwriting is on the title page of " Antiquities, Book 3rd," which contains *The Unknown Knyght* and *Battle of Hastings* (I), not later, apparently, than March 6, 1768, where the designation " parish preeste St. John's " goes to show that the writer was familiar with the brass to Thomas Rouley, merchant and sheriff, in St. John's Church.

What led to the choice of a person bearing these two names as the author of the bulk of his antiques is again conjecture ; the coincidence of the Christian name with his own may have helped, but we should rather look for a clue in the relationship between Thomas Rowley and William Canynges (whom, probably for metrical reasons, Chatterton usually calls Canynge in the poems), his patron or Mæcenas.

Now Canynge is more than this in Chatterton's poetical scheme, more even than the illuminated merchant prince, a

Medici of fifteenth century Bristol, five times its mayor, who, as tradition and John Halfpenny's engraving told him, at a great expense new covered, glazed and repaired the church of St. Mary Redcliff, and not merely subscribed with other merchants towards its restoration, as did the historical William Canynges, like his grandfather before him in Edward III's reign. He is the being chosen by Providence to rear and finish "the pride of Bristowe and the westerne lande." The burden of *The Parlyamente of Sprytes* is that not Simon Burton alone, the church's legendary founder, has been outvied, but all Bristol's benefactors who raised churches and charitable foundations; St. Mary Redcliff will fall "onlie in the wrecke of nature," and, rising at the Last Judgment, Canynge will find "he chose on erthe a lyfe the beste." Rowley's admiration for Canynge is the poet's most intimate and personal expression of his own devotion to the glorious building for which his forefathers laboured and under whose shadow he was born and dreamt his earliest dreams.*

It was natural, then, that he should select for the purpose of this homage some person whose name he found near that of William Canynges (and here we touch on the Shakespearean limit of his genius, what has been called "that power of artistic self-effacement"); thus the Muniment Room, with its coffers, and in particular "Mr Canynges' Cofre" takes its place as a formative influence in the poetic conception. The existence to-day of that lease, evidently from this source, bearing date 1475 and mentioning the tenement of William Canynges, gentleman, and Thomas Rowley, sheriff, as one of the witnesses, is sufficient confirmation of Sir Daniel Wilson's guess in 1869 as to the whereabouts of the finding, nor need we suppose Chatterton to have been conversant, before he met Barrett, or during his schooldays, with the *Kalendar* of Robert Ricart, where, under 1467, he could have read:

* Oh worke of hande of heav'n,
Where Canynge sheweth as an instrumente,

he exclaims in *The Storie of William Canynge*, where the merchant's childhood is identified with his own. Bacon's definition of Poetry as "Historiae Imitatio ad Placitum" (*De Aug.* II. 13) comes to mind.

Maiores.	Vicecomes.	Ballivi.
Willelmus Canynges.	Johannes Gaywodde.	Thomas Rowley.
		Walterus Grymstede.

as well as the statement " This yere the said William Canynges Maire shulde haue be maried, by the kyng our souerain lordes commaundement as it was saide. Wherefore the said Canynges gave vp the worlde, and in al haste toke ordirs vpon hym of the gode Bisshoppe of Worcestre callid Carpynter, and was made preest and sange his furst masse at Our Lady of Redeclif the yere folouyng."*

Now *this* circumstance Chatterton has thrice turned to account: in the last stanza of *The Storie of William Canynge*—

> I saw the myndbruch† of hys nobille soule
> When Edward meniced a seconde wyfe ;
> I saw what Pheryons‡ yn hys mynde dyd rolle
> Nowe fyx'd fromm seconde dames a preeste for lyfe ;

in the prose correspondence between Rowley and Canynge, where the latter writes (" 1467 ") " Now, broder, yn the chyrche I amme safe, an hollie prieste unmarriageable," and (" 1468 ") " I bee now shutte uppe ynne mie College of Westburie ; come mie Rowlie and lette us dyspende our remaynynge yeeres togyder "§ ; and in Rowley's *Memoirs*, apparently the first of the antiques submitted to Catcott, where it is thus concluded: " On Sunday sung his first mass in the church of our ladie to the astonishing of Kyng Edward, who was so furiously madd and ravyngs withall that Master Cannings was wyling to give him 3000 marks, which gave him peace again, and he was admyted to the presence of the Kyng, staid in Bristow and partook of all his pleasures and pastimes till he departed the next year."|| He could have read it, however, on John Half-

* That Chatterton was familiar with the existence of the Society of Kalendaries, of which Robert Ricart was a member, is plain from p. 456 of Barrett's *History*, where an extract from Rowley, which accompanied a drawing of the house, is quoted—" Inne itte was 8 hundredthe bookes, in the bochorde meinte Saxonne Hystorie and Lege."

† " A hurting of honour and worship." Kersey.

‡ i.e. Pheons, " The barbed head of a dart, or arrow." Kersey.

§ *History of Bristol*, p. 636. *Works* III, p. 324, 5.

|| *Works*, III, p. 80.

penny's engraving ; and, according to Tyrwhitt, it was also to be seen in Latin and English as part of Canynges' epitaph in the church.* From Canynges' English epitaph he has, incidentally, drawn inspiration for the speech of " Lanyngetonnes spryte " :

But yette in sothen to rejoyce I muste
That I dyd not immeddle for to buylde ;
Sythe thys quaintissed† place so glorious,
Seemeynge alle chyrches joyned yn one guylde,
Has nowe supplied for what I had done,
Whych toe mie cierge‡ is a gloryous sonne.

Over the monument to Canynges in priest's habit may still be read, inscribed on a board (or " in a table," as the phrase was), just as in Chatterton's time :

A Lantern cleere settes forth a candell light
A worthy act declares a worthy wight
The Buildings rare that here you may behold
To shrine his Bones, deserves a tombe of gold
The famous Fabricke that he here hath donne
Shines in its sphere as glorious as the sonne.

So far, then, so good ; we have the groundwork of a romance ; the wealthy, generous, illuminated mayor of Bristol, William Canynge, who renounced the world, and his schoolfellow, friend, and protégé, Thomas Rowley, priest of St. John's ; one element is lacking, the poetry. Was there a precedent for a poetical monk of the fifteenth century ?

There was, indeed, in John Lydgate (1370?-1451?), the monk of Bury, the most voluminous as well as the most famous versifier of his age, who was not only the poet of his monastery, as Warton says,§ but of the world in general, and wrote pageants for the Mercers' and Goldsmiths' Companies, ballades to the sheriffs and aldermen of London, verses for the Queen's marriage, and satires on women and their headgear, as well as his

* *Vindication*, p. 113, the part relating to the 3,000 marks only, not the proposed marriage.

† Curiously devised.

‡ Candle.

§ *The History of English Poetry*, Section XXI.

Fall of Princes, *Troy Book*, and *Siege of Thebes*. That Chatterton knew of his existence is plain by the lines of Rowley on sending him the *Songe to Ælla*, as "a bowtynge matche"; they were, apparently, well acquainted:

> Lette ytt ne breakynge of oulde friendshyppe goe,
> Thys ys the onelie all-a-boone* I crave.

Lydgate is described, passing well, as "a priest in London," and his answer is in a plain ballad measure, where, however, in one verse the spirit of his more catalogic style has been caught, by chance or design:

> Amonge the Greeces Homer was
> A Poett mouche renownde,
> Amonge the Latyns Vyrgilius
> Was beste of Poets founde.

with which compare *Fall of Princes* (ed. Bergen) IX, 2245 sqq.:

> Mong Siciliens first Theodorus,
> For pacience hadde in gret reuerence;
> Among Grekis, the stori tellith vs,
> Anaxerses for his magnificence,†

There is no evidence that the West Countryman read the East Anglian to any appreciable extent; he dipped into him as he dipped into Chaucer, but rather less. *The Siege of Thebes*, *The Black Knight* and other Lydgatian pieces were printed in Speght, whose glossary he did not neglect; and a copy of the *Fall*, in one of the four pre-Elizabethan editions, may very well have been on Mr. Green's shelves. Rime royal, the fifteenth century measure *par excellence*, is used but thrice in the Rowley Poems (though the Miltonic measure of *Elinoure and Juga* and the *Balade of Charitie* is really rime royal, with an alexandrine

* Favour.

† Oddly enough the only other passage in Lydgate I have come across which seems to look forward to Rowley is in the same book (848 sqq.) where the Kings of Lombardy are described:

> Ther shon wer racid fresshli to the ton,
> Richeli transuersed with gold weer, &c.

This puts one in mind of the "Abbote of Seyncte Godwynes convente" in the *Balade of Charitie*, whose "Shoone pyke a loverds mighte have binne."

as the last line), namely, in the fourth stanza of *The Worlde, On Happienesse*, and the " Entroductionne " (two stanzas) to *Ælla*. No, it was the character, rather than the verse-practice, that was taken over, and only the outer shell of that. He may have known of Lydgate's description of his wild youth in the *Testament;* it is not necessary that he should, for Rowley embodies his creator's quite individual spirit of mischief.

For instance, in *Battle of Hastings* (II., stanza 5), glossing the line :

Fierce as a ryver burstynge from the borne

Rowley notes that Lydgate, not knowing of the violent bursting forth of Holywell in Turgot's time, left out one line*; from which an innocent reader draws the natural inference that both Lydgate and Rowley translated Turgot's *Battle of Hastings*, and only the latter's version, the more accurate, has come down to us.

Rowley's lines *To John Lydgate* afford a more convincing proof of Chatterton's artfulness than even *The Execution of Sir Charles Bawdin*. He brought them to Barrett, as may be seen by the MS. (5766B, f. 11) as *To John Ladgate*; Barrett, says Dean Milles (p. 376), convinced him from the original that " he had mistaken it for *Lidgate*," and in the parchment, in Sir William Rose Smith's possession, " Lydgate " is written. The Dean adds, evidently on Barrett's authority, " it was not easy, however, to make him acknowledge an error." So much for Lydgate.

But Chatterton's idea went farther than throwing back to the fifteenth century a happy picture of a monkish poet and his patron—the patron he himself was never to find—Canynge doing duty for Humphrey Duke of Gloucester in this case. There was a little group of poets, of whom Canynge was not the least; John a Iscam, i.e. Josephus Iscanus, from Gibson's Camden (ed. 1695, p. 65), who collaborated with Rowley in *The Parlyamente of Sprytes*, and wrote *The Merrie Tricks of Laymyngetowne*, Sir Thybbot Gorges (Sir Theobald Gorges died

* " In Turgott's tyme Holenwell braste of erthe so fierce that it threw a stone-wall carrying the same awaie. J. Lydgate ne knowynge this lefte out o line."

10 Edw. IV, possessed of Wraxall, where, incidentally, Barrett bought a house in 1766*), who wrote one of the songs in *Ælla*, and Bishop Carpenter, whose modest contribution is an inscription for the cover of a Mass Book at Westbury (*Works*, III, p. 312). They took lines from one another ; Iscam's " flouretts straughte with dewe," according to one of Chatterton's notes on *The Parlyamente of Sprytes*, was borrowed from Rowley's " Like kynge-cuppes brasteynge with the mornynge dew." They were feasted by Canynge in the Rudde House, now 97 Redcliff Street, a famous Bristol mansion† ; they acted before and with him, and in a poem engraved by Joseph Strutt for the early editions of Rowley as a specimen of the " originals," Canynge, presiding at a mayoral banquet, while the aldermen sit around and snuffle up the pleasant steam,

> Lyke asses wylde ynne desarte vaste
> Swotelye the morneynge ayre doe taste,

complains of the absence of his fellow bards :

> Thus echone daie bee I to deene
> Gyf Rowley, Iscamm or Tyb. Gorges be ne seene.

This is all, with hardly a shadow of a doubt, an idealization (unconscious, it may be, in the first place) of an insupportable milieu. Chatterton lived in a world of bustling, get-rich-quick, tradesfolk, and swaggering prentices, who preened themselves on their talents, spouting clubs, and effusions in the Bristol newspapers and the London magazines. He was one of them, and indeed corrected the efforts of one John Lockstone, a linen draper, so that there is still a doubt as to the authorship of

* Milles, p. 178, citing Dugdale *Bar.* II, 267 ; *Bristol Times*, Mar. 19, 1859. The name would be familiar to Chatterton. Sir Ferdinando Gorges had occupied The Great House in 1642. See also Leland, *It.* VII, 98.

† " Memorandum in mansione pulcherrima de le bak ex posteriore parte de Radclyf-strete super aquam de Avyn est pulcher turris per Willelmum Canyngis edificata, continet 4 fenestras vocatas Bay-wyndowes ornatissimo modo cum cameris, continet circa 20 virgas, in longitudine 16 virgas." William of Worcester, *It.* ed. 1778, p. 254.

It is called " Canynges place " in a deed of 1500 bearing Barrett's endorsement (Bickley, *op. cit.*, no. 281) and by Chatterton in his sketch map of Redcliff, 5766B. f. 38. See also *Works*, III, p. 337.

From Skelton's " Etchings " (Pl. xlviii).

CANYNGE'S PLACE, 97 REDCLIFF STREET, BRISTOL.

face p. 162

some of the pieces signed "Asaphides."* Here reigned the simmering friendship, the petty grudge, the hint in time, and the pretence of boldness that has characterized a thousand groups of writers since his day, callow mediocrities with office jobs, who fraternize in a restaurant or teashop between their business and their homes. He saw this, felt it, expressed it in his satires, and, in the pieces ascribed to Rowley and his circle, escaped from it. *There,* like Troilus in his posthumous exaltation, he could laugh " in himselfe " at that world, secure in the knowledge that no member of it, not even his best friend, gave him credit for being more than the transcriber of ancient manuscripts, and " the mad genius " or " young villain "—both terms were used of him in Bristol then. When in his "Will " he leaves to his native city all his spirit and disinterestedness, parcels of goods unknown on her quay since the days of Canynge and Rowley, it is as much as to say that he sees both worlds at once, fairly and squarely. Yet even into the ideal world, so sane is he, some raillery must creep. There is the bore on current topics ; Canynge writes :

ONN JOHNE A DALBENIE

Johne makes a jarre boute Lancaster and Yorke ;
Bee stille, gode manne, and learne to mynde thie worke.

There is the descendant of Suffenus :

Hee synges of seynctes who dyed for ther Godde
Everych wynter nyghte afresche he sheddes theyr blodde . . .
Yette Vevyan ys ne foole, behynde hys lynes.

there is the person who belongs to a school of poetry, or turns it out to pattern ; this might also serve, by anticipation, for his criticism of a later mediævalist, William Morris :

* Lockstone is the " haberdasher " of *A Bristol Spouting Club* (*T. and C.M.*, June, 1771), identified by the " Jack Touchstone, the haberdasher, who had just been murdering the majesty of Alexander," in *Cosmopolitus Detected* (*ibid.*, July, 1771). He admitted that Chatterton corrected the lines on Mr. Alcock, the miniature painter (*T. and C.M.*, Feb., 1769). See Gregory, p. 48, *n.* Nothing signed *Asaphides* after Aug., 1770, can be admitted as Chatterton's, except perhaps *Cutholf* (*Lady's Magazine*, Jan. 1771), which the 1803 editors accepted as his on internal evidence. *The Lady's Magazine*, in particular, has execrable imitations of Chatterton's work under this signature.

Geofroie makes vearse, as handycraftes theyr ware ;

and there is the intellectual snob :

Whoever speketh Englysch ys despysed,
The Englysch hym to please moste fyrste be Latynized.*

Strange creature ! One gift, besides patience, was denied him, to laugh at his helplessness among these earthworms ; but Chatterton was not the sort ever to admit that he was helpless : he had stared upon the sun, and, unable thereafter to bear the gloom of the cave, exulted in his silent priesthood. Hear William Smith :

" He was always very fond of walking in the fields, and particularly in Redcliffe meadows ; and of talking about these manuscripts and reading them there. *Come,* he would say, *you and I will take a walk in the meadow. I have got the cleverest thing for you, that ever was. It is worth half a crown merely to have a sight of it ; and to hear me read it to you.* When we were arrived at the place proposed, he would produce his parchment ; shew it, and read it to me. There was one spot in particular, full in view of the church, in which he always seemed to take a peculiar delight. He would frequently lay himself down, fix his eyes upon the church ; and seem as if he were in a kind of extasy or trance. Then, on a sudden and abruptly, he would tell me, *that steeple was burnt down by lightning : that was the place where they formerly acted plays* : (meaning, if I remember right, what is now called the Parade). I recollect very assuredly, that he had a parchment in his hand at the very time, when he gave me this description : but whether he read this history out of that parchment, I am not certain."†

But note that he did not hesitate to lie to this friend. Lort has a note :

" Mr Smith says that C mentioned to him the original MS of Sir Charles Baldwyn as being in his possession, and said he could not read it then, but that he was determined to be able to do it."‡

If such be not what Plato calls the noble lie, it is at any rate

* Or be it by young Yeatman criticized,
Who damns good English if not Latinized.
Happiness.

† Bryant, p. 530.
‡ 11457.

not the lie in the soul, of which William Barrett and George Catcott were guilty.

To resume, of this poetic band Rowley is the chief, and about him we are told most. According to the first note to the *Balade of Charitie* he was born at Norton Malreward, that is to say in the neighbourhood of primitive remains, under the shadow of Maes Knoll, educated at the convent of St. Kenna (an imaginary house, put, maybe, for the Abbey of Black Canons) at Keynsham, and died at Westbury. But this bare statement is supplemented by his *Memoirs*, the *Lyfe of Canynge*, and their correspondence; we have the MS. of the two latter in 5766B. In "1418" he "emprooved hys Leore" with Canynge at the White Friars (site of Colston's Hospital); about "1430" he was inducted into holy orders and became father confessor to William Canynge, whose money-loving father and brother had both died, leaving him their wealth. Canynge, after his father's obit, went to Gloucester, and in "1431" married Johanna Hathwaie* (a name not necessarily suggested by Shakespeare's Anne Hathaway, as Sir Daniel Wilson thought, but a local one, to be found in the Redcliff register of marriages, under 1644, and still current in the city), who died in childbirth. Thereafter he returned to the "greete rudde House neere to the Waterre," where he was born, and made it a Freemasons' Lodge, of which Rowley was a member. Canynge opened it formally on the vigil of Epiphany "1432"—over his seat was depicted Architectura in a Saxon habit—and spoke of the "use of the Artes to emproove the Trade." The Friars enlarged, the gentlemen attended, and the councilmen fell asleep. Canynge's speech was approved, and framed "ynn eguilten Frames," possibly like Mr. Colston's "Orders" for the regulation of his Hospital. The body met every Thursday, and Rowley was soon commissioned to write an interlude with a great part for Iscam on the laying of the foundation stone of St. Mary's. *Ælla* was the result ("1432"); Canynge's letter to Iscam on the performance is as follows:

"I heerebie sende youe mie thankes for the goode parte you haveth plaied yn the whyche the Auctoure and yourselfe seemed one.

* Barrett has corrected the surname to "Young" (5766B, f. 35).

Celmondes rageynge yn the Warre dydd excelle thoughte of Phantasie —Rowleie alleyne culde have plaied Ælle soe fyne—all enseemed properre. no strained Voice ne wrythinge of boddie ne dystortynge of Face, when Ælla saieth

O ! speack ne moe : mie hearte flames yn its keste
I once was Ælle nowe bee nott hys Shade
Han all the Fhuyr of Mysfortunes wylle
Felle onne mie* benned Head I han beene Ælle stylle
Thys alleyn was unburld of all mie Spryghte
Mie Honoure Hounoure frownd at the dulce Wynd
That stealed onne ytte.

Thenne was the Actyone united wythe the Wordes—I saie ne moe—botte next to Rowleies Ælle was Iscammes Celmonde—ne dyd Byrtha Magnus or the rest speak alleyne—you wylle take thys heerew[th] as a smalle tokenne from W[m.] C.

This criticism on his own work by the poet is incidentally in marked contrast to Thomas Warton's comment on the dialogue (ll. 1146-1175) between Ælla and Egwina : "A better scene for shewing the shrug and the start to the greatest advantage never appeared at Drury Lane Theatre" (*Enquiry*, p. 89).

In "1435" the church's body was arched, and there was a discourse at the Lodge, "of Peyncteynge," but Canynge adds "the Freeres kenne littel thereofe" ; and "1443" saw the building finished and dedicated by Carpenter ; *The Parlyamente of Sprytes* was written for this occasion, Iscam contributing 58 lines. The correspondence then jumps, in Chatterton's MS., to "1461," when Canynge announces the King's command that he marry again with the generality "Lyfe ys a Sheelde where ne Tyncture of Joie or Tene haveth preheminence."† Then comes the retreat to his college at Westbury (which the historical Bishop Carpenter had refounded‡), whither in "1467" he invites Rowley, who

* Chatterton has written quite unmistakably "bie," through the attraction of "benned," or possibly to suggest a miscopying of his "original." Barrett(?) has scratched through the first two letters and written "mie" above. Cf. l. 1084, "Bie thankes," and Tyrwhitt's note, p. 307 (ed. 1777).

† The web of our life is of a mingled yarn, good and ill together.
All's Well, Act IV, Sc. 3.

‡ See Pryce, *Memorials of the Canynges*, p. 163. John Halfpenny's engraving has "he was dean of Westbury certain years where he founded an almshouse for six poor women."

refused the offer of "a Cannon's place" there, his pains making him to stay at home, but we gather that Rowley lived with him at Westbury for six years; this may be one of the inconsistencies that troubled Mr. Barrett. In 1474, unimpeachable year, William Canynges died; and it is a pathetic commentary on what has gone before that there is no mention of Rowley in his extant and genuine will (P.C.C. Wattys, 17) dated Nov. 12, and proved Nov. 29, 1474. To meet this difficulty, Chatterton has provided a deed (unantiquated) made on the eve of Canynge's retirement to Westbury, where Thomas Rowley priest and William Rowley merchant are given all his lands in trust, for Canynge's sons, &c., Thomas Rowley while living to have the manors of Wye and Westbury on Trym (5766B, f. 17). William Rowley, "bailiff," it may be mentioned, is witness to a genuine lease (271 in Mr. Bickley's *Calendar*) by Nicholas Pyttes, vicar of St. Mary de Redclyf, 15 Edw. IV (1475), which can be presumed to have come from "Mr. Canynges Cofre," and this further substantiates Sir Daniel Wilson's theory of the place where Chatterton found the name*; it bears Barrett's endorsement.

Rowley seems to have passed some part of the rest of his life in Bristol; he had a house "on the hyll" (Redcliff Hill), where "the ayer was mickle keen," but he secured a house by the Tower, which had not been repaired "since Robert Consull of Gloucester repayrd the castle and wall," at a very small rate, on a 99 years repairing lease; hither he transferred his chattels and "livd warm." Of his death at Westbury we have no account.

He certainly deserved a substantial legacy, for his duties were not merely those of a father confessor, but a secretary, or factor. In "1431," on the occasion of Canynge's marriage, he is instructed to "Release the Dets of my Tenauntes . . . yeve [give] newe whyte Garmentes & Marks to the needie & lette the Fyddlers scrape the Crowd bee not unpleasaunt atte my makeynge you a Servitoure the Friende wylle allowe of ytte." He might even have set the fiddlers the tune, for Catcott tells us that Chatterton "informed me that his father

* *Chatterton* (1869), pp. 133, 156.

(who took a great delight in musical compositions) had a book of that sort composed by Rowley, but I do not recollect whether his son ever had it in his possession."*

But his chief occupation was acting as itinerant antiquary and collector of drawings and MSS. for his patron: "Fadre, quod he, I have a crotchett in my brayne that will need your aide. Master William, said I, if you command me I will go to Roome for you. Not so far distant said he: I ken you for a mickle learned priest, if you will leave the parysh of our ladie, and travel for me, it shall be mickle to your profits." This must have been about "1430," and on the Monday following the interview Rowley started on his travels. Peterborough, Coventry, Durham, Cirencester (for "Fryar Rycharde's" papers), York, and even Ireland ("wheere ys twayne of your Famylie buryed") were visited, with good fortune. At first drawings only were bargained for. Before he went to Durham, Canynge sent for hin: "Fadre, you have done mickle well, all the chatills are more worth than you gave; take this for your paynes: so saying, he did put into my hands a purse of two hundreds good pounds, and did say that I should note be in need, I did thank him most heartily." It was this episode in the *Memoirs* that Barrett found so hard to believe. An extract relating to *Battle of Hastings* can conclude these specimens of Rowley's prose:

"I gave master Cannings my Bristow tragedy, for which he gave me in hands twentie pounds, and did praise it more than I did think my self did deserve . . . and now haveing nought to do and not wyling to be ydle, I went to the minster of our Ladie and Saint Goodwin, and then did purchase the Saxon manuscripts, and sett my self diligently to translate and worde it in English metre, which in one year I performd and styled it the Battle of Hastings; master William did bargyin for one manuscript, and John Pelham, an esquire of Ashley, for another—Master William did praise it muckle greatly, but advised me to tender it to no man, beying the menn whose name were therein mentioned would be offended. He gave me 20 markes, and I did goe to Ashley, to master Pelham, to be payd of him for the other one I left with him.

But his ladie being of the family of the Fiscamps, of whom some

* *Monthly Review*, May, 1777.

things are said,* he told me he had burnt it, and would have me burnt too if I did not avaunt. Dureing this dinn his wife did come out, and made a dinn to speake by a figure, would have oversounded the bells of our Ladie of the Cliffe ; I was fain content to get away in a safe skin."

One might be tempted to regard the aspect of Rowley as itinerant collector for Canynge as the last accretion to the character, suggested by the more than weekly supplying of Barrett with parchments, draughts, and "transcripts" for his history, but for the fact that the *Memoirs* appear first in the list of pieces produced after the "Bridge" article, and before the introduction of the surgeon. Unfortunately we have not Chatterton's thin quarto copy-book containing them; the handwriting of the *Lyfe of William Canynge*, and of the correspondence, approximates to that of the accounts of Bristol churches, which were certainly written for Barrett's benefit; it is more cursive and mature than that of "Antiquities, Book 3rd," and more hurried certainly. On the extant evidence, the travels of Macpherson, financed by the Faculty of Advocates in Edinburgh, must be adjudged the original of Rowley's suspicious two hundred pounds.

The historical allusions in the correspondence (which, *inter alia*, differentiate it from the Paston Letters) are laid on in bold journalistic colours, and Henry VI, Margaret, and the Kingmaker tricked out in Tussaud garb. Rowley was a Yorkist, though he could feel for Bawdin's fate ; and a footnote to the *Balade of Charitie*—which shows that the sources of laughter were not wholly dried up at that particular moment—states that it would have been *charitable* if the author had not pointed at personal characters, the Abbot of St. Godwin's at the time of its composition being Ralph de Bellomont, "a great stickler for the Lancastrian family." Where note that one William de Bello Monte appears as witness to three grants, *temp*. Hen. III, numbered 2, 4, and 12 in Mr. Bickley's *Calendar*. "Mr. Canynges Cofre" had doubtless afforded the surname.

* Behynde the erlie Fiscampe did advaunce,
Bethoghte to kill him with a stabbynge knife &c.
Battle of Hastings I, l. 443.

"His historic works" are not exhausted, though the reader's patience may well be. Of two among them "Of the Auntiaunt Forme of Monies," and "Englandes Glorye revyved in Maystre Canynge," which comprise what Chatterton himself called *Yeloue Rolle,* a modern text is actually available*; but the Rowley prose pieces have small value save as curiosities or sidelights on the poet's nature and environment. They lend no loveliness to the antique poems, and are hardly illuminated thereby, though they are a little nearer his heart than the Ossianics and the political letters; but the intrinsic Rowley is complete without them.

2. THE MATERIALS

This, then, was the Bristol Lydgate, as his creator displayed him. That such a priest as Thomas Rowley had no existence, or that the real fifteenth century William Canynges played no such part in the enlightenment of Bristol is neither here nor there.† The picture of a guild of craftsmen eager "to advaunce the glorie of thys oure Towne," with the mayor at their head, and his school friend and confessor leading the poetic van is, however crudely expressed, that of an idealist and a dreamer, and no doubt partly the reason why D. G. Rossetti, with the Pre-Raphaelite Brotherhood in his mind, vowed so uncompromising a devotion to Chatterton, declaring him as great as any English poet whatever.‡ A MS. note of Blake (1826) on Wordsworth's *Supplementary Essay* is also in point: "I believe both Macpherson and Chatterton that what they say is ancient, is so." For these later poets, citizens of no "city of pigs" but a New Jerusalem, the "forgeries" were sentences of truth, as they could not be for Catcott, Barrett, Bryant and Dean Milles, or even for Tyrwhitt, Malone, and Thomas Warton.

The relation of the Rowley Poems to the Rowley Romance,

* Sir Ernest Clarke, *New Lights on Chatterton,* pp. 34-37.

† For the historical William Canynges see H. J. Wilkins, *Westbury College* (1917), Ch. VIII.

‡ Sir Hall Caine, *Recollections of Dante Gabriel Rossetti* (1882), p. 185.

or Idea (as I have called it), may perhaps be expressed by the analogy of that of a castle's keep to its curtain wall. Supposing ourselves to have crossed the drawbridge, that article in *Felix Farley*, casually glanced at some of the bastions, the drawings and parchments, and inspected the two-towered gatehouse, Rowley's *Memoirs* and *The Lyfe of W. Canynge*, it is our next business to examine the fabric of the keep from outside before entering it. There are buttresses, machicolations, and turrets, and the architecture is perverse and fantastic in the extreme: "Gyff theie have anie, itte ys roughe made art." And first, where was this stone quarried?

(*a*) *Words*

This question has been roughly answered under Oct. 1, 1768. Ironically enough the main source of the Rowley vocabulary was stumbled on, as early as 1781, by Jacob Bryant, the Rowleian, whose words are worth quoting:

> "As these" [i.e., Skinner's Etymologicum and a Saxon dictionary] "did not answer his purpose, he got Speght's Chaucer for the sake of the glossary, and Kersey's dictionary. In the latter of these he used to hunt in a most servile manner. This may be perceived in a strange bombast letter to his friend Smith, which he wrote about a fortnight before he died.* It consists of many high-sounding and uncommon terms; borrowed from the Greek, and relating chiefly to different sorts of poetry. These are all to be found in Kersey, and, I believe, in no other English dictionary. That he had them from this source, is certain from his copying the very errors of the author; such as *Ogdastick*, for *Ogdoastick*, a mistake, which occurs in Kersey; also *Cephalophonia* for the *head-ache*, instead of *Cephaloponia*; which is to be found in the same author. In like manner he has *cherisaunei* for *cherisaunce*" [*Ælla*, Entroductionne, l. 1] "borrowed in the same manner."†

Bryant's solemn conclusion "This gives room to suspect, that he sometimes altered the originals, which he had before him, upon the authority of these etymologists" was thus turned against him by Tyrwhitt: "In my opinion it gives much more

* *Vide inf.* p. 430.
† *Obs.*, p. 561.

room to suspect that it was upon the authority of these etymologists that he composed his pretended originals." (*Vind.*, p. 186.)

In 1838, C. V. le Grice, Charles Lamb's friend, independently, as it seems, traced all but three words in the letter to Smith to Nathaniel Bailey's dictionary, the book mentioned in the poet's talk with Edward Gardner.* And indeed Chatterton may well have used both dictionaries, not to speak of the glossaries to Percy's *Reliques*, Hughes's *Spenser*, Hearne's *Robert of Gloucester*, Verstegan's *Restitution*, and, it may be, many another Old English work.†

The well-known *Essay* of Skeat (1871) in essence did little more than reaffirm Bryant's unwitting discovery of ninety years before, but it had the advantage and disadvantage of being written by an etymologist. Hence, while Chatterton's use of Kersey, and formation of a MS. glossary by entering the words in reverse order (e.g. " *cause*, gare "—Barrett, by the way, showed Lort a glossary of Chatterton's " with ye old words first "), and the blunders consequent on such a system, where a verb might be mistaken for a noun, or the wrong meaning assigned, as well as his copying his lexicographer's errors, producing a ghost English, and altering spellings and terminations to suit pleasure, convenience or rhyme ; while all this is expounded with irrefragable logic, the conclusion is reached that to edit the Rowley Poems to the most advantage we must " do away with the needless disguises, and give them as far as possible in modern English," substituting the words in

* *Gentleman's Magazine*, Aug., 1838.

† Both Bailey and Kersey have "cherisaunei (O) comfort." E. Coles (1732) has " cherisaunce."

Gif, for if, is not in Speght, Kersey or Bailey, but in Verstegan.

Loverd, for lord, *do*. Coles has " Loverd, Lav—, O. *a lord*." Chatterton uses both forms.

Selinesse, is not in Kersey or Bailey, but in Speght, " felicity."

Ghastnesse, *do.*; gastnes, " terror."

If he used Urry's *Chaucer*, he found Abroden in the Glossary. In Urry, but not in Speght, he would find a note on the Y " prefixed to verbs in perfect tense."

In Hughes's *Spenser* he would find encouraging notes on " made words," words " writ by poetick License " or " put for the sake of Rhime," on the final N and the prefix Y, Saxon words, and words used with two different meanings.

Chatterton's footnotes for his words in the text, where they are metrically equivalent, and leaving them, or rewriting the text, where they are not, or the rhyme forbids. Skeat honestly thought that thus we approximated more closely to the original text as conceived by the poet, yet at the same time he notes that the hard words sometimes come in clotted masses so as "to increase the labour of perceiving his first thoughts."

The plain fact is that Chatterton, even less than any other true poet or artist, asks for his work to be touched up by another hand, and the kindly Skeat performed a service for him analogous in results to that performed by George Catcott, in his transcripts for eighteenth century noblemen, where the poems were made more antiquated to satisfy the taste of that day. When he wrote, glossing "gites" by "robes, mantles":

> Throwe halfe hys joornie, dyghte yn gites of goulde

are we seriously to suppose that the true text is

> Through half his journey, dight in robes of gold

substituting, that is, one kind of alliteration for another, in another limb of the line, and destroying a forcible assonance? And gite happens to be a good old English poetic word,* found for example in Fairfax's translation of Tasso, which Cibber says (1753), "is in everybody's hand":

> And donned a gite in deepest purple dyed
> Book XIII, St. 54.

This particular instance is chosen because it is that adduced by Skeat himself in justification of his method; that method's sole justification is as a proof that the baffling spirit of English poetry shines through professorial fogs. It is astonishing that Tyrwhitt's successor in the editorship of Chaucer should have ventured on such textual liberties,† but they are part of the

* *Cf.* also "And wered upon my gaye scarlet gytes." *Wife of Bath's Prologue* (ed. Skeat, l. 559).

† Even the excuse that, as the poems were originally composed in eighteenth century English, Chatterton's glossary as often as not gives the text as it entered his head, cannot justify the rewriting (e.g.) of

> Chauntynge owte so blatauntlie,[1]
> Tellynge lecturnyes[2] to mee,

as

[1] loudly. [2] lectures.

dismal tradition that Chatterton was but a boy, and his poetry but a " copy " of verses, up for correction. And that truly is the appearance of Skeat's text, with footnotes on every page informing the reader how this or that word should have been formed, or what was the " proper word," when the poet's spare glossary, plus common sense on his reader's part, is enough to make his meaning, in nine cases out of ten, as plain as ever he meant to make it ; and this editor can remark in good faith, " Chatterton's editors have, in fact, done but little for him."

It must not be thought, however, that I belittle Skeat's aperçu as to the slightness of Chatterton's knowledge of Anglo-Saxon, or many of his notes, or his efforts (the first) to print the acknowledged poems in chronological order ; but if Rowley is to be read at all, he must be read as his creator produced him.

The poet's four methods of forming words, according to Skeat—and it is hard indeed to cavil at him here—were :

1. To copy exactly what he found in Kersey, &c. e.g. *cherisaunei.*
2. To take a groundwork, but alter the termination, e.g., *adrames* (*adraming*, Kersey).
3. To alter spelling capriciously, e.g. *anere,* for *another.*
4. To coin words at pleasure (a) from some intelligible root, e.g. *hopelen* for *hopelessness.* (b) from imagination, e.g. *bayre* for *brow.*

His rhyming is careless ; in the same stanza *run* rhymes with *gone,* and *ryne* (for *run*) with *twyne* ; *night* he spells *nete, twain, twaie* ; *banèd* is found in the first line of a stanza and *bante* in the last, and *words* close to *wordès.* Sometimes singular rhymes with plural, e.g. *Thys Celmonde menes* with *bewreene*; and no grammarian would have written *glare* in the *Songe to Ælla.* But it is hopeless to criticize him on these lines.

His was an eager, impressionistic, unscholarly mind, alive to sound and colour ; Kersey was his paint-box, and he mixed

Chaunting forth so lustily,
Telling warning tales to me.

See on this point Buxton Forman, *Chatterton and his latest editor* (1874). Skeat is just as amazing on the modern poems ; e.g., additional notes, vol. 1, p. 368, " ' Displays his bigot blade, and thunders *draw* ' ; (i.e. draws forth his thunders)." This, when the line itself thunders " Draw ! " at him.

the tints he found there with others of his own fancy. No proceeding could be more opposed to eighteenth century formality. He will write *theie pyghtes*, where the verb, glossed *pluck*, seems to derive from Kersey's "*pight* (O), propped, settled." From *ardour*, *blanch*, and *duress* he produces *ardurous*, *emblaunchèd*, and *duressèd*. The joy in sound is paramount always. Kersey gives him "*hanten* accustom"; he coins *unenhantende*, knows exactly where to place it, and throws off the sonorous

> Brendynge perforce with unenhantende fyre.

It is a shaping mind, his; to get a certain emphasis in the middle of a line, he does not shrink from sheer invention:

> To gayne so gayne a prize wyth losse of breathe

where the adjective is glossed "great, advantageous."

He contracts *garden* to *gorne*; renders *hermit's errmmietts*; strikes out *cleme* for *sound* (clamour); forms *gyttelles* from *gites*, possibly with *mantles* in his head, and *ybroched*, of the moon, from Kersey's "*broch* or *brooch*, an old fashion'd peeked ornament of gold"; hits on weird compounds like *gronfers* (*gron*, fen + fires), *eynegears* (eye-tackles, hence *objects*), and *unwers* (for unweathers, *tempests*). He will even, in a line already quoted, take a musical term, spelt *dulce*, as an epithet for the wind. *Quenched* appears as *quansed*, *lethal* as *lethlen*, *renown* as *rennome*; and, perhaps strangest of all, in the line

> Ne seyncte yn celles, botte, havynge blodde and tere

tere, glossed *health*, is a pillage from Kersey's "*teres major* (in *Anat.*) a round smooth muscle of the arm."

Examine the MS. of the opening stanza of his first English Eclogue, *Roberte and Raufe*; see what it yields:

> Whanne Englonde smeetheynge from her lethal Wounde,
> From her galled Necke dyd twytte the chayne awaie;
> Kennynge her leegeful Sonnes falle all arounde,
> Myghtie theie fell 'twas honoure led the fraie,
> Thanne inne a Dale bie Eve's dark Surcote graie,

Twayne lonelie Shepsterres dyd abredden flie;
The rostlyng Liff dothe theyr whytte hartes affraie,
And wythe the Owlette trembled and dyd crie;
Firste Robert Neatherde hys sore boesom stroke,
Then fellen on the Grounde and thus yspoke—

Smeetheynge is glossed thus: "*smoking*, in some copies *bletheynge*, but in the original as above." Coined out of *smoking* and *seething*, it is what Humpty Dumpty might have called "a portmanteau."* But note the happy effect of the sounds *smeeth* and *leth*, packed between *onde* and *wounde*! *Twytte* is Kersey's "*twitch*, to pinch or pluck"; *kennynge* is used in the second sense Kersey gives—"to spy out at some distance"; *leegeful* is a coinage, i.e. *lawful*, through the attraction of *legal*; *shepsterres* and *surcote* are again from Kersey. *Abredden* has this note, "*abruptly*, so Chaucer, Syke he abredden dyde attourne." Urry glosses the word Abroden "set free, delivered"; Kersey has "*abraid*, upstart, recovered. *Chaucer*"; but the line Chatterton gives is not in Chaucer, and may very well be Rowley's.†

His idiom is often crude, ungrammatical, and of the people; but it is *spoken*. He must have written much, even of his antique verse, with impetuous fury; hence there are frequent inversions and ellipses:

She nillynge to take myckle aie dothe hede

means, as Mr. Hare says, "She, not willing to take much, ever doth heed not to take much," but is "nonsense," according to Skeat; yet Shakespeare, in his last period, wrote things of this sort:

like one
Who having into truth, by telling of it,
Made such a sinner of his memory,
To credit his own lie,

* "Well, '*slithy*' means 'lithe and slimy.' 'Lithe' is the same as 'active.' You see it's like a portmanteau—there are two meanings packed up into one word." *Through the Looking Glass*, Ch. VI.

† The final couplet is coloured by a remembrance of Fairfax's eclogue, *Eglon and Alexis*, which he could find in Cibber's *Lives* (I, p. 225) or Elizabeth Cooper's *Muses Library* (p. 364):

Crowned with a wreath of Heban branches broke:
Whom good Alexis found, and thus bespoke.

The line in *Battle of Hastings* (I) :

> Who, love of hym, han from his country gone

owes all its strangeness and pathos to the omission of a word before " love." In the flyting of the Danish chiefs in *Ælla*, Magnus piles words on words :

> Mie shielde, lyche sommere morie gronfer droke,
> Mie lethalle speere, alyche a levyn-mylted oke.

One does not always ask for intelligibility or construction, when a writer's genius is dramatic ; effects like

> Gyf thou anent a wolfynnes rage wouldest staie,
> 'Tys here to meet ytt.

or,

> None touch mie rynge who not in honour live

are their own defence. A systematic grammar of his usages could hardly be compiled, because he is everywhere a law unto himself. *Lissedd** is used in the sense of " limited " (glossed *bounded*) in *The Tournament* (l. 97) ; but in the second line of that poem *lysse* is glossed " sport or play." And the reader falls back on Skeat's remark about the entering of words in reverse order in his MS. glossary, and *bounded* being the cause of the mistake ; but that does not wholly satisfy ; one suspects that, had the mood so taken him, Chatterton might have given this word half a dozen other meanings. In short, the words are more important than what they literally stand for. *Wailed* in Kersey is explained as " wine, choice wine " ; in *Ælla* (l. 11)

> Orr scarlette, wythe waylde lynnen clothe ywreene[1]
>
> [1] Covered.

the unglossed word apparently means " choice."

And there are words which actually defied Tyrwhitt and Skeat, and still await their etymologist. *Tochelod* (*Ælla*, l. 205) is one ; it is glossed by Dean Milles " Tackeld or joined to," Chatterton not having condescended to explain it ; Skeat

* This word shows that Kersey's dictionary was used, in Bailey's it is spelt " listed," with the same meaning, " bounded."

says "possibly it is an error for *tochered*, endowed, from the Scottish *tocher*, a dower." The line is

Tochelod yn Angel joie heie Angeles bee

May be Kersey's "*Takel* (O), a feather or arrow," gives the clue; a poet might have written "Takeled," meaning feathered, with an angel's wings in mind. *Bercie* (*Storie of William Canynge*, l. 8) and *trerdie* (*Sancte Warbur*, l. 31) are others; of course they may have been printed incorrectly: and there is the mysterious *ente*, glossed by Chatterton "a purse or bag" (*Ecl.* III, 57), and used several times, which may be a purely mischievous invention.*

Not seldom the incongruous waits at the heels of the heroic, and never more so than when the formal cut of eighteenth century idiom peeps from Kersey's veneer, as in

Hear from mie groted[1] harte the lover and the friende,

[1] Swollen (for *agroted*).

or in ignorantly made compounds like *proto-slene* (first slain, on the analogy of Kersey's "*proto-plast*, first made"), or in the frequent personifications of Terror, Hope, Victory, etc., on which the Anti-Rowleians were not slow to pounce as evidences of the age in which the poems were composed, no less than on anachronisms like knitted stockings.

Rowley's spelling will probably never find an enthusiast; final *e*s are tacked on, *y*s are freely put for *i*s, *ie*s for final *y*s, and *e*s and consonants (*d*, *l*, *m*, *n*, *t* in particular) are as freely doubled; in this childish procedure, even more than in his "originals," Chatterton enjoys the doubtful honour of paving the way for W. H. Ireland's Shakespearean forgeries of 1795. Still, no fair-minded editor would now alter this spelling, as stanzas and lines would be left with a patchy appearance; besides, the reader who turns naturally to Rowley soon gets used to it. We do the author of *Ælla* no service by modernizing

* Wright's *Dialect Dictionary* has "Ent., Glo., Brks., Dor., Cor. to empty, pour out. Enties, empty bottles, empties, Cor." Remembering "The Compleint of Chaucer to his empty purse," I think this meaning may have been in Rowley's mind.

his antiques to the slightest extent. If, for instance, we write *honour* for his *honnoure*, we are losing the weight of the first syllable and the resonance of the second.

Hong pendaunte bie thy swerde and craved for thy morth

is ruined, as word music, when replaced by

Hung pendant by thy sword &c.

No! leave the "oulde rouste" alone, and read him aloud, not with the eye merely, and out of that barbarous incantation emerges the indisputable form and stature of an English poet.*

(*b*) *Prosody*

In his choice of a vocabulary, his errors, and his coinages, it would seem, then, that Chatterton is a pioneer, deserting the conventionally prim parterres of his century for "the shores of old romance," and anticipating the "new bower of England's art," so dear to us in Coleridge, Keats and Rossetti. No eighteenth century poet, not Thomson, not Collins, not even Blake, possesses this specifically *romantic* appeal. *The Seasons*, with their "flood of corn," are a thing apart, and the "Hebrid Isles" of *The Castle of Indolence* soon fade into personifications; Collins, in the best of his *Odes*, has an innate Hellenism, of which Chatterton was incapable, no less than an exquisite gift of word-painting, as it were on an ivory fan, in his *Oriental Eclogues*, beside which the Bristol scarlets and ochres show as the glare of a Van Goch flower piece beside a Brabazon or a Fantin Latour; and Blake's angelic vision, overcoming the spectre of Death itself, had no need of a borrowed tongue, albeit developed and individualized. True, there is Burns, in whom lyric art ranged coextensive with humanity, and Gray, who by a miracle, with a single poem, has won an immortal home in the heart of every normally constituted Englishman:

* Whether Chatterton had any philosophy of language or composition I doubt, but in Hooke's *Bristollia* (1748, Dissertation, p. 47 *n*), he could have read, "All languages are, in fact, equally *learned*. Words in their own Nature are only arbitrary signs of ideas, coin'd by custom, and made current by popular authority; and consequently can be no part of real knowledge."

but Romance is an evasive fairy; she abstracts from humanity, too proud to subsume it.

In the prosodic sphere—the assertion is sanctioned by the labours of Professor Saintsbury—Chatterton and Blake are the illuminati, and Chatterton, though he never achieved the miraculous scheme and cadences of the *Mad Song*, was first on the field.

And here be it noted that, although the author of Rowley's Poems is the morning star of Bristol's poetry, verse actually written by a Bristolian of Rowley's alleged period has come down to us. In Elias Ashmole's *Theatrum Chemicum Britannicum* (1652) will be found *The Ordinall of Alchimy*, dated at the end 1477, and from the first word of the proem and the first syllable of each of the six following chapters the author's name and place of residence are obtained, adding to which the first line of the seventh chapter we have

> Tomas Norton of Brisetow
> A perfect Master ye maie him trowe.*

It may also be mentioned that Ashmole's notes refer to William Canynges as the builder of Redcliff Church and augmenter of Westbury College (p. 441), and to Bishop Carpenter as the founder of the latter (p. 474). Here are twenty-six consecutive lines from the *Ordinall* (Chap. II):

> An other Ensample is good to tell,
> Of one that trusted to doe as well
> As *Raymond Lully*, or *Bacon* the Frier,
> Wherefore he named himself *saunce peere*;
> He was *Parson* of a little Town,
> Not farr from the Citty of *London*,
> Which was taken for halfe a Leach,
> But little cunning had he to Preach;
> He weened him sure this Arte to finde;
> His Name he would have ever in minde
> By means of a *Bridge*, imagined in dotage,
> To be made over *Thames* for light passage:

* He built what is now St. Peter's Hospital as his residence (*Official Guide to Bristol*, 1928, p. 16). William of Worcester speaks of "Norton magistri ecclesiae de Radclyff," i.e., as master mason, who may be the same man. *It.*, p. 244 (ed. 1778).

Whereof shulde grow a Common ease,
All the Countrey thereabout to please.
Yet though he might that warke fulfill,
It might in no wise suffice his will;
Wherefore he would set up in hight,
That *Bridge* for a wonderfull sight,
With Pinacles guilt shining as goulde,
A glorious thing for men to beholde.
Then he remembred of the newe,
How greater fame shulde him pursue,
If he mought make that *Bridge* so bright,
That it mought shine also by Nighte.
And so continue and not breake,
Than all the Londe of him would speake.

And here is the whole of one of the less disguised of the Rowley Poems, possibly that in which Mary discovered her brother's "stile":

ONN OURE LADIES CHYRCHE

As onn a hylle one eve sittynge,
At oure Ladie's Chyrche mouche wonderynge,
The counynge handieworke so fyne,
Han well nighe dazeled mine eyne;
Quod I; some counynge fairie hande
Yreer'd this chapelle in this lande;
Fulle well I wote so fine a syghte
Was ne yreer'd of mortall wighte.
Quod Trouthe; thou lackest knowlachynge;
Thou forsoth ne wotteth of the thynge.
A Rev'rend Fadre, William Canynge hight,
Yreered uppe this chapelle brighte;
And eke another in the Towne,
Where glassie bubblynge Trymme doth roun.
Quod I; ne doubte for all he's given
His sowle will certes goe to heaven.
Yea, quod Trouthe; than goe thou home,
And see thou doe as hee hath donne.
Quod I; I doubte, that can ne bee;
I have ne gotten markes three.
Quod Trouthe; as thou hast got, give almes-dedes soe;
Canynges and Gaunts culde doe ne moe.

Chatterton's comment on this, which was in the thin quarto copybook containing Rowley's *Memoirs*, is "N.B. I think this piece abounds with more true poetry and sentiment, than is commonly to be met with in Monkish writers, tho' much inferior to the generallity of Rowlie's compositions." In it the eighteenth century could only see two lines from Gray's *Long Story*:

> Employ'd the power of fairy hands
> To raise the cieling's fretted height.*

That Chatterton was acquainted with the *Ordinall* I am inclined to believe from other lines in the same chapter, *e.g.*:

> *Thomas Dalton* this good man height
> He served *God* both day and night

and

> The *Kinge* gave to *Daulton* Marks foure
> With liberty to goe where he would that houre.

but it makes small odds whether he was or was not, the point being that in his poem above quoted he has caught the prosody and movement of genuine fifteenth century Bristol verse, adding thereto a beauty and a strangeness all his own.

Now this type of verse, of which *The Unknown Knyght* is "another ensample," was not, as Coleridge stated apropos of *Christabel*, founded on a new principle, but on one as old as the hills, or at least as the early middle-English poem *Genesis and Exodus* (*c.* 1300), namely, that of equivalent substitution of feet in the octosyllabic couplet:

> Man og /to luven /that ri /mes ren
> The wis /seth wel /the loge /de men
> Hu /man may /him /wel loken
> Thog he /ne be le /red on /no boken

or as Spenser has it in *February*:

> In fine the steele had pierced his pitth,
> Tho downe to the earth he fell forthwith:
> His wonderous weight made the grounde to quake,
> Thearth shronke vnder him, and seemed to shake.

* Warton, *Enquiry*, pp. 30, 1. Helene Richter compares Scott's *Lay of the Last Minstrel*, II, 11. "Thou wouldst have thought some fairy's hand," &c.

There lyeth the Oake, pitied of none.
Now stands the Brere like a Lord alone,*

Spenser, whom Chatterton studied, more carefully even than is supposed (for the *manner* of the glosses beneath the antique poems is clearly derived from *The Shepheardes Calender*), admits the decasyllable,

Tho on the flore she sawe the merchandise,
Of which her sonne had sette to dere a prize.
May.

Nor was the art lost in the seventeenth century :

If all's praescription, and proud wrong
Hearkens not to an humble song,
For all the gallantry of him
Give me the suff'ring Seraphim ;
His be the bravery of all those bright things
The glowing cheekes, the glistering wings.

The Annians, with their *correct* prosody, had been deaf to these cadences, though Pope, the correctest of them, declared, so Doctor Johnson was told, that the couplet by which his ear was most gratified was :

Lo ! where Maeotis sleeps, and hardly flows
The freezing Tanais through a waste of snows.
Dunciad, III.

The Doctor was honestly puzzled, for he adds " But the reason of this preference I cannot discover." We can, perhaps ; for Pope, though his influence went far to banish it temporarily, was quite aware of substitution, as is seen by his *Imitation of Chaucer*, " done by the author in his youth." Still, this is only saying that Pope is the exception which proves the rule of

* *Cf.* So have I sene a mountayne oak that longe
Has caste his shadowe to the mountayne syde,
Brave all the wyndes, tho' ever they so stronge ;
And view the briers belowe with self-taught pride ;
But, whan throwne downe by mightie thunder stroke,
He'de rather bee a bryer than an oke.
Battle of Hastings (I).

Another proof of his study of the *Shepheardes Calender* is the epithet "lordynge," for the toad (*Tournament*, l. 51) taken from *December* (l. 70).

the school of Pope. In the prosodic sphere Chatterton is a reactionary force :

> I kenne Syr Roger from afar
>   Tryppynge over the lea ;
> Ich ask whie the loverds son
>   Is moe than me.

Where in the eighteenth century can you find *anything* like that, before Blake, who uses the equivalenced octosyllabic in his *Everlasting Gospel* ?

Professor Saintsbury, who calls that quatrain from the Third Eclogue, " a breath from heaven," says " the prosodic afflatus is all over the Rowley Poems."*

Take, for instance,

> But now the worde of Godde is come,
> Borne of Maide Marie toe brynge home
>   Mankynde hys shepe
>   Theme for to keepe
> In the folde of hys heavenlie kyngdome.

and note how the cadence of the second line prepares the ear for the resolutions in the last ; or (from *The Storie of William Canynge*), a strict decasyllabic couplet,

> Sweetnesse was yn eche worde she dyd ywreene,[1]
> Tho shee strove not to make that sweetnesse sheene.

[1] Display.

He is describing the apparition of Truth ; every word in the second line, as you say it over, has the true and full value, yet the whole is a musical unit.

Or :

> Bie oure ladie her yborne,[1]
> To-morrowe, soone as ytte ys day,
> I'll make thee wyfe, ne bee forsworne,
> So tyde me lyfe or dethe for aie.

[1] Son.

For such primitive beauty we have to go back to

* *History of English Prosody* (1923), Vol II. p. 520 sqq.

My ghostly father, I me confesse
First to God and then to you;

it is not in the Elizabethans even.

But the ten line stanza, the Rowley measure *par excellence*, awaits examination. Its growth can be determined to some extent on the assumption (for which evidence has been given) that *Battle of Hastings* (I) is one of the earliest of the antiques.

This is in a ten line decasyllabic stanza, *a b a b c d c d e e*, but three stanzas end with alexandrines of the strict later pattern, with a cæsura, *e.g.*:

Fitz Broque, who saw his father killen lie,
Ah me! sayde he; what woeful syghte I see!
But now I muste do somethyng more than sighe;
And then an arrowe from the bowe drew he.
Beneth the erlie's navil came the darte;
Fitz Broque on foote han drawne it from the bowe;
And upwards went into the erlie's harte,
And out the crymson streme of bloude gan flowe.
As fromm a hatch,[1] drawne with a vehement geir,[2]
White rushe the burstynge waves, and roar along the weir.

[1] Pen or lock. [2] Turn, or twist.

Now this is precisely the measure of Prior's *Ode to the Queen* (1706), which Prior in his "Preface" rather light-heartedly regards as a development of the Spenserian—"having only added one verse to his stanza, which I thought made the number more harmonious," whereas the relation it bears to that stanza is that the lines are decasyllabic, except the last, and the start is *a b a b*, Spenser rhyming on three sounds (*a b a b b c b c c*), and Prior on five.*

Chatterton had the wit or instinct to see this, and in *Battle of Hastings* (II) goes back to Spenser and produces a measure, not so far removed from his, rhyming on four sounds, i.e., *a b a b b c b c d d*, a sort of compromise between the sixteenth and the eighteenth century, but nearer the former, and, like Spenser, occasionally "running over" in the alexandrine, as here:

* This was realized early; see Mathias, *Essay* (1783), p. 67; the aperçu was Malone's, *Cursory Observations* (1782), p. 15.

A standarde made of sylke and jewells rare,*
Wherein alle coloures wroughte aboute in bighes,[1]
An armyd Knyghte was seen deth-doynge there,
Under this motte,[2] He conquers or he dies.
This standard rych, endazzling mortal eyes,
Was borne neare Harolde at the Kenters heade,
Who chargd hys broders for the grete empryze
That straite the hest[3] for battle should be spredde.
To evry erle and knyghte the worde is gyven,
And cries *a guerre* and slughornes shake the vaulted heaven.†

[1] Jewels. [2] Motto. [3] Command.

This is the Rowley measure, and though our ears may crave for that of *The Eve of St. Agnes* or *The Faerie Queene*, we are closer to it than at any time during the eighteenth century, and I am not forgetting Thomson. It is a coarser fabric than Spenser's, admitted, but better adapted, thanks to the comparative looseness of its texture, for dramatic use.

But, having hit on this modification of the Spenserian, Chatterton does not plump for it at once. There is a decasyllabic tenth line (l. 60), and even a fourteener (l. 320), in the first 520 lines of *Battle of Hastings* (II) ; and of the twenty stanzas of the continuation only three close with an alexandrine, one of which " runs over." Moreover in the 183 lines preceding the chorus of the fragment *Goddwyn*, strict alexandrines and decasyllabics share the honours of concluding the stanzas,

* Compare the stanza beginning " First, in the Kentish streamer was a wood " in Drayton's *The Battle of Agincourt* (ottava rima).

† In a recent reading of *The Castle of Indolence* I counted fourteen alexandrines of this type, six in the first, and eight in the second, canto. Thomson knew what he was about, the opening stanza of both cantos has one, and note—

" Ne had my master Spencer charmed his Mulla's plain."

The Schoolmistress, on the other hand, does not show one, and *The Minstrel* has two, one in either canto. Chatterton, also, is sparing of them ; there are four in the whole of *Hastings*, one in *Ælla*—

" Botte leave the vyrgyn brydall bedde for bedde of warre,"

none in *Goddwyn, Laymyngetowne*, or *Englysh Metamorphosis*. In *The Eve of St. Agnes* there are two, one in the first stanza ; none in *The Revolt of Islam* or *Adonais* ; none in *Childe Harolde ;* but four in the twenty (Miltonic) stanzas of *Resolution and Independence*. Of the six stanzas of Blake's early *An Imitation of Spenser* not one is actually a Spenserian, and the last has ten lines.

and so they do in the lovely third eclogue: only in *Ælla*,* *The merrie Tricks of Laymyngetowne*, and the piece called *Englysh Metamorphosis*, does the alexandrine hold undisputed sway at the close of the ten line scheme.

I think this goes to show: (1) the care with which *Ælla* was composed, not *necessarily* that it is one of the latest of the antiques, and (2) the impetuosity with which the greater number of them were thrown off. Take *The Gouler's Requiem*; it is in two stanzas of the metre under discussion; the first ends in a decasyllabic line:

O storthe[1] unto mie mynde! I go to hell.

[1] Death.

the second with an alexandrine:

I kenne notte botte for thee I to the quede[2] must goe.

[2] Devil.

I am not so perverse an admirer of this poet as to suppose that here is an emotional climax that calls for autocratic prosody; I imagine the poem came out of his head just so, and he left it, knowing that the "slow length" of an alexandrine makes a good end, as it did to Rowley's three *Eclogues*: but with *Ælla* it was far otherwise. In passing, I have often wondered whether the alexandrine that closes the second stanza of the *Nightingale* ode:

And with thee fade away into the forest dim

is not a divine inadvertence; nothing short of torture can make it a resolved decasyllable. Present in the MS., the word "away" was excised in the first printing (in Elmes' *Annals of the Fine Arts*, July, 1819), but restored in the 1820 volume.

A final word on Chatterton's modification of the Spenserian; if the two last lines be removed, and they are not, as in Spenser,

* One stanza in *Ælla* ends in a pair of alexandrines, arranged thus:

O thou, whatteer thie name,
  Or Zabalus or Queed,
Comme, steel mie sable spryte,
  For fremde and dolefulle dede.

Dryden's opera, *The State of Innocence*, also ends with a pair.

always an integral limb, what is left is *a b a b b c b c*, one of Chaucer's metres ; in fact *The Monkes Tale, The Former Age,* and *L'Envoy to Bukton* are written in it, apart from its use, with a refrain, in Balades :

> But yit, lest thou do worse, tak a wyfe ;
> Bet is to wedde, than brenne in worse wyse.
> But thou shalt have sorwe on thy flesh, thy lyf,
> And been thy wyves thral, as seyn these wyse :
> And if that holy writ may nat suffyse,
> Experience shal thee teche, so may happe,
> That thee were lever to be take in Fryse
> Than eft to falle of wedding in the trappe.

And here is one entire speech of Birtha, the concluding couplet, *Ælla's* answer, omitted :

> Love, doe notte rate your achevmentes soe smalle ;
> As I to you, syke love untoe mee beare ;
> For nothynge paste wille Birtha ever call,
> Ne on a foode from Heaven thynke to cheere.
> As farr as thys frayle brutylle flesch wylle spere,
> Syke, and ne fardher I expecte of you ;
> Be notte toe slacke yn love, ne overdeare ;
> A smalle fyre, yan a loud flame, proves more true.

The advantages of an eight line scheme seem to have occurred to Chatterton, though he uses ottava rima once only (*Letter to the Dygne Master Canynge*). Not least among his trophies are the three verses on St. Mary Redcliff in a stanza which may perhaps be regarded as a rearrangement, coloured by *The Faerie Queene*, of the scheme of Spenser's *June*. They were tucked away in the latter part of Rowley's " Emendals to Turgotte," and have survived their environment.* One cannot regret too much that he has not left us an interlude in this proud self-knit measure, which his dramatic genius would have redeemed from the charge of monotony :

> Well maiest thou be astound but view it well
> Go not from hence before thou see thy fill

* Add. MS. 24891, f. 7b.

And learn the Builder's Vertues and his name
Of this tall Spyre in every Countye telle
And with thy Tale the lazing Rychmen shame
Showe howe the Glorious Canynge did excelle
How hee good Man a Friend for Kynges became
And gloryous paved at once the Waie to Heavn and Fame*

(c) *Method and Manner*

The strange words then are dictionary-begotten and modified at pleasure, the metres for the most part, the outcome of an instinct for antiquity, the Spenserian stanza, and an ear that could be un-eighteenth century when it chose; what of the subjects, or rather (since the poems remain to be discussed *as* poems), how did Chatterton go to work, apart from his "red book," the MS. glossary? The answer is: much as Shakespeare did.

Of *Bristowe Tragedy* he told his mother: "I found the argument and versified it."† The subject was local history and partly accessible in Stow's *Annales*.‡ The theme of *Godwynn* is the burden of the first few pages of Hooke's *Bristollia*, a work, which, as Tyrwhitt saw (*Vindication*, p. 149, n.), afforded a basis for Turgot-Rowley's *Discorse on Brystowe*. The Battle Abbey Roll in Fuller's *Church History*, and a variant in *Holinshed*, afforded names for *Battle of Hastings*. Poetry of all periods, English only, was floating in his receptive brain, moreover. The earlier critics, and Skeat, whose object (fair play to him) was to lay the ghost of the Rowleian hypothesis for ever, contented themselves with pointing out passages where poets later than the fifteenth century are echoed. That procedure is, to some extent, unnecessary to-day, but the problem of Chatterton's sources is still interesting.

The central figure of his masterpiece will serve to justify this assertion. Suppose a person, who had just read *Ælla*, and knew little or nothing of the history of Bristol, went thither,

* Chatterton has placed a comma after "thou" in the first line of this verse.

† *Works*, III, p. 524. Here is his statement to Mary that he wrote *Onn oure Ladies Chyrche*.

‡ "Probably taken from Howe's chronicle," Chatterton's note, transcribed by G. Catcott, B.5344, i.e. the 1615 edition of Stow, with Howe's continuation.

and asked what, apart from the Rowley Poems, was known of Ælla himself, the Saxon Keeper of the Castle, who was mortally wounded in a battle against the Danes at Watchet; it is unlikely that he would learn much. A Bristolian, up in Barrett, might refer him to Ellbridge Street near the site of the Castle, with the warning that Barrett was suspect on this, as on other matters*—and rightly, since Ellbridge Street has nothing whatever to do with Ælla, the ancient name for this locality being apparently "le Weere"†—and he might add that there was nothing in Seyer's *Memoirs of Bristol* about Ælla.‡ But then the enquirer would be perplexed, for Ælla is the very core of Chatterton's Saxon Bristol, its martial hero; and as Canynge and Rowley have some sort of basis in the city's annals, why not he? In reply he would probably be sent back to the play, and to "the marvellous boy." But the basic material for Ælla, in his relation to the city, is deducible from the silence of Hooke, and two passages in Camden's *Britannia*, a copy of which stood in Lambert's office.

One is where, speaking of Bristol, Camden says (ed. 1695, p. 73)§:

"At what time, and by whom it was built, is hard to say: but it seems to be of a late date, since in all the Danish plunders, it is not so much as mention'd in our Histories. For my part, I am of opinion it rose in the decline of the Saxon Government, since it is not taken notice of before the year of our Lord 1063, wherein Harald (as Florence of Worcester has it) set sail from *Brystow* to Wales with a design to invade it."

The other is printed in italics at the end of his account of

* *History of Bristol*, p. 204, and 32-33, where also Corn Street may be traced back to Coernyke, Small Street to one Smallaricus, and (no doubt) Wine Street to Egwyn, with Rowley's good help. Leofwynne's Charter on p. 33 is derived from Edward the Confessor's grant to Ralph Peperking in Camden's *Britannia* (ed. 1695, p. 344).

† William of Worcester, *It.*, p. 208.

‡ In chapter III, § 10 Seyer says the two sons of Ella, King of Sussex, were slain in the battle of Badon, A.D. 520.

§ I judge the edition used to have been that of 1695 (or 1722) with Bishop Gibson's additions, partly because of the "additions" to Heylin's Heraldry, &c., in "Antiquities, Book 3rd," and partly because Kenric is first mentioned in the 1695 edition (additions to Wiltshire, p. 100) as son of Cerdick, and Chatterton wrote Ossianics on both these worthies.

Sussex (*ibid.* pp. 179, 180), "the Kingdom of the South Saxons," which "31 years after the coming in of the Saxons, was begun by Ælla, who, according to Bede, 'First amongst the Kings of the English Nation ruled all their Southern Provinces, which are sever'd by the River Humber, and the adjacent limits'."

Now Chatterton always "saw something further and saw something more"; and, resolving to *create* a Saxon Bristol, took the chance afforded by the second extract of making Ælla its lord, and drew the main features of the character, the fire, the impetuosity, and the "honnoure," from Harold, himself, and Shakespeare's Hotspur. It is not implied that he was ignorant of the Northumbrian Alla in *The Man of Law's Tale*, or the passage in Thoresby's *Ducatus Leodiensis*,* one of the books referred to in the De Bergham pedigree, about Alla's Hill, "now called Allice hill," where the remains of the Northumbrian Kings were dug up, or that he did not transfer Alfred's wars with the Danes to his own creation; the suggestion is only that the initial spur from without to invent Bristol's ideal Saxon guardian and warrior was yielded by the then supposed blank in the early history of the city to which Camden alludes. And having written the play and the *Songe to Ælla* to please himself, he could then write Rowley's "Emendals to Turgotte" and make drawings of the cover of Ælla's coffin (5766B, ff. 42, 104, 105) to please Barrett.

Asserius, Ingolphus, Torgotte, Bedde, Birtha (Celmonde, as Warton saw, is, like Ælla, in Fuller's *Church History*†), Magnus (in Macpherson's *The Highlander* also), Hurra (Hubba), and the raven standard of the Danes (not only in *Alfred, a masque*, 1740) are in Camden; and it is not going too far to say that this folio was his North's *Plutarch*.

Two lines in *Battle of Hastings* (I) are a fair example of the use he had for it.

* Ed. 1713, p. 343. cf. Thy countrymen shall rere thee on the playne
A pyle of carnes, as anie grave can boaste:
Ælla, ad fin.

For other sources for the name see Richter, *Thomas Chatterton*, pp. 124, 5. The D.N.B. *sub* "Ælla (d. 514 ?)" says, "Ælla was looked on as the head of all the Teutonic settlers in Britain, and is reckoned as the first Bretwalda." In drawing him Chatterton was expressing his conception of the ideal Englishman.

† Ceolmund, Bishop of Selsey, p. 108, ed. 1655.

So fell the myghtie tower of Standrip, whenne
It felte the furie of the Danish menne.

Dean Milles (p. 46) has a characteristic note here: "By *the tower of Standrip* must be meant Staindrop, in the bishoprick of Durham, the only place of that name in England; for though there is neither the appearance nor tradition of a castle there, a tower might have antiently stood on that spot, and have been destroyed by the Danes; an event too inconsiderable to be recorded by historians, though perhaps important enough to be preserved in that neighbourhood by tradition." Looking at Gibson's Camden, however, (p. 773) we read: "*Standrope* (which is also called *Stainthorp*, that is to say a stony village) a small market town," &c. The next sentence runs: "Bordering upon this stands *Rabye*, which King Cnute or Canutus the Dane gave to the Church of Durham, with the land about it, *and Stanthorp, to have and to hold freely for ever.*" Thus we get "Standrip" and "the Danish menne." Half-way down the second column (numbered p. 774) comes a description of wells called Hell-Kettles: "For we find in the Chronicle of *Tinmouth that in the year of our Lord* 1179. *upon Christmas-day, at Oxenhall in the out-fields of Darlington in the Bishoprick of Durham, the Earth rais'd itself up to a great height in the manner of a lofty tower, and remain'd all that day till the evening* (*as it were fixed and unmoveable*) *in that posture*; *but then it sunk down again with such a horrid noise that it terrified the neighbours,*" &c.

Chatterton has combined and adapted for his poetic purpose three statements which he found on a single page, thus bearing out his own words:

Wee wylle ne cheynedd to one pasture bee,
Botte sometymes soare 'bove trouthe of hystorie.

Apropos of Weever's *Ancient Funerall Monuments*, another of his sources, it should be noted that probably the only hint, apart from *The Shepheardes Calender*, that he can have had for writing his interludes in *stanzaed* verse (the Miracle plays not yet having been printed*) must have come from the dialogue

* He doubtless had access to Robert Dodsley's *Old Plays*, 1744.

in rime royal between a secular priest and a friar at the grave of Dame Johan of Acres (p. 734 sqq.), which Weever says he copied out of an ancient roll ; this piece is actually mentioned in the Essay on the Antiquity of Christmas Games.*

One more example of his use of prose books before passing to his debt to the poets. In the *Epistle to Mastre Canynge on Ælla,* Rowley writes :

> Playes made from hallie tales I holde unmeete ;
> Lette somme greate storie of a manne be songe ;
> Whanne, as a man, we Godde and Jesus treate,
> In mie pore mynde, we doe the Godhedde wronge.

Voss is thus quoted in Cibber's life of Francis Goldsmith (*Lives*, Vol. II, p. 14) :

> "I am of opinion it is better to chuse another argument than sacred. For it agrees not with the majesty of sacred things, to be made a play and a fable. . . . These things have place, especially when we bring in God, or Christ speaking, or treating of the mysteries of religion."

This aperçu was Michael Lort's.

The Rowley poems being largely dramatic, it is hardly surprising that some attention was paid to Shakespeare. Chatterton no more than Milton has escaped the lure of the line of three words, whose kingdom began with "Unhousel'd, disappointed, unaneled."† The dirge in *Ælla* harks back to Ophelia's and Desdemona's songs, taking *The Friar of Orders Gray* in its stride; and the battle pieces in that tragedy derive from *Henry V*. The Anti-Rowleians took a delight in pointing out such glaring plagiarisms as

> O forre a spryte al fiere
>
> O, for a muse of fire.

* *T. and C.M.*, Dec., 1769.

† "Unburled, undelievre, unespryte." *Goddwyn*, l. 27.
The couplet in his "Will" :

> But happy in my humbler sphere had mov'd
> Untroubled, unrespected, unbelov'd.

is coloured, I suspect, by the Bristol Collins's :

> But right or wrong disdaining to be mov'd,
> Unprincipl'd, unloving, and unlov'd.
>
> MONIMIA to PHILOCLES (*Miscellanies*, 1762).

What opportunities his apprenticeship allowed him of *seeing* Shakespeare at the theatre in King Street (which his master had helped to erect) we do not know,* but a natural inference from the poems to Powell and Holland is that he had witnessed their performances. Twelve days after his indentures were drawn, *Othello* was played with Powell and Mrs. Hopkins (July 13, 1767), and on the 30th *Romeo and Juliet*, with Powell as Romeo, Holland as Mercutio, and Mrs. Barry as Juliet.† On June 20, 1768, *Hamlet* (with Holland), July 29, *Romeo and Juliet* (Romeo Holland, Juliet Mrs. Barry), Aug. 3 *Lear* (Lear Powell, Cordelia Mrs. Barry), and Aug. 24 (ominous day !) *The Merry Wives of Windsor*, Shuter's benefit, " never acted before," with Shuter as Falstaff, and Mrs. Barry as Mistress Page. The adjective *ouphante*

Ouphante fairie lyghte youre fyres

is derived from this play—" Strew good luck, ouphes, on every sacred room " (Act V, Sc. 5) ; you will find neither *ouph* nor *ouphante* in Speght, Kersey, or Bailey.‡ There was a play every night this summer, during the Fair.

* Thanks to *Felix Farley* and Richard Smith's collection of playbills in the Bristol Library, we have a fair conspectus of the theatre's work. It opened on May 30, 1766, and during that summer *Othello, Lear, Cymbeline, Hamlet, Romeo and Juliet, Much Ado, Merchant of Venice, Macbeth, Richard III, King John* (" never acted here "), as well as the farce, *Catherine and Petruchio, Venice Preserv'd*, and *Cato* were played. The Colston boy must have heard of these performances, which doubtless gave an impetus to the " Juvenile Club," though he cannot have attended them ; they must have been the talk of Bristol.

† But most thy softer tones our bosoms move
When Juliet listens to her Romeo's love.
To Mr. Powel.

His Macbeth and Richard are praised in *Clifton*.

‡ I came on the following note of Chatterton's transcribed by Catcott (in Richard Smith's *Chattertoniana*) after I had written the above ; the original was in the " thin quarto copy book," apparently, the references being to *Battle of Hastings* (I) :

" The above simile [As from a Hache drawne with vehement geire] is (I think) elegant, but the following is a little mystic :

As ouphant Fairies whann the Moone sheenes bryght
Ynne lyttle circals dangle on [" daunce upon," ed. 1777] the green
All lyvyng creatures flye farr fromm theyre Syghte
Ne bie the race of destinie be seene
For whatt he be thatt ouphant Fairies strike
Theyre sowles wyll wanderr to Kynge Offa's Dyke.

This opinion of the Fairys, I never before met with, Shakespeare speaking

Not wholly frivolous, I trust, is the following parallel, though it may not prove that Chatterton saw *Othello* in King Street before he wrote *Ælla*. Few spectators of the former can have missed the amazing dramatic effect of the bell in Act II, Sc. 3, when Cassio, by Iago's contrivance, has wounded Montano. Roderigo has just run out, and Iago shouts :

> Help, masters ! Here's a goodly watch indeed !
> [*Bell rings.*
> Who's that which rings the bell ? Diablo, ho !
> The town will rise :

Then Othello enters, the bell ringing continuously while he addresses the combatants, until he exclaims :

> Silence that dreadful bell : it frights the isle
> From her propriety.

The issue having been explained to him, and Cassio cashiered, enter Desdemona :

> Look, if my gentle love be not raised up !

In *Ælla*, immediately after the protagonist has stabbed himself, comes this passage :

SERVITOURE

> Ælla ys sleene ; the flower of Englande's marrde !*

ÆLLA

> Be stylle : stythe[2] lette the chyrches rynge mie knelle.
> Call hyther brave Coernyke ; he, as warde
> Of thys mie Brystowe Castle, wylle doe welle.
> [*Knelle ryngeth.*

[2] ? If Chatterton did not write "swythe," "quickly."

of Queen Mab, says, 'her Waggoner a small greycoated gnatt.' We all allow, I suppose, a gnatt to be a living creature, then this opinion in part corresponds with Shakespear in the Merry Wives of Windsor,

> They are Fairies, he that speaks to them shall die,
> I'll wink and couch, no men their works may eye.

But the opinion of the Soul's wandering to King Offa's Dyke, I never before heard of."

* The King is slain, the kingdom overthrown.
Tennyson, *Harold*, Act V, Sc. 2.

ÆLLA, EGWINA, SERVYTOURE, COERNYKE

ÆLLA

Thee I ordeyne the warde ; so alle maie telle.
I have botte lyttel tym to dragge thys lyfe ;
Mie lethal tale, alyche a lethalle belle,
Dynne yn the eares of her I wyschd mie wyfe !
Botte, ah ! shee maie bee fayre.[3]

[3] Innocent.

EGWINA

Yatte shee moste bee.

ÆLLA

Ah ! saie notte soe ; yatte worde woulde Ælla dobblie slee.

ÆLLA, EGWINA, SERVYTOURE, COERNYKE, BIRTHA, HURRA

ÆLLA

Ah ! Birtha here !

BIRTHA

Whatte dynne ys thys ? Whatte menes yis leathalle knelle ?

Here the bell is not silenced, but apparently continues ringing till the end of the play, thirty-nine lines later ; " this proceeding," to quote Longinus, " is not plagiarism ; it is like taking an impression from beautiful forms or figures or other works of art."*

Of other Elizabethan or Jacobean dramatic influence little or none can be detected. There is no trace, for example, that *Bonduca* was read, or that Marlowe, through whose greatest plays runs the conception of a finite mind grasping at infinite power, shaped the eighteenth century poet's proud imaginings ; the resemblance of style in one passage, hereafter to be quoted, is doubtless accidental. Chatterton, with far less sensuousness than the Kentish genius,

Had in him those brave translunary things
That the first poets had,

but when he writes of the seven deadly sins his kinship is

* *On the Sublime*, XIII. (ed. Rhys Roberts, p. 81.)

hardly with the scholar-poet of *Faustus* but with an unknown fifteenth century writer, whose work he could by no possibility have seen.

Next to the Shakespearean afflatus comes that of Dryden. Mr. Oswald Doughty in his book on the eighteenth century lyric has dealt with Dryden's influence on the acknowledged pieces, but in Rowley too the manly vigour and superb directness of this master have saved Chatterton from the falsetto of Pope's disciples. His power is felt prosodically also; the four line scheme (*a b b a*, three decasyllabics followed by an alexandrine), which Ælla shares twice with Celmonde, is used in *The State of Innocence* (Act I); nor do I think the two following resemblances accidental:

> No more; it cannot, was not, must not be.
> *Conquest of Granada* (Part I) Act V.
> Ytte cannotte, must notte, naie ytte shall not bee.
> *Ælla*, l. 16.
> "True priests," he said, "and preachers of the word
> Were only stewards of their sovereign Lord,
> Nothing was theirs.
> *The Character of a good Parson.*
> We are Goddes stewards all, nete of oure owne we beare.
> *Baladé of Charitie.*

The hint for the attempted seduction of Birtha by Celmonde is afforded by a like situation (harking back to Silvia and Proteus), in a wood too, in Act IV of *Amboyna*.* Both scenes should be read in full to gauge the difference in likeness, but two passages may suffice here:

Ysabinda. Come, Sir, which is the way? I long to see my love.
Harman Junior. You may have your wish, and without stirring hence.
Ysab. My Love so near? Sure you delight to mock me.

* Not only in Chatterton can *Amboyna* be traced; Towerson's last words in Act V:

> Till, at the last, your sapped foundations fall,
> And universal ruin swallows all.

have helped to usher out the drama of *The Dunciad*:

> Thy hand, great Anarch! lets the curtain fall,
> And universal darkness buries all.

BIRTHA

Saiest thou for love ? ah ! love is far awaie
Faygne would I see once moe the roddie lemes of daie.

CELMONDE

Love maie bee nie, woulde Birtha calle ytte here.

BIRTHA

How, Celmonde, dothe thou mene ?

Har. Jun. You are a Woman ; have enough of love for him and me ; I know the plenteous Harvest all is his : he has so much of joy, that he must labour under it. In Charity you may allow some gleanings to a Friend.

CELMONDE

O ! do nete nowe to Ælla syke love bere
Botte geven some onne Celmondes hedde.

How far apart is the tongue of the two dramatists ! The one speaks nervous realism ; the other romance !

With these guides the poet, in his antiques, largely succeeded in escaping his age, though Fairfax, Milton, and doubtless others, played their part in the work of release : still it may fairly be said that a thorough self-education in Spenser, Shakespeare and Dryden is the core of Chatterton's poetic mystery, inspiration excepted.

And how much *is* inspiration (though that word covers what has just been alleged), in its popular sense of sheer originality ? Something should be said on this score before the poems are looked at as wholes. Here an obvious, but necessary, comment suggests itself ; because, for instance, three consecutive lines in Celmonde's first speech :

Ah ! Birtha, whie did Nature frame thee fayre ?
Whie art thou all that poyntelle[1] canne bewreene ?[2]
Whie art thou notte as coarse as others are ?

[1] A pen. [2] Express.

resolve themselves into :

Why are you made so excellently fair ?
So much above what other beauties are,
Aureng-Zebe, Act IV, Sc. 1.

and

Is she not more than painting can express?
The Fair Penitent, Act III.

because, in other words, pre-existing verse was for ever running in Chatterton's head, and may be found to have gone to the making of well-nigh all he wrote, he is not therefore to be criticized adversely; much the same might be said of Vergil. Only from one, and that a secondary, point of view are the three lines derivative; for they are stamped with the character of their speaker; they are *Celmonde's*, and therefore Chatterton's, not Dryden's and Rowe's. A sentence from his first biographer deals adequately with this very point: "He knew that original genius consists in forming new and happy combinations, rather than in searching after thoughts and ideas which never had occurred before."*

Now, judged by the test of simile and metaphor, these poems respond but grudgingly to a modern mind. The similes almost always seem to have been drawn from a common poetic stock, embellishments hung round their context: the flower or plant and its mainstay—thrice in one poem of 180 lines:

Soe the tall oake the ivie twysteth rounde . . .
Arounde theire heaulmes theie greene verte doe entwyne . . .
Ynn hys armes hee dydd herr hente
Lyche the merk-plante[1] doe entwyne.

[1] Night-shade. *The Tournament.*

a current increased by the stoppage of a stone:

So have I seene a dolthead place a stone,
Enthoghte to staie a driving rivers course;
But better han it bin to lett alone,
It onlie drives it on with mickle force.
Battle of Hastings (I).

the *bore* of the Severn:

As Severnes hyger lyghethe[2] banckes of sonde
Pressynge ytte downe binethe the reynynge streme,
Wythe drearie dynn enswolters the hyghe stronde,
Beerynge the rockes alonge ynn fhurye breme[3].

[2] Lodgeth. [3] Fierce. *Ælla.*

* Gregory, *Life*, p. 103.

storm, lightning, thunder and earthquake, soldiers standing on a hillside " lyche yonge enlefed trees," the morning sun drinking the dew; the last seems to have impressed him deeply and may point to early Sunday walks in the low lying meadows. The image of the blood-red-haired Danes:

Lyche kynge-cuppes brastynge wythe the morning due

of which he was justly proud, is as entirely his as its archetype:

Like vernal hyacinths in sullen hue

applied to the " locks divinely spreading " of the Athenian tyrannicides, is William Collins's.

The kingcup, by the way, is probably the common buttercup (not specifically the marsh marigold) for which " kingcup " or " gold cup" was in his time the usual term. " Buttercup " he does not use, and the *New English Dictionary* gives 1777 as the earliest date for it. Besides, a vast martial array is more likely to have been compared to a field of buttercups than to a dazzling clot of marsh marigolds, which do not stand up in such serried profusion. In one place (*Ælla*, l. 739) sunlight on dew is declared to be

Lyche gottes of blodde whyche doe blacke armoure steyne
Sheenynge upon the borne[1] whyche stondeth bie.

[1] Burnish.

His most original simile is where the nut-brown hair of Truth on her milk-white body is compared to " veynes of brown hue yn a marble cuarr " (quarry), and his finest, that in *Goddwyn*:

Stylle toe the kynge
Theie rolle theire trobbles, lyche a sorgie sea.

" I assure you I can scarce bear any poetry that I have taken up after it," the Rev. Thomas Twining wrote to his brother in April, 1777. " What think you of this image of a discontented, murmuring, remonstrating people ? "*

* *A Country Clergyman in the Eighteenth Century* (1882), p. 49.

But I would not lay too much stress on these, nor on his metaphors, occasionally of a grave recondite beauty :

> The stagge ys ouch'd wythe crownes of lillie flowerrs.
>
> *The Tournament.*

where his gloss reads :

> " *from* ouch, *a chain worn by Earls round their necks* "

or, more often, of a lurid vehemence :

> Theyre throngynge corses shall onlyghte the starres ;
>
> *Ælla.*
>
> Fell ys the Cullys-yatte of mie hartes castle stede.
>
> *Eclogue* I.

glossed " *alluding to the portcullis, which guarded the gate, on which often depended the castle.*"

> Botte falleynge nombers sable all the feelde.
>
> *Eclogue II.*

His poetry, as Mr. Hare has well said, is " a pageant staged by an impressionist," and the images must not, as in the generality of poets, be pursued too exactly, but judged by their immediate impression.

And here there must always be vast divergence of taste. Skeat thought the epithet *deft* (glossed " neat, cleanly ")—

> As when a bordelier[1] onn ethie[2] bedde,
> Tyr'd wyth the laboures maynt[3] of sweltrie daie
> Yn slepeis bosom laieth hys deft headde,
>
> *The Storie of William Canynge.*

[1] Cottager. [2] Easy. [3] Many.

singularly unsuitable, as applied to a labourer of Rowley's alleged time ; but why a labourer, even in the fifteenth century, should not have a well-shaped head, or a poet, of any century, should necessarily fail to perceive it, if he had, I confess I am at a loss to understand.

The salient feature of his images is the pleasure he takes in light, and (what almost may be said to fall in the category of light), sudden impact.

I saw hym eager gaspynge after lyghte

he says in the most autobiographical of the "old Rowleys"; the clash of armies,

> Speres bevyle speres; swerdes upon swerdes engage;
> Armoure on armoure dynn, shielde upon shielde.*
>
> *Eclogue* II.

the fall of a rock, the splashing of spray, the spurt of blood, the golden shower of leaves in Autumn and the invisible hand that sends it; his ecstasy is made up of these, and they are presented raw and uncouth. Take the earthquake stanza in *Battle of Hastings* (II):

> As when the erthe, torne by convulsyons dyre,
> In reaulmes of darkness hid from human syghte,
> The warring force of water, air, and fyre,
> Brast from the regions of eternal nyghte,
> Thro the darke caverns seeke the reaulmes of lyght;
> Some loftie mountayne, by its fury torn,
> Dreadfully moves, and causes grete affryght;
> Nowe here, now there, majestic nods the bourne,
> And awfulle shakes, mov'd by the almighty force,
> Whole woods and forests nod, and ryvers change theyr course.

There is no construction here, the stanza is an anacoluthon, possibly more than one, but the effect is right; and it sweeps along even the prosaic "causes grete afryght" in its avalanche. Similarly in the speeches of Magnus and Hurra an end is proposed, and formal grammar and common sense turned topsy-turvy to attain it. Analogies between the arts are desperately unsure, but have we not in much of the music of Berlioz a comparable procedure?

Thus it is that seldom only, in Chatterton, does a verb or adjective force itself on the attention as a separate beauty, as in

> The boddynge flourettes *bloshes* atte the lyghte;

and

* In *The Constabiliad* (Oct. 30, 1769), he parodies this:

> Sauces encountred sauces, Bottles smashed;
> Butter with Butter swims, Knives with Knives clashed.

Pope's *Iliad* has influenced both passages:—

> Now shield with shield, with helmet helmet clos'd;
> To armour armour, lance to lance oppos'd.
>
> IV, 447.

Wynter and *brownie* hylles wylle have a charme for thee.

His great (and, it may be, unconscious) effects are as the sudden impact of a dazzling object on the retina :

The Sarasen lokes owte : he doethe feere,

or, with his much loved device of anaphora :

See ! the whyte moone sheenes onne hie ;
Whyterre ys mie true loves shroude ;
Whyterre yanne the mornynge skie,
Whyterre yanne the evenynge cloude ;

This must be the manner that so won on Keats that he wrote, after a spell of *Paradise Lost*, in the third week of September, 1819 :

" The purest English, I think—or what ought to be the purest—is Chatterton's. The language had existed long enough to be entirely uncorrupted by Chaucer's Gallicisms, and still the old words are used. Chatterton's language is entirely Northern. I prefer the native music of it to Milton's, cut by feet."

We begin to tread his " castle stairs," to inhale the peculiar fragrance of these poems, which the dictionary language conceals but superficially, their complete lack of affectation—their Saxonism, if you like—their stark vision, a presenting of the object seen with no " poetical " trappings. Here Chatterton abuts on Blake, the Blake of

O Rose, thou art sick !

and

I saw you and your wife

no less than on the poetical reformers of 1798, though he wrote no prefaces, and most effectually breaks through the imprisoning canons of the eighteenth century poets in general, who, as Matthew Arnold said (developing Wordsworth), composed " without their eye on the object."* He was conscious of this power in himself, as of his pride and whither that

* *Thomas Gray* (*Essays in Criticism*, 2nd Series).

pride would lead him. An unprinted note by him on the first verse of *Bristowe Tragedy*,

> The feathered songster chaunticleer
> Han wounde hys bugle horne,
> And tolde the earlie villager
> The commynge of the morne :

runs " In my humble opinion, the foregoing lines are far more elegant and poetical than all the Parade of Aurora's whipping away the night, unbarring the gates of the East, &c., &c."* The first stanza of the third *Eclogue* is almost a confession of his poetical principles. " Haveth your mynde a lycheynge of a mynde ? " he asks ; " Would it kenne everich thynge as it mote be ? " He glosses *mote* " might," and adds " The sense of this line is, Would you see every thing in its primæval state." He is, in fact, a primitive.

So, in this poet, you will get line after line with no graces or epithets, gradus or other, yet a cadenced beauty and a poignant cry of *truth*, as here :

> I ryse wythe the Sonne,
> Lyche hym to dryve the Wayne
> And eere mie Wurche is don,
> I synge a Songe or twayne.
> I followe the Plough tayle,
> Wythe a longe jubb of ale. . . .
>
> On everyche Seynctes hie daie,
> Wythe the mynstrelle am I seen,
> All a footeynge it awaie,
> Wythe Maydens on the Greene—
> But oh—I wyshe to be moe greate,
> In rennome Tenure and Estate.

Could a better anticipation of the theory and practice of the *Lyrical Ballads* be desired ? In him, too, you will find the glory of the monosyllabic, or all but monosyllabic, line, with a handling that only independence and self-education can give:

* Transcribed by Catcott, B.5344. It did not escape Lort, who quotes it with the variant : " Clipping the wings of Night " in 11457, and, as above, in his copy of Tyrwhitt's 1777 ed. (B.11060).

Thie name alleyne wylle put the Danes to flighte,
The ayre that beares ytt woulde presse down the foe.

Mie race of love, mie race of lyfe ys ronne.

Hane Englande thenne a tongue butte notte a stynge ?

" Nature," wrote Maurice Morgann, " condescending to the faculties and apprehensions of men, has drawn through human life a regular chain of visible causes and effects : but poetry delights in surprise, conceals her steps, seizes at once upon the heart, and obtains the sublime of things without betraying the rounds of her ascent. True Poesy is *magic*, not nature ; an effect from causes hidden or unknown."* Let the bigger pieces of the Rowley cycle be inspected from this point of view.

3. THE POEMS†

Elinoure and Juga

(First printed in *The Town and Country Magazine*, May, 1769.)

The difficulty in dating this, the only one of his antique poems which Chatterton saw in print, has been touched on in Chapter VI. With respect to the names, the ballad of Lord Thomas and Fair Ellinor (imitated in Sir Thybbot Gorges's song in *Ælla*) was not only in Percy's but the earlier collection of old ballads ; while Juga is to be found in Camden (ed. 1695, p. 345) as the founder of a monastery at Dunmow in 1111 ; that this name was drawn hence is probable from the fact of Chatterton having elsewhere adapted the rhyming charter of Edward the Confessor which stands in the column opposite (p. 344), but the circumstance is hardly enough to date this composition subsequent to his apprenticeship.

Modernity will hardly echo Dr. Gregory's opinion that this complaint of two young females for their lovers slain in the Wars of the Roses is " one of the finest pathetic tales I have ever read." It is a charming but rather stilted piece, coloured

* *Essay on the Dramatic Character of Sir John Falstaff* (ed. 1912), p. 70.

† The Clarendon Press *Rowley* (ed. M. E. Hare, 1911), the only edition now (1929) in print, does not include more poems than were in Tyrwhitt's third edition (1778).

by Gray's *Elegy*, in the stanza beginning " No moe the miskynette shall wake the morne," but the movement is gracious, and there is one magnificent line :

O mai ne sanguen steine the whyte rose peyncte,

nor is the play on Rudborne (red water) unbecoming :

And Rudborne streeme be Rudborne streeme indeed.

The night picture he was to improve in *The Parlyamente of Sprytes*, and in his tragedy :

Whan mokie[1] cloudes do hange upon the leme,[2]
Of leden[3] moon ynn sylver mantels dyghte ;
The tryppeynge faeries weve the golden dreme
Of selyness,[4] whyche flyethe with the nyghte :
Thenne (butte the seynctes forbydde !) gif to a spryghte
Syrre Rychardes forme is lyped[5]; I'll holde dystranghte
Hys bledeynge clai-colde corse, and die eche daie yn thoughte.

[1] Black. [2] Light. [3] Decreasing (" to leden (O) to languish," Kersey). [4] Happiness. [5] " Lipopsychia, a small swoon." Kersey.

The *Faerie Queene* has helped to fashion the alexandrine, as Helene Richter observed :

Dying each day with inward wounds of dolour's dart.
III, 12, 16.

The Unknown Knyght or the Tournament

(MS, at Bristol Museum in " Antiquities Book 3rd." First printed in *A Supplement to Chatterton's Miscellanies*, 1784.)

This is the poem that was sent to Baker on March 6, 1768; and more need not be said about its prosody, except to note, with Professor Saintsbury, that as in Spenser's *February*, the decasyllable is admitted :

So great the shock their senses did depart,

It is hard to believe that when Coleridge began the second part of *Christabel* with

Each matin bell, the Baron saith,

and continued it with "trump and solemn heraldry" and the "tourney court," he had not in mind, if not the whole, at least the two opening stanzas, of this joyous thing.

The Matten Belle han sounded longe,
The Cocks han sang their morning songe,
When lo, the tuneful Clarion's sound,
Wherein all other Noise was drownd,
Did echo to the Rooms around,
And greet the Ears of Champyons stronge—
Arise, arise from downie Bedde,
For Sunne doth gin to shew his Hedde.

Then each did done in seemlie Gear,
What Armour eche beseem'd to wear:
And on ech Sheelde devices shon,
Of wounded hearts, and Battels won,
All curious and nice echon—
With manie a tassild Spear,
And mounted echone on a Steed,
Unwote made Ladies hartes to blede—

The last line of this "fyrst cento" ("And then one Howre was gone and past") looks back to Fairfax's "And of the day ten hours were gone and past." *Tasso*, XX. 1.

Battle of Hastings

(MS. of Part I at Bristol Museum, in "Antiquities Book 3rd"; first printed by Tyrwhitt in 1777.)

"What I sickened my poor brother with, I remember very well, was my inattention to the Battle of Hastings, which before he used to be perpetually repeating." Thus Mrs. Newton, to whom the antiques were "all a mere blank, I had no kind of relish for them. This my brother used sometimes to perceive, would grow angry, and scold at me for want of taste."* He submitted the home circle to an unnecessarily severe test,

* Milles, p. 8. "One of the poems on Our Lady's Church" was also read to her. "His own poems" were barred owing to their satirical tendency, the mother and grandmother "fearing that they should involve him in some scrape." He read *Ælla* to his sister "when he was communicative."

perhaps. This poem consists of two parts, the first 564 lines, avowed to be his, the remainder, 709, Rowley's. The whole can be roughly defined as the effect on a young, impetuous, creative brain of a perusal of Pope's *Iliad*,* but the effect is not in the least like Pope. The peculiarly fresh touch of the Bristol poet is seen quite at the start (the actual opening " O Chryste, it is a grief for me to tell " derives from the *Reliques*†) in:

Soone as the erlie maten belle was tolde,
And sun was come to bid us all good daie,

and

The clarions[1] then sounded sharpe and shrille;
Death doeynge blades were out intent to kille.

[1] " sharp slughornes " in MS.; " clarions " crossed through.

No time is lost in beginning the fray:

And now the Battle closde on everich side,
And Face to Face appeared Knyghtes full brave;
They lifted up their Bylles with mickle pride,
And manie wounds unto the Normans Gave.
So have I see two Weirs at once give[2] ground
White foameynge high to roarynge Combat runne;
In roarynge Din and Heaven breakynge sound;
Burst waves on waves and spangle in the sunne;
And when their myghte in burstyng waves is fled
Like Cowards steal along their owzy Bedde.

[2] " gave " MS.

The tone is boyish and bloodthirsty, but not more so than Michael Drayton's *The Battle of Agincourt*, which has this stanza:

Their cuirases are unriveted with blows
With horrid wounds their breasts and faces flasht;
There drops a cheek; and there falls off a nose,
And in one's face his fellow's brains are dasht:

* Helene Richter has noted eleven parallel passages (*Thomas Chatterton*, pp. 97, 98).

† O Christ, my very heart doth bleed
With sorrow for thy sake;
The more Modern Ballad of Chevy Chase (also in Ambrose Philips's *A Collection of Old Ballads*, 1723.)

Yet still the better with the English goes ;
The earth of France with her own blood is washt ;
They fall so fast, she scarce affords them room,
That one man's trunk becomes another's tomb.

The second part, which opens with an invocation to Truth (balancing the first's to Christ) is much finer, and the picture of Harold's camp by night nobly conceived :

With ale and vernage[1] drunk his souldiers lay ;
Here was an hynde,[2] anie an erlie spredde ;
Sad keepynge of their leaders natal daie !
This even in drinke, toomorrow with the dead !
Thro' everie troope disorder reer'd her hedde ;
Dancynge and heideignes[3] was the onlie theme ;
Sad dome was theires, who left this easie bedde,
And wak'd in torments from so sweet a dream.
Duke William's menne, of comeing dethe afraide,
All nyghte to the Great Godde for succour askd and praied.

[1] A sort of wine. [2] Peasant. [3] Dances. " Haydegines (O) a country dance or round," Kersey.

Dawn's approach is described in these terms :

And now the greie-eyd morne with vi'lets drest,
Shakyng the dewdrops on the flourie meedes,
Fled with her rosie radiance to the West :
Forth from the Easterne gatte the fyerie steedes
Of the bright sunne awaytynge spirits leedes :
The sunne, in fierie pompe enthrond on hie,
Swyfter than thoughte alonge hys jernie gledes,[1]
And scatters nyghtes remaynes from oute the skie :
He sawe the armies make for bloudie fraie,
And stopt his driving steedes, and hid his lyghtsome raye.

[1] Glides.

That the poet intended to better his previous work is clear from the description of Salisbury Plain and Stonehenge (ll. 521-540), far superior to that in the first part (ll. 301-320).* Here note that the epithet " dreare " or " derne " is peculiar to him, and seems, from its recurrence in the poems which he acknowledged, to be an image of his recurrent state of mind :

* The latter was quoted in his first communication to Catcott.

Where fruytless heathes and meadowes cladde in greie,
Save where derne[1] hawthornes reare theyr humble heade,
The hungrie traveller upon his waie
Sees a huge desarte alle arounde hym spredde,*
The distaunte citie scantlie to be spedde,[2]
The curlynge force of smoke he sees in vayne,
Tis to far distaunte, and his onlie bedde
Iwimpled[3] in hys cloke ys on the playne,
Whylst rattlynge thonder forrey oer his hedde,
And raines come down to wette hys harde uncouthlie bedde.

[1] Melancholy. [2] For "spied," as in Drayton. [3] Covered.

A wondrous pyle of rugged mountaynes standes,
Placd on eche other in a dreare arraie,
It ne could be the worke of human handes,
It ne was reared up bie menne of claie.
Here did the Brutons adoration paye
To the false god whom they did Tauran name,
Dightynge[1] hys altarre with greete fyres in Maie,
Roastynge theyr vyctualle round aboute the flame,
'Twas here that Hengyst did the Brytons slee,
As they were mette in council for to bee.

[1] Dressing.

Chatterton had an uncle living in Salisbury, but he probably had in mind the engraving of Stonehenge by Johannes Kip (1653-1722) in Gibson's *Camden*, where the stones indeed look like rugged mountains, and in the background, exactly as he says:

Near on a loftie hylle a citie stands,
That lyftes its scheafted[1] heade ynto the skies,

[1] Adorned with turrets.

The mention of Adhelm, "a knyghte," introduces, by way of contrast to the bloodshed, a picture of his lady, Kenewalcha,† whom he has left for the wars, in four stanzas. Here, among much that is extravagant, cold, or even absurd, such as

* The weary traveller with wild surprise
Sees the dry desert all around him rise.
Addison, *Cato*.

† From "Kenewalch, King of the West Saxons" (Gibson's *Camden*, p. 120), Adhelm may have been grafted on to Turgot ("the lov'd Adhelme by thie syde") on the analogy of Aldwin (*ibid.* p. 783); he comes, however, from Fuller's *Church History*, Cent. VIII, Book II, if not from *Camden* (p. 86).

White as the chaulkie clyffes of Brittaines isle,
Red as the highest colour'd Gallic wine,

which Mr. Hare calls " a study in Burgundy and whitewash," are the eyes of the poet himself :

Greie as the morne before the ruddie flame
Of Phebus charyotte rollynge thro the skie ;
Greie as the steele horn'd goats Conyan made tame,
So greie appeard her featly sparklyng eye ;

The fighting recurs, and Harold's death is not reached.

Brystowe Tragedy or The Dethe of Syr Charles Bawdin

(MS. in Bristol Museum, not in Chatterton's hand, I think ; a transcript, in G. Catcott's hand, in Bristol Library, 5343 ; for account of a MS, apparently holograph, of the first 168 lines, then in possession of Mr. S. G. Perceval, see *Bristol Times and Mirror*, June 27, 1904 ; the last is identical with the text as first printed in 1772.)

This virile, direct, and fiery piece of 392 lines can be regarded as a case of Chatterton having "exerted all his might" to produce a ballad that could vie with some of those in Percy's *Reliques*. With great appropriateness, on its publication two years after his death, it was dedicated to the Duchess of Northumberland, and bore on the title page the motto *Durat opus Vatum*. Its historical basis is that in 1461 Sir Baldwin Fulford, a Lancastrian, who had undertaken, "on paine of loosing his head, that he would destroy the Earle of Warwicke, but when he hadde spent the King (i.e. Henry VI) a thousand markes in money, he returned againe" (Stow's *Annales*, ed. 1615, p. 406), was with two others, after capture, imprisoned in Bristol castle, tried (William Canynges being Mayor), and suffered a traitor's death, Edward IV being in Bristol at the time. The poet, possibly following a tradition, has availed himself of a note in St. Ewen's Churchwardens' book* to make Edward watch the condemned man's passage to his fate, from

* "Item, for washynge the church payven against K. Edward 4th is comynge to Brystow iiij d. ob."

the great window of the church in Broad Street. The verse is fourteeners, almost wholly free from resolutions, the language straightforward, with hardly an admixture of Kersey,* and the touch everywhere dramatic. For instance, when Canynge starts his intercession, the King says:

> Justice does loudlie for hym calle,
> And hee shalle have hys meede:
> Speke, Maister Canynge! Whatte thynge else
> Att present doe you neede?

Sir Charles represents the noble and heroic character; he even paraphrases Pope's *Universal Prayer* at one point, but there is no falsetto:

> Ynne Londonne citye was I borne,
> Of parents of grete note;
> My fadre dydd a nobile armes
> Emblazon onne hys cote. . . .
>
> Hee taughte mee justice and the laws
> Wyth pitie to unite;
> And eke hee taughte me howe to knowe
> The wronge cause fromm the ryghte. . . .
>
> And none can saye, butt all mye lyfe
> I have hys wordyes kept;
> And summ'd the actyonns of the daie
> Eche nyghte before I slept.

The young Shelley reproduced the last two lines in *Queen Mab* (ll. 176-8):

> Nor that ecstatic and exulting throb
> Which virtue's votary feels when he sums up
> The thoughts and actions of a well spent day.

The characteristic note of the poem is defiance—"Hee can ne harm my mynde"; but it is when the procession is reached

* The name of Sir Charles's wife, Florence, is glossed "a proper name of women" in Kersey; and if "Who tuned the Psaume bataunt" be read in ll. 276, 292 (Bristol Museum MS.) the strange word must come from Kersey's "batauntly, (O) boldly." "Syr Canterlone" is probably formed from Cantlow (in Holinshed and Baker), the person who captured Henry VI.

that "the true dayspring of Romantic poetry" shines most clearly:

> The Freers of Seincte AUGUSTYNE next
>   Appeared to the syghte,
> Alle cladd ynn homelie russett weedes,
>   Of godlie monkysh plyghte.
>
> Ynne diffraunt partes a godlie psaume
>   Moste sweetlie theye dydd chaunt;
> Behynde theyre backes syx mynstrelles came,
>   Who tun'd the strunge bataunt.
>
> Thenne fyve-and-twentye archers came,
>   Echone the bowe dydd bende,
> From rescue of Kynge HENRIE's friends
>   Syr CHARLES forr to defend.
>
> Bolde as a lyon came Syr CHARLES,
>   Drawne onne a clothe-layde sledde,
> Bye two blacke stedes ynn trappynges white,
>   Wyth plumes uponne theyre hedde:
>
> Behynde hym fyve-and-twentye moe
>   Of archers stronge and stoute,
> Wyth bended bowe echone ynne hande,
>   Marched ynne goodlie route:
>
> Saincte JAMESES Freeres marched next,
>   Echone hys parte dydd chaunt;
> Behynde theyre backes syx mynstrelles came,
>   Who tun'd the strunge bataunt.

This unintelligible instrument may have developed into the "loud bassoon" of *The Rime of the Ancient Mariner*, which was itself slightly "antiquated" on its first appearance, but the *varia lectio* "psaume bataunt" seems to be the poet's.

The great dramatic climax comes at the close of the hero's speech:

> "Thye pow'r unjust, thou traytour slave
>   Shall falle onne thye owne hedde"—
> Fromm out of hearyng of the Kynge
>   Departed thenne the sledde.

Kynge EDWARDE's soule rush'd to hys face,
  Hee turn'd hys hedde awaie,
And to hys broder GLOUCESTER
  Hee thus dydd speke and saie :

" To hym that soe-much-dreaded dethe
  Ne ghastlie terrors brynge,
Beholde the manne ! hee spake the truthe,
  Hee's greater thanne a Kynge ! "

Chatterton is too considerable an artist to leave matters there ; two stanzas later we have the sunlight on the axe, before the ballad ends the four quarters of Sir Charles, and also his head, are disposed of on various Bristol sites ; and not till then the poet cries :

Thus was the end of BAWDIN's fate :
  Godde prosper longe oure kynge,
And grante hee maye, wyth BAWDIN's soule,
  Ynne heav'n Godd's mercie synge !

There is a wonderful *brightness* maintained throughout, and the reader is made to feel that the events, tragic and pitiable as they are, pass in broad daylight. Blake's early *Gwin King of Norway* where Godred (cf. Chatterton's *Godred Crovan*) is a character, seems to owe something to this poem, especially in such lines as

O what have kings to answer for
  Before that awful throne ;

and

Gwin fell : the sons of Norway fled,
  All that remained alive ;
The rest did fill the vale of death,
  For them the eagles strive.

Another, though vaguer, instance of its power may be cited. A writer in *Notes and Queries* (Aug. 24, 1872), signing himself J.H.C., says he only saw Keats once, but then he read some lines from *Bristowe Tragedy*, " such as could only be felt by a poet and which true poetry only could have excited."

Chatterton seems to have returned to the subject of this

poem, in his own person, if the following statement can be trusted; it is found in an anonymous *Essay on the Rowley Controversy*, dated 30 March, 1783, possibly in the early handwriting of Samuel Seyer, one of Richard Smith's MSS., in the Bristol Library (5199, f. 42): "Once indeed (an anecdote I do not remember to have been noticed before) he attempted—he compleated a Dramatic poem of the subject of Sir Charles Bawden—This was shewn to the Rev[d] Mr Catcott by Mr Geo. Catcott, who had it in his possession, and condemned by him as miserable stuff unworthy even the other compositions of Chatterton. It was in three acts, and Mr G. C., who had copied the Tragedy of Ellae and the other works of Rowley with avidity, did not think it worth the pains of transcribing a single Page."

Songe to Ælla

(MS. (paper) in British Museum, 5766 B, f. 11 (parchment) *penes* Sir William Rose Smith; first printed in *The Westminster Magazine, Jan.* 1775.)

This is in "Rowleyfied Pindaric," which Professor Saintsbury finds "rather terrible"; but the piece is made by its fire:

Oh thou, orr what remaynes of thee,
Ælla, the darlynge of futurity,
Lett thys mie songe bold as thie courage be,
As everlastynge to posteritie.

That opening either carries you away completely or leaves you completely cold; no hedging is possible concerning it; and though, later in the piece, the metre of the *Nativity Ode* and the phrasing of stanza six of *On the death of a fair Infant* are echoed in one and the same stanza:

O thou, whereer (thie bones at reste)
Thye Spryte to haunte delyghteth beste,
Whetherr upponne the bloude-embrewedd pleyne
Or whare thou kennst* fromm farre
The dysmall crye of warre
Orr seest somme mountayne made of corse of slayne.

* "hearste" in the paper MS.

the utterance is Chatterton's, not his models'. The last line, too,

Tylle ynne one flame all the whole worlde expyre

may be analysed as begotten on Milton's

That till the world's last end shall make thy name to live

by Gray's

Till wrap'd in flames, in ruin hurl'd,
Sinks the fabric of the world.

one of whose parents is a line, already quoted, from Dryden. Descent in English poetry, it cannot be repeated too often, is spiritual. Pindaric is also used in *On the Mynster* (19 lines).

The Storie of William Canynge

(MS. of ll. 1-34 on a parchment in the British Museum, 5766A, f. 3; first printed by Tyrwhitt in 1777; an engraving of the "original" faces p. 637 of Barrett's *History of Bristol.*)

None of the antiques surpasses this in sheer loveliness. The Middle-English convention of a dream or "sweven" is followed. The poet represents himself as lying beside a brooklet, tributary to the Avon, listening to the water, and gazing at the osiers, alders, and reeds. These bring to his thought "hardie champyons knowen to the floude," and first among them Ælla, who fought the Danes on its banks, and he regrets that this hero's actions are left "so spare yn storie." Then "holie Wareburghus," and "eche dygne buylder" pass through his fancy, when the apparition of a maid arises from the stream:

Ne browded[1] mantell of a scarlette hue,
Ne shoone pykes[2] plaited o'er wyth ribbande geere,
Ne costlie paraments[3] of woden[4] blue,
Noughte of a dresse, but bewtie dyd shee weere;
Naked shee was, and loked swete of youthe,
All dyd bewryen[5] that her name was Trouthe.

[1] Embroidered. [2] Picked (i.e. peaked) shoes. [3] Robes of State. [4] Dyed with woad. [5] Declare.

She comes close to him, "dreste up yn naked viewe," but

he takes a crucifix from his pocket and looks on her with eyes as pure as angels. She tells him that many champions, men of lore, painters and carvers, have gained good name,

> But there's a Canynge, to encrease the store,
> A Canynge, who shall buie uppe all theyre fame.
> Take thou mie power, and see yn chylde and manne
> What troulie noblenesse yn Canynge ranne.

He falls into a trance—remember, it is no youth, but Rowley, *an old man*,* who is speaking—

> Strayte was I carryd back to tymes of yore,
> Whylst Canynge swathed yet yn fleshie bedde,
> And saw all actyons whych han been before,
> And all the scroll of Fate unravelled;
> And when the fate-mark'd babe acome to syghte,
> I saw hym eager gaspynge after lyghte.
>
> In all hys shepen[1] gambols and chyldes plaie,
> In everie merriemakeyng, fayre or wake,
> I kenn'd a perpled[2] lyghte of Wysdom's raie;
> He eate downe learnynge wyth the wastle[3] cake.
> As wise as anie of the eldermenne,
> He'd wytte enowe toe make a mayre at tenne.†

[1] Innocent.

[2] This is from Kersey's "Disparpled or Disperpled (in Heraldry) loosely scattered, or shooting itself into several parts," and has nothing to do with "the purple light of love" in Gray's *Progress of Poesy*. Chatterton does not seem to have provided this poem with a glossary.

[3] Cake of the whitest bread.

This is more than an inspired self-portrait; if it is not as lovely a miniature of childhood as has been painted in words since Catullus's

Torquatus volo parvulus,

* In St. Mary Redcliff, crawling from the feet of the effigy of William Canynges in his priest's robes are the head and shoulders of an old man apparently in great agony, which may be figurative of Canynges's putting off the old man. Chatterton haunted this tomb, and the little figure ("bieneth your fote ylayn") may have helped him in the association of another person with the church's fifteenth century benefactor. He had an eye for the minutiæ of sculpture, e.g., he noted the ram playing a violin in the Elder Lady Chapel of Bristol Cathedral. (*T. and C. M.*, Suppl. 1770, p. 704).

† Everich, for the wisdom that he can
Was shaply for to been an alderman.
Canterbury Tales, Prol. l. 371.

it is at least lovelier and more human than the two lame sections of Wordsworth's famous *Ode*, where the " Six years' Darling of a pigmy size " is hailed as " Mighty Prophet ! Seer blest ! "

The life of Canynges is traced till " Edwarde meniced a seconde wyfe," and his consequent retreat to Westbury ; and the dreamer is awakened by the bell for Evensong.

The Parlyamente of Sprytes

(MS. in British Museum, 5766B, ff. 5-10 ; first printed in Barrett's *History of Bristol*, 1789, p. 600.)

This, one of Chatterton's earliest communications to Barrett, is in effect a pæan of 268 lines to St. Mary Redcliff and Canynge, owing little to Chaucer beyond the hint for its title. The church is represented as finished. Queen Mab speaks a prologue, preparing the spectator (this is an acted piece) for the appearance of " the sprytes of valourous menne " who

Agleeme along the þarbed halle,
Pleasaunte the moltrynge banners kenne,
Or sytte arounde yn honourde stalle.

An address to Carpenter, who dedicated the church, follows, in which the accent of Lydgate's rime royal is caught :

Learned as Beauclerk, as the Confessour
Holie ynne lyfe, lyke Canynge charitable,
Busie in holie chyrche as Vavasour,
Slacke yn thynges evylle, yn alle goode thynges stable*

Next the " sprytes " appear, a grotesque collection, Nimrod, Assyrians, Ælla, Bythrycke (" an Anglo-Saxon, who in William the Conqueror's time had Bristol ")†, Burton, Segowen (" a

* A footnote on a line in this address gives another poem of twenty lines, in fourteeners, a processional:—

Arounde the highe unsaynted chyrche withe holie relyques wente;
And every door and poste aboute wythe godlie thynges besprente.

In most editions of Chatterton this is printed in eight and six, like *Brystowe Tragedy*.

† " 'Tis said, that about the Norman Invasion, one Bithrick, a Saxon, was lord of Gloucester." Gibson's *Camden*, p. 242.

usurer, a native of Lombardy"), imaginary founder of St. Thomas Church,* Fitzharding, who founded the Abbey of St. Augustine's, now the Cathedral, Frampton (Walter Frampton's tomb is in his foundation, St. John's Church, not far from the Rouley brass), Gauntes (Maurice de Gaunte), a Knight Templar, and Lanyngeton (Lamington), the Robin Hood of the Rowley Poems, each stating his good works in and out of Bristol, and how far Canynge has excelled them. The jumble of the two scriptural names with the rest is somehow Gothic, and one or two of Nimrod's lines carry one back to the *Romaunt of the Rose*:

> The rampynge lyon, felle tygere,
> The bocke that skyppes from place to place,
> The olyphaunt and rhynocere
> Before mee throughe the greene woode I dyd chace.†

The legend of Nimrod as builder of the Tower of Babel he may have taken from the first chapter of Verstegan's *Restitution*. The piece is full of colour, and about a third of the way through settles into the ten-lined decasyllabic stanza; there are but two alexandrines in the whole. The poet's directness of vision is displayed in

* This name puzzled Barrett; he "examined Chatterton very strictly on this subject," who told him Segowen was "an *Elenge*, a foreign merchant." Milles, p. 188. Kersey glosses Elenge "(O) strange, foreign." I think Segowen may have been taken from Segovia, the province of Old Castile.

† Cf. *R. R.* 1401-1408 (ed. Skeat); the "buk" is in *The Parlament of Foules* (l. 194). Chaucer's influence is most plainly seen in the *Balade of Charitie*. On a sheet of paper (5766 B. f. 71) Chatterton has jotted down seven quotations from Chaucer, one from the *Plowman's Tale*, and an extract from Speght about Chaucer beating a friar in Fleet Street; two of the quotations are used in his essay on Christmas games. The extract was worked up into the *Anecdote of Chaucer*, and appeared in the *Town and Country* for Jan. 1770. The original draft (5766B. f. 31) reads thus: "When Chaucer had distributed Copys of the Tale of Piers Plowman, the first of his Performances, a Franciscan Friar wrote a Satyric Mommery (the Comedy of the Age) upon him, which was acted at every Monastery in London & at woodstock before the Court: Chaucer not a little nettled, at the poignancy of the Satyre, and the popularity of it, meeting his Antagonist in Fleet Street; beat him with his Dagger, for which he was fined two Shillings, as appears by a record of the Inner Temple where Chaucer was a Student." Thomas de Quincey, in his copy of Chatterton's *Miscellanies* (1778), where the *Anecdote* is reprinted from the magazine, at p. 137, has made this note: "N.B. This anecdote was a pure fiction [or, to use Mr Ritson's expression, a *Hum*] of Thomas Chatterton's: there is no truth in it. Indeed it disproves itself; for Chaucer was not the author of Piers Plowman."

There sytte the canons ; cloth of sable hue
Adorne the boddies of them everie one
The chaunters whyte with scarfes of woden blewe,
And crymson chappeaus for them toe put onne,
Wythe golden tassyls glyttrynge ynne the sonne ;
The dames ynne kyrtles alle of Lyncolne greene,

and his word-music in the stanza on Temple Church (Bristol's leaning Tower of Pisa), where the *Reeve's Tale* has lent him an adjective belonging properly to the nose :

Maint[1] tenures fayre, and mannoures of greete welthe,
Greene woodes, and brooklettes runnynge throughe the lee,
Dyd menne us gyve for theyre deare soule her helthe,
Gave erthlie ryches for goodes heavenlie.
Ne dyd we lette oure ryches untyle[2] bee,
But dyd ybuylde the Temple chyrche soe fyne,
The whyche ys wroughte abowte so bismarelie[3]
Itte seemeth camoys[4] to the wondrynge eyne ;
And ever and anon when belles rynged,
From place to place ytte moveth yttes hie heade :
Butte Canynge from the sweate of hys owne browes
Dyd gette hys golde and rayse thys fetyve howse.

[1] Many. [2] Useless. [3] Curiously. [4] Crooked upwards, Lat. simus.

Here note the internal echoings, culminating with "sweate" "gette" and "owne" "golde" in the last couplet.

A gloss on "oliphaunt" betrays his Puckish humour :

" Elephant—so an ancient anonymous author :
The olyphaunt of beastes is
The wisest I wis,
For hee alwaie doth eat
Lyttle store of meat."*

This is the author himself, who " never touched meat, and drank only water, and seemed to live on the air."† Few of the poems suffer more from partial quotation than this, because of the fusion of quaintness with exalted rapture.

* Contrast D. H. Lawrence :—
Oldest they are and the wisest of beasts
So they know at last
How to wait for the loneliest of feasts
For the full repast.
Pansies (1929), p. 56.

† Mr. and Mrs. Walmsley's niece's testimony ; *L. and M.*, p. 191.

The Tournament, an Interlude

(MS. in the Bristol Museum; first printed by Tyrwhitt in 1777.)

This spirited dramatic piece (to be distinguished from *The Unknown Knyght*) is found at the other end of the first copybook containing the De Bergham pedigree—Syrr Johan de Berghamme is one of the tilters—and it is reinforced by a parchment in the British Museum (5766A, f. 7), on which Chatterton has written a life of Symonne de Byrtonne, and, as here, made him vow to build a church to St. Mary on the site of the tournament. The ten-line metrical scheme is used; alexandrines, save in the second stanza, being reserved for the minstrels' first song, of King William's hunting, with the much-varied refrain:

> Lett thie floes[1] drenche the bloode of anie thynge botte menne.

[1] Arrows.

We are on the way to *Ælla*, the lines and stanzas are broken up:

KYNGE

Now to the Tourneie; who wylle fyrste affraie;

HERAULDE

Nevylle, a Baronne, bee yatte Honnoure thyne:

BOURTON

I clayme the Passage—

NEVYLLE

I contake[2] thie Waie—

BOURTON

Thenne theers mie Gauntlette on mie Gaberdyne[3]—

[2] Contest. [3] A piece of armour.

HEREHAULDE

A Leegefulle Challenge, Knyghtes and Champyons dygne,
A leegefulle Challenge, lette the slughorne sounde.
[Syr Simonn *and* Nevylle *tylte.*
Loverdes, how doutyghttilie the tylters jyne,
Nevylle is goeynge Manne and Horse, to grounde!
[Nevylle *falles.*

Ye Champyones : heere Symon de Bourtonne fyghtes,
On hee ha'the quaced,[1] assayle hym yee Knyghtes.*

[1] Vanquished.

Browning, by the way, has followed Chatterton in making " slogan " an instrument, in

Dauntless the slughorn to my lips I set,
And blew, '*Childe Roland to the dark Tower came.*'

Twice in *Harold* Tennyson puts one in mind of this poem ;

" I should be there, Malet, I should be there."—Act II, Sc. 2.

with which compare

" Annodherr launce, Marshalle, annodherr launce."—l. 130.

and in Act V, Sc. 2, where William says :

I vow to build a church to God
Here on the hill of battle

recalling Bourtonne's

Bie thee Seyncte Marie, and thy Sonne, I sweare,
That yn whatte place yon doughtie Straungere fall
Anethe the Stronge Pushe of mie straughte out Speare,
There sal aryse a hallie chyrchys Walle.

The second, and final, minstrels' song has a delightful change from iambic to trochaic rhythm, which more than atones for the lifting of an image from Collins's *Ode to Mercy :*

Whan Battle smetheynge wythe nue quickend Gore,
Bendeynge wythe Spoyles and bloddie droppynge Heads;
Dydde the merke wode of Ethe and Rest explore,
Secheynge toe lie onne Pleasures downie Beds
Pleasure Dauncynge fro her Wode,
Wreathed wythe Floures of Aiglentyne ;
From hys Vysage washed the Blode,
Hylte hys Sworde and Gaberdyne.

* Buxton Forman (*Chatterton and his latest Editor*, p. 30), on grounds of metre and common sense, first arranged this stanza thus, lines 7 and 8 being inverted in all the editions ; the MS. confirms him here, though not in his conjecture " blodd-ydroppynge " at l. 162. (p. 31, n.)

The Worlde

(MS. of ll. 1-12 in British Museum, 5766B, f. 37 (v.); first printed in Barrett's *History of Bristol*, p. 629.)

This is given entire, that the reader may compare it with an entire fifteenth century English poem on the same subject. Kersey helps to gloss the hard words, in the absence of a gloss by Chatterton. It purports to be the work of William Canynge, whose father " loved money, as hys charie joie " (in the Rowley Romance), and going to court, " but kenneynge he mote ne goe there wydoute a guift, he took a brasse chaine and giltynge the same lyke unto goulde gave ytte to the Queene." This will illustrate the circumstance of the interlude. Chatterton could not have known the lovely fifteenth century poem, *The Child of Brystow*, in which the son of an avaricious father sells himself to his master, a Bristol merchant, and strips himself bare to save his father's soul from hell, as it was then in mansucript only (Harl. 2382, f. 118 sqq.); neither, I think, could he have known Dunbar's masterpiece, nor the following, taken from Wright's *Reliquiæ Antiquæ* (Vol. I, p. 136), as during his time, and indeed till 1841, it was accessible only in a MS. in the library of Jesus College, Cambridge.

DE SEPTEM PECCATIS MORTALIBUS

SUPERBIA

Who that wylle abyde in helle,
He most do as me hym telle.
I bost and brag ay with the best;
To mayntene syn I am full prest;
Myn awn wylle I wylle have ay,
Thof God and gode men alle bid nay.

INVIDIA

I am full sory in my hert
Off other mens welefare and whert;
I ban and bakbyte wykkedly,
And hynder alle that I may sikerly.

IRA

I chide and feght and manas fast;
All my fomen I wylle doun cast;
Mercy on thaym I wylle none have,
Bot vengeance take, so God me save!

ACCIDIA

I yrk fulle sore with Goddes servyse ;
Godenes wyrk I will on no wyse ;
Idelnes and slepe I luf ay best,
For in thaym I fynde most rest.

AVARITIA

I covet ay, and wyles oft cast,
How that I may be riche in hast ;
Full fast I hald alle that I wynne,
Alle if my part be left thereinne.

GULA

I luf my wombe over all thynge ;
Hym most to plese is my likynge ;
I have no rest nyght nor day,
To he be served alle to his pay.

LUXURIA

I luf foulle lust and lichory,
Fornification and adowtry ;
For synfulle lust I wylle not fle,
If I for it in helle ay be.

THE WORLDE

FADRE. SONNE. MYNSTRELLES.

FADRE

To the Worlde newe and ytts bestoykeynge[1] Waies
Thys Coistrelle[2] Sonne of myne ys all mie Care
Ye Mynstrelles warne hymme how wyth rede[3] he straies
Where guiled Vyce dothe spredde her mascilde[4] Snare
To gettyng Wealthe I woulde he shoulde be bredde,
And Couronnes of rudde Goulde ne Glorie, round hys head.

FIRST MYNSTREL

Mie Name is Intereste 'tis I
Dothe ynto alle Boosoms flie
Echone hylten[5] secretes myne
None so wordie goode and dygne,
Butte wylle fynde ytte to theyre Coaste
Intereste wylle rule the roaste.*
I to everichone gyve lawes,
Selfe ys fyrst yn everich cause.

[1] Betraying. [2] A young lad. [3] Counsel. [4] "Mascle (F. in Heraldry) a kind of short lozenge that is voided, or has a hole in the middle, representing the mash of a net," hence meshed. [5] Hidden.

* But int'rest is the most prevailing cheat,
The Hind and the Panther, III. 394.

SECOND MYNSTREL

I amme a faytour[1] flame
Of lemmies[2] melancholi,
Love somme behyghte mie name,
Some doe anemp[3] me follie ;
Inne sprytes of meltynge molde
I sette mie burneynge sele ;
To mee a goulers[4] goulde
Doeth nete a pyne avele[5] ;
I pre upon the helthe,
And from gode redeynge flee,
The manne who woulde gette wealthe
Muste never thynke of mee.

[1] Vagabond. [2] Flames. [3] Name. [4] Usurer. [5] Pin avail.

THIRD MYNSTREL

I bee the Queede[1] of Pryde, mie spyrynge heade
Mote reche the cloudes and stylle be rysynge hie,
Too lyttle is the earthe to bee mie bedde,
Too hannow[2] for mie breetheynge place the skie ;
Daynous I see the worlde bineth me lie
Botte to mie betterres, I soe lyttle gree,
Aneuthe[3] a shadow of a shade I bee,
Tys to the smalle alleyn that I canne multyplie.

[1] Devil. [2] Narrow. [3] Beneath.

FOURTH MYNSTREL

I am the Queed of Goulers ; look arounde
The ayrs aboute mee thieves doe represente,
Bloudsteyned robbers spryng from oute the grounde,
And airie vysyons swarme around mie ente[1] ;
O save mie monies, ytte ys theyre entente
To nymme[2] the redde Godde of mie fremded[3] sprighte,
Whatte joie canne goulers have or daie or nyghte ?

[1] Purse. [2] Rob. [3] Strange.

FIFTH MYNSTREL

Vice bee I hyghte, onne golde full ofte I ryde,*
Fulle fayre unto the syghte for aie I seeme ;
Mie ugsomness[1] wythe goldenne veyles I hyde,
Laieynge mie lovers ynne a sylkenne dreme ;
Botte whan mie untrue pleasaunce have byn tryde,
Thanne doe I showe all horrownesse[2] and row,[3]
And those I have ynne nette woulde feyne mie grype eschew.

[1] Terribleness. [2] Nastiness. [3] Ugly.

* And greedy Avarice by him did ride
Upon a camel loaden all with gold. *F. Q.* I., 4, 27.

SIXTH MYNSTREL

I bee greete Dethe, alle ken mee bie the name,
Botte none can saie howe I doe loose the spryghte,
Goode menne mie tardyinge delaie doethe blame,
Botte moste ryche goulerres from mee take a flyghte;
Myckle of wealthe I see whereere I came,
Doethe mie ghastness mockle multyplye
And maketh hem afrayde to lyve or die.

FADRE

Howe, villeyn Mynstrelles, and is this your rede,
Awaie: Awaie: I wyll ne geve a curse.
Mie sonne, mie sonne, of this mie speeche take hede,
Nothynge ys goode thatte bryngeth not to purse.

Englysh Metamorphosis

(First printed by Tyrwhitt in 1777, from a single sheet in Barrett's possession.)

This is Chatterton's "Imitation of Spenser"; it consists of eleven Rowley stanzas, with strict alexandrines. A note says: "Booke 1st. I will endeavour to get the remainder of these poems." Ovid has suggested the title, and (as Skeat saw) the "Chronicle of Briton Kings" in *The Faerie Queene* (II. x., st. 5-19) most of the matter. But, though not so far from Spenser as Blake's "Imitation," it is farther than Keats's. The poet's object is to improve on the mythological derivation of the Severn from Sabrina, daughter of Locrine and Estrild, whom he calls Elstrid. In her flight the latter dons man's gear and names herself Vyncente. "Gendolyne," the outraged wife of Locrine, sends a giant after them, who throws a mountain, which overwhelms the mother with the child in her arms; but the gods change Elstrid into St. Vincent's Rock, and Sabrina into the river:

Sabryna's floode was helde ynne Elstryd's bones,
So are theie cleped; gentle and the hynde
Can telle that Severnes streame bie Vyncentes rocke's ywrynde.[1]

[1] Hid, covered.

The giant, while on his return to Gendolyne, is struck by

lightning, falls " an hepe of ashes on the playne " and emerges as Snowdon. Hence we have *three* metamorphoses, Spenser being content with " Which of her name now *Seuerne* men do call " merely ; the proceeding is typical of Chatterton's attitude to existing literary matter. The infidelity of Locrine is thus beautifully worded :

The gentle suyte of Locryne gayned her love ;
Theie lyved soft momentes to a swotie[1] age ;
Eft[2] wandringe yn the coppyce, delle, and grove,
Where ne one eyne mote theyre disporte engage ;
There dydde theie tell the merrie lovynge fage,[3]
Croppe the prymrosen floure to decke theyre headde ;
The feerie Gendolyne yn woman rage
Gemoted[4] warriours to bewrecke[5] her bedde ;
Theie rose ; ynne battle was greete Locryne sleene ;
The faire Elstrida fledde from the enchafed[6] queene.

[1] Sweet. [2] Oft. [3] Tale. [4] Assembled. [5] Revenge. [6] Heated.

Eclogues

(MS., "a thin copy book in quarto " in British Museum, Add. 24890, ff. 2-11 ; first printed by Tyrwhitt in 1777.)

There are three poems with this title, though *Elinoure and Juga* is, properly speaking, an eclogue. The first, *Robert and Raufe* (60 lines) is a dialogue between two shepherds on the miseries of war ; the opening, and finest, stanza, has been quoted ; the piece contains such beautiful lines as

Farewell the verie Shade of fayre disporte . . .
I amme duressed unto Sorrowes blow . . .
Now from een Logges[1] fledden is Selyness

[1] Cottages.

The second, *Nygelle* (48 lines), which employs the device of a refrain, learnt from Collins's *Hassan and Abra*,

Sprytes of the Bleste ! the pious Nygelle sed,
Poure owte yer pleasaunce, onn mie Fadres hedde.

is, for the most part, a sea piece, the time being that of the Crusades. Considering that the author was native of a seaport it is strange that the sea plays so small a part in these poems, only here, in *Laymyngtowne*, and *Ælla* (where the Danish fleet is fired). The painting is crude, like an early English secular illumination :

> The Bollengers and Cottes,[1] soe swyfte yn fyghte,
> Upon the Sydes of everich Barke appere ;
> Foorthe to his Office lepethe everych Knyghte,
> Eftsomes hys Squyer, with hys Shielde and spere.

[1] Different kinds of boats.

and the excitement of the writer communicates itself in :

> The Fyghte is wonne : Kynge Rycharde Master is ;
> The Englonde Banner kisseth the hie Ayre ;

That " Englonde " is pure Chatterton ; anyone else would have written " English."

Of the third, *Manne, Womanne, Syr Rogerre* (94 lines, of which fifty are in the Rowley stanza—two alexandrines—and the rest in various measures) enough perhaps has been said. It is a fresh treatment of the English pastoral, and, except prosodically, has had no influence on subsequent poets ; though one of our time, the late Edward Thomas, wrote "The speech of the woman in his third eclogue, doomed to work thinking of the jewelled dame buried in the church, comes near to a romantic earthiness and implies a deep sympathy."* The lines are these :

> Howe harde ys mie Dome to Wurch !
> Moke is mie Woe :
> Dame Agnes, whoe lies ynne the Chyrche
> With Birlette, golde,
> Wythe gelten aumeres stronge ontolde,
> What was shee, moe than me, to be soe ?

Goddwyn

(In the same MS. as the preceding, ff. 12-21b ; first printed by Tyrwhitt in 1777.)

This inchoate tragedy of 212 lines is chiefly remembered for the chorus which concludes the second scene, but it contains

* *The Feminine Influence on the Poets*, p. 284.

at least one superb stanza besides, and one or two dramatic strokes of the *Bristowe Tragedy* sort. The verse is less uniform than *Ælla*, including stanzas of four, six, and eight lines, besides many decasyllabic closes.*

The theme is the growing power of the Normans who make up the Court of Edward the Confessor. Harold stands forth as a Saxon champion (he was played by Rowley himself), and the piece opens with a vivid and nervously written scene between him and his father Godwin, whose character, according to the prologue, has been blackened because "he gyfted ne the churche"—the latter preaching moderation to the hot-brained hero:

GODDWYN

Awayte the tyme whanne Godde wylle sende us ayde.

HAROLDE

No, we muste streve to ayde ourselves wyth poure!
Whan Godde wylle sende us ayde! tis fetelie[1] prayde:
Moste we thosen calke[2] awaie the lyvelonge howre?

[1] Nobly. [2] Cast.

Unlike Coriolanus, the ties of kin incite him further.

GODDWYN

Thie Suster.

HAROLDE

Aye, I knowe she is his Queene;
Albeyette dyd shee speche her foemen fayre:
I wulde dequace[3] her comlie Semlykeene,[4]
And foulde mie bloddie Anlace[5] yn her hayre.

[3] Mangle. [4] Beauty. [5] An ancient sword.

Godwin is not for deposing the king, but raising the country; and at last Harold, who is ready to kill himself to free England (Wilkes and Liberty!), condescends to listen.

HAROLDE

I will to the West, and gemote[1] alle mie Knyghtes,
Wythe Bylles that pancte for blodde, and Sheeldes as brede[2]
As the ybroched[3] Moon, when blaunch[4] she dyghtes[5]
The Wodeland Grounde or water-mantled mede;

* One unrelated line "What tydynge withe the foulke?" of the exclamatory sort found in *Ælla*.

Wythe hondes whose myghte canne make the doughtiest blede,
Who efte have knelte upon forslagen[6] foes,
Whoe wythe yer Fote orrests[7] a Castle stede,
Who dare on Kynges for to bewreck[8] yiere Woes;
Nowe wylle the menne of Englonde haile the daie,
Whan Goddwyn leades them to the ryghtfulle fraie.

[1] Assemble. [2] Broad. [3] Horned. [4] White. [5] Decks. [6] Slain. [7] Oversets. [8] Revenge.

In the second scene the queen weakly protests against the Normans, " these browded strangers," but Edward tells her to go in while he says his prayers; and, as she goes out, a knight enters with tidings of popular discontent and the depleted treasury.

KYNGE

Thenne guylde the Weste.

HUGHE

Mie Loverde, I dyd speke,
Untoe the mitte Erle Harrolde of the thynge;
He raysed hys Honde, and smote* me onne the Cheke,
Saieynge, go beare thatte Message to the Kynge.

This is in the manner of Cyril Tourneur.

Castiza: Oh they shall thanke you sir,
Whence this,
Vindice: Oh from a deere and worthy friend,
mighty!
Cast.: From whome?
Vin.: The Dukes Sonne!
Cast.: Receive that! [*A boxe ath eare to her Brother.*
I swore I'de put anger in my hand,
And passe the Virgin limits of my selfe.
To him that next appear'd in that base office,

The Revengers Tragedy (1607), Act II, Sc. 1.

The knight flatters his sovereign that the English Earls are unworthy of him, and the two go in to prayers, Edward promising that all Normans shall be fed from his land—" Theie alleyn have syke love as to acquyre yer bredde." And then, following perhaps the example of *Gorboduc*, Chatterton bursts

* Chatterton has written " smoke," perhaps by the attraction of " Cheke." 24890 f. 19. b.

into a lyric, where, with the fullest possible use of his century's personifications, perversely disguised, that century's bonds are broken asunder, and the ecstasies of the poets who, after the French Revolution, wrote *France: an Ode*, *Hellas*, and *The Isles of Greece* are anticipated from afar.

CHORUS

Whan Freedom dreste, yn blodde steyned Veste,
To everie Knyghte her Warre Songe sunge;
Uponne her hedde, wylde Wedes were spredde,
A gorie Anlace bye her honge.
She daunced onne the Heathe,
She hearde the Voice of Deathe;
Pale-eyned Affryghte hys harte of Sylver hue,
In vayne assayled[1] her bosomme to acale[2];
She hearde onflemed[3] the shriekynge Voice of Woe,
And Sadnesse ynne the Owlette shake the Dale.
She shooke the burled[4] Speere,
On hie she jeste[5] her Sheelde,
Her Foemen all appere,
And flizze[6] alonge the Feelde—
Power, wythe his Heafod[7] straughte[8] ynto the Skyes,
Hys Speere a Sonne beame, and his Sheelde a Starre;
Alyche twaie brendeynge Gronfyres[9] rolls hys Eyes,
Chaftes[10] with hys Yronne Feete, and soundes to War—
She syttes upon a Rocke,
She bendes before hys Speere;
She ryses from the Shocke,
Wieldynge her owne yn Ayre.
Harde as the Thonder, dothe she drive ytte on;
Wytte scillye wympled gies[11] ytte to hys Crowne,
Hys longe sharpe Speere, hys spreddynge sheelde ys gon,
He falles and fallynge rolleth thousandes down—
War, goare faced War, bie Envie burld,[12] arist,[13]
Hys feerie Heaulme[14] noddynge to the Ayre;
Tenne bloddie Arrowes ynne hys streynynge fyste—

[1] Endeavoured. [2] Graze. [3] Undismayed. [4] Pointed. [5] Hoisted on high. [6] Fly. [7] Head. [8] Stretched. [9] Two flaming meteors. [10] Stamps. [11] Closely mantled guides. [12] Armed. [13] Arose. [14] Helmet.

Liberty had been sung by William Collins, with Sophoclean dignity and calm, little under a generation before; but

She daunced onne the Heathe
She hearde the Voice of Deathe

was a strange note in the ears of the Age of Reason, that of "the savage war dance"*; it was the personifications that were admired, and the Roubillac-like handling of the group. Blake has not escaped from the first line in one of the songs in *An Island in the Moon* beginning

> When Old Corruption first begun,
> Adorn'd in yellow vest,

and it cannot have been far from Coleridge's mind when he wrote, in February, 1798:

> When France in wrath her giant-limbs upreared,
> And with that oath, which smote air, earth, and sea,
> Stamped her strong foot and said she would be free,
> Bear witness for me, how I hoped and feared!

This particular feat of Bristol's Muse has perhaps been over-praised (lines 94-100 of *Goddwyn*, quoted above, are finer to my ear), but it has passed unquestioned from 1777 till now.

Sir Daniel Wilson thought that the "Prologue" was strong evidence that *Goddwyn* was completed†; Buxton Forman did not, but conceived the poet stopping at "hys streynynge fyste" with "There, that's enough to waste upon that ignoramus Catcott!"‡ The appearance of Chatterton's MS. inclines me to agree with the former. The copy-book ends with "Tenne bloddie Arrowes ynne hys streynynge fyste," with what looks like a dash under the final *e*. Someone, not, I think, the author, (possibly George Catcott), has added "219 lines" under the last two words. Underneath is the glossary, separated from the text by a line drawn across the page, and the next page is the inner side of the back cover; but there is no indication of the play *coming to an end* fragmentarily, and the natural inference is that it was continued in another note-book. When a piece in the book ends, it is marked by lines thus ═══. Moreover 24890 is evidently a fair copy (there is hardly a correction), and the Dramatis Personæ contain the names "Elwarde" and "Alstan," neither of whom appears in

* Edward Gardner, *Miscellanies*, Vol. II, p. 157.
† *Chatterton*, p. 149.
‡ *Chatterton and his latest Editor*, p. 25.

the extant portion. It is perhaps a fair deduction from *Heraudyn A Fragmente* that when Chatterton intended a Rowley Poem to end fragmentarily, he said so. Finally, the title of the copy-book is

Eclogues, and
other Poems
by
Thomas Rowley—
with
A Glossary, and Annotations
by
Thomas Chatterton

The Bristol literati may not have been curious for "the remainder of these poems." Certainly, so far as *Goddwyn* is concerned, this marble-covered exercise-book was all that George Catcott vouchsafed to Thomas Tyrwhitt.

The subject was again treated as a play by Ann Yearsley, the Bristol milkwoman, in 1791, eighty-five years before Tennyson touched it. It is perhaps worth noting that Henry Jones, the bricklayer poet (1721-1770), author of *Clifton*, and *Kew Garden*, brought, somewhere about 1767, a tragedy called *Harold* to a publisher, one John Cooper; the play has disappeared, but Chatterton may have known of this fact (see *European Magazine* for April, 1794).

Ælla

(First printed by Tyrwhitt in 1777 from a MS. in the possession of George Catcott, who had written in it "Chatterton's Transcript, 1769." It was "a folio quire in gilt marble covers," Catcott wrote to Dean Milles on Nov. 24, 1778, "all in Chatterton's hand," and then in Mr. Payne's—the publisher's—or Tyrwhitt's possession.)

We have reached Chatterton's citadel. Of its importance he makes no secret; *Ælla* (1,248 lines) is fenced about with three preliminary pieces, namely, an "epistle" of 48 lines. a "letter" of 56, and an "entroductionne" of 14, before the "Personnes Representedd".

The epistle (in a six line decasyllabic stanza *a b a b c c* with final alexandrine) is in praise of rhyme, which, according to Rowley, has now fallen from its high estate; he enumerates the professors of it whom he knows, comments on them, and submits his work to Canynge's correction, much as Chaucer submitted *Troilus* to moral Gower and the philosophical Strode, remarking (Rowley was something of a latitudinarian) that plays should not be made from holy tales, but rather "somme greate storie of a manne."

The "Letter to the Dygne Mastre Canynge" which follows (in ottava-rima, Fairfax's measure), elaborates the decline of Poetry from a different angle; History has ousted her:

> Heie pycke up wolsome[1] weedes, ynstedde of flowers,
> And famylies, ynstedde of wytte, theie trace;
> Nowe poesie canne meete wythe ne regrate[2]
> Whylste prose, and herehaughtrie,[3] ryse yn estate.

[1] Loathsome. [2] Esteem. [3] Heraldry.

Rowley prays for an admixture of what we should term Romance with History:

> Instedde of mountynge onn a wynged horse,
> You onn a rouncy[1] dryve yn dolefull course
> Canynge and I from common course dyssente;
> Wee ryde the stede, botte yev[2] to hym the reene;
> Ne wylle betweene crased[3] molterynge[4] bookes be pente
> Botte soare on hyghe, and yn the sonne-bemes sheene;
> And where wee kenn somme ishad[5] floures besprente,[6]
> We take ytte, and from oulde rouste doe ytte clene;
> Wee wylle ne cheynedd to one pasture bee,
> Botte sometymes soare 'bove trouthe of hystorie.*

[1] Cart horse. [2] Give. [3] Broken. [4] Mouldering. [5] Broken. [6] Scattered

* cf. Spenser's *October*.

> O pierlesse Poesye, where is then thy place?
> If not in Princes pallace thou doe sitt;
> (And yet is Princes pallace the most fitt)
> Ne brest of baser birth doth thee embrace,
> Then make thee winges of thy aspyring wit,
> And, whence thou camst, fly backe to heaven apace.

This is not unlike the address to Boccaccio in *Isabella*, where Keats writes :

> There is no other crime, no mad assail
> To make old prose in modern rhyme more sweet.

And indeed, when Keats employed enjambement to the extent he did in *Endymion*, he may well have had in mind Chatterton's criticism

> A keppened poyntelle restynge at eche lyne

of formal eighteenth century versification. " Poyntelle " is glossed " a pen, used metaphorically, as a muse or genius " ; and " to keppen (O) " in Kersey stands for " to hood-wink."

Then comes a line, which would serve as an answer to those critics who, with Hazlitt at their head, declare that Chatterton is no considerable poet because he has not produced lines that come readily to mind :

> Vearse maie be goode, botte poesie wantes more

Ælla must be its own defence, and with a message of health and happiness to Canynge from Bishop Carpenter, the " gode Prieste " takes his leave.

The " Entroductionne " consists of two stanzas of rime royal rousing up Ælla from the grave, where all his faults are buried, to tell, before Judgment Day, " howe hee sojourned in the vale of men."

The plot is this. Ælla, Saxon " warde " of Bristol Castle, has just married Birtha, and is holding his wedding feast there, when a messenger announces that the Danes, under Magnus and Hurra, have landed. Ælla parts from his wife, who in vain urges him to stay, and send Celmonde, his friend, a " wordhie knyghte," to fight in his place ; honour rules him. A battle takes place near Watchet, and the invaders are routed, Magnus, a craven, being killed. Ælla is wounded, and desiring only to die in his wife's sight, commands a horse to bear him to Bristol. Meanwhile Celmonde, who secretly loves Birtha, goes to Bristol by night, and announcing himself to a servitor as a stranger, persuades her to accompany him to " Wedecester's walled toune" where, he says, Ælla is dying of his wounds. She leaves Bristol with him, giving no word to Egwina her maid, or to anyone. As they pass through a wood, where Hurra and some Danes are ambushed, Celmonde reveals his love, and attempts to ravish Birtha. She is rescued by them (Celmonde being killed by Hurra in the brawl), and magnanimously conducted back to Bristol Castle. Thither Ælla has come, and learning from Egwina and the servitor of his wife's flight with a stranger, stabs himself in a passion of wounded honour, appoints a new "warde," and dies, just after she has entered with Hurra, but in time to learn that she has been true to him. Birtha faints on his dead body.* The action takes three days, being concluded on the morning of the third.

Fatal impetuosity is the theme of this tragedy; but it is important to recognize, as not all critics seem to have done, that the tragic hero is mortally wounded, *or thinks he may be*, some hours before his suicide; that is surely clear from the lines:

> Curse onn mie tardie woundes! brynge mee a stede!
> I wylle awaie to Birtha bie thys nyghte;
> Albeytte fro mie woundes mie soul doe blede,
> I wylle awaie, and die wythynne her syghte.

At the same time his readiness to assume that the woman he has just married is unfaithful, merely because she has left the castle secretly with a strange man, may strike a twentieth century reader as quaint. But this is the heroic ideal, and what we find in the Icelandic Sagas. There trivial occasions are the motiving of men.

> Greatly to find quarrel in a straw
> When honour's at the stake

is the supreme law of conduct. "The tempers of men," says

* This is more natural than Edith's *death* at the end of *Harold*. With

> Oh! ys mie Ælla dedde?
> Oh! I wyll make hys grave mie vyrgyn spousal bedde.
> [Birtha *feyncteth*.

compare

> And thou,
> Thy wife am I for ever and evermore.
> [*Falls on the body and dies*.

Professor Ker, " are easily stirred ; they have a general name (*Skapraun*, lit. *test of condition*) for the trial of a man's patience, applied to anything that puts a strain on him, or encroaches on his honour. The trial may come from anything—horses, sheep, hay, women, merchandise. . . . Anything almost is enough to set the play going."* Is not this exactly Ælla's " rennome " or " myndbruche," a word glossed by Kersey " S " (for Saxon) " a hurting of Honour and Worship," which we meet in *The Storie of William Canynge*, when " Edwarde meniced a seconde wyfe " ? Cleopatra's "A Roman thought has struck him " is the same trait.

> Ælla, bie nete moe thann hys myndbruche awed,
> Is gone, and I moste followe, toe the fraie.

says Celmonde. Celmonde also is impetuous, although he is not ruled by honour. It is worth while examining him somewhat closely, as he is the mainspring of the plot.

Ælla's friend, and second-in-command, speaks the first lines of the play and shares a metrical scheme with him :

> Before yonne roddie sonne has droove hys wayne
> Throwe halfe his joornie, dyghte yn gites of goulde,
> Mee, hapless mee, hee wylle a wretche behoulde,
> Mieselfe, and al that's myne, bounde ynne myschaunces chayne.

A lover,† and a warrior, he first plans to poison Birtha, Ælla and himself on the wedding night (l. 20) and makes an ironical admission to Ælla (ll. 83, 84) :

> I, as a token of mie love to speake,
> Have brought you jubbes of ale, at nyghte your brayne to breake.

who says he will drink the ale after supper ; but the announcement of the Danish invasion, just as they are going in to supper, defeats this plan. He gives sound military advice (l. 268 sqq.). Birtha's

> He's gon, he's gone, alass ! percase he's gone for aie.

* *Epic and Romance*, p. 230.
† In marriage, blessynges are botte fewe, I trowe. l. 154.

suggests his plot ; for his soliloquy, opening with the beautiful image of

> Hope, hallie suster, sweepynge thro' the skie,
> In crowne of goulde, and robe of lillie whyte,

follows directly on it. He will wait till the war is over ; he has now something other than Birtha to occupy him, and is in his native element :

> Celmonde canne ne'er from anie byker[1] staie.
> Dothe warre begynne ? there's Celmonde yn the place.

[1] Contest.

At l. 730 (Tyrwhitt's line-numeration) he acts as chorus, relating the battle, and assumes that Ælla is not mortally wounded (ll. 814, 815) :

> Ælla ys woundedd sore, and ynne the toune
> He waytethe, tylle hys woundes bee broghte to ethe.[2]

[2] Ease.

Celmonde has a conscience, but Birtha is the prize ; he will make "the vyctore yn hys vyctorie blethe," despite of "rennome aeterne," which vexes him. He defends his treachery by heredity :

> The qualytyes I fro mie parentes drewe,
> Were blodde, and morther, masterie, and warre ;
> Theie I wylle holde to nowe, and hede ne moe
> A wounde yn rennome, yanne a boddie scarre.
> (ll. 828-831.)

So, giving himself out for dead (l. 809), he decides on abduction. His "Wythoute your syghte, he dyes"* (l. 945) is a masterstroke, it precipitates Birtha's flight from Bristol, without leaving word whither or with whom ; thus she too falls a victim to impetuosity. He dies fighting against numbers, "a wordhie knyghte (Hurra echoes Ælla's praise of him), and his last words are affectionate :

* Without your much-lov'd sight, I cannot live.
Dryden, *The State of Innocence*, Act V.

Oh ! I forslagen be ! ye Danes, now kenne,
I amme yatte Celmonde, seconde yn the fyghte,
Who dydd, atte Watchette, so forslege youre menne;
I fele myne eyne to swymme yn æterne nyghte ;—
To her be kynde. [*Dieth.*

I do not think that Glenalvon in Home's *Douglas* has inspired this conception to any extent.* Celmonde's creator had clearly studied Edmund and Iago, the latter in particular (ll. 405, 819)—and indeed *Othello* has been drawn on not only for points in Ælla's heroic simplicity, but for his violent language in the scene with Egwina (l. 1166) ; but there is in Celmonde a strain of nobility ; he is, and was intended for, an epic personage.

In Birtha, Chatterton, abstracting, maybe, from the women he knew, what he conceived to be a woman's finest traits, has produced a clinging, tender, trustful being :

thou dydst cheese mee for thie swote to bee,
Enactynge ynn the same moste faiefullie to mee,

She does not expect too much of her man :

Be notte toe slacke yn love, ne overdeare ;

and uses all her sex's instinctive artfulness and flattery to keep him with her on the marriage night :

Thou nedest notte goe, untyll thou haste command
Under the sygnette of oure lord the kynge.

and

Lett Celmonde yn thie armour-brace be dyghte ;
And yn thie stead unto the battle goe ;

She has fire ; she answers his " Rouze all thie honnoure " with

Rouze all thie love ; false and entrykyng wyghte !
Ne leave thie Birtha thos uponne pretence of fyghte.

These are primitive characters, with primitive emotions ; she can speak beautiful words over Celmonde's corpse :

* See Gregory, *Life*, p. 155.

Maie ne thie cross-stone of thie cryme bewree !
Maie alle menne ken thie valoure, fewe thie mynde !

Her tragedy, impetuosity apart, is that she can only make her husband's *grave* her "vyrgyn spousal bedde," and that is primitive too.

Ælla is a solitary dramatic monument in its century, a sort of Stanton Drew ; it bears no spiritual relation to any literary works near it. *The Ghost of Abel* (1822) is more akin to it than is *Elfrida* (1752) or *Caractacus* (1759), poems which its author must have known. Since Coleridge's time it has been unfashionable to cry up *Caractacus* ; still, though Mason be not the high poet his friend Gray thought he was, that work is informed by a valiant strain.* But Chatterton's stanzaed interlude has one huge advantage over the dramatic poem à la grecque in that it is continuous, and the lyrical measures are woven into the texture of their environment. In fact, the treatment of the Chorus in *Ælla*, or rather the dividing of its functions throughout the action, is not the least astonishing or original of its beauties.

The play starts with festal rejoicing ; everyone is happy but Celmonde, who conceals his misery. What more natural than a succession of songs ? The minstrels sing three. The first is a duet between a man and a woman, a picture of rural courtship :

MANNE

Sytte thee, Alyce, sytte, and harke,
Howe the ouzle chauntes hys noate,
The chelandree, greie morn larke,
Chauntynge from theyre lyttel throate.

WOMANNE

I heare them from eche grene wode tree,
Chauntynge owte so blatauntlie,
Tellynge lecturnyes to mee,
Myscheefe ys whanne you are nygh.

* ELIDURUS
Ah ! what discover ?
Say, whom must I betray ?
EVILINA
Thy brother.
ELIDURUS
Ha !

HURRA
Saie, who bee you ?
BIRTHA
I am greate Ælla's wyfe.
HURRA
Ah !

closing with the Church's blessing on the pair, who will live in a cottage, "Hailie, thoughe of no estate."*

The second is divided between three minstrels, and has the famous opening:

> The boddynge flourettes bloshes atte the lyghte;
> The mees be sprenged wyth the yellowe hue;
> Ynn daiseyd mantels ys the mountayne dyghte;
> The nesh yonge coweslepe bendethe wyth the dewe;

The burden of these eight beautiful stanzas is that the glories of nature are not enough to satisfy the desire of man:

> I laie mee onn the grass; yette, to mie wylle,
> Albeytte alle ys fayre, there lackethe somethynge stylle.

The description of Autumn that follows is more than a halfway house between *The Seasons* and Keats's *Ode*:

> Whanne Autumpne blake[1] and sonne-brente doe appere,
> Wyth hys goulde honde guylteynge the falleynge lefe,
> Bryngeynge oppe Wynter to folfylle the yere,
> Beerynge uponne hys backe the riped shefe;
> When al the hyls wythe woddie sede ys whyte;
> Whanne levynne-fyres[2] and lemes[3] do mete from far the syghte
>
> Whanne the fayre apple, rudde as even skie,
> Do bende the tree unto the fructyle grounde;
> When joicie peres and berries of blacke die,
> Doe daunce yn ayre, and call the eyne arounde
> Thann, bee the even foule, or even fayre,
> Meethynckes mie hartys joie ys steynced[4] wyth somme care.†

[1] Naked. [2] Flashes of lightning. [3] Meteors. [4] Stained.

* There is a miserable pastoral, based on this, "Dick and Dolly," in *Boddely's Bath Journal* (May 14, 1770) signed T.R. The Rowleian writer of *Remarks on . . . Warton* (1779) says "That he wished to put off some of his own poems for Rowlie's is certain; I myself have seen some written with such a design . . . they are the worst even of Chatterton's own compositions." Here is an unimpeachable example, in Chatterton's handwriting (5766B. f. 89):

> There was a Broder of Orderys Blacke
> In mynster of Brystowe Cittie
> He layd a Demoisell onne her Backe
> So guess yee the Taile of mie Dittie
>
> T. R.

† In *Battle of Hastings*, II, l. 551, the *gales* of autumn are the point of the simile:

> So when derne Autumne with hys sallowe hande
> Tares the green mantle from the lymed trees,

and the leaves "flie in whole armies."

But the next two stanzas are a thing alone in English poetry. Chatterton may have read " Womman is mannes joye and al his bliss " in *The Nonne Preestes Tale*, or found in Thomas Usk's *The Testament of Love* (II. 3) " Without women, the being of men were impossible. They conne with there swetnesse the crewel hate ravisshe, and make it meke, buxom and benigne, without violence mevinge," before he wrote, in the third,

> Albeytte, wythout wommen, menne were pheeres[1]
> To salvage kynde and wulde botte lyve to slea,

[1] Fellows.

but all the sweetness, all the love, in his lonely nature, with an added something that no *experience* can give, seem to have gone to the making of lines 190-201, and left in him nothing spiritual to bestow, thereafter, on any actual woman :

> Angelles bee wrogte to bee of neidher kynde ;
> Angelles alleyne fromme chafe[1] desyre bee free ;
> Dheere ys a somwhatte evere yn the mynde,
> Yatte, without wommanne, cannot stylled bee,
> Ne seyncte yn celles, botte, havynge blodde and tere[2],
> Do fynde the spryte to joie on syghte of womanne fayre :
>
> Wommen bee made, notte for hemselves, botte manne,
> Bone of hys bone, and chyld of hys desire ;
> Fromme an ynutyle[3] membere fyrste beganne,
> Ywroghte with moche of water, lyttele fyre ;
> Therefore theie seke the fyre of love, to hete
> The milkyness of kynde,[4] and make hemselfes complete.

[1] Hot (a verb in Kersey). [2] Health. [3] Useless. [4] Nature.

" Bone of his bone, and child of his desire "—what a line to have been written in the eighteenth century ! Truly did Edward Thomas remark on this passage " Where there is no appearance or profession of personalities, he writes of women and love in a far different tone."*

The third song (not by Rowley, but Syr Thybbot Gorges, and no doubt intentionally inferior) is a solo, d'Urfey-like and of this world. Warton traced it back to " The Vicar of Taunton Dean." It need not be quoted, save one line which shows how

* *The Feminine Influence on the Poets, loc. cit.*

deliberately Chatterton could set down the pegs that made his music: a woman is speaking:

> I stylle wanted somethynge, botte whatte ne coulde telle.

The pitch is lowered, because the personages are about to go in to their ale and wine.

Now the mirth darkens; a messenger announces the Danes, the feast is shattered; and, after his scene with Birtha, Ælla departs for Watchet. Celmonde's four stanzas of soliloquy have the effect of a grave choric ode.

The second episode introduces the enemy, who are consulting the omens. A high priest sings to the gods, in the metre of the *Macbeth* incantations, a spell pregnant with havoc and tempest:

> Whanne the oundynge[1] waves dystreste
> Stroven to be overest,[2]
> Sockeynge yn the spyre-gyrte towne,
> Swolterynge wole natyones downe,

[1] Foaming, undulating. [2] Uppermost.

At the close he falls down and, rising, speaks an ambiguous oracle.

Then follows a hundred lines of altercation between the two Danish chiefs, quite the most primitive feature of the play. The action stops completely for the flyting bout, and generally Magnus and Hurra have a stanza each. The manner here is Marlowe's; though the "fen vapours" are Caliban's, and the contention of Achilles and Agamemnon in Pope's *Iliad* (Book I) has not been forgotten:

MAGNUS	BAJAZET
Eternalle plagues devour thie baned tyngue!	Go, never to return with victory.
Myrriades of neders pre upponne thie spryte!	Millions of men encompass thee about,
Maiest thou fele al the peynes of age whylst yynge,	And gore thy body with as many wounds!
Unmanned, uneyned, exclooded aie the lyghte,	Sharp, forked arrows light upon thy horse!
Thie senses, lyche thieselfe, enwrapped yn nyghte,	Furies from the black Cocytus lake,

A scoff to foemen and to beastes a pheere!
Maie furched levynne onne thie head alyghte,
Maie on thee falle the fhuyr of the unweere:
Fen vapours blaste thie everiche manlie powere
Maie thie bante boddie quycke the wolsome peenes devoure.

Ælla, ll. 513-522.

Break up the earth, and with their firebrands
Enforce thee run upon the baneful pikes!
Volleys of shot pierce through thy charmed skin,
And every bullet dipt in poisoned drugs!
Or, roaring cannons sever all thy joints,
Making thee mount as high as eagles soar.

Tamburlaine, Part I, v. 2.

Apropos of this passage one is reminded of a statement of Professor Ker to the effect that, in the Lay of Helgi, disproportionate length is given to an interlude of vituperative dialogue between two heroes, Sinfiotli, Helgi's brother, and Gudmund, son of Granmar, the warden of the enemy's Coast: "this passage of *Vetus Comoedia*," he writes, "takes up fifty lines, while only six are given to the battle, and thirteen to the meeting of Helgi and Sigrun afterwards!"* Chatterton, with an instinctive sense of primitive manners, has here written an interlude within his interlude.

A remarkable effect is obtained by the introduction of fourteen lines of blank verse divided between two messengers, who announce Ælla's approach with the Saxon army. They give the suggestion of *tidings*, though the usual explanation of them is that the boy, either through ignorance or impudence, desired to show Rowley as Lord Surrey's precursor in the invention of this measure.

The third episode opens with a new day and Ælla's speech to his soldiers (ll. 589-693). Of this I will only say that I regard it as the touchstone of this poet's rank among our poets. The scene is quoted in full at the end of this book,† so that the reader may conveniently form his own unaided opinion on that matter.

The battle is skilfully managed; two stanzas (twenty lines) are divided between three flying Danes, and Hurra speaks

* *Epic and Romance*, p. 111.
† Appendix F.

sixteen lines in dispraise of Magnus, and urging a retreat "yn tyme to fyghte agenne." He is followed by Celmonde, who, as chorus (ll. 730-803), *describes* the fighting, after which he came away, "in odher fieldes to fyghte a moe unequalle fraie": tragedy now sets in apace.

The fourth episode—the word is not strictly appropriate, as the scene changes from Bristol to Watchet, thence to Bristol again, and thence to a wood—is the abduction. It starts quietly with Birtha lamenting for her absent mate; Egwina summons the minstrels to chase away her grief—they have not appeared since the interrupted wedding feast—and they sing the lyric by which Chatterton is remembered best:

O! synge untoe mie roundelaie,
O! droppe the brynie teare wythe mee
Daunce ne moe atte hallie daie,
Lycke a reynynge[1] ryver bee;
Mie love ys dedde,
Gon to hys deathe-bedde,
Al under the wyllowe tree.

Blacke hys cryne[2] as the wyntere nyghte,*
Whyte hys rode[3] as the sommer snowe,
Rodde hys face as the mornye lyghte,
Cale[4] he lyes ynne the grave belowe;
Mie love ys dedde, &c.

[1] Running. [2] Hair. [3] Complexion. [4] Cold.

Swote hys tyngue as the throstles note,
Quycke ynn daunce as thoughte canne bee,
Defte[5] hys taboure, codgelle stote,
O! hee lies bie the wyllowe tree:
Mie love ys dedde, &c.

[5] Neat.

Harke! the ravenne flappes hys wynge,
In the briered delle belowe;
Harke! the dethe-owle loude dothe synge,
To the nyghte-mares as heie goe;
Mie love ys dedde, &c.

* Chatterton echoes this rhythm in one of his Ossianics: "Brown is his face as the sun-burnt heath; strong his arm as the roaring sea."—*Godred Crovan.* Aug. 10, 1769.

See ! the whyte moone sheenes onne hie ;
Whyterre ys mie true loves shroude ;
Whyterre yanne the mornynge skie,
Whyterre yanne the evenynge cloude ;
Mie love ys dedde, &c.

Heere, uponne mie true loves grave,
Schalle the baren fleurs be layde,
Nee one hallie[6] Seyncte to save
Al the celness[7] of a mayde.
Mie love ys dedde, &c.

Wythe mie handes I'lle dente[8] the brieres
Rounde his hallie corse to gre,[9]
Ouphante[10] fairie, lyghte your fyres,
Heere mie boddie stylle schalle bee
Mie love ys dedde, &c.

Comme, wythe acorne-coppe and thorne,
Drayne mie hartys blodde awaie ;
Lyfe and all yttes goode I scorne,
Daunce bie nete,[11] or feaste by daie.
Mie love ys dedde, &c.

Waterre wytches, crownede wythe reytes,[12]
Bere mee to yer leathalle tyde.
I die ; I comme ; mie true love waytes.
Thos the damselle spake, and dyed.

[6] Holy. [7] Coldness. [8] Fasten. [9] Grow. [10] Elfin. [11] Night.
[12] Water-flags.

" The remarkable thing about this," says Professor Saintsbury, " is the almost unerring skill with which the variations of the metre are adapted, and the still more wonderful judgment with which the vowel values adjust themselves."*

Its musical quality seems to have been recognized early, for in 1783 it was modernized and set as a song for three voices by Stephen Paxton (d. 1787), and forms part of his *Op*. 5. Twice in his *Juvenilia* Shelley has echoed the fourth stanza, in the fragment *Omens* (1807), and in *Ghasta* (1810) ; the latter opens :

Hark ! the owlet flaps her wing,
In the pathless dell beneath,
Hark ! night ravens loudly sing
Tidings of despair and death.

* *A History of English Prosody*, Vol. II., p. 522.

"Methinks," wrote Bailey in his recollections of Keats, I now hear him recite, or *chant*, in his peculiar manner, the following stanza of the Roundelay sung by the minstrels of Ella: *Come with acorn cup and thorn* [&c.). The first line to his ear possessed the great charm."* If it be not desecration to analyse what Keats loved, perhaps one may say that the alliteration (so difficult to manage successfully with a hard *c*) and the internal rhyme contribute not least to the effect here.

The scene in the wood, which opens with Hurra and his loyal remnant taking covert by the oak, and closes with the dead Celmonde on the ground and the rescued wife of Ælla under chivalrous convoy, passes from the depth of night to the approach of dawn.

The mornynge 'gyns alonge the Easte to sheene;
Darklinge the lyghte doe onne the waters plaie;
The faynte rodde leme[1] slowe creepeth oere the greene,
Toe chase the merkyness of nyghte awaie;
Swifte flies the howers thatte wylle brynge oute the daie;
The softe dewe falleth onne the greeynge[2] grasse;
The shepster mayden,[3] dyghtynge[4] her arraie,
Scante[5] sees her vysage yn the wavie glasse;
Bie the fulle daylieghte wee scalle Ælla see,
Or Brystowes wallyd towne; damoyselle, followe mee.†

[1] Ray. [2] Growing. [3] Shepherdess. [4] Preparing. [5] Scarce.

This ten line speech of Hurra has the force of a chorus or aubade.

The last episode takes place in broad daylight. Ælla, who wished to die in Birtha's sight, standing outside his palace, feels a throb of hope and life:

Nowe, Birtha, wyll thie loke enhele mie spryte,
Thie smyles unto mie woundes a baulme wylle prove;
Mie ledanne bodie wylle bee sette aryghte.

Earlier he has exclaimed:

* Colvin, *Life of Keats*, p. 146.

† Cf. Awake! arise! my love, and fearless be,
For o'er the southern moors I have a home for thee.
The Eve of St. Agnes, xxxix.

Yee goddes, howe ys a loverres temper formed!
Sometymes the samme thynge wylle bothe bane, and blesse;*

The shock of the empty room, with the news of her flight, destroys the desire to live at one blow:

nowe wyth rage Im pyghte[1]
A brondeous unweere[2] ys mie engyned[3] mynde.
Mie hommeur[4] yette somme drybblet[5] joie maie fynde,
To the Danes woundes I wylle another yeve[6];
Whanne thos mie rennome and mie peace ys rynde[7]
Itte were a recrandize[8] to thyncke toe lyve.

[1] Tortured. [2] Tempest [3] Racked. [4] Honour [5] Inconsiderable. [6] Give. [7] Ruined. [8] Cowardice.

Suicide from the compulsion of wounded honour is a mediæval notion, and found in the Knight in *La Chastelaine de Vergi*†; but *Othello* has afforded the hint here. From the hero's entrance to Birtha's fainting on his dead body there are only 101 lines: the action is concentrated and white-hot, without room for lyrical emotion. The single stanza of epilogue spoken by Coernyke, the new lord of Bristol, resembles the closing philosophical anapæsts of some Greek tragedy, in its final cadence, though not in choric rhythm:

Further, a just amede to thee to bee,
Inne heaven thou synge of Godde, on erth we'lle synge of thee.

There remains, if the Laymyngetowne "Discoorses" be excluded,‡ but one more Rowley Poem, of any length, to be discussed, the *Balade of Charitie*. A MS. of this, according to Tyrwhitt, bore date July 4, 1770; it may be dealt with later, therefore. If Flaubert be right, and the man is nothing, his work everything, Chatterton's life, with this exception, ends here, since (in the present writer's opinion) there is nothing in

* Cf. Altamont in *The Fair Penitent*, "With what unequal tempers are we form'd," etc. Act IV., *ad init.*

† Ker, *Epic and Romance*, p. 414. Here the lady has died of a broken heart, at the thought that the Knight has betrayed her.

‡ See Chapter XIII. They are fragmentary, though we have "the whole" of them.

the acknowledged poems, even the *African Eclogues*, or the astronomics of *Resignation*, really comparable to *Rowley*.*

* The following Rowley fragment, designated "worthless," by Skeat, has not yet found a place in print, barring the first line:—

"In the merry merye vale
Where leavis gre grene & longe
Eclyped of Eld Ayerdale
Of Guillaume de Pictevongue
A Cisterce Freere dhere baied[1]
Whychen . . .
&c."

5766 B. f. 89.

[1] "To Obay (O.), to abide." Kersey.

Chapter XII

DODSLEY AND WALPOLE

Chatterton seems to have made up his mind within three months of the " Bridge " article that, whatever else they might be, his Bristol patrons were not patrons of poetry, for on Dec. 21, 1768, we find him writing to the publisher of Percy's *Reliques* as follows :

" Sir,

I take this method to acquaint you, that I can procure copies of several ancient Poems ; and an Interlude, perhaps the oldest dramatic piece extant ; wrote by one Rowley, a Priest in Bristol, who lived in the reigns of Henry VIth and Edward IVth.— If these Pieces will be of service to you, at your command, copies shall be sent to you, by,

Your most obedient Servant,

D. B.

Please to direct for D.B. to be left with Mr. Thomas Chatterton, Redclift Hill, Bristol.

For Mr. J. Dodsley, Bookseller, Pall Mall, London."

In 1764 R. and J. Dodsley had published *Some Specimens of the Poetry of the Antient Welsh Bards* by the Rev. Mr. Evan Evans, which contained explanatory notes " in order to give the curious some idea of the taste and sentiments of our ancestors and their manner of writing." Chatterton used this book as certainly as he used the *Reliques*.

A Mr. John Tandey, Barrett's father-in-law, died early in the new year (Jan. 5) and the poet wrote an elegy on him in his lamest eighteenth-century manner for insertion in one of the Bristol journals, but it " was suppressed at the particular request of Mr. Tandey's eldest son." This fact was duly appended by the author to his MS.*

On Feb. 15 he wrote to Dodsley again†:

"SIR,

Having intelligence that the Tragedy of Ælla was in being, after a long and laborious search, I was so happy as to attain a sight of it. Struck with the beauties of it, I endeavoured to obtain a copy to send to you; but the present possessor absolutely denies to give me one, unless I give him a Guinea for a consideration. As I am unable to procure such a sum, I made search for another copy, but unsuccessfully.—Unwilling such a beauteous Piece should be lost, I have made bold to apply to you: several Gentlemen of learning who have seen it, join with me in praising it.—I am far from having any mercenary views for myself in this affair, and, was I able, would print it on my own risque.‡ It is a perfect Tragedy, the plot clear, the language spirited, and the Songs (interspersed in it) are flowing, poetical, and elegantly simple. The similies judiciously applied, and though wrote in the reign of Henry VIth, not inferior to many of the present age. If I can procure a copy, with or without the gratification, it shall immediately be sent to you. The motive that actuates me to do this, is, to convince the world that the Monks (of whom some have so despicable an opinion) were not such blockheads, as generally thought,§ and that good poetry might be wrote in the dark days of superstition, as well as in these more enlightened ages. An immediate answer will oblige

* First printed in *Works* I, p. 185. There is a copy by Seyer "from the original in Miss A[nna] Barrett's possession," 4533 f. 128, in Bristol Library. Seyer notes "not a stop thro' the whole." It has the following variants: l.1, tuneful; l.3, melting; l.7., who; l.26, judgment solid, sense refin'd; l. 29, god-like; l.36, th' unfeigned. *Felix Farley* of Jan. 7, 1769, has five heroic couplets on Mr. John Tandey, senior.

† The letters to Dodsley were found at the clearing out of his counting house; they were first printed in John Britton's *History of Redcliffe Church* (1813), p. 40. A facsimile of one of them is in *The London Miscellany* for Jan., 1839.

‡ For instances of writers publishing on their own account with profit see *Genuine Memoirs of Mr. Charles Churchill* (1765): "Tristram Shandy was offered to divers booksellers for fifty pounds, and they offered seven. The author printed the first edition on his own account and cleared upwards of two hundred pounds by the sale. Mr. Dodsley then purchased the copy, and has gained much money by it." (p. 132).

§ Chatterton may have in mind the introduction (p. 1) to Hooke's *Bristollia*: "Whoever reflects on the situation and peculiar circumstances of the place . . . and the prevailing taste of the monkish writers, will have little cause to wonder that Bristol has not been more frequently mention'd by those original English historians."

me. I shall not receive your favour as for myself, but as your agent.

I am, Sir,
Your most obedient Servant,
T. Chatterton.

P.S. My reason for concealing my name, was, lest my Master (who is now out of Town) should see my letters, and think I neglected his business.
Direct for me on Redclift Hill."

The stanza of Ælla's address to his soldiers beginning " Ye Chrystyans, doe as wordhie of the name" accompanied the letter, with the note : " The whole contains about 1,000 lines. If it should not suit you, I should be obliged to you if you would calculate the expenses of printing it, as I will endeavour to publish it by subscription on my own account."

The unworldliness of this attempt to win the suffrage of a London publisher has been much commented on. It is not known whether Dodsley replied, but from Chatterton's speaking of him, in his letter to Mr. Stephens, as his correspondent, and his mention of him to his mother as one of the publishers whom he visited on his first day in London, I infer (with the editor of the 1842 edition of the poems) that he did. The same method, offer of a sample in advance, was adopted here as in approaching Catcott. Probably, too, he did not wish to dispose rashly of his MS. Making another copy of a play nearer 1,300 than 1,000 lines long would have been tiresome, when the writing hand was employed day and night on other matters.

Besides, a new magazine, *The Town and Country*, had started in the last week of January, not hereafter to be neglected by one who " loaded the press with his contributions." The first number (nothing in it can be identified as Chatterton's) contained an *Essay on Fame*, the second a letter on Saxon Tinctures signed " D.B., Feb. 4," and a poem to Mr. Alcock, miniature painter of Bristol, signed "Asaphides," and dated Jan. 29 (in which the phrases " ethereal blue " and "chorded shell" suggest William Collins's *Ode to Pity*) both doubtless by a reader of that essay. In the March number were two contributions from D.B. of Bristol sent on the 4th, the one a " copy of a manuscript written three hundred years ago by one Rowley a monk" to show how court dress came "from a Brystoe imagerie"—Henry II having been mentioned as the introducer of the Court Mantle in an article on the ancient and modern dresses of the English which had run through the first two numbers—the other *Ethelgar, a Saxon Poem,* i.e. imitation of Ossian, into which the name of Birtha's maid, Egwina, was introduced. Before this number was published, however, an audacious step had been taken, if not at Barrett's advice, followed up, undoubtedly, with his connivance.*

Chatterton's attempt to make Walpole his patron has always been a favourite theme with the poet's apologists. Both Wilson and Ingram (the latter particularly) in their zeal for the *boy,* have strained the facts to meet their theory of an inexperienced plebeian's encounter with a heartless man of the world; but Chatterton's action in this matter was for the most part less that of a distressed poet than a bold, presumptuous decoy duck, on his mettle, and Walpole is to be pitied rather than blamed, at any rate up to 1789, when the problem, such as it is, emerges; before that date there are few historic doubts of importance.

Horace Walpole was now turned of fifty-one, and had resigned his seat in Parliament in May, 1767, abandoning himself to a career of polite dilettantism. Chatterton may or may not have known that he affected Republican sentiments and that the death-warrant of Charles I, inscribed "Major Carta," hung on one side of his bed at Strawberry Hill.† In 1765 his *Anecdotes of Painting,* published three years before, had passed into a second edition. These contained (Vol. I, p. 48) a memorandum copied from the minutes of the Antiquarian Society for 1736, an extract from one of the church books of St. Mary Redcliff relating to an Easter Sepulchre delivered by Canynges—wrongly transliterated "Cumings"—on July 4, 1470, to the vicar, Nicholas Pyttes (printed "Bettes"), and three procu-

* The statement in Rowley's *Memoirs* "but I was onley to bargayne for drawyngs" inclines me to suspect that the author of the *Anecdotes of Painting* was in Chatterton's mind before he was introduced to Catcott or Barrett.

† Letter to G. Montagu, Oct. 14, 1756.

rators.* Chatterton was certainly aware of this document, for he has imitated it in a Painter's Bill (5766B, f. 4 *v.*) of "Wm Dove" to "Mr. Canynge" which is printed before the genuine relic at p. 303 of his *Works* (ed. 1803, Vol. III). It may be observed, too, that on p. 2 of the first volume of the *Anecdotes* there is a footnote remarking that since the first edition of the work the author has been informed by a curious gentleman that Saint Wolstan, Bishop of Worcester in 1062, or Erwen his master, was the earliest English painter.

Here was an opening for an approach to a writer who, apart from his authorship of *The Castle of Otranto*, avowed himself none too critical,† and whose chief eagerness appeared to be to please and divert mankind.

Accordingly, on a Saturday, when probably he had plenty of time on his hands, Chatterton sent from Lambert's office, on foolscap paper, the following letter (5766B, f. 44), which bears the postmark 

"Sir

Being versed a little in antiquitys, I have met with several Curious Manuscripts among which the following may be of Service to you, in any future Edition of your truly entertaining Anecdotes of Painting—In correcting the Mistakes (if any) in the Notes you will greatly oblige

Your most humble Servant

Thomas Chatterton.

Bristol March 25th

Corn Street."

Immediately below, filling the rest of the sheet and one side

* Lort has a note: "Mr. W. told me that among other things C sent him up the paper concerning Mr. Canning's gifts to Redcliff Church, which he himself had already printed." 11457.

† e.g., on p. 29, Vol. I of the *Anecdotes*, apropos of an altar-table at Chiswick and the likelihood of Van Eyck learning oil-painting in England, he starts a long note: "I cannot help hazarding a conjecture (though unsupported by any of the writers on painting)," and ends it: "However I pretend to nothing more in all this than meer conjecture." Hence the justice of the description of "Baron Otranto" as one "who has spent his whole life in conjectures." (*Memoirs of a Sad Dog*, 1770)

23

Eche of the Pyctures of Ymageries: wherynne he saieth, the Saxonnes dyddo throwe a mengleleð over theyr Colowres to clowe them fro the Weder. Nowe methynketh steinede Glasse moste nede ne vyle a carvinge, botte Oile alleyne.. botte alleyth ne Peyncteynge of the Saxonnes bee in Oyle, botte Water, or as whylome called Eau. Chatelion a Frenchmanne learned, Oyle Peyncteynge of Abbot John. Carvellynge ynne hys daies, gederèd newe beauties, botte moche was wasted in smalle and dribblet Pieces, the ymageries beeynge alle cladde ynne longe Rowmentes, whan the Glorie of a Carveller shulde bee in unpremented Ymagerie, therebie shewinge the semblamente to Kynde. Roberte of Glowster lysed notte his Knyghte too Sowe, ne Learneynge; botte was the Sunne, under whose Raies, the Floweretts of the Fielde shotte ynto Lyfe: Gilles a Brygstowe was hyghelie noticed, bie hymme whoe depycted notablie yn Oyle. Henrie a Thonton was a grave Depycter of Countenaunces, he paynted the Walles of Master Canynge hys Howse, whar bee the Councelrowme atte Dynnere; a moste daintie ande feetyve performaunce nowe Ygravede beeynge done ynne M.C.C.I. Henrie a Londre was a curyous broderer of Sanctes ynne Sylver ande Golde, and other dinner of hues. Childeborle Weste was a Depycter of Countenaunces: botte aboove alle was the Peyncter, Johne de Bohun whoe Workes maie be seene yn Westmynster Halle. Of Carvellers and other Peyncters I shal saie hereafter, depot Englysheynge fro the Latynne dere to wrytte; Peyncteynge unproveth the Mynde and smoothethe the rowghe Face of oure Spryghtes—

Poetry. On King Richarde 1st.

Harte of Lyone! shake thie Sworde,
Bare thie mortheynge steinede honde:
Quace whole Armies to the Queede,
Worke thie Wylle yn burlie bronde.
Barons here on bankers-browded,
Fyghte yn Furres gaynste the Cale;
Whilest thou ynne thonderynge Armes,
Warriketh whole Cyttyes bale.
Harte of Lyon! Sound the Beme!
Sounde ytte ynto inner Londes,
Feare flies sportinge ynne the Cleembe,
Inne thie Banner Terror stondes—

11 I have the Lives of several Eminent Carvers, Painters, &c. of Antiquity but as they all relate to Bristol may not be of Service in a general History; if they may be acceptable to you they are at your Service

British Museum.

PART OF CHATTERTON'S FIRST LETTER TO WALPOLE.

(Reduced.)

face p. 234.

of another* is "The Ryse of Peyncteynge yn Englāde, wroten bie T. Rowleie, 1469 for Mastre Canynge."

This, one of the poorest of the prose Rowleys, traces English painting from the Britons, who "dyd depycte themselves, yn sondrie wyse, of the fourmes of the Sonne and Moone wythe the hearbe Woade," to "Henrie a Thornton," who "payncted the Walles of Master Canynge hys House, where bee the Councelmenne atte Dynnere; a moste daintie and feetyve performaunce nowe ycrasede beeynge done ynne M.CC.I.," and introduces Hengist as the bringer of heraldry into England, "whyche dydde bryngе Peyncteynge." Worked into the middle is a short Ossianic piece on "Afflem" a glass painter, who was taken by the Danes and carried to Denmark. Though in the Rowley dialect, it may serve as a specimen of Chatterton's imitations of Macpherson.

"Inkarde a soldyer of the Danes was to slea hym [Afflem]; onne the Nete before the Feeste of Deathe hee founde Afflem to bee hys Broder. Affrighte chaynede uppe hys Soule, Gastnesse dwelled yn his Breaste. Oscarre the greate Dane gave hest hee shulde bee forslagene, with the commeynge Sunne: no Teares colde availe, the morne cladde yn roabes of ghastness was come; whan the Danique Kynge behested Oscarre, to araie hys Knyghtes eftsoones for Warre: Afflem was put yn theryre flyeynge Battailes [ships], sawe his Countrie ensconced wythe Foemen, hadde hys Wyfe and Chyldrenne brogten Capteeves to hys Shyppe, and was deieynge wyth Sorrowe; whanne the loude blautaunte Wynde hurled the Battayle agaynste an Heck [rock]: Forfraughte wythe embolleynge Waves, he sawe his Broder Wyfe and Chyldrenne synke to Deathe: himselfe was throwen, onne a Banke ynne the Isle of Wyghte, to lyve hys Lyfe forgard to all Emmoise [comfort]—thus moche for Afflem."

Walpole's remark "I then imagined, and do still, that the success of Ossian's poems had suggested the idea"† is a warrantable inference from this passage, and confirmed by "Antiquities, Book 3rd."

The essay ends with the sentiment "Peyncteynge improveth the Mynde and smootheth the rough Face of oure Spryghtes."

* The verso of the second sheet is the address "For Horace Walpole Esqr to be left with Mr. Bathoe Bookseller near Exeter Change Strand London."

† *Letter to the Editor of Chatterton's Miscellanies*, (1779), p. 30.

As a specimen of the abilities of "Johne seconde Abbate of Seyncte Austyns Mynsterre the fyrste Englyshe Paynctere yn Oyles," twelve lines on King Richard I^st^ were included.* The action of *The Castle of Otranto* takes place at this period. There were also the notes following on Rowley and Canynge:

"T. Rowleie was a Secular Priest of St. Johns, in this City: his Merit as a Biographer Historiographer is great, as a Poet still greater: some of his Pieces would do honor to Pope; and the Person under whose Patronage they may appear to the World, will lay the Englishman, the Antiquary, and the Poet, under an eternal Obligation.

"The Founder of that noble Gothic Pile, Saint Mary Redclift Church in this City: the Mecenas of his time: one who could happily blend the Poet, the Painter, the Priest, and the Christian—perfect in each; a Friend to all in distress, an honor to Bristol, and a Glory to the Church."

On March 26, while this packet was in the post, Walpole wrote from Strawberry Hill to his Eton crony George Montagu in jocose terms of the Wilkesian "rebellion" in London, adjourned till April 13, "when Wilkes and Colonel Luttrel are to fight a pitched battle at Brentford," adding "I tremble for my painted windows, and write talismans of Number 45 on every gate and postern of my castle." Tremble he well might, for he was about to be saddled with a human problem which was, with intermissions, to vex and tease him to within five years of his death.

Two days later he answered the Bristol communication, possibly in haste, though the handwriting is leisurely enough, from his town house:

"Arlington street
March 28 1769.

Sr,

I cannot but think myself singularly obliged by a Gentleman with whom I have not the pleasure of being acquainted, when I read your very curious & kind letter, which I have this minute received. I give you a thousand thanks for it, & for the very obliging offer you make me of communicating your MSS. to me.

* See end of chapter. The "Saxone achevements" in the "Ryse," which necessitated a glossary, bore fruit afterwards in the *Town and Country* for May.

Arlington Street
March 28. 1769.

Sr

I cannot but think myself singularly obliged by
Gentleman with whom I have not the pleasure of being acquainted,
hen I read your very curious & kind letter, which I have this minute
ceived. I give you a thousand thanks for it, & for the very obliging offer
u make me of communicating your MSS to me. What you have already
t me is very valuable & full of Information; but instead of correcting
u, Sr; you are far more able to correct me. I have not - happiness
understanding the Saxon Language, & without your learned notes, should
t have been able to comprehend Rowley's text.
s a second Edition of my Anecdotes was published but last year, I must
t flatter myself that a third will be wanted soon; but I shall be happy
lay up any notices you will be so good as to extract for me & send me
your leisure; for as it is uncertain when I may use them, I would by
means borrow & detain your MSS.
Give me leave to ask you where Rowley's poems are to be found. I should
t be sorry to print them, or at least a specimen of them, if they have never
n printed.
he Abbot John's verses, that you have given me, are wonderfull for their
rmony & spirit, tho there are some words I do not understand. You do not point

sh Museum.

WALPOLE'S FIRST LETTER TO CHATTERTON.

(*Slightly reduced.*)

face p. 256.

out exactly the time when he lived, which I wish to know, as I suppose it w[as]
long before John ab Eyck's discovery of oil-painting. If so, it confirms wha[t]
I had guessed, & have hinted in my Anecdotes, that oil-painting was known
here much earlier than that Discovery or revival.

I will not trouble you with more questions now, Sr; but flatter mysel[f]
from the humanity & politeness you have already shown me, that you
will sometimes give me leave to consult you. I hope too you will forgi[ve]
the simplicity of my Direction, as you have favoured me with no other.

I am Sr
yr much obliged and
obedient humble servt
HorWalpole

P.S.
Be so good as to direct
to Mr Walpole in
Arlington street.

112.

What you have already sent me is very valuable & full of Information; but instead of correcting you, Sr; you are far more able to correct me. I have not the happiness of understanding the Saxon language, & without your learned notes, shoud not have been able to comprehend Rowley's text.

As a second Edition of my Anecdotes was published but last year, I must not flatter myself that a third will be wanted soon; but I shall be happy to lay up any notices you will be so good as to extract for me & send me at your leisure; for as it is uncertain when I may use them, I woud by no means borrow & detain your MSS.

Give me leave to ask you where Rowley's poems are to be found. I shoud not be sorry to print them, or at least a specimen of them, if they have never been printed.

The Abbot John's verses, that you have given me, are wonderfull for their harmony & spirit, tho there are some words I do not understand. You do not point out exactly the time when he lived, which I wish to know, as I suppose it was long before John ab Eyck's discovery of oil-painting. If so, it confirms what I had guessed, & have hinted in my Anecdotes, that oil-painting was known here much earlier than that Discovery or revival.

I will not trouble you with more questions now, Sr; but flatter myself from the humanity & politeness you have already shown me, that you will sometimes give me leave to consult you. I hope too you will forgive the simplicity of my Direction, as you have favoured me with no other.

I am Sr.

Yr much obliged and obedient humble Sert

HOR WALPOLE

P.S. Be so good as to direct to Mr Walpole in Arlington street."*

In this letter (which Walpole never got back to re-edit), surely one of the most courteous acknowledgments ever penned, three points are to be noted:

* Add MS. 40015, f. 11. The wrapper with the "direction" has gone, but a red seal remains intact, an anchor with the motto ESPÉRANCE. Irony indeed! As for the history of the letter, it seems to have passed from Chatterton to his mother, according to Walpole (Letter to the Countess of Upper Ossory, July 17, 1792): "The lad's mother died last autumn, and in her custody was found that answer, which some of the lad's partisans printed. I had kept no copy, but it perfectly agreed with my account, and I am persuaded was genuine." This is not conclusive, for (Oct. 28, 1789) Dr. Glynn says he gave it to Barrett. It certainly passed back to Glynn. (*Gent. Mag.*, Feb., 1797). But copies were doubtless abroad (Chatterton himself made one). G. Catcott in a postscript, Nov. 6, 1789, asks Glynn for it; Glynn sends it, Feb. 6, 1790. Catcott (Letter-book, p. 472) says Glynn had it in June, 1793. In 1803 Southey and Cottle printed it as "furnished by Mr. Catcott." On April 10, 1920, the British Museum acquired the original from Messrs. Maggs, by whom it had been priced at £52.

1. The writer assumes the good faith of his correspondent.
2. He misdates the second edition of his own work, the *Anecdotes of Painting.*
3. He offers to lay up any notices his correspondent sends him, evidently regarding " The Ryse of Peyncteynge," as such. This is important, as it affects the charge of detaining MSS., no less than the treatises on painting coming to hand.

This was not printed till Feb., 1792, in the *European Magazine,* despite Walpole's publicly expressed desire that all his correspondence with the poet should be produced; and it is the only letter of his *sent* to Chatterton that has been printed to this day.

Its arrival must have filled the recipient with a delirious joy that he seldom knew. All his desires, apparently, were granted. What he had already sent was very valuable, his correspondent desired more, and actually volunteered to print Rowley. Chatterton's description of "Canynge's Cabynet" in the *Yellow Roll* shows that he could visualize an interior of the Strawberry type.* Of that citadel he must have felt himself already an inmate, seeing *Ælla* set up like Gray's *Odes* with the " Fari quæ sentiat " device on the title page. Clearly he was a select candidate for the noble author's capricious benevolence. Had not Henry Jones, the bricklayer of Drogheda (author of *Kew Garden, Clifton,* and *The Earl of Essex*), been rescued from servitude by Lord Chesterfield? What was impossible in an era of patronage?

He lost no time in replying; but we have not his reply (5766B, ff. 46-7) as he sent it; a piece has been cut off at the top after the S of " Sir " in his hand, and the eight lines of antique verse which covered the back of the missing portion have been copied by him in a cramped hand at the foot of the

* " Cannynge too must be furnished with a cabinet of coins and other rarities; and there being a private printing-press at Strawberry-Hill (the only one perhaps in England,) the Bristol Mayor must likewise have one. It is in one of his letters that has not yet been printed, that Chatterton mentions his having read an account in the Rowley MSS of Cannynge's intention to set up a *printing-press* at Westbury." Malone, *Cursory Observations,* 1782 (p. 24, *n.*). In a further note (p. 60) Malone gives an extract from this Rowley document, which was dated " 1451."

page.* The rest of the letter runs exactly thus, the words underlined not being in his hand—"peyncters" is certainly in Barrett's; and it had this appearance when Lort saw it in 1777, *teste* his letter to Walpole of July 20, 1778, printed in Nichols's *Literary Illustrations* (Vol. VII, p. 538): N.B. The "ed" in "offered" and "am" before "peyncters" have been scratched through with a pen.

"Sr . . .

you
I offered ^ some further Anecdotes and Specimens of Poetry & am peyncters [erasure] an[d]
am Your very humble & obedient Servt.

THOMAS CHATTERTON.

March 30—69 Corn Street
Bristol"

Thereafter follows on the lower portion, back, and both sides of the next sheet "Historie of Peyncters yn Englande bie T. Rowley." Here are introduced two stanzas of "Ecca Byshoppe of Hereforde yn D.LVII" englished by Rowley, a night piece and a description of spring respectively, and one, as an example of "ghastlieness," by "Elmar Byshoppe of Selseie" (like one of Magnus's stanzas in *Ælla*), as well as *The Warre* ("Of Warres glumm Pleasaunce doe I chaunte mie Laie"), as a "larger" specimen of the Abbot John's work—"inducted Abbot in the year 1186—and sat in the Deis 29 Years—as you approve of the small Specimen of his Poetry," all in the Rowleian ten line stanza with alexandrines. The last, "tho' admirable," is declared to be "inferior to Rowley whose Works when I have Leisure I will fairly Copy and send you." One footnote states that none of Rowley's pieces were ever made public, being till 1631 shut up in an iron chest in Redcliff Church; and another that nothing is so much wanted as a history of the antiquity of the violin "nor is any Antiquary more able to do it than Yourself—such a Piece would redound to the Honor of England

* In the letter to Walpole beginning "Sir, as I am now fully convinced" (5766 B. f. 48), in Chatterton's hand, and marked by him "Never sent," a piece is cut off also. This makes it practically certain that Chatterton, not Walpole, was responsible for the mutilation, after the letter was returned to him, his motive being, I take it, concealment (through pride) of the statement concerning his status and condition.

as Rowley proves the use of the Bowe to bee knowne to the Saxons and even introduced by them."

A letter signed *Civis* in the *Town and Country Supplement*, 1770, should be mentioned in this connection; it speaks of the carving of a ram playing the violin with a long bow, in Bristol Cathedral, and a P.S. adds "MSS. may be doubted in this age of infidelity but facts are obstinate arguments and not to be invalidated by the conjectures of the greatest antiquaries."

These three letters are eloquent. On the one hand they show the poet assailing Walpole as a connoisseur, but using every opportunity to force his own poetry to the forefront—"Botte nowe wee bee upon Peyncteynge sommewhatte maie be saide of the Poemes of those daies, whyche bee toe the Mynde what Peyncteynge bee toe the Eyne: the Couloures of the fyrste beeynge mo: dureynge" (this is in the letter of March 30); on the other the uncritical dilettante grateful to a country correspondent, and asking for more.

The Arlington Street document *looks* as if the writer, who knew less of Anglo-Saxon than did Chatterton, and to whom a date had no significance whatever,* was completely hoodwinked; but, though we may not believe Walpole when he writes ten years later "At first I concluded that somebody having met with my Anecdotes of Painting had a mind to laugh at me,"† its effect, at any rate, was to give the other side rope, always a sure method of detecting an imposition.‡ But Walpole could hardly have expected the second letter from Bristol to take quite the shape he tells us it did, for here, because of the mutilation, we are dependent on his testimony:

* "I have often said it of myself, and it is true, that nothing that has not a proper name of a man or a woman to it, affixes any idea upon my mind. I could remember who was King Ethelbald's great-aunt, and not be sure whether she lived in the year 500 or 1500." Letter to Sir H. Mann, Dec. 13, 1759.

† *Letter* (1779), p. 30.

‡ A sentence in a letter from Barrett to Lort (Feb. 1, 1772) makes this abundantly plain, and proves that the attempt on Walpole was doomed to failure from the beginning: "Had not Mr. W. too hastily condemn[d] y[e] poetry as an Imposture, he might at this time have had y[e] originals to my knowledge in his own possession, as Chatt[n]: told me at y[e] time he intended." 11457.

"I wrote according to the inclosed direction, for farther particulars. Chatterton, in answer, informed me that he was the son of a poor widow, who supported him with great difficulty; that he was clerk or apprentice to an attorney, but had a taste and turn for more elegant studies; and hinted a wish that I would assist him with my interest in emerging out of so dull a profession, by procuring him some place, in which he could pursue his natural bent. He affirmed that great treasures of ancient poetry had been discovered in his native city, and were in the hands of a *person*, who had lent him those he had transmitted to me; for he now sent me others, amongst which was an absolute modern pastoral in dialogue, thinly sprinkled with old words."*

This is perfectly credible; it is the Baker story over again, as Michael Lort in effect observed, writing to Walpole on July 20, 1778, "What he wrote to you about getting the poems from another person, he asserted also at first to Messrs. Barrett and Catcott." The Pastoral, by the way, exactly answers to the description of *Elinoure and Juga*, which appeared two months later in the *Town and Country*. Sir Ernest Clarke was of opinion that an early MS. of this poem, formerly belonging to Percy, and now in the writer's possession, was the actual document sent to Walpole, but that (I fear) is hardly more than a pretty conjecture.† Note that here, just as in the correspondence with Dodsley, Chatterton becomes tactlessly ingenuous as soon as the ice is broken.

Walpole, then, however imprudent his letter of March 28 may have been, acted, if we accept his word (and I do not see why we should not) with real forethought. He wrote to a "relation at Bath, a noble lady"—Ingram, I know not on whose authority, says the Countess of Ossory (p. 168, *n.*)—to inquire into the situation and character of Chatterton according to his own account of himself; nothing was returned about his character, but his story was verified. Meanwhile he communicated with Gray (who, no doubt, could discern traces of his own *Elegy* in *Elinoure and Juga*) and Mason.

* *Letter* (1779) p. 33.

† *New Lights* pp. 20, 1. There are no grounds for supposing that the *Balade of Charitie* was sent to Walpole, as Lort first thought. 11457. The note on "glommed" was the cause of the confusion. See Nichols, *L. I*, VII, p. 538.

They saw the poems at his house, so Mason told Michael Tyson ten years afterwards, and at once pronounced them " modern forgeries," advising Walpole to return them without any further notice.*

Thus armed, he wrote a letter to the poet, which has never been produced; maybe Chatterton destroyed it in fury without communicating the whole to Barrett†: but in fairness to the sender it must be borne in mind that from the beginning of 1779, when he printed his *Letter to the Editor of the Miscellanies of Thomas Chatterton*, to March 16, 1792, the date of his " Last declaration respecting Chatterton" (*Works of Lord Orford*, Vol. IV. p. 239) Walpole continued to demand the production of this second letter. It was, he says, written with as much kindness and tenderness as if he had been his guardian: " I undeceived him about my being a person of any interest, and urged; that in duty and gratitude to his mother, who had straitened herself to breed him up to a profession, he ought to labour in it, that in her old age he might absolve his filial debt; and I told him, that when he should have made a fortune he might unbend himself with the studies consonant to his inclinations. I told him also, that I had communicated his transcripts to better judges, and that they were by no means satisfied with the authenticity of his supposed MSS."‡

The first clause inclines one to sneer at Walpole; but indeed, though he could hardly know this, a person would have to be of enormous interest to find a post, then or now, in which Chatterton would have felt at home. I do not throw this out provocatively, it is based on his own admission of his liberty as an apprentice; and Walpole was jully justified in writing " Chatterton was neither indigent nor distressed at the time of his correspondence with me. He was maintained by his mother, and lived with a lawyer. His only pleas to my assistance were,

* M. Tyson, letter to W. Cole, Feb. 4, 1779, Add. MS. 5826 f. 51 b. " As I owed to you and Gray the confirmation of my doubts at first." Walpole, to Mason, Aug. 2 [6?] 1778.

† Though a writer in the *Gentleman's Magazine* for Feb., 1797, challenges Dr. Glynn to produce Lord Orford's *answers* as well as Chatterton's letters.

‡ Southey and Cottle (III, 395) imply that Chatterton wrote a third letter before Walpole wrote casting doubt on the authenticity of the poems, &c.: this is not necessary.

disgust to his profession, inclination to poetry, and communication of some suspicious MSS."* One may hate Walpole, but he had not seen his correspondent, nor, if he had, might he have been able to convince himself that Thomas Chatterton was acting alone in the matter.

The poet answered the second letter as follows:

"SIR,

I am not able to dispute with a person of your literary character. I have transcribed Rowley's poems, &c &c. from a transcript in the possession of a gentleman who is assured of their authenticity. St. Austin's minster was in Bristol. In speaking of painters in Bristol, I mean glass-stainers. The MSS. have long been in the hands of the present possessor, which is all I know of them.—Though I am but sixteen years of age, I have lived long enough to see that poverty attends literature. I am obliged to you, sir, for your advice, and will go a little beyond it, by destroying all my useless lumber of literature, and never using my pen again but in the law.

I am

Your most humble servant,

THOMAS CHATTERTON.

Bristol, April 8, 1769."

This, which, with the two subsequent letters *sent* to Walpole, was printed for the first time in the *Works of Lord Orford* (1798, Vol. IV, p. 236), is surely a pathetic document, despite the artfulness in stating the transcript was made from a transcript, so as to avoid having to produce an "original." Walpole obscured the sting in the first line by paraphrasing it "He wrote me rather a peevish answer and said he could not contest with a person of my learning"; but the thrust is at *Otranto*. Too little attention has been paid to the last sentence but one, which is the cry of an embittered literary *man*, to whom vocation is vocation.

Six days later he wrote again, demanding the papers back for the first time:

"SIR,

Being fully convinced of the papers of Rowley being genuine, I should be obliged to you to return the copy I sent you,

* *Letter* (1779), p. 23.

having no other. Mr Barrett, a very able antiquary, who is now writing The history of Bristol, has desired it of me; and I should be sorry to deprive him, or the world indeed, of a valuable curiosity, which I know to be an authentic piece of antiquity.

Your very humble servant,

THOMAS CHATTERTON.

Bristol, Corn St, April 14, 1769.

P.S. If you will publish them yourself, they are at your service."

There are two drafts for this particular note in the British Museum, showing that a longer and controversial letter was first intended; one (5766B, f. 48, 9) is in Chatterton's hand, the other (*ib.* f. 50) entirely in Barrett's, who has started to sign it "Wm Bar" and written "T. Chatterton" over that; and both are marked by the poet "Never sent." Chatterton's, mutilated in two places, is as follows:

"SIR,

As I am now fully convinced that Rowleys Papers are genuine: should be obliged to you, if you'd send Copys of them to the Town & Country Magazine; or return them to me for that Purpose:—as it wd be the greatest Injustice, to deprive the World of so valuable a Curiosity—

I have seen the original from whence the Extracts first sent you were first Copyed—

The Harmony is not so extraordinary:—as Joseph Iscan is altogether as Harmonious—

The Stanza Rowley wrote in, instead of being introduc'd by Spencer was in use 300 Years before [lower part of sheet cut away] by Rowley—tho' I have seen some Poetry of that Age—exceeding Alliterations without Rhyme—

I shall not defend Rowleys Pastoral: its merit can stand its own defence—

Rowley was employ'd by Canynge to go to the Principal Monasterys in the Kingdom to Collect drawings, Paintings & all MSS relating to Architecture—is it then so very extraordinary he should meet with the few remains of Saxon Learning—'Tis allow'd by evry Historian of Credit, that the Normans destroy'd all the Saxon MSS, Paintings &c that fell in their Way; endeavoring to suppress the very Language—the want of knowing what they were, is all the Foundation you can have for stiling them a barbarous Nation.

If you are not satisfied with these conspicuous Truths [lower part of sheet and portion of upper part of next cut away] the Honor to be of my opinion

I am

S^{r} y^{r} very hble & ob^{t} Servt

T. CHATTERTON.

Bristol Corn Street. April 14th 69 "

This, which bears a direction to Arlington Street, leads one to suppose that Bryant's picture of the poet as "choleric beyond description" may not be greatly exaggerated.

Barrett's, as will be seen, embodies the version that was used; the phrase "a very able antiquary," in the latter, was no doubt Chatterton's addition:

" SIR,

Being fully convinc^{d} of the papers of Rowley being Genuine, I should be oblig^{d} to you to return ye Copy, I sent you having no other; Mr Barrett, who is now writing the History & Antiquities of ye City of Bristol, has desir^{d} it of me, & I should be sorry to deprive him or the World indeed of a Valuable Curiosity; wch I know to be an authentic peice of Antiquity. However Barbarous ye Saxons may be call^{d} by our Modern Virtuosos, it is certain we are indebted to to [*sic*] Alfred & other Saxon Kings for ye wisest of our Laws & in part for ye British Constitution—The Normans indeed destroy'd [" all " erased] ye MSS, paintings &c of ye Saxons that fell in their way; but some might be & [" were " erased] certainly were recover^{d} out of ye Monasteries &c, in wch they were preserv^{d}—Mr Vertue could know nothing of ye Matter—'twas quite out of his Walk—I thought, Rowleys pastoral had ["some " erased] a degree of merit, that would be its own Defence. *Abbot Johns* Verses were translated by Rowley out of the Greek; & there might be [" some" erased] poetry of his Age something more than meer Alliterations, as he was so great a Scholar. The Stanza if I mistake not, was us^{d} by Ischan, Gower, Ladgate &c—long before Spencer. Glumm is us^{d} by John a Beverly, Gower & Ladgate in ye Same Sence as by Rowley, & ye Modern Gloomy seems but a refinement of ye Old Word—Glommung in Anglo Saxon is ye Twilight—*

from Sr Y^{r} Very Hble Servt

T. CHATTERTON."†

The spelling "Ladgate" is odd if Barrett had not

* See "GLOOMY" in N. Bailey's Dictionary (1721).

† Both drafts are printed in Chatterton's *Works* (1803) III, pp. 399-401.

Chatterton at his elbow. The defence of "glumm,"* in the first line of *The Warre,* was used afterwards in the notes on the *Balade of Charitie.* In these drafts I see the surgeon trying to water down the poet's exasperation, and persuade him into sending a letter which would not have the effect of alienating the great man in London altogether.

At this point, Michael Lort not having helped Walpole (who had mislaid his Chatterton papers) to any dates,† there is a slight difficulty.

> "When I received this letter [that of Apr. 14] I was going to Paris in a day or two, and either forgot his request of the poems, or perhaps not having time to have them copied, deferred complying till my return, which was to be in six weeks. I protest I do not remember which was the case; and yet, though in a cause of so little importance, I will not utter a syllable of which I am not positively certain; nor will charge my memory with a tittle beyond what it retains.
>
> Soon after my return from France, I received another letter from Chatterton, the style of which was singularly impertinent. He demanded his poems roughly; and added, that I should not have *dared* to use him so ill, if he had not acquainted me with the narrowness of his circumstances."‡

Now Walpole's letters of this year, as chronologically arranged in Volume VII of Mrs. Paget Toynbee's edition, show that he did not leave England till on or after Aug. 15.§ He wrote from Calais on Aug. 18 to George Montagu, and returned from Paris on Oct. 11.|| It follows therefore that either

1. Chatterton's letters were returned before Walpole went to France; i.e., that the date of their return, Aug. 4,

* This proves, in the absence of the postmark, that Chatterton's letter of March 30, which contains *The Warre,* reached Walpole.

† "I find I can help you to some dates for y^r Narrative from memorandums I took at Bristol last year when Mr. Barret showed me part of the two first letters which C sent to you." Letter to Walpole. July 20, 1778. Cf. Lord Orford's *Works* (Preface, Vol. I, p. 14). "This letter," [i.e. Chatterton's of July 24, 1769] "which his Lordship had not been able to find, with the others, was recovered by his executors from amongst a quantity of waste paper"; and *ibid.* (Vol. IV, p. 228, *n.*).

‡ *Letter* (1779) pp. 36, 7.

§ "I shall set out on the fifteenth of next month, and return the first week in October." Letter to Sir H. Mann, July 19, 1769.

|| "I arrived the night before last." P.S. (Oct. 13) to letter to Sir H. Mann, Oct. 8, 1769.

1769, as given in Walpole's *Works* (Vol. IV, p. 237) may, perhaps, be followed;

or,

2. If Walpole's statement, given above, in his letter to the editor of Chatterton's *Miscellanies* be followed, they were not returned till after Oct. 11.

But, *in either case*, the "singularly impertinent" letter (July 24) must have reached Walpole before he left England, and his conscience or his memory faulted him in this particular, for he was "in town yesterday and found the parcel arrived very safe" (Letter to Cole, Strawberry Hill, Aug. 12, 1769).*

This document, which the editors of 1803 called "dignified and spirited," ran thus:

"SIR,

I cannot reconcile your behaviour to me, with the notions I once entertained of you. I think myself injured, sir; and, did not you know my circumstances, you would not dare to treat me thus. I have sent twice for a copy of the MS.:—No answer from you. An explanation or excuse for your silence would oblige.

THOMAS CHATTERTON.

July 24th."

All to be said here is that if Chatterton had written twice already for his MSS., a letter has been lost. Walpole says his heart did not accuse him of insolence to Chatterton. He wrote an answer "expostulating with him on his injustice, and renewing good advice," but on second thoughts reflecting that "so wrong-headed a young man" might print it, he flung it into the fire, and wrapping up both his poems and letters, without taking a copy of either, "for which I am now sorry," he returned all to him and thought no more of him or them, till about a year and a half after.†

In 1783 or 1784 he found he had not burnt his unfinished

* "I sincerely do not recollect why I did not return the first papers; I have spoken strict truth to the best of my memory, and cannot tell whether I forgot or reserved them to transcribe." Letter to the Countess of Upper Ossory, Feb. 1, 1779. The difficulty did not escape the eighteenth century; see *The Genuine copy of a Letter found near Strawberry Hill* (1783), p. 13.

† *Letter* (1779), p. 37. A year and a half after Oct. 11, 1769, the date of Walpole's return from France, is April 11, 1771. The Academy Banquet was on the 23rd.

reply,* and it was printed in Vol. IV of his *Works*. It is the restrained letter of an incensed eighteenth-century public man, alive to imposition, but quite justified; and must be given, in fairness to both parties.

" SIR,

I do not see, I must own, how those precious MSS. of which you have sent me a few extracts, should be lost to the world by my detaining your letters. Do the originals not exist, from whence you say you copied your extracts, and from which you offered me more extracts? In truth, by your first letter, I understood that the originals themselves were in your possession by the free and voluntary offer you made me of them, and which you know I did not chuse to accept. If Mr Barrett (who, give me leave to say, cannot know much of antiquity if he believes in the authenticity of those papers) intends to make use of them, would he not do better to have recourse to the originals, than to the slight fragments you have sent me? You say, sir, you know them to be genuine; pray let me ask again, of what age are they? and how have they been transmitted? In what book of any age is there mention made of Rowley or of the poetical monk, his ancient predecessor in such pure poetry? poetry, so resembling both Spenser and the moderns, and written in metre invented long since Rowley, and longer since the monk wrote. I doubt Mr Barrett himself will find it difficult to solve these doubts.

For myself, I undoubtedly will never print those extracts as genuine, which I am far from believing they are. If you want them, sir, I will have them copied, and will send you the copy. But having a little suspicion that your letters may have been designed to laugh at me, if I had fallen into the snare, you will allow me to preserve your original letters, as an ingenious contrivance, however unsuccessful. This seems the more probable, as any man would understand by your first letter, that you either was possessed of the original MSS. or had taken copies of them; whereas you now talk as if you had no copy but these written at the bottom of the very letters I have received from you.

I own I should be better diverted, if it proved that you have chosen to entertain yourself at my expence, than if you really thought these pieces ancient. The former would show you had little opinion of my judgment; the latter, that you ought not to trust too much to your own. I should not at all take the former ill, as I am not vain of it; I should be sorry for the latter, as you say, sir, that you are very young, and it would be pity an ingenious young man should be too early prejudiced in his own favour.

* Four or five years after he wrote and published the letter to the editor of the *Miscellanies*, he says, *Works*, IV, p. 234.

N.B. The above letter I had begun to write to Chatterton on his redemanding his MSS. but not chusing to enter into a controversy with him, I did not finish it, and, only folding up his papers, returned them.

HOR. WALPOLE."

That is the sum of the issue as between Walpole and Chatterton, *in the latter's lifetime*, and the only charge to which the former can possibly be amenable is that of the retention of Chatterton's MSS. (parts of two letters to some extent) for less than nine months,* a retention which might have been interpreted, however mistakenly, by some authors, as evidence that not all interest was lost in their creations.

But the incontrovertible point is that made by Lort: "His youth and situation could not lead Mr. Walpole to suppose he was himself the author and contriver, more especially as he had asserted them to be the property of a person at Bristol then alive. He had indeed represented himself as a lover of the muses, but had given no specimens of his *own* compositions."†

Walpole may well have suspected, though perhaps not *immediately* on receiving Chatterton's second letter, that he was being made a butt, for (apart from his having been drawn into the Ossian business) three years before this, one of his own *jeux d'esprit* in Paris had been a mock letter from Frederick the Great to Rousseau, offering him an asylum in his dominions, which, besides delighting the Anti-Rousseau party, passed to England, and had its effect on the quarrel between Rousseau and Hume.‡ A note of Lort's develops this probability: "Therefore he had to conclude that the whole was a fiction contrived by some or more literary wags who wished to impose on his credulity and to laugh at him if they succeeded, and that C. was only the instrument employed to introduce and recommend these old writings."§ The reference, in the letter of April 14, to Barrett and his History of Bristol, coupled with

* Personally, I am satisfied that the MSS. were returned shortly after Chatterton's demand of July 24; otherwise, I fancy, he would have made more capital out of their retention.

† Gregory, *Life*, p. 63, *n*.

‡ See article *Horace Walpole*, by Austin Dobson, in the *D.N.B.*

§ 11457.

Chatterton's admission of his own youth, confirmed as that was by enquiry, must indeed have led Walpole to believe that his correspondent was the decoy-duck or catspaw of a gang, though not perhaps of so infamous a gang as had threatened his brother Edward in 1751.* And in fact, though he wanted to get Rowley before the world, Chatterton may have been used as Barrett's tool in this matter (to some extent), for the suffrage of Horace Walpole would have materially assisted the *History of Bristol.*

However that may be, Chatterton repeatedly told George Catcott that he was despised by Walpole from the moment he made known his dependent situation, and bitterly regretted that he had not concealed it from his obsequious correspondent.† Such a gesture, in the circumstances, was only to be expected of him; and it must be owned that the poetry, by being proved modern, did not thereby forfeit all claims to the wonderful harmony and spirit which Walpole had, on a first glance, professed to find in it; though even that argument has to be set against the risk the dilettante ran of making himself publicly ridiculous, had he given it, or the Bristol painters, the *imprimatur* of Strawberry Hill.

I think it likely that the poet may have been much baited and teased by the Juvenile Club and his 'prentice acquaintance over this fiasco. Who can doubt that he had bragged of the March 28 letter wherever he went? His biographers are silent on this point, but John Broughton's preface to the *Miscellanies* (Redcliff testimony) takes us just a little of the way, in the last six words of the extract: "Although he was of a profession that might be said to accelerate his pursuits in antiquities, yet so averse was he to that profession, that he could never overcome it. One of his first efforts to emerge from a situation so irksome to him was an application to a gentleman well known in the republic of letters which unfortunately for the public and himself, met with a very cold reception; and which the disappointed author always spoke of with a

* See *The Tryal of John Cather* [and others] *for a conspiracy against the Hon. Edward Walpole, Esq.* Dublin, 1751.

† Chatterton's *Works*, Vol. III, p. 387, *n.*

high degree of acrimony, whenever it was mentioned to him." This was written in 1778, when there were plenty of people in Bristol who remembered Chatterton.

The following lines, in his autograph, are at the Bristol Museum* :

Walpole ! I thought not I should ever see
So mean a Heart as thine has proved to be ;
Thou, who in Luxury nurs'd behold'st with Scorn
The Boy, who Friendless, Penniless, Forlorn,
Asks thy high Favour,—thou mayst call me Cheat—
Say, didst thou ne'er indulge in such Deceit ?
Who wrote Otranto ? But I will not chide,
Scorn I will repay with Scorn, & Pride with Pride.†
Still, Walpole, still, thy Prosy Chapters write,
And twaddling Letters to some Fair indite,
Laud all above thee,—Fawn and Cringe to those
Who, for thy Fame, were better Friends than Foes
Still spurn the incautious Fool, who dares — —
— — — — — — [so in MS.
Had I the Gifts of Wealth & Lux'ry shar'd
Not poor & Mean—Walpole ! thou hadst not dared
Thus to insult. But I shall live & Stand
By Rowley's side—when *Thou* art dead & damned
THOMAS CHATTERTON
1769
I intended to have sent the above to Mr. Walpole
but my Sister persuaded me out of it.
T. C.

The punctuation shows that *this* copy was not hastily put to paper ; and indeed it is tantamount to a confession that Rowley is Chatterton. The last couplet may be coloured by the last lines

Your *Fate* is written by an *unseen Hand*,
But his *Three Books* with the *Three worlds* shall stand.‡

* The poet's sister was governess in the family of Philip George (Sheriff 1808, 1813, 1815) about 1783, and gave him the MS. about 1783. It remained in the possession of the George and Swan families, and was presented to the City by W. E. George in 1906. There is a facsimile in *The True Chatterton*, at p. 172. The lines were first printed in Dix's *Life* (1837), p. 102.

† Then, crouch no more on suppliant knee,
But scorn with scorn outbrave.
Wordsworth.

‡ First printed in *Anthropoposophia Theomagica* (1650), p. 53.

of Thomas Vaughan's encomium on Cornelius Agrippa's *Occult Philosophy*, translated by J.F. (1651).

Whatever hopes may have been raised by Walpole's first letter, the poet certainly made the most of his repulse. If he did not write the scandalous "Tête à Tête" in the *Town and Country* for December, 1769, where Walpole and the comedian Kitty Clive* (1711-1785) appear as Otranto and Mrs. Heidelburgh, he certainly wrote in *The Advice* (*ibid.* Suppl. 1769):

To keep one lover's flame alive
Requires the genius of a Clive,
With Walpole's mental taste.

and in one of his "Exhibitions" (*Middlesex Journal*, May 26, 1770):

"*A Piece of Modern Antiquity by Horace Walpole*
This is no other than a striking portrait of the facetious Mrs. Clive. Horace, finding it too large to be introduced in his next edition of Virtu, has returned it on the town."

Walpole also appears as "Horatio Otranto" in the short piece *The Polite Advertiser* (*T. and C.M.*, July, 1770), "Horatio Trefoil" in *The Woman of Spirit*, and "Baron Otranto" in the *Memoirs of a Sad Dog* (*T. and C.M.*, July-Aug., 1770), where he is represented as reading a broken stone, once inscribed "James Hicks lieth here, with Hester his wife," as "Hic jacet corpus Kenelmæ Sancto Legero Requiescat, &c., &c."

This incident, long afterwards reinvented in *The Pickwick Papers*, is derived from a letter signed "Theates Aoratus" in the same magazine for Oct., 1769.†

Michael Lort's comment on the affair, twenty years afterwards. in a letter to Walpole, is:

"Chatterton having met with such easy credit at Bristol, where every thing he produced seems to have been received as gospel, and by everybody, no wonder he wished to extend the scene of his

* Walpole had written a farewell epilogue for her (*T. and C. M.*, Apr. 1769) and given her a house near Strawberry Hill.

† "Chatterton did draw me under the title of Baron of Otranto, but unluckily the picture is more like Dr. Milles, and Chatterton's own devotees, than to me." Letter to Cole, Aug. 22, 1778.

forgeries, nor any wonder that a rebuff from a quarter should irritate and inflame so proud and presumptuous a spirit as he represents his own to be, and what had well nigh drawn him to put an end to his being, when he was in no want of the necessaries of life, which has been assigned, though I think improperly, for committing this act afterwards. Had he done it the first time, there might have been a much better foundation for all the clamour that idle people raised of a great and promising genius lost to the world for want of patronage and encouragement."*

It will be convenient to pursue the story of Walpole and Chatterton in this place, so that the reader may form an undistracted opinion of both parties.

Walpole heard no more of his Bristol correspondent from July 24th, 1769, till the evening of Apr. 23, 1771, when he attended the first Annual Banquet of Sir Joshua Reynolds's newly organized Royal Academy. There Goldsmith drew the company's attention to an account of ancient poems lately discovered at Bristol, and expressed enthusiastic belief in them, for which he was laughed at by Dr. Johnson, who was present. Walpole informed Goldsmith that this was no novelty to him, and, had he pleased, he might have "had the honour of ushering the great discovery to the learned world." Then, on his asking about Chatterton, Goldsmith informed him that he had been in London and had destroyed himself, mentioning that he went by the name of "the young villain" in Bristol. Walpole seems to have been genuinely shocked, for the moment anyhow.†

In 1772, *Bristowe Tragedy* was published, and he wrote to Mason on May 25: "Somebody, I fancy Dr. Percy, has produced a dismal dull Ballad called *The Execution of Sir Charles Bawdin*, and given it for one of the Bristol poems called Rowley's —but it is a still worse counterfeit than those which were first sent to me." A lull of five years followed.

At the beginning of 1777 Tyrwhitt published the Rowley Poems, and Walpole wrote to Mason on Feb. 17: "He does not give up the antiquity, yet fairly leaves everybody to ascribe them to Chatterton. . . . Mr. Tyrrwhit seems to have dreaded

* Aug. 4, 1789. Nichols, *L.I.* Vol. VII, p. 555.
† *Letter* (1779), p. 37. Letter to Cole, March 13, 1780.

drawing himself into a controversy, which joys me, who dreaded being drawn into one too."

But his joy was to be of short duration. He writes to Cole on June 19 that he did see the *Monthly Review*, but hopes one is not guilty of the death of every man who does not make one the dupe of a forgery—" I believe Macpherson's success with *Ossian* was more the ruin of Chatterton than I." This is the earliest reference in Walpole's correspondence to the charge of hastening the poet's decease. What then had happened?

The authorship of Rowley was now being canvassed, and Catcott and Barrett were in communication with the cognoscenti. The book was noticed in the *Monthly Review* of April, and one paragraph ran: " Hitherto it appears that the personal evidence of the authenticity of these poems rests entirely on the faith of Chatterton, on the faith of a vagrant, living by expedients, and equally destitute of property and principle. We have been credibly informed that this young man carried his MSS. to Mr. Horace Walpole, and that he met with no encouragement from that learned and ingenious gentleman, who suspected his veracity: a circumstance which certainly does not speak in favour of the originality of these productions."

This was followed up in the May number by a long account of the discovery of the poems, furnished by " Mr. George Catcott, a learned antiquary of Bristol," one of whose remarks was: " In 1770 Chatterton went to London, and carried all this treasure with him, in hopes, as we may very reasonably suppose, of disposing of it to his advantage: he accordingly applied, as I have been informed, to that learned antiquary, Mr. Horace Walpole, but met with little or no encouragement from him: soon after which, in a fit of despair, as it is supposed, he put an end to his unhappy life, having first cut to pieces and destroyed all the MSS. he had in his possession."

This, it need hardly be said, was a perfectly monstrous accusation, considering that Walpole never saw Chatterton, whose application to him was made over a year before he came to London, and seventeen months before his death. Accordingly, on May 23, 1778 (observe that he did not act precipitately) Walpole addressed a long private letter to William Bewley, "an obscure surgeon" of Massingham, Norfolk, a constant contributor to the *Monthly Review*, and friend of Dr. Burney, a letter which formed the nucleus of his *Letter to the Editor of the Miscellanies of Thomas Chatterton*, giving an account of his relations with the poet, beginning "I am far from determined to publish anything about Chatterton," and ending "You are my confessor; I have unburdened my soul to you, and I trust you will not enjoin me a public penance"; and on June 3, probably stimulated by the appearance of Tyrwhitt's *Appendix*, he tells Cole that he has drawn up an account of his "transaction with that marvellous young man."*

The publication of the *Miscellanies* forced his hand; for the preface (dated June 20, 1778) contained this sentence: "Perhaps he ["the reader"] may feel some indignation against the person to whom his first application was made, and by whom he was treated with neglect and contempt. It were to be wished that the public was fully informed of all the circumstances attending that unhappy application; the event of which deprived the world of works which might have contributed to the honour of the nation, as well as the comfort and happiness of this unfortunate author."

On July 24, 1778, he wrote at length to Mason on the subject: "I am at last forced to enter into the history of the supposed Rowley's poems. I must write on it, nay, what is more, print, not directly, controversially, but in my own defence. Some jackanapes at Bristol (I don't know who) has published Chatterton's Works, and I suppose to provoke me to tell the story accuses me of treating that marvellous creature with contempt; which having supposed, contrary to truth, he invites his readers to feel indignation at me." In the same letter he speaks of Chatterton as a consummate villain who had gone to enormous lengths before he destroyed himself; and for some little time, as his correspondence shows, vacillated, hating unnecessary

* The identification of W. B. as William Bewley was due to the late Sir Ernest Clarke, whose *New Lights* (1916) was the first effort to unravel this particular tangle. See Walpole's Letters (ed. Toynbee) *Suppl.* I, p. 260.

publicity, as a fastidious man naturally would, yet (though he does not say so) resenting the imputation of cowardice if he remained in the background. On Aug. 25 he writes to Mason: "You have put an end to my thoughts of publishing my narrative, for you have said in four lines all that I have been trying to say in thirty pages." However, by the new year he had enlarged his letter to William Bewley, and sent part of the MS. to Thomas Percy, the then Dean of Carlisle, with the following, hitherto unpublished, letter :

"Arlington street
Jan. 11. 1779.

DEAR S^r^

As I shoud be very unwilling to take any step in the affair of Chatterton without your good advice and direction, I take the liberty of submitting to you my Narrative of that strange history, & of begging that you will honour me with any remarks, additions or corrections that you shall think necessary, except to facts, which I mention on memory ; & which, tho they may not be perfectly exact, I had rather give as they occurred to me, as a proof of my veracity, tho, shoud they be wrong, I will add a note to say that I am informed of my mistake, if you observe any such.

My Intention is to print only 200 Copies, & give them away, not to publish for sale ; for as this is only the justification of a private character, I think it is impertinent to suppose that the Public in general is concerned about an Individual, tho he has been so publickly & so very unjustly accused. As every page that is printed about this story adds something to it (the common Case of Lies) the Monthly Review of last November* (of which I was told but last week, for I very rarely read reviews) seems to suppose that I saw *all* Chatterton's forgeries, or (which woud have been a little severe upon me) that I *ought* to have done so ; tho the Truth is, that I certainly did not receive *from Him* half a dozen of them, before he resented my doubts—It woud be excellent indeed, if every Man on whom a forgery is attempted, were in Duty bound to examine *all* the forgeries of such an Impostor—& for what purpose ?—not to detect him, but to find out whether he were not a great Genius !—are not Reviewers admirable & just Judges ?

I will beg, dear S^r^, to have my MS. returned as soon as you can conveniently, because I have no other tolerably fair copy, & wish to put it to the Press as soon as I can, my Illness having delayed it too long already. I must beg your pardon too for imposing this trouble on you, but you have accustomed me to y^r^ Indulgence ; &

* Review of Chatterton's *Miscellanies*, p. 395.

tho gratitude is not very common, it is apt to be a little intruding, especially when it hopes for more Obligations.

I am with great regard, Sr

Yr most obedient and obliged humble Sert

HOR WALPOLE.

To Dr. Percy Dean of Carlisle

Jan. 24

Dear Sr

the foregoing letter I sent to Northumberland House a fortnight ago, as you will see by the Date ; but as you was not in town, I was forced to begin printing, and therefore can only send you now the MS. as far as it is printed off, on which I shall be very glad to be honoured with your remarks."*

The two hundred copies were duly printed and distributed privately, but by 1782 the Rowley Controversy, what with the publication of *Love and Madness* (1780), Bryant's *Observations* (1781), Dean Milles's *Rowley* (1782), and the rain of literature which that was evoking, had reached such a pitch that, in April, Walpole sent this note to John Nichols :

" As it is said to be so much desired, the author consents to let the whole of the letter on Chatterton be printed in the *Gentleman's Magazine*, but not in a separate pamphlet."

Accordingly in four numbers of that periodical (Apr.-July, 1782) the letter to the Editor of Chatterton's *Miscellanies* made its first *public* appearance.

But, except in discerning minds, it did not leave the effect intended ; for it contained at least one magnetic phrase which invoked on its maker a temporary obloquy not unlike that which a phrase concerning his " spiritual home " invoked on a public man of the twentieth century : "All of the house of forgery are relations ; and though it is just to Chatterton's memory to say that his poverty never made him claim kindred with the richest, or more enriching branches, yet his ingenuity in counterfeiting styles, and I believe, hands, might easily have led him to those more facile imitations of Prose, promissory notes."

* The original was given to me in 1925 by Mr. H. C. Wallace, Sir Ernest Clarke's executor.

This is not even yet forgotten. " Oh, ye who honour the name of man," wrote Coleridge, at a time when he was hot with the French Revolution, " rejoice that this Walpole is called a Lord ! "* No writer on Chatterton has troubled to quote, " I do not mean to use the term *forged* in a harsh sense," or to recognize that the author of *Otranto* (whether intentionally or not, does not matter) is here claiming kinship with the author of *Ælla*. Again, so far as I am aware, nobody quotes : " It is that fierce and untamable spirit, that consciousness of superior abilities, that inattention to worldly discretion, and its paths, that scorn of owing substance or reputation to anything but the ebullitions of genius that I regret not having known, that I lament not having contributed to rescue from itself."

There can be few poets worth the name who would not welcome neglect and contumely during their lives, on the condition of wresting such an epicede from the personage supposed responsible therefor.

But it is rarely other than a mistake, especially in literary matters, to defend one's conduct, and *a fortiori* when it needs no defence ; and when Walpole writes, referring to the receipt of Chatterton's first letter, " Such a spirit of poetry breathed in his coinage as interested me for him," etc., he is forgetting that he could not know at that time that Chatterton was the author of the "Abbot John's" lines ; he knew him merely as the sender of copies of manuscripts. Thus he has stood in his own light, and become the butt of sentimentality, and unintelligent journalism, for nigh a hundred and fifty years.

But he was to do himself even greater harm. In 1789 Dr. Gregory's life of the poet, drawn up for the *Biographia Britannica*, appeared, to which Lort had added notes signed "O", which put both Chatterton's and Walpole's conduct in the clearest light possible ; and Walpole had only to remain silent to be acquitted of blame by all fair-minded judges.† But, later in the year, Barrett's *History of Bristol* was published, and there, for the first time, Chatterton's two letters to Walpole of March 25, and March 30, 1769 (with " The Ryse of Peynct-

* Cottle, *Early Recollections* (1837) Vol. I. p. 35.

† See Lort's letter to Walpole of Nov. 10, 1788, in Nichols *L. I.* VII, p. 553.

eynge" and "The Historie of Peyncters yn Englande" appended), which the latter sent back to him, were printed, in their then entirety, at pages 639 and 642. Two days after seeing the book, Horace Walpole wrote the following surprising letter to Michael Lort:

"Strawberry Hill,
July 27, 1789.

DEAR SIR,

Mr Barrett in his new history of Bristol has inserted two letters which he says Chatterton sent to me with an account of the rise of painting in England. I do assure you solemnly upon my honour and veracity that I never received such letters. Chatterton in his *first* address, I think, offered me an account of *great painters at Bristol**—but not a word about the rise of painting. The offer was so utterly incredible that I believed it much less than the poetry, and did not in the least encourage the offer; nor did he mention painting more. This might easily be proved, if my letters and his with their dates, if preserved, were to be produced, for he had mine certainly and I returned his. And were the two letters now printed, suddenly demanded, I am persuaded they would have no postmarks —unless counterfeited. My letters they have shamefully kept suppressed—yet it will be no wonder, if after my death, spurious ones are produced, which candour will not trust, as, tho' called on by me, they have unhandsomely concealed them.

I do not say that Chatterton would not have sent me the two letters now exhibited, if I had been his dupe and had encouraged him to send them; and Mr Barrett is a goose to take his argument for a good one, that Chatterton would not have ventured to send them to me, unless he had strongly supposed them authentic. As he did *not* send them, what becomes of that argument! Still I do not believe that that was Chatterton's reason for not sending them. What forgery of the kind did he not risk!"

Then, after laughing at the prints of Bristol Castle at p. 196 of the *History*, at Chatterton's ascribing the introduction of heraldry to Hengist, and at the bringing of painted glass to England by Afflem, he concludes:

"As I have declared I will meddle no more with that preposterous controversy, which tho' detected over and over, still has its partisans,

* "I have the Lives of several Eminent Carvers, Painters, &c. of Antiquity, but as they all relate to Bristol, may not be of Service in a General Historie. If they may be acceptable to you, they are at your Service." Chatterton's note at end of "Ryse of Peyncteynge," March 25, 1769.

I shall leave Mr. Barrett's foolish new documents to confirm the faith of Chatterton's proselytes : but I thought, dear Sir, you would not be sorry to learn from me the absolute falsehood of my having seen those letters till the day before yesterday."*

Barrett had introduced the letters thus : "The following are printed from the very originals in Chatterton's hand-writing, sent in two letters to Horace Walpole Esq.," but the remark which must have infuriated Walpole was—"However much he might impose upon others, he never would have chosen such a one for the first trial of his imposition."

Lort, who, as an antiquary, was far more interested in the effect the Chatterton matter in Barrett's *History* would have in extending the triumph of the Anti-Rowleians, than whether Chatterton had or had not sent the letter of March 30 to Walpole, replied on Aug. 4 :

> "Having lent Barrett's book to a friend, and not receiving it back till this morning was the reason of my not having replied sooner to your favour of the 27th. I wished to see again the observations that Barrett made on the correspondence between you and Chatterton ; and the more so, as when I read the passage you allude to, it did not appear to be of much consequence whether the letter had been really sent to you, or only intended to have been sent ; for, whatever opinion you or any one else might have formed of the discovery of a series of Bristol painters and carvellers, the series itself now produced to the world must stagger the belief of all but the most prejudiced or most ignorant, and be rejected at once as fictitious.
>
> "I will write to a friend at Bristol to try if he can find out whether the letter has got the postmark, or seems only intended or the copy of one intended to have been sent."

Note that he says "letter," for, as we have seen, that of March 25, containing "The Ryse," has the postmark, though there is not a shadow of doubt that Walpole received both.

On the 7th he wrote to Walpole, "Mr. Stephens [Steevens] called on me yesterday and to him I communicated what you wrote to me concerning Chatterton ; it cannot be in better hands."†

* Printed in *Walpole's Letters*, ed. Toynbee, Supplement, Vol. II, p. 33.

† Lort's letters to Walpole are in Add. MS. 12527 ; they are all printed in Nichols, *L. I*, Vol. VII.

The matter did not stop there, unfortunately. In two letters to Hannah More (Sept., Nov. 4, 1789) Walpole speaks respectively of "two letters pretended to have been sent to me, and which never were sent," and of his rejoicing that he did not "publish a word in contradiction of the letters which he [Barrett] said Chatterton sent to me," as he was advised to do. Nay more, writing to the Countess of Upper Ossory (July 17, 1792)—"Poor Barrett, author of the *History of Bristol*, printed there two letters to me found among Chatterton's papers, and which the simple man imagined the lad had sent to me, but most assuredly never did, as too preposterous even for him to venture, after he found that I began to suspect his forgeries."

As for Steevens, he gave Dr. Farmer of Emmanuel College, Cambridge, the following information: "Mr. Walpole has authorized his friends to declare that he never saw those letters from Chatterton, which Mr. Barrett has printed, till they appeared in the new History of Bristol. Mr. W. also expresses his apprehensions that, after his death, some pretended answers to them will be produced."

In 1792 this developed into a report that Walpole had had no correspondence with Chatterton*; and his last declaration (March 16 of that year) was an admission that he wrote the letter of March 28, 1769.

It is, I think, barely possible to make a case here for the injured dilettante. Walpole, who in 1789 was seventy-two, *may* have confused the two letters printed in Barrett which he did receive, with the two letters marked by Chatterton "Never sent." On July 20, 1778, when helping him to some dates for his narrative, Lort mentioned that Barrett showed him part of the first two letters Chatterton sent to Walpole (Lort, who was writing from notes, gave their dates March 26, March 30, and apparently confused the Abbot John's verses with the second Eclogue) adding, "Mr. Walpole having made some objections to the authenticity of the poems, Mr. Barrett drew up an answer, which Chatterton did in part adopt, but never sent." There is no mention of the "The Ryse of Peyncteynge" or "Historie of Peyncters" in Lort's letter; and it is con-

* *Gentleman's Magazine*, Apr.-May, 1792. Nichols *L. I*, vii. 554.

ceivable, since the Rowley *Poems* had been the main staple of controversy till Barrett was published, that Walpole forgot twenty years later that spurious prose matter had been sent to him with the poetry. Still it is a very lame case, for how could the author of *Anecdotes of Painting* forget that two suspicious treatises on painting had been submitted to him? Besides, in 1782 he had made public admission of having received Chatterton's first two letters, and these extant documents shew that the treatises on painting are written underneath them.

Nothing has prejudiced Walpole more severely than this denial, as it has been interpreted as taking a despicable advantage of Chatterton when he was in his grave; and this is the only real problem in his relations with the poet, for the date of his returning the MSS. is of trivial importance beside it.

The curiously blended strands of the feminine, the mischievous, and the petty in Horace Walpole's composition can blind no sane critic to the fact that he was a genius. One genius's opinion of another, if biassed, is generally interesting, and Walpole, though hardly a judge of Rowley's real merits (his remark that Chatterton's poems were ten thousand times more curious for not being old* disposes of him as a critic of *Rowley*; it is the mot of a bric-à-brac collector) can be said to have had a rational view of his correspondent's attainments, while regarding him as a dual personality. "He had generally genuine powers of poetry; often wit, and sometimes natural humour. . . . He was an instance that a complete genius and a complete rogue can be formed before a man is of age" he wrote to Mason (July 24, 1778); and to the Countess of Upper Ossory (July 4, 1785): "For Chatterton, he was a gigantic genius, and might have soared I know not whither. In the poems avowed for his is a line that Rowley nor all the monks in Christendom could or would have written, and which would startle them all for its depth of thought and comprehensive expression from a lad of eighteen:

Reason, a thorn in Revelation's side! [*The Defence*]"

Though this may say little for the critical powers of the writer,

* Letter, addressee unknown, March 4, 1777. *Suppt.*, Vol. III, p. 26.

it says something for his sincerity. His autograph marginalia in Dean Milles's *Rowley* were possibly intended for no eye but his own, or for his own primarily : take three of them !

p. 26.	*Dean Milles* :	The style of Chatterton never rises to the dignity of Rowley.
	Horace Walpole :	Not true.
p. 160.	*Dean Milles* :	It is not in the power of nature or genius to confer this knowledge.
	Horace Walpole :	Shakespeare is a contradiction to almost all this pedantic definition.
p. 161.	*Dean Milles* :	To the claim of originality is opposed that of a youth of the age of seventeen.
	Horace Walpole :	Was a monk of the most savage Period, who it is not in the least probable had ever seen a Greek Tragedy or a translation of one, more likely to light on simplicity and nature than a poetic youth ? Which has most prejudices to struggle with ?

"An owl mangling a poor dead nightingale " was Coleridge's word on the Dean of Exeter's lucubration* ; would he have taken back his word on Lord Orford, had these side-notes been put before him ?

Finally, to descend to a lower level of esteem, " Baron Otranto " paid " the young villain " the compliment of modernizing the Abbot John's verses. Here, in true *Town and Country Magazine* fashion, is the tête-à-tête :

ON KING RICHARD Ist.

Harte of Lyone ! shake thie Sworde,
Bare thie mortheynge steinede honde :
Quace whol Armies to the Queede,
Worke thie Wylle yn burlie bronde.
Barons here on bankers-browded,

AN ODE MODERNIZED FROM CHATTERTON.

Heart of lion, shake thy sword ;
Bare thy slaughter-stained hand :
Chase whole armies with thy word,
Work thy will in holy land.

Barons here, with coursers prancing,
Boldly breast the pagan host :

* Cottle, *Early Recollections*, Vol. I, p. 36.

Fyghte yn Furres gaynste the Cale ;
Whilest thou ynne thonderynge Armes,
Warriketh whole Cyttyes bale.
Harte of lyon ! Sound the Beme !
Sounde ytte ynto inner Londes,
Feare flies sportinge ynne the Cleembe,
Inne thie Banner Terror stondes—5766B, f. 45.*

See, thy thund'ring arms advancing
See, they quail ! their city's lost !

Heart of lion, sound the trumpet !
Sound the charge to farmost lands !
Fear flies sporting o'er the combat ;
In thy banner terror stands.
Lord Orford's Works,
Vol. IV, p. 235.

* John, Abbot of St. Augustine's, is the first witness to a grant (No. 1 in Mr. Bickley's *Calendar*) by Robert de Berkeleia at the instance of William "Capellanus" of the church of St. Mary de Redecliue, to the said church, of a well called Rugewelle, with a proviso that the hospital of St. John the Baptist, Radecliue, shall have a pipe " ad mensuram vnius mediocris pollicis" for carrying water to their building, *s.d.* [1207 (?)]. This Barrett quotes (*History of Bristol*, p. 594), and the charter is endorsed in his hand, "John Abbot of St. Augustin Witness." Its provenance was doubtless "The Treasury" ; and thence Chatterton may be judged to have taken his "Abbot John." See also Milles, p. 189, against which, in his copy, Walpole has made the note, " Why shd Chatterton not have seen the deed ? " That Chatterton knew of its contents is indicated by "Fytz-Hardyinge's" speech in *The Parlyamente of Sprytes* :

The pypes maie sounde and bubble forth mie name,
And tellen what on Radclefte syde I dyd.

Dugdale (*Baron.*, I, p. 351) tells us that Robert Fitzharding's descendants assumed the surname of Berkley ; and see Leland, *Collect.*, I, p. 621 (ed. 1715).

Chapter XIII

ELEGIES

So far as is known, Chatterton made no further effort to obtain patronage, other than that of a magazine, for his antiques. On July 20, 1769, he wrote to a relation at Salisbury, a Mr. Stephens, styled breeches-maker by his later biographers, who about a year previously had called on the family at Bristol, when the poet talked about nothing else but Rowley's poems.* As a sprightly piece of mocking arrogance, he never produced another letter to match it. The torn original can be seen in the Bristol Library (the missing words are supplied from the edition of 1803),† and on the back Walpole's polite answer of March 28 is transcribed in his hand.

"Corn Street Bristol July 20. 1769.

Sir,

If you think Vanity is the Dictator of the following Lines, you will not do me Justice. No, Sir, it is only the desire of proving myself worthy your Correspondence, has induced me to write. My partial Friends flatter me, with giving me a little uncommon share of Abilitys, tis Mr Stephens alone whose good Sense disdains Flattery whom I must appeal to. It is a Maxim with me [that compliments of friends] are more dangerous than railing of Enemys. You m[ay inquire, if you please, for the] Town and Country Magazines, wherein all signed D.B. and Asaphides [are m]ine. The Pieces called Saxon‡

* Milles, p. 8.

† Vol. III, p. 410.

‡ The "Saxon" pieces are :—Letter on Saxon Tinctures, Feb. 4. *T. and C.M.*, Feb., 1769. Signed D.B.

Ethelgar, March 4. *T. and C.M.*, March, 1769. D.B.

Kenrick, *T. and C.M.*, April, 1769. D.B.

Cerdick, May 20. *T. and C.M.*, May, 1769. D.B.

Saxon Atchievements, May 15, a letter with woodcut illustration, the hint taken from Kip's plate of curiosities in Gibson's *Camden* (ed. 1695, p. 697). *Ibid.*, D.B.

are originally and totally the product of my [M]use tho I should think it a greater Merit to be able to translate Saxon. As the s[d] Magazine is by far the best of its Kind I shall have some Pieces in it every Month and if I vary from my said Signatures, will give you notice thereof. Having some curious Anecdotes of Paintings and Painters I sent them to M[r] Walpole Author of the Anecdotes of Painting, Historic Doubts, and other Pieces well known in the learned World. (His answer I make bold to send you.) Hence began a Literary Correspondence, which ended as most such do. I differed with him in the age of a MS he insists upon his superior Talents, which is no proof of that Superiority. We possibly may publickly engage in one of the periodical Publications tho' I know not who will give the onsett: of my proceedings in this Affair I shall make bold to acquaint you. My next Correspondent of Note is Dodsley, whose Collection of modern and antique Poems are in every Library. In this City my principal Acquaintance are—M[r.] Barrett, now writing at a vast expence An Ancient & modern History of Bristol a task more difficult than the cleansing the Augean Stable many have attempted but none succeeded in it, yet will this Work when finished please not only my fellow-Citizens, but all the World—M[r] Catcott, Author of that excellent Treatise on the Deluge and other Pieces to enumerate which would Argue a supposition you was not acquainted with the Literary World. To the studys of these Gentlemen I am always admitted,* and they are not below asking my Advice in any matters of Antiquity. I have made a very curious Collection of Coins and Antiques. As I cannot afford to have a gold Cabinet to keep them in I commonly give them to those who can. If you can pick up any Roman Saxon English coins or other Antiques, even a sight of them would highly oblige me. When you quarter your Arms, in the Mullet say Or a Fess Vert by the name of Chatterton. I trace your Family from Fitz-Stephen Son of Stephen Earl of Aumerle in 1095 Son of Odo Earl of Bloys & Lord of Holderness.

I am y[r] very hble Serv[t]

THO[s] CHATTERTON"

Godred Crovan, Aug. 10. *T. and C.M.*, Aug. 1769. D.B.
The Hirlas (1), Nov. 17. *T. and C.M.*, Nov. 1769. D.B.
The Hirlas (2), Jan. 3, 1770. *T. and C.M.*, Suppl., 1769. D.B.
Suggested by Evan Evans's *Specimens of the Welsh Bards* (1764), Poem I.
Gorthmund. *T. and C.M.*, Sept., 1770. D.B.
Cutholf. *Lady's Magazine*, Jan., 1771, signed Asaphides.

* "I have observed before that Chatterton was by no means of an open or ingenuous disposition, and his so positively asserting he had free access to my late good and learned brother's study, is a glaring proof of it, for even his own family were excluded that privilege." George Catcott to Dr. Glynn, May 29, 1793. But Chatterton may not be using "studys" in the sense of "rooms."

This was written before his letters were returned to him by Walpole, but nearly two months after the *Town and Country* had printed *Elinoure and Juga*,* which was modernized by "S.W.A., aged 16" in the June number. This version is generally supposed to be Chatterton's work, but Cottle (*Works*, III, p. 511, n.) gives it to a Westminster scholar unnamed. The young Bristolian was working up a Magazine connection, and by November, among the "Acknowledgments to our Correspondents" may be read "D.B. *of* Bristol's *Favours will be gladly received*." He could be said, then, to be enjoying his rising fame, but his real state of mind is divulged by a poor, but vehement, poem, dated in the MS. (5766B, f. 77, v.) "Aug. 12, '69," the same day as the fragmentary Burletta *Amphitryon*, out of which his London Burletta *The Revenge* was developed. Little office work can have been done at Corn Street on that Saturday.

ELEGY ON M[R] W[M] SMITH.

Ascend my Muse on Sorrows sable Plume
Let the soft number meet the swelling Sigh
With Laureated Chaplets deck the tomb,
The bloodstaind Tomb where Smith & Comfort lie.

I lov'd him with a brothers ardent love,
Beyond the Love which tendrest brothers bear,
Tho savage kindred bosoms cannot move,
Friendship shall deck his Urn & pay the tear.

Despis'd: an alien to thy Fathers breast,
Thy ready Services repaid with Hate
By Brother Father Sisters, all distrest:
They push'd thee on to Death they urgd thy Fate.

Ye Callous breasted Brutes in human form
Have you not often boldly wishd him dead?
Hes gone ere yet his Fire of man was warm
O may his Crying blood be on your head

+ Happily mistaken having since heard
from good Authority it is Peter

This is, on the face of it, the first cry of real grief from a person aged sixteen and three-quarters, who has learnt that his best

* Reprinted from the *T. and C.M.*, unsigned, in the June 8 issue of *The Weekly Magazine* (Edinburgh). Scotland was aware of Rowley in Chatterton's lifetime.

friend is dead, and by his own hand. When the lines are written, he learns that the suicide is not his friend but that friend's brother; and he lets them stand, adding an explanatory note, as he did to the elegy on Mr. Barrett's father-in-law, in January. The extravagance of the language justifies the inference that he is identifying himself with the object of his grief, and in

Thy ready Services repaid with Hate

the discredited correspondent of Horace Walpole is manifest.

But a letter in the *Gentleman's Magazine* for Dec., 1838, by Richard Smith the younger, nephew of William and Peter, tells us more. He says: "Peter Smith was another *bon compagnon*, and incurred by his irregularities with Chatterton, the displeasure of his father, so that he was most severely lectured; of which such was the effect, that he retired to his chamber, and set to his associate an example that was but too soon followed.* Richard Smith [the "brother" of l. 11 of the *Elegy*] was my father, a gentleman of great abilities, who died the senior surgeon of the Bristol Infirmary in 1791. At first Chatterton and himself were good friends, but the unhappy affair of his brother Peter estranged them, as Mr. Smith attributed the wretched catastrophe to congenial opinions in morals and religion. . . . William Bradford Smith was Chatterton's bosom friend."

Now this Richard Smith the elder, who broke with Chatterton (who was some seven years his junior), is, if family gossip is to be trusted, an instance of a wild, high-spirited Bristol youth who made good early, and found the road to happiness and prosperity; so that a glance at his life till his twenty-sixth year will hardly come as a digression here. He was the son of one Richard Smith, a brewer, Tory, and President of the Dolphin Society in 1766, and Elizabeth Bradford, and was born in 1745† in a house with a freestone front opposite the Baptist

* Temple Church Register gives Peter Smith's baptism as July 21, 1748, and his burial "in a vault in ye chansell" Aug. 14, 1769. Interest may have secured this favour for his remains; his brother Richard married the vicar's sister, Augusta Catcott, at this church on Sept. 23, 1771.

† Bapt. July 26, 1745 (*Temple Register*). See also G. Munro Smith, *History of the Bristol Royal Infirmary*, Appendix B., p. 460, *sqq*.

Chapel in the Counterslip, at no great distance from the bottom of Redcliff Street and Bristol Bridge. At nine he was sent to the Grammar School in Christmas Street, and before Sept., 1758, to the Grammar School at Warminster, his father's native place, from which he ran away " with a small bundle of clothes," and was found, several days after, working with some masons who were building a house. This long afterwards went among his friends by the name of " the house that Dick built." He was then sent to Winchester, where according to one of his school-fellows* he was very idle and " pretty regularly flogged." He took part in punch-drinking to the Pretender in an ale-house, fights with the townsfolk, and orchard and farmyard raids. He had, however, a good voice, and was selected to chant the graces " Benedic nobis, Domine " and " Benedictus sit Deus in donis Suis" at a College Visitation. He left Winchester on May 29, 1762, and on Sept. 9 was " bound " to John Townsend, surgeon to the Infirmary, then practising in Broad Street, with a side door in Cider House Passage, not far from one of the bookshops which Chatterton frequented, who makes Townsend speak of his apprentice in *The Exhibition* (May, 1770) as :

> that thing of flatulence and noise,
> Whose surgery is but a heap of toys,
> That thing once slave to me, who boasts he's got
> A treatise on the matrix piping hot.

Other testimony speaks of Townsend's own surgery as " calculated to strike terror into all beholders," and as resembling the torture room of the Spanish Inquisition. There were difficulties, but Dick overcame them. For instance, in the third year of his indentures he came home one night just at the point of eleven. Townsend had locked the door, and growled at him to " go about his business, that no one should come in after eleven." " Sir," said the apprentice, " the quarter-boys are

* George Wilkins, afterwards rector of St. Michael's. Both were scholars of Winchester, Wilkins being 21st and last name on the Election Roll of 1757 (16 Sept., 1757–2 Oct., 1761), and Richard Smith, " de Temple Bristoliæ," 11th on that of 1758 (9 Sept., 1758–20 May, 1762). Wilkins matriculated at St. John's College, Oxford, 2 Dec., 1761, aged 18 ; his testimony, if correctly reported, is that of a typical senior boy.

now going, and Christ Church has not finished striking." "My clock has struck," returned the master, "and that's enough for me." Dick Smith called the watchman and bade him take notice he was at the door before the Parish Clock had struck. The next morning Townsend would neither receive him, nor return any portion of his fees. A lawsuit followed; the apprentice pleaded for himself, got a verdict; and, it is said, remained on good terms with the surgeon afterwards. In *The Exhibition*, after Barrett's speech, Chatterton writes:

He ended, and a murmur of applause
Drop'd from each carcase-butcher's wither'd jaws,
From all but Townsend, always Townsend had
A soul for opposition good or bad.
Of contrarieties and whims compos'd
He never in a friendly treaty clos'd.

Richard Smith next did his midwifery course at the Borough Hospital, London, and was once stopped by the lecturer as he was "going to a labour" with a scarlet cloak and a sword, as was then the mode with students. Dr. Colin Mackenzie pointed out the "impropriety of a man's going armed to bring a being into the world, when such a weapon could only serve to send a person out of it." In 1768 he returned to Bristol, and began practice at his father's house at Counterslip; and on Aug. 11, a year and a day before Chatterton's elegy, inspired by his brother's suicide, he was elected Surgeon to St. Peter's Hospital, being not long turned of twenty-three. Thirteen months after the poet's tragedy, he married George Catcott's sister, Augusta; he had moved to the last house in Charlotte Street, at the corner of Queen Square, opposite the gable end of the Mansion House, early that year.

His sister Elizabeth told her nephew that "when Brother Dick came from London, patients poured in upon him so fast that his father gave him a sort of Cock-loft in the Brewery, which he fitted up as a Surgery; and up there used to mount men and women, gentle and simple, such a cataband that there was no end to them." Such was the brother of Peter and William Smith.

In *The Exhibition*, where Chatterton falls foul of the Bristol clergy and doctors, Richard Smith is deputed " in his accent great " to bring the culprit to the bar, and, in the course of a long speech, represented as boasting of amorous excesses :

Hot in the furnace of a youthful fire ;

At the end, his speech is thus characterized :

Empty and without meaning he display'd
His sire's loquacity in his array'd.

This, no doubt, was the poet's revenge on the young man, better educated than himself (whose name was blown about Bristol as a popular healer), for ceasing to know him.

Aug. 12, 1769, is one of the crucial dates for us in Chatterton's short life, for it affords the first indication of his reckless and embittered spirit. Whether he was or was not well acquainted with Peter Smith is of small consequence in view of this extract from a letter of the Rev. D. Debat to Lort : " He [i.e. Catcott, probably George] said there was a juvenile society all the years you mentioned, composed of such profligate youths, as may now probably all be dead or obliged to quit this city. One Wm. Smith was an intimate and is still living, but where to be found his relations know not. The last transaction I heard of him was selling one wife and marrying another."*

It is tempting but uncritical to assign to this period the three " discoorses " that make up *The merrie Tricks of Laymyngetowne*† "by Maystre John a Iscam," which, fragmentary in appearance, is complete according to its author's intention, and formed part of Rowley's " Emendals to Turgotte." We do not know when this fiction was given to Catcott except that it was " shortly after " the three *Eclogues* and *Goddwyn*, and, if we did, we should not be much nearer discovering the date of its composition. Its sole basis in reality is a carved

* Aug. 2, 1778. 11457.

† The MS. of " Discoorse " I and II (to " pensmen sayes ") is in British Museum Add. 24891 (*A Discoorse on Brystowe by Thos Rowleie*), that of " Discoorse " II (from " Home newes well let alone ") and III (to l. 22), in the Bristol Museum, presented to the city by Richard Smith, Jun., in 1838 ; the whole was first printed in the Cambridge edition of 1842.

coffin lid representing a priest, with his head on a pillow or cushion and hands joined in prayer, inscribed under the feet in Gothic letters JOHES: LAMINGTON (doubtless for Lauington), which was removed from the demolished chapel of the Holy Ghost in Redcliff Churchyard while Chatterton was at Colston's, and is still to be seen in the south aisle of the church. A general pardon from Henry IV or V (1402 or 1415) to John Lavyngton and Thomas Godefelewe, Chaplains of St. Mary Redclyve, with the great seal, in green wax, is numbered 218 in Mr. Bickley's *Calendar*, and bears an endorsement in Barrett's hand. This may very well be one of the parchments which had "large seals of green wax with the impression of a bishop in his robes" of which Mrs. Chatterton spoke, *teste* Palmer (Apr. 1773).

Chatterton's myth is as follows*: "Johannes Laymyngetone Esquier" was employed by Henry VI, when prince, in "honourable servitudes," but wasted a hundred marks a year, and then took to evil courses. He was condemned to death, pardoned and banished, but stayed in England and played his former knaveries. Taken again, he was again condemned, and pardoned on condition of rebuilding Simon de Burton's church; but he was slow, and the King threatened death unless he was faster. So he pulled down Burton's church, leaving only "the chamber of oure Ladie, ybuylden by his Cognamesakes Lamyngton," saying "Aftertymes maie think ytt mie warke, if I dyen before this is edone"; thinking to possess the "renome" of another, who was a good man and a priest. But having pulled down, he was in no haste to build up, complaining that no large stone was to be got. When the stone was got, he built and pulled down till the Wars of the Roses began; then he left the church, a wall three ells in height and three in length, so slight, that a man might push it down with ease. Joining the Yorkists, he was slain in battle, and buried in the common barrow, "a meet Dome for so great a Ungrace." The church lay in ruins till William Canynge rebuilt the same, not where Burton's stood, but on a new place, employing not one stone that was not his own.

* It can be read in Milles, pp. 180-1, where there is an engraving of the stone. The MS. is Add. 24891. Chatterton spells the name in at least eight ways;

In *The Parlyamente of Sprytes* Lanyngetonne's says:

Lette alle mie faultes bee buried ynne the grave* ;
Alle obloquyes be rotted wythe mie duste ;
Lette him fyrst carpen that no wemmes[1] have :
'Tys paste mannes nature for to bee aie juste—

[1] Faults.

Chatterton, too, was buried in a common barrow, far from Redcliff.

The three " Discoorses," 121 lines in all, deal solely with the " banished man" motif. The first is a soliloquy ; the hero's servant Ralph has but one line. The sentence of exile has just been pronounced, but Laymyngetowne will stand his ground. He is represented as a swashbuckling Timon of Bristol, who loves his city, though she has flattered and sucked him dry, so that he has become " a bloudie foe in arms, gaynst all mankynde," and as freebooter and pirate, though not in foreign lands, will make "cheating Londons pryde to digner Bristowe rolle." The sentiments betray Chatterton's desire to leave Bristol and make his fortune in the capital ; and I hardly think (though this is perilous ground) that—I will *not* say before his written encounters with Dodsley and Walpole—but before his experience of the manners of the local literati he would have written quite in this manner :

Unfaiful Cockneies-dogs ! your God is gayne.
When in your towne I spent my greete estate,
What crowdes of citts came flockyng to my trayne,
What shoals of tradesmenne eaten from my plate.
My name was alwaies Laymyngeton the greate ;
But whan my wealth was gone, ye kennd mee not,
I stood in warde, ye laughed at mie fate,
Nor cared if Laymyngeton the Great did rotte.†
But know, ye curriedowes,[1] yee shall soon feele
I've got experience now, altho' I bought it weele.

[1] Flatterers.

* Let all his faults sleep in his mournful chest. Nash, *Piers Penniless. ap*. Cibber, *Lives*, I, p. 348.

† The MS., which is neatly written, reads :
I stood in warde, he laughed at mie Fate—
Not cared if Laymyngeton the Great did rotte
Was not this done wilfully, to suggest miscopying from an original ?

The second " Discoorse " is a dialogue between two " cockneies," Philpot and Walworth,* creditors of Laymyngetowne, concerning the selling of his goods ; here some Latin tags from *Cato's Disticbes* and the *Sentences of Publilius Syrus*, for many years, with Lilly's Grammar, the first Latin primer. Tyrwhitt, who perceived this, has a good remark, "Though I do not suppose that he ever made any great progress in that language, I really think that he might have attained to these quotations."† The same is true of the quotation from St. Cyprian in Rowley's Sermon.

In the third " Discoorse " the hero speaks a little over two stanzas, one of which describes the dangers of the sea, to one Robynne, who has thought on all and is resolved to go and " bee a pick-hatch of the wave " :

Goods I have none, and lyfe I do disdayne
I'll be a victoar, or I'll break mie gallynge chayne.

Such is the spirit of the piece. I deal with it here because it reflects Chatterton's mind at this juncture ; but all the available evidence goes to show that it must come earlier in the story.

The summer of '69 was not without events at Bristol. In June, at the Cock Inn, St. James's Churchyard, a party of forty-five Wilkesites had sat down to a feast of 45 fowls, a 45 lb. ham, 45 lb. rump of beef, 45 cabbages, 45 cucumbers, 45 loaves, 45 tarts, 45 gallons of ale, 45 glasses of brandy, and 45 papers of tobacco ; and, a month later, at the Guildhall, Henry Cruger, Thomas Cary's master, presided when a strongly worded protest was made against the Commons' action in declaring the member for Middlesex, now a prisoner in the King's Bench, unseated.‡

In the first week of July, Powell the actor, on whom Chatterton had in 1768 written some lines, closing :

Though great thy praises for thy scenic art,
We love thee for the virtues of thy heart.§

* Sir John Philpot and Sir William Walworth, respectively citizen and Mayor of London, from Stow (ed. 1615), pp. 281, 289.

† *Vindication*, p. 208.

‡ Latimer, *Bristol in the Eighteenth Century*, p. 391.

§ *European Magazine*, Dec., 1791.

had died at 7 o'clock, just before the play began, in his lodging next to the theatre (the ends of King Street being hung with chains during his illness) and was buried in the Cathedral. He is lamented in *Clifton*.* Charles Holland, the poet's favourite actor, was billed to play Richard III at the time of his death. The lines on *him* in the *Town and Country* are dated July 21. On the 10th of that month he had played Romeo, and on the 19th Macbeth. He also died before the year was out.† In writing on actors Chatterton was following Churchill's lead.

"Ended Sat: Even 30 Sept 1769" is the date appended to the "tedious lengthening" *Journal 6th*, addressed to Baker, which is written in four parallel columns on both sides of a large sheet of paper 19½ by 15 inches, possibly a wrapper (5766B, f. 55), with very few stops. This, barring one of the Hoyland effusions, is the first of Chatterton's poems in which the orthodox Church is attacked. The manner of the first 258 lines, Hudibrastics, is that of Prior's *Alma*, which Churchill had affected in *The Ghost* (1762) and *The Duellist* (1763); and the poet rambles on from a dialogue between a dean and a rector, where Burgum, who has sent the latter a ticket, is held up to admiration:

That Man you mention answers Dean
Creates in Priests of Sense the Spleen
His Souls as open as his hand
Virtue distrest may both Command
That ragged Virtue is a Whore
I always beat her from my Door
But Burgum gives & giving shews
His Honor leads him by the Nose
Ah! how unlike the Church divine
Whose feble lights on mountains shine;
And being placd so near the Sky—
Are lost to every human Eye.
His Luminarys shine around
Like Stars in this Cimmerian ground.

* Henry Jones, the Bricklayer Poet (1721–1770), had published a poem in two cantos with this title at Bristol in 1757. In Chatterton's, as well as the scenic beauties, the Cenotaph to the officers of the 79th Regiment, who fell in the Indian campaign of 1759-60, is celebrated.

† Some verses "On the death of Mr. Holland" (*London Magazine*, Dec., 1769), signed *Bristoliensis*, may be Chatterton's.

to a discussion on love (Chapter VIII, p. 93). Then, " changing for a Shandeyan stile," i.e. that of a Burletta (he calls it " Ode ") made up of recitatives and airs, with a swinging skill that looks forward to Coleridge's *The Rash Conjuror* and the *Ingoldsby Legends,* he draws a vigorous Hogarthian design of the Penn Street services, to show that he is as indifferent to Nonconformity as to the Establishment :

In his wooden Pallace jumping
Tearing sweating bawling thumping
Repent Repent Repent
The mighty Whitefield cries
Oblique Lightning in his Eyes
Or die and be damnd all around
The long-eard Rabble grunt in dismal sound
Repent Repent Repent
Each Concave Mouth replies
The Comet of Gospel the Lanthorn of Light
Is rising and shining
Like Candles at Night
He shakes his Ears
He jumps he stares
Hark he's whining
The shorthand Saints prepare to write
And high they mount their Ears

In one section of this rhapsody the preacher descends to the infernal regions, indicating that Chatterton has London, rather than Bristol, in mind :

Well in I walk'd and what dye think*
Instead of Sulphur fire and Stink
Twas like a Masquerade
All Grandeur all Parade
Here stood an Amphitheatre
There stood the small Haymarket house
With Devil Actors very clever
Who without blacking did Othello†

* The two preceding lines, as given in all the editions,
We have here a stranger just come in,
A brother from the triple tree,
contain a misreading of the MS., which has " Broker " unmistakably.

† Just above we have, " Out comes Mr. Porter Devil." Cf. " I'll devil-porter it no further." *Macbeth,* Act II, Sc. 3.

And truly a huge horned Fellow
Told me he hop'd I would endeavor
    To learn a Part and get a Souse[1]
For Pleasure was the Business there.

[1] "Sous, a *French* penny." Kersey.

Shelley may have known this piece; the third part of *Peter Bell the third* (1819), beginning with the famous "Hell is a city much like London," is written in the same mood; his eleventh stanza:

Thrusting, toiling, wailing, moiling,
Frowning, preaching—such a riot!
Each with never-ceasing labour,
Whilst he thinks he cheats his neighbour,
  Cheating his own heart of quiet.

is not unlike

Now he raves like brindled Cat
    Now tis Thunder
        Rowling
        Growling
        Rumbling
        Grumbling
Noise and Nonsense Jest and Blunder
    Now he chats of this and that

The last few days of October seem to have been very fruitful in verse. A small oblong vellum-bound notebook, whose cover bears Chatterton's name and rude heraldic drawings, among the Phœnix collection in the Library of Columbia University, contains, with one new poem, the original text of five poems which the editors of 1803 printed from transcripts supplied by Thomas Hill, to whom the MS. then belonged. Mr. T. O. Mabbott, who first made this fact public,* has shown that three of these poems, "Interest, thou universal god of men" (Oct. 27), "Far from the reach of critics and reviews" (Oct. 27, 28), and "Hervenis, harping on the sacred text" (Sunday, Oct. 29) are complete poems, not "fragments," as entitled by Southey and Cottle, and he has noted the variations from the printed text. The Stanton Drew *Elegy* is dated "27 [Oct.],"

* A new poem by Thomas Chatterton, *Modern Language Notes*, xxxix, 4, April, 1924.

and the early version of the *Elegy on Thomas Phillips* " 28 [Oct.]." The new poem, through which the poet has drawn his pen, as a mark of cancellation, follows this. Mr. Mabbott gives it thus—the subject is quite certainly the pupil-teacher of Colston's :

ELEGY OCT 29.

Muse ascend on Sorrows sable Plume
Soar like the heavn ascending Wing
Of the great Bard you sing
With twisted Wreath of silverd Yew
Deck the laureld Poets Tomb,
The bard whose total Soul was God.

[Sickness prevents the grateful Lay
I End unknowing what to say
To speak his worth ; my feeble Lyre
Cannot to such a Pitch aspire.]

The first and fifth lines hark back to the first and third of the Aug. 12 *Elegy*; but there is another bond between the two poems, the impetuosity with which they were composed. In William Smith's case the death was contradicted after the elegy was written ; in Thomas Phillips's case, this little poem, as the lines to Clayfield, and the elegy proper, in its first form, must have been written while the death was expected. The poet, not unlike the professional necrologist, had his work ready beforehand, and was frank besides ;

Sickness prevents the grateful Lay

and (in the lines to Clayfield*) :

O may he live, and useless be the strain

prove, even if we did not have T. Stephenson's letter to Clayfield of Nov. 1 announcing Phillips's death " ab[t] one o'clock " that morning, that the end had not yet come.

* The version of these lines in 5766 B. (f. 56) differs from the printed version in having variants in the sixth and penultimate lines, and six new lines, an invitation to Clayfield to correct the Phillips *Elegy*, to take the place of ll. 11-18 inclusive ; these are all printed by Skeat (Vol. I, p. 57, *n*.). It is dated " Monday Evng. Oct[r]. 30–69." On the verso are the first three stanzas of the elegy, with the variant " Soul rack Muse" in l. 10, and half the first line of a fourth, " Say Soul unsullied."

At the same time, unless manners have altogether changed, I imagine Michael Clayfield, distiller (or tobacconist, as he is styled in the 1775 Directory) of 71 Castle Street, Bristol, to have been a little perturbed by the arrival of the Redcliff youth's elegy, with the poetical query " Say, is he mansion'd in his native spheres " before the fatal news had arrived from Fairford. This, it is supposed, was Chatterton's introduction to his notice.

Although the postscript " To the Reader " of the first version states :

> Observe in favour to an hobbling strain
> Neat as Exported from the Parent brain
> Are each & evry Couplet I have pend :
> But little labord & I never mend.

the poet subjected the *Elegy to the Memory of Mr. Thomas Phillips, of Fairford*, to considerable revision ; and there are certainly three versions of it :

1. That in the Columbia MS. (*Works*, Vol. I, p. 214), in three parts : (*a*) Invocation to the Muse, three heroic couplets ; (*b*) the elegy, in thirty-three quatrains ; (*c*) the postscript.
2. That in 5766B, ff. 57, 58, thirty quatrains, of which those beginning " Immortal shadow " (XIII) and " Black Melancholy " (XX) are scratched through. This is addressed, on the back of the second leaf, " To Anthony Gavin Smock Alley Dublin." There are two exclamation marks, one full stop, and one dash in the whole ; no other punctuation, and no marginal comments.
3. That in the *Town and Country Magazine* (*Suppl.* 1769). Twenty-eight quatrains dated Dec. 5 (*Works*, Vol. I, p. 22).

This and the *African Eclogues* are generally considered the best of the non-Rowley poems ; and, though the description of the seasons cannot compare with the Minstrels' Song in *Ælla*, the personification of Winter is beautiful enough. In the earlier (the longer) version Chatterton, writing at the end of October, begins with " golden autumn wreathed in rip'ned corn," expunges as " unconnected " the quatrain opening " With rustling sound the yellow foliage flies," goes on to

Spring, Summer, Winter, and returns to " The rough October." In the British Museum MS. some variants, including "The rough November," are introduced. In the magazine version he takes the seasons in their proper order, beginning with Spring, and returns to " The rough November," Winter's place being unchanged:

> Pale rugged Winter bending o'er his tread
> His grizzled hair bedropt with icy dew;
> His eyes, a dusky light congealed and dead,
> His robe, a tinge of bright ethereal blue.
>
> His train a motley'd sanguine sable cloud,
> He limps along the russet dreary[1] moor,
> Whilst rising whirlwinds, blasting keen and loud
> Roll[2] the white surges to the sounding shore.*

[1] Dreary russet. 5766 B. [2] Rolls. 5766 B.

Later in the piece the quatrain

> Wet with the dew the yellow hawthorns bow;
> The rustic whistles thro' the echoing cave,[3]
> Far o'er the lea the breathing cattle low;
> And the full Avon lifts the darkned wave.

[3] Altered to " Dell." 5766 B.

is marked " expunged as too flowery for grief " in the Columbia MS. The last line of this quatrain gave some trouble; the British Museum MS. shows that "And the swoln Severn rolls the dashing Wave" was first written, crossed through, and "The clamors of the flying Screech Owl swell" substituted. In the magazine version it stands as "And the shrill shriekings of the screech-owl swell," a savage onomatopoeia, and the first line has the reading " yellow'd."

The autumnal stanza and the line " But see! the sick'ned glare of day retires."† mildly anticipate

> The breath of winter comes from far away,
> And the sick west continually bereaves
> Of some gold tinge,

* " How do the s's hiss in the last couplet, as the sense demands! How large and open the vowel sounds!" Hon. Roden Noel, *Essays on Poets and Poetry* (1886), p. 38.

† " Lamp of Day," 5766 B., scratched through, nothing substituted.

in *Isabella*; and the last line of the vivacious vignette of

> Fancy, whose various figure-tinctured vest
> Was ever changing to a different hue;
> Her head, with varied bays and flowerets drest,
> Her eyes, two spangles of the morning dew.

foreshadows

> A blooming girl, whose hair was wet
> With points of morning dew.

in *The Two April Mornings.*

Every lover of Shelley is moved at the end of *Adonais* by the poet's prescience of his fate in the Bay of Spezia:

> The breath whose might I have invoked in song
> Descends on me, &c.

So here, in a quatrain marked "Too plain" in the Columbia MS., crossed through in 5766B,* and omitted altogether from the magazine version, is a deathbed picture foreboding the top room in Brooke Street:

> Immortal shadow of my much-loved friend!
> Clothed in thy native virtue meet my soul,
> When on the fatal bed, my passions bend,
> And curb my floods of anguish as they roll.

Oct. 30 is the date on the MS. of *The Constabiliad* (5766B, f. 63), a tediously brutal picture of a free fight at a vestry dinner. This was developed into the political piece, *The Consuliad* (Jan. 4, 1770), printed in the *Freeholder's Magazine* for January, and brought the author 10/6 from Fell, the editor. It is a mock-heroic *Battle of Hastings*:

> With straining Arms uprears a Loin of Veal
> In these degenerate days for three a Meal
> In days of old as various Writers say
> An Alderman or Priest eat three a Day . . .

* Which reads:

> meet my Shade
> When this Mortality has found its End
> O bear me where a real Friendship's made

The quatrain before has the unforgettable line, "Farewell the Lawrel now I grasp the Yew."

He thunders senseless to the sandy Ground
Prest with the Steamy Load that ooz'd around . . .
The fight is gen'ral Fowl repulses fowl
The Victors Thunder and the vanquished howl
Here flows a Torrent of resistless Beer
Here broken Tarts with bloody Wounds appear.

The *Elegy*, "Joyless I seek the solitary shade," dated Nov. 17, three days before his seventeenth birthday, and printed without signature in the *Town and Country* for that month, probably derives from Phillips's death; it contains the bold personification " Self-frighted Fear," the beautiful arrangement of v and s sounds in

The distant forest, and the dark'ned wave
  Of the swol'n Avon ravishes my sight.

and the tragic evening landscape :

A dreary stillness broods o'er all the vale,
  The clouded Moon emits a feeble glare ;
Joyless I seek the darkling hill and dale,
  Where'er I wander Sorrow still is there.

CHAPTER XIV

RELIGION AND THE TEMPLE VICAR

The clock strikes eight ; the taper dully shines ;
Farewell, my Muse, nor think of further lines :
Nine leaves, and in two hours, or something odd,
Shut up the book ; it is enough by God.*

THE dates of the poems mentioned in the last chapter, in one of which the above lines occur, give an idea of the haste with which Chatterton composed when the fit was on him, or the moon at full, leading many of the early disbelievers in his genius to doubt that it was physically possible for him to write Rowley in the time at his disposal. Add his prose essays and his love epistles, and it will be plain that he taxed his mind and emotions to some purpose, even when Rowley was laid by.

Moreover he was now of " the age when all become geniuses for a season ".† He had studied assiduously since he was ten, and Nature was now loosening the bonds of his personality, to expose it far more intimately to the world around him. Few, clever or stupid, pass through adolescence without some mental and physical disquiet ; for him that period was to prove fatal :

* Cf. The clock strikes Eight ! No friendly feet explore
The gloomy passage to the mourner's door ;
In vain your well-known step does Fancy hear,
In vain, I wait, no Jefferies comes here,
The darkling Lamp emits a dying light
And sympathizes with me as I write.
E. Collins, *Miscellanies* (1762), p. 34.

and The bell strikes *One*. We take no note of time
But from its loss.
Young, *Night* I, quoted in *T. and C.M.* (Oct., 1769)
in " A letter consisting entirely of monosyllables in answer to an elaborate epistle full of sesquipedalia verba," a criticism of the *Night Thoughts*.

† Stanley Hall, *Adolescence*. Vol. I, p. 187.

he was dead nine months and five days after his seventeenth birthday. From this point the familiar sentence in the preface of the great poem dedicated to his memory is of peculiar application to this life: "The imagination of a boy is healthy, and the mature imagination of a man is healthy; but there is a space of life between, in which the soul is in a ferment, the character undecided, the way of life uncertain, the ambition thick-sighted." Poetry, a spiritual issue, depends not on bodily vicissitudes. The only symptom of extreme youth in the Rowley Poems is their barbarous verbal medium, which goes far to exclude even the finest of them from the category of perfect compositions. Had their author lived to subdue his pride, the work of reducing them to normal English, *while preserving their magical and primitive beauty*, remained for him. This, surely, a reader has a right to observe, and, as surely, that the work was for no hand but Chatterton's : yet the simplicity, the strength, ay, the very crudeness, of their themes, and the vivid empassioned treatment, these are no accidents of boyhood, but the essentials of inspired art.

Most folk recognize that a curiosity about life and a scepticism about religion are concomitants of adolescence. At this time, too, an average youth of parts is apt to fall in the way of one or more older persons, who encourage him to think for himself (or, rather, as they think) and, maybe, to question accepted beliefs. Such an one, I take it, was Michael Clayfield,* friend of Chatterton's poetical mentor Thomas Phillips, who comes into his life, as we have seen, on Phillips's death, and to whom, in his "Will", the poet leaves "the sincerest thanks my gratitude can give."

Mrs. Newton's testimony for this epoch is as follows:

"Mr Barrett lent him many books on surgery and I beleive he bought many more as I remember to have packt them up to send to him when in London and no demand was ever made for them. About this time he wrote several saterical poems, one in the papers on Mr. Catcot's putting the pewter plates in St. Nicholas tower. He began to be universally known among the young men. He had

* Barrett calls Clayfield "a worthy, generous man." *History of Bristol*, p. 646.

many cap acquaintance but I am confident but few intimates. At about 17 he became acquainted with Mr. Clayfield disstiller in Castle-street, who lent him many books on astronomy. Mr. Cator* likewise assisted him with books on that subject, from thence he applyd himself to that study."†

Clayfield, who kept his books in a glass case, told Dr. Glynn that he only lent Chatterton Martin's *Philosophical Grammar* and one volume of Martin's *Philosophy*; the latter, he thought, was merely borrowed for the verses prefixed.‡ A glance at Benjamin Martin's *Young Gentleman's and Lady's Philosophy* (1755), Vol. I, shows that Chatterton really borrowed the book for the plate of the "Copernican or Solar System" at p. 23, which enabled him to write his fine poem, *The Copernican System* (Dec. 23, 1769)—"The sun revolving on his axis turns"—printed in the *Town and Country* for that month.§ The epithets here are used with Popelike precision:

Now the just Ballance weighs his equal force,
The slimy Serpent swelters in his course;
The sabled Archer clouds his languid face;
The Goat, with tempests, urges on his race;
Now in the Wat'rer his faint beams appear,
And the cold Fishes end the circling year.

but the imagery was to serve him for a still nobler flight. It is possible that he may have cast his horoscope about this time, for Ebenezer Sibly, at the end of the century, who quotes this poem in his *Illustration of the Occult Sciences* (Vol. II, p. 811), says: "I have many reasons to believe that his knowledge of the uranical part of Astronomy had enabled him to foresee, by his own geniture, the evils he had to combat, and the fatal termination of a life, which his own folly had rendered

* Henry Kater of St. Thomas, Sugar Baker, married Ann Collins, of Redcliff, by licence 25 Jan. 1777. *Redcliff Register*.

† *L. and M.*, p. 145.

‡ Bryant, *Obs.*, p. 533.

§ Dix (*Life*, p. 63), on the authority of a Mr. Corser of Totterdown, has an anecdote which may well be true, of Chatterton reading an unfinished treatise on astronomy, which he had just written, and intended to make the subject of a poem, in Temple Churchyard on a Sunday morning when the bells were chiming for service, shortly before the publication of this poem. Temple Churchyard had a double row of trees in 1768.

insupportable." His father, the schoolmaster, had been superstitiously inclined, and was not Dryden a believer in Astrology ?*

To return to Clayfield: he had heard Chatterton speak of Rowley, but not often, and heard him read Milton and Thomson; "but he seemed more fond of his own verses; and these turned chiefly on satire." Chatterton, he thought, was of too volatile a turn to read much, and had not abilities for such a performance as Rowley. "Sir," quoth this friend, "take my word for it, they were no more his composition than mine." Clayfield was, I fancy, something of a freethinker at this time, though President of the Tory Dolphin Society, a Colstonian institution, in 1782; and one of the first-fruits of the intimacy was the *Epistle to the Reverend Mr. Catcott* (Dec. 16).

George Catcott's eldest brother, Alexander,† a Winchester and Wadham man, Vicar of Temple or Holy Cross from July, 1766, to his death, thirteen years later, has been denied the credit due to his intelligence by the poet's biographers. Not only did he refuse to believe that there were ever "any papers of the poetical or historical kind" in Canynges' chest,‡ but he frequently told George that Chatterton was capable of writing anything attributed to Rowley, and that he was upon the whole the most extraordinary genius he ever met with.§ Chatterton was not with him more than five, or at most six, times in his life, and never more than an hour together‖; and Dean Milles, Rowleian as he was, wrote to George Catcott (March 6, 1779): "I am told that your brother observed when Chatterton came to him that he turned his quick and penetrating eye on whatever book lay open before him in order to build a forgery." One of Lort's memoranda confirms this: "Mr. A. Catcott

* See Appendix B., Chatterton's horoscope.

† Born Nov. 2, 1725, at the Grammar School; admitted scholar at Winchester 8 Sept., 1739 (5th name); Matric. Wadham Coll. 24 Oct., 1744; B.A. 1748; Lecturer at St. John's Church, Bristol; Chaplain to the Earl of Buchan; d. June 18, 1779.

‡ George Catcott to Dean Milles (Feb. 22, 1781); George adds sagely, "tho' we well knew there were both."

§ The same to the same (Sept. 11, 1780); confirmed by Dean Milles: "Your late good brother . . . used frequently to say that Chatterton was equal to anything." (Aug. 30, 1780).

‖ The same to the same (Apr. 8, 1779).

told me that, his suspicions being awakened, Chatterton was aware of this, and much on his guard; he had a large full gray eye, the most penetrating Mr. Catcott had ever seen, and the eye of his understanding seemed no less penetrating. He would catch hints and intelligence from short conversations, which he would afterwards work up, and improve, and cover in such a manner that an attentive and suspicious person only could trace them back to the source from whence he derived them."*

A mind at last, among these credulous Bristolians, but unfortunately it had no taste for poetry. An anonymous MS. essay on the Rowley Controversy, dated 30 March, 1783, and attributed to Samuel Seyer,† states that George fully believed that if Alexander had survived him he would have burnt the poems instead of publishing them. The writer goes on to say that at this period A. Catcott had "relinquish'd all works of taste" and confined himself to works of divinity alone, and these were constantly read to him, as from a weakness in his eyes he was unable to continue at his book for any length of time. He continually reproved his brother for his attention to these poems, which, he said, took up too much of his time; he should be "employed on more serious subjects." An anecdote relative to his putting a copy of Barclay's *Ship of Fools* (ed. 1509 or 1570) in the kitchen to be torn up for domestic purposes is given in the same place and repeated by Wilson (p. 192).

Nevertheless the Vicar was a man of learning and industry, who had followed his father, the headmaster of the Grammar School, in his dedication to the Hutchinsonian philosophy, and like him, had written on it. His *Treatise on the Deluge*, published in 1761, had passed into a second edition, in 1768, and Chatterton's copy of it, enriched with poems in manuscript, is in the Bodleian Library.‡ The *Treatise* is an example of a class of work, common enough in its time, which sought to invent some system as a scientific basis for the Mosaic account

* 11457. See Gregory, *Life*, p. 180.

† 5199, in the Bristol Library, one of Richard Smith's MSS.

‡ MS. Eng. poet., e. 6. With two exceptions, these poems were first printed in the *Supplement* to the *Miscellanies* (1784).

of the Creation. Thomas Burnet's *Telluris Theoria Sacra* (1681) is the best remembered of these, but John Ray, John Woodward, William Whiston, and Benôit de Maillet, vied with John Hutchinson in contemporary esteem.* Alexander Catcott came a little later in the day ; he was an enthusiastic geologist, and liked to square his hobby with his calling. The printed volumes which he gave to the Bristol Library, and his MS. notebooks, leave on a mind fresh from his brother and Barrett the effect of a scholarly oasis in an uncritical desert. He has set down an "Encomium" on the study of fossils—"it contributes to health, gives no disturbance to anyone ; the greatest men have employed their talents this way," &c., and he left his "Fossilary," at which the poet pokes fun, to the city ; it stands to this day on the first floor (geological section) of the Bristol Museum, with its original contents.†

On November 6, a month and ten days before Chatterton addressed the *Epistle* to him, he went with the churchwardens

* See an article by G. R. Potter in *Modern Language Notes*, xxxix, June, 1924. One is reminded here of the "Father" in *Father and Son.*

† An extract from his will (March 24, 1778), further illustrates the assailable side of the Vicar : "I will also that that copy of the second edition of my Treatise on the Deluge which contains an extract of this my will respecting the disposal and preservation of the aforesaid fossils and books fairly written on the first loose leaves thereof and which contains some additions on the loose leaves at the end of the said book both which extracts and additions may be printed in if there should be any call for a third edition of the said book be always preserved open or visible on the lower shelf of the said Fossilary I will also that one of the keys of the aforesaid Fossilary be kept by the Librarian of the aforesaid Library for the time being for ever and that after the Fossilary and fossils are once placed therein and the key delivered to the present or any future Librarian (which I could humbly wish might be done by the hand of the Mayor or of one of the Aldermen of the said City) that the said Librarian give his word that he will not knowingly or wilfully permit any of the aforesaid fossils or papers to be taken away hurt or injured by any person whatsoever and that whensoever he should have occasion to shew the said fossils especially if it be to persons unknown to him he will take all possible care that the spectators do not transgress the Eighth Commandment (for curious persons make no scruple of stealing curiosities) I will also that the other key of the Fossilary be kept by the Chamberlain of the aforesaid City for the time being for ever and I request the favour of him that he would once or twice in the year when business may call him that way and he can conveniently spare the time visit the said Library and examine the state of the Fossilary and fossils just to see that everything be kept clean and neat and in particular that the above mentioned book with the extract of this part of my will be preserved in the place above appointed and that the inward curtains or blinds be drawn over the glass in the Fossilary."

P. C. C. Warburton, 293.

to view the spring head of Temple Pipe Water at Totterdown, and he was clearly as much interested in his church's reservoir as in its services. Of course, when he showed his treasures to the ladies, he enquired triumphantly whether the ammonites, &c., did not plainly prove a Deluge. The point about him, which the poet realized to the full, was that here in Bristol, among the clergy, was a brain with which he had the opportunity of crossing swords, while lavishing on him a Rowleian account of his church, still among its archives* (the Vicar gave the parchment "original" to Barrett, and it went with Dr. Glynn's bequest to the British Museum, 5766A, f. 9), and part of a Sermon on the Divinity of the Holy Spirit (see *Gentleman's Magazine*, Apr., May, 1782), for which Rowley was mainly indebted to one on the same subject by the Rev. Caleb Evans of Bristol (1766), tacking on to it a line of Greek to be found in a 1639 edition of St. Gregory of Nazianzus.† In a letter to Tyrwhitt of Feb. 22, 1777, and one to Dean Milles, of March 24, 1777, George Catcott expressed himself much perturbed at the omission of Rowley's Sermon before the poems, in Tyrwhitt's edition, as the piety of it would have proved that Chatterton did not write the latter.

The bachelor brothers, Alexander and George, lived together in the roomy parsonage,‡ still standing, close to the west door and leaning tower of Holy Cross ("Temple Church Pavement"), and my impression is that Martha Catcott, "the rose of virginity," kept house for them. It was William Bradford Smith

* See *Thomas Chatterton and the Vicar of Temple Church* [W. George]. 1888. The sexton of Temple Church, when showing me this relic, remarked that if Chatterton had remained in Bristol "they would have clapped him in irons." This might have been said in the eighteenth century.

† Chatterton, according to George Catcott, never gave the Vicar more than a fragment of the sermon because he did not want any more. George could not prevail on Chatterton either to give or sell *him* the rest of the sermon. Letter to Dean Milles. Apr. 8, 1779.

From George Catcott's letter to Milles, of Aug. 21, 1777, the Vicar seems also to have been given (in 1769) the Proclamation by Canynge and Rowley respecting disputes "concerning the Unity in Trinity" between the Prior of St. James and Johann a Milverton. *Works*, III, p. 307; the MS. is 5766 B. f. 30.

‡ John Wesley, who married a couple in this church on Sept. 5, 1785, stayed here and wrote two Latin hexameters on a pane of glass in one of the upper rooms, it is said; underneath which George Catcott has written two more, signed and dated 1770.

in the autumn of 1768 who told George (his future relative) about Tom Chatterton finding the old writings in Redcliff Church, and the tragedy of Peter Smith may have called attention to "the wild expences of a poet's brain." The writer of the MS. essay above cited says: "He [the Vicar] very soon found Chatterton was not a lad of veracity, and when he examined him concerning the account of the rebuilding Temple Church, he found him vague and evasive in his answers, and thinking him a lad of bad morals, declared he would have nothing more to say to him." At any rate we may be sure of this, that the *Epistle* was not written until Chatterton had taken full stock of the Rev. Alexander Catcott, whose acquaintance he had certainly made through the geologist's "wild antique and sputt'ring brother," at some date after the "Bridge" contribution to *Felix Farley*.

The model for this curious piece is possibly the Drydenian argumentative satire (e.g. *Religio Laici*), but Churchill has crept in and marred the Olympian tone somewhat. The poet jests at the literal interpretation of the Bible, after commenting on "These nice distinctions in the preaching trade" and doctors disagreeing, apropos of the Vicar's *Remarks on the second part of the Bishop of Clogher's Vindication* (1756), which was bound up with his copy of the *Treatise on the Deluge*:

Attentive search the Scriptures, and you'll find
What vulgar errors are with truths combin'd.
Your tortur'd truths, which Moses seemed to know,
He could not unto Inspiration owe;
But if from God one error you admit,
How dubious is the rest of Holy Writ!

The Vicar of Redcliff, Thomas Broughton, and Stephen Penny, a devotional accountant, are thrown into the scale with the author of the *Treatise*, and he proceeds:

Some may with seeming arguments dispense,
Tickling your vanity to wound your sense:
But Clayfield censures, and demonstrates too,
Your theory is certainly untrue;
On Reason and Newtonian rules he proves
How distant your machine from either moves.

But my objections may be reckon'd weak,
As nothing but my mother-tongue I speak ;
Else would I ask, by what immortal Pow'r
All Nature was dissolv'd as in an hour.*

Chatterton is neither an atheist, nor a pantheist, as the following lines show :

'Twas the Eternal's fiat, you reply ;
And who will give Eternity the lie ?
I own the awful truth, that God made all,
And by His fiat worlds and systems fall;
But study Nature ; not an atom there
Will unassisted by her powers appear.
The fiat, without agents, is, at best,
For priestcraft or for ignorance a vest.
Some fancy God is what we Nature call,
Being itself material, all in all ;
The fragments of the Deity we own,
Is vulgarly as various matter known.
No agents could assist Creation's birth :
We trample on our God, for God is Earth !

The implication is clear, he does not believe in a God who sets the world going and remains aloof, or in a God identical with Nature, but a God working endlessly through natural laws ; and this must be his meaning when, four months later, he leaves the Rev. Mr. Catcott some little of his freethinking, " that he may put on the spectacles of reason and see how vilely he is duped in believing the Scripture literally."

After this the poem becomes personal, an attack on " learning," i.e. intellectual snobbery, after an address to himself :

Restrain, O Muse, thy unaccomplish'd lines,
Fling not thy saucy satire at Divines ;
This single truth thy brother Bards must tell—
Thou hast one excellence, of railing well ;
But disputations are befitting those
Who settle Hebrew points, and scold in prose.

Henry Burgum, George Catcott's partner, is contrasted favourably with " rigid Christians," and worse, the visitors

* My view of the nature of Clayfield's influence on the poet is based on this passage.

to the sanctum are vignetted—women's praise plainly meant nothing to this poet :

> The Ladies are quite ravish'd as he tells
> The short adventures of the pretty shells ;
> Miss Biddy sickens to indulge her touch,
> Madam more prudent thinks 'twould seem too much.
> The doors fly open, instantly he draws
> The sparry lode[1], and—wonders of applause ;
> The full dress'd Lady sees with envying eye
> The sparkle of her di'mond pendants die ;
> Sage Natural Philosophers adore
> The fossil whimsys of the numerous store.

[1] Spelt "lood" in MS.

With one last stab at the petit maître, characterized elsewhere as "heavy with hereditary pride," the poem concludes:

> Where is the priestly soul of Catcott now ?
> See what a triumph sits upon his brow !
> And can the poor applause of things like these,
> Whose souls and sentiments are all disease,
> Raise little triumphs in a man like you,
> Catcott, the foremost of the Judging few ?

and the last four lines describe the Temple Vicar's "great brother" George emptying his pint and sputtering his decrees at Llewellin's pot-house by way of comparison.* *Après moi le déluge* is the note, truly.

A prose postscript of Dec. 20 vainly endeavours to palliate the effects of what has gone before : "Mr. Catcott will be pleased to observe that I admire many things in his learned Remarks : this Poem is an innocent Effort of Poetical Vengeance, as Mr. Catcott has done me the honor to criticise my Trifles. I have taken great Poetical Libertys, and what I dislike in Verse possibly deserves my approbation in the plain Prose of Truth.—The many Admirers of Mr. Catcott may, on Perusal of this, rank me as an Enemy : but I am indifferent in

* There was more than one MS. of the *Epistle* ; as the 1784 text mentions "Renounce" written over "You're a" in l. 240, and the Bodleian MS. has the latter only. The Bodleian MS. has very few stops, and hardly any at the ends of lines.

all things ; I value neither the Praise or Censure of the multitude."

This is not unlike what Blake wrote at the end of his annotated copy of Lavater's *Aphorisms* : " I hope no one will call what I have written cavilling because he may think my remarks of small consequence. For I write from the warmth of my heart," &c.* But Alexander Catcott was not his brother, he could not see a compliment where ridicule was intended ; and though the satire on the pewterer in a December issue of *Felix Farley* made Chatterton talked of through the winter of '69 (we can infer this from his sister's notice of that poem), it is pretty generally admitted that he lost the Vicar's favour, if he ever had it, by the *Epistle*.† His marginal comments include " Hum the 1st " on the first page of the dedication in the *Remarks* and " Hum the last " on page 416 of the *Treatise*.‡

Of the poems on the fly-leaves, two are in blank verse, the only examples of the measure in his acknowledged work ; both shed light on his state of mind at this time.

SENTIMENT

Since we can die but once, what matters it,
If rope or garter, poison, pistol, sword,
Slow-wasting sickness or the sudden burst
Of valve arterial in the noble parts,
Curtail the miserys of human life ?
Though varied is the Cause, the Effect's the same :
All to one common Dissolution tends.

There is but one stop in the MS., at the end. The lines may possibly have been intended as a counterblast to the opening of John Pomfret's *A Prospect of Death :*

* *Writings of William Blake*, Nonesuch Press, Vol. II., p. 116.

† In the account of two Bristolian oddities in the *T. and C. M.* for June, 1771, we read " The eldest, Sandy Catskin, formerly made his appearance in the literary world, he having endeavoured to prove, with great learning and profound judgment, what may be known full as well by reading the seventh and eighth chapters of Genesis." He is here described as being imposed on with part of an old brass kettle, which, he declares, " has the sound, colour, taste and consistency of the true Corinthian brass," by one of the colliers and miners, "who often taste of his liberality for supplying him with minerals, &c."

‡ At the bottom of p. 17 "(Preliminaries)," Sig., C., he has added "hatterton" and a heraldic shield, or, a fesse [vert].

Since we can die but once, and after death
Our state no alteration knows ; &c

a poem of sufficient practical use in its day to be reprinted at the end of a book of dying men's admonitions called *Fair Warnings to a Careless World*.* The reviewer of the *Supplement to Chatterton*'s *Miscellanies* in the *Gentleman's Magazine* for Nov., 1784, remarks " The following 'Sentiment' dated '1769' will shew that his exit was then premeditated, and that, like a true disciple of Hume, he argued much in the same absurd manner." But it is doubtful if Hume's suppressed *Essay on Suicide* can have come his way, though its arguments were broadcast.

The other blank verse piece† runs thus :

If wishing for the mystic Joys of Love
Is by eternal Justice deem'd a fault
Tell me ye Pow'rs what Woman's Innocent.
O how extensive is the Power of God !
Conceiv'd in Sin we Sin by God's decree
And for such forc'd iniquity are damnd
For who can say his Nature is his own !
Who formed the Mind and who instill'd the Soul ;
Who gave us Passions which we must obey
But the Eternal Justice of the God.
And for such forc'd iniquity we're damnd.

There is a similar thought in Fitzgerald's *Omar* :

What ! out of senseless Nothing to provoke
A conscious Something to resent the yoke
  Of unpermitted Pleasure, under pain
Of Everlasting Penalties, if broke !

O Thou, who didst with pitfall and with gin
Beset the Road I was to wander in,
  Thou wilt not with Predestined Evil round
Enmesh, and then impute my Fall to Sin !‡

Michael Lort speaks of the piece as "some lines seemingly a

* By Josiah Woodward, D.D. (3rd ed. 1717).
† First printed in the *Times Literary Supplement*, March 2, 1922.
‡ Rubáiyát, lxxviii, lxxx (Golden Treasury ed. p. 53). I owe this parallel to my friend Mr. Robin Flower.

paraphrase on those of Ld. Brooke quoted by Abp. Tillotson, ' O wearisome condition of humanity '," i.e. the famous chorus of priests in *Mustapha*.

Chatterton, though not a Deist or Socinian, was certainly heterodox. The MS. of the *Romance of the Knight*, in the de Bergham copybook, after

> May all thy sins from Heaven forgiveness find!
> May not thy body's crimes affect thy mind!

closes with four hitherto unprinted lines of comment, in red ink,

> (For howsoever Casuists disagree
> It is a Tenett Orthodox with me
> That Crimes which merely from the blood arise
> Are held no Crimes in the Immortal's eyes)*

How he reconciled this tenet, which apparently justifies rape, homicide, or any crime short of premeditated murder, and perhaps even that, with belief in a personal Deity, will be seen in the next chapter.

For he undoubtedly believed in God (i.e. a Person, superior to human beings, by Whom they are pardoned and redeemed) at all periods of his life. In *The Defence*, a poem addressed to William Smith, recommending tolerance in religious matters, and copied on to a fly-leaf in A. Catcott's *Treatise*, he writes:

> I own a God, immortal, boundless, wise.
> Who bid our glory of creation rise;
> Who form'd His varied likeness in mankind,
> Centring His many wonders in the mind;
> Who saw religion a fantastic night,
> But gave us reason to obtain the light.

Some lines on Immortality,† written down extempore in the presence of the same friend, and betraying the influence of Young's *Night VII*, end:

* This poem, it will be remembered, describes the rescue of a damsel from a discourteous knight, the theme of the wood scene in *Ælla*.

† First printed in John Evans's *Chronological Outline of the History of Bristol*. (1824), p. 288. Chatterton kept the original, and gave Smith a transcript; the date is stated as "some time previous to his departure from home."

Oh, may our portion in that world above,
Eternal Fountain of eternal Love,
Be crown'd with peace, that bids the sinner live.
With praise to Him who only can forgive—
Blot out the stains and errors of our youth ;
Whose smile is mercy, and whose word is truth.

The accent of sincerity here, through the formal phrasing of his age, cannot be mistaken ; nor can it in the thirty-two lines of unknown date called *The Resignation*, which were shown to Croft by the poet's mother* :

O God, whose thunder shakes the sky ;
Whose eye this atom globe surveys ;
To thee, my only rock, I fly,
Thy mercy in thy justice praise. . . .

If in this bosom aught but thee
Incroaching sought a boundless sway ;
Omniscience could the danger see,
And mercy look the cause away.

Then why, my soul, dost thou complain,
Why drooping seek the dark recess ?
Shake off the melancholy chain,
For God created all to bless.

Again an echo of *Night VII*† :

Heaven is all love ; all joy in giving joy :
It never had created but to bless.
ll. 877, 8.

While in Bristol, he carried in his pocket, so it would appear from the folds in the MS. (5766B, f. 51), a creed of his own composition. This he mounted on a bit of parchment (nearly six and a half inches square) like more than one of the Rowley drawings and the bill from Rowley's executors to George Catcott, cutting away a piece for the paper's endorsement, the title, to be seen. He brought it to George Catcott one day in 1769.‡

* *L .and M.*, p. 157.
† The writer of the monosyllabic *Letter* in the *T. and C. M.* for Oct. 1769, quotes twice from this *Night* on the subject of pride : " The proud run up and down in quest of eyes." and " Parts push on to *pride*, and *pride* to *shame*."
‡ Letter-book, p. 19.

hat God being incomprehensible ; it is not required of 51
us, to know the mysterys of the Trinity &c &c &c &c

That it matters not whether a Man is a Pagan Turk
Jew or Christian if he acts according to the Religion he professes

hat if a man leads a good moral Life he is a
Christian

hat the Stage is the best School of Morality
and
The Church of Rome (some Tricks of Priestcraft
excepted) is certainly the true Church

T. Chatterton

sh Museum.

CHATTERTON'S CREED.

face p. 316.

The first article appears in an unantiquated proclamation by Canynge and Rowley respecting the disputes between the Prior of St. James and Johann a Milverton (i.e. John Milverton, a historical person, *teste Magna Britannia*, 1717, Vol. IV, p. 742*) thus: "As What is above human Comprehension can neither be proved nor disproved by human Arguments, it is vain for the Will of Man to pretend to unfolde the dark Covering of the Ark of the Trinity, lest like those of Old he be stricken dead, and his Reason lost by breathing in an Element too fine and subtle for the gross Nature." For the last article the poet's love of mediæval pageantry may be partially responsible†; but the Shakespearean performances in King Street, coupled with dissatisfaction at the professors of formal religion in Bristol (which was to reach its height in the satires of his last year), is beyond doubt at the back of the article about the stage:

THE ARTICLES OF THE BELIEF OF ME THOMAS CHATTERTON

That God being incomprehensible it is not required of us to know the mysterys of the Trinity &c &c &c &c
That it matters not whether a Man is a Pagan Turk Jew or Christian if he acts according to the Religion he professes.
That if a man leads a good moral Life he is a Christian
That the Stage is the best School of Morality
and
That The Church of Rome (some Tricks of Priestcraft excepted) is certainly the true Church

T: CHATTERTON

* Chatterton no doubt read of him in *Weever*, p. 438.

† Into the tale *One Hour after Marriage* Chatterton has introduced a curious passage on Transubstantiation. A Protestant clergyman says "Look ye, here d'ye see; here's a piece of dough, well; I kneaded it up, well; I bake it into bread, very well; and will any man say that in his conscience it is not dough now under the alteration of bread?" "True," replied Eugenius; "but let us reason candidly on the matter: Do not the Roman catholics allow the sacrament to be the real presence, under the appearance of bread? Why, Lord, how you talk! Why d'ye see? Why egad, I believe you are a rank *papish*: but I am sure I am right!" *T. and C.M., Suppl.*, 1770.
Chatterton's attitude to the Roman Church is not unlike Charles Meryon's. Dr. Foley said of the etcher: "Il penchait vers le Catholicisme, mais il avait horreur de sa discipline, le vrai motif était son ancienneté." Meryon's own words are "Mais il faudrait donner trop de peine pour le suivre. Cela ne m'empêche pas de l'aimer." Geffroy, *Charles Meryon* (1926) pp. 119, 120.

Chapter XV

BREAKING AWAY

The New Year, 1770, opened with a love poem, *The Advice*, to Maria Rumsey (Jan. 1), which included an attack on Jack Fowler. Two days later, while perhaps still under the spell of jealousy, he copied the first of his three *African Eclogues* on to the end leaves of the *Treatise on the Deluge*; the last six lines can still be read on the inside of the back cover, the rest of the poem having been torn out. The initial inspiration must have come from William Collins,* but the colours are more glaring and warmth more torrid than in the exquisite *Persian Eclogues*. In *Heccar and Gaira*, a negro chief, whose wife and children have been captured by slave dealers while he was hunting, aments his agony to a fellow chief, "King of warring Archers," who promises to join in his vengeance. Sir Sidney Lee has remarked of this poem, and of *Narva and Mored*, that in them Chatterton employs recondite proper names with the sonorous effect of which only the greatest poets have the mastery.†

> Cawna, o Cawna! deck'd in sable charms,
> What distant region holds thee from my arms?
> Cawna, the pride of Afric's sultry vales,
> Soft as the cooling murmur of the gales,
> Majestic as the many-colour'd snake,
> Trailing his glories through the blossom'd brake:

* The *Town and Country* for Oct. 1769 contains "Observations on the manners &c. of the Africans" from a Bristol correspondent unnamed (Oct. 10), in which the dance, the macaws, and the calamus are mentioned. Thistlethwaite imitated Chatterton in *Bambo and Giffar* (*Everyman's Magazine*, Sept. 1771), signed S.E.

† Preface, p. x. Methuen's Standard edition.

Black as the glossy rocks where Eascal roars
Foaming thro' sandy wastes to Jaghir's shores;
Swift as the arrow, hasting to the breast,
Was Cawna, the companion of my rest.
The sun sat low'ring in the Western sky,
The swelling tempest spread around the eye;
Upon my Cawna's bosom I reclin'd,
Catching the breathing whispers of the wind:
Swift from the wood a prowling tiger came,
Dreadful his voice, his eyes a glowing flame;
I bent the bow, the never-erring dart
Pierc'd his rough armour, but escap'd his heart;
He fled, tho' wounded, to a distant waste,
I urg'd the furious flight with fatal haste;
He fell, he dy'd—spent in the fiery toil,
I strip'd his carcase of the furry spoil,
And, as the varied spangles met my eye,
"On this," I cried, "shall my lov'd Cawna lie."

It was sent to the newly started *Court and City Magazine* of which Chatterton wrote, in *The Art of Puffing* (July 22, 1770):

The "Town and Country" struck a lucky hit,
Was novel, sentimental, full of wit:
Aping her walk, the same success to find,
The "Court and City" hobbles far behind.

There it appeared, in the second (February) number, signed C, and dated Bristol, Dec. 12, 1769. I think this poem may have haunted Coleridge's imagination during the composition of *Lewti, or the Circassian Love-Chaunt* (1798), where, as one of the original drafts (Add. MS. 35343, f. 2) shows, the name first chosen was "Cora."

The same day (Jan. 3) is the date appended to the letter signed "Astrea Brokage," where a Bristol boarding-school Miss invites the editor of the *Town and Country* to decide whether, in the event of her marrying her father's choice Bob Barter, the buck, she is obliged to hate "a young author who has read more than Magliabechi, and wrote more love-letters than Ovid." The self-portrait continues: "is continually invoking the nine to describe me; but he never pays a compliment to my person, without a concomitant one to my understanding. Though I have ten thousand pounds, he never mentions marriage* ; and when it is forced into his discourse, rails against it most religiously: but he intrigues like a Jesuit to be made happy with a tête-à-tête conversation ; or a walk in the wood ; but, thank my stars ! I have always courageously denied. He has sentiment in his common conversation ; and is reported to have ruined three young ladies of fortune."†

The next day, Jan. 4, appears on *The Consuliad*, the recast of *The Constabiliad*, where he has turned a local squib into a satire on the Grafton ministry, with the Earl of Sandwich, " Jemmy Twitcher," as the central figure. The poem, in both its versions, contains a reference to his magical interests, in the person of the lawyer who stays the tumult :

Tyro, for necromancy far renown'd,
A greater adept than Agrippa found.

We have reached the period of the long satirical poems and the political letters. His impetuous headstrong nature, angry for fame, had been embittered by Walpole's snub and the sparse rewards—though it is uniformly agreed that he was not mercenary—of the local patrons. It seems clear that at one section of his Bristol life he dressed fashionably,‡ and the paper, and possibly the postage (for the cost of a letter, single sheet, to the metropolis was fourpence in those days§), for the contributions, with which he loaded the London press, must have been items of expense, besides printed books and notebooks; and he was earning nothing. From his schooldays he had shown a tendency to satire, the specific, though not invariable, mark of a young poet. " Memorandum," notes John Aubrey speaking of the author of *Hudibras*, " satyricall witts disoblige whom they converse with, &c., consequently make to themselves many enemies and few friends, and this was his manner and

* Sometimes indeed it is a middle state,
Neither supremely blest nor deeply curst ;
A stagnant pool of life, a dream of fate :
In my opinion, of all states the worst.
To a friend, on his intended marriage.

† *T. and C. M.*, Jan. 1770.

‡ Southey, letter to John Britton, Nov. 4, 1810, in Bristol Museum.

§ *ex inf.* G. H. G. Smith, Esq., G.P.O.

case."* Rowley apart, his environment stimulated him mainly to poetic reprisals, and his friend Cary gives him credit for abusing without blackmailing, having Thistlethwaite, it may be, in view:

Sharp-visag'd satire own'd him as her lord
  Exclusive of her hand-maid in her train,
Ill-nature—curst attendant of the board
  Of those who stigmatize mankind for gain.

Martha Catcott's "sad wag of a boy" was probably the kindest word Bristol could find for him; Broderip, the organist of Redcliff (d. 1779), to whom (Jan. 25, 1769) he had addressed a flattering poem in *Felix Farley*, had turned him out of the organ loft for talking too much†; Barrett was advising him to stick to his desk, though fate had ordained that he should write; George Catcott, whose hero was Charles the Martyr, could hardly fail to take him to task for his Wilkesian principles; while he was lucky if the vicars of Redcliff and Holy Temple regarded him as no worse monster than a Deist. On Redcliff Hill plenty of advice was going, we may be sure; "the dear unhappy boy had faults enough I saw with concern" his sister could write eighteen years later.‡ Both she and Mrs. Chatterton, who supported him—not to mention the grandmother who lived with them—must have pointed out that a due decorum better befitted the lawyer's apprentice, who would be a free man on July 1, 1774, than "darting lightnings from his

* *Lives of Eminent Men* (ed. 1813, Vol. II., p. 264.)

† Ah, blame me not, Broderip, if mounted aloft,
  I chatter and spoil the dull air.

A Song to Mr. G. Catcott, 1769.

Lort was told that Broderip, being disturbed whilst he was playing by some boys in the organ loft, turned them all out, and that Chatterton was among the number. The poem in *F.F.J.*, which is signed "Chatterton Asaphides" (11063 f. 109), affords an example of his alternate praise and abuse of individuals; he writes there:

"Through diapason's solemn key
Sage melancholy does convey
  Her precepts to mankind."

but, in *Kew Gardens*, contrasting Broderip unfavourably with Allen:

"Sacred to sleep, in superstitious key
Dull doleful diapasons die away.

"On Mr. Broderip's excellent performance on the organ," may of course be by John Lockstone (Asaphides), but I hardly think so. See Appendix C.

‡ *L. and M.*, p. 146.

vengeful eye"; and the favourite uncle, Richard Phillips, the sexton, to whom the corner house (1 Colston's Parade) had been let by the Vestry in 1765,* may have added his injunctions to theirs. Might not someone have even said: "Think, Tommy, of what good Mr. Walpole wrote to you"? Conjectures, no doubt; but the young impatient soul, goaded by its maturing body, was beginning to find not only environment, but existence, a torment, and to excogitate means, even physical, of release.

Peter Smith's suicide gives a date for the introduction of this motif, but a letter in *Felix Farley's Journal* of Dec. 3, 1768, signed "T," has a bearing on it. Beginning "The frequency of Self Murder naturally leads me to consider from what cause they proceed; and I think that upon a little Reflection we shall find it to be generally disappointed Pride. Pride seems to be the remote cause, even of those self-murders that are reputed to proceed from Lunacy."—it ends "To reason with people under the influence of this ridiculous and extravagant Pride would be utterly hopeless; for it is a species of madness, and if it can be cured at all, it must be either by contempt or ridicule." The object of this quotation is to suggest that the method of cure put forward by "T", whoever he was, may actually have been tried on the attorney's clerk by those who knew something of him and read *Felix Farley.*

Die Leiden des jungen Werthers was not published till 1774 (English translation, 1779), and Wertherism is scarcely in point here; for this is an English life. Chatterton's pride, which had become spleen by the time he reached London, if not before, was indeed nothing strange in a century which tolerated duelling; but his externals, at least, were familiar to the ordinary Georgian observer. The reader is referred to an anonymous pamphlet of 1748, *An earnest appeal to Passionate People, wherein the Rise, Progress, and Consequence of that unhappy Disposition of Mind are fully displayed.* The section in point is where it is argued that the disposition, whose chief source is "Pride and Self-conceit," is less excusable in high life, but more dangerous in low life: "How many Instances must

* *Redcliff Vestry Book,* No. 1. Minute of Aug. 22, 1765.

occur to the Reader, of Tradesmen, Mechanicks, and Publicans, who have fretted themselves out of a flourishing Trade, and scolded themselves into a Jail! Whereas, if they had put a reasonable Restraint upon their Tempers, they might have lived and died in Plenty and Reputation" (p. 40). This must be exactly how many contemporary ex-Colston lads, and others* who were making good in their several spheres, judged of their more gifted, but less amenable, schoolmate. Moreover, Chatterton was not the only young man, turned of seventeen, in Bristol or out of it, whose poetry was appearing in London periodicals, though truly he might be the most ambitious to be known. Very well for him to write:

> The tail-bud 'prentice rubs his hands and grins,
> Ready to laugh before the tale begins:

but was not he a 'prentice still? The Juvenile Club, Lort tells us, were "all Patriots,"† but, we can tell ourselves, they were not all passionate.

It was the political crisis that gave the first, the fatal, turn to this acrimonious mood of self-assertion. Junius's "Address to the King" had appeared in the *Public Advertiser* for Dec. 19, 1769, the days before Wilkes's release were being eagerly counted by his supporters, and on Jan. 28 the Duke of Grafton resigned the Premiership. Edmunds, editor of the *Middlesex Journal*, had on New Year's Day sworn an affidavit that he would not declare the name of any person or persons who sent papers to the publications in which he was concerned. Chatterton, who, if Thistlethwaite is to be trusted, had written letters to several booksellers in London, who made him liberal offers of assistance and employment if he would settle there,‡ and—it is pretty certain—was planning his emancipation from Lambert's office, celebrated February by a satirical elegy bearing the name of the month§ (enlarged from one called

* Capel was one; (Bryant, *Obs.* p. 523) he "might have been very intimate, but the young man's pride disgusted him."

† 11457.

‡ Milles, p. 460.

§ *February* was not his first satirical elegy. "Haste, haste, ye solemn messengers of night," which ends "For—Lady Betty's tabby cat is dead" (Apr. 4, 1769) had appeared in the *T. and C. M.* for that month, signed Asaphides. Both were reprinted in *The Weekly Magazine* (Edinburgh), for May 15, 1769, and March 15, 1770, which contained "the essence of all the magazines . . . printed in Great Britain."

"Elegy on the demise of a Great Genius," 5766B, f. 78, "the pension'd muse of Johnson," taking the place of a nonentity, one Laurence) for the *Town and Country*, and a letter *To the Duke of Grafton*, dated Feb. 16, for the *Middlesex Journal* (Feb. 24), signed *Decimus*, accusing him, *inter alia*, of being the "pack-ass" of Bute. Nothing can have been more consoling to the "slave" than this elevation to the status of an anti-ministerial writer, unknown, but dictating to the country.

For some reason, which psychologists can perhaps determine, though afire to have his name blown about, not a single printed contribution by him stands signed with it. "J. F—r" and "J. T—t—w—e" are familiar Bristolian signatures in the magazines of the period, and, often enough, the skeleton surnames resolve themselves into "Fowler" and "Thistlethwaite"; but this author, even after breaking his indentures, seldom seems to have advanced nearer his surname than the inital C (T.C. were also the initials of his friend Cary), and, when not anonymous, rejoiced in a plurality of pseudonyms. It may be that, conscious of his genius, he wished to give posterity the trouble of looking for him, but that explanation is not wholly satisfying. The theory of an "inferiority complex" has recently been argued by E. P. Ellinger.*

At any rate there is no doubt about the identity of *Decimus*, for his pocket-book, still preserved at Bristol, gives in his handwriting the titles of some of his political letters: other signatures used in this connection were *Probus*, *Libertas*, *A Briton*, and *The Moderator*, according to that witness.

The political is the last literary phase of Chatterton, and perseveres to within ten days of his death. I think it was, for him, the happiest form of spiritual relief, when Rowley was set aside, though it has no value for us beyond that of a tiresome curiosity. *Junius* is hardly read to-day, except by a historian; what room then can there be for a mere shadow of that shade? But Chatterton, it must be remembered, was not just a poet, but a *writer*; writing was his natural expression, and his hand never seems to have tired. Political hackwork would not only bring in money; his ungovernable fury against the world in general—his "one excellence, of railing well"—could there

* *Thomas Chatterton . . . to which is added "The Exhibition"* (1930).

find almost perfect vent in attacks on dignitaries whom he had never seen. England would not hear the voice of *Rowley;* that of *Decimus* she would, and should, obey.*

His chief activity between February and April appears to have been the composition of *Resignation* and *Kew Gardens*† ; the latter, according to Dr. Gregory,‡ was transmitted to Edmunds at 73 Shoe Lane in different packets. Lort and Gregory say the poem was above thirteen hundred lines ; what we have is 1092 lines. At the bottom of the first packet, which contained about 300 lines, was a postscript in Chatterton's hand : " Mr. Edmunds will send the author, Thomas Chatterton, twenty of the Journals, in which the above poem (which I shall continue) shall appear, by the machine, if he thinks proper to put it in ; the money shall be paid to his orders." The signature was "Decimus, March 19, 1770," Lort says. The second part, commencing " Hail Inspiration " (? line 263), about 250 lines, was dated March 28, and concluded : " I catch the pen and publish what I think " (l. 1092) ; and the third, characterized by Lort as " much ridicule on Bp. Newton and his prophecies," concluded : "Men will not bear the ridicule of boys" (l. 984). The *Middlesex Journal* did not print the poem.§

* Not long ago, a solicitor's clerk of seventeen, born in the shadow of a cathedral, whose father, a music master, had died when he was seven, was tried for sending letters of terrorism, signed " A British Communist," to titled and wealthy people (and copies of them to several newspapers), threatening to kidnap their sons, unless money were paid to some charitable institution. The style of these letters was by no means undistinguished. A prison doctor found that the youth had been encouraged to believe himself " exceptionally talented," and still felt a certain satisfaction at having created a stir in the world. It is not suggested that here was a second Chatterton, but that adolescent vanity played its part in both cases ; and the parallel seems to me as forcible, in regard to this epoch of the poet's career, as is Masson's of James McBey (the Aberdeenshire idiot, who formed a strong affection for the bell in the ruined church of Ruthven, which he called " wow ") in regard to his absorbing passion for St. Mary Redcliff. (*Chatterton, A Biography*, ed. 1899, p. 43).

† Composed, respectively, after Jan. 28, 1770 (Duke of Grafton's resignation) and, in part, after Jan. 29, 1770. (" If Musgrave could not prove it, how can I ? " l. 676. Dr. Samuel Musgrave's examination for having sold the peace of 1762 took place in the Commons on that date) ; ll. 247-262 of *Kew Gardens* are repeated, with slight changes, from the *Epistle to the Rev. Mr. Catcott*, ll. 213-228.

‡ *Life*, p. 77. Lort's notes are in B.11063.

§ The first 376 lines appear, without title-page, as an undated pamphlet of sixteen pages, headed " Supplement to Chatterton's Miscellanies, Kew Gardens " ; this was probably printed off as the first item in the *Supplement* (1784), and then cancelled; the sig. is B, in fours. The poem as we have it

It will be convenient to discuss this work, with its variant *The Whore of Babylon*, and *Resignation* (252 lines of which appeared in the *Freeholder's Magazine* for April, and 158 more in the May number) in the same place, with some remarks on the obligations to Churchill, which go perilously near to robbing these pieces of independent value.

Kew Gardens (the title is in scoffing emulation of the bricklayer poet, Henry Jones*) is most generously defined in Dr. Gregory's words as "a satire on the Princess Dowager of Wales, Lord Bute, and their Friends in London and Bristol, but particularly on those in Bristol who had distinguished themselves in favour of the Ministry."† Chatterton's position is simply the "patriotic" one—that George III's mother, backed by Bute, and Bute's satellites, is ruining and enslaving England. Bristol, as the second city in the Kingdom, reflects everything that passes in the capital; hence the justification for exploiting private spleen in the sketches of local personages.

As the poetic ally of Wilkes and the popular party, he was starring himself as a new Charles Churchill (who had died in 1764); and Churchill's influence on Chatterton's satire is generally admitted by biographers, though nowhere, so far as I am aware, examined. There are three bare references to his name in Sir Daniel Wilson's very full work, and it is omitted from the index of Ingram's; but the entire tone, style, and even topics of the pieces under notice are taken over from him; and the influence can, I verily believe, be rated as high as this: that, one passage only excluded, they contain nothing, save the Bristol vignettes, the immediately topical allusions, such as change of ministry, and the mentions of himself as the *boy* satirist, that does not derive from Churchill, whose poems are

was first printed by Dix (1837), but there are only 120 lines in this version which are not included in the undated publication, and in *The Whore of Babylon* (*Works* Vol. I, p. 159).

* *Kew Garden; A Poem in Two Cantos.* 1767. Chatterton characterizes this blank verse effort as

Where cabbages, exotic'ly divine,
Were tagg'd in feet and measur'd with a line.

One of Jones's lines is

Banana next, sustaining plant, behold.

† *Life*, p. 77.

characterized by Hazlitt as "strong, coarse, and full of an air of hardened assurance."*

And first, take the much quoted passage from *The Whore of Babylon*:

†Damned narrow notions! tending to disgrace
The boasted Reason of the Human Race.
Bristol may keep her prudent Maxims still,
But know, my saving Friends, I never will.
The Composition of my Soul is made
Too great for servile, avaricious Trade:
When raving in the Lunacy of Ink
I catch the Pen, and publish what I think.

This occurs also in *Kew Gardens*, with "notions which disgrace" in the first line, and the couplet

Since all my vices magnified are here,
She cannot paint me worse than I appear,

in place of the "The composition of my soul," &c. Now the denunciation of Prudence is the burden of Churchill's *Night* (1762), where it is declared to be synonymous with hypocrisy, though "of old a sacred term":

Would'st thou, my son, be wise and virtuous deem'd,
By all mankind, a prodigy esteem'd?
Be this thy rule; be what men *prudent* call,
Prudence, almighty Prudence, gives thee all.
Keep up appearances, there lies the test,
The world will give thee credit for the rest.
Outward be fair, however foul within;
Sin if thou wilt, but then in secret sin.
This maxim's into common favour grown,
Vice is no longer vice, unless 'tis known.

and the point urged on his companion, Robert Lloyd, to whom *Night* is addressed, is that whatever follies we commit we should not be at pains to conceal. "Prudent" comes into almost every poem of Churchill's with this ironical meaning:

* *On the English Poets*, Lecture VI.
† Mean narrow maxims, which enslave mankind,
Prophecy of Famine.

"And prudent dullness marked him for a mayor."
The Rosciad.

Chatterton's last couplet, expressing his pride in improvisation, is a condensed version (an improvement possibly) of the lines in *Gotham*, Book II:

> When the mad fit comes on I seize the pen;
> Rough as they run, the rapid thoughts set down,
> Rough as they run, discharge them on the town.

but derivative beyond question.

In *The Prophecy of Famine* (1763) "a Scots Pastoral," inscribed to Wilkes, Churchill dedicates himself to Nature, in bitter humour invites the Tweed to

> correct that blood
> Which mutinies at call of *English* pride,
> And, deaf to prudence, rolls a *patriot* tide.

and satirizes the incursion of the Scots into public offices, in a dialogue between Jockey and Sawney*:

> *Thence* issued forth, at great Macpherson's call,
> That *old, new, epic pastoral,* Fingal;

There are some good nature passages in this poem, and the section in *Resignation* (l. 77 sqq.) describing the humble cottage of Bute, and his progress from Scotland to the English court, is modelled on the hints there given.

Then there are the "catamites." A reader of *Kew Gardens*, though aware that Savage had written of Bristol:

> Still spare the catamite and swinge the whore,
> And be whate'er Gomorrah was before.

is puzzled, till, turning to *The Times* (1764), where Churchill undertakes to defend woman against the prevailing vice, he

* Hence probably the satirical dialogue of Hobbinol (from *The Shepheardes Calender*) and Thyrsis, 5766, B. f. 56, first printed by Ingram (*The True Chatterton*, p. 200).

realizes that Chatterton has taken them over with the rest of his hero's satirical furniture, and that the line and a half which, it may be, struck him, on a first perusal, as the panting ecstasy of amorous youth:

> Woman, of every happiness the best,
> Is all my heaven!

is, actually, the impression left on the Bristolian's receptive mind by the section beginning

> Woman, the pride and happiness of man,
> Without whose soft endearments Nature's plan
> Had been a blank,

in that extremely unpleasant piece.

Similarly, though there was good cause for a Wilkesite attacking Dr. Johnson in 1770 as the author of *The False Alarm*, it is doubtful if the Doctor would have taken up the room he does in *Kew Gardens*, had he not appeared as Pomposo in *The Ghost* seven years before.*

A smaller point! In *The Candidate*, and *Independence*, particularly, Churchill has a trick of starting successive paragraphs with the same apostrophe, e.g. " Come, Panegyric" or " Hail, Independence "; this will be found in *Resignation* and *Kew Gardens*.

Of these *Resignation*, though less interesting, is the better poem, because the subject is strictly adhered to; it starts with Grafton's resignation and ends with an invitation to his successor in the premiership, North, to follow his example. The most inspired passage is where the imagery of Chatterton's lines on the Copernican System is applied to politics:

* " I'm not another Fanny of Cock Lane " (l. 802) comes three lines before the fifty lines on " pension'd Johnson," which conclude:

> Irene, wondrous composition, came
> To give the audience rest, the author fame;
> A snore was much more grateful than a clap,
> And pit, box, gallery, prov'd it in a nap.
> Hail, Johnson! Chief of Bards, thy rigid laws
> Bestow'd due praise, and critics snor'd applause.

As Bute is fix'd eternal in his sphere
And ministers revolve[1] around in air,[2]
Your infamy with such a lasting ray
Glow'd thro' your orb in one continued[3] day,
Still ablest politicians hold dispute
Whether you gave, or borrow'd light from Bute.[4]
Lost in the blaze of his superior parts,
We often have descry'd your little arts.
But at a proper distance from his sphere
We saw the little villain disappear,
When drest in titles, the burlesque of place,
A more illustrious rascal shew'd his face.
Your destin'd sphere[5] of Ministry now run
You drop'd like others in the parent sun;
There as a spot you purpose to remain
And seek protection in the Sybil's swain.[6]
Grafton his planetary life[7] began,
Tho' foreign to the system of the clan;
Slowly he rolld around the fount of light,[8]
Long was his day, but longer was his night,
Irregular, unequal in his course,
Now languid he revolves,[9] now rolls with force;
His scarce[10] collected light obliquely hurl'd
Was scatter'd ere it reach'd his frozen world.

ll. 313-336.*

[1] revolv'd, 5766 B. f.75.
[2] Four lines added in Magazine version:
He gilds the flying orbs, his venal force,
Supports their conscience in the fiery course;
H-ll-nd thy talent wanted no supply,
Thy conscience ne[v]er gave thy purse the lie.
Your infamy, etc.
[3] continual, 5766B.
[4] Whether you shone self-lighten'd, or by Bute.
Freeholder's Magazine.
[5] race, *ib.*
[6] Safe when protected by the Sybil's swain, *ib.*
[7] state, *ib.*
[8] Slowly he circumscrib'd the fount of light, *ib.*
[9] revolve, 5766B.
[10] loose, *Freeholder's Magazine.*

You will not find anything as good as this (which indeed owes nothing to Churchill, and approximates to Dryden's abstract manner) in *Kew Gardens*. The picture of the provincial dance

* The MS. (5766 B. ff. 72-76) has the lines numbered, by Chatterton, in hundreds ("822" at end) and betrays, by the cramped hand, his lack of paper; there are very few stops. See also Skeat, Vol. II, pp. 370-3.

hall, as foreshadowing the poet of *The Borough*, should perhaps be given:

A mean assembly room, absurdly built,
Boasted one gorgeous lamp of copper gilt;
With farthing candles, chandeliers of tin,
And services of water, rum, and gin;
There in the dull solemnity of wigs,
The dancing bears of commerce murder jigs;
Here dance the dowdy belles of crooked trunk,
And often, very often, reel home drunk
Here dance the bucks with infinite delight,
And club to pay the fiddlers for the night.

Nor is the contrast between the two organists wholly devoid of merit, where the " slow variety " of Broderip's tones evokes:

How unlike Allen! Allen is divine!
His touch is sentimental, tender, fine;
No little affectations e'er disgrac'd
His more refin'd, his sentimental taste:
He keeps the passions with the sound in play,
And the soul trembles with the trembling key.

The following lines are a fair specimen of the poem and its twin sister, *The Whore of Babylon*:

O Prudence! if, by friends or counsel sway'd,
I had thy saving institutes obey'd;
And, lost to every love but love of self
A wretch like Harris,* living but in pelf;
Then happy in a coach or turtle feast,
I might have been an alderman at least.
Sage are the arguments by which I'm taught
To curb the wild excursive flights of thought.
Let Harris wear his self-sufficient air,
Nor dare remark, for Harris is a mayor;
If Catcott's flimsy system can't be prov'd,
Let it alone, for Catcott's much belov'd;
If Burgum bought a Bacon for a Strange,
The man has credit, and is great on 'Change;
If Camplin† ungrammatically spoke,
'Tis dang'rous on such men to break‡ a joke;

* Thomas Harris, merchant, Mayor, 1769-70.

† Rev. John Camplin, Precentor of Bristol Cathedral, first Librarian of the Cathedral Library, and vicar of St. Nicholas; his haughty accent and stride are satirized in *The Exhibition*. He also held a lectureship at St. Mary Redcliff.

‡ pass, *The Whore of Babylon*.

If you from satire could withhold the line,
At every public hall perhaps you'd dine.
I must confess, exclaims a* prudent sage,
You're really something clever for your age;
Your lines have sentiment, and now and then
A dash of satire stumbles from your pen;
But ah! that Satire is a dang'rous thing,
And often wounds the writer with its sting;
Your infant Muse should sport with other toys,
Men will not bear the ridicule of boys.
Some of the aldermen (for some, indeed,
For want of education cannot read;
And those who can, when they aloud rehearse
What Collins,† happy genius! titles verse,
So spin the strains sonorous through the nose,
The hearer cannot call it verse or prose,)
Some of the aldermen may take offence
At your maintaining them devoid of sense;
And if you touch their aldermanic pride,
Bid dark reflection tell how Savage died!

ll. 959-994.

But (excepting that planetary passage) compared with Churchill's brilliants, Chatterton's are but Bristol diamonds.

It is hard to believe that he could have maintained a steady behaviour at the office in Corn Street while writing thus impetuously; and both Lort and Gregory state that long before he left Bristol he repeatedly told Lambert's servants that he meant to take his own life.‡ Among Samuel Seyer's MS. memoranda at Bristol is the following: "When Chatterton lived in Bristol he constantly carried a loaded pistol in his pocket and oftentimes when walking with Dr. A. Broughton§ has taken it out of his pocket, and putting it to his mouth said he wished he could persuade himself to draw the trigger. Arthur Broughton told me this."‖ Seyer's informant was probably the "Mr. A. Broughton," whom, in the postscript to his letter of May 6, 1770, the poet advises with J. Broughton

* rejoins the, *ib.*

† Fowler, *ib.* Emanuel Collins is meant.

‡ 11457. *Life*, p. 74.

§ Possibly the A. Broughton M.D., who published *Observations on the Influenza* in 1782; he was physician to the Bristol Infirmary.

‖ 4533, f. 121.

(who wrote the preface to his *Miscellanies*) and others to read the *Freeholder's Magazine*. This is Redcliff testimony, and not to be despised. A more highly coloured version is given in C. B. Willcox's memoir (1842), where the scene is laid at an evening gathering, when suicide was under discussion; in either case the theatricality is apparent.

But he had given his views on the propriety of suicide to the world in an unsigned short story, *The Unfortunate Fathers*, which immediately follows *Astrea Brokage* in the *Town and Country* for Jan., 1770. They are expressed in the guise of a letter written by a young man, George Hinckley, to his father, who has financially ruined the father of the girl, Maria Sladon, to whom he is engaged, and forbidden the match, not scrupling to employ agents to suggest to Mr. Sladon that the lover was privy to his ruin, whereby Maria is induced to return a love-missive unopened. Young Hinckley, who unites to the most refined notions of honour and morality an absolute contempt for religion, on hearing that his letter is returned, raves "to the utmost extravagance of madness," then, appearing calm, sits down, writes a letter, seals it, leaves it on the table, goes into his chamber, and shoots himself. The apologia runs thus:

"I shall not accuse your conduct, for you are my father; I shall only endeavour to vindicate the action I am about to perpetrate. This will be easily done. There is a principle in man (a shadow of the divinity) which constitutes him the image of God; you may call it conscience, grace, inspiration, the spirit, or whatever name your education gives it. If a man acts according to this regulator, he is right: if contrary to it, he is wrong. It is an approved truth, that this principle varies in every rational being. As I can reconcile suicide to this principle, with me it is consequently no crime. Suicide is sometimes a noble insanity of the soul: and often the result of a mature and deliberate approbation of the soul. If ever a crime, it is only so to society: there indeed it always appears as an irrational emotion: but when our being becomes dissocial, when we neither assist or are assisted by society, we do not injure it by laying down our load of life. It may seem a paradoxical assertion, that we cannot do wrong to ourselves, but it is certain that we have power over our own existence. Such is my opinion, and I have made use of such power."

Though Chatterton cunningly adds: "This seeming philosophy was lost on old Hinckley," the sentiments must be his own; nor is it stretching probability too far to connect the magazine article with the death of Peter Smith not six months before. Hume had written: "A man who retires from life does no harm to society, he only ceases to do good"; but the *Essay on Suicide*, where this sentence appears, was suppressed, and not generally accessible till 1777.*

The poet, though an adolescent, well knew what he was about at this juncture. Kill himself he might, but he would cut himself loose from Bristol first, and somewhere near the date of Wilkes's enlargement was a convenient time for the young partisan, who had been contracting with the popular press, to change his quarters from the second city in England to the first; and in order that he might get away most cleanly, what better plan than that his master should be terrorized into dismissing him? John Sherwen, the Rowleian (*teste* his note in a copy of Davis's *Life of Chatterton* in the BritishMuseum) was informed by an acquaintance of the poet that the "Will" was merely a ruse for this purpose.†

It is plain, though the biographers (all but Dix, oddly enough) gloss this, that he made two distinct attempts in this direction. The first is that referred to by Barrett in his *History of Bristol* (p. 646), when Lambert found on his apprentice's desk a letter addressed to Clayfield stating "his distresses, and that on Mr. Clayfield's receiving that letter, he (Chatterton) should

* *The Unfortunate Fathers* was printed as Chatterton's in the *Miscellanies* (1778), it faintly adumbrates Mr. Sedley and George Osborne's father in *Vanity Fair* (1848).

† Eighteenth century apprentices were well up in strategy of this sort. Take these two pieces of evidence from a case in the Sessions Papers for 1754 (Part II, No. III, 186):

> *John Mariot.* I worked journey-work with the Prosecutor, I have known Abbot the apprentice break his work, and then lay a stick in his master's way, in order that his master might beat him, that he might get his indentures sued out by his uncle. I have heard him say several times, he would get away either by fair or foul means.
>
> *Sidney Williams.* Abbot the apprentice has said to me several times, provided I did not tell his master, he would tell me so and so. He said, he had a mind to sue out his indentures, and had a scheme that would do, and then he could work for himself, and could earn a great deal of money, and that he had brought the youngest apprentice into his own way. He said once to me, his master had struck him, thinking he had put tallow into a marrow-bone for his master to eat.

be no more." Lambert, alarmed, sent it to Barrett, thinking he might dissuade him, an interesting point as proving that the attorney regarded Barrett as Chatterton's good angel. Barrett, on his own showing, sent at once for Chatterton, questioned him closely on the occasion in a tender and friendly manner, but forcibly urged on him the horrible crime of self-murder, "however glossed over by our present libertines," blaming the bad company (note this) and principles he had adopted. The poet seemed to take the advice to heart, and shed tears, but denied that he was in pecuniary distress. The next day he sent Barrett the following letter, now in the British Museum (5766B, f. 91); Barrett's comment on which is that it shows "the prevailing temper of this unhappy youth." It was folded, sealed, addressed "Mr. Barrett" on the verso, and evidently handed in at 41 St. Augustine's Back:

"SIR,

Upon recollection, I don't know how Mr Clayfield, could [a second "could" scratched through] come by his Letter, as I intended to have given him a Letter but did not. In regard to my Motives for the supposed rashness, I shall observe, that I keep no worse Company than *myself*; I never drink to Excess, and have, without Vanity, too much Sense to be attached, to the mercenary retailers of Iniquity.—No; It is my PRIDE, my damn'd, native, unconquerable Pride, that plunges me into Distraction. You must know that the 19/20th of my Composition is Pride I must either live a Slave, a Servant; to have no Will of my own, no Sentiments of my own which I may freely declare as such;—or DIE—Perplexing Alternative! But it distracts me to think of it—I will endeavor to learn Humility, but it cannot be here. What it may cost me in the Trial Heaven knows!—I am

Yr much Obliged, unhappy
hble Sert.
T. C.
Thursday Eveng"

"Thursday evening" shows that the attempts are distinct, for the "Will," immediately on the discovery of which he was dismissed, is dated "Saturday." There is both more and less in this letter than meets the eye. The first sentence I take to be a dignified rebuke for the interception of his letter to Clayfield, though doubtless it was exposed on his desk purposely. But it is more important to note that some of the expressions used, however applicable to the writer and to Barrett's knowledge of him (the clause about drinking, for instance, is a thrust, for Barrett could never make him drink), are also catchwords of the Wilkesites. Compare these lines from an address " *To* Junius " in the *Middlesex Journal* for Oct. 10, 1769 :

> What is it to be slaves ?—'Tis to resign
> Each faculty that makes a mortal shine ;
> 'Tis to pluck up our reason by the roots,
> And level human nature with the brutes ;
> 'Tis to make royal tyranny our law,
> And live, of kings, more than of God, in awe ;
> All moral sense extinct, it is to hear
> The tales of priests with reverential ear ;
> Under the sacerdotal rule to groan,
> Which only knits us to an earthly throne ;
> 'Tis hardly to retain the human mien,—
> 'Tis to commence an animal machine.
> What is it to be free ?—'Tis to maintain
> Not one weak man's, but reason's sovereign reign ;
> It is to scorn to draw ignoble breath,
> And rather than be slaves, to rush on death !*

" Rushed out of life," by the way, is Barrett's phrase for the poet's exit. One need not dispute the remark about pride, which Rossetti, in his sonnet, turns to such noble account :

> And kin to Milton through his Satan's pride,
> At Death's sole door he stooped and craved a dart ;

but the rest is politics.

The second attempt, with which this is usually conflated, was perhaps some weeks later,† though this cannot be ascertained ; it is that mentioned by Gregory (p. 74). Mrs Lambert, the attorney's mother, was unable to persuade her son of the reality of the apprentice's threats till on April 14 (on which day the *North Briton* was published, glowing with poetry in

* Signed " Cassius " ; there is no reason to suppose that this is a pseudonym of Chatterton's.

† " Some few weeks after this he planned the scheme of going to London." *Barrett*, p. 647.

anticipation of the triumphant release of the member for Middlesex on the Tuesday following) he found by accident " upon his desk " a " Last Will and Testament " which announced Chatterton's design of committing suicide on the very next day, Easter Sunday, " the feast of the resurrection." This, Gregory was informed from good authority (almost certainly Lort), *was* occasioned by pecuniary distress, i.e. the refusal of a gentleman—Henry Burgum, it would appear—whom he had occasionally complimented in his poems, to accommodate him. A far more startling document than the letter to Clayfield can have been, it achieved its purpose at once. John Lambert dismissed the difficult apprentice who had been in his service two years, nine months, and thirteen days.

Even at this distance of time, and with the knowledge that it is based on Samuel Derrick's (theBath Master of Ceremonies) mock will* in the *Town and Country* for April, 1769, in which number two contributions by Chatterton appeared, Chatterton's testament, now in the Bristol Museum—Lambert gave it many years later to his friend John Paget, whose son gave it to the City in 1830—is a startling enough affair. It is written on small quarto paper, 8½ by 6½ inches, possibly the leaves of a copybook, and falls into five sections ; it is of course possible that the prefatory matter, or some of it, may have been written last, and the leaves have got out of order.

1. An introduction ; the other side of the leaf is blank :

> All this wrote bet 11 & 2 oclock
> Saturday in the utmost Distress of Mind

2. A caveat, on a new leaf :

NOTA BENE

In a dispute concerning the Character of David it was argued that he must be a holy Man from the Strains of Piety that breathes thro' his whole works—Being of a contrary Opinion and knowing that a great Genius can affect every thing—endeavoring in the foregoing Poems to represent an Enthusiastic Methodist intended to send it to

* Which derives from " Isaac Bickerstaff's " will in the *Tatler*, No. 7 (Apr. 26, 1709).

Romaine & impose it upon the infatuated World as a Reality but thanks to Mr Burgum's Generosity I am now employ'd in matters of more Importance.

This is, by anticipation, an answer to George Catcott's remarks on Rowley's Sermon, and an indirect way of intimating that the "gode prieste" is Thomas Chatterton. A great genius may, or may not, "affect every thing," but an English poet will, and does. Keats wrote, on Nov. 22, 1817, "If a sparrow come before my window I take part in its existence and pick about the gravel." What "poems" are referred to is unknown. William Romaine (1714-1795) was the revivalistic vicar of St. Anne's, Blackfriars, and in a letter written in 1766, and not published till 1809, he had drawn the portrait of "a very very vain, proud young man" who "knew almost everything but himself and therefore was mighty fond of himself" and "met with many disappointments to his pride, till the Lord was pleased to let him see and feel the plague of his own heart" (*Works*, VIII, p. 188).* "Mr. Burgum's Generosity" means, no doubt, Mr. Burgum's tightfistedness, and the "matters of more Importance" are the making of the will.† As to David, Chatterton was no doubt aware of Peter Annett's *The Life of David, the History of the Man after God's own Heart*, which was printed anonymously in 1761, and reprinted five years later; and the "dispute" may well have been one in which members of the Juvenile Club engaged, apropos of this Deistic tract. In his *Epistle* to the Temple Vicar, speaking of Inspiration, he writes "If David found thee in a sea of blood."

3. Fifty-four lines of verse headed "Saturday April 14 . 70" on the verso of the caveat, and two leaves (the verso of the last leaf being blank), as thus:

> Burgum I thank thee thou hast let me see
> That Bristol has impress'd her Stamp on thee
> Thy genrous Spirit emulates the May'rs,
> Thy gen'rous Spirit with thy Bristol's pairs

* "He had not lived long in Wales before he became a very popular preacher, and was followed there as much as Romaine is here."
Genuine Memoirs of Mr. Charles Churchill, p. 89.

† Wilson (p. 245) supposes that Burgum had changed his mind; Ingram (p. 195, n.), as I do, that the allusion is sarcastic.

Gods ! what would Burgum give to get a name
And snatch his blund'ring Dialect from Shame
What would he give to hand his Mem'ry down,
To times remotest Boundary—a Crown.
Would you ask more ? his swelling Face looks blue
Futurity he rates at Two pounds Two.
Well Burgum take the Laurel to thy brow
With a rich saddle decorate a Sow
Strut in Iambics totter in an Ode
Promise and never pay & be the Mode
New page in MS.] Catcott for thee : I know thy heart is good
But ah ! thy Merit's seldom understood
Too bigotted to Whimsys which thy Youth
Receiv'd to venerate as Gospel Truth
Thy Friendship never could be dear to me
Since all I am is opposite to thee
If ever obligated to thy Purse
Rowley discharges all ; my first chief Curse
For had I never known the antique Lore
I ne'er had ventur'd from my peaceful Shore
To be ye wreck of promises and hopes
A Boy of Learning* and a Bard of Tropes
But happy in my humbler Sphere had mov'd
Untroubled unrespected unbelov'd†
New page in MS.] To Barrett next—He has my Thanks sincere
For all the little Knowledge I had here
But what was Knowledge could it here succeed
When hardly twenty in the Town can read
Could Knowledge bring in Int'rest to maintain
The wild Expences of a Poet's Brain
Disinterested Burgum never meant
To take my Knowledge for his Gain Per Cent
When wildly squand'ring every thing I got
On Books and Learning and the Lord knows what
Could Burgum then my Critic, Patron, Friend,
Without security attempt to lend

* I wonder if this phrase gave Crabbe a hint for his tale of *The Learned Boy*, which is directed against the mischiefs of freethinking ; its moral is " Hadst thou been humble." *The Patron*, where Chatterton is named, comes in the same Series (*Tales*, 1812).

† Cf. If mine no glorious work may be,
Grant Heaven ! and 'tis enough for me,
(While many squally sails flit past,
And many break the ambitious mast)
From all that they pursue, exempt,
The stormless bay of deep contempt !

Landor, *Miscellaneous Poems* (1846), xcix.

No! that would be imprudent in the Man
Accuse him of Imprudence if you can
He promis'd I confess and seem'd sincere
Few keep an honorary Promise here,
New page in MS.] I thank thee Barrett; thy Advice was right
But twas ordain'd by Fate that I should write
Spite of the Prudence of this prudent Place
I wrote my Mind nor hid the Authors face
Harris e'er long (when reeking from the Press
My Numbers make his self importance less)
Will wrinkle up his Face and damn the Lay
And drag my Body to the Triple Way
Poor superstitious Mortals! wreak your hate!
Upon my cold remains

Three points are of special importance in these lines: their indicating that the immediate occasion for the will was Burgum's refusal to accommodate him with money, thus differentiating the document from the letter to Clayfield; his speaking of himself as "the wreck of promises and hopes" *before* he left Bristol*; and his insistence on *Kew Gardens*, the "lay" in question, showing his almost complete metamorphosis into the politico-satirical character.

4. The will proper†:

This is the last Will and Testament—of me Thomas Chatterton of the City of Bristol being sound in Body or it is the Fault of my last Surgeon—The Soundness of my Mind the Coroner and Jury are to be judges of—desiring them to take notice that the most perfect Masters of Human Nature in Bristol distinguish me by the Title of the Mad Genius‡ therefore if I do a mad action it is conformable to every Section of my Life which all savored of Insanity—§

* "In my own view, the untimely fate of poor Chatterton lies at the door of his middle-aged friends and bad advisers, Barrett and Catcott."
Sir E. Clarke, *New Lights*, p. 28.

† A facsimile in Stanley Hutton, *Bristol and its famous Associations*, pp. 72-78.

‡ "The modern acceptation of the word [genius] by which it signifies a very silly young fellow, who from his extravagance and debauchery has obtained the name of a genius, like *lucus a non lucendo*, because he had no genius at all." *The Connoisseur*, No. 90, 5th Ed., 1767.

§ Southey's remark (letter to John Britton, Nov. 4, 1810) that there was a taint of insanity in the Chatterton family, manifesting itself in Mrs. Newton, who was at one time in an asylum, and in her daughter, and that this is the key to the poet's eccentricities and suicide, is usually quoted on this passage. As regards Chatterton himself *credat Judaeus Apella, non ego.*

Item. If after my Death which will happen tomorrow night before 8 oClock being the feast of the resurrection, the Coroners & Jurors bring it in Lunacy I will and direct that Paul Farr Esq[r] & M[r] Jn[o] Flower* do at their joint Expence Cause my Body to be interred in the Tomb of my Fathers and raise the Monument over my Body to the Height of 4 feet 5 Inches placing the present Flat stone on the Top & [new page] adding six Tablets on the first to be engraven in old English Characters—

Vous que par ici pasēt
Pur l'ame Gualeroine Chatterton priet
Le cors de oi ici gist
Le Ame receyve Ihu CCrist. MCCLX† [The date in Gothic lettering]

On the Second Tablet in Old English Characters

Orate pro animabus Alanus Chatterton et Alicia uxoris ejus qui quidem Alanes obiit X die mensis Novemb. M.CCCC. XV. Quoram animabus propitietur Deus.

On the Third Tablet in Roman Character
Sacred to the Memory of Thomas Chatterton Sub Chanter of the Cathedral of this City whose Ancestors were residents of S[t] Mary Redclift since the year 1140
He dyed the 7th of August 1752

[New page] On the Fourth Tablet in Roman Characters.
To the Memory of Thomas Chatterton. Reader Judge not: if thou art a Christian, believe that he shall be Judged by a Superior Power, to that Power only is he now answerable—

On the 5th & 6th Tablets which shall front each other, Atchievm[s] viz. on the one Vert a Fess Or Crest a Mantle of Estate Gules sup-

* One Paul Farr was master of the Merchant Venturers, 1775-6; President of the Anchor Society, 1776; Warden of St. Stephen's Ringers, 1779; d. Dec. 27, 1794. (Beaven, *Bristol Lists*). The Bristol Polling List of 1774 gives two John Flowers, coach-wheeler and lime-burner respectively, and one, a rope-maker, in Bedminster. I presume the persons mentioned in the "Will" to have been Redcliff officials, possibly churchwardens.

† The mythical ancestor's epitaph is taken from the same source as the drawing of him with a church in his hands (5766 B. f. 118), namely Weever's *Funerall Monuments* (1631); it is that of Sir John Peyton in Tendringhal Chapel, Stoke by Neyland, Suffolk (p. 776):

Vous qe par ici passet
Pur l'ame Sire Iehan de Peytona priet.
Le cours de oi ici gist;
L'ame receyue Ihu crist. Amen.

The monuments of the Howards in this portion of Weever seem to have had a remarkable fascination for Chatterton; "Alicie uxoris eius" is to be found "in old English characters" on p. 773, and "qui quidem" comes on p. 771.

ported by a Spear Sable headed Or on the Other Or a Fess Vert Crest a Cross of Knights Templars—
And I will and direct that if the Coroners Inquest bring it in—Felo de se the s[d] Monument shall be notwithstanding erected—And if the s[d] Paul Farr & Jn[o] Flower have Souls so Bristollish as to refuse this my Bequest they will transmit a Copy of my Will to the Society for supporting the Bill of Rights whom I hereby empower to build the said Monument according to the aforesaid Directions. And if they [New page] the said Paul Farr & Jn[o] Flower should build the said Monum[t] I will and direct that the Second Edition of my Kew Gardens shall be dedicated to them in the following Dedication —To Paul Farr & John Flower Esq[rs] this Book is most humbly dedicated by the Author's Ghost—

Item I give and bequeath all my Vigor and Fire of Youth to M[r] George Catcott being sensible he is in most want of it—

Item From the same charitable motive I give and bequeath unto the Rev[d] M[r] Camplin Sen[r] all my Humility. To M[r] Burgum all my Prosody & Grammar likewise one Moiety of my Modesty, the other moiety to any young Lady who can prove without blushing that she wants that valuable Commodity. To Bristol all my Spirit and Disinterestedness parcells of goods unknown on her Key since the days of Canynge and [New page] Rowley. Tis true a Charitable Gentleman one Mr Colston smuggled a Considerable quantity of it, but it being prov'd that he was a Papist the worshipful Society of Aldermen endeavor to throttle him with the Oath of Allegiance—* I leave also my Religion to D[r] Cutts Barton Dean of Bristol hereby impowering the Subsacrist to strike him on the head when he goes to Sleep in Church†—My Powers of Utterance I give to the Reverend M[r] Broughton‡ hoping he will employ them to a better Purpose than reading Lectures on the immortality of the Soul—I leave the Rev[d] M[r] Catcott some little of My freethinking that he may put on the Spectacles of reason and see how vilely he is duped in believing the Scripture literally I wish he and his Brother would know how far I am their real Enemy but I have an unlucky way of railing and when the strong fit of Satyre is on me Spare neither Friend nor Foe. This is my Excuse for what I have said of them elsewhere [New page] I leave M[r] Clayfield the sincerest thanks my Gratitude can give and

* The only reference to Colston in Chatterton's extant works. The Rev. H. J. Wilkins writes to me : "The Council had a majority of Whig Dissenters ; they loved neither Colston, a High-Church Jacobite, nor his gifts. I think that the reference is in praise of Colston."

† This is the "lazy dean" (1763-1780) "who gave the cross to Hoare." In *The Exhibition*, besides somnolence, he is charged with drunkenness and habitual swearing.

‡ Vicar of St. Mary Redcliff, from 1744 to 1772, author of the fine libretto to Handel's *Hercules* (1745) ; Chatterton is thinking of his four dissertations, *A Prospect of Futurity* (1768). He was buried Dec. 24, 1774. *Redcliff Register*.

I will and direct that whatever any Person may think the Pleasure of reading my Works worth they immediately pay their own valuation to him since it is then become a lawful Debt to me & to him as my Executor in this Case—I leave my Moderation to the Politicians on both Sides the Question—I leave my Generosity to our present Right Worshipful Mayor Thomas Harris Esqr.—I give my Abstinence to the Company at the Sheriffs annual feast in General more particularly to the Aldermen—

Item I give and bequeath unto Mr Mat. Mease* a Mourning Ring with this motto Alas ! poor Chatterton—Provided he pays for it himself.

Item I leave the young Ladys all the Letters they [New page] have had from me assuring them that they need be under no Apprehensions from the Appearance of my Ghost for I dye for none of them

Item I leave all my Debts in the whole not five Pounds to the Payment of the Charitable and generous Chamber of Bristol On Penalty if refused to hinder every Member from ever eating a good Dinner by appearing in the form of a Bailiff—If in Defiance of this terrible Spectre they obstinately persist in refusing to discharge my Debts Let my two Creditors apply to the Supporters of the Bill of Rights.

Item I leave my Mother & Sister to the protection of my Friends if I have any

Executed in the presence of Omniscience
this 14th day of April 1770
T : CHATTERTON

5. The "Codicil," on the verso of the last leaf :

* Vintner, of the Bush in Corn Street. He is the "Mat. Mixum." of the tale *One Hour After Marriage* (*T. and C. M.*, Suppl. 1770) where he is described as "a jolly fellow, and a very cheerful companion, especially when you was drinking his wine . . . as he had seen a little of the world at the bar, he laughed at everyone's jests but his own ; and found accomplishments everywhere but in himself." He is also "the laughing Mease" of *Kew Gardens*, who "inserts this item in his bill—

Five shillings for a jest with ev'ry gill."

on which Chatterton remarks :

"How commendable this, to turn at once
To good account the Vintner and the dunce,
And by a very hocus pocus hit,
Dispose of damag'd claret and bad wit."

His autograph may be seen in the Redcliff Register, March 14, 1776, when he was a witness to the marriage of his sister Catherine to Francis Gold of Christ Church. He was succeeded at the Bush by John Weeks, who married another sister. It was to the Bush that Mr. Winkle fled from the wrath of Mr. Dowler.

It is my Pleasure that Mr Cocking & Miss Farley
print this my Will the first Saturday after my Death
T. C.

This, like a lady's postscript, reveals the truth of the matter. He wanted to make a stir in the world, and imagined, no doubt, at the moment of writing, the consternation of his native place at seeing (whenever he died) the will printed in *Felix Farley*. Sure, in his heart, of fame, he was at all times sufficiently human, or " Bristollish," to desire some notoriety as well. For the elaborate directions about the monument are of the place no less than of the poet. Compare this extract from the life of Lord Keeper North (I. p. 234) quoted in Southey's *Commonplace Book* : " In a word pride and ostentation are publicly professed [*sc.* in Bristol] ; Christenings and burials pompous beyond imagination. A man who dies worth three hundred pounds will order two hundred pounds of it to be laid out in his funeral procession." An unsentimental reader will probably suspend judgment as to the whole of the farrago having been written in the utmost distress of mind, and a musical one will reflect that Mozart, then not much over fourteen, was more profitably employed during Easter week, 1770, in taking down the *Miserere* of Allegri while the Sistine choir were singing it, and merely correcting one or two passages at the repetition on Good Friday : but Mozart had a father alive.

In the periodical publications of this year there is one mock will, at least, which has a claim to be considered hackwork of Chatterton's ; it is that of Beckford (*Universal Magazine*, July ; *General Evening Post*, July 24 ; *Boddely's Bath Journal*, July 30) where the penultimate bequest is " my fame to the four winds." Another in the *General Evening Post* for Sept. 15 three weeks and a day after the poet's death, is that of " Matthew Moonshine, Prisoner in the Fleet." Here one of the bequests is " my debts to the supporters of the Bill of Rights," and another, " my castles, edifices, and other buildings in Nubibus and elsewhere to the Earl of C[hatham?] and my sincerity to the Prime Minister for the time being."

As Chatterton did not commit suicide on Easter Sunday, it is hardly an affront to his intelligence to suppose that his dismissal from Lambert's postponed that plan. The *Middlesex Journal* of Tuesday (17th) contained a letter by him to the Princess Dowager of Wales, styled, à la Churchill, " Princess of Gotham," on the subject of woman's intrusion into politics ; Charles I and George III, we there read, were both misled, and both by women. " What shall we say," the tirade concludes, " but that we are slaves, and ever shall be so, till we know how to free ourselves ? " It is dated " Bristol, April 20, 1770 " ; this need not be a printer's error or editorial correction for " March 20 " or " April 10," for the writer may have post-dated the contribution in view of its not being inserted immediately ; in any case it must have been written before the " Will." Both he and Wilkes were now free ; and if the disciple chose to die, death at the hub of events was preferable to death in a " mercenary cell."

Mrs. Newton is responsible for the statement that "a few months before he left Bristol he wrote letters to several booksellers in London I believe to learn if there was any probility of his getting an employment there but that I can't affirm as the subject was a secret at home "* ; and Barrett says that some few weeks after the " perplexing alternative " letter he planned the scheme of going to London, " and there writing for the booksellers, &c."† in which case there must have been quite a considerable interval between the letter and the " Will." Now he was *in* London by Thursday, Apr. 26, so that it is clear, at all events, that what arrangements he had made with the booksellers were made previously to the " Will." The ten days after it must have been an anxious bustling period for his family at least. As for him, he had broken off the affair with Esther Saunders on the 9th, and, as he intended to die for none of the ladies, the Miss W, then " in chase," must have been relinquished speedily. Thistlethwaite, as we have seen, repeating perhaps what Chatterton had told him, says the booksellers had added to their praises and compliments " the most liberal promises of assistance and employment," if he removed to the capital, but Thistlethwaite received the following answer

* *L. and M.*, p. 146.
† *History of Bristol*, p. 674.

from the author of *Apostate Will*, on questioning him as to his plan on arrival there : " My first attempt shall be in the literary way : the promises I have received are sufficient to dispel doubt ; but should I, contrary to my expectations, find myself deceived, I will, in that case, turn Methodist preacher : Credulity is as potent a deity as ever, and a new sect may easily be devised. But if that too should fail me, my last and final resource is a pistol."*

This, in substance, I believe to have been said ; it is far enough from a hopeful outlook, and Chatterton, according to my view, started for London in no exalted mood of confidence, save at having escaped from Bristol, but rather " as a soldier marches up to a battery."†

Before leaving it is probable that he made the renderings of two odes of Horace (I. 5, 19) from David Watson's translation, first published in 1741, lent to him by Edward Gardner.‡ In rendering the Ode to Pyrrha he was following Milton's lead, but his work is less a paraphrase than a free fantasia on the prose version he used, in either case ; both end on the note of escape.

> Thank Heav'n I've broke the sweet but galling chain
> Worse than the horrors of the stormy main.

and

> Sweet gentle peace may still be mine ;
> This dreadful chain be broke.

thus reflecting his own mood at this time.

Money, now more than ever, was a necessity, and he sold his masterpiece, we do not know for what sum. " The last thing I had of him," George Catcott wrote to Dean Milles (Sept. 21, 1778), " was the *Tragedy of Alla*, which I purchased about a week prior to his going to London." This fact is important, as it negatives in part Catcott's statement that the poet " carried all this treasure with him " to the metropolis.§

* Milles, p. 459.
† Keats to Shelley (Aug., 1820).
‡ *Works*, I, p. 349.
§ Catcott was, of course, thinking of the parchments. (*Monthly Review*, May, 1777.)

Certainly it proves that, unless he had made another copy, the biggest piece in the Rowley cycle was marketable only in Rowley's city.

Bristol gave him a send off; according to Barrett most of his friends and acquaintance contributed a guinea apiece towards his journey, an indication perhaps that Barrett's contribution was a guinea.*

At Corn Street a few *disjecta membra* were left behind; copies of them are kept at the Bristol Museum—two and a half folio sheets, dated Jan. 1769, of banter on the birth of a child, representing it as a stranger newly arrived at a house, nine lines of a probably satirical *March, an Elegy*,† a scrap with musical notes, two drawings of seals of Johannes Berkelei, and on the reverse five lines beginning "Eternal Vengeance,"† a drawing of a shield with sixty-nine quarterings, a calendar beautifully designed on parchment with a figure of Time in the centre, signed and dated on the back, in black-letter, Aug. 3, 1768, and, a vanished volume, his father's Book of Magic. The Devil had been raised; Thomas Chatterton was free.

* *History of Bristol*, p. 647. George Cumberland, late in 1808, learned from a Mrs. Stephens, daughter (he believed) to Richard Phillips, that when Chatterton was going to London, he took leave of her and others on the steps of Redcliff Church very cheerfully, and, at parting, saying he would give them some gingerbread, went over the way to Mr. Freeling's, to buy some. This witness also remembered him getting on these steps at eleven years old and repeating poetry to his favourite play-fellows. (*Cumberland MS., circ.* 1827). William Colmer, in the *Bristol Mirror* (July 23, 1836), stated that Chatterton was in the habit of buying tarts at Mr. Freeling's, a gingerbread baker (i.e., confectioner) at the foot of Redcliff Hill, leading into Redcliff Street. This was the father of Sir Francis Freeling (1764-1836), secretary to the G.P.O. and a trustee of Chatterton's sister's estate (P. C. C. Heseltine, 681).

† See Appendix C.

CHAPTER XVI

SHOREDITCH AND LIBERTY

THUS opens the third and last era of the poet's life; he is seventeen and five months, and has not quite four months more to live. His works apart, the sources now dwindle to practically one, Letter 49 in Croft's *Love and Madness*. There is mystery near the end, but no desperate problem, like the dating of *Elinoure and Juga*; in fact it is a consistent story, and reconcilable at almost every point with what has gone before.

The prospect was not wholly without hope. Chatterton had shown himself admirably fitted for imposing on the credulity and interest of others by a current style assumed for the nonce, for journalism, in a word. He could write verses of well-nigh any description, stories, political letters, antiquarian notes, and topical essays; "he seems to have wanted nothing but time," as Professor Ker says, "to establish a good practice as a literary man,"* and—a healthy sign—he knew, not only what he could do, but that poverty attends literature. He was abstemious, no great eater, and, so far as is known, robust; moreover, unlike Crabbe, ten years later, he had made his capabilities well known to the booksellers beforehand. There was a risk of starvation, but less so, surely, than in a score of cases, thanks to his improvisatory and chameleon-like faculties: the trouble, the only trouble, was his state of mind.

"Chatterton, *I* think, was mad," Byron wrote to Leigh Hunt, and Southey wrote much the same to John Britton, instancing Mrs. Newton and her daughter; but there is nothing in Chatterton's career, unless it be argued that suicide denotes a

* *Cambridge History of English Literature*, X, p. 237.

habit of insanity, to warrant that reading of his character. No ; his pride, i.e. sense of superior attainments, had been fed by an intensive system of silent self-education lasting over many years ; his environment had taught him that beauty bakes no bread, that a poet, in order to see himself successful and esteemed, must make men feel his power by qualities less ethereal than poetry. Soured and exasperated as he was by the refusal of Bristol and Walpole to accept him on his intrinsic merits, his native anger directed itself against all mankind, and party-writing appealed not merely, as his first biographer suggests, to his vanity, by elevating him into immediate notice,* but to his soul, as affording a trumpet for that thwarted and famished organ to blow its grievance against the encircling walls of commercial industry and worldly prudence. How could it matter who was the reigning power ? As a political satirist, " indifferent in all things," he could attack everyone ; and in the secrecy of solitude applaud his pseudonymous shafts. Imagine such a temper, whetted by Spartan rigour in food and drink, inwardly justified and exalted by the thought that the great work, the work that would be remembered three hundred years later, was actually written, though its author had done, and was doing, his utmost to deny himself the glory of swift recognition ; imagine this, add thereto the urge and disquiet of adolescence, bearing into the mind symptoms properly of the body ; add to that the momentary rapture at having broken his chain, at being henceforth accountable to no human being but himself, and you have a faint representation of the youth now bound for the first city in England.

The jaunty, swaggering tone of his London correspondence, possibly the earliest missives he had sent to his folk, covers, in my idea, an almost complete disillusionment, an ingrained pessimism, coupled with a desire to keep Bristol at bay. If he returned, it would be as a conqueror ; but his purpose was hardly to return, rather to live no longer than he could help, and—to change the pronoun in Marvell's lines :

* Cf. " On account of some political pieces he published, his fame was now in its meridian. He was regarded as a skilful politician, as well as a great poet."
Genuine Memoirs of Mr. Charles Churchill, p. 155.

tear his pleasures with rough strife
Thorough the iron gates of life—

then, possibly, to be done with a life which he hated: "*cælum non animum mutans*"—*there*, I believe, Barrett wrote the truth. "Few are the pleasures Chatterton e'er knew," the poet had confessed in his Elegy on Thomas Phillips; away from Bristol he would know some, at least, before the end: thus much of happiness, but no more, informs those pathetic and untrustworthy tokens of his freedom, the private letters of his last months.

The first of these is dated April 26, a Thursday, possibly the day after his arrival:

"DEAR MOTHER,

Here I am safe, and in high spirits.—To give you a journal of my tour would not be unnecessary. After riding in the basket, to Brislington, I mounted the top of the coach, and rid easy: and agreeably entertained with the conversation of a quaker *in dress*, but little so in personals and behaviour. This laughing friend who is a carver, lamented his having sent his tools to Worcester, as otherwise he would have accompanied me to London. I left him at Bath, when finding it rained pretty fast, I entered an inside passenger to Speenhamland, the half way stage, paying seven shillings: 'twas lucky I did so, for it snowed all night, and on Marlborough downs the snow was near a foot high.

At seven in the morning I breakfasted at Speenhamland, and then mounted the coach box for the remainder of the day, which was a remarkable fine one.—Honest gee-ho* complimented me with assuring me that I sat bolder and tighter than any person who ever rid with him.—Dined at Stroud most luxuriantly, with a young gentleman who had slept all the preceding night in the machine; and an old mercantile genius whose school-boy son had a great deal of wit as the father thought, in remarking that Windsor was as old as *our Saviour's time*.

Got into London about 5 o'Clock in the evening—called upon Mr. Edmunds, Mr. Fell, Mr. Hamilton and Mr. Dodsley. Great encouragement from them; all approved of my design; shall soon be settled.—Call upon Mr. Lambert, shew him this, or tell him, if I deserve a recommendation, he would oblige me to give me one—if I do not, it would be beneath him to take notice of me. Seen all

* i.e., Jehu. Perhaps written so by confusion with the Bristol "Gee-hoes" or sledges, or, by transference, the cry for the crier.

aunts, cousins—all well—and I am welcome. Mr T. Wensley is alive and coming home.—Sister, grandmother, &c. &c. &c. remembered.—I remain,

Your dutiful son,

T. CHATTERTON."*

The letter indicates that he was an economical traveller, and could probably be trusted to make a little go a long way in London. The following advertisement from the *Felix Farley* of his last Saturday in Bristol (April 21) will serve as a commentary:

" The *London*, *Bath*, and *Bristol*
MACHINES
IN ONE DAY

Set out from the Rummer-Tavern, Bristol, on Sunday next the 15th Instant April 1770 and continue every night (Saturdays excepted) precisely at Nine o'clock; and from the Greyhound and Shakespeare Inn in the Market place Bath, every night (Saturdays excepted) at Eleven for London; and return from the Swan Inn Holbourn Bridge, every Sunday, Tuesday, and Thursday Night, at Ten o'clock, and from the Three Cups in Bread Street every Monday, Wednesday, and Friday, at the same Hour, for Bath and Bristol. . . .

All lie the first Night at the George and Pelican Inn Speenhamland [near Newbury] . . .

Inside to and from Bristol in one day 1 . 10 . 0 . . .†

Children and outsides in the above Machines half-price.

Half the money to be paid on taking the places, the other half on entering the machines :—Inside passengers to be allowed 14 lb, and children and outsides 7 lb weight of luggage; all above to pay in the One day machine and post coaches Three halfpence per pound, and in the Two day machines one penny per pound.

They all call at the Black Bear and New White Horse Cellar Piccadilly . . ."

The discomfort of the overhanging back compartment on the outside is celebrated in *She Stoops to Conquer* (1773), where

* *L. and M.*, p. 168.

† The Two-day machine was three shillings less, and the post-coaches threepence per mile. Five years after Chatterton's ride John Weeks of the Bush advertized that the original Bristol Diligence or flying postchaise would thenceforth make the journey to London in 16 hours at 3d. per mile, 10 lb. luggage a head being allowed; these coaches only carried four passengers each.

Latimer, *Bristol in the Eighteenth Century*, p. 418.

Tony Lumpkin exclaims, apropos of his riding by night, "It has shook me worse than the basket of a stage coach" (Act II, Sc. 2).

The break from home was not absolute. He lodged in Shoreditch with a relation, one Mrs. Ballance,* who was herself a lodger in the house of one Walmsley, a plasterer with wife, nephew and niece; from a statement of the niece it would appear that he took his meals with Mrs. Ballance. A sewer-rate book of 1779 in the London County Council's possession shows (p. 143) that one William Walmsley occupied a house, the yearly rent of which, for rating purposes, was £21, in Shoreditch High Street, the first going citywards at which the collector called, as he came out of Webb Square. This would appear to be the house (or to have stood on the site of the house) marked 48 High Street in Tallis's *London Street Views* (1839), being one of two built over the entrance to Webb Square. The site is now occupied by the Bishopsgate Goods Station (L.N.E.R.), and the Committee of the London County Council, on July 8, 1927, decided not to commemorate it.† Croft, who, in 1779, was landlord of the plasterer's house,‡ collected the testimony of these people concerning Chatterton.

He had not much luggage§; and it is interesting to compare his case with Crabbe's, who came to London in April, 1780, "master of a box of clothes, a small case of surgical instruments, and three pounds in money," with an introduction to a Mrs. Burcham, who had been in early youth a friend of Miss Elmy, his sweetheart, and was married to a linendraper in Cornhill. The Aldeburgh poet, who lodged at a hairdresser's near the Exchange, had never heard of the Bristol one, and was often warned by the Burchams of Chatterton's fate. He was supported by his future wife's family—"they have from time to time supplied me with such sums as they could possibly

* In 1779 one Thomas Ballance occupied a house (£45 rental) in Shoreditch High Street, nearer the City than Walmsley's, on the same side. The same book shows one Daniel Chatterton occupying a house (£6 rental), the 47th after the collector crosses to Kingsland Road.

† The facts are complicated by the recurrence of the name "Walmsley" on p. 139 of the sewer-rate book, at what is probably another part of the street.

‡ See his letter to George Steevens, Feb. 5, 1782, *ap.* Gregory, *Life*, p. 179.

§ *L. and M.*, p. 208.

spare, and that they have not done more arose from my concealing the severity of my situation"—for nearly twelve months (i.e. till Burke relieved him), and "hardly ever tasted butcher's meat except on a Sunday," when he dined usually with a tradesman's family, and thought their leg of mutton, baked in the pan, the perfection of luxury. But Crabbe was twenty-six, and had had experience of humanity as a hedge doctor.*

The editors mentioned in the letter, whose names, latterly at any rate, were no doubt familiar to the home circle, lived at some distance from Shoreditch and one another. Edmunds, of the *Middlesex Journal*, was in Shoe Lane, Fell of the *Freeholder's Magazine* in Paternoster Row, Hamilton of the *Town and Country* (who had another printing office on the road between Highgate and Finchley) at St. John's Gate, Clerkenwell, and Dodsley of the *Annual Register* in Pall Mall. If these four persons and his relatives were all interviewed on the first evening, he must have gone to bed tired.

On the day he wrote his first letter home the *Middlesex Journal* printed in its Poets' Corner *The Hag* (signed "Q," and dated "Bristol, April 10"), 72 lines, an attack on the Princess Dowager, the first twenty lines of which are all but identical with *Fables for the Court*† ; this has not been reprinted, and a single couplet,

> Was ever nation rul'd before
> By an old stallion and a whore?

will show the libellous nature, even for that age, of the style he now chiefly favoured.‡

* *Life of Crabbe*, by his son, prefixed to the *Works*, Chapters II and III; *Correspondence of Sir T. Hamner*, p. 393.

† Addressed to Clayfield; introduction and part of one fable only, "The Shepherds," remain. The title was suggested by *Fables for Grown Gentlemen: for the Year* 1770, printed for J. Dodsley. ("And if we credit Dodsley's word" l. 3): ll. 15 to 30 are absent from *The Hag*, the rest of the introduction to which has some insertions and variants referring to Bristolians:

> Let Patriotic Cruger vote
> On 't'other side and turn his coat

and The patriotic taste of Mease.

‡ "The colour and character of them [i.e., Chatterton's poems] may be found in the uneasiness expressed by his mother and sister for his safety."
Essay on the Rowley Controversy (MS. 1783) B.5199. p. 42.

Before his next letter he had written three poems, the first portion of *Resignation* had appeared in the April *Freeholder's*, and a piece called *The Candidates* (note the influence of Churchill), which Ingram mistakenly calls the first published after his arrival in town, in the *Middlesex* of May 1. It is dated "Bristol, April 27, 1770"; the "Bristol" was kept up after he left that city, as it appeared on the MS. of the *Balade of Charitie*, sent to the *Town and Country* in July.

The first of the Shoreditch Poems is *The Exhibition, a Personal Satyr*. There are two MSS. at Bristol, eighteenth century copies*; they assert that it was begun on May 1 and finished on May 3. The 444 lines of Book I, probably all that was written, contain two extracts, 34 lines in all, from *Kew Gardens*, dealing with the assembly room and the rival organists. After a prelude of sixteen lines dissociating this Exhibition from that of the *Incorporated Society of Artists* in Spring Gardens, which the King had visited (*vide* poem in *Middlesex Journal*, May 19, signed "C, May 9, 1770"), 174 are devoted to an attack on the Bristol clergy, starting with Alexander Catcott:

If holy Gospel might be dignify'd
By his set Phiz, austerity and Pride
How can these attributes be sound within
When Satan tempts the inward man to sin
Fly hence Temptation Catcott's heavenly Heart
Is never mov'd but in the better part
Devotion only warms his freezing blood
Lust never melted up the sizy flood
And should his lost degeneracy of mind
Be to the pleasures of the world inclin'd
Sickly desire is all his little crime
For Catcott's stretch'd beyond his toying time
Like his dull brother frigid cold and dead
He'd sleep unsullied in a Harlot's bed.

ll. 41-54.

Two months later the same hand was to write

Look in his glommed face, his sprighte there scanne;
Howe woe-begone, how withered, forwynd, deade!

* B. 5374, in the Bristol Library, is in George Catcott's hand, and the better text; the other is at the Museum, and has been printed in E. P. Ellinger's *Thomas Chatterton* (1930).

So close together dwelt ugliness and beauty in this proud brain.*

The Bishop, Thomas Newton, who had (presumably) confirmed him, and against whom about this time he conceived a bitter hate, the Dean, Cutts Barton, the Precentor, Camplin, and Broughton, the Vicar of Redcliffe, are arraigned, with others, and dismissed scornfully:

Now to the Exhibition we proceed,
And let the reader who can read it read,

a necessary caution, the subject being the arraignment of a clergyman, guilty of indecency, before a panel of Bristol doctors. Possibly this stupid stuff was written to please Barrett, for he alone seems to be mentioned in terms of praise. It was, one would imagine, completely unsuited to a London periodical, even of the *Town and Country* type, and would certainly have been thrown out of *Felix Farley*; an odd occupation, truly, for the first days of party writing in London.

The picture of a Bristol twilight is arresting:

Flying on silken Wings of dusky Grey
The cooling evening clos'd a sultry day
The cit walk'd out to Arno's dusty Vale†
To take a smack of Politicks and ale
Whilst rock'd in clumsy coach about the town
The prudent Mayor jogg'd his dinner down
ll. 197-202.

and the couplet

O Inspirations rising in my Scull
A certain token that the moon's at full

bears out his sister's testimony that he wrote best at this time.‡

* The difference in likeness between Chatterton and Rowley often hits one in the face:

Hie at the deys, lyke to a kynge on's throne
Dyd I take place, and was myself alone.

he writes, in *The Parlyamente of Sprytes*; and, in *Resignation*:

The sceptred King, who dignifies a throne,
Should be in private life himself alone.

† An inn at Brislington, on the Bath Road.

‡ On March 18, 1802, George Catcott wrote to Joseph Cottle objecting to the inclusion of *The Exhibition* in the *Works*. Ingram gives portions of it in

It is pleasanter to turn to the second African Eclogue, *Narva and Mored*, which bears the date May 2, while *The Exhibition* was in the making. This is the first of the only two pieces which the poet had "the vanity to call poetry," and appeared in the *London Magazine* at the end of the month.

The description of the subterranean river here, and in *The Death of Nicou*, may have influenced the imagery of *Kubla Khan ;*

So, when the splendor of the dying day
Darts the mad lustre of the wat'ry way, [? "on "]
Sudden beneath Toddida's whistling brink
The circling billows in wild eddies sink,
Whirl furious round, and the loud bursting wave
Sinks down to Chalma's sacerdotal cave,
Explores the palaces on Zira's coast,
Where howls the war-song of the chieftain's ghost ;
Where the artificer in realms below,
Gilds the rich lance, or beautifies the bow,
From the young palm-tree spins the useful twine,
Or makes the teeth of elephants divine ;
Where the pale children of the feeble sun,
In search of gold, thro' every climate run :
From burning heat to freezing torments go,
And live in all vicissitudes of woe.

The Coleridge parallel (no less than the resemblance between the last eight lines of the quotation and *Isabella*, stanzas xiv and xv) was first noted by Theodore Watts Dunton,* and indeed I cannot think of any other place in English Literature besides *Kubla Khan* where the tumult of waters is associated with a war-song.

Nor perhaps is it a fancy to see in the opening of *Hyperion* a tiny hint taken from the Priestess's lines :

Far from the burning sands of Calabar ;
Far from the lustre of the morning star ;
Far from the pleasure of the holy morn ;
Far from the blessedness of Chalma's horn :

The True Chatterton (Appendix B) ; he is wrong in saying that Sir Daniel Wilson probably never read it, for Wilson had a transcript made of it (*penes me*) in 1869 for his own use.

* Essay on Chatterton in Ward's *English Poets*, Vol. 3.

Now rest the souls of Narva and Mored,
Laid in the dust, and number'd with the dead.
Dear are their memories to us, and long,
Long, shall their attributes be known in song.
Their lives were transient as the meadow flow'r
Ripen'd in ages, wither'd in an hour.
Chalma reward them in his gloomy cave,
And open all the prisons of the grave.
Bred to the service of the Godhead's throne,
And living but to serve his God alone,
Narva was beauteous as the op'ning day
When on the spangling waves the sunbeams play,
When the Mackaw ascending to the sky
Views the bright splendor with a steady eye.*

It is idle to ask whether Chatterton is one of the great poets of the world; of course he is not that, but he is not the least of English poets, as these lines prove, and precursor no less of the great Romantics of the early nineteenth century than of poets like Leconte de Lisle.

The conception of Mored, as that of Birtha, is in contrast with his addresses to actual women:

Where the soft Togla creeps along the meads,
Thro' scented Calamus and fragrant reeds;
Where the sweet Zinsa spreads its matted·bed
Liv'd the still sweeter flow'r, the young Mored;
Black was her face, as Togla's hidden cell;
Soft as the moss where hissing adders dwell.

The young Blake seems to have remembered this in his *An Imitation of Spenser*†:

If thou arrivest at the sandy shore
Where nought but envious hissing adders dwell.

* Mr. Matt. Richardson thinks that the epithets "compact" and "beautous", applied to Narva, may have suggested "In form and shape compact and beautiful." *Hyperion*, II, l. 209.

† This was printed in *Poetical Sketches* (1783). In *An Island in the Moon* (1784 or 1787) Blake refers to Chatterton and the Rowley Controversy (Chapters 3, 5, and 7), imitates *Goddwyn* in Quid's song on "Surgery," and the essay on the Antiquity of Christmas games in that of Steelyard, the Lawgiver:—

. . . old English hospitality is long since deceased.
Chatterton.

Good English hospitality, O then it did not fail!
Blake.

The poet's interest in negroes at this period seems to me spiritually akin to Rimbaud (1854-1891)—the Rimbaud of the *Saison en Enfer*—who wrote " Oui, j'ai les yeux fermés a votre lumière. Je suis une bête, un nègre. Mais je puis être sauvé." It is part and parcel of his disgust with the only civilization he knew. I like to think of these *African Eclogues* as gropings after the divine truth of " The Little Black Boy " (*Songs of Innocence*, 1789).

In the *Court and City Magazine* for July, 1770, without date or signature, is the following piece, which reveals itself as his by the matter as well as by the burletta style ; it is here reprinted for the first time.

AN AFRICAN SONG

Haste, ye purple gleams of light,
  Haste and gild the spacious skies ;
Haste, ye eagles, take your flight,
  Haste and bid the morning rise.

Now the eastern curtain draws ;
  Now the red'ning splendor gleams,
Now the purple plum'd maccaws,
  Skim along the silver streams.

Now the fragrant-scented thorn,
  Trembles with the gummy dew ;
Now the pleasures of the morn,
  Swell upon the eager view.

Whither does my archer stay ?
  Whither is my Narva fled ?
What can keep his soul away,
  From the transports of Mored ?

AIR changes

He comes, he comes ! I see him nigh,
Rapture dancing in his eye ;
Swift as the wolf, or hunted fawn,
He sweeps the flow'ry mantled lawn :
Black, as the glossy fruits which grow,
Where Toyla's* rapid waters flow.

* Probably a misprint for " Togla's."

AIR changes.

God of my life, thy beauteous form,
Makes every wishing bosom warm,
And kindles fierce desire :
Why didst thou leave me all the night
To curse the langour of the light,
And in my flame expire.

HE

Far where the clouds of Bonny spread,
I sought the beauties of Mored
But ah ! I sought in vain !
And thro' the ling'ring darkness trac'd,
The wild inhabitable waste
To Chelmar's burning plain.

But now ! propitious to my love,
The guardian Deities above
Have led me to thy arms !
But now ! I'll shun the coming heat,
And in yon darkened, close retreat,
Enjoy those godlike charms.

Black is that skin as winter's skies* ;
Sparkling and bright those rolling eyes,
As is the venom'd snake ?
O let me haste ! O let me fly !
Upon that lovely bosom die,
And all myself forsake.

It does not respond to the beauty of its opening, but it has more feeling than the third Shoreditch poem, *A song to Miss C—am of Bristol* (May 4), which appeared in the *Court and City* for June, signed "C" :

Then come, my dear charmer, since love is a flame
Which polishes nature, and angels your frame,
Permit the soft passion to rise in your breast,
I leave your good nature to grant me the rest.

* Blacke hys cryne as the wyntere nyghte,
Whyte hys rode as the sommer snowe.
Ælla, ll. 851, 2.

Two days later, on Sunday morning, he wrote again to his mother, whose neglect of her son, at this moment in particular, is curious* :

"Shoreditch, London, May 6, 1770

DEAR MOTHER,

I am surprized that no letter has been sent in answer to my last. I am settled, and in such a settlement, as I would desire. I get four guineas a month by one magazine : shall engage to write a history of England and other pieces, which will more than double that sum. Occasional essays for the daily papers would more than support me. What a glorious prospect ! Mr. Wilkes knew me by my writings since I first corresponded with the booksellers here. I shall visit him next week, and by his interest will ensure Mrs. Ballance the Trinity House. He affirmed that what Mr. Fell had of mine could not be the writings of a youth : and expressed a desire to know the author. By the means of another bookseller I shall be introduced to Townshend and Sawbridge. I am quite familiar at the Chapter Coffee-house, and know all the geniuses there. A character is now necessary ; an author carries his character in his pen. My sister will improve herself in drawing. My grandmother is, I hope, well. Bristol's mercenary walls were never destined to hold me—there, I was out of my element ; now, I am in it—London ! Good God ! how superior is London to that despicable place Bristol† —here is none of your little meannesses, none of your mercenary securities which disgrace that miserable Hamlet.—Dress, which is in Bristol an eternal fund of scandal, is here only introduced as a subject of praise ; if a man dresses well, he has taste ; if careless, he has his own reasons for so doing, and is prudent. Need I remind you of the contrast. The poverty of authors is a common observation, but not always a true one. No author can be poor who understands the arts of booksellers.—Without this necessary knowledge, the greatest genius may starve ; and, with it, the greatest dunce live in splendor. This knowledge I have pretty well dipped into. The Levant man of war, in which T. Wensley went out, is at Portsmouth ; but no news of him yet. I lodge in one of Mr. Walmsley's best rooms. Let Mr Cary copy the letters on the other

* But the post was apt to be erratic in these times ; e.g., "The London mail did not arrive so soon by several hours as usual on Monday, owing to the postman's getting a little intoxicated on his way between Newbury and Marlborough, and falling from his horse into a hedge, where he was found asleep by means of his dog." *Bristol Journal*, Nov. 3, 1770, *ap.* Latimer, *Bristol in the Eighteenth Century*, p. 395.

† "But, Good God ! what a contrast ! Pomp and splendor are the characteristics of our church." Letter of Churchill, *ap. Genuine Memoirs*, p. 150.

side, and give them to the persons for whom they are designed, if not too much labour for him.

I remain, yours, &c.

T. CHATTERTON.

P.S. I have some trifling presents for my mother, sister, Thorne, &c."

"For Mr. T. Cary.

I have sent you a task. I hope no unpleasing one. Tell all your acquaintance for the future to read the Freeholder's Magazine. When you have any thing for publication send it to me, and it shall most certainly appear in some periodical publication. Your last piece was, by the ignorance of a corrector, jumbled under the considerations in the acknowledgments. But I rescued it, and insisted on its appearance.

Your friend,

T. C.

Direct for me, to be left at the Chapter Coffee-house, Paternoster-row."*

This, as Masson remarks, is pretty well after only ten days in London.† We hear nothing more of the History of England in the letters home, or of Mr. Wilkes (for next week Mr. Fell was safe in the King's Bench), or the two aldermen, nor is the Chapter Coffee House‡ (in Chapter House Court, a famous meeting place for publishers, where in 1777 a scheme was arranged for offering Dr. Johnson the editorship of the British poets) mentioned again, save once in a most incredible connection; moreover the writer does not add that he *shares* one of Mr. Walmsley's best rooms with his host's nephew; but he has bought presents for his family, and that is as much as to say that his fortune is made.

The letters on the other side, which, to save postage from London to Bristol, Thomas Cary is instructed to copy, are addressed to Henry Kator, a sugar baker, William Smith, a Mrs. Baker, one Mason, and Matthew Mease, of whose name

* *L. and M.*, p. 170.

† *Chatterton* (ed. 1899) p. 157.

‡ "The conversation here naturally turns upon the newest publications; but their criticisms are somewhat singular. When they say a *good* book, they do not mean to praise the style or sentiment, but the quick and extensive sale of it." *The Connoisseur*, No. 1, Jan. 31, 1754. For other literary associations of the Chapter Coffee House, including Johnson and Charlotte Brontë, see Wheatley, *London Past and Present*, Vol. I, pp. 350, 351.

he had made public use lately, maybe in *Kew Gardens*, (which was doubtless circulated among his acquaintance), telling them to read the *Freeholder's Magazine*, and send any pieces they have for publication to him at the Chapter Coffee House. Mrs. Baker is asked to give him John "Rymsdyk's," the Bath painter's, address, and Mason to send a short prose description of the situation of Nash (this cannot be Beau Nash, who died in 1761). Cary must tell thirteen other specified persons and an &c. to read the *Freeholder's Magazine*; this is quite understandable; Chatterton was the only person writing poetry in the April number.* The generalissimo-like orders remind one forcibly of Mrs. Newton's early recollection of her brother as presiding over his playmates "as their master and they his hired servants."

Whatever effect this letter may have had on the home party, the opening of the next, eight days later, must have given Mrs. Chatterton a fright, and such may well have been her son's intention, for he could have written it from Shoreditch.

"King's Bench, for the present, May 14, 1770.†

DEAR MADAM,

Don't be surprized at the name of the place. I am not here as a prisoner. Matters go on swimmingly: Mr Fell having offended certain persons, they have set his creditors upon him, and he is safe in the King's Bench. I have been bettered by this accident: His successors in the Freeholder's Magazine, knowing nothing of the matter, will be glad to engage me, on my own terms. Mr. Edmunds has been tried before the House of Lords, sentenced to pay a fine, and thrown into Newgate. His misfortunes will be to me of no

* As for the piece of his friend which the poet claims to have rescued, I can only tentatively suggest that it may be some lines "On Miss P.L." in the April *Town and Country*. "The fair one's name" is given in the last line as "L-t-y." Polly Lutley was Cary's flame. Dated "Bristol, April 7," the piece is signed "S.Y.," the last, instead of the first, letters of "Thomas Cary." The identification is perhaps not quite so far-fetched as it seems, as James Thistlethwaite (*teste* Lort) on occasion signed his effusions "S.E."; it may serve to show the difficulties a modern "hunter of oddities" in the magazines of the period has to contend with.

† The necessary "good address" in this century was provided by the coffee house or tavern. Johnson was told before he came to London in 1737 few people would enquire where he lodged, and if they did, it was easy to say, "Sir, I am to be found at such a place." In "King's Bench" Chatterton is scoffing at convention, maybe.

little service. Last week being in the pit of Drury-Lane Theatre, I contracted an immediate acquaintance (which you know is no hard task to me) with a young gentleman in Cheapside; partner in a music shop, the greatest in the city. Hearing I could write, he desired me to write a few songs for him: this I did the same night, and conveyed them to him the next morning. These he showed to a doctor in music, and I am invited to treat with this doctor, on the footing of a composer, for Ranelagh and the gardens. *Bravo, hey boys, up we go!*—Besides the advantage of visiting these expensive and polite places, gratis; my vanity will be fed with the sight of my name in copper-plate, and my sister will receive a bundle of printed songs, the words by her brother. These are not all my acquisitions: a gentleman who knows me at the Chapter, as an author, would have introduced me as a companion to the young Duke of Northumberland, in his intended general tour. But alas! I speak no tongue but my own!—But to return once more to a place I am sickened to write of, Bristol. Tho', as an apprentice none had greater liberties, yet the thoughts of servitude killed me: now I have that for my labour, I always reckoned the first of my pleasures, and have still, my liberty. As to the clearance, I am ever ready to give it; but really I understand so little of the law, that I believe Mr. Lambert must draw it.* Mrs. L brought what you mention. Mrs. Hughes is as well as age will permit her to be, and my cousin does very well.

I will get some patterns worth your acceptance;† and wish you and my sister would improve yourselves in drawing, as it is here a valuable and never-failing acquisition.—My box shall be attended to; I hope my books are in it‡—if not, send them; and particularly Catcott's Hutchinsonian jargon on the Deluge, and the M.S. Glossary, composed of one small book annexed to a larger."

Then comes a long passage, dealt with earlier in this book (Chapter VIII), about his female acquaintance, which shows, unless it is a part of his singularity, that the conversation at home must have been unrestrained on these topics. Ending "I promised before my departure to write to some hundreds, I believe," he continues:

* This I take to be sarcasm. He had received no legal instruction at Corn Street; he was merely the office drudge; but Lambert might argue, "He copied precedents; he should be able to draw a clearance."

† "She [Mrs. Chatterton] keeps a small school drawing patterns." Lort, *Memorandum*, Aug. 14, 1777, 11457.

‡ According to Croft (*L. and M.*, p. 142) many books were sent, in languages and in "hands" which Mrs. Newton could not understand, and with them a catalogue of the books he had read to the amount of many hundreds.

" but, what with writing for publications, and going to places of public diversion, which is as absolutely necessary to me as food,* I find but little time to write to you.—As to Mr. Barrett, Mr. Catcott, Mr. Burgum, &c. &c. they rate literary lumber† so low, that I believe an author, in their estimation, must be poor indeed! But here matters are otherwise; had Rowley been a Londoner, instead of a Bristowyan, I could have lived by copying his works.—In my humble opinion, I am under very few obligations to any persons in Bristol; one, indeed, has obliged me, but, as most do, in a manner which makes his obligation no obligation.—My youthful acquaintances will not take it in dudgeon that I do not write oftener to them, than I believe I shall: but as I had the happy art of pleasing in conversation, my company was often liked, where I did not like: and to continue a correspondence under such circumstances, would be ridiculous. Let my sister improve in copying music, drawing, and every thing which requires genius: in Bristol's mercantile style those things may be useless, if not a detriment to her; but here they are highly profitable.—Inform Mr Rhise that nothing shall be wanting on my part, in the business he was so kind as to employ me in; should be glad of a line from him to know whether he would engage in the marine department; or spend the rest of his days, safe, on dry ground.—Intended waiting on the Duke of Bedford, relative to the Trinity House; but his Grace is dangerously ill. My grandmother, I hope, enjoys the state of health I left her in. I am Miss Webb's humble servant. Thorne shall not be forgot, when I remit the small trifles to you. Notwithstanding Mrs B's not being able to inform me of Mr. Garsed's address, thro' the closeness of the pious Mr. Ewer, I luckily stumbled upon it this morning.

I remain, &c. &c. &c. &c.

THOMAS CHATTERTON.

Monday evening.

(Direct for me, at Mr. Walmsley's, at Shoreditch—only.) "‡

The misfortunes of the editors of the *Freeholder's Magazine* and the *Middlesex Journal* did not affect him much, no doubt, as Hamilton took over the latter; but the remark about his youthful acquaintances suggests that he is no longer able to serve them, and is in marked contrast with the instructions to

* " He frequented taverns and coffee-houses, places of public diversion, got acquainted with bucks and bloods, and people of all sorts of characters; and, in order to see low as well as high life, did not disdain sometimes to go into obscure public-houses, the better to observe the different scenes which different places could afford." *Genuine Memoirs of Mr. Charles Churchill*, pp. 127, 128.

† " My useless lumber of literature." Letter to Walpole, Apr. 8, 1769.

‡ *L and M.*, p. 174.

Cary. At the Chapter House he had probably been told that he was not of sufficient importance to have letters addressed to him there. The remark about speaking no tongue but his own we have met in the *Epistle to the Rev. Mr. Catcott*, and that about Rowley being a Londoner, Bryant tells us, he occasionally made to his sister at Bristol.* The promise in the previous letter to ensure Mrs. Ballance a pension as a sailor's widow seems to have been taken up by his mother, and we are now flattered with a vision of the Duke of Bedford, a still remoter personage than Mr. Wilkes.

The Drury Lane incident must have led to the composition of *The Revenge.* What he saw there is matter for conjecture. On May 7, *The Provoked Husband* and *The Ladies' Frolic* (music by William Bates), an adaptation of *The Jovial Crew*, playing (May 9) at Covent Garden with Mr. Reinhold as Hearty, were given, on the 8th *Romeo* (Brereton's Benefit), and on the 9th *As you like it.*† The music shop was possibly John Longman and Co., 26 Cheapside (established 1767), and the doctor of music Dr. Samuel Arnold, of whom more later. The references to Lambert in this and the first letter are high-spirited enough, but the high spirits are but a veil for savage mockery and contempt, qualities which must for ever distinguish the familiar letters of Chatterton from those of many another young provincial journalist who has come up to London to set the Thames on fire.

"All goes on swimmingly." Wilkes had been enlarged on the night of April 17. "The Lord Mayor had enjoined tranquillity as Mayor," Walpole wrote to Sir Horace Mann two days later; "as Beckford, his own house in Soho Square, was embroidered with '*Liberty*' in white letters three feet high. Luckily the evening was very wet, and not a mouse stirred." However, on the 24th Wilkes was sworn in as an alderman for the Ward of Farringdon Without, and banqueted famously. By the time Chatterton reached London news of the Boston

* *Obs.*, p. 522.

† The other plays at Drury Lane for this week were *Jealous Wife* (10), *Double Falsehood* (11), *Cymon*, followed by *The Minor*, "with a grand procession of knights of different orders of chivalry" (12).

Riot (March 5) had come in, and was illustrated by a copper-plate of American citizens being shot down, in the *Freeholder's* for May. This presage of war with the Colonies forms the subject of Decimus's letter to the Earl of H[illsborough], third Secretary of State for American affairs, in the *Middlesex*, for May 10, dated " Bristol, April 27 " :

" Think of the recent murders at Boston. O, my lord ! however you may force a smile into your countenance, however you may trifle in the train of dissipation, your conscience must raise a hell within."*

On May 1, Chatham in the Lords renewed a motion " to appeal and rescind the resolution of the House of Commons in regard to the expulsion and incapacitation of Mr. Wilkes," which was lost by forty-six votes ; and, before Parliament was prorogued on the 19th, measures, as we have seen, had been taken to put a check on the editors of the anti-ministerial journals.

Notwithstanding, the voice of Decimus was still heard in the *Middlesex* ; the notices to correspondents under dates May 3, 17 and 24 respectively, have :

" Decimus has our sincere thanks, and may depend on our making use of the precautions he requires.

" Decimus may be assured his two last essays are in the Editor's hands, and will be published in due time.

" The address to the Freeholders of Bristol, is come to hand."

The 15th saw the publication of a long letter to the Princess Dowager, dated "May 10," and the 22nd that of one to Lord North, dated "May 15." There is something grotesquely comical to us now in an unknown minor addressing the Premier as follows :

" You may be a good husband—a good father—I cannot deny it,

* I take this opportunity of stating that the Letter to the Earl of Dartmouth (*Political Register*, Oct., 1772) signed " Probus " cannot possibly be Chatterton's, as Lord Hillsborough resigned the Secretaryship of State for the Colonies on Aug. 10, 1772. It is reprinted, with a doubt only, in Skeat, Vol. I, p. 320.

I know nothing of your concerns ; but private virtues, or private vices, in a minister are of no public account*. . . .
. . . Is there one honest man now in the administration of public affairs ? If there is, let him be pointed out, for the author cannot find him ! . . .
Fly to the council, with your face whitened with fear : tell them, that justice is at the door, and the axe will do its office."

Immediately under this letter is printed "A Card. To old Slyboots" (a writer in the *Public Advertiser* and *General Evening Post*) signed "Libertas," dated "May 16," and beginning, "Sir, if your affected comicality will permit you to peruse seriously what an honest heart dictates, you may not repent you have given a few moments to advice." This, which has escaped the editors, is undoubtedly Chatterton's, for it appears in the autograph list of his political letters in his pocket-book—" Libertas to old Slyboots" It invites the "hireling of the Minister" to confine himself "to the humble sphere of a literary harlequin."

On the 23rd an event took place which raised the Lord Mayor to equal popularity with Wilkes, who was not present on the occasion. This was his "humble remonstrance" to the King in person at his rejection of the Corporation of London's petition (March 14) against excluding the member for Middlesex from the Commons. On the King declaring that his sentiments on that subject continued the same, Beckford *answered* the royal reply by an informal and (as it reads now) perfectly harmless assertion of the City of London's loyalty, still legible in gilt letters on the base of his statue in the Guildhall.† This flagrant breach of official etiquette, which reduced George III to answer

* Compare the passage in Macaulay's *Essay on Milton* beginning, "For ourselves, we own that we do not understand the common phrase, a good man, but a bad king."

† "Wondrous loyal and respectful, but being an innovation, much discomposed the solemnity" (Walpole, to Sir H. Mann, May 24, 1770). It is well known that Horne Tooke claimed to have written the rejoinder (Sam. Rogers's *Table Talk*, ed. 1903, p. 102). Sir William Treloar (*Wilkes and the City of London*, 1917, p. 98) says, "I believe that Beckford made no rejoinder to the King, or merely muttered a few indistinct words, and the speech was concocted afterwards." But the two letters of Sheriff Townsend to the Earl of Chatham (May 23, 25, 1770), the first of them written on the same day, seem conclusive as to a rejoinder having actually been made. (See *Chatham Correspondence*, III, p. 460, and *D.N.B.*, Art. William Beckford.)

extempore, "no part of the royal trade," as Walpole observed, "or sit silent," is characterized by Chatterton thus:

Hence, honest to his Prince, his manly Tongue,
The PUBLIC WRONG and LOYALTY convey'd,
While TITLED TREMBLERS, ev'ry Nerve unstrung,
Look'd all around, confounded and dismay'd.

Look'd all around, astonish'd to behold
(Train'd up to Flatt'ry from their early Youth)
An ARTLESS, FEARLESS Citizen unfold
To ROYAL Ears, a MORTIFYING Truth.

Elegy on William Beckford.

It must be remembered that "Wilkes and Liberty" had been the political topic *par excellence* since April 23, 1763, when Number 45 of the *North Briton* was published, before the poet was eleven, and Beckford's extempore speech of 1770 may have struck him (for one moment, at any rate) as a coming to life of his fifteenth century patriot, who so boldly faced Edward IV:

Beholde the manne! hee spoke the truthe,
Hee's greaterr thanne a Kynge!

The day after the Remonstrance (May 24) the *Middlesex* printed "Probus's" letter to the Lord Mayor, dated the 18th, advising Beckford how to approach the King: "Should you address again, my Lord, it would not be amiss to tell his Majesty, that you expect *his* answer, and not the answer of his mother or ministers." This letter was reprinted in the *Political Register* for June, though, one would have thought, even more out of date by that time.

Among the political letters of Chatterton in MS. which Michael Lort saw, and of which there is a note extant in Lort's hand, was one to Lord North signed "The Moderator" (May 26, 1770), an encomium on the administration for rejecting the Remonstrance, beginning, "My Lord, it gives me a painful pleasure." Horace Walpole instances this* to show that

* *Letter to the Editor of Chatterton's Miscellanies*, p. 51, based on Lort's memoranda, 11457. Wilkes himself wrote on both sides of the question, e.g., to *The Auditor* praising "Floridan peat," and exposed it in the *North Briton*. *Cambridge History of English Literature*, X, 392.

Chatterton alternately flattered and satirized all ranks and parties, a statement which, with Broderip, Burgum, and Barrett in mind, no less than the remark in the poet's letter of May 30, four days ahead, one is hardly inclined to dispute. It is confirmed by an extant transcript, in Lort's hand, of the letter's conclusion : " Mr. Wilkes now shines at the head of the patriots. He is the epitome of the faction ; self-interested, treasonable and inconsiderable. That minister must be virtuous who is opposed by such pretended Patriots. Their approbation is Infamy, and the way of truth is only known as being opposite to the course they take." This has, I believe, never yet found a place in a life of Chatterton.

Lort also saw an " Introductory Essay to the Moderator," a paper, apparently, set up by Chatterton, which, he says, was in favour of the Government, as well as a Letter to Lord Mansfield beginning " My Lord, I am not going to accuse you of pusillanimity," with many passages cancelled, and a marginal comment " Prosecution will lye upon this," which, as we shall see, was afterwards printed. Another of these MS. letters had a note of payment at the rate of half a guinea a column.

On the 26th Decimus, under date May 17, appears as a critic of an exhibition of sign paintings. There are several articles of this type in the newspapers of the time,* and as Chatterton in his letter to George Catcott of Aug. 12 speaks of " one of my exhibitions " he may be held responsible for more than one. An exhibit has already been quoted in the chapter dealing with Walpole ; here are three more :

" 11. *The Genius of Bristol, by Bonner,*—Represents a fish-woman sleeping on a cask : her shield a cheese, with her arms blazoned ; three hogs couchant in the mire ; her lance a spit, with a goose on it. There are several smaller figures in the groupe ; a turn-spit dog, a sleeping Alderman, and a Welch rabbit.

" 20. *The Earl of Bute.*—The English and Scotch disagree concerning this figure. The connoisseurs of the latter assert, that it is not perfect, because it wants a head ; whilst the opposite party as strenuously maintain that it could not be perfect unless it wanted a head.

* e.g., *Boddely's Bath Journal,* May 29, 1769, June 18, 1770 ; *Bingley's Journal,* Aug. 4, 18, 1770 ; *General Evening Post,* Aug. 28, 1770.

"24. *The last Peace,*—modelled in gingerbread, and ready to fall in pieces with the slightest touch."

The description of exhibit 1 shows that his poem *The Whore of Babylon* was intended directly to reflect on the Princess Dowager. The letter to the Freeholders of Bristol (dated May 21), urging them to follow the lead of the "humble remonstrance," appeared on the 31st; to make a fair close, the Rowley Romance is resuscitated:

'Remember the speech of the glorious COMYNGE (*sic*), in whose repeated mayoralties, honour and virtue were not unknown in the corporation. When the unhappy dissentions first broke out between the house of Lancaster and York, he immediately declared himself for the latter. His Lady, fearful of the consequences, begged him to desist, and not ruin himself and family. "My family," replied the brave citizen, "is dear to me: Heaven can witness how dear! But when discord and oppressions begin to distract the realm, my country is my family, and THAT it is my duty to protect."'

This speech, ascribed to "Sir John de Beauchamp," appears in the *Town and Country* for June, as a separate article. Immediately above the letter, in the "Poet's Corner" of the *Middlesex*, is the brilliant Swiftian piece *The Prophecy*, without date or signature, the last three stanzas of which run:

When George shall condescend to hear
The modest suit, the humble prayer;
A Prince, to purpled pride unknown!
No fav'rite to share the throne!*
   Look up, ye Britons! sigh no more,
   For your redemption's at the door.

When time shall bring your wish about,
Or sev'n years lease *you sold* is out;
No future contract to fulfill;
Your tenants holding at your will;
   Raise up your heads, your rights demand,
   For your redemption's in your hand.

Then is the time to strike the blow,
And let the *slaves* of Mammon know,

* The version in the *Political Register* (June, 1770) has "No favourites disgrace the throne."

Britain's true sons A BRIBE can scorn,
And die as FREE as they were born.
VIRTUE again shall take her seat,
And your redemption stand compleat.

On the previous day he had written home, possibly, but by no means certainly, from "Tom's" in Devereux Court, Strand, the coffee-house frequented by Akenside*; here, at least, good care is taken not to alarm by the name of the place:

"Tom's Coffee House, London, May 30, 1770.

DEAR SISTER,

There is such a noise of business and politicks, in the room, that my inaccuracy in writing here, is highly excusable. My present profession obliges me to frequent places of the best resort. To begin with, what every female conversation begins with, dress. I employ my money now in fitting myself fashionably†; and getting into good company; this last article always brings me in interest. But I have engaged to live with a gentleman, the brother of a Lord (a Scotch one indeed) who is going to advance pretty deeply into the bookselling branches: I shall have lodging and boarding, genteel and elegant, gratis: this article in the quarter of the town he lives in, with worse accommodations, would be 50 l. per annum. I shall have, likewise, no inconsiderable premium: and assure yourself, every month, shall end to your advantage: I will send you two silks this summer‡: and expect, in answer to this, what colours you prefer. My mother shall not be forgotten. My employment will be in writing a voluminous history of London, to appear in numbers the beginning of next winter: as this will not, like writing political essays, oblige me to go to the Coffee-house; I shall be able to serve you the more by it.§ But it will necessitate me to go to Oxford, Cambridge, Lincoln, Coventry, and every Collegiate Church near; not at all disagreeable journeys, and not to me expensive. The Manuscript Glossary, I mentioned in my last, must not be omitted. If money flowed as fast upon me as honours, I would give you a portion of

* Thornbury (*Old and New London*, Vol. II, p. 173) thinks Tom's in Birchin Lane, the rendezvous of young merchants at 'Change time, is the place meant; there was another Tom's in Russell St., Covent Garden.

† He had "a shabby genteel dress." Oldham's testimony, *ap.* Lort, 11457.

‡ This was the season for silks:—

Now new vamp'd silks the mercer's window shows,
And the spruce prentice wears his Sunday clothes.
"Description of May in London," *Public Advertiser*, May 2.

§ The history of England has turned into this. J. Noorthouck, who published *A New History of London* (1773), denied having seen Chatterton. Gregory says "the scheme appears not to have been proceeded in." *Life*, p. 85, *n*.

5000 l. You have, doubtless, heard of the Lord Mayor's remonstrating and addressing the King: but it will be a piece of news to inform you that I have been with the Lord Mayor on the occasion.* Having addressed an essay to his Lordship, it was very well received; perhaps better than it deserved; and I waited on his Lordship, to have his approbation, to address a second letter to him, on the subject of the remonstrance, and its reception. His Lordship received me as politely as a citizen could: and warmly invited me to call on him again. The rest is a secret.†—But the devil of the matter is, there's no money to be got of this side the question. Interest is of the other side. But he is a poor author, who cannot write on both sides. I believe I may be introduced (and, if I am not, I'll introduce myself) to a ruling power in the court party. I might have a recommendation to Sir George Colebrooke, an East India director,‡ as qualified for an office no means despicable; but I shall not take a step to the sea, whilst I can continue on land. I went yesterday to Woolwich, to see Mr. Wensley; he is paid to-day. The artillery is no unpleasing sight; if we bar reflection; and do not consider how much mischief it may do. Greenwich Hospital, and St. Paul's Cathedral are the only structures which could reconcile me to any thing out of the gothic. Mr. Carty will hear from me soon: multiplicity of literary business must be my excuse.—

I condole with him, and my dear Miss Sanford, in the misfortune of Mrs. Carty: my physical advice is, to leach her temples plentifully: keep her very low in diet: as much in the dark as possible. Nor is this last prescription the whim of an old woman: whatever hurts the eyes, affects the brain: and the particles of light, when the sun is in the summer signs, are highly prejudicial to the eyes; and it is from this sympathetic effect, that the head ach is general in summer. But, above all, talk to her but little, and never contradict her in any thing. This may be of service. I hope it will.§ Did a paragraph appear in your papers of Saturday last, mentioning the inhabitants of London's having opened another view of St. Paul's,|| and advising the Corporation, or vestry of Redclift, to procure a more compleat view of Redclift church? My compliments to Miss Thatcher; if I am in love, I am; tho' the devil take me, if I can tell with whom it is; I believe I may address her in the words of

* Note "on the occasion," though it is instantly modified by the next clause.

† The only confirmation of this interview is Chatterton's extravagant despair on Beckford's death.

‡ There is a letter attacking him, signed "Probus," in the *Public Advertiser* of April 23.

§ The sole evidence we have of Barrett's tuition.

|| Chatterton referred to this in a destroyed letter to Catcott; Letter-book, p. 42.

Scripture, which no doubt she reveres ; if you had not plowed with my heifer (or bullock rather), you had not found out my riddle.* Humbly thanking Miss Rumsey, for her complimentary expression, I cannot think it satisfactory. Does she, or does she not, intend coming to London ? Mrs O'Coffin has not yet got a place ; but there is not the least doubt but she will in a little time.

Essay writing has this advantage, you are sure of constant pay ; and when you have once wrote a piece, which makes the author enquired after, you may bring the booksellers to your own terms. Essays on the patriotic side, fetch no more than what the copy is sold for. As the patriots themselves are searching for a place, they have no gratuities to spare. So says one of the beggars, in a temporary alteration of mine, in the Jovial Crew.

A patriot was my occupation,
It got me a name, but no pelf :
Till, starv'd for the good of the nation,
I begg'd for the good of myself.
Fal, lal, &c.

I told them, if 'twas not for me,
Their freedoms would all go to pot,
I promis'd to set them all free,
But never a farthing I got.
Fal, lal, &c.†

—On the other hand, unpopular essays will not even be accepted : and you must pay to have them printed, but then you seldom lose by it—Courtiers are so sensible of their deficiency in merit, that they generally reward all who know how to daub them with an appearance of it. To return to private affairs.—Friend Slude may depend upon

* Judges xiv. 18. Beyond the comparison of himself to Samson, the allusion, I suspect, is past finding out.

† This is altered from Air xvii of *The Jovial Crew* (1731, the opera based on Richard Brome's play), which was probably sung at both Drury Lane and Covent Garden in the week beginning May 7, 1770 ; the first verse runs, with Bates's accompaniment :—

I once was a Poet at London, I keep my Heart still full of Glee, There's no Man can say that I'm undone, for Begging's no new trade to me, tol de rol *etc.*

It is conceivable that this is the song which he "*poetted*" about the streets, for it was popular, and has gone to the making of "Sir Wisdom's a fool when he's fou" in Burns's cantata *The Jolly Beggars*. See Burns, centenary edition (Henley and Henderson), Vol. II, p. 294, and *Times Literary Supplement*, Dec. 13, 1923.

my endeavouring to find the publications you mention. They publish the Gospel Magazine here. For a whim I write in it: I believe there are not any sent to Bristol; they are hardly worth the carriage: Methodistical and unmeaning.* With the usual ceremonies to my mother, and grandmother: and sincerely, without ceremony, wishing them both happy; when it is in my power to make them so, they shall be so; and with my kind remembrance to Miss Webb, and Miss Thorne, I remain as I ever was,

Yours, &c. to the end of the chapter,

THOMAS CHATTERTON.

P.S. I am this minute pierced through the heart, by the black eye of a young lady, driving along in a hackney coach.—I am quite in love: if my love lasts till that time, you shall hear of it in my next."

There is little to comment here, save that the saga of success rings a trifle hollow, the Scotch lord's brother being altogether too good to be true; the sole actualities that emerge, *l'affaire Beckford* apart, are the writer's lack of funds, and his readiness to appear as a man of fashion, reflection, learning, and experience, a universal genius, in fact, on all occasions.

We now come to the matter of payments. The articles sent from Bristol, it is supposed, were not paid for, but met with a few copies of the paper served; and the only *unimpeachable* evidence of earnings in London is the receipt still in existence (*Add. MS.* 12050, f. 18 v.) for *The Revenge* (July 6). This five guineas, out of which it is inferred that he bought the presents for his mother and sister, is *not* entered in Chatterton's pocket-book, a calendar for 1769, without cover, and lacking pages at the beginning and end, which was found on him at death, and given by his sister on her deathbed to Joseph Cottle; it contains entries for May, 1770, only. These tell a sad tale. £10 . 17 . 6 is set down as "due from others"; he has written "gratis" for the *Court and City*, and there is no payment from "Mr. Hamilton as a writer in the Middlesex Journal," or from Mr. Mortimer under "May 1"; neither is there payment from "Mr. Coote in the Oxford Magazine," nor from the *London*

* The lines "found written on a blank leaf in Lucas's *Enquiry after Happiness*" appeared in the *Gospel Magazine* for Nov., 1770, signed D.B.; *The Retreat*, signed T.C. (*ibid.* March, 1766), is probably not his. See Wilson, p. 271.

Magazine. Fell has paid him 10/6 for *The Consuliad* (published in January),* and the same amount for "Resigned" (*Resignation*). One "B" has paid him £1.2.3. Against "Middlesex Journal" is written "8.6," and underneath, "9th London Packet" with no corresponding sum; and there is a note "Recd. to May 23 of Mr. Hamilton for Middlesex £1.11.6," which works out at half a guinea each for the political letters that appeared on May 10, 15, and 22. Hamilton has also paid him two shillings for "Candidate" (*The Candidates* is 34 lines long) "and Foreign Intelligence," and half a guinea on the 16th, where there is a note of "Songs," and no corresponding payment. Therefore he would seem to have made £4 15s. 9d.; and four shillings are entered in all as having been lent by him, sixpence being lent on May 2 when the two shillings were paid,† The only dates he mentions are "May 1, May 2, 9th, 16th, May 23."

These entries, be it observed, are not made in the proper spaces of the calendar for April 24–May 7; a leaf has been torn out of the book, and he has written across the present double pages subsequent to its abstraction; moreover "£2 12s. 6d." appears without any explanation or date in the left hand corner of the week May 8–17, an item unmentioned by the biographers, though duly noted in the catalogue of the Bristol Museum, where this relic is preserved.

Most practising literary men know that magazine payments are at all times apt to be irregular, and sometimes even a twelve-month after the contribution has been accepted or printed. Chatterton, who knew the art of Curlism pretty well, cannot have been unaware of this; and indeed Mr. Hamilton's settlement on May 2 of the two shillings for the poem, &c., published only the previous day, must, though the sum was

* Magazines were then published *at the end* of the month whose name they bore.

† "When twelve years of age, he could not bear to hear of anyone suffering; and passing over the Drawbridge, where at that time many beggars plied, she has seen him distribute all the halfpence he had in his pocket, and do without what he was going to purchase for himself." Mrs. Edkins, *ap.* Cumberland (*circ.* 1828), who also says that Cary grieved Chatterton greatly by once reminding him of a debt of twenty shillings before her, a sum so large as to make both anecdotes suspicious.

small, have been cheering to a soul that craved for immediate justice. With the deepest sympathy for the poet's fate, I do not think any stable conclusion as to payments can be drawn from this pocket-book, except that he seems to have depended mainly on the Mr. Hamilton who edited the *Middlesex Journal*, one of the two Archibald Hamiltons,* father and son; the latter conducted the *Town and Country*, of which periodical the pocket-book tells us nothing.

The *Court and City* has yielded us *An African Song*, the *Oxford Magazine* for April yields us an unsigned contribution, not as unmistakably by Chatterton as that piece, but his, I think:

The BACCHANALIAN.

Ye sordid wretches! chain'd to rules,
As asses dull, and obstinate as mules;
Whose minds ne'er knew one lib'ral thought,
Back to your sneaking miserable cells!†
Where narrowness of thinking dwells,
With not one social sense of feeling fraught.

There, free from tumult, free from strife,
In silence doze, nor snuff the wick of life:
But slowly let it waste away
Whilst cunning Prudence plauds the saving scheme,‡
Nor let its flame so much as seem
To cast a glimpse of one eccentric ray.§

Give me the man of blither soul,
Whose spirits thro' an ampler channel roll,
Who, spite of Method's drowsy plan,
Will plunge alert into a sea of joy,
And float on active Fancy's buoy,
And snatch at fleeting pleasure whilst he can.

* See Nichols, *L. A.*, III, p. 399. Lort interviewed them both in 1777; 11063, p. 425.

† But bred in Bristol's mercenary cell,
Compell'd in scenes of avarice to dwell,
Kew Gardens.

‡ Bristol may keep her prudent maxims still,
But know, my saving friends, I never will.
The Whore of Babylon.

§ Ne lette a flame enharme the grounde,
Tylle ynne one flame all the whole worlde expyre.
Songe to Ælla.

See yonder festive jocund band !
A nectar'd goblet gracing ev'ry hand ;
Mirth opes the storehouse of the soul,
And on Ill-nature turns the polish'd key :
Sullen the demon limps away,
Nor dares exert the function of controul.

Thither let me bend in haste,
And embrace the bottle's waist,
Charms Anacreontic prove,
Quaffing to the god of love ;
Brighter blushes paint his face,
And he looks a fresher grace,
When with Bacchus he reclines
Underneath his purple vines.
How the jolly hunting song,
Emblematic, loud, and strong,
On Attention's organ dwells,
And the force of care dispels.
Till the full-voic'd, bursting chorus
Sets the fox and hounds before us.
Sons of sorrow ! quit your beds,
Seek the path which Bacchus treads,
Drown your avaricious notions
In the claret's lively potions :
Mind not what the Miser says,
Folly 'tis to earn his praise ;
Or his constitution fails,
Or his avarice prevails,
Else he'd laugh, and quaff, and be
Airy, tipsy, gay as we.*

Here I see, not only the deft ringer of metrical changes, but the lawyer's apprentice who, his indentures cancelled, has thrown himself on the metropolis.

Such was the mood of this proud, fighting heart at this juncture ; and whatever degree of untruth there may be in the letters to Bristol, the sanguine determination to appear victorious at all costs (however imprudent and ill-suited to the literary character) compels enthusiasm and perhaps regard. Unworldly Goldsmith, or Elia, humorously and humbly grateful for a

* Compare the two "Bacchanalians" for Mr. Reinhold, appended to *The Revenge*. This piece was first reprinted in the *Times Literary Supplement* for May 31, 1923. The last 16 lines are miserably imitated by a writer signing himself "S. S." in the *Town and Country Magazine*, Suppl., 1771.

"noble goose," is the English beau ideal of a brother of the quill, not a Kastril, even though he happens to have written an *Ælla.* The question that arises next is how did the gray-eyed, laborious, fiery being appear to his new associates; and, thanks to Croft, who interviewed the five parties at Shoreditch within ten years of the Brooke Street suicide, it can be answered satisfactorily.*

"Mrs. Ballance says he was as proud as Lucifer. He very soon quarrelled with her for calling him 'Cousin *Tommy*,' and asked her if she ever heard of a poet's being called *Tommy*: but she assured him she knew nothing of poets, and only wished he would not set up for a gentleman. Upon her recommending it to him to get into some office, when he had been in town two or three weeks,"—quite clearly when his affairs were put out of gear by the arrest of Edmunds and Fell—"he stormed about the room like a madman, and frightened her not a little, by telling her, he hoped, with the blessing of God, very soon to be sent prisoner to the Tower, which would make his fortune"—like Wilkes, in fact, after the publication of *No.* 45. "He would often look stedfastly in a person's face, without speaking, or seeming to see the person, for a quarter of an hour or more, till it was quite frightful; during all which time (she supposes, from what she has since heard), his thoughts were gone about something else." This procedure is not *wholly* explained by the "extasy or trance" William Smith speaks of, when Chatterton's eyes were fixed on St. Mary Redcliff,† or by the old female relation's statement that he was "very absent in company,"‡ for, if correctly reported, it would not appear to be characteristic of an abstracted person, who does not *stare* at his interlocutor. Possibly the poet wanted to give Mrs. Ballance good cause for remembering him, unless this was a mere impish prank, a means of defence while she was holding forth. "He frequently said he should settle the nation before he had done; but how could she think her poor cousin Tommy was so great a man as she now finds he was? His mother should have written

* *L. and M.*, pp. 189-193.
† Bryant, *Obs.*, p. 530.
‡ *L. and M.*, p. 148.

word of his greatness, and then, to be sure, she would have humoured the gentleman accordingly." It is easy to imagine how much he must have disliked taking meals alone with this worthy creature, having come to London partly to escape from good advice.

"Mr. Walmsley saw nothing of him, but that there was something manly and pleasing about him, and he did not dislike the wenches"; in other words he struck a British working man as not in the least abnormal.

"Mrs. W.'s account is, that she never saw any harm of him—that he never *mislisted* [? molested] her; but was always very civil, whenever they met in the house by accident—that he would never suffer the room, in which he used to read and write, to be swept, because, he said, poets hated brooms—that she told him she did not know anything *poet folks* were good for, but to sit in a dirty cap and gown in a garret, and at last to be starved." Her ideas were possibly formed from Hogarth's print of the Distressed Poet. "That, during the nine weeks he was at her house, he never staid out after the family hours, except once, when he did not come home all night, and had been, she heard, *poetting* a song about the streets. This night, Mrs. Ballance says, she knows he lodged at a relation's, because Mr. W.'s house was shut up when he came home."

He was, as we should say, "in good hands" at the Walmsleys', and no doubt kept in touch with his London relations, for quietness' sake.

Then comes the younger people's testimony.* "The niece" (a girl of between seventeen and eighteen in 1770) "says, for her part, she always took him more for a mad boy than any thing else, he would have such flights and *vagaries*—that, but for his face and her knowledge of his age, she should never have thought him a boy, he was so manly, and *so much himself*—that no women came after him, nor did she know of any connexion; but, still, that he was a sad rake, and terribly fond

* I follow Masson (p. 128) not Wilson (p. 251, *n.*) as to their ages. Croft says "the latter" (the niece) "as old as C. would be now, the former three years younger," speaking of the time when he interviewed them, 1779.

of women, and would sometimes be saucy to her—that he ate what he chose to have with his relation (Mrs. B.) who lodged in the house, but he never touched meat, and drank only water, and seemed to live on the air." This fits in well enough with Martha Catcott's "sad wag of a boy." She added: "He was good-tempered, and agreeable, and obliging, but sadly proud and haughty; nothing was too good for him, nor was any thing to be too good for his grandmother, mother and sister, hereafter, —that he used to sit up almost all night, reading and writing; and that her brother said he was afraid to lie with him; for, to be sure, he was a *spirit*, and never slept; for he never came to bed till it was morning, and then, for what he saw, never closed his eyes."

"The nephew" (between fourteen and fifteen in 1770, and Chatterton's bedfellow "during the first six weeks he lodged there") "says, that, notwithstanding his pride and haughtiness, it was impossible to help liking him—that he lived chiefly upon a bit of bread, or a tart, and some water; but he once or twice a week saw him take a sheep's tongue out of his pocket—that C. to his knowledge never slept while they lay together; that he never came to bed till very late, sometimes three or four o'clock, and was always awake when he (the nephew) waked; and got up at the same time, about five or six—that almost every morning the floor was covered with pieces of paper not so big as sixpences, into which he had torn what he had been writing before he came to bed."

The united testimony of the household was that no one would have taken him from his behaviour, &c., to have been a poor boy of seventeen—and a sexton's son (which he was not)—they never saw such another person before nor since (this must be taken *cum grano*, as wisdom after the event)—he appeared to have something wonderful about him. He gave no reason for quitting their house—Mrs. Ballance, surely, was *reason* enough—and they found the floor of his room covered with little pieces of paper, the remains of his *poettings*, as they termed it.

What comes out of this evidence as a whole is that Chatterton wished to impress these good folk with the fact that he was a poet; it is only his relative who mentions the political connection.

Some time in June he changed his lodgings; the last *African Eclogue* bears the note "Brooke Street, June 12," but the statements of Mrs. Walmsley and the nephew cannot wholly be disregarded, though given nine years later,* and Gregory (p. 95) dates the move "early in July." If the locale of the scene described in his next letter be the Upper Liberty of St. Andrew's, Holborn, he was domiciled in that parish on Monday, June 18. We do not know whether during the last three weeks at Shoreditch he had a room to himself, but somewhere about June 21 there was a to-do in that house, which came about thus.

We have seen that, according to his own account, he waited on the Lord Mayor "to have his approbation to address a second letter to him on the subject of the Remonstrance." This letter, according to Michael Lort, who saw it,† he seems to have lost no time in writing. It was dated May 26, signed "Probus," like the first, and accepted by Bingley, proprietor of the *North Briton*. A tirade against the Government for rejecting the Remonstrance, it began, "When the endeavours of a spirited people to free themselves from an insupportable slavery." Apparently he set great store by its publication, although no money was to be got this side of the question; but on June 21, quite unexpectedly, the father of the author of *Vathek*, "that noisy vapouring fool," as Walpole called him,‡ died of a cold, the result of hastening up to town from Fonthill. Let Mrs. Ballance be heard again: "When Beckford died, he was perfectly frantic, and out of his mind; and said he was ruined." This, her words imply, was a far more violent outburst than when she suggested an office job in May. One might therefore, with a degree of reason, expect suicide at this point. But no, the letter, directed to Cary, which Lort saw, bore this endorsement:

* Nine weeks from April 26 (his first letter home) is June 28, one day before the date of the postscript to the letter of June 19.

† Ingram, who was evidently unacquainted with Lort's memorandum (11457), and took the information from Walpole's *Letter to the Editor of Chatterton's Miscellanies* (p. 51), casts doubt (*The True Chatterton*, p. 243) on its authenticity, but no fair-minded judge can follow him.

‡ Letter to the Earl of Strafford, July 9, 1770.

Accepted by Bingley, set for, and thrown out of the N Briton, 21 June, on account of the Lord Mayor's death

	£	s.	d.
Lost by his death on this essay	1	11	6
Gained in Elegies	2	2	0
,, ,, Essays	3	3	0
Am glad he is dead by	3	13	6

This, incidentally, is the only evidence for payments in June.

Though taken by surprise, the poet, as usual, elegized promptly. The *Public Advertiser* announces on June 25*:

In a few days will be published,

AN ELEGY on the much-lamented Death of WILLIAM BECKFORD, Esq. late Lord-Mayor of, and Representative in Parliament for the City of London.

'Titles to him no Pleasure could impart,
'No Bribes his rigid virtue could controul:
'The Star could never gain upon his Heart,
'Or turn the Tide of Honour in his Soul.

Vide the POEM.

Printed for George Kearsly at No. 1, Ludgate Street.

In the following Saturday's (June 30) issue it is advertised as published that morning, price one shilling, and the *Middlesex Journal* follows suit on July 3. The poem is anonymous, and was included in the *Miscellanies* of 1778.† It is supposed (but see note at end of chapter) to be the only separate publication by the poet in his lifetime, and, probably, he did not consider it poetry; no more of the twenty-eight stanzas than the astronomical one need be quoted:

* On Monday, June 25, he addressed a letter, unpreserved, to Cary, containing "a remarkable adventure at Marybone Gardens," a song set for Mr. Bannister and Mrs. Thompson to be sung in the Gardens, "Lucy, since the knot was tied," and a glee for the Queen's Arms, beginning "Since man, as says each bearded sage" (*The Revenge*, ll. 209-216). That is to say *The Revenge* was written already, with one of its "additional songs." "List of Chatterton's letters in MSS.," not in Lort's hand. 11457.

† These contain an engraving of a statue of Beckford, which faced the "Essay on Sculpture" in the *T. and C.M.* for Aug., 1770. A writer in the *Critical Review* for June, 1782 (p. 422) denies that Chatterton is responsible for either drawing or essay.

He, as a Planet with unceasing Ray,
Is seen in one unvaried Course to move,
Through Life pursu'd, but one illustrious Way,
And all his Orbit was his Country's Love.

Extracts appeared in the *General Evening Post* for July 10 and the *London Magazine* for July.

To assign other elegies on this subject to him were an unkindness; *Bingley's Journal* is particularly rich in them; and the *Middlesex* for June 28 announces "We cannot possibly find room for any more elegies on this subject." Of those I have read *The Lamentation of Liberty and Britannia* (Bingley's Journal, July 28), signed "R.," is most like Chatterton; it is in dialogue, with a refrain:

Lament, lament, your mighty loss deplore,
Beckford, your pride, your glory is no more.

of which the second line is varied, and it contains a paraphrase of the stanza on the title-page of the *Elegy*.

The Lord Mayor's death, and its consequences, temporary paralysis and pressure of work, serve to explain the gap of ten days between the next letter home and its postscript. The *Elegy* was published by the time this sheet reached Bristol; but the writer had now reached a lodging where death was to find him before two months were out.

NOTE ON "THE AUCTION"

On the last leaf of the *Elegy on William Beckford* is the following printed notice:

This day is published, Price 2s.

THE AUCTION, A POEM; A familiar Epistle to a Friend, sent with the Head of HARPOCRATES, the God of Silence, in a Ring.

It had, in fact, been published before, and advertised, e.g. in the *Middlesex Journal* (Apr. 24). The *Monthly Review* of February, 1770, dealt with it in these terms: "This Poem has considerable merit, the language is pure, the numbers harmonious, the expression animated, the sentiments just. Harpocrates, the God of Silence, being brought from Egypt by a travelling peer, is sold among the rest of his Lordship's effects, when his affairs are ruined by his vices. This deity gives an account of the auction." The "advertisement" to the poem says that part of it was printed off before the death of Mr. Holland (Dec. 7, 1769), "otherwise the Author would in a different manner have given his opinion of the goodness of that valuable Actor's heart." Charles Holland was Chatterton's favourite actor (See R. Jenkins's *Memoirs of the Bristol Stage*, 1826, and compare the last line of the poem *To Mr. Powel* "We love thee for the virtues of thy heart"). The unexpanded first version appeared as *A familiar Epistle to a Friend* in the *London Magazine* for Feb. and March, 1769, also in the *Annual Register*, and the supplement to the *Oxford Magazine* for that year; Chatterton contributed to all three periodicals. Other reasons for connecting it with him are:

1. The author is anti-ministerial, and speaks of Grafton, Bedford, and Mansfield much as Chatterton does; e.g.:

Where Grafton, *ever honour'd* name,
Immortal on the roll of fame;
Who like an Atlas, bears the weight,
Attendant on a mighty state;
Ne'er leaves the council, *ne'er* attends
Newmarket, and his jockey-friends,
Who when the fascinating die,
Bids ample patrimonies fly,
Ne'er mingles in the guilty train,
Damn'd to variety of pain:
Where Grafton stands, *unaw'd* by fear,
Tho' faction thunder in his ear;
Let fear the guilty mind deform,
The *virtuous* man defies the storm. p. 30.

Cf. *Resignation*, ll. 7-8, 39-44, 351-360, 736-738.

2. The subject matter is akin to Decimus's Exhibition of Sign-paintings.

3. These lines suggest Chatterton:

Who came, his orders to obey,
Bowing and smirking all the way. p. 4.

The modern bards, as yet whose rhyme,
Is not with value stamp'd by time,
Were indiscriminately sold
For nothing, as they were not old. p. 6.

When Phaeton, whose thirst of fame,
Had nearly set the world on flame, p. 8.

4. The choice of the two painters, Barrett and Berghem:

Happy the painter who can find,
A patron of exalted mind;
This to his tints fresh vigour gives,
By this the lifeless canvas lives:
And hence when Barrat meets our eyes,
We see another Bergham rise. p. 14.

5. The resemblance between:

(a) At first, he claim'd the promis'd place
He earn'd by pimping for his grace: p. 3.

and

Since pious Chudleigh is become her Grace,
Martin turns pimp, to occupy her place.
Kew Gardens, ll. 593, 594.

(b) Last came an urn which L[an]gf[or]d feign'd
Was carv'd when good Aurelius reign'd;
But which to me and all appear'd,
The work of days far less rever'd. p. 36.

A catalogue was quickly made,
Prefac'd with pomp and much parade;
Of urns, from Herculaneum brought
(In fact not worth a single groat)
Of headless trunk and noseless bust,
Tarnish'd by artificial rust;
Of medals brought from Rome and Greece,
Who know to pluck your English geese; p. 4.

and

When you knocked down Lord Rust with the bust of Marcus Aurelius, you looked the very picture of the Alecto last taken out of the Herculaneum. *The Woman of Spirit*, Act I, Sc. 1.

Yes, Sir, you must know, this morning, Mr Latitat had invited all his antiquated friends, Lord Rust, Horatio Trefoil, Col.

Tragedus, Professor Vase, and Counterfeit the Jew, to sit upon a brass half-penny, which being a little worn, they have agreed, Nem. Con. to be an Otho.

Ibid., Sc. 2.

6. The use of the cant term " waddle " of an unfortunate speculator (at " Jonathan's," footnote in *Annual Register* version):

Behind it stands that famous place,
Where modesty ne'er shows her face;
Where ign'rance, if she chance to come,
Is certainly sent wadling home,
Whose lawless sons avow this creed
By lies and fraud we best succeed;
And meet tumultuous ev'ry day,
On each unwary fool to prey. p. 40.

which occurs in *The Memoirs of a Sad Dog* and *A Hunter of Oddities*, No. X (*Works*, Vol. III, p. 216); also the resemblance between this passage and a description of Corn Street, the Exchange end (*Kew Gardens*, ll. 395-402).

7. The cry to be delivered from " this detested modern Babel " (p. 41), which fits no writer of 1770 so aptly as Chatterton.

If the attribution be accepted, *The Auction*, not the Beckford *Elegy*, is the poet's first separate publication. That he nowhere mentions it is hardly a fatal objection, since he makes no specific reference to the *Elegy*; indeed we do not know on what grounds that poem was attributed to him by the editor of the *Miscellanies*, " gained in elegies " being the sole indication we have from Chatterton that he wrote verse on Beckford's death. A more serious objection is the silence of Lort. Still, there do not seem to be other candidates for the authorship of *The Auction*. I cannot think it is by James Cawthorn (whose *The Antiquarians* is in the same genre), because of the " patriotic " bias. It falls into the same category as *Journal 6th*; the immediate model is the Hudibrastic efforts of Churchill, *The Duellist* and *The Ghost*, but the closing lines are clearly based on the end of Prior's *The Conversation* (1721).

From a Sketch in the Writer's possession.

39, BROOKE STREET (1825).

face p. 387.

Chapter XVII

BROOKE STREET

"June 19, 1770.

Dear Sister,

I have an horrid cold—The relation of the manner of my catching it, may give you more pleasure than the circumstance itself.—As I wrote very late Sunday night (or rather very early Monday morning), I thought to have gone to bed pretty soon last night: when being half undressed, I heard a very doleful voice; singing Miss Hill's favorite bedlamite song;—the hum-drum of the voice so struck me, that, tho' I was obliged to listen a long while, before I could hear the words, I found the similitude in the sound. After hearing her with pleasure drawl for above half an hour, she jumped into a brisker tune, and hobbled out the ever-famous song, in which poor Jack Fowler was to have been satyrized.—" I put my hand into a bush: I prick'd my finger to the bone: I saw a ship sailing along; I thought the sweetest flowers to find": and other pretty flowery expressions, were twanged with no inharmonious bray. —I now ran to the window, and threw up the sash, resolved to be satisfied whether or no it was the identical Miss Hill, in propria persona.—But, alas! it was a person whose twang is very well known, when she is awake, but who had drank so much royal bob* (the gingerbread baker for that, you know), that she was now singing herself fast asleep; this somnifying liquor had made her voice so like the sweet eccho of Miss Hill's, that if I had not considered that she could not see her way up to London, I should have absolutely imagined it her's.—There was a fellow and a girl in one corner, more busy in attending to their own affairs, than the melody.

[*This part of the letter, for some lines, is not legible.*]

. . . the morning) from Marybone gardens; I saw the fellow in the cage at the watch-house, in the parish of St. Giles's†; and the nymph is an inhabitant of one of Cupid's inns of court.—There was one similitude it would be injustice to let slip. A drunken fishman,

* Gin.

† A map of the parish of St. Giles's in the fields in Stow's *Survey* (ed. 1755, Vol. II, p. 76) shows this watchhouse in the middle of the roadway, High Holborn, at the point where it is joined by Newton Street.

who sells souse mackarel, and other delicious dainties, to the eternal detriment of all twopenny ordinaries; as his best commodity, his salmon, goes off at three half-pence the piece: this itinerant merchant, this moveable fish-stall, having likewise had his dose of bob-royal, stood still for a while; and then joined chorus in a tone, which would have laid half a dozen lawyers pleading for their fees, fast asleep: this naturally reminded me of Mr. Haythorne's song of

"Says Plato, who oy oy oy should man be vain?"*

However, my entertainment, though sweet enough in itself, has a dish of sour sauce served up in it, for I have a most horrible weezing in the throat: but I don't repent that I have this cold; for there are so many nostrums here, that 'tis worth a man's while to get a distemper; he can be cured so cheap.

June 29th, 1770.

My cold is over and gone: if the above did not recall to your mind some scenes of laughter, you have lost your ideas of risibility."†

Whether the body of this letter was written at the Walmsleys' or Mrs. Angel's, and the reference to "Cupid's inns of court" points in favour of the latter, he was, with the publication of the Elegy on Beckford (which the *Monthly Review* of July praised as breathing alike the spirit of Poetry and Liberty) in strange quarters. Shoreditch might be a poor neighbourhood, but the eyes of friends—troublesome friends, doubtless—were upon him, and there remained something more than an illusion of home life; but in moving to the Upper Liberty of St. Andrew's Holborn, and to the front top room of a sacque maker's in particular, he had stepped into the forefront of eighteenth century London's temptations.

That parish is perhaps most familiar to us in the pages of *Oliver Twist*, but the easterly end of it was a haunt of rough

* *Plato's Advice* (*New Universal Magazine*, June, 1758, with music, and often reprinted):—

Says Plato why should Man be vain since bounteous Heav'n has made him great.

† *L. and M.*, p. 182.

and doubtful characters before 1838. In 1820, when some of the rookeries were so dangerous that the clergy of St. Andrew's had to be accompanied by plain-clothes police officers on their pastoral visits,* Brunt, the Cato Street conspirator, had a lodging in Fox Court (where in 1697 Richard Savage, the poet, was born), and the gang met in a room behind the White Hart in Brooks Market.† The evidence of the parish beadle in 1817 reveals that the state of the district, on Sunday morning in particular, was most riotous, from three to five hundred of the low Irish—the main population—being drunk and rolling about the streets; and the witness hardly knew an instance but what their children were brought up in such a way that the boys mostly became thieves and the girls prostitutes.‡ A century earlier its reputation was much the same. "This parish," writes the author of *A View of London and Westminster or The Town Spy* (1725, p. 28) "has rendered its name famous to all succeeding ages for retaining the ashes of that great and wonderful woman Mrs. Sarah Salisb[ur]y."§ The same authority adds (p. 29), which is to our purpose, "I am sorry to hear that towards *Redlyon street*, &c., so many pretty gentlewomen are retain'd for the use and behalf of too many gentlemen in this great Protestant city and suburbs, and that a certain lady not forty miles from *Lamb's-Conduit* . . . should lately be surpriz'd in bed between two *Grays-Inn attornies* at her mantua-makers." This, the West End, towards Queen's Square, was the abode of fashion; Chatterton, naturally enough, had set up in the poorer part.

It is not suggested that he walked bitterly or wilfully into this region, though he had, as the reader must have realized, a habit of inviting the world to put the worst construction on what he said and wrote about himself. He had come from the city where Savage died, with whom he felt a spiritual kinship, having written in *Kew Gardens*:

* *Events of interest in the history of St. Andrew's Church, Holborn*, p. 14.

† G. T. Wilkinson, *History of the Cato Street Conspiracy*, pp. 118, 300.

‡ *Report on the Police of the Metropolis* (1819), pp. 350, 351.

§ *Select Trials* (1743, Vol. I, p. 328) elucidates: "the most eminent Punk that ever the Hundreds of *Drury* could boast of."

My prudent neighbours (who can read) can see
Another Savage to be starv'd in me,

and he may have wished to be close to Savage's birthplace; or in eyeshot of the ancient street front of Staple Inn; or nearer Marybone Gardens, Shoe Lane, and Mr. Hamilton Junior, than he had been at the plasterer's; or to escape from Mrs. Ballance; or, as Gregory suggests, to hide the approach of indigence from his friends who had only heard his boasts of greatness*; or, not least important, to have a room to himself with no one over his head. Still, whatever the motives, "at Mrs. Angel's, sack-maker, Brook-street, Holborn"—and between a sacque and a mantua, in this connection, there is about as much difference as between the Johnsonian louse and flea—always allowing that Mrs. Angel, who was not to be found when Croft sought her, may have been a wholly respectable matron, *that* address could have conveyed to the Shoreditch household, if not to his Bristol correspondents, a poetic licence disquieting enough.† Nor do I think that Mrs. Chatterton could have derived comfort from the reflection that the Rector of St. Andrew's was the Dean of Bristol, Dr. Cutts Barton, as he was one of the foremost objects of her son's satire, and in the "Will" had been left "my religion."

The house, which by the aid of a poor-rate book for 1772,‡

* *Life*, p. 95. Gregory adds, "Pride was the ruling passion of Chatterton, and a too acute sense of shame is ever found to accompany literary pride."

† As far back as Jacobean times a dressmaker's was associated in the popular mind with a house of resort, as is evident from the scenes in Cyril Tourneur's *Atheist's Tragedy* (1611) laid in Cataplasma's dwelling. R. Campbell, in *The London Tradesman* (3rd ed., 1757, p. 227), speaking of the mantua-maker, says, "Their profits are but inconsiderable, and the wages they give their journeywomen small in proportion; they may make a shift with great sobriety and economy to live upon their allowance; but their want of prudence, and general poverty, has brought the business into small reputation."

‡ I have seen this and some of its fellow rate books, from which it appears that three people living on the west side of Brooke Street occupied the same houses in 1757 as in 1772, Adrian Marsh, Francis Martin, Robert Wolfe (next door but one to the poet's lodging). The last house on this side was tenanted in 1767, 8 by W. Manlove; in 1772 "Frederick Angell" is crossed through, and "Gregory" substituted in pencil. The rent charge was "16." One James Angell lived in the fifth house in Fox Court on the collector's way from Holborn, as he turned out of Gray's Inn Lane, in 1767 (not in 1764), but he was gone by 1768. The Town Clerk of Holborn is the present guardian of these records. Thanks are due to the Prudential Assurance Company, the owners of the site, for letting me consult their magazine, *The Ibis*.

Moy Thomas identified as No. 39 (*Athenæum*, Dec. 5, 1857) was the first house from Holborn on the west side of the street, and was pulled down in May, 1880; on Sept. 27, 1928, the Corporation of the City of London affixed a memorial plaque to the house now on its site.* It is described by Thomas Maurice who, with Sir William Jones, visited it in 1779, as "a dreary place," and everything on the spot presented "a miserable appearance."† The life prefixed to the Cambridge edition of 1842 seems to have been responsible for the mistaken notion that the house was No. 4 (p. 135), the houses not being numbered in the rate books.

A very different change of residence from Crabbe's, who, when Mr. Vickery, the hairdresser, removed with his family to Bishopsgate Street, accompanied them‡; but Chatterton was hardly "a quiet, amiable, genteel young man," though his hours at Shoreditch had been regular.

The passage in his last letter to George Catcott (Aug. 12), where he indicates that he paid at first six shillings a week for his room, savours of braggadocio. Six shillings for a garret, even with two windows, as this seems to have had, was too much before the great rise in prices of 1795. The rent of a furnished room in a poor district, according to Mrs. Eric George's calculations,§ varied from two shillings to three and six (cellars and garrets being often cheaper) with a tendency to rise as the century went on. It may be argued that his landlady was fleecing him, but he must have had at least six weeks' experience of town prices before he settled in. Mrs. Angel was a shopkeeper with assistants; letting lodgings was her by-industry, and most working people lived in a furnished room. The inventory of a half a crown a week room occupied by an unmarried clerk in a public office with £50 a year, in 1767, "two pair of stairs forwards in Grub Street, Golden Lane, Moor Lane, Fee Lane, Rag Fair, or the Mint," contains "a half-tester bedstead with

* As the result of a letter from Mr. G. W. Wright, of Stockwell.

† Maurice was an Oxford undergraduate at the time, and communicated his information to Croft, with whom he and his friends dined almost daily at the White Hart. *Memoirs*, Pt. 2, pp. 156, 160.

‡ *Life of Crabbe*, by his son. Ch. III.

§ *London Life in the 18th Century*, p. 92.

brown linsey-woolsey furniture, a bed and bolster half flocks, half feathers, a green glazed chamber-pot, a small wainscot table, two old chairs with cane backs and bottoms, a small looking-glass six inches by four in a deal frame painted red and black, a red linsey-woolsey window curtain, an old iron stove, poker, shovel, tongs, and fender, an iron candle-stick mounted with brass, a tin extinguisher, a wooden wash-hands bowl, a quart bottle for water, a tin pint pot, a tin pepper-box, a vial for vinegar, and a stone white tea-cup for salt. Also two large prints cut in wood and coloured, grained with deal, but not glazed, *viz.* : (1) Hogarth's Gate of Calais, or the Roast Beef of Old England; (2) Queen Esther and King Ahasuerus: with the fate of tyranny and oppression, or The just punishment of the proud and hard-hearted Haman."* The room's appearance sixty-one years later, before a partition was put up, dividing it into two, is given by a writer in *Adversaria* (Dec. 1857) : it was square, and large for an attic, with a couple of dormer windows ; outside ran the gutter, and a low parapet, over which you could look into the street. The roof was low, with a long slope from the middle down to the windows. Mrs. Jefford, the wife of the occupier, a plumber, is there stated to have been in the service of Lord Orford as a girl. Croft, unfortunately, describes, not the room, but his own emotions in it ; the second window may perhaps be inferred from " in that window he loitered for some hours before he retired to his last rest."† The garret represented in Hogarth's *Distressed Poet* is roomy enough ; for such a room as is suggested by Henry Wallis's famous picture, " Chatterton," in the Tate Gallery, true, I think, in the detail of St. Paul's, and surely right in that of the *Middlesex Journal* on the floor, six shillings a week would, in 1770, have been excessive.

Shops were in the vicinity ; of the names in the 1772 poor-rate book, Holden's *Directory* for 1802-4 gives the professions of three—Wolfe, tobacconist, at No. 37 ; Marsh, silk-dyer, at No. 33, and Ducroz, flower and ostrich feather manufacturer,

* *Considerations on the Expediency of raising . . . the wages of servants that are not domestic*, 1767. Pp. 6, 7.

† *L. and M.*, p. 198.

at No. 27*; these ran northwards from Mrs. Angel's on the same side of the street.

The Death of Nicou, structurally the weakest of the *African Eclogues,* is the first Brooke Street poem; in outline vague and Ossianic, in colour masterly. The subterranean river reappears, described thus:

On Tiber's† banks, Tiber, whose waters glide
In slow meanders down to Gaigra's side;
And circling all the horrid mountain round,
Rushes impetuous to the deep profound;
Rolls o'er the ragged rocks with hideous yell;
Collects its waves beneath the earth's vast shell:
There for a while in loud confusion hurl'd,
It crumbles mountains down and shakes the world.
Till borne upon the pinions of the air,
Through the rent earth the bursting waves appear;
Fiercely propell'd the whiten'd billows rise,
Break from the cavern and ascend the skies:
Then lost and conquer'd by superior force,
Through hot Arabia holds its rapid course.

The resemblance to *Kubla Khan* is even closer here than in the *Narva and Mored* passage; "crumbles mountains down" balances "huge fragments vaulted," and "slow meanders" "five miles meandering with a mazy motion," the epithet "mazy" being actually used later in the poem, of the lamp of midnight.

The "scarlet jasmines" and "purple aloes" increase the exotic effect, and the jungle picture is superb:

Where, when the sun is melting in his heat,
The reeking tygers find a cool retreat;
Bask in the sedges, lose the sultry beam,
And wanton with their shadows in the stream,

* The number of houses between Marsh and Ducroz is the same in the *Directory* as in the poor-rate book; a Ducroz occupied No. 27 in 1768.

† "Tiber" is wilful, I fancy, though Bryant (*Obs.*, p. 477) suggests that Chatterton misread Tigris "Tibris," the map of Africa which he saw comprehending part of Asia, particularly Arabia and Syria as far as the Tigris. Bryant supposes that he took the names Zira, for Zaira, Gaigra, for Gaga, Lupa and Lorbar, for Cape Lopo, the people of Banny, for the Binni, *viva voce* from the mouth of a foreigner, with small regard to the spelling; he makes no allowances for undisciplined imagination working on book-lore.

In the contest between Vichon and Narada the poet seems to be harking back to his picture of Power in the chorus to *Goddwyn* :

> There Vichon sat ; his armour on his bed,
> He thought Narada with the mighty dead.
> Before his seat the heavenly warrior stands,
> The lightning quiv'ring in his yellow hands.
> The God astonish'd dropt ; hurl'd from the shore,
> He drop'd to torments, and to rise no more.

At the end of the poem the couplet

> He drew his army forth : O ! need I tell
> That Nicou conquer'd, and the Lover fell.

betrays the memory of Dryden's

> The process of the War I need not tell,
> How Theseus conquer'd and how Creon fell.
> *Palamon and Arcite.*

The lines to Miss Bush, printed in the June *Town and Country*, in which he conceives himself afloat :

> In the wild element the sea,
> I'll drown the softer subject, thee,

were probably composed about this time, and show that the project of going aboard a Guinea ship had occurred to him some while before he applied to Barrett for a recommendation.

On Sunday, July 1, he sent a chatty rambling letter to Cary.* He begins by rallying him on his love for Polly Lutley, and urging a multiplicity of mistresses, as a sure defence against the injuries of the eyes of one—" a general love never hurts any person." Then, after a passage about Maria Rumsey, already quoted, he goes on : " The following poetic letter which I drew up in Bristol, but altered it here and addressed it to a young linendraper, has been well rec'd and by some officious admirer convey'd to the Court and City Magazine, but as I am concern'd in that Publication I was happy enough to throw it out

* MS. (a copy) " To Mr. Cary, No. 2," at Bristol Library, 11063, f. 113. Lort (*ibid.*, p. 431) gives the date. First printed in Dix's *Life* (1837), p. 272.

From Skelton's "Etchings" (Pl. xlix).

ST. MARY REDCLIFF, INTERIOR.

face p. 395

after it had been set." Sixty-two lines, "An Epistle to a Friend," follow, beginning "Dear Arran, now prepare the smile" (part of this, including the close, has been given in Chapter VIII); he then relapses into prose: "But, by the Lord, I have business of more importance than poetry. As I wanted matter for a sheet in the Town and Country Magazine, you will see this in print metamorphosed into high life." The "second self" did not see it so till his friend had been sixteen months in a nameless grave. (*T. and C.* Suppl., 1771.)

Cary, apparently, had been reading *Kew Gardens* or *The Exhibition*, and had accused Chatterton of partiality in his panegyric of Allen the organist, which comes in both poems. The poet explains his point by an analogy from a sister art, and very sound musical criticism it is. He objects to embellishments, such as until quite recently have disfigured the scores of Handel, and clearly would have disapproved of Mozart's additional accompaniment to *The people that walked in darkness*; but his manner of expressing himself reveals what is nearest his heart:

". . . Step into Redclift Church, look at the noble arches, observe the symmetry, the regularity of the whole; how amazing must that idea be which can comprehend at once all that magnificence of architecture; do not examine one particular beauty or dwell upon it minutely, take the astonishing whole in your *empty* ["your last letter" in margin] *pericranium* and then think, what the architect of that pile was in building is Allen in music.* Step aside a little and turn your attention to the ornaments of a pillar of the chapel; you see minute carvings of minute designs, whose chief beauties are deformity or intricacy. Examine all the laborious sculpture; is there any part of it worth the trouble it must have cost the

* I cannot forbear quoting, apropos of this passage, and one in the letter of May 30, Thomas Warton's note on "And love the high embowed roof," in *Il Penseroso*. "Old saint Paul's cathedral, from Hollar's valuable plates in Dugdale, appears to have been a most stately and venerable pattern of the Gothic style. Milton was educated at saint Paul's school, contiguous to the church; and thus became impressed with an early reverence for the solemnities of the antient ecclesiastical architecture, its vaults, shrines, iles, pillars, and painted glass, rendered yet more aweful by the accompaniment of the choral service. Does the present modern church convey these feelings? Certainly not. We justly admire and approve sir Christopher Wren's Grecian proportions. Truth and propriety gratify the judgment, but they do not affect the imagination." *Poems . . . by John Milton* (1785), p. 90.

artist, yet how eagerly do children and fools gaze upon these littlenesses. If it is not too much trouble, take a walk to College-gate, view the labyrinths of knots which twist round that mutilated piece, trace the windings of one of the pillars, and tell me if you don't think a great genius lost in these minutiæ of ornaments. Broderip is an exact copy of the ornamental carvers; his genius runs parallel with theirs, and his music is always disgraced with littlenesses, flowers, and flourishes. What a clash of harmony Allen dashes upon the soul. How prettily Broderip tickles their fancy by winding the same dull tune again. How astonishingly great is Allen when playing an overture from Handel. How absurdly ridiculous is Broderip when blundering in, and new-modelling the notes of that great genius; and how emptily amusing when torturing and twisting airs which he has stolen from Italian operas. . . ."

In *The Exhibition* he speaks of "the heavenly harmony of Boyce," and musical notes are found among his scribbles.* Here too he was self-taught, but something of the father's faculty had descended to the posthumous child.

The rest of the letter is as follows:

"A song of mine is a great favourite with the town, on account of the fulness of the music. It has much of Mr. Allen's manner in the air. You will see that and twenty more in print after the season is over. I yesterday heard several airs of my burletta sung to the harpsichord, horns, flutes, bassoons, hautboys, violins, &c., and will venture to pronounce, from the excellence of the music, that it will take with the town. Observe, I write in all the magazines. I am surprised you took no notice of the last London; in that, and the magazine coming out tomorrow, are the only two pieces I have the vanity to call poetry. Mind the Political Register, I am very intimately acquainted with the editor, who is also editor of another publication. You will find not a little of mine in the London Museum, and Town and Country.

The printers of the daily publications are all frightened out of their patriotism, and will take nothing unless 'tis moderate or ministerial. I have not had five patriotic essays this fortnight, all must be ministerial or entertaining.

I remain, yours, &c.,

T. CHATTERTON."

The last clause can be dealt with first. Between the first

* e.g., In *Add. MS.* 5766 C ("The Rolle of Seyncte Bartlemeweis Priorie"), f. 16, perhaps copied from an old musical MS.

week of June and the third week of July three editors, Almon of the *London Museum*,* Woodfall of the *Public Advertiser*, and Miller of the *London Evening Post*, had stood their respective trials on Junius's account; and the *Middlesex* from June 12 to July 19 had consoled the readers of its back page with the correspondence in the crim. con. case of the Duke of Cumberland and Lady Harriet Grosvenor, where the lady's husband was awarded £10,000 damages.† Chatterton could write entertaining articles as easily as political ones, though, maybe, no promotion was to be looked for that way.

As for the periodicals mentioned: the *Political Register* for June printed *The Prophecy* and Probus's letter to the Lord Mayor; the *Town and Country* two short stories, *Maria Friendless* (adapted from "Misella" in *The Rambler*, Vol. IV, No. 170‡) and *The False Step*, also the lines to Miss Bush. Nothing in the *London Museum* for May, June or July can with any degree of certainty be attributed to him.§ The estimate of the two *African Eclogues* in the *London Magazine* is one with which few students of the poet will quarrel, though some may prefer *Heccar and Gaira* to them.

The song that took the town was, without a doubt, *The Invitation* ("Away to the woodlands, away") one of the additional songs to his burletta. It was published, as *May*, by Charles and Sarah Thompson, 75 St. Paul's Churchyard, who published for Luffman Atterbury, to whom the copyright of *The Revenge* was sold; and the air and words are reprinted in a collection called *Vocal Music* (1772, Vol. II, p. 9). It is set for voice, two violins and 'cello, and was sung by a boy, Master Cheney.‖ The composer is not known. Dr. Samuel Arnold (1740-1802), who became proprietor of Marybone Gardens in

* See *Public Advertiser*, June 30, "Atticus" on Mr. Almon's Prosecution.

† Cupid's :— I undermin'd it all; see, here's the letter:
Could Dukes spell worse, whose tutors spell no better?
You know false spelling now is much the fashion,

in *The Revenge* (Act I, sc. 3) refers to this case, and it finds a place also in *The Adventures of a Star*.

‡ See Bryant, *Obs.*, p. 487, for a comparison between the two pieces.

§ The most likely is the letter from Ninon de l'Enclos in the Shades (July; cf. *A Hunter of Oddities*, No. 8).

‖ See Appendix D.

1769,* was doubtless the doctor of music with whom Chatterton was invited to treat; but F. H. Barthélémon, the violinist (1741-1808), was also a composer for the Gardens, and is referred to in the *Memoirs of a Sad Dog*.

Not a trace remains of the music to *The Revenge* itself, and the burletta has not been run down in the newspaper advertisements of Marybone Gardens. The burlettas for 1770 were the Gardens' *cheval de bataille, Serva Padrona, The Magic Girdle, The Noble Pedlar*, and *The Madman*. The *Gentleman's Magazine* for May, 1799 expressly says it was never acted there; and in the *Monthly Mirror* for Sept., 1803, a letter of Dr. Arnold to T. Park may be read to this effect, recalling the payment of the five guineas by Atterbury, who had a joint share in the Gardens with the Doctor (Feb. 24, 1799).

Free admission to this famous pleasure resort, which extended from the Rose of Normandy on the east side of High Street, Marylebone, as far east as Harley Street, comprising about eight acres, must have been appreciated.† Performances took place at 6.30, and doors opened at 5, the prices on the big nights, when there were fireworks by Rossi and Clanfield, and the Temple of Apollo was illuminated, with a ball to wind up, being 3/6. The work now to be considered bears all the marks of rapture and excited certainty of applause; moreover, it shows what a good literary workman Chatterton could be, when an opportunity came.

The fragment of *Amphitryon, a Burletta* (Aug. 12, 1769),‡ consisting of recitatives, twelve airs, and one line of a thirteenth (in all, two scenes and part of a third), is little more than a childish and miserable adaptation of Dryden's Plautine comedy; but *The Revenge*, while keeping two whole airs of *Amphitryon*, is a spirited piece, that need not be extravagantly praised,

* Worth, *The London Pleasure Gardens of the Eighteenth Century*, p. 103.

† J. T. Smith (*Nollekens and his Times*, Ch. 2) states that the orchestra stood on the site of the house in Devonshire Place numbered, in 1828, "17."

‡ MS. 5766 B. (ff. 79-86). Lines 1-16, 37-46 ("sits still," *Amphitryon*), 147-154, 497-500 ("Mortals and immortals hear," *Amphitryon*, spoken by Jupiter) of *The Revenge* are found in *Amphitryon*, assigned to the same speakers, Jupiter and Juno, with the exceptions noted. Dean Milles quotes ten lines of *Amphitryon* from another MS. in Chatterton's hand on two pages, given to him by Rudhall (p. 521), containing the first two scenes, and an extract is given by Ingram (*The True Chatterton*, pp. 251, 252).

but can stand on its own feet. The plot is slight enough ; the revenge is Cupid's : Jupiter has laid a thunderbolt across his back because he stopped his lordship in a hurry, so he promptly tells Juno of the Thunderer's assignation with Maia. Bacchus, with a bowl, meets Cupid, vainly urges him to partake, and ends by throwing the contents in his face : the God of Love, left alone, vows to maul him with his best arrow. Thus ends Act I. A dark room enables Bacchus, now amorous of Maia, to court her, as he supposes, assuming Jupiter's voice ; but jealous Juno has " stept in her room," and, after the Thunderer has arrived, sudden light reveals the lovers " all at clapper clawing." Cupid, as *deus ex machina*, sets the matter right, and the four characters (Maia does not appear at all), to be played by Mr. Reinhold, Mr. Bannister, Mrs. Thompson, and Master Cheney, address the audience severally, and in chorus, Cupid making an allusion, apposite enough in Marybone Gardens, to " Handel's lofty flight."* There is, by the way, no singer's name opposite Juno in the MS.

Two extracts will give an idea of the style :

JUNO

RECITATIVE [*Aside*

Ah ! I'm quite out here—plaguily mistaken—
The man's in earnest. I must save my bacon :
Since scolding but provokes him,
A method I'll pursue,
I'll soothe him, tickle, coax him,
Then I shall have my due.†

AIR

Ah, cruel, cruel Jove,
And it is thus a love,
So pure, so chaste, so strong as mine,
Is slighted disrespected,
Unnoticed‡ and neglected,
Return'd with such a love as thine ?§

* It was in these Gardens that Dr. John Fountayne of the Manor House School, being asked by Handel his opinion of an air the band was playing, said, " It's very poor stuff," to which Handel replied, " You are right, Mr. Fountayne, it is very poor stuff. I thought so myself when I had finished it." Thomas Smith, *History of Marylebone*, p. 34.

† " And chouse him of my due " was first written.

‡ " Unregarded " first written.

§ " And thrown away a Prey for Swine " first written.

JUPITER

AIR

Did the foolish passion teaze ye
Would you have a husband please ye,
Suppliant, pliant, am'rous, easy;
Never rate him like a fury:
By experience I'll assure ye,
Kindness, and not rage, must cure ye.

JUNO

RECITATIVE [*Aside*

He's in the right on't—hits it to a tittle—
But Juno must display her tongue a little.

AIR

I own my error, I repent;
Let thy sparkling eyes behold me,
Let thy lovely arms infold me;
Let thy stubborn heart relent.

Act I, Sc. 2, ll. 103-126.

BACCHUS

RECITATIVE

Ah! Master Cupid, 'slife I did not s'ye,
Tis excellent champagne, and so here's t'ye:
I brought it to these gardens as imported,*
'Tis bloody strong, †you need not twice be courted.
Come drink, my ‡boy—

CUPID

Hence, monster, hence! I scorn thy flowing bowl,
It prostitutes the sense, degenerates the soul

BACCHUS

Gadso, methinks the youngster's woundy moral!
He plays with Ethics like a bell and coral

* "I bought it in these gardens as imported" first written; "as" altered to "just."

† "I" first written.

‡ "Son" first written.

AIR

'Tis madness to think,
To judge ere you drink,
The bottom all wisdom contains :
    Then let you and I
        Now drink the bowl dry
We both shall grow wise for our pains

CUPID

* Pray keep your distance, beast, and cease your bawling,
Or with this dart I'll send you catterwauling.

AIR

† The charms of wine cannot compare,
With the soft raptures of the fair ;
Can drunken pleasures ever find
A place with love and woman kind

Can the full bowl pretend to vie
‡ With the soft languish of the eye ?
Can the mad roar our passions move
Like gentle breathing sighs of love ?

Act. I, Sc. 6, ll. 217-241.

Echoes of Dryden's " Tyrant Jealousy " (*Love Triumphant*) and a parody of Addison's " O the pleasing, pleasing anguish " (*Rosamond*) add a piquancy to the gay trifle, which belongs to the same order of things as *Ixion in Heaven.*

Chatterton's MS.,§ written, like Rowley's *Eclogues*, in a plain small quarto exercise book, has had a curious history, being recovered by William Upcott, librarian of the London institution in 1827 from the counter of a cheesemonger's in the City,‖ whither it had found its way after its first publication in 1795,

* " Hence " first written.

† " O can the charms of Wine compare " first written.

‡ cf. " Their eyes' blue languish." W. Collins, *Agib and Secander*.

§ British Museum, Add. 12050, lacking original covers and ll. 25-52 (this leaf is at the Bristol Museum) and ll. 445-497 (probably two leaves), " a marble-covered copy-book superscribed ' Marybone Gardens. Volume I,' " *Gentleman's Magazine*, May, 1799, where it is stated that Luffman Atterbury was a joint-proprietor of the Gardens.

‖ *Evening Standard*, Oct. 20, 1827 ; *Gentleman's Magazine*, Oct. 1827. In 1824 it seems to have escaped destruction " as waste paper," *ibid*. Feb., 1825. The British Museum acquired it from the Rev. Thomas Butler in July, 1841.

from Egerton's printing office, where it was declared lost.* It shows several marks, many in pencil, of having been corrected for performance; e.g., "End the Act here" (l. 275), "No Business here" (l. 372), "To be alter'd" (l. 508), and interesting improvements, mainly in the poet's hand†: for instance, Cupid's passionate recitative, quoted above, in which one can almost hear Chatterton speaking, was conceived first as an air, thus:

Hence, Monster, hence,
I scorn thy Ivy Crown;
Thy full flowing bowl,
Degenerates the Soul;
It puts our Judgments down,
And prostitutes our Sense.

Here he has subjected his own lines to the same treatment as, in *The Whore of Babylon*, he meted out to Churchill's praise of woman. On the verso of f. 18, before the first two additional songs (all that appear in the MS.) is the following receipt signed by him:

"Receiv'd July 6th; 1770 of Mr Luffman Atterbury, Five Pounds, Five Shillings, being in full for all the Manuscripts contain'd in this Book, of which I am the Author: for which consideration of Five Pounds, Five Shillings I hereby give up my sole right & property in, and the liberty of printing & disposing of the same to the said Luffn Atterbury only, and in such a manner as he thinks proper—As witness my Hand this 6th Day of July 6th: 1770.

T. CHATTERTON.

Witness—
James Allen"

But for the preservation of the manuscript, this payment to the poet would have remained completely unknown, as indeed

* "A Burletta in MS. written by the late Thos. Chatterton, to be disposed of; apply to T. Egerton, Bookseller, Whitehall." *The Star*, Oct. 8, 1793; see Joseph Haslewood's note in *Works* (III, p. 537) and *Monthly Mirror*, Sept., Oct., 1803. Catcott, mentioning the advertisement to Dr. Glynn (Dec. 28, 1793), supposed the burletta was *Amphitryon*, which Chatterton had given him.

† In the margin of the opening of Act I, Sc. 4 Chatterton has written "Shorten or throw in an Air—." The last line of the Burletta is corrected and rewritten in another hand.

it appears to have been to Lort, Croft, and Dr. Gregory; in the consideration of the causes of his suicide, no less than of the alleged meanness of his London patrons, it is a factor of some importance.

The character of Juno may have suggested the shrewish, passionate Lady Tempest in the unfinished burletta, *The Woman of Spirit* (first printed in the supplement to his *Miscellanies*, 1784), which he wrote at this time. It is cast thus :

*Distort	Mr Bannister
†Counsellor Latitat	Mr Reinhold
Endorse	Master Cheney
Lady Tempest	Mrs. Thompson.

The lady, who forgot her quality and married " a tautology of nothing," has turned a whole synod of antiquaries out of her house, insisting on her privilege as an English wife ; some attempt has been made to calm her before the second scene ends abruptly. The opening is conceived in the manner of the famous debate between Sir Peter and Lady Teazle.‡

LATITAT

I tell you, Lady Tempest— .

LADY TEMPEST

And I tell you, Mr. Latitat, it shall not be.—I'll have no Society of Antiquaries meet here : none but the honourable members of the Coterie shall assemble here—you shall know.

Lady Tempest and Latitat also occur in a prose piece, *The Happy Pair* (the title of one of the additional songs to *The Revenge*) in the *Town and Country* Supplement for 1771, signed " Z.A." This story is unmistakably Chatterton's, the exordium being a sort of paraphrase of his lines on Happiness ; the allu-

* The name is Churchillian, taken from the description of Foote in *The Rosciad* :

His strokes of humour, and his bursts of sport
Are all contain'd in this one word *Distort*.

† The name "Charles Latitat" occurs in "An Uncommon Love-letter from a lawyer to his mistress " in the *Universal Museum* for Jan., 1763 ; the article was reprinted in *Felix Farley's Journal* for Feb. 5, 1763.

‡ *The School for Scandal* (1777), Act II, sc. 1.

sion to " my grand mother's tobacco pipe " helps perhaps to place it among the efforts of this summer, and a phrase in the tale itself, " angelized his bosom," recalls " angels thy frame " in the *Song to Miss C—am* of May 4.

Two days before he signed the receipt for the five guineas, which *The Revenge* had brought him, he had sent to the *Town and Country** a poem of a very different character, the last of his Rowleys, on a single sheet, with the following letter prefixed:

" To the Printer of the Town and Country Magazine

SIR,

If the Glossary annexed to the following piece will make the language intelligible ; the Sentiment, Description, and Versification, are highly deserving the attention of the Literati.

July 4, 1770. D. B."

We learn from one of Lort's notes† that the manuscript of this, " the pretty ballad of Charity, which they had not made use of," was given to Tyrwhitt, who first printed it in 1777, by one of the Hamiltons ; another draft, of which the 1803 editors made use, seems to have been in Barrett's possession, " who received it from Chatterton " ; the two versions are identical, even to the spelling mose (for moste) in l. 7. It is presumed from the poet's demand for his old Glossary in the letters of May 14, 30, that it was composed in London, and it is, with some degree of justice, regarded as his swan song.‡

* Archibald Hamilton, Junior, was the editor of this magazine, but according to a note of Lort (11457) it was " conducted " by a Mr. Beaufort, who lived by St. John's Gate and frequented a coffee-house near it ; it was he who, in common with a Mr. Caracioli, wrote the *tête à têtes* which Sheridan has immortalized.

† 11063, p. 425. In a letter of Aug., 1779 (probably to Steevens) Lort speaks of it as seeming " to have been thrown by neglected till it was produced by one of them to Mr. Tyrrwhyt." 11457. Among the acknowledgments in the August *Town and Country* is "The Pastoral from Bristol, signed D.D (*sic*) has some share of merit: but the author will, doubtless, discover upon another perusal of it, many exceptionable passages." Chatterton was dead by the time this appeared.

‡ It is always possible, however, that the *Balade* was composed in Bristol, for Lort writes to Walpole (Aug. 4, 1789), " It does not appear that after he left Bristol he wrote anything under the character of Rowley." Nichols *L. I.*, vii, p. 555. At any rate he was always aware that Rowley was not a Londoner, and it is quite uncritical to make its rejection a prime cause of the suicide, for the *Town and Country* had printed no Rowley poem since May, 1769 (*Elinoure and Juga*). See also Wilson, p. 282.

AN EXCELENTE BALADE OF CHARITIE

As wroten bie the gode Prieste THOMAS ROWLEY, 1464.

In Virgyne the sweltrie sun gan sheene,
And hotte upon the mees[1] did caste his raie ;
The apple rodded[2] from its palie greene,
And the mole[3] peare did bende the leafy spraie ;
The peede chelandri[4] sunge the livelong daie ;
'Twas nowe the pride, the manhode of the yeare,
And eke the grounde was dighte in its mose defte aumere.[5]

[1] Meads. [2] Reddened. [3] Soft. [4] Pied goldfinch. [5] Neat mantle.

The sun was glemeing in the midde of daie,
Deadde still the aire, and eke the welken[6] blue,
When from the sea arist[7] in drear arraie
A hepe of cloudes of sable sullen hue,
The which full fast unto the woodlande drewe,
Hiltring attenes[8] the sunnis fetive[9] face,
And the blacke tempeste swolne and gatherd up apace.

[6] Sky. [7] Arose. [8] Hiding at once. [9] Beauteous.

Beneathe an holme, faste by a pathwaie side,
Which dide unto Seyncte Godwine's covent lede,
A hapless pilgrim moneynge did abide,
Pore in his viewe, ungentle[1] in his weede,
Longe bretful[2] of the miseries of neede,
Where from the hail-stone coulde the almer[3] flie ?
He had no housen theere, ne anie covent nie.

[1] Beggarly. [2] Filled with. [3] Beggar.

Look in his glommed[4] face, his sprighte there scanne ;
Howe woe-be-gone, how withered, forwynd,[5] deade !
Haste to thie church-glebe-house,[6] asshrewed[7] manne !
Haste to thie kiste,[8] thie onlie dortoure[9] bedde.
Cale,[10] as the claie which will gre[11] on thie hedde,
Is Charitie and Love aminge highe elves ;
Knightis and Barons live for pleasure and themselves.

[4] Clouded. [5] Sapless. [6] The grave. [7] Accursed. [8] Coffin. [9] A sleeping-room. [10] Cold. [11] Grow.

The gatherd storme is rype ; the bigge drops falle ;
The forswat[12] meadowes smethe,[13] and drenche[14] the raine ;
The comyng ghastness do the cattle pall,[15]
And the full flockes are drivynge ore the plaine ;
Dashde from the cloudes the waters flott[16] againe ;
The welkin opes ; the yellow levynne[17] flies ;
And the hot fierie smothe[18] in the wide lowings[19] dies.

[12] Sunburnt. [13] Smoke. [14] Drink. [15] Fright. [16] Fly. [17] Lightning. [18] Steam. [19] Flames.

Liste ! now the thunder's rattling clymmynge[1] sound
Cheves[2] slowlie on, and then, embollen,[3] clangs,
Shakes the hie spyre, and losst, dispended, drown'd,
Still on the gallard[4] eare of terroure hanges ;
The windes are up ; the lofty elmen swanges ;
Again the levynne and the thunder poures,
And the full cloudes are braste[5] attenes in stonen showers.

[1] Noisy. [2] Moves. [3] Swelled. [4] Frighted. [5] Burst.

Spurreynge his palfrie oere the watrie plaine,
The Abbote of Seyncte Godwynes convente came ;
His chapournette[6] was drented with the reine,
And his pencte[7] gyrdle met with mickle shame ;
He aynewarde tolde his bederoll[8] at the same ;
The storme encreasen, and he drew aside,
With the mist[9] almes craver neere to the holme to bide.

[6] A small round hat. [7] Painted. [8] He told his beads backwards, cursing. [9] Poor.

His cope was all of Lyncolne clothe so fyne,
With a gold button fasten'd neere his chynne ;
His autremete[10] was edged with golden twynne,
And his shoone pyke a loverds[11] mighte have binne ;
Full well it shewn he thoughten coste no sinne ;
The trammels of the palfrye pleasde his sighte,
For the horse-millanare his head with roses dighte.

[10] A long, white robe, worn by priests. [11] Lord.

An almes, sir prieste ! the droppynge pilgrim saide,
O ! let me waite within your covente dore,
Till the sunne sheneth hie above our heade,
And the loude tempeste of the aire is oer ;
Helpless and ould am I alas ! and poor ;
No house, ne friend, ne moneie in my pouche ;
All yatte I call my owne is this my silver crouche.

Varlet, replyd the Abbatte, cease your dinne ;
This is no season almes and prayers to give ;
Mie porter never lets a faitour[12] in ;
None touch mie rynge who not in honour live.
And now the sonne with the blacke cloudes did stryve,
And shettynge on the grounde his glairie raie,
The Abbatte spurrde his steede, and eftsoones roadde awaie.

[12] Vagabond.

Once moe the skie was blacke, the thounder rolde ;
Faste reyneynge oer the plaine a prieste was seen ;

Ne dighte full proude, ne buttoned up in golde ;
His cope and jape[1] were graie, and eke were clene ;
A Limitoure he was of order seene ;
And from the pathwaie side then turned hee,
Where the pore almer laie binethe the holmen tree.

[1] A short surplice.

An almes, sir priest ! the droppynge pilgrim sayde,
For sweete Seyncte Marie and your order sake.
The Limitoure then loosen'd his pouche threade,
And did thereoute a groate of silver take ;
The mister pilgrim dyd for halline[2] shake.
Here take this silver, it maie eathe[3] thie care ;
We are Goddes stewards all, nete[4] of oure owne we bare.

[2] Joy. [3] Ease. [4] Naught.

But ah ! unhailie[5] pilgrim, lerne of me,
Scathe anie give a rentrolle to their Lorde.
Here take my semecope,[6] thou arte bare I see ;
Tis thyne ; the Seynctes will give me mie rewarde.
He left the pilgrim, and his waie aborde.
Virgynne and hallie Seyncte, who sitte yn gloure,[7]
Or give the mittee[8] will, or give the gode man power.

[5] Unhappy. [6] A short under-cloak. [7] Glory. [8] Mighty, rich.

Here he has returned to the Miltonic measure of *Elinoure and Juga* (the first, it may be, of the cycle), but the music is both graver and sweeter, besides voicing a directly personal appeal, which does not, however, destroy the antique manner. Notwithstanding, the piece is rich in echoes, apart from the striking one from Dryden's *Character of a good parson*, and aptly illustrates Gregory's remark that Chatterton knew that original genius consists in forming new and happy combinations.

The subject is taken from the Parable of the Good Samaritan (Luke x). The account of the storm is coloured by the thirteenth book of Fairfax's Tasso, which helped in shaping Celmonde's first speech in *Ælla* ; for instance :

Still was the air, the rack nor came nor went, [Stanza 56.

—a lightning flash outbrake,
And coming drops presaged with thunders shrill : [Stanza 74.

and

A sudden cloud, as when Helias prayed,
Not from dry earth exhaled by Phoebus' beams,
Arose, moist heaven his windows open laid,
Whence clouds by heaps out rush, and watery streams,
The world o'erspread was with a gloomy shade,
That like a dark and mirksome even it seems ;
The crashing rain from molten skies down fell,
And o'er their banks the brooks and fountains swell.
[Stanza 75.

the final apostrophe, too, is not unlike

O happy zeal ! who trusts in help divine
The world's afflictions thus can drive away,

in the stanza (80) which closes this book of *Godfrey of Bulloigne.*

The description of the pilgrim is clearly modelled on that famous picture of Despair, which is said to have roused Sir Philip Sidney's interest in the poet of the *Faerie Queene* to the extent of a gift of two hundred pounds ; this is quoted in Cibber's *Lives of the Poets* (1753, Vol. I, p. 102), where the anecdote is told (p. 92) :

The darksome cave they enter, where they find
That cursed man, low sitting on the ground,
Musing full sadly in his solemn mind ;
His greasy locks, long growing and unbound,
Disordered hung about his shoulders round,
And hid his face ; through which his hollow eyne
Look'd deadly dull, and stared as astound ;
His raw-bone cheeks thro' penury and pine,
Were shrunk into his jaws, as he did never dine.
F. Q., I, IX, 35.

Nor has the Prologue to the *Canterbury Tales* been forgotten ; the Monk's habit has helped to fit out the "Abbote of Seyncte Godwynes" :

And, for to festne his hood under his chin,
He hadde of gold y-wroght a curious pin.
Prol., ll. 195, 196.

and the Abbote's words derive from the description of the Frere (who wore a semicope) :

For un-to swich a worthy man as he
Accorded nat, as by his facultee,
To have with seke lazars aqueyntaunce.
It is not honest, it may nat avaunce
For to delen with no swich poraille,
But al with riche and sellers of vitaille.
Prol., ll. 243-248.

But this is no more than saying that Chatterton was an artist; his work is his own. He did not scorn to add a home touch or two. Dean Milles tells us that *shooting* was pronounced *shettynge* in Devonshire in that day (1782). The word "gallied," according to the 1803 editors, was still used in the sense of "frighted" in the country round Bristol; neither it nor "gallard" are in Kersey or Bailey.* He glosses "horse-millanare" thus: "I believe this trade is still in being, though but seldom employed"; but one morning in 1776, when Steevens was in Bristol with Tyrwhitt, he saw a saddler's shop, in a public part of the city, inscribed "Horse-Milliner," with a wooden horse dressed out with ribbons outside one of the windows.† John Davis in his *Life of Chatterton* (1806, p. 90, *n.*) says the saddler's name was John Wells, and that the poet passed the shop every day when he walked out with the bluecoat boys. The eighteenth century can show few poems more beautiful than this, and none more moving.

However desperate was his state of mind when he penned this myth of Poetry's relation to Humanity, within a few days of sending it to Hamilton he had fulfilled the promise of his childhood, reiterated in the third and fourth letters home, and despatched a box of presents to his mother and sister. It may be presumed, though he does not say so, that the five guineas received for his burletta enabled him to do this. On

* Cf. The wrathful skies
Gallow the very wanderers of the dark,
King Lear, Act III, Sc. 2.
and "We've all been gallied at the dairy at what might ha' been a most terrible affliction." Hardy (*Tess*, p. 287, ed. 1895.)

† *Works*, II, p. 365, *n.* Sir Walter Scott uses the word in *The Heart of Midlothian*: "in my wretched occupation of a saddler, horse-milliner, and harness-maker." I, 12, p. 186. (Border edition.)

the sister's part, I fancy, there had been a little restiveness about these presents, a wonder whether they were ever coming, for his remark about the songs, followed by the list of his magazine articles, looks like an answer to some question of hers. The patterns would be of use to his mother in her sewing school, and the British herb snuff was possibly Rowley's, which was much advertised in *Felix Farley* and *Boddely's Bath Journal* at this time.* The Shoreditch people were evidently made aware of this munificence, for the plasterer's niece told Croft that " he had *such a proud spirit* as to send the china, &c., at a time when she knew he was almost in want."† The episode has won many a heart to the boy, if not to the poet ; but the acute Lort, in a note to be found in Kippis's *Biographia Britannica* (IV., p. 588), observed—and bear in mind that this antiquary never mentions the burletta, but bases his conclusions solely on the letters home—that there had been too much flourishing about affection to relations and these presents, which did not seem (to Lort) to have been expensive, or sent when he was in want ; and though we may not agree with him that abstention from suicide would have been a greater kindness to the mother and sister, the poet no doubt counted on the presents being shown, and his name being blown about Bristol as a successful author.

The letters in the case are as follows; that to his mother was written on a Sunday, and the five guineas were received on the Friday before, so that he can have lost small time :

" DEAR MOTHER—

I send you in the box—

Six cups and saucers, with two basons, for my sister. If a China teapot and cream-pot is, in your opinion, necessary, I will send them ; but I am informed they are unfashionable, and that the red China, which you are provided with, is more in use.

A cargo of patterns for yourself, with a snuff-box, right French, and very curious in my opinion.

* An advertisement in the latter (Aug. 6, 1770) states that the son of Mr. Cross, apothecary in Primrose Street, near Bishopsgate Street, London, going blind, was cured by it, and could see the notes of a pianoforte. This may be a clue to the identity of the Cross whom Chatterton knew, whose name I cannot find in the poor-rate books for Brooke Street and that neighbourhood.

† *L. and M.*, p. 192.

Two fans—the silver one is more grave than the other, which would suit my sister best. But that I leave to you both.

Some British-herb snuff in the box: be careful how you open it. (This I omit, lest it injure the other matters.) Some British-herb tobacco for my grandmother, with a pipe. Some trifles for Thorne. Be assured whenever I have the power, my will won't be wanting to testify, that I remember you.

Yours,

T. CHATTERTON.

July 8, 1770.

N.B. I shall forestal your intended journey, and pop down upon you at Christmas.

I could have wished, you had sent my red pocket-book, as 'tis very material.

I bought two very curious twisted pipes, for my grandmother, but, both breaking, I was afraid to buy others lest they should break in the box; and, being loose, injure the China. Have you heard any thing further of the clearance? Direct for me, at Mrs. Angel's, sackmaker, Brook-street, Holborn."

"DEAR SISTER,

I have sent you some china, and a fan. You have your choice of two. I am surprised that you chose purple and gold*; I went into the shop to buy it; but it is the most disagreeable colour I ever saw; dead, lifeless, and inelegant. Purple and pink, or lemon and pink, are more genteel and lively. Your answer in this affair will oblige me. Be assured, that I shall ever make your wants, my wants: and stretch to the utmost to serve you. Remember me to Miss Sanford, Miss Rumsey, Miss Singer, &c. &c. &c.

As to the songs, I have waited this week for them, and have not had time to copy one perfectly; when the season's over, you will have 'em all in print. I had pieces last month in the following Magazines:

†Gospel Magazine,
Town and Country, viz.
Maria Friendless.
False Step.
Hunter of Oddities
To Miss Bush, &c.

* I think, with Wilson and Ingram, that he refers to the two silks promised in his letter of May 30.

† *The Gospel Magazine* for June contains an unsigned poem on the nature and perfections of God, but there is nothing beyond this letter to connect it with Chatterton, and the reference is generally supposed to be to the lines printed in the November number. The *Christian Magazine* I have not yet been able to trace.

Court and City. London. Political Register, &c &c.
The Christian Magazine, as they are not to be had perfect, are not worth buying—I remain,

Yours,
July 11, 1770. T. CHATTERTON "*

It looks as if there were some anxiety on his account at home, which is hardly to be wondered at; the "horrid cold" letter of June 19 had contained no information whatever, and its postscript of ten days later, stating that the cold had gone, was laconic and disquieting. It may even be that Mrs. Chatterton had heard from Mrs. Ballance of the scene after Beckford's death. Nevertheless her intended journey to London does not, from the context, seem immediate. This letter of July 8th is the last to his mother that we have, and the first to give the Brooke Street address.

On the same day as he wrote to Mary he sent a stupid list of wants, "The Polite Advertiser," to the *Town and Country*, which was printed in the July number.

If further commentary be needed, here is the opening of *The Happy Pair*:

"Many and learned are the dissertations on happiness and contentment; but of all the writers who have said a great deal on the premises, there has been very little said to the purpose. Contentment is like a man's hobby-horse, undefineable; the simile holds good farther; content is a perfect hobby-horse, which carries every different possessor a different way, and whether you ride backward or forward, with a saddle or without one, with one foot in the stirrup or both, you are still in the road to contentment on your own hobby-horse. Pray, Mr. Reader, do me the honour to take a step with me to the grand road of contentment, and take a view of all the by-ways which lead to it. See yonder! clish, clash; dish, dash; through thick and thin comes a curate riding on a bishoprick. What a sacerdotal face he has! look at him again. By my grandmother's tobacco pipe, it is the religious W[arburto]n!† What divinity sits on his haughty brow! how prettily he kicks the mud and filth without daubing his lawn-sleeves in the least: well, heaven preserve us, there is never a tythe priest in canonicals can excommunicate with half his charity. He is on the high road to contentment, but he will

* *L. and M.*, pp. 184-186, both letters.

† William Warburton (1698-1774), Bishop of Gloucester: see *Kew Gardens*, l. 779.

never reach his journey's end, though he obtains a primacy—unless he tickles his conscience asleep. What piece of solemnity is that riding on a ten-headed beast through the dark wood there? O! pardon me Revelation, it is the infallible Newton,* sounding a halfpenny rattle, which he mistakes for the trumpet of fame. He is now posting through the bog of literary reputation where he will find as much filth, as Wheble's† authors can throw on him: I pity him; he has no internal merit which might oil his sacerdotal habiliments, so as to make the filth slip off again. He spurs his mysterious steed like a bishop, but he will never reach the cottage of content, until the destruction of the whore of Babylon is accomplished. Look on the other side; here comes a Patriot; he is riding on a black rod; let him ride on; I believe he begins to find he rides backwards. Behind him comes a Cit, jolting on an immoderately large country house; but, at the same time, casting many retrograde looks at his little pitiful compter. See an amorous widow, riding on her seventh cuckold, a lawyer on the bench; and but just turn yourself round and you will see me, the identical writer of this, galloping to the highway of content, on a monument in Westminster Abbey."‡

* Thomas Newton(1704-1782) Bishop of Bristol, author of, *inter alia*, an edition of Milton, and *Dissertation on the Prophecies* (1754-1758). See *Kew Gardens*, ll. 722-770. He said that Milton's "Cherub contemplation" had the gaiety of a cupid, on which T. Warton remarks "As Milton's Satan is not a monster with cloven feet, horns, and a tail, so neither are his cherubs Cupids."

† The *Middlesex Journal* was printed for J. Wheble, 20 Paternoster Row.

‡ There is yet another *Happy Pair*, a short prose piece, in the *T. and C.M.* Supplement for 1770, unsigned.

CHAPTER XVIII

SUICIDE

THE payment of the five guineas for his burletta, a fact unknown to the early biographers, and not revealed till after its publication in 1795,* must have been as important as any event in Chatterton's brief life; and though the sum was at once reduced by the purchase of the presents, "trifling" as these may have been, and, it may be, by the settlement of outstanding debts to his landlady, tailor, and others, he could not but have realized that fortune's gale did not always blow adverse, and that the arrest of patriot editors or a lord mayor's death was no more fatal to literature than the frown of a Walpole or the meanness of a Burgum. Rowley, it is true, was useless lumber, and political essays for the moment unlucrative; but his brain was by no means crippled, and he could do work that was wanted. In short, native pride and the ups and downs of hack journalism are insufficient to explain the tragedy now so close at hand; though the continual strain of working through the night, and denying his adolescent body its due quota of nourishment must have gone far to keep his mind out of healthy paths. Still, if loose and scurrilous, the tone of his prose work is not morbid, and except for a certain fixed hatred of sacerdotalism (in itself no symptom of insanity) it is hard to find in the Chatterton of 1770 any traces of a mind unhinged. On the contrary it is his objectivity, so unexpected in youthful work, that extorts surprise, and even praise; compared with him Shelley, as often as not, is a luxurious egotist, Coleridge a dreamful hypochrondriac. One looks in vain for self-pity in that last

* The advertisement, stating the payment, which is found in some copies of *The Revenge*, was, according to Joseph Haselwood, written some time after the work was printed. *Works*, III, p. 537.

Rowley poem, all is subdued to the romantic exigencies of the scene described :

> " Knightis and barons live for pleasure and themselves "

is statement, not invective, and the pilgrim, " withered, forwynd, deade," as impersonal, despite his pathos, as the bedesman, " meagre, barefoot, wan," in the *Eve of St. Agnes*.

Most of his periodical essays, though they cannot be ranked high, have the same trait. The gallery of "oddities", which set an example for many years to the *Town and Country's* contributors, Dick Flighty, Eolus, Flirtilla, Jack Shift, Tom Goosequill, Tony Selwood, and the rest, are pieces of detached observation, and he can write of himself, as if the subject were a complete stranger :

> " Tom was therefore compelled once more to have recourse to his pen; but instead of pursuing the melodious harmony of numbers, he engaged in the jarring discord of politics. Though Tom was a writer on either side, as convenience suited, and though he never wrote gratis for the Gazetteer or the Public, it was but very rarely he produced a five and threepenny essay—he skirmished in the still lighter parts of literature." *A Hunter of Oddities*, No. X.

His best prose effects are got quite shortly : Jack Spangle has been lectured by his father on the subject of expensive mistresses :

> " Jack heard this admonition with a sheepishness natural enough to the choice spirits of the city, when they are under the rod of correction : but the old gentleman producing a bill at the end of his harangue, Jack's countenance brightened up ; he received it, and bowing respectfully, stammered out, ' 'Tis very true, Sir, as you say, Sir.' " *Adventures of a Star.*

The object is always *seen* :

> " My sister Biddy's gown was as heavy as a modern novel : upon a moderate computation it had above three pounds of silver, in its embroidery : the colours indeed were faded, but that defect was made up in the length of the train, which afforded the cat a five minutes play while Miss Biddy was turning the corner."
>
> *Tony Selwood.*

The most diverting of these skirmishes is *The Memoirs of a Sad Dog.**

Harry Wildfire, who hopes to earn a dinner by relating his adventures, is the youngest son of a sparing father; he sets out in life with a fortune of five thousand pounds and an old book, *The Way to Save Wealth.*† When the legacy is paid him, he bids his brother adieu, drinks three bottles of claret with his brother-in-law, Sir Stentor Ranger, and drives to London in his phaeton and four—"Honour was the only book I ever honoured with a perusal." He gambles away a fifth, and wenches away a fourth, of his total, and then resolves to turn fortune-hunter. He "dresses at" a girl who, a month later, takes a trip to Scotland with her father's footman. This creates in him an absolute aversion to matrimony, and soon after he becomes the cicisbeo of an alderman's wife, at which point we are treated to a digression:

"'Behold! thou art happy; but soon, ah! soon, wilt thou be miserable. Thou art as easy and tranquil as the face of the green-mantled puddle; but soon, ah! soon, wilt thou be tumbled and tossed by misfortunes, like the stream of the water-mill. Thou art beautiful as the cathedral of Canterbury; but soon wilt thou be deformed like Chinese palace-paling. So the sun rising in the east gilds the borders of the black mountains, and laces with his golden rays the dark-brown heath. The hind leaps over the flowery lawn, and the reeky bull rolls in the bubbling brook. The wild boar makes ready his armour of defence. The inhabitants of the rocks dance, and all nature joins in the song. But see! riding on the wings of the wind, the black clouds fly. The noisy thunders roar; the rapid lightnings gleam; the rainy torrents pour, and the dropping swain flies over the mountain: swift as Bickerstaff, the son of song, when the monster Bumbailiano, keeper of the dark and black cave, pursued him over the hills of death, and the green meadows of dark men.' O Ossian! immortal genius! what an

* *T. and C. M.* July, Aug., 1770. Cottle (*Early Recollections*, Appendix, p. 293 *n.*), denies that this piece is by Chatterton, but does not specify his "fresh sources of information"—whitewashing, I suspect. Its presence in the *Miscellanies* (1778) does not prove its authenticity, of course, but no one but the 1803 editor has doubted it.

† The book referred to is *The way to save wealth, showing how a man may live plentifully for two-pence a day . . . Likewise how to make a hundred noble dishes.* (2nd ed., 1697.)

invocation could I make now ! but I shall leave it to the abler pen of Mr. Duff, and spin out the thread of my own adventures."*

The husband breaks in, and the frolic costs the hero £2,000. He schemes a despicable revenge, seduces the alderman's daughter, and when her father bids her prepare to marry Mr. Lutestring, the mercer, by the next week, is almost persuaded to love her in earnest :

" But I had not yet accomplished my revenge. Steeled in impudence as I am, I blush to write the rest ; but it shall be out. I informed Mr. Lutestring of my intimacy with his future spouse, and advised him not to unite himself to a woman of such principles. I made certain of receiving a challenge, and a string of curses for my information ; but, alas ! I knew not the city. 'Sir,' replied the mercer, 'I thank you for your intelligence, this day received : but your advice is not worth a yard of tape ; you say Sabina has been faulty, I allow it ; but will her father give me any thing the less for her fortune on that account ? On the contrary, were not my notions

* *Critical observations on the writings of the most celebrated Geniuses in Poetry*, by W. Duff, was reviewed in the *General Evening Post* of June 19, 1770. In the *Gazetteer* (June 13), the paper to which Tom Goosequill contributed, is an essay signed " A Dreamer," describing an auction at Christie's, and beginning " It has ever been a custom with me since I passed the mystic meridian Forty-five, to indulge myself with a nap after dinner." When the head of " Gentle Naso " has been sold, as well as those of Johnson and Goldsmith, " the leviathan of literature, the colossus doctor, and his friend the head of the press, a technical pair to fill up any lady's library," styled also " the incomprehensible Holofernes and the impenetrable Goodman Dull," and " the immaculate contemporaries," the auctioneer proceeds : " But here is the *Rara Avis* ; the Highland Nightingale ! the gawke on the bust ! the solemn solon goose ! (which is as big as any poetical swan whatsoever !), this is the true *Fingal* ! the Port of the Arck ! the English Chaldean ! This is he that composed such sweet words to the sweeter bagpipe ! This is he that made the English language dance a Highland reel ! His verse is as rough as the waves of the rock, and dances like a cock-boat in a storm : His genius is as fertile as the summits of the highest hills, and sublime as the weed in the vale : His words flow like waters in a standing pool, and coarse as the shores of his fathers. His works are marvellous on earth, and have travelled from Scotland into Ind. He is the Homer of the Highlands, and deserves a good price for his poem. He kneaded poetical paste up for Zingis [a tragedy, by Alexander Dow, 1769], and sprinkled it with the juice of poppies ; he threw his lethargic hearers in a trance, and went off with the profits of the sale ; he is the baker of blank verse, and the gingerbread baker of rhime ; he is the poetical Tiddidoll of his day ; but still there is *Dough* in whatever he handles ! But such as he is I recommend him to you."

" In the midst of this," the essay immediately concludes, " the Governor of Pensacola rushed in, seized Fingal by the arm, and swore no pensioner of Scotland should be sold—*And I awaked*."

This piece reappears without signature, and prefaced by a quotation from the *Dunciad*, closing " The field of glory is a field for all," in the *Court and City Magazine* for July, 1770.

of honour very refined, I might make it a means of raising my price.' I slunk away, astonished at this reply, reflecting how various are the species and refinements of honour."

He has now not five hundred pounds left, and throws himself on his brother-in-law. Sir Stentor, who at the nineteenth bottle confuses a colt and a filly, is admirably drawn, foreshadowing, though dimly, Thackeray's Hampshire baronet :

" 'Adad, thou art in the right, Hal, nobody knows these things better than me. There's my lord Grosvenor's filly, Long Dick ; he would have it, that he was got by his own horse, Thunder, when I, by the mere make of his pastern, found 'um out, to be got by Sir George Blunt's white horse, Duke. Dost thou know any thing of dogs ? Canst train a pointer, or a hawk, or such like thing ? "

Then comes the skit on Walpole (Baron Otranto) and the broken stone. Harry clears eight thousand on racing with Sir Stentor, and goes to Paris to " glitter in all the splendour of an Englishman." There he marries a poor marquise, has to settle her debts, and is thrown into prison ; he returns to his brother-in-law, whose fortune he had made, but comes off with nothing better than a bill of £100 and " my bay gelding Jockey." After turning stockjobber he sets up as an author :

" The first fruits of my pen, were a political essay and a piece of poetry: the first I carried to a patriotic bookseller, who is, in his own opinion, of much consequence to the cause of liberty ; and the poetry was left with another of the same tribe, who made bold to make it a means of puffing his Magazine, but refused any gratuity. Mr. Britannicus, at first imagining the piece was not to be paid for, was lavish of his praises, and I might depend upon it, it should do honour to his flaming patriotic paper ; but when he was told that I expected some recompense, he assumed an air of criticism, and begged my pardon ; he did not know that circumstance, and really he did not think it good language, or sound reasoning.

" I was not discouraged by the objections and criticisms of the bookselling tribe ; and as I know the art of Curlism, pretty well, I make a tolerable hand of it. But, Mr. Printer, the late prosecution against the booksellers having frightened them all out of their patriotism,* I am necessitated either to write for the entertainment of the public or in defence of the ministry."

* Almost the same phrase as in the letter to Cary of July 1 ; who can doubt that the *Sad Dog* is Chatterton's ?

There we leave him "throned in a broken chair within an inch of a thunder-cloud."

The yarn may be slipshod and coarse, as Masson says, but it moves with ease and gusto, proving undeniably that with patience (experience he hardly needed) Chatterton could have written a breezy picaresque book, less earthy than any of Smollett's, and full of types he knew, with a hero perhaps, not so far removed from "Equality Jack"; for the matter of that, the "Sad Dog," in his desire for getting even with his environment, is scarcely a distant relation of the anti-hero of Marryat's early *Frank Mildmay* (1829). Rowley is beyond regrets, but the eighteenth century Bristol autobiography he could have given us, when his precious spleen had mellowed, if not vanished, is one of the real losses to our literature.*

The remark about Curlism is borne out by his journalistic practice. In some lines dated July 22, 1770, "The Art of Puffing,"† he writes:

> The honourable Boswell writes, 'tis true,
> What else can Paoli's supporter do?
> The trading wits endeavour to attain,
> Like booksellers, the world's first idol, gain.
> For this they puff the heavy Goldsmith's line,
> And hail his sentiment, tho' trite, divine‡;
> For this, the patriotic bard complains,
> And Bingley binds poor liberty in chains:
> For this was every reader's faith deceiv'd,
> And Edmunds swore that nobody believ'd:
> For this the wits in close disguises fight;
> For this the varying politicians write;
> For this each month new magazines are sold,
> With dullness fill'd and transcripts of the old.

Maria Friendless, as already mentioned, is *Misella* over again; the essay on Sculpture (which may not be Chatterton's) is quarried out of Ephraim Chambers's *Cyclopædia*. S. R.

* A Scotsman once said to me, with all the gravity of his nation, "Chatterton should have remained in Bristol."

† First printed in the *T. and C.M.* for Jan., 1783, with an engraved facsimile of the MS., which had lain in the editor's hands for twelve and a half years.

‡ *The Deserted Village* was the outstanding poetical success of this year.

Maitland traced "A dissertation on the virtues and abilities of Caligula's horse" (*Annual Register*, 1770) to a periodical called *Common Sense* (Feb. 6, 1742)*; and it is used again in the *London* for May, 1770 (signature "Centaur") and in the *Freeholder's* for August ("letter to Lord North," signature "T.C."). The little "Anecdote of Lord Chancellor Jeffries," printed in *Works* (III, p. 93) appeared in the *Town and Country* for June, *Universal Museum* for July, and the *Annual Register* (1770). Magazines may have copied from one another, but the Caligula article, in two of its appearances, shows changes that must come from the author; and other instances have been given. This, of course, was the practice of the time: the *Middlesex* printed letter after letter signed "Lucifer" during this summer, which were extracted from a book called *A Sure Guide to Hell*, published many years before. That his newspaper connection was intimate is evidenced by his mention of "London Packet" and "Foreign Intelligence" in his accounts for May; he must have been something more than an occasional freelance writer.

Lort's memoranda tell us of now vanished works in MS.† and of his London friends. There was a poem, *The Flight*, addressed to a great man, Lord Bute, in forty stanzas of six lines each, endorsed "Too long for Political Register. Curtail'd in the digressions, given to Mr. Mortimer" (one imagines it a piece like *The Prophecy*); and a scene and a half of a tragedy, *The Dowager*; "Dramatis Personæ Prs. D. of W. Ld Bute and the D. of Cumberland," a satirical performance clearly, and, it may be, identical with, or akin to, the "unsuccessful attempt in the dramatic style" which Thistlethwaite saw a few weeks before the London journey, and thought unworthy of Chatterton's pen; of that effort there were two or three acts, and it was "political in its plan," though described as a comedy or farce.‡

* *Chatterton, an Essay*, pp. 55-61.

† 11457; Walpole, *Letter* (1779), p. 49.

‡ Milles, p. 522. Malone (*Cursory Observations*, p. 37, *n.*) speaks of "a *Manks Tragedy*, which, if his forgeries had met with a more favourable reception than they did, he would doubtless have produced as an ancient composition."

There was an apothecary named Cross, resident in Brooke Street, according to Warton* ; hardly a morning or evening would pass but the poet would step into his shop to chat. Cross found his conversation, "a little infidelity excepted," most captivating. Lort says this man had several pieces of Chatterton's, a MS. of *Kew Gardens*, which he lent to Dr. Percy, and "an elegy or soliloquy of a man in his cell addressed to a crucifix," which he had lost.†

Other London friends were a Mr. John Oldham, a button-seller, of the button and silk warehouse, 25 Lombard Street, who married John Lambert, the attorney's, sister Beliza, two years after Chatterton's death‡ (in Holden's 1802-4 Directory, and the Post Office Directory for 1809, the business is carried on at the same address under her name), his brother a surgeon, one Baylis, also a surgeon, and Booth a journeyman to Oldham. John Oldham was in Chatterton's company two or three times ; his testimony, as given by Lort (July 21, 1777) is as follows : "Mr. O. says that he had a particular spleen to the present Bishop of Bristol§ to whose patronage he had been early recommended but did not profit from it. He had wonderful faculty for writing and would exhibit some pieces to his acquaintance without mentioning the author, only asking how

* *Enquiry*, p. 108, *n*.

† Immediately following the letter to Lord North in the *Freeholder's* for August is "A remarkable account of a converted Jew," Joachim Engelberger. The prison scene on the denial of a reprieve may have a bearing on this "elegy," as well as on Rowley's *Apostate* : "This pretended proselyte, transported with despair, cast a wooden crucifix which he held in his hand on the ground and broke it to pieces, crying, that since he must die, he declared he died a Jew, and publicly renounced the Christian religion, having always remained a Jew in his heart." It is unsigned :

But be his outward what it will,
His heart was an apostate's still.

‡ *Ex. inf.* the Rev. R. W. Oldham, great-grandson of Joseph, brother of John Oldham (the latter died in 1789, *Gentleman's Magazine*, 1789, p. 1058) ; Beliza Oldham died in 1812 (*ibid.*, 1812, p. 594, Vol. II), their seven children o. s. p. John Oldham's age in 1770 has not been ascertained ; his father, Nathaniel Oldham, was born in 1712. See *Times Literary Supplement*, Apr. 6, 1922.

§ "Tom" Newton, the noted preferment hunter, is thus characterized in Boswell's *Life of Johnson*, under June, 1784 :

DR. ADAMS. 'He was a very successful man.'

JOHNSON. 'I don't think so, Sir. He did not get very high. He was late in getting what he did get ; and he did not get it by the best means. I believe he was a gross flatterer.'

he liked them. Mr. O. said that in appearance he seemed to be at least twenty years of age and had a shabby genteel dress."

Croft was informed that he wrote no more letters home after that of July 20 to his sister, which Mrs. Chatterton suffered the author of *Love and Madness* to retain " as a curiosity " :

" I am now about an Oratorio, which when finished will purchase you a gown. You may be certain of seeing me, before the 1st of January, 1771.—The clearance is immaterial.—My mother may expect more patterns.—Almost all the next Town and Country Magazine is mine. I have an universal acquaintance : my company is courted everywhere ; and, could I humble myself, to go into a compter, could have twenty places before now ; but I must be among the great : State matters suit me better than commercial. The ladies are not out of my acquaintance. I have a deal of business now, and must therefore bid you adieu. You will have a longer letter from me soon—and more to the purpose.

Yours,

20th July, 1770."* T. C.

This is an ominous document, and must have struck the recipient as such. No trace of the oratorio remains ; though there is a note of Barrett's (1778) " Dr. Glynn has lately found out a woman with whom Chatterton lodged in London ; she gave him part of a Burletta which he was writing for Marybone Gardens, and told him she wished he had call'd a day sooner for she had just burn'd some old thing in the black letter because she could not read it."† The latter statement, vague and unsatisfactory as it is, is the only indication we have that any of the Rowley " originals " were actually brought to London.

As for the boast about the July *Town and Country*, only three contributions, none poetical, have been laid to him,‡ but there is no doubt that many of his pieces, including the articles reflecting on Bristolians, were held over ; the Supplement for 1771 is particularly rich in them.

* *L. and M.*, p. 187. † 11457.

‡ The trashy anonymous *Alonzo to Celia* (cf. the story of Thomas de Blunderville in *Rowley's Memoirs*, which is incidentally the plot of *The Mysterious Mother*) may be his ; it is only interesting metrically, as ringing the changes between decasyllables, alexandrines (four of which run over) and octosyllables ; another doubtful piece is *On Modern Fribblism*, Suppl. 1770, signed " Castigator," where Warburton is attacked (l. 16) ; this is more likely to be his than the other.

The clause about humbling himself carries us back to the "Thursday evening" letter to Barrett, and receives confirmation from a sentence in the *Sad Dog*: "I know by woeful experience, that when an author resolves to think himself in the right it is more than human argument can do to convince him he is in the wrong." Only too accurately had he gauged his own nature.*

There is little means of discovering what fresh disappointments befell him in July and August beyond the indisputable fact that his burletta was not performed. *The Magic Girdle* was announced for July 10, but postponed, and played on July 17; on Aug. 4 two new burlettas were advertised as "being preparing" for Mr. Bannister's night, Aug. 14, and Mr. Barthelemon's, Aug. 21; but these dates were not adhered to. I cannot believe that the rejection, or rather non-publication, of the *Balade of Charitie* can have affected him as much as this, which involved the holding up of the printing of his songs, as he did not depend on Rowley now that he was in London.

On Aug. 8 he dated a letter to Lord Mansfield for the *Middlesex*, which has escaped his editors; it is one of those which Lort saw in MS., is signed "Menenius" (a name taken from *Coriolanus*), and begins "My Lord, I am not going to accuse you of pusillanimity." On the same day George Catcott addressed the following letter to him, in answer to one which we have not.† This is the only letter received by Chatterton, with the exception of those of the two females and Walpole's of Apr. 28, 1769, that is forthcoming; the spire in question was for St. Mary Redcliff:

"Bristol August 8, 1770

SIR

I have your's of the 10 Ult. now before me, which shou'd

* When I was in Bristol during the winter of '28 I was reminded of this clause by seeing faintly chalked across the first storey of a house, two hundred years old at least, in St. Jude's parish, "This is penniless corner all on this corner goes out looking for work but *prays* to God they wont get It."

† Catcott says the poet had told him, "in a letter long since unfortunately destroyed, that the inhabitants of London intended removing the obstacles that obscured the magnificent west view of St. Paul's Cathedral." Letter-book, p. 42.

have been answer'd sooner, cou'd I possibly have found a Leisure Hour to do it in.

As to the Gothic Dome which you so much commend, I must inform you I have seen one in the Possession of Mr Webb in Guiney Street,* drawn by Hogarth, & is I suppose the same you mention. I must candidly own the Design is really elegant, & at first Sight struck me much, but when I view'd that of Mr. Marshe's, the latter appear'd to me so lofty & bold, that I thought the other by no means worthy of being compar'd with it; it differs very much from the modern Steeples, is entirely Gothic, and agrees perfectly well with the present Edifice. I wish I had Time & Ingenuity enough to send you a drawing of it, but as that is Impossible, I will endeavor to the best of my small abilities, to describe it. That part of the Steeple already built, will be taken down, & a light 4 Square airy Building erected in its Room, rather higher than the present, & the disposition of the Lights so contriv'd, that the Clock Bell (the present Tenor), will be plainly visible from the Ground. Above this rises the Spire, in which are 12 Windows, so admirably contriv'd, as to enlighten every part of it. The exact height of it I have forgot, but I think including the Tower its altitude from the Ground, will be 278 feet; & as I observ'd in the printed paper enclos'd† will be by far the most elegant Structure of its kind in England. I am always open to Conviction, & ready to retract my Opinion, when convinc'd of my Error; But I really think there's no Impartial Person whatever who has the least Skill in Architecture, but must give it the preference to any of the preceding Designs laid before the Vestry, & I am persuaded you wou'd coincide with my Sentiments, cou'd you have a sight of it. I have promis'd in the Name of my Partner & Self, to subscribe (for that is the method by which they propose raising the Money)‡ 10 Guineas, if I may be permitted to lay the top Stone, & put an Inscription there. I was once very sanguine in my Expectations of living to see it executed, but this like most other undertakings of a similar nature in Bristol, seems to be dying away, & I really believe will never be executed.§

You will undoubtedly be not a little pleasd when I inform you, Mr Barratt has been lucky enough to rescue from Oblivion a large Box full of valuable Manuscripts relating to Bristol, which have been in a Gentleman's Family a few Miles from this City, (whose Father intended publishing them ever since the year 1708. Mr Barratt wou'd be glad to hear from you, & desires to be inform'd what way you are in; I am told you're employ'd sometimes as a political, &

* "Webb John, capt. 22, Guinea-street." *Directory*, 1775.

† "One of the Bristol Journals for June 4." Catcott has transcribed his letter to it (B. 6490, f. 125).

‡ The expense of Henry Marsh's ("an ingenious ship carver") scheme was a thousand guineas. Letter-book, pp. 31, 33.

§ He was almost a prophet; the spire was not completed till 1870.

at other Times as a poetical Writer, at a Salary of 2 Guineas a Week.

Since you are got under the Tuition of an Angel, shou'd be glad to be inform'd, whether he belongs to the Prince of Darkness, or the Regions of Light, I sincerely hope the latter.

I am inform'd the blundering Bridge Commissioners are going to take down the 2 new Houses lately built by Mr Gay, the end of Bridge Street, & make only one rank, if that is the Case, we may boast of having the best Row of Tradesmen's Houses in England. See the Bristol Gazett for Thursday July 26. 1770, where you will find a Plan laid down for them to pursue, of which I shou'd be glad to have your opinion. I am Sir

Your obedient Servant

GEORGE CATCOTT.

If you send any more Letters, be sure don't omit sealing them as you did the first."

[Wrapper "Mr Thos Chatterton, at Mrs. Angel's Sack maker, Brooke Street Holborn London. Single Sheet"; also "S" "San" "Sang," in Chatterton's hand.]*

There is an absence of the Temple Vicar's name; if *The Exhibition* had got round, he would certainly have no message for its author. On May 7, the day after the poet's second letter home, he had set out with a friend on a tour through South Wales, fossilizing, but he was back in Bristol by June.† His brother and Barrett usher out Rowley's tragedy, as they ushered it in.

The above letter bears postmark Aug. 11. The *Middlesex* for that day has two significant paragraphs in its acknowledgments:

"The Essays signed Probus and Decimus, we should have inserted with pleasure, if they had been sent us in due season; but the writer must be sensible they are out of date, we must therefore beg leave to return them.

"Menenius to Lord M——d will appear in the first page as soon as we have room for so long an address."

One essay accepted anyhow! The next day, Sunday, he answered the pewterer:

* At the Bristol Museum, Richard Smith's bequest (1838).

† MS. Diary, 6495, in Bristol Library.

"London, August 12, 1770

SIR,

A Correspondent from Bristol had raised my Admiration to the highest Pitch, by informing me that an appearance of Spirit and generosity, had crept into the Niches of Avarice and Meanness: That the murderer of Newton, Ferguson,* had met with every Encouragem^t Ignorance could bestow; that an Episcopal Pallace, was to be erected for the Enemy of the Whore of Babylon†; and the present turned into a Stable for his [ten-]headed Beast. That a spire was to be patched to St Mary's; & the Streets kept cleaner, with many other Impossibilities: but when Mr Catcott the Champion of Bristol doubts it, It may be doubted. Your description of the intended Steeple struck me: I have seen it: but not as the invention of Mr Marsh; all that he can boast, is Gothicizing it: give yourself the trouble to send to Webleys, Holborn,‡ for a View of the Church of St Mary de la Annunciada in Madrid§; and you will see spire almost the Parallel of what you describe. The Conduct of your Bishop is no more than what I expected: I had received information that he was absolutely engaged in the defence of the Ministry; and had a Pamphlet on the Stocks, which was to have been paid with a translation. In consequence of this information, I inserted the following in one of my Exhibitions.

Revelation Unravelled, by Dr Newton Bishop of Bristol—The Ministry are indefatigable in establishing themselves; they spare no Expence, so long as that Expence does not lie upon them. This Piece represents the Tools of Administration offering the Doctor, a Pension or translation, to new-model his Treatise on Revelations & prove Mr Wilkes to be Antichrist.

The Editor of Boddely's Bath Journal has done me, the honor to murder most of my Hieroglyphics, that they might be abbreviated for his paper. Whatever may be the political Sentiments of your inferior Clergy, their Superiors are all flamingly ministerial. Should your Scheme for a single row take place; Conscience must tell you, that Bristol will owe even that Beauty to Avarice; since the absolute impossibility of finding Tenants for a double row, is the only occasion of your having but one. The Gothic Dome I mentioned was not designed by Hogarth; I have no great opinion of him, out of his ludicrous Walk; there he was undoubtedly inimitable. It was designed by the great Cypriani. The following Description may give you a faint Idea of it. From a Sexagonal Spiral Tower (such

* James Ferguson (1710-1775), whose *Astronomy explained on Sir Isaac Newton's Principles* was published in 1756.

† Bishop Newton.

‡ Henry Webley, bookseller near Chancery Lane, Holborn. *Kent's London Directory*, 1770.

§ *The European Magazine* for Apr., 1792, says the print does not exist; in which case Chatterton was hoaxing Catcott.

I believe Redclift is) rose a similar Palisado of Gothic Pillars, three in a cluster on every Angle ; but single and at an equal distance in the angular Spaces. The Pillars were trefoliated (as Rowley terms it) and supported a majestic oval Dome ; not absolutely circular, that would not be Gothic ; but terminating in a point ; surmounted with a Cross: and on the top of the Cross a Globe. The two last Ornaments may throw you into a fit of religious reflection, and give rise to many pious meditations. Heaven send you the Comforts of Christianity ; I request them not, for I am no Christian. Angels, according to the Orthodox Doctrine, are Creatures of the Epicene Gender, like the Temple Beaux : the Angel here, is of no such materials ; for staggering home one Night from the Jellyhouse,* I made bold to advance my hand under her covered way, and found her a very very Woman. She is not only an Angel, but an arch Angel ; for finding I had Connection with one of her Assistants, she has advanced her Demands from 6s to 8s 6 per Week, assured that I should rather comply than leave my Dulcinea, & her soft Embraces.† I intend going abroad as a Surgeon, Mr Barratt has it in his Power to assist me greatly, by giving me a physical Character : I hope he will. I trouble you with a Copy of an Essay I intend publishing—

I remain

Yr much obliged Servant,

Direct at Mrs Angel's."‡ THOs CHATTERTON.

The remarks about the Bishop of Bristol bear out John Oldham, and in them Masson sees " traces of over-excitement of brain, and of that morbid spirit of hatred to persons which results from it " (a far cry from insanity, however). The contri-

* For a description of a jelly-house see Richard King's *New London Spy* [1781], p. 76 ; he says, " There was formerly a greater number of these ; but as there is a fashion in all things, so the taverns, bagnios and genteel night-houses, have taken away great part of their business."

† " I am far from charging all milliners with the crime of connivance at the ruin of their apprentices ; but fatal experience must convince the public, that nine out of ten of the young creatures that are obliged to serve in these shops, are ruined and undone. Take a survey of all the common women of the town, who take their walks between *Charing Cross* and *Fleet Ditch*, and, I am persuaded, more than one half of them have been bred milliners, have been debauched in their houses, and are obliged to throw themselves upon the town for want of bread, after they have left them. Whether then it is owing to the milliners or to the nature of the business, or to whatever cause it is owing, the facts are so clear, and the misfortunes attending their apprentices so manifest, that it ought to be the last shift a young creature is driven to." R. Campbell, *The London Tradesman*, p. 209.

‡ At the Bristol Museum, with the letter to Bishop Newton, both in the poet's hand. Richard Smith's Bequest (1838). First printed in the *European Magazine*, Apr., 1792.

bution to which the poet refers is " Exhibition of SIGN PAINTINGS, at the West End of the Town," in *Boddely's Bath Journal* for June 18, and the Bishop is the fifth exhibit.* The essay sent, at the Bristol Museum, and unprinted, so far as I am aware, in any periodical of the time, is headed " To Dr. Newton Bishop of Bristol," and begins "When we examine the Annals of this Kingdom we find Prelacy to have been the nurse of every Rebellion & Civil discord fomented here." He denounces Newton for speaking against Wilkes in his last charge to the clergy of his diocese—the charge, in fact, was a political harangue : " Excommunicate me, my Lord, if I reason deistically if submission is one of the Orthodox Articles to be subject to the wicked Ministers of an innocently misled King. I am a Nonconformist." This he says, carrying out what he had told James Thistlethwaite. He concludes, in what reads to-day as an almost blackmailing tone, " My honest warmth may offend you ; I court not your Smile tho' by what I know I might command that Smile. I only wish you would see the Blessings of Independence, and disdain for a miserable Pittance to sell your Genius, your Conscience, your Country, & your King." The signature is "Decimus."† There are anti-ministerial letters on Bishop Newton's charge in the *General Evening Post* for Aug. 7, signed " Verax, Bristol, Aug. 1," the same issue containing Chatterton's "Eolus" (a *Hunter of Oddities*, No. 3), and in the *Political* Register for September, signed "Atticus, Aug. 16,"

* No. 4 is " PIETY, by a country curate—This represents Dr. C[u]tts B[art]on, Dean of B[ri]st[o]l, sleeping on his Prayer-Book. The painter, envious of the confidence the Doctor enjoys, has sketched beyond Truth, and painted him rather muzzy with drink than sleeping." I must thank the proprietors of the *Bath Chronicle* for giving me access to the files of this periodical, which is only to be found in their office.

† Ingram suggests (p. 277), on no grounds whatever, that the essay sent was " The Gallery and School of Nature," a MS. presented to the Bristol Museum in 1905 ; this I do not believe to be Chatterton's, the handwriting is unlike his, and the only voucher for its authenticity is the inscription, " Autograph of Thomas Chatterton, presented by John Dix to Dr. Mackenzie." Whoever examines the MSS. of the letter to Catcott and that to Bp. Newton will have little hesitation in deciding that they always formed a pair ; their transcripts form a pair in Catcott's Letter-book, pp. 34-38. See *Poetical Works*, ed. 1842, Vol. I, p. 317. Chatterton's letter was enclosed in the Essay to Newton, the verso of which is addressed to Catcott, and bears postmarks " 13 Au," " 15 Au " ; the address seems to be " Mr G. Catcot near the Bridge Bristol."

the same number containing " Menenius to Lord Mansfield." "Atticus " concludes thus : " But the prospect of a beneficial translation supersedes every other consideration, and though the road to *fame* be *infamy itself*, yet you *piously* determine on inflexible perseverance. Go on, my Lord. *Finis coronat omnia*."

Barrett in his *History of Bristol* makes no remark on Chatterton having applied to him for a recommendation as a surgeon's mate,* or on his having given the poet any instruction, but that something was looked for from this quarter is clear from Mary Chatterton having (if we believe her) packed up the books on surgery, before he went to London, and hints of the project are in his letter of May 30 and the lines to Miss Bush. All biographers regard this as the last hope, and Ingram, in particular, makes much capital out of " I hope he will " ; all but the same words are used apropos of the physical advice to Mrs. Carty. On this score Barrett can hardly be blamed ; Dr. Gregory, indeed, argued that the refusal even reflected honour on him, as he could not in conscience be the instrument of committing the lives of a considerable number of persons to one totally inadequate to the charge† ; we need not perhaps go so far as this.

Two other points are worth noticing in this letter to Catcott : (1) That the piece of news about Barrett's latest antiquarian haul is not taken up, except by the bare reference to Rowley ; and (2) the paragraph before " I intend going abroad," an instance doubtless of

> Since all my actions magnified are here,
> She cannot paint me worse than I appear ;

* It is customary to instance Goldsmith and the author of *Roderick Random* (1770) here (see Wilson, p. 293), but an extract from the *Life of Gill Smith*, a criminal (1738, p. 8), may serve, for a change: "This was the first time they had ever heard any complaint of him. And his master, notwithstanding the ill treatment he had received from him, sent him to sea, as surgeon of a ship, and he went to Barbadoes."

† *Life*, p. 97, *n*. Seyer has this note : " Ch. at London wrote to Mr Barrett telling him he intended to go to the coast of Africa, & wished he could pick up knowledge to qualify him to act as a surgeon. Mr B took the opportunity in his answer to ask him, if the account of T. Canning the L. Mayor of London was authentic. The next account he heard of him was that he had killed himself." B. 4533, f. 117.

Thomas Canynges was Lord Mayor of London in 1456. Pryce, *Memorials of the Canynges*, p. 146.

but of importance in view of the tragedy so close at hand. The fairest way of dealing with statements like " I am no Christian " is in relation to their writer's life as a whole.*

About this time I would place a letter which is generally given earlier in the story, but Bryant, who first made use of it, in 1781, explicitly says " which he wrote about a fortnight before he died."† It has been rightly characterized as the Key to the Rowley Poems, for all the hard words are in Kersey ; the signature is " Thomas Chatterton " anagrammatized :

" Infallible Doctor,

Let this apologize for long silence. Your request would have been long since granted, but I know not what it is best to compose : a Hendecasyllabum carmen, Hexastichon, Ogdastich, Tetrametrum or Septenarius. You must know I have been long troubled with a poetical Cephalophonia,[1] for I no sooner begin an Acrostick,[2] but I wander into a Threnodia.[3] The poem ran thus : the first line, an Acatalectos[4] ; the second an Aetiologia[5] of the first ; the third an Acyrologia[6] ; the fourth an Epanalepsis[7] of the third ; fifth, a Diatyposis[8] of beauty ; sixth, a Diaporesis[9] of success ; seventh, a Brachycatalecton[10] ; eighth, an Ecphonesis of Ecplexis.[11] In short, an Emporium[12] could not contain a greater Synchysis[13] of such accidents without Syzygia.[14] I am resolved to forsake the Parnassian Mount, and would advise you to do so too, and attain the mystery of composing Smegma.[15] Think not I make a Mycterismus[16] in mentioning Smegna. No ; my Mnemosyne[17] will let me see (unless I have an Amblyopia[18]) your great services, which shall always be remembered by

HASMOT ETCHAORNTT."‡

[1] A pain or heaviness in the head. [2] A poem so ordered, etc. [3] A mournful, or funeral song. [4] A verse exactly perfect. [5] A showing of a cause or reason. [6] An improper way of speaking, a bull. [7] Repetition. [8] A description. [9] A doubting. [10] A verse that has a syllable wanting in the end. [11] An exclamation of astonishment. [12] A mart-town. ; *in Anatomy* the *common sensory* in the brain. [13] Confusion. [14] A joining together. [15] Soap. [16] A disdainful gibe or scoff. [17] Memory. [18] Dulness or dimness of sight.

He appears to be telling his friend William Smith, to whom

* Compare the profession of Rimbaud, aged eighteen and a half : " Je n'ai jamais été de ce peuple-ci ; je n'ai jamais été chrétien ; je suis de la race qui chantait dans la supplice ; je ne comprend pas les lois ; je n'ai pas le sens moral. Je suis une brute : vous vous trompez." *Une Saison en Enfer* (1873).

† *Obs.*, p. 561. Mozart, on one occasion, gave his surname as " Trazom."

‡ First printed in *Works*, III, p. 409, " furnished by Mr. Catcott " ; see *Gentleman's Magazine*, Aug., 1838, and Skeat, I, pp. xxxi-xxxiii.

the missive is addressed, to take to soap-boiling, Smith once having advised him, for reasons equally practical, to study French instead of Latin ; but it is a gesture of revelation as well, as on Redcliff meadow, perhaps even a farewell one; yet never interpreted, though the friend survived him nearly sixty-six years. Bryant did not see Smith; he had left Bristol, perhaps for Bristol's good, when the book of 1781 was preparing ; but much later he is described as doorkeeper or prompter to the theatre,* and according to his nephew, while never ceasing to pour out verses himself, always refused to believe that Tom Chatterton wrote Rowley—there was a mystery about the poems, but Tom no more wrote them than he did.†

On Aug. 16 the letter to Lord Mansfield was printed on the back page of the *Middlesex* ; the poet has now eight more days to live.

Even with our knowledge of how little he ate, it is difficult not to read the dialogue between Jack Shift and the Shire Lane landlady as autobiography :

Shift. What can I have for dinner today, madam ?
Landlady. 'Pon my word I do not know, Sir.
Shift. Is there any fish ?
Landlady. I believe not.
Shift. Can't I have a rump steak ?
Landlady. I am afraid not.
Shift. A veal cutlet then ?
Landlady. I do not think it is to be had.
Shift. Well, I don't mind, I can put up with mutton-chops.
Landlady. There are none in the house.
Shift. What cold meat have you ?
Landlady. Why, to tell you the truth, Mr. Shift, I do not chuse to trust you any longer. Your score is now seven and thirty shillings; and I think it is time it should be cleared.
Shift. Oh ! if that's the case, I can take a hint as soon as another : and so good day to you, madam.
[*Exit* Mr. Shift.‡

* George Cumberland's MS., written *circ.* 1827 ; but the time referred to may be 1807.

† *Gentleman's Magazine,* Dec., 1838.

‡ *A Hunter of Oddities,* No. 9. *T. and C.M.*, Sept., 1770.

In *The Festival of Wit* (1783, p. 8) are two anecdotes which come in fitly here. An old gentleman, who professed a respect for men of uncommon literary talents, and frequently conversed with the poet at the Cyder Cellar in Maiden Lane (famous for its political debates), asked him to supper at his house. When the cloth was removed, some very sour wine was placed on the table, which the host praised extravagantly as he was filling Chatterton's glass, requesting him to drink a bumper to the memory of Shakespeare. Chatterton had not finished his glass when the tears stood trembling in his eyes and instantly rolled down his cheeks. " God bless me," said the other, " you are in tears, Mr. Chatterton." "Yes, sir," said the poet, "this *dead* wine of yours compels me to shed tears, but by Heaven they are not the tears of veneration."

The second relates that he was amusing himself with a friend readinge pitaphs in St. Pancras Churchyard, and was so deep in thought that he stumbled into a grave just dug. His friend helped him out, observing that he was happy in assisting at the resurrection of genius. Chatterton smiled, and taking him by the arm, replied, " My dear friend, I feel the sting of a speedy dissolution. I have been at war with the grave for some time, and find it is not so easy to vanquish it as I imagined; we can find an asylum to hide from every creditor but that." His friend tried to divert his thoughts, but three days later he poisoned himself.*

On Tuesday, Aug. 21, the first of the new burlettas, not Chatterton's, but *The Noble Pedlar*, was performed for the first time at Marybone Gardens, " Mr. Barthelemon's night."

How long before the end he accepted Cross the apothecary's invitation, after previous persistent refusals, and partook of a barrel of oysters (a bad month for oysters, August), when he was observed to eat voraciously,† does not appear; but Mrs.

* This will be found in Dix's *Life* (p. 290), derived from this source, as the wording shows. It finds a place too in George Cumberland's MS., as told in a letter from Chatterton to his mother, a week before she heard of his death; here it concludes, " But he added, in his humorous way, ' It was not the quick and dead together '; for he found the sexton under him, who was digging a grave." There is no mention of a companion. (Dix, Appendix, p. 311.)

† *Enquiry*, p. 108, *n.*

Wolfe, the barber's wife, who lived two doors away, remembered his proud and haughty spirit, and told Croft that he appeared, both to her and Mrs. Angel, as if he was born for something great. She said that Mrs. Angel told her, after his death, that as she knew he had not eaten anything for two or three days, she begged he would take some dinner with her on the 24th of August; but he was offended at her expressions, " which seemed to hint he was in want," and assured her he was not hungry.*

This refusal may not have been wholly due to pride. More than a half a century later at the inquest (held at the Horseshoe and Magpie, Saffron Hill) of a man who died in a lodging-house in West Street, Saffron Hill, in the same parish, the landlady said in evidence, " There was plenty of *grub* in the house if he liked to have asked for it ; but I thought if I asked him to have victuals he would be offended, as he might receive it as a hint for the few nights' lodging that he owed me."†

Mrs. Wolfe, who lived till 1820, told Thomas Maurice in 1779 that a baker in Brooke Street, with whom Chatterton dealt, having refused to trust him with an additional loaf, he immediately went home and committed suicide‡ ; and this agrees with Horace Walpole's " poisoned himself on being refused a loaf of bread,"§ and Thomas Warton's " died for want of bread."

That night was his last ; either then, or previously, he is supposed to have addressed the following lines to a friend, who, on returning from the East Indies, sent them to the *Bristol Mercury* (" as a compliment to the city that gave him birth ") where they first appeared, on the twenty-fifth anniversary of the tragedy, Aug. 24, 1795 ; their authority is questionable, however :

Naked and friendless to the world expos'd
Now every scene of happiness is clos'd ;

* *L. and M.*, pp. 194, 195.
† *Morning Herald*, Feb. 11, 1834, *ap.* John Ashton, *The Fleet*, p. 157.
‡ *Memoirs* (1820), Pt. II, p. 161.
§ *Letter* (1779), p. 25.

My mind[1] distress'd, and rack'd with anguish drear,
Adown my cheek oft rolls the falling tear;
My native place I ne'er again shall see;
Condemn'd to bitter want and penury.[2]
Life's thorny path incautiously I've trod,
And bitterly I feel the chastening rod:
O! who can paint the horrors of my mind,
The stings which guilty conscience[3] leave behind:
They rage, they rend, they tear my aching heart,
Increase the torment, agonize the smart.
What shall I do, whither[4] speed my way,
How shun the light of the refulgent day?
Each coming morn but ushers in fresh grief;
No friend at hand[5] to bring me sweet relief:
The sigh I stifle, and the smile I wear,
In secret, but increase my weight[6] of care.
One comfort's left, and that's in speedy death,
What! rob myself of my own vital breath;
Yes! for my frame's so torn, I can't abide,
Of keen reflection the full flowing tide;
Then welcome death: O God my soul receive,
Pardon my sins, and this one act[7] forgive:
*I come! I fly? O how my mind's distrest;
Have mercy Heaven! When shall I find rest.†

[1] mind's, Cumberland MS. [2] misery, *ibid.* [3] pleasures, *ibid.* [4] O whither, *ibid.* [5] friendly hand, *ibid.* [6] the weight, *ibid.* [7] last act, *ibid.*

No one familiar with the works of Richard Savage can read these without being reminded of the lines closing "And when she pities, who can be distress'd?" of which the first dozen run:

Hopeless, abandon'd, aimless and opprest,
Lort to delight, and every way distrest,
'Cross his cold bed, in wild disorder thrown,
Thus sigh'd Alexis, friendless and alone—
Why do I breathe? What joy can being give,
When she, who gave me life, forgets I live?

* I die; I comme; mie true love waytes. *Ælla*, l. 902.

† George Cumberland, who (Nov. 4, 1808, he thought) copied these lines from a version in the possession of Richard Phillips's (the Redcliff sexton's) son, Stephen Chatterton Phillips, to whom the poet's mother had presented them, was given to understand that they were found just after the poet's death, addressed to Stephen Phillips, his cousin, a few days before he died; he adds, "but I have heard say were intended for a Mr. Baker, of Charles Street [i.e., Charleston] and after all they may not be his." There is no proof that Cumberland saw a MS. in Chatterton's hand; the resemblance to Savage says a little for their authenticity, but not nearly enough.

Feels not those wintry blasts—nor heeds my smart,
But shuts me from the shelter of her heart!
Saw me expos'd to want! to shame! to scorn,
To ills!—which make it Misery to be born!
Cast me, regardless, on the world's bleak wild,
And bade me be a wretch, while yet a child!

These had been printed in the *Life of Richard Savage* (1727, p. 15): the tragedy that began in Fox Court, Holborn, ended in Bristol Newgate; the tragedy that began under the shadow of St. Mary Redcliff ended in Brooke Street.

When the room was broken open the next day it was found, like the room at Shoreditch, covered with little scraps of paper. Croft, who says so, saw the Coroner, who had no minutes, could recall none of the circumstances, but produced a "memorandum." The witnesses, as thereby appeared, were Frederick Angell, Mary Foster, William Hamsley. As Croft adds, "none of whom I have been able to find out," one hesitates before identifying the last with William Walmsley, who occupied premises in High Street, Shoreditch, in 1779, and was presumably Croft's tenant; still it is natural to suppose that someone may have been called from the poet's last place of residence to identify the body. The finding was that Chatterton "swallowed arsenick in water, on the 24th of August, 1770; and died, in consequence thereof, the next day."*

It is not an unlikely supposition that the inquest took place at a public-house.† The writer in *Adversaria* (Dec. 1857), already referred to, states that in his boyhood there was a public-house next door to the house in which Moy Thomas had found that Chatterton lodged called The Three Tons [Tuns], two doors out of the city, a resort of disreputable characters, and afterwards suppressed. It is worth remarking, perhaps, that in Tallis's *London Street Views* (1839) a corner house numbered "143, The Cordwainers Arms," is shown on the

* *L. and M.*, pp. 196, 197.

† A spurious account of the inquest, stating that it took place at a public-house called *The Three Crows*, was exposed by Moy Thomas in the *Athenæum* (Dec. 5, 1857): this was a fabrication of Dix; see also *Athenæum* for Jan. 23, 1858.

north side of Holborn, where it joins with the west side of Brooke Street.

The coroner's memorandum must be taken as final as regards the manner of the death; it is not incompatible with Barrett's statement in the *History of Bristol* (1789, p. 647): "The same pride, the same principles impelled him to become his own executioner. He took a large dose of opium, some of which was picked out from between his teeth after death, and he was found the next morning a most horrid spectacle, with limbs and features distorted as after convulsions, a frightful and ghastly corpse." Barrett, if anyone, would know that opium could not produce these appearances; but *Love and Madness* had been published nine years before, and been reprinted several times; and he may well have assumed that the world in general knew that Chatterton had taken arsenic, and have mentioned a fresh fact that had come to his knowledge.* Opium may have been taken to deaden the pain of the arsenic, and the constricting effects of the latter have prevented its assimilation; Sibly, at the end of the century, speaking of the fatal draught, uses the phrase "which he prepared with his own hand."†

If he poisoned himself *immediately* after the refusal of the loaf, he must have had the means of death handy; and, apart from the threats of self-destruction at Bristol, and the pistol incident, there are two suspicious items, in this regard, in journals to which he contributed, after his arrival in London.

In the *Oxford Magazine* for July (which contains his short story called "The False Step" in the *Town and Country* for

* I submitted the evidence to my friend. Dr. O. H. Gotch; he writes as follows:—"Opium, however taken or administered, cannot possibly cause the appearances of contortion, &c., found in Chatterton's case. Acute arsenical poisoning by itself will explain the appearances found after death, since the symptoms, vomiting and diarrhœa, sweating, accompanied by great pain and tenesmus, would of course cause the victim to show evidences of his suffering after death took place. The finding of opium between his teeth is perfectly possible, since opium in the raw state is a coarse powder, sometimes made into sticks, sometimes in seed-like form." Robert James (*A Medical Dictionary*, 1745), after stating that opium is brought from the Levant and the East Indies in round flat cakes . . . covered with leaves . . . to prevent them running or sticking together, adds "but what I have seen here is covered with the flowers, seeds, chaffy husks, stripped from the stalks of some of the Lapatha or dock kind." I have to thank Professor Singer for referring me to this book.

† *Illustration of the Occult Sciences*, p. 810.

June), under the head "Old Bailey Intelligence Extraordinary for 1770," is the following paragraph; that Chatterton is responsible for it is likely from the mention of "Paul Vamp" in the paragraph before, "Vamp" being the signature appended to "The Art of Puffing" (July 22):

"John Cordial, Apothecary, was indicted for killing, with malice prepense, Abel Chance, by selling to the said Chance arsenic instead of magnesia. Proved by the prosecutor the sale of the arsenic by Cordial's man, while Cordial himself was asleep in the said shop. The jury would have found the facts specially, but the court declared the sale of the servant was the sale of the master, and the law in such a case presumes the malice. The jury brought in their verdict *guilty*, and Cordial was hanged when awake for what he never dreamt of in his sleep."

Now whether this (1) refers to some contemporary affair, or (2) is pure fiction, or (3) a piece of autobiography worked up, it shows that, if Chatterton wrote it, his thoughts were running on the purchase of arsenic at least three weeks (the magazine being published at the end of the month) before he took it.

In the *General Evening Post* for Aug. 21, these two extracts appear, not consecutively, in an article headed "Humorous effects by cross-reading the Newspapers":

"Yesterday a sermon was preached by the Bishop of B——
——on the New Essay on the Venereal disease.
Yesterday a young gentleman cut his throat——
——a most effectual remedy against the spleen."

with which compare two couplets, not consecutive, of the poem of Oct. 27, 28, 1769:

Anti-venereal medicines cheek-by-joul
With Whitfield's famous physic for the soul;

Sage Gloster's bishop sits supine between
His fiery floggers, and a cure for spleen.

This leads to a more debatable matter, the reason for the suicide. For myself, I am satisfied that, apart from the denial of the loaf, his constitutional melancholy, exasperated by lack of sleep, delays in payment, and the agony, at this juncture, with the burletta unperformed, of keeping up the farce of brilliant success which had run through all his letters home, drove him to this, not the least among the regular objects of his contemplation.* But he might, according to my view, have taken his life almost at any time after breaking his indentures. The death of a Beckford, a short purse, refusal to sponge or steal, these were unnecessary; adolescence and the burden of genius unrecognized were enough. Shelley, during his last few weeks, certainly contemplated self-destruction.† The poetic consciousness has its abyss, as well as its height, and existence can, at any moment, be envisaged as the former.

Nevertheless, at the risk of being tedious, it will be well to look at some of the authorities.

Tyrwhitt, in the preface (p. x) of the 1777 *Rowley*, says, "He was soon reduced to real indigence; from which he was relieved by death (in what manner is not certainly known), on the 24th of August, or thereabout." John Broughton, in the preface to the *Miscellanies* (p. xix) next year, is more precise: "Every effort appears to have been insufficient to ward off the approach of poverty; and very soon after he settled in London, his distress became so great, that he meditated a design of going to Senegal. This intention he never executed. He continued drudging for the booksellers a few months, when at last, oppressed with poverty and disease, in a fit of despair, he put an end to his existence in the month of August, 1770, with a dose of poison." Here it is my impression that "disease"

* W. P. Ker, not the least of whose merits was understatement, wrote: "He had come to a point of bad luck, and his pride and ambition would not allow him to get over the difficulty by begging or sponging; so he killed himself." *Cambridge History of English Literature*, X, p. 237. Blake's jocose explanation in *An Island in the Moon* should, perhaps, be added: "Then Aradobo began, 'In the first place I think, I think in the first place that Chatterton was clever at Fissie Follogy, Pistinology, Aridology, Arography, Transmography, Phizography, Hogamy, Hatomy, & hall that, but, in the first place, he eat every little, wickly—that is, he slept very little, which he brought into a consumption; & what was that that he took? Fissic or somethink,—& so died!'"

Writings of William Blake, ed. Keynes, I, p. 66.

† "On June 18th [1822] Shelley requested Trelawney to secure for him a small quantity of 'Prussic acid, or essential oil of bitter almonds.' 'I need not tell you,' he wrote, 'I have no intention of suicide at present, but I confess it would be a comfort to me to hold in my possession that golden key to the chamber of perpetual rest.'" W. E. Peck, *Life of Shelley*, Vol. 2, p. 279, *n.*

bears a more positive meaning than if the paragraph were written to-day ; I mean, that the word would not have been used then merely as a synonym for general ill-health.

Next comes Croft (1780), with a statement astonishing in a sentimental chronicler : " That he should have been driven to it by *absolute want*, though I don't say it was *not* so, is not very possible ; since he never indulged himself in meat,* and drank nothing but water " ; and a note comments on Tyrwhitt's sentence thus : " Now, the manner is certainly known ; the cause (*real* indigence) is not. Can any one be sure he was not determined to seal his secret with his death ? "† Now this is really the last conclusion one would have expected from the only man who took the trouble to seek out the Shoreditch people, and who obtained Mrs. Wolfe's testimony ; and full weight must be given to it. Of course it is true that Chatterton could live on very little ; that in itself may have hastened the end.

The Hamiltons, whom Lort saw in 1777, are next ; they said they occasionally paid Chatterton a few guineas for what he had sent them.‡ However, in the notice of *Love and Madness* in the *Critical Review* for June, 1782, a notice written with considerable knowledge of the poet, and mentioning the poorness of his drawings, there is this emphatic statement : " We can only say with confidence that he *did not die for want*. He sent, we believe, the day before the fatal termination of his existence to a very respectable friend for some money, and pledged his honour, that he would return an equivalent in a few days. The money was sent, with an assurance that he might have more, if he wanted it ; but two or three days afterwards his friend was informed that he was dead and buried."

The writer continues : " We are well convinced that he wished to seal his secret with his death. He knew that he and

* But ? the sheep's tongue.

† *L. and M.*, p. 196.

‡ 11063, p. 425. In a letter, probably to Steevens (Aug., 1777), Lort says, " I am much surprised at what you tell me of the very little intelligence the two Hamiltons are able to communicate concerning Chatterton and his publications in their magazine." 11457.

Rowley were suspected to be the same ; his London friends spoke of it with little scruple, and he neither confessed nor denied it. He might fear somewhat from himself ; might dread the effects of increasing obligation ; and be struck with horror at the thought of a public detection. He sometimes seemed wild, abstracted, incoherent ; at others he had a settled gloominess in his countenance, the sure presage of his fatal resolution. In short, this was the very temperament and constitution from which we should, in similar circumstances, expect the same event."

Now this coincides well enough with the Bristol testimony, though no man *there* but Alexander Catcott suspected the identity of Rowley and Chatterton. Still, a caveat is necessary ; the *Critical Review* was a publication of the elder Hamilton ; in fact Chalmers speaks of this very article as having been written under Hamilton's inspection by one who knew Chatterton well in London, adding that Archibald Hamilton senior was the benefactor mentioned.* In the *Gentleman's Magazine* for April, 1799, Hamilton is stated to have admitted in a letter to the 1782 reviewer that he sent the money (a guinea) with promise of more, and also that from his conversations with Chatterton he had no doubt that he had written all Rowley's poems. Moreover, there was nobody in a position to contradict the statement ; true or false, it could be made (one would imagine) with perfect immunity.

Chalmers says that Archibald Hamilton (who died in 1793, five months after his son, who edited the *Town and Country*†) was a man of well known liberality, both of mind and purse ; the only other statement I have come across concerning him is that of Joseph Brasbridge, the silversmith, who used to meet him at the Globe tavern in Fleet Street, and says he had a mind fit for a lord chancellor,‡ whatever that may mean. Be it hoped that he did send the poet that money, before it was too late : it may be that the gift was intercepted.

Finally, or rather penultimately, this memorandum of

* *Works of the English Poets* (1810), Vol. XV, p. 376.
† *Gentleman's Magazine*, March, 1793.
‡ *The Fruits of Experience* (1824), p. 34.

Michael Lort: "Mr. Cross says he had the foul disease which he wd cure himself and had calomel and vitriol of Cross for that purpose who cautioned him against the too free use of these particularly the latter. He loved talking about religion and to argue against Christianity, saying that he meant to turn Mahometan. This circumstance Cross turned after his death to some account, for being found dead in his bed and to all appearance poisoned, when the Jury sat on the body Cross urged this among other things to prove he was out of his senses."*

It is true that Cross's name is not among the witnesses in the Coroner's memorandum, but that was admittedly an imperfect document; the rest of this testimony squares with the letter to George Catcott. He might reasonably boast to the "Knight of the Spit" of salacious exploits which had never occurred, but would he obtain these medicines of Cross in the same spirit? The *Critical* reviewer remarks that a person particularly acquainted with him in London said he was "guilty of no other follies and foibles than most young men are, at his age."† For this disease the cure was, in those days, of an extremely painful nature—"a salivation"; he, who was poor, and with whom self-help was always paramount, might be expected to attempt to cure himself.‡ A complete explanation of the suicide, from sheer physical torment, with no mental complex whatever, is afforded by the hypothesis that he had severe untreated gonorrhœa, for the calomel which Cross gave

* 11457. Robert James (*op. cit.*) says calomel in the common acceptance is *mercurius dulcis*; "it is most commonly mixed with other purging medicines and some chuse to give it in this manner every other day, in order to cure the pox without spitting." Of vitriol he says, "at present [1745] it is used as an emetic, vermifuge, styptic, detergent, and antiphlogistic, but is seldom given inwardly without preparation." Perhaps it should be added that under "Arsenic" he mentions a preparation, for external use only, called the *Arsenical Magnet*, a caustic for breaking venereal buboes.

† A tiny point; the tenth line of "Naked and friendless" in the Cumberland MS. is "The stings which guilty pleasures leave behind"; in the version sent to the newspaper in 1795 by the "friend" the reading is "guilty conscience."

‡ W. R. Barker's catalogue of the Chatterton relics at the Bristol Museum notes (p. 29) that a deep stain as of some strong acid has penetrated the last leaf of the poet's pocket-book, and may be traced through nineteen leaves. In the absence of a chemical examination this cannot be pronounced the action of vitriol.

him would act as a purgative only, unless it were an ointment, which would not relieve the pain to any extent.

At the end of the century Ebenezer Sibly, the astrologer, found in the poet's horoscope evidence of certain ruin by means of wicked and debauched women, Venus being in conjunction with Saturn, the Anareta or destroyer of life. His words are: "Finding himself encompassed with private enemies, surrounded with the evils of poverty, and destitute of every means of subsistence, he quitted Bristol, to try his fortune in the metropolis. Having fixed himself in private lodgings, he sought for bread through the medium of his literary talent, which falling short of his expectations, as well as of his merit, he most unfortunately fell into the hands of the lower order of prostitutes, by whom he was duped, diseased, and finally deserted! In this deplorable situation he continued a few months, occasionally drudging for the booksellers, who neither having the generosity to reward him as he deserved, nor spirit to advance upon the credit of his future productions, he at length, oppressed with poverty and disease, and overcome by despair, put an end to his existence, in the month of August, 1770, by a dose of poison, which he prepared with his own hand."*

Dr. Richard Garnett, commenting in 1882 on the hour of Chatterton's birth, wrote "Sibly was a Bristol man, and very likely to be well informed upon a point to which he would attach great importance."†

As I have tried to show, there is abundant motive for the poet's fate *without* this: nor do I think that this, even if it could be proved the solution, degrades his character; for, in spite of his sister's and Thistlethwaite's testimony to his correctness, in spite of his own statement in his sole extant letter to Barrett, is it likely that a mind so ardent, hasty, and inquisitive would be content to meet death wilfully, with no previous experience, at first hand, of the sexual adventure?

In the room where he died was found the Temple Vicar's

* *Illustration of the Occult Sciences*, p. 810. See Appendix B.

† *Athenæum*, Jan. 14.

Treatise on the Deluge, with MS. poems on the blank leaves at either end. His London friends (Lort, possibly in error, includes Thistlethwaite among them*) came to see the corpse, and Oldham bore the book away† ; it seems to have passed to his brother Joseph, who, twenty-two years later, as an inscription in it attests, gave it to one Christopher Jeaffreson. In 1858 it was discovered on a bookshelf in an inn parlour at Clifton Hampden by the Rev. W. D. Macray,‡ from whom the Bodleian Library purchased it on Nov. 1, 1877, for fifteen pounds ; and it is now MS. Eng. poet. e. 6. *Habent sua fata libelli.* George Catcott's letter, with some other papers, was in the poet's pocket-book, and conveyed to his mother, who, according to Catcott, " seeing my name subscribed thereto, sent it me again in a very mutilated condition."§

The 24th was a Friday ; on the following Tuesday the body was neither dragged "to the triple way" nor interred " in a vault in ye chansell " like Peter Smith's, but enclosed in a shell destined for the burial ground of Shoe Lane workhouse.‖ The register of St. Andrew's Holborn shows (not in the handwriting of Dr. Cutts Barton) that two other persons, a man from " Safforn Hill " and a woman from " Bartholomew's Hospital " were buried on the same day, and on the next day one John Wilkes, from Wards Rents. Like his father the poet was entered among the burials under a wrong Christian name— " William Chatterton Brook's Street 28 " ; " the poet T. Mill " is added in a later hand, which has noted on the flyleaf of the

* " When C lay dead in his room some young fellows of his acquaintance came to see the corpse. Among these Cross believes was one Thistlethwaite a Bristol Poet who has written a very severe satire agt. the court called Liberty [1776]. T had been employed at the last election at Bristol [1774] by Mr. Burke's party to write in their favour, he has been some time in the King's Bench prison or the Marshalsea, he has some pieces composed by C and talks of printing them together with some memoirs of the writer." 11457. In Palmer's testimony, as transcribed by Lort (*ibid.*) is " Relations here went to see the corpse ; so did Thistlethwayte and others of his acquaintance." I can hardly believe anyone came up from Bristol between the 24th and the 28th on this account, but apostles of the reinterment theory can make the most of this.

† " C had Catcott's book of the Deluge, Mr O has it, found in his room after his death." 11457.

‡ *N. and Q.*, Sept. 4, 1858.

§ Letter-book, p. 31.

‖ *L. and M.*, p. 196.

volume " Chatterton the poet was buried on the 28th of August 1770 as appears by this Register Book. T.A.M."

The work-house stood on the site of premises now known as 41 to 43 Shoe Lane, that is to say slightly north-east of the present arched entrance to Robin Hood Court, and it is indicated between 40 and 42 Shoe Lane in Horwood's map of 1799. The burial ground was at the east end, behind the building; in Roque's map of 1746 it appears to be bounded on the south by Eagle and Child Alley and on the north-east by the Angel Inn. A stone bas-relief of the Last Judgment, which stood over the archway of the burial ground, is still preserved on the outer side of the north wall of St. Andrew's Church, facing Holborn. The remains were deposited in a pit which admitted of many bodies, and the entrance for them was by a door like a horizontal cellar door. So it had been pointed out " many years ago " to C. V. le Grice, writing in 1838, ten years after the work-house had been demolished, and the new Fleet Market erected over it and the burial ground. He had wished to stand on Chatterton's grave, the precise spot: " That," said the sexton, " cannot be marked."* It is well to remember that this enthusiast characterized as " perfectly absurd " the legend of the poet's reinterment in St. Mary Redcliff churchyard.

On the same date, Aug. 28 (irony of circumstance !), the second of the new burlettas was performed at Marybone Gardens—Mr. Bannister's night—for the first time, *The Madman.*

Where does Chatterton lie to-day ? Mr. G. W. Wright has tried to answer that question. If the bodies were removed in 1828, his may be among those in the additional burial ground for St. Andrew's, opened in 1754, and closed a hundred years later, in Gray's Inn Road. If they remained till the market site was sold in 1892—it is now crossed by Farringdon Avenue

* *Gentleman's Magazine,* Aug., 1838. In *Notes and Queries* for Aug. 1, 1857, Le Grice gives the date of this visit as sixty-five years ago, i.e., in 1792. There he says, " The sexton showed me quite acquiescently the part of the ground where his body was interred with others in a pit; and his sister, whom I called upon at Bristol, heard my account of my attention without any hint of any removal, but was pleased with my account." The legend was denied also by Benjamin Purnell, who was engaged to Chatterton's niece. See Pryce, *Fact versus Fiction* (1858), p. 69 *sqq.*

—they should be in the City of London Cemetery at Little Ilford, consecrated Nov. 16, 1857.*

A more profitable line of enquiry, perhaps, is what MSS. did the poet destroy. Of the two books specially commanded from Bristol on May 14, one, as we have seen, still exists, with poems written in his own character; the other, the glossary, we are at liberty to imagine among the written papers torn into small pieces, though Barrett certainly had *a* glossary of Chatterton's.† At Shoreditch, according to Croft, he used frequently to say that he had many writings by him which would produce a great deal of money if they were printed. To this it was once or twice observed that they lay in a small compass, for he had not much luggage. But he said he had them nevertheless. When he talked of writing something which should procure him money to get some clothes, to paper the room in which he lodged, and to send some more things to his sister, mother, and grandmother, he was asked why he did not enable himself to do all this by means of these writings which were "worth their weight in gold." His answer was that they were not written with a design to buy old clothes, or to paper rooms, and that, if the world did not behave well, it should never see a line of them.‡

On these grounds§ it has been surmised that the scraps on the garret floor, among which, Tyrwhitt was "credibly informed," were no parchments,|| included Rowley Poems, possibly *The Apostate, The Justice of Peace,* "which Master Cannings advisd me secrett to keep, which I did," and the

* *N. and Q.*, Dec. 15, 1928. This does not exhaust all possibilities:—"Sextons of parish-churches, privately digging up, and sending to the houses of surgeons, the bodies of such people who were buried the preceding night, that died young, and after a short illness, to be anatomized." *Low-Life* (ed. 3, 1764), p. 16.

† "With ye old words first," 11457. Possibly *not* a copy of Chatterton's Glossary; Seyer says, "He had made out a double alphabet which Mr. B[arrett] now has, one part the ancient and modern alphabetically, the other modern and ancient alphabetically." 4533, f. 117.

‡ *L. and M.*, p. 208.

§ It should be added that Lort in a note of 1772 writes: ". . . which Mr. Barrett refusing to do [i.e., give him a character as a surgeon], and he in great distress, he first employed himself a whole day in tearing all his manuscripts to pieces, and then poisoned himself." 11063, f. 405.

|| Preface (1777), p. x.

rest of *Goddwyn*. It may be so, but I cannot easily believe it. Chatterton was far too avid of fame to destroy, even in his death agony, pieces which would entitle him to posthumous renown. What he did destroy he, no doubt, thought bad; and he seldom made a mistake in judging of his work. If we had not evidence already of torn up matter written overnight, we might well be alarmed for those fragments, which the broom swept away when there was no voice to forbid; indeed, of what was swept away there may, even now, exist duplicates: *The Balade of Charitie* does not appear to have been entrusted solely to the printer's office near St. John's Gate, Clerkenwell. No, he did not destroy Rowley; he died that Rowley might live: but that he wrote more poems in the character of the "gode prieste" than have come down to us is a possibility which no one, acquainted with his industry, would be disposed altogether to exclude.

He would have been eighteen on the 20th of November.*

NOTE ON "LAST VERSES"

In the 1857 Boston (U.S.A.) reprint of the 1842 edition of Chatterton's *Poetical Works* the following lines, "never before published," are printed, as "politely communicated" by J. R. Dix Esq, "which he states to have been found in Chatterton's pocket-book after his death. They were given to Mr. Dix by Joseph Cottle, who received them from Mrs. Newton, but too late for insertion in his edition of Chatterton's works" (p. cxxvi). The note introducing them is signed "C."

* Ill-omened Brooke Street! On Sept. 21, 1628, in Brooke House, from which it takes its name, Sir Philip Sidney's friend, the poet Fulke Greville, 1st Lord Brooke, was, at the age of seventy-four, fatally stabbed by his servant, Ralph Haywood (unmentioned in his will) who straightway withdrew to another room and killed himself. The names of Beauchamp Street and Greville Street, hard by, also preserve the memory of this nobleman.

THE LAST VERSES WRITTEN BY CHATTERTON

Farewell, Bristolia's dingy piles of brick,
Lovers of Mammon, worshippers of trick!
Ye spurned the boy who gave you ancient lays,
And paid for learning with your empty praise.
Farewell, ye guzzling aldermanic fools,
By nature fitted for Corruption's tools!
I go to where celestial anthems swell;
But you, when you depart, will sink to Hell.
Farewell, my mother!—cease, my anguished soul,
Nor let Distraction's billows o'er me roll!—
Have mercy, Heaven! when here I cease to live,
And this last act of wretchedness forgive.

August 24, 1770 T. C.

Were it not for the provenance, one might be inclined to pass these, though Chatterton never, I think, calls Bristol "Bristolia"; and "trick" without the article (for "fraud, trickery") is marked "rare" in the N.E.D., with only one instance given, and that as late as 1833. Still, there is a splenetic ring in the lines, which are admitted into Skeat's edition (I, p. 266), and resemble "Ye sage, Broughtonian, self-sufficient fools," &c., in *Kew Gardens*, and a parallel passage in the *Epistle to the Rev. Mr. Catcott*; and "aldermanic" is Chattertonian. Moreover, the sentiment of two of them is right English, and even fifteenth century:

We dreden nat /we han greet auantage,
Whethir we lyue /or elles slayn be we,
In Crystes faith /for up to heuenes stage,
If we so die /our soules lift shult bee;
And on that othir part /yee feendes /yee
In the dirke halke of Helle shul descende.
And yet with us abit this charitee,
Our desir is /that yee yow woulde amende.

Occleve to Sir John Oldcastle (1415), Stanza 60.

Mrs. Newton died in 1804, Cottle in 1853, four years before these lines were published, for the first time, as we are told. Cottle was a publisher; and in 1829 the fourth edition of his *Malvern Hills* contained Chatterton matter, but *not* these "last verses," which, *ex hypothesi*, he had received too late to print in the 1803 *Works*. We are not told when he gave the MS. to Dix, but evidently too late also for insertion in Dix's *Life of Chatterton* (1837). That is the worst difficulty; and until some proof can be obtained of their existence, not only before Dix sent them to "C" (presumably the editor of the Boston edition), but before Cottle gave them to Dix, they must remain, *me judice*, completely unauthenticated. They were repudiated as "totally unworthy of Chatterton's genius" by J. A. Symonds in his review of Skeat's edition (*Academy*, Dec. 15, 1871).

CHAPTER XIX

YEARS OF CONTROVERSY

RARELY is an English poet's death good journalistic copy, a starving youth's suicide is better; but the public prints of August, 1770, found no place for the tragedy of Brooke Street. An over-driven bullock that tossed and gored a butcher's boy with a tray full of meat, and broke both his legs, running down Cannon Street into Tower Street on Friday the 24th, was reported,* also a poor widow who stabbed herself fatally in Cock Alley, Carnaby Market, on Sunday the 26th,† and a country salesman who dropped dead bargaining at the door of the Red Cow in Smithfield on the 27th.‡ The silence of newspapers is occasionally an omen of fame; "If you saw this town," wrote Walpole to Sir Horace Mann on the 31st, "you would not think there could be any news in it. It is as empty as Ferrara."

Chatterton perished, unsung for the moment, except by Cary, his school mate, whose elegy, dated "October," appeared in the *Town and Country* for that month. It sheds no light on the manner of his end; "The wonder of our drooping isle is dead" is its burden, and the Rowley cycle characterized thus:

> Antiquity! bewail his cruel fate,
>   He paid thy hoary head the rev'rence due;
> Thy valu'd acts reviving out of date,
>   Recalling ages past to present view.
> To truths long dead, he gave a second birth,
>   Rescuing from oblivion occult stores;

Thus was the torch of the Great House handed on; Thomas

* *Lloyd's Evening Post*, Aug. 27.
† *Middlesex Journal*, Aug. 28.
‡ *London Evening Post*, Aug. 28.

Chatterton had elegized Thomas Phillips, and Thomas Cary elegized him.

But already the learned world was astir, and to the credit of Chatterton's native place be it stated that a former Bristol Grammar School boy was the first person to interest himself in him when it was just too late. This was the President of St. John's College, Oxford, Dr. Thomas Fry,* who visited the city at the end of August, and, hearing of the ancient poetry, had the intention of patronizing Chatterton, whether discoverer or author merely.† He was told that the young man had within a few days destroyed himself in London, and, calling on Barrett and George Catcott (he had been a pupil of the latter's father), he received from them on loan specimens of the Rowley Poems, "transcripts" in Chatterton's writing, promising to return them after making a glossary; he also undertook to show no copies made from them to others. On Sept. 25, 1770, Dr. Fry returned Rowley's Sermon, *Ælla* and "two quarto volumes" to Catcott‡ (who says this was the first letter he received about Rowley), and on Nov. 30 Dr. Francis Woodward,§ also a Grammar School boy and member of Fry's College,—he was then practising at Bath—asked his friend George for a copy of *Bristowe Tragedy*, for which he would pay, promising not to give a transcript to anyone. This is the dawn of that trade in Chattertoniana which Catcott indulged in till the end of his life, but most lucratively up to 1776, when he sold the Rowley MSS. for Payne's London publication.‖

* Son of Thomas Fry, Pipe Lane, Bristol, pleb. St. John's Coll., matric. 30 June, 1732, aged 14, B.A. 1736, M.A. 1740, B.D. 1745, D.D. 1750. Pres. 1757 until his death, 22 Nov., 1772. Foster, *Alumni Oxonienses*.

† *L. and M.*, p. 201.

‡ The source of nearly all the letters written to or by George Catcott, quoted in this chapter, is the large quarto into which he copied them, numbered 5342 in the Bristol Library; the originals of some that he received are among Richard Smith's Chattertoniana at the Bristol Museum.

§ He matriculated, according to Foster, March 23, 1737-8, aged 16; was present (*teste* Lort) at Chatterton's father's deathbed in 1752, and held the post of physician to the Bristol Infirmary from 1757 to 1769, when he migrated to Bath; Fanny Burney calls him "a chatty, agreeable man" (*Diary*, ed. Dobson, I, p. 332). He died, aged 74, on Oct. 12, 1785. See G. M. Smith, *History of Bristol Royal Infirmary*, p. 81 sqq.

‖ Lort has a note "It is said that Messrs. Tyrwhyt and Stevens gave Catcot 60 guineas for this collection." 11457.

Great secrecy and mystery was made about these relics, by him (not so much by Barrett) from the very first. Moreover, not content with transcribing " Rowley," Catcott antiquated him, so that no reliance can be placed on the spelling of his transcripts; they are distorted in countless instances. Really it is a wonder that Chatterton's " transcripts " were allowed to survive, but then most of them lacked parchment " originals."

To continue; on Sept. 29, 1771, Dr. Fry wrote to Catcott offering to supply a glossary, and on Apr. 10, 1772, Catcott told him that he had consented to the publication of *Bristowe Tragedy*, hoping that it would spur Mr. Barrett on to publish his History. Dr. Fry (Apr. 14) was sorry about this: " It will do no honour to Mr. Rowley's memory by appearing in that manner, and I can assure you with very great certainty that it will not hasten Mr. Barrett's publication in the least "; he was right in the second particular.

On May 3 Catcott wrote to Dr. Fry that he was much surprised to hear from Barrett that copies of Rowley's poems were current in Oxford. Barrett had heard this from " a gentleman of Oxford." Catcott desired further information on the point, and added that he had ordered eight copies of *Bristowe Tragedy* to be sent down to Bristol.

On May 8 " Rowley's midwife " informed Dr. Woodward that five hundred copies of this poem, thanks to Mr. Thomas Eagles (a Bristolian literary character, 1746-1812, who " knew Chatterton well "*) had been published by Newbery in St. Paul's Churchyard† at half a crown; two shillings, he thinks, would have been enough. We have already seen how Horace Walpole characterized this publication. The reviews, also, were sceptical: " We cannot think," said the *Monthly* for August, " on account of the smoothness of the numbers, that the Poem is of so early a date as is suggested. There is, however,

* So Eagles wrote to John Britton, Dec. 21, 1811, quoted in a catalogue of Messrs. Maggs, 1929; and cf. Catcott to J. C. Walker, June 24, 1797, Letter-book, p. 511. Catcott's letter to Woodward is among Richard Smith's Chattertoniana in the Bristol Museum.

† The British Museum has a copy with two title pages, one stating it to be sold by W. Goldsmith, at No. 20 Paternoster Row, the other by F. Newbery: my copy has the Goldsmith imprint. See Clarke, *New Lights*, p. 22.

a natural pathos, and a beautiful simplicity in it, which cannot but recommend it to the lovers of antique poetry." The *Critical* for September was more caustic: "We do not find in it, however, any characteristic of the manner of those *venerable ancient song inditers* . . . but the intention here being only to convey the writer's sentiments, it might have succeeded as well, had the modern orthography been adopted." This reviewer, too, complained that the sentiments were clothed in too vulgar a dress to make him either admire Sir Charles Baudin's fortitude, or drop a tear for his misfortune.

Interest was by this time excited in another quarter. On Apr. 24, 1771, the day after the Royal Academy banquet, when Goldsmith broke the news of Chatterton's death to Walpole, Lord Hardwicke wrote to the former, on the eve of his trip to Bath, suggesting five points in the enquiry he proposed making at Bristol about the poems lately discovered there; the fourth was "The circumstances of the young man's history who sent some of the poems to Mr. Walpole will greatly tend to clear up this matter. It may easily be traced thro' what hands any of them came into his possession. He may either have been the forger or the mender [?] of them."*

Goldsmith, who may have begun Rowleian,† had been favoured with a letter of introduction to Catcott (Apr. 5) from Dr. Woodward, which said "he has a proper relish for those excellent compositions; but is *doubtful* of their antiquity, at least being so far back as their date."‡ The Citizen of the World, however, was no match for the pewterer, who remarked, when purchase was suggested, "Alas, Sir! I fear a poet's note of hand is not very current upon our Exchange of Bristol."§

* Add MS. 35350 f. 41.

† Else Johnson would hardly have laughed at him on this score, if the incident is reported truly. Joseph Cradock says (*Memoirs*, p. 206): "I was witness to an entire separation between Percy and Goldsmith about Rowley's poems": yet Woodward's letter, in which he says he has read some of the poems to Goldsmith, is dated eighteen days *before* the Academy banquet.

‡ Letter-book, p. 92.

§ *European Magazine*, Feb. 1792. Catcott wrote to Dean Milles on June 29, 1775: "The late Dr. Goldsmith offered me in presence of several witnesses, before I had digested them in the order they now stand, or made any glossary or notes, £200 for my MSS, which I refused solely because I would not hurt the sale of Mr. Barrett's *History of Bristol*; but as I have reason to think

On Dec. 15, 1771, the Rev. Mr. Chapman, rector of Weston, writes to the antiquary, Dr. Ducarel, that Catcott is waiting in hopes some gentleman will buy his poems, it is said he has refused £200 for them* ; and on Sept. 12 of the following year, to the same, that Catcott offered him *Ælla*, *The Tournament*, and the three *English Eclogues* for £50 and, Chapman believed, would have taken £40 for them. The other pieces in his possession are intended to be inserted in Barrett's history of Bristol, and for that reason Catcott chooses not to part with them, though, he says, Barrett's behaviour to him does not deserve this compliment. After mentioning that Barrett has "a noble poem of the epic kind" (*Battle of Hastings*), he concludes, "You must know that this Catcott is a pewterer and though very fond of scribbling, especially since he has got Rowley's Works, is extremely ignorant and illiterate. He is, however, very vain, and fancies himself almost as great a genius as Rowley himself."† As a matter of fact on May 6 of this year (1772) Catcott had inserted in a Bristol newspaper a puff preliminary of Barrett's History.‡

This autumn, through the offices of Dr. Woodward, who attended Lady Charlemont medically, a noble fish was hooked. Lord Charlemont (for ever famous as having asked Dr. Johnson, *aet.* 72, if it was true that he was taking dancing lessons of Vestris) had called on Catcott in September and negotiated for transcripts of *The Tournament* and *Ælla* for fifteen guineas, promising never to permit them to be transcribed or learnt by heart. Catcott insisted on a written "promissory memorandum," and on Oct. 12 this was given, in the course of a morning call.§

he will never publish it, I am now willing (altho' I well know they are worth more than 4 times that sum) to dispose of them for 50 guineas, provided the purchaser will publish them with my introduction, which the noble Lords *Camden and Dacre* assur'd me woud bare the public eye." Letter-book, p. 265.

* *Gentleman's Magazine*, May, 1786.

† *Ibid.* July, 1786. William Cole (Add. MS. 5811, f. 59 b.) describes Catcott thus: "a pewterer also of the same city who is half mad, has also a great collection of them, but is as chary as the other [*sc.* Barrett]." Chatterton is described as "an ingenious person, but very debauched," who "made some profit" of the Rowley MSS. "in order to furnish him with recruits for his pleasures." These are notes of a conversation with Lort on Sept. 18, 1773.

‡ Richard Smith's Chattertoniana, p. 351.

§ Letter-book, pp. 173, 174.

On Nov. 22, Dr. Fry died, whether in the faith of Rowley or Chatterton I do not know, but suspect the former; Catcott tells us in the *Monthly Review* for May, 1777, that Dr. Fry commenced Anti-Rowleian "on account of the elegance of the language," but ended "thoroughly convinced." His patronage would not have been of great duration, and it is more than likely that the poet would have fallen foul of it before long. Adolescents who are "choleric beyond description and given to the most violent sallies of passion" (Bryant*) are not, as the world goes, likely to form lasting or profitable friendships with Oxford dons.

The late Sir Ernest Clarke possessed a book into which Dr. Fry had roughly copied some of the Rowley Poems and made the beginnings of a glossary†; this I saw. He was under the impression that it was the book which the President of St. John's was in the habit of showing to his friends, greatly to Catcott's annoyance when he heard of it; but *that* volume, a vellum-bound quarto, is in the Bristol Library (6493). There the poems are copied fair. It is thus inscribed in the pewterer's hand: "The *Extracts* in this Book were written by Dr. Thomas Fry, the late learned President of Saint John's Oxford," and above: "George Catcott's Book, July 5, 1773." It would seem to have been restored to Catcott through Dr. Woodward after Fry's death, *teste* a letter of Dec. 17, 1772, from the doctor to him.‡

In November, 1772, also, a set of circumstances arose which made the Bristolian literati still more secretive and tenacious. Lord Dacre, one of Dr. Woodward's patients, paid a visit to Bristol from Bath in order to see Rowley's poetry, and, to the annoyance of Catcott, was allowed by Barrett to borrow two of the parchments, the "Songe to Ælla" and the "Yellow Roll,"§ with a view to obtaining expert opinion on their

* *Obs.*, p. 500. Because Bryant is an obstinate Rowleian, it does not follow that he is not a trustworthy authority for Chatterton's appearance and behaviour.

† *New Lights*, p. 8.

‡ Letter-book, p. 95.

§ i.e. "Of the Auntiaunt Forme of Monies" and "Englandes Glorye revyved in Maystre Canynge"; the parchment is endorsed "Yeloue Rolle" in Chatterton's Rowleian script. *Vide supra*, Ch. IX p. 123.

authenticity. He sent them to Thomas Percy, then Domestic Chaplain to the Duke of Northumberland at Alnwick Castle. Percy submitted them to Thomas Butler, the Duke's agent, "one of the best judges in England of old writings," who immediately pronounced them spurious, "for the characters uniformly resemble the writing of no Aera whatever, nor are in any degree consistent with themselves." Mr. Justice Chambers, recently appointed a judge to the East Indies, also examined them, with the same result.

Writing to Lord Dacre to this effect on Sept. 6, 1773, Percy said, in the course of a long postscript :

"With regard to Mr Barett I leave to your Lordship to communicate to him in whatever manner you think proper, the above Sentence passed on these Specimens. As he seems a Man of a liberal ingenuous Mind, & open to conviction, I flatter myself that upon recollection he will be glad to have had the forgery detected before he had reposed too securely upon these Writings . . . yet still it may be highly deserving of Publication, not only on account of the Poetical Merit of the Poems, but also to show what human Invention is capable of performing: And I am persuaded that if all the undoubted Pieces of Chatterton were collected into a Volume they would prove him not only capable of writing these Poems attributed to Rowlie, but considering his early youth & the disadvantages of his Education, to have been one of the greatest Geniuses that ever existed in the World.—For my own part, I would subscribe to such a publication with as much pleasure as if the Pieces could be proved to be Rowlie's own ; and would lend all the assistance in my power to promote the sale and formation of such a Work."*

Percy regarded this letter as important, and desired it to be preserved and shown to Lord Camden (another patient of Dr. Woodward, who had been recommended to Catcott) ; but not trusting the documents to the post, he sent them back to Lord Dacre through the medium of Chambers, who was travelling south on the way to his judgeship. They never reached Bristol, however, for Chambers mislaid them. This put the editor of the *Reliques* in a terrible plight ; he was afraid to see Lord Dacre again, till reassured by him ; Barrett,

* Add. MS. 32329, f. 75.

no doubt, did not matter so much* ; and Catcott assured Lord Charlemont that the fact that the parchments had " never yet been return'd, and most probably never will " was " a very striking proof of their authenticity " (Oct. 30, 1774)†, but it is noticeable that Percy does not figure as one of the disputants in the Rowley Controversy, where some of the foremost antiquaries in England took sides.

On March 9, 1778, on the eve of the publication of Tyrwhitt's *Appendix*, he wrote to Chambers : " I should be particularly happy if accidentally dipping into some of your books you should have found the two pieces of parchment attributed to Rowley (the supposed Bristoll-Poet). His pretended poems have run through two editions, and are received as genuine by a large party of pseudo antiquaries and critics : who make a great clamour about the disappearance of these two parchments : and it would be a most fortunate circumstance, if they could at last be produced, with all the evidence they carry of fraud and imposture. At no distance of time would they be the less valuable or decisive."‡

Eleven years later (Nov. 9, 1789), when Barrett was dead, and Percy Bishop of Dromore, Sir Robert Chambers, from Calcutta, wrote to him suggesting two ways in which the parchment (he forgot there were two ; both had been printed by this time from the *real* " originals," i.e. Chatterton's " transcripts ") might have been lost, either " carried away from my Chambers in the Temple by some attorney's clerk . . . by mistake for a *Bailpiece* . . . or . . . lost at sea, in a portfolio which my servant, in a sudden roll of the ship, let fall from my cabin window, being obliged to employ both his hands in saving himself."§

A century passed before their return to life was publicly made known ; they were then,‖ as now (1929), in the possession

* Catcott writes to a Dr. William Smith on May 25, 1775, " Had they been my property, I should by no means sit down so tamely under their loss as Mr. Barrett does." Letter-book, p. 152.

† Add. MS. 39168, f. 81.

‡ Clarke, *op. cit.*, p. 10.

§ Add. MS. 32329, f. 126 b.

‖ *Athenæum*, June 8, 1889 ; letter of Mr. C. G. Crump.

of Sir William Rose Smith, to whom they had ultimately come, through Archdeacon Nares (who attended Sir Robert Chambers's funeral in 1803), enclosed in a paper wrapper sealed with black wax, and inscribed by the widow and executrix:

About the Bristol Parchments
Song of Ella qu Chatterton

N.B. I found these Parchments & letters at different times lately among letters to Sir Robert Chambers.

FRANCES CHAMBERS

The story was first told by Sir Ernest Clarke in his *New Lights on Chatterton* (1916); it bears a curious affinity to Walpole's demand that all his letters to Chatterton should be published.

Thus from 1773 to Aug. 1776, when Catcott got his sixty guineas (having asked seventy) for Chatterton's MSS. from Tyrwhitt and Steevens, expert examination of the poems, the so-called "originals" in particular, was hedged about with more difficulties than ever.

Meanwhile what of the fortunes of the Chattertons? The poet's mother, who, according to Cottle,* always predicted that her poor boy would one day lose his senses, was, it is said, permitted to return to the Pile Street Schoolhouse, which was in 1771 "lett by the Treasurer for the use of the charity," the master, Mr. Love, being permitted "to reside in any part of St. Mary Redcliff parish as he shall think fit." There, supposedly, she remained till March, 1778, when Stephen Love was succeeded by Nathaniel Cope, who, as a married man, required the schoolhouse; the widow was then forced to move out, and lost certain perquisites such as "the making of the bands" for the scholars.† She is said to have burnt

* *Early Recollections*, Vol. II, p. 294 *n.*, where it is stated: "His insanity does not admit of a doubt; produced, as it was, by great mental distress."

† Ingram, *The True Chatterton*, p. 289, 290, *ex inf.* H. P. Stokes. I have been able to verify this in part only. Stephen Love's address is given as 3 Guinea St., in the 1775 Directory; he was buried March 18, 1778 (Redcliff Register). On Aug. 14, 1777, when Lort visited Mrs. Chatterton, she and her daughter lived in Pile Street; "she keeps a small school, drawing patterns" (11457). In 1780 Croft believed the two women kept "little day-schools" (*L. and M.*, p. 187). Cottle says Mrs. Newton's sole means of support was "teaching infants their letters at three pence per week." (*Early Recollections*, I, p. 257.)

" lapsfull " of the poet's papers on hearing of his death,* and later to have brought out copybooks and bedewed them with tears.† One of George Cumberland's informants‡ remembered her having an oval box full of his writings, which she showed to enquiring strangers ; and some certainly, betraying no marks of exuberant genius, were, for a gratuity, disposed of to Thomas Maurice and his friends, as mementoes, in 1779.§ Some papers may have been destroyed in a preliminary access of grief, no doubt ; but much, we may be sure, was kept, the lines on Walpole, for instance. Among the Braikenridge " Collections for Bristol " in the Bristol Library is a torn blazoned coat of arms (similar to those in 5766B in the British Museum), given to a Bristolian by Mrs. Newton as a relic of her brother, a fragment which one would hardly have thought the family could have set any store by at any time. At some date after August, 1770, the Vestry of St. Mary Redcliff reclaimed from the Chattertons the depredations of the schoolmaster antiquary‖ ; but this can hardly have been before the literary controversy drew attention to their existence. The following document is more eloquent than the statements of biographers :

" To the Gentlemen of the Vestry of the Parish of St Mary Redcliffe.

The humble Petition of William Chatterton of the parish of Saint Mary Redcliffe (and the son of John Chatterton who was Sexton of the said parish upwards of Thirty Years) most humbly

Sheweth

That your Petitioner has a family of a Wife and Child, and thro' Misfortunes am obliged to be a Ticket porter at the Tolsey

And as there is now a Vacancy if my Brother in Law, Richard Phillips accepts of being Clerk in the Room of Mr Colstring dec[d]

Most humbly prays you would be pleased to appoint me a Sexton

* Miss Newton's fiancé's testimony, *ap.* Pryce, *Fact versus Fiction*, 1858, p. 99.

† John Taylor, letter to Sir Daniel Wilson, Oct. 31, 1869, *penes me* ; see Wilson, p. 319.

‡ Mrs. Stockwell, *circ.* Oct. 1808.

§ *Memoirs* (1820) Pt. 2, p. 157.

‖ Pryce, *Memorials of the Canynges*, p. 297 ; among them is said to have been the MS. Accounts of Canynge's Chantries (1509-1534). See Ch. IX, p. 122.

thereof and If I am so happy as to Gain such appointment will discharge the Duty therein by a Diligent Attendance therein.

And your Petitioner as in
Duty bound shall for
Bristol Jany. 22nd 1772. ever pray &c.

WM. CHATTERTON."*

The appearance of Bristol was now altering. The demolition of St. Leonard's Church had been ordered in May, 1770, of Redcliff Gate in June, 1771, the construction of Union Street in the same month; and Redcliff Parade, on a site known as Adderclift, was a-building. In emulation of London, where the Corporation had introduced flagged pathways, the Council, on Sept. 28, 1771, decided on a paved pathway, seven feet wide, before the Exchange, in full view of Lambert's Office, and the removal of the four brass pillars, standing on one of which the eldest scholar of the Grammar School used to make a Latin oration to the mayor on Nov. 5, a ceremony which Chatterton may have watched enviously, from over the way. Already Clare Street and College Street were begun, St. Stephen Street opened, and stage coaches plied between Bristol and Hotwells at sixpence a head. In June, 1772, through the medium of the *Bristol Journal*, the ladies returned thanks to the magistrates for " encouraging the accommodation of their feet " with smooth paved streets, but complained that four-wheeled carriages called trucks were allowed to be driven along the footways. At the close of this year the Bristol Library Society was formed; there had been a Library in the Marsh since 1613, and in King Street, without wing, since 1740. Had the poet served out his indentures, he would have found himself in the midst of a rapidly changing city, which was to lose much of its trade by the American War.†

* *Ibid*, p. 299. Whether the applicant was William Chatterton the potter, I cannot say, but the petition failed, according to Pryce, " probably through the breach of confidence of which other members of the family had been guilty anterior to his time."

† Latimer, *Bristol in the Eighteenth Century*, pp. 393-5, 403. Barrett, *History of Bristol*, p. 702; Evans, *Chronological Outline* (1824) says, under 1772, " the new paving began all over the city " ; " A Sojourner " in *Felix Farley* for Oct. 26, 1771, speaks of " the paved foot passages so commendably begun in several of the streets."

On Monday, Apr. 29, in the year before Tyrwhitt's *Rowley* appeared, Boswell was entertained with seeing Dr. Johnson enquire upon the spot into the poems' authenticity, as he had seen him do in the case of Ossian. According to Catcott, who met them at their inn (which " was so bad that Boswell wished to be in Scotland ") they were not in Bristol more than four, or at most five, hours, and returned to Bath that evening.* The pewterer " with a triumphant air of lively simplicity called out, 'I'll make Dr. Johnson a convert.' Dr. Johnson, at his desire, read aloud some of Chatterton's fabricated verses, while Catcot stood at the back of his chair, moving himself like a pendulum, and beating time with his feet, and now and then looking into Dr. Johnson's face, wondering that he was not yet convinced." This was presumably at the inn; they next called on Barrett (who had been enrolled as F.S.A. on Nov. 9, 1775, as one whose credentials were taken as granted), Catcott obviously going with them, where they saw the " originals " (and no doubt heard some comments on the two " pretended to be lost "), which, Boswell says, " were executed very artificially," a judgment which does not surprise, from the person who, not twenty years later, exclaimed, apropos of the Shakespearean imposture, "I now kiss the invaluable records of our bard: and thanks to God that I have lived to see them."† They then proceeded, part of the way possibly by ferry, from 41 St. Augustine's Back to Redcliff,‡ and further yet:

" Honest Catcot seemed to pay no attention whatever to any objections, but insisted, as an end of all controversy, that we should go with him to the tower of the church of St. Mary, Redcliff, and *view with our own eyes* the ancient chest in which the manuscripts were found. To this, Dr. Johnson good-naturedly agreed; and though troubled with a shortness of breathing, laboured up a long flight of steps,§ till we came to the place where the wonderous chest stood. '*There*, (said Catcot, with a bouncing confident credulity)

* P.S to letter to Dr. Glynn, July 18, 1791. Letter-book, p. 490.

† W. H. Ireland, *Confessions* (1805), p. 96.

‡ Barrett, *History of Bristol*, p. 703.

§ They had already, supposedly, climbed the steps *outside* the church, on the N.W.

there is the very chest itself!' After this *ocular demonstration*, there was no more to be said."*

If anything could make the ghost of Chatterton smile, it would have been the sight of Pomposo and his Scottish conductor† ascending to the "Treasury" in the wake of "incomparable Catcott." Dr. Johnson's remark, "This is the most extraordinary young man that has encountered my knowledge. It is wonderful how the whelp has written such things," was not followed by any further exertion in the poet's favour. George Catcott, for some reason or other, did not regard the passage in the *Life* with the same favour as the lines on *Happiness*; "Boswell," he wrote to Dr. Glynn on July 18, 1791, "has been kind enough to carricature me in his second volume of Johnson's Life, but he cannot place me in a more ridiculous light than he has himself, therefore with all Xian charity I freely forgive him."

The Rowley Poems appeared on Feb. 8 (*v. The Gazetteer*) 1777, price five shillings, with no suggestion of partisanship in Thomas Tyrwhitt's preface, which insisted that the decision must finally depend upon the internal evidence. It closed, "Whether the Poems be really antient or modern; the compositions of Rowley, or the forgeries of Chatterton; they must always be considered as a most singular literary curiosity." Horace Walpole, as we have seen, wrote to Mason on Feb. 17: "Mr. Tyrrwhit has at last published the Bristol poems. He does not give up the antiquity,‡ yet fairly leaves everybody to ascribe

* Boswell's *Life of Johnson* (Oxford edition), II, p. 34.

† The noun, used in this connection, is not mine; See Percy's letter to Sir R. Chambers, quoted in G. B. Hill's *Johnson's Letters*, Vol. I, p. 285, *n*.

‡ In 1775 Tyrwhitt was certainly a Rowleian. See the *Essay* in Vol. IV of his edition of the *Canterbury Tales*, p. 87 *n*., where he says: "Rowley, who wrote in the reigns of Henry VI and Edw. IV with an uncommon harmony of numbers, has made the last verse of the stanza [rithme royall] an alexandrin, and so has Milton in some of his juvenile compositions," and *ibid*, p. 252, where he quotes two lines of *Elinoure and Juga* to explain "levesell" in "The Reves Tale." N.B. his "additional note" on this, Vol. III, p 273. On May 16, 1776, after the visit to Bristol, Johnson wrote to Mrs. Thrale: "Stevens seems to be connected with Tyrwhitt in publishing Chatterton's poems; he came very anxiously to know the result of our enquiries, and though he says he always thought them forged, is not well pleased to find us so fully convinced." Steevens, on the publication of the Thrale correspondence, inserted an unsigned letter in the *Gentleman's Magazine* for March, 1788, in which he asserted that he always thought

them to Chatterton if they please." This is how they struck a scholarly and musical country clergyman of the time, who took no part in the controversy, and wrote to his brother about them in April: "I read the Rowley poems through after you left me, and found them full of genius. There are touches here and there that Mr. Gray would not have been ashamed of. The tragic interlude of Ælla is fine almost all through. In short, the book I think is full of uncommon beauties; and I have settled it in my mind that it is partly forged, and partly not. There are many things which it is in the highest degree improbable that Chatterton should have thought of. He must have found some old fragments, at least, which led and assisted his invention, gave him ideas, and put him in the way. Lines left out, or illegible, he supplied, and rough ones, I suppose, he polished and harmonised."

In June, the same writer, the Rev. Thomas Twining, in a letter to Dr. Burney, after enquiring what Mr. Mason thinks of them, continues: "Whatever he may think of their authenticity, if he did not allow them to be full of genius I should scarce be able to think him sincere. What a fuss people make whether Rowley or Chatterton wrote them, as if the whole merit of the poetry depended on that point! Nothing will do but a rarity; but I know of no greater rarity than such genius as appears in those poems. Aye, but the precious mould and the cobwebs! For my part, I have made up, long ago, my creed about these things: I believe they are neither all old nor all modern;" &c.*

the poems forged, and that Mr. Tyrwhitt, before he printed them, had arrived at the same conclusion. Nichols, however, in a note on this statement (*L. A.* IX, 530), says that Tyrwhitt changed his mind after the volume was actually completed at the press, and cancelled *several sheets*, which had been printed to demonstrate that the poems were genuine. Catcott tells Dean Milles (Apr. 8, 1779), that Tyrwhitt printed one sheet of prose MSS., but afterwards suppressed it, "at the particular desire of Mr. Barrett, who engaged to insert the whole in his History of the City, an engagement I never expect to see fulfilled"; and Lort has a note (11457): "It is said . . . that Mr. T. had printed the prose as well as verse, and had cut wooden blocks to accompany them, but afterwards cancelled the sheets and gave the blocks to Barret." Blake's comment, put into the mouth of Quid the Cynic, comes in aptly here: "Chatterton never writ those poems! A parcel of fools, going to Bristol! If I was to go, I'd find it out in a minute, but I've found it out already." *An Island in the Moon*, Ch. VII.

* *Recreations and Studies of a Country Clergyman* (1882), pp. 49, 53.

Even now, after Skeat's complete proof that Chatterton was the sole author of the poems, people of Thomas Twining's opinion are occasionally to be found.

An attack, probably the first, on the genuineness of the poems, by the Rev. G. Ashby, appeared in the *Gentleman's Magazine* for May, which reviewed them in June, and in August printed a remarkable letter, signed "A detester of literary imposture but a lover of good poetry," in which their style was declared to be modern (the writer notes in particular the rhetorical device of anaphora, and the use of compound adjectives), the beauty of a line such as:

> The swote ribible dinnynge yn the dell (*Ecl.* I, l. 25),

where sound is accommodated " as echo to sense," is dwelt on, the use of dictionaries suggested, and the conclusion reached that " whether a poem was written three centuries ago by a Romish priest, in real old English, or seven years ago, in fictitious old English, by a lawyer's clerk, surely cannot either enhance or diminish its merit, considered merely as a poem."

On Nov. 30 of this year (1777) Chatterton's sister took to herself a husband; the Redcliff register reads: " Thomas Newton of this Parish Glasscutter and Mary Chatterton spinster."

In a year Tyrwhitt's *Rowley* went through two editions, and with the third (1778) was issued, price sixpence, an appendix* (paged to bind in with the book) proving the poems to be wholly Chatterton's work from one part only of the internal evidence, their language. In the same year appeared the second volume of Thomas Warton's *History of English Poetry*, where (Section VIII) the same conclusion was reached from an examination of the two lost parchments (i.e. Percy's letter to Lord Dacre of Sept. 6, 1773), that of *The Accounte of W. Canynges Feast*, which had been admirably engraved by Isaac

* " Mr. Tyrwhit, I hear, has actually published an appendix, in which he gives up Rowley." Walpole to Cole, June 10, 1778. A copy of the third edition, with William Blake's autograph on the title page,—it afterwards belonged to Samuel Palmer—is in the possession of Mr. S. C. Cockerell, who tells me he has found in it no marks of any sort (other than the signature) by Blake. In condemning Barrett one should remember that *Tyrwhitt* let the poems go through *two editions* before definitely ascribing them to Chatterton.

Strutt to face p. 288 of Tyrwhitt's *Rowley*,* anachronisms, and various points of style. On Jan. 25, 1776, Warton had written to Percy: "As to Chatterton, I have considered that subject pro and con, not professing to enter *minutely* into the controversy, but just as much as the *general* nature of my work properly required. I own, I lean to the side of the forgery: but if you could find me *only one capital* argument in favour of the genuineness of Rowlie's poems, I should accept it most thankfully."† This is an early use of the term " controversy " in this connection, for at the time of writing Tyrwhitt's edition had not appeared. Warton was aware of Chatterton's admission that he wrote *Bristowe Tragedy*, and reinforces his results with an *ex pede Herculem* argument; nay, more, he adds "This youth, who died at eighteen, was a prodigy of genius; and would have proved the first of English poets, had he reached a maturer age," and ventures a conjecture as to Chatterton's motives: " It will be asked, For what end or purpose did he contrive such an imposture? I answer, From lucrative views; or perhaps from the pleasure of deceiving the world; a motive which, in many minds, operates more powerfully than the hopes of gain. He probably promised himself greater emoluments from this indirect mode of exercising his abilities; or, he might have sacrificed even the vanity of appearing in the character of an applauded original author, to the private enjoyment of the success of his invention and dexterity." (p. 158)

The authorship of Rowley had, therefore, been settled by the two greatest authorities in the kingdom on our old poetry, not to speak of Percy, Lort, Gray, Mason, and Johnson,‡ before the middle of 1778, and was virtually *res judicata* long before the so-called controversy began; but at this point George Catcott, who had already appeared in print on the subject,

* Warton had had the parchment " original " (5766, A f.6) of Barrett; see his letter to Percy of July 29, 1774 (Add. MS. 32329, f. 76), where, asking for " what you know about Rowlie's Poems of Bristol," he says Barrett " rather embarrasses than clears the subject." There are evidences in Catcott's letter-book that this loan was regarded with the utmost disfavour.

† 32329, f. 83.

‡ Johnson's opinion, according to Letitia Hawkins (*Memoirs*, I. p. 270), was that they were not genuine, but not Chatterton's; " If Chatterton had any hand in them *at all*, he must have had very great assistance."

could not allow antiquity to be impugned by a person who had not visited the city of Rowley, and whose enquiries he would "have been happy to assist"; and in August sent a letter to "Sylvanus Urban" beginning, "It may seem strange to you that I, who have been bred to trade, should interfere in a literary dispute," and proceeding to raise objections to certain statements in the *History of English Poetry*; one of them was:

> "Page 140 and 158 he says the poems were deposited in an iron chest. It is a *wooden* one, and the construction of it attended with such peculiar circumstances, as serve to confirm the general evidence. N.B. The chest was made in the room."

The pewterer was indeed a nuisance to the cause of poetry and criticism just then; for, not content with ascribing Chatterton's death to Horace Walpole (*Monthly Review*, May, 1777), he had contradicted his own statements to Tyrwhitt, and fixed his first meeting with the poet at the beginning of 1768. The scholar took him to task for this, and he put the date forward to three weeks or a month after Oct. 1, 1768, in which most, including the present writer, have been content to follow him (*Gentleman's Magazine*, Sept., 1778).*

Chatterton, then, was already in people's mouths. At the end of August, 1778, at the Thrales' house, "Dr. Lort produced several curious MSS. of the famous Bristol Chatterton; among others his Will, and divers verses written against Dr. Johnson as a placeman and a pensioner, all which he read aloud with a steady voice and unmoved countenance, I was astonished at him; Mrs. Thrale not much pleased; Mr. Thrale silent and attentive; and Mr. Seward was slily laughing; Dr. Johnson himself listened profoundly, and laughed openly." So Fanny Burney.† Lort's last visit to Bristol was probably in Aug. '77;

* In the Bristol Library there is a letter from Tyrwhitt to Catcott (Sept. 5, 1778) telling him peremptorily to write to the *Gentleman's Magazine* and correct his error. 11457, and Letter-book, p. 141.

†*Diary*, ed. Dobson, I, pp. 97, 92. Her description of Michael Lort, "who is reckoned one of the most learned men alive," is a typically feminine judgment on a man concerned only to discover the truth: "His manners are somewhat blunt and odd, and he is altogether out of the common road, without having chosen a better path."

about a month before this reunion at Streatham he had written to Walpole to help him to some dates for his narrative.*

The review of the *Miscellanies* (published this year at three and sixpence) in the *Gentleman's Magazine* for Sept., 1778, starts : " The name of Chatterton, like that of Sterne, is now become so famous that trash and garbage, if cooked by him, it is supposed will be greedily swallowed by the undiscerning public." Soon after their publication, Anna Seward spoke of Chatterton to Dr. Johnson with admiration, but he would not hear her, exclaiming, " Pho, child ! don't talk to me of the powers of a vulgar uneducated stripling. He may be another Stephen Duck. It may be extraordinary to do such things as he did, with means so slender ;—but what did Stephen Duck do, what could Chatterton do, which, abstracted from the recollection of his situation, can be worth the attention of learning and taste ? Neither of them had opportunities of enlarging their stock of ideas. No man can coin guineas, but in proportion as he has gold."† It need not perhaps be added that, except that both were West Countrymen, and came of poor parents, there is no parallel whatever between Chatterton and Stephen Duck, who drowned himself, in a fit of dejection (1756) at the age of fifty-one, after many years of royal patronage. Walpole's " all of the house of forgery are relations " is a compliment beside this illiberal, ruthless, and pedantic sneer, one reason for which is obvious : Dr. Johnson had not forgotten Michael Lort's reading from *Kew Gardens*.

Note that Miss Seward was not referring to *Rowley*, for she believed that the *Miscellanies*, which she calls " stupendous," were all that Chatterton left behind. Her quotation (in this

* Add. MS. 12527, f. 35.

† *Letters of Anna Seward*, V, p. 270. To Thomas Park, Jan. 30, 1800. Miss Seward's enthusiasm for the poet was grounded ; on July 1, 1800 she contrasts a thunderstorm in the *Farmer's Boy* unfavourably with that in the *Balade of Charitie*, and on March 7, 1803, writing to Hayley about his *Life of Cowper*, she is severe on Cowper for stating that Burns was the only poet since Prior's time, whose compositions stand in no need of allowance from the recollected obscurity of birth and education: "He must have heard of Chatterton, and if he wanted all generous curiosity to look into his verse, he had no right to make such an assertion," etc. I am not aware that her *veracity*, as regards Dr. Johnson, has been questioned, but see E. V. Lucas, *A Swan and her Friends*, Ch. XII.

letter) from Coleridge, her praise of the historian of English Poetry, and her remarks on Dr. Johnson's not allowing Chatterton "a place in those volumes in which Pomfret and Yalden were admitted" incline one to agree for once with Sir Walter Scott's high opinion of her critical attainments.

In July, 1778, there came to Bristol a young man of twenty-seven, the result of whose enquiries was to bring about, in an odd fashion, Southey and Cottle's three volume edition of Chatterton's works not quite twenty-five years later. This was Herbert Croft, not yet in orders, or a baronet. He called on Catcott (who showed him his MSS., including *The Exhibition*), Barrett, then on Mrs. Newton (now living apart from her mother, in Somersetshire Square, Redcliff), and Mrs. Chatterton, saw the poet's letters—they had been lent to Steevens in 1777, and extracts of them printed in Tyrwhitt's preface—and prevailed on both parties—he gave one a half a guinea and the other a guinea—to lend them to him "for one hour," as it would be too painful to his feelings to read them in their presence. Neither of them saw him again, nor did they know the name of their visitor; but on July 27, according to both accounts (a fortnight after the visit, according to Southey's), he wrote saying that all the little treasure would be faithfully returned. In the autumn the letters were actually returned, except the last, which, he said, Mrs. Chatterton suffered him to keep along with two of her son's drawings. He also, by letter of Aug. 24, prevailed on Mrs. Newton to draw up a memorandum of her recollections of her brother; this she sent, and it is dated Sept. 22, 1778.

Not two years later* the women had the shock of seeing all the borrowed letters printed entire in *Love and Madness*, an ingenious Wertherian novelette, published at three and sixpence, in epistolary form, based on the murder, in April, 1779, of Lord Sandwich's mistress, Martha Reay, by James Hackman, a

* Southey, who got his information from Mrs. Newton, says "in the following July (i.e. 1779)," but *Love and Madness* was not published till March, 1780. Southey's date must be wrong, it is only two months after Miss Reay's murder: between Croft and Mrs. Newton precision is hard to arrive at. The authorities are *Monthly Magazine*, Nov. 1799; *Gentleman's Magazine*, Feb., March, April, 1800; Gregory, *Life*, p. 182.

hare-brained clergyman, who was hanged for the offence. One letter only, the 57th, was genuine, in the non-Chatterton part, and the book was censured by Dr. Johnson in 1783 on the score of " mingling real facts with fiction."* The Chatterton section, inserted in one of the murderer's supposed letters (49), and well over a third of the whole, undoubtedly helped to sell the farrago, of which a second edition was announced by the *Public Advertiser* of Apr. 19, 1780, only five weeks after the first. Mrs. Chatterton wrote to Croft, indignantly denouncing his breach of trust, and received from him ten pounds (March 22, 1781), through Rudhall, it seems, to be divided between her and her daughter, by way of compensation, with the assurance that the family of Thomas Chatterton would " never be forgotten by H.C." Two other letters appear to have been sent by Croft, and in one (Nov., 1780) he had asked for a statement of Mrs. Newton's circumstances, as he was about to promote a public subscription for her. In April he wrote for an acknowledgment of the money, and on the 20th of that month (1781) Mary Newton gave it, saying that the only benefits they had reaped from the " labours of her dear brother " were what they had received from him.† There *that* matter rested till June 19, 1796, when Mrs. Newton was persuaded to take it up again. As far as Chatterton's biographers are concerned, Croft's unprincipled action in publishing the letters, is, like his London researches into the poet's life, a fortunate occurrence.

Meanwhile Rowley and Chatterton was the literary topic *par excellence*, Early in May, 1780, Fanny Burney was at Bath —" much talk among us of Chatterton." Dr. Harrington (either the compiler of *Nugæ Antiquæ* or his father) surprised her by declaring that the poet was " no impostor," and the

* Boswell *Life*, ed. cit. II, p. 472, " Great part of the book," says the reviewer in the *Gentleman's Magazine* (June, 1780) "resembles an ordinary's account, or a sessions-paper."

† A gross untruth. Not only is there a note in the Bristol Museum that J. M. Gutch possessed a letter from Mary Chatterton (19 July, 1771) thanking Steevens for five pounds, but a letter in her autograph is extant in the British Museum (C. 39 h 20) thanking Steevens for five guineas received " by Mr. Catcott," dated " Pile Street, Bristol, Feb. 19th, 1777." See note at end of chapter.

poems fifteenth century productions. "A book however is preparing," she notes in her diary, "that is entirely to clear up this so-long-disputed and very mysterious affair, by Dr. Mills, Dean of Exeter."*

This ponderous obscurantist (1714-1784), President of the Society of Antiquaries, and described by Coleridge as "a priest, who, though only a Dean, in dulness and malignity, was most episcopally eminent,"† had been, from Sept. 24, 1774, one of George Catcott's correspondents, and wrote to him sympathetically about *Love and Madness* on July 3, 1780,‡ for Croft had published the lines on Happiness without Catcott's permission, "as well as letters from the poor boy's sister written in confidence, in order to throw the innocent part of his family into fresh uneasiness." The Dean's sublime conclusion, in this letter, is that the advocates of Rowley have shown themselves the best friends to Chatterton's family. And, ironically enough, there was great truth in this; for while the Anti-Rowleians were concerned only in examining the parchments, *penes* Barrett, or pronouncing on the impossibility of the poems being of the fifteenth century, by internal evidence, the Rowleians took every opportunity of informing themselves of the humble and ignorant condition of the dead poet, to show how impossible it was for such an one to have been any more than the inaccurate transcriber of ancient documents. This line of research, unlike the other, involved visits to the family, where a gratuity was the thing; and honestly it was thought

* *Diary*, ed. Dobson, I, p. 357.

† Cottle, *Early Recollections*, I, p. 36.

‡ In answer to Catcott's of June 27, which says that about eighteen months ago Croft paid him a visit from Bath. "The very instant he entered our compter" Catcott had finished his remarks on Mr. Warton's eighth section. Mrs. Newton thought Catcott and Barrett had been very scandalously used. Croft wrote to him for a copy of *The Exhibition* without the names, in Aug. 1778, which he did not send him; Croft gave Mrs. Chatterton half a guinea. On Aug. 18 he writes to the Dean that Mrs. Newton informed him that her mother has been and still continues "greatly indisposed and is frequently thrown into the most violent hystericks occasion'd by the unfortunate publication . . . nothing subsequent to her late unhappy brother's death had given 'em both so much uneasiness." Writing to Dr. Glynn on July 24, he says Mrs Newton "desir'd I would thank you in her own and mother's name for the many favors received at your hands. I could wish you would write poor Mrs. Chatterton a letter of condolence, I can assure you she stands greatly in need of it."

that *something* was due to Chatterton for having perceived the value of these relics. The two women, who are described as, in 1778, thanks to the humanity of certain curious enquirers, ready "to believe that injured Justice demanded their lives at Tyburn, for being the mother and sister of him who was suspected to have *forged* the Poems of Rowley,"* trimmed their sails according to the prevailing view, and many more than one enquirer must have come away under the impression that he was their sole benefactor. In 1777, when returning Chatterton's letters and MSS. to George Steevens, Mrs. Newton spoke of "the poems my brother copied from Rowley"; but years later Cottle left it on record that once when he mentioned to her that her brother was the writer of the *whole* of Rowley, her face suddenly lightened, and, with a singularly arch smile, she replied, "Aye, to be sure; anybody might have seen that with half an eye."†

But to the matter in hand, the Rowley Controversy.

Dr. Johnson, an Anti-Rowleian, who took no part in it, speaking, as usual, *ex cathedra*, said: "It is a sword that cuts both ways. It is as wonderful to suppose that a boy of sixteen years old had stored his mind with such a train of images and ideas as he had acquired, as to suppose the poems, with their ease of versification and elegance of language, to have been written by Rowlie in the time of Edward the Fourth."‡

This pronouncement adequately interprets the fascination which a problem, to all intents and purposes solved by 1778, exercised over the public mind for some years, and in 1781-2 went far to exclude all other literary interests.

The battle began in 1780 (?) with an undated anonymous pamphlet (probably by Henry Dampier) attacking Warton's eighth section, to which many years later, an undated reply issued from Sherborne§; and in 1781 Jacob Bryant, slightly

* *L. and M.*, p. 139.

† *Malvern Hills* (ed. 4, 1829) p. 412, and see *Early Recollections*, I. p. 257.

‡ Birkbeck Hill, *Johnson Miscellanies*, II, p. 15 (Sir. J. Hawkins).

§ *Remarks upon the Eighth Section of the Second Volume of Mr. Warton's History of English Poetry*; London, for T. Payne, 1s. A note by J. Haslewood in the British Museum copy suggests an alternative ascription to Dr. Woodward. *An Examination of the Poems attributed to Thomas Rowley and William Canynge. With a Defence of the opinion of Mr. Warton*; Sherborne, for R. Goadby, 1s. 6d.

assisted by Dr. Glynn of King's College, Cambridge, published his *Observations*, in two parts, one volume of 602 pages, at 8/6. This monument of perverted ingenuity, the profits of which were promised to Mrs. Chatterton, " a good woman, who has been starving while the booksellers have been fattening on the spoils or discoveries of her unfortunate son,"* is grounded on the assumption that a person who (1) does not understand the context of a learned composition which he transmits to another, and (2) has, in transcribing, varied any of the terms through ignorance, the true meaning appearing from the context, cannot be the author. Fifty-six examples of such " mistakes and ignorance " are adduced from the Rowley Poems, and in the second part the testimony of the Bristol youths is marshalled to show that, zealous of fame as Chatterton was, he never claimed the authorship of what, it is supposed, would have put it in his grasp, the inferiority of his acknowledged pieces to Rowley being dwelt on to some effect.

It is easy to laugh at this procedure now, but the difficulty of the Rowleians was, at bottom, a psychological one ; Bryant, whose picture of the poet generally is convincing enough (he *may* exaggerate the irascibility, but I hardly think so), expresses it thus :

> " If a young lad of little or no principle should find a treasure of old poetry, and put it off for his own ; I should not much wonder. But that such a person should compose to this amount, and then give the credit of it to another, is past my comprehension. It is repugnant to nature, and contrary to all experience." p. 502.

Such a judgment one would sooner have suspected in an age of publicity like ours than in that of Bertram and Macpherson. It never occurs to Bryant that Chatterton copied the mistakes of the dictionary in which " he used to hunt in a most servile manner," and in fact this Rowleian left little work for Skeat ninety years later except to follow Tyrwhitt's lead and turn his arguments the other way, since it is *he* (p. 561) who declares

* *Gentleman's Magazine*, Jan. 1782. Southey used practically the same words fifteen years later to John May ; *Life and Correspondence*, I, p. 319.

that all the words in the " Infallible Doctor " letter are to be found in Kersey, and Kersey alone.*

The *Observations* were reviewed respectfully in the *Gentleman's Magazine* for Jan., 1782, and small time was allowed to the Anti-Rowleians for a riposte. This new year ushered in the President of the Society of Antiquaries' long-promised guinea quarto, which was clearly intended to be the last word. Textually it is a reissue of Tyrwhitt, with two of the *Laymyngetowne* " Discoorses " and the prose account of Laymyngetōwne (pp. 180-6), the songs of Seyncte Warburghe and Seyncte Baldwynne (pp. 433-5), and three stanzas from *The Parlyamente of Sprytes* (pp. 185, 189), embedded in the explanatory matter. The commentary is characterized by Skeat (*Essay*, p. xxxvii) as " the most surprising trash in the way of notes that has ever perhaps been penned."† James Thistlethwaite's letter of Apr. 4, 1781, appeared for the first time as " additional evidence" (pp. 454-461), and preceded the Dean's answer to Tyrwhitt's *Appendix*. " Rowley," says the reviewer in March, " here steps forth armed at all points as a classic and attended by his commentator with notes *variorum*." On Jan. 3, 1782, Walpole (who had written to Mason on Apr. 14, 1781, " Dean Milles is going to revive Rowley, yet so as by laudanum ") complained to him that he was " suffocated by Milles's waggon load of notes."

The credit of the tome was destroyed, however, on the instant of its appearance by a Cambridge sharpshooter, a young fellow of Trinity, John Baynes (1758-1787), parody being the missile employed. Even now *An Archæological Epistle to Jeremiah Milles*,‡ especially the Rowleyizing of " To be or not to be " :

> To blynne or not to blynne the denwere is ;
> Gif it be bette wythin the spryte to beare
> The bawsyn floes and tackels of dystresse

* The words " queed " and " goule " were traced to Bailey's Dictionary by Samuel Badcock, editor of the *Monthly Review*, an Anti-Rowleian (Letter, Feb. 25, 1782, in *Gentleman's Magazine*, Sept. 1788).

† For a specimen, see Chapter XI, p. 192.

‡ Published at a shilling, it was printed in the format of Milles's *Rowley*, and went into a second edition ; it was also inserted with Chatterton's works in Anderson's *Poets*, Vol. XI. *An Etymological Epistle to Jacob Bryant, Esq.*, by the same author, was promised, but, apparently, not published.

is good fun. It did not stand alone ; a travesty by "B. R" of the *Songe to Ælla*, in the *European Magazine* of this April, is sound criticism, as well as diverting :

Oh thou, orr what remaynes of thee,
Rowley, thou preacher of antiquitye,
Lett thys mie songe, like Hastings' battle be,
A subject of debate for all posteritye.

Whanne artful Chatterton, of bloude-red hue,
Hys stockings streaming wythe the morning due,
Upponne the lethale daie,
To Redcliffe took his waie,
Wythe antiquarian Barrett for hys guide ;
Than dydd hys furiouse hande
Steale monie deeds of lande,
Not even myghty Milles hys guilte can hide.

Rowley and Chatterton in the Shades, by George Hardinge (1743-1816), the Welsh Judge, was another nameless squib of 1782, and Henry Maty, in *A New Review* (April), reviewed the controversy in the form of a trial of Chatterton for uttering the poems " against the so frequently disturbed peace of Parnassus."

With Dean Milles the Rowleian heavy artillery had exhausted itself, but the public mind was aware of controversy only.* Dr. Johnson aptly sums up the situation in a letter to Edmund Malone, acknowledging the latter's *Cursory Observations*, one of the earliest, no less than the cheapest (1/6), of the Anti-Rowleian replies : " I think this wild adherence to Chatterton more unaccountable than the obstinate defence of Ossian. In Ossian there is a national pride, which may be forgiven, though it cannot be applauded. In Chatterton there is nothing but a resolution to say again what has once been said." (March 7, 1782†).

* Lort writes to Cole (Dec. 24, 1783) " As to the Rowleian controversy I suppose Dr. Glynne thinks that since the publication of Mr. Bryant's and Dean Milles' books, there can be but one opinion concerning it, and that the infidels are totally routed—yet I am told that there are still some remaining who mean to rally and return to the attack." Add. MS. 5993, f. 60.

† Boswell, *Life, ed. cit.* II, p. 438. By " Chatterton," as the context and Malone's note *ad loc.* show, he means the subject of the controversy, i.e., " Rowley."

It was Malone who showed that, if the antiques were written in eighteenth century English, and the *African Eclogues* in the language of the antiques, no one would be able to distinguish between Chatterton and Rowley.*

The publication of Thomas Warton's *Enquiry* (2 /–) and Tyrwhitt's *Vindication* of his Appendix (3 /6), both before the year was out, left the Rowleians—T. J. Mathias,† Rayner Hickford,‡ and E. B. Greene are three names that occur to one—without an argument ; yet there are Rowleian pamphlets as late as 1809 (John Sherwen) and 1857 (S. R. Maitland) ; and indeed it is impossible to quarrel with Skeat's statement in 1871 that no amount of argument would ever convince a true Rowleian.

Early in the autumn of 1783, within nine days of one another, Thomas and Mary Newton buried their two little boys, Thomas Chatterton Newton (bapt. July 15, 1779, bur. Sept. 13, 1783) and Isaac Henry Newton (bapt. Jan. 10, 1782, bur. Sept. 21, 1783) ; a baby daughter Marianne (bapt. June 26, 1783) was left to the couple.§

The project of a monument to Chatterton is glanced at and repudiated in a letter of Dean Milles to George Catcott of Sept. 30, 1780, Catcott having written on the 11th that he had heard that the Dean, Dr. Glynn, and a third intended erecting one in Bristol Cathedral, and hoped the information was not true. The reply is worth quoting, as typical of the Rowleian state of mind :

" Exeter, Sept 30th 1780

SIR,

I am obliged to you for your letter, & beg you will contradict any report that you hear concerning my being engaged to erect a Monument to Chatterton. Though I must acknowledge upon the authority of all his friends that he was a most surprising Genius,

* *Cursory Observations*, p. 48.

† Mathias's *Essay* (1783) is rather a handbook to the controversy than a piece of partisanship ; still, as it implies that there is a *lis pendens* at this late hour, I include it with the unilluminates. For a brief synopsis of the arguments used in the controversy, taken mainly from Gregory's *Life*, see the Clarendon Press *Rowley* (1911), Editor's Introduction, pp. xlii-xliv.

‡ Who emended " Whyte hys rode as the sommer snowe " to " Whyte his TOTHE as somned snowe." This was published before Tyrwhitt's *Vindication*, and included remarks on his *Appendix*, by John Fell.

§ Redcliff Register.

yet when I consider how much he abused that Genius, & rebell'd by his Principles & conduct agst that great and good Being wch gave him his Faculties, the best thing I could wish for his credit is that ye Remembrance of him and his Vices was blotted out of ye minds of mankind ; for so young and so great a rebel to God and Religion has rarely been seen. Though you confirmd yr Bros high opinion of his abilities you do not account for his putting no Faith in his Rowleyan Productions when you put so much. Did you ever endeavour to convince yr Bro, or could he give any good reason to justify his scepticism.

I am Dear Sr
Yr faithfull
Humble Servant
JER. MILLES.

P.S. To establish the Authenticity of Rowley's Poetry (wch he produced as such) is ye best monument wch can be raised to his memory ; those who extoll his genius only to show how artfully he imposed on mankind, are not friends to his Fame."*

In 1783, however, a monument had actually been erected by private enterprise on the estate of Philip Thicknesse (1719-1792), The Hermitage, Lansdowne, Bath ; it was a profile in relief, backed by a much broken lyre, over a rude but substantial Gothic arch, raised between the bosom of two hills under the spreading roots of an ash tree, a laurel being planted by its side ; the inscription was partly taken from a sentimental writer (Vicesimus Knox). Engraving and description appear in the *Lady's Magazine* for Feb., 1784, and Thicknesse, who was proud of being the first to celebrate the poet thus, set out the particulars in full in an anonymous Bath publication, *A Sketch of St. Catherine's Hermitage* (1787),† and in his own memoirs (1788). It has now completely disappeared, though the dingle which sheltered it is part of the garden of 9 Lansdowne Crescent. Impossible to say whether the relief was taken from an *ad vivum* likeness, but this seems extremely unlikely. In July of the previous year (1782) a picture of Chatterton (in a garret, writing in

* Richard Smith's Chattertoniana, Bristol Museum.

† I am indebted to Mr. R. N. Green-Armytage for knowledge of this rare pamphlet. In his *Memoirs* (Pt. II, p. 154) Thicknesse says of Chatterton : " Poor fellow ! he thought that the writings of a young bluecoat boy could not attract notice, but he hoped that *his writings* under an antient and borrowed name might." The engraving is reproduced in Ingram's *The True Chatterton*, at p. 335.

front of a turned up strung bedstead), which claimed to be the work of a friend, was engraved for the *Westminster Magazine* under the title "The Distressed Poet," and this (with a different face) appears, surrounded by verse and prose, on a handkerchief, printed alternatively in red and blue, specimens of which are in the British and Bristol Museums, without date, but doubtless also of that controversial year. This again, in spite of the assurance "this friend drew him in the situation in which he is represented—anxieties and cares had advanced his life, and had given him an older look than was suited to his age," would seem to be a fanciful representation. It has not hitherto been noticed that in Cary's memorial lines of Oct., 1770, the writer at the close regrets that "plastic means" are wanting to assist the paintings of fancy. On Friday, Dec. 3, 1784, a concert in commemoration of the poet, previously announced for Nov. 2, was held at the Assembly Rooms, Princes Street, Bristol. The programme has an engraving by Nicholas Pocock of "Genius conducting Chatterton in the habit of a Blue-coat boy, to her altar." St. Mary Redcliff is in the background, the child's face podgy, quite devoid of expression, and the design clearly an emblematic one.*

Four days (July 31, 1778) after the publication of the *Miscellanies*, at 3/6 sewed, by Fielding and Walker, a second part was announced as "in the press," and owners of original pieces were invited to supply them to complete the works of "that extraordinary genius." The supplement did not make its appearance till 1784, at 2/, printed for T. Becket in Pall Mall.† Lort wrote to Percy on July 27, "There is a supplemental volume of Chatterton's works just published; among these his will, as curious a morceau as any that has yet appeared; whether this will revive the sleeping controversy or not, I do not know."‡

* Richard Jenkins, *Odes, Songs, Choruses, etc., for the Concert in Commemoration of Chatterton*, 1784.

† It included two Rowley Poems, both headed "In imitation of our old poets," *The Unknown Knyght* and *Sancte Warbur* (called "On oure Ladyes Chirch"), *Heccar and Gaira*, all but one of the pieces written in the *Treatise on the Deluge*, the Hoyland Poems, the "Will," *The Woman of Spirit, Burlesque Cantata*, and *Fanny of the Hill*; the first 326 lines of *Kew Gardens* seem to have been printed off as the first item and then cancelled.

‡ Nichols, *L. I.*, VII, p. 465.

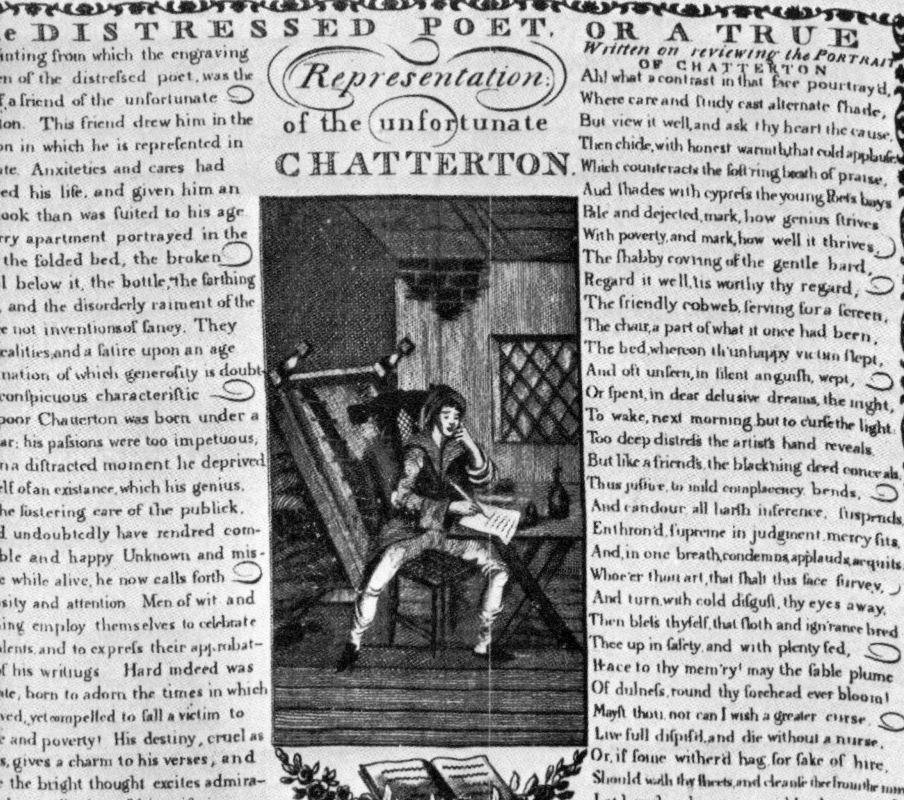

e DISTRESSED POET, OR A TRUE

Representation of the unfortunate CHATTERTON.

inting from which the engraving
en of the diſtreſsed poet, was the
, a friend of the unfortunate
ton. This friend drew him in the
on in which he is repreſented in
ate. Anxieties and cares had
ed his life, and given him an
ook than was ſuited to his age
rry apartment portrayed in the
the folded bed, the broken
l below it, the bottle, the farthing
, and the diſorderly raiment of the
e not inventions of fancy. They
ealities, and a ſatire upon an age
nation of which generoſity is doubt-
conſpicuous characteriſtic
poor Chatterton was born under a
ar; his paſsions were too impetuous,
n a diſtracted moment he deprived
elf of an exiſtance, which his genius,
he foſtering care of the publick,
d undoubtedly have rendred com-
ble and happy. Unknown and mis-
e while alive, he now calls forth
sity and attention. Men of wit and
ing employ themſelves to celebrate
alents, and to expreſs their approbat-
f his writings. Hard indeed was
ate, born to adorn the times in which
ved, yet compelled to fall a victim to
e and poverty! His deſtiny, cruel as
s, gives a charm to his verses, and
the bright thought excites admira-
the recollection of his miſeries
ens a tender ſimpathy and ſorrow.
would not wiſh that he had been
rtunate, as to relieve a fellow
ure ſo accompliſhed, from wretch-
ſs, deſpair, and ſuicide?

Written on reviewing the PORTRAIT OF CHATTERTON

Ah! what a contraſt in that face pourtray'd,
Where care and ſtudy caſt alternate ſhade,
But view it well, and ask thy heart the cauſe,
Then chide, with honeſt warmth, that cold applauſe,
Which counteracts the foſt'ring breath of praiſe,
And ſhades with cypreſs the young Poet's bays
Pale and dejected, mark, how genius ſtrives
With poverty, and mark, how well it thrives,
The ſhabby cov'ring of the gentle bard,
Regard it well, 'tis worthy thy regard,
The friendly cobweb, ſerving for a ſcreen,
The chair, a part of what it once had been,
The bed, whereon th'unhappy victim ſlept,
And oft unſeen, in ſilent anguiſh, wept,
Or ſpent, in dear deluſive dreams, the night,
To wake, next morning, but to curſe the light.
Too deep diſtreſs the artist's hand reveals,
But like a friend's, the black'ning deed conceals,
Thus juſtice, to mild complacency bends,
And candour, all harſh inference, ſuspends,
Enthron'd, ſupreme in judgment, mercy ſits,
And, in one breath, condemns, applauds, acquits.
Whoe'er thou art, that ſhalt this face ſurvey,
And turn, with cold diſguſt, thy eyes away,
Then bleſs thyſelf, that ſloth and ign'rance bred
Thee up in ſafety, and with plenty fed,
Peace to thy mem'ry! may the ſable plume
Of dulneſs, round thy forehead ever bloom!
May'ſt thou, nor can I wiſh a greater curſe,
Live full diſpis'd, and die without a nurſe,
Or, if ſome wither'd hag, for ſake of hire,
Should with thy ſheets, and cleanſe thee from the mire,
Let her, when hunger peeviſhly demands
The dainty morſel from her barb'rous hands,
Inſult, with helliſh mirth, thy craving maw,
And ſnatch it to herſelf, and call it law,
Till pinching famine waſte thee to the bone,
And break, at laſt, that ſolid heart of ſtone.

xample in the British Museum.

THE CHATTERTON HANDKERCHIEF.

(Reduced.)

face p. 476.

In 1785 Mrs. Newton lost a daughter Hannah, christened on the 17th of that February, and her man; the burials in the Redcliff Register recording "June 14, Hannah Newton" and "Oct. 31, Thomas Newton"; the family tombstone gives the date of the husband's death Sept. 29, and his age 40. Her little Marianne, christened in 1783, and her mother, a woman of 54, were all that were left now to Chatterton's only sister.

The affairs of George Catcott, whose brother, the Temple Vicar, had died in June, 1779,* three months before he called his creditors together, were now in a saddish way; for though he lived at Temple Back, cared for by "the rose of virginity," his sister Martha (he never set his hand on matrimonial pewter, in spite of the poet's advice), the business had failed, thanks of course to the "musico-maniac" Burgum, though George was left in charge of it, and he was forced to go as assistant to Messrs. Richard and Thomas Hales, pewterers, in the Back, at 12/ a week, his occupation being to serve in the shop, assist in papering and packing up the goods, and collecting their debts.† By this date he had paid 17/9 in the pound, as against 14/ at the second meeting of creditors (letter of Dec. 17, 1782), who behaved with great civility, and did not ask a single question. "Burgum," he adds complacently, "will not pay a shilling in

* Alexander left George an estate in Fulham, inherited through his father and grandfather, or, if George died childless, to his next brother Thomas, on condition that ten pounds a year should be paid out of it to one Elizabeth Nash (P. C. C. Warburton, 293).

† To Dr. Glynn, Nov. 8, 1783. "My time is now so entirely engrossd," he there says, "that I have not half a days vacation in 3 or 4 months together. I commonly at this time of year rise by break of day, and seldom or ever leave the shop till between 8 and 9 at night. Add to this my employers, who are both rigid Presbyterians, and whose Republican principles I heartily detest, now appear in their proper colours, and behave wth much less respect than when I first offerd my services. It was but a few days ago, I received a very severe reprimand for reading a newspaper in the shop, being asked in a very imperious manner, if I could find no better employment for my time. It is very trying, my dear Sir, for a person of my time of life [56] and (I will add, as I justly may) so much respected, to be reduced to a state of servitude, and the more so, as I am well known to be a person of uncommon curiosity, and don't like confinem^{nt} . . . I believe I might thro' the interest of Mr. Sheriff Blake (who married the Dean of Exeter's sister) & some other gentleman, get a land waiter's place in our custom (alias c-r-d House)." Catcott did not do so badly out of his Rowleian correspondents; there is a payment of thirty guineas from Dr. Glynn on Apr. 17, 1787, *ibid.* p. 438.

the pound" (March 17, 1783); but Burgum, so far as is known did not receive £20 from Jacob Bryant in June, 1782,* after writing a letter full of his miseries. The creditors seem to have behaved with forbearance, for they gave their word ("I wish they had given it under their hands") that they would not break in upon Catcott's private property, "which, God knows, is little enough, not exceeding at the best of times £50 per annum" (Jan. 18, 1783). "We have now," he writes in this letter, "about £1100 to pay, £1000 of wch bears an interest of 5 per cent." Integrity is his only satisfaction; he says that his partner took up £12,000 in his name in less than eighteen months.

Dr. Woodward, however, obliged him by dying in the autumn of 1785, a year after the Dean of Exeter, and leaving him "the sum of ten guineas for his natural life." "Had the sum been doubled," was the legatee's comment to Dr. Glynn, "it would with great frugality (but not otherwise) have enabled me to retire from the noise and hurry of business. . . . I am very thankful for what I have, which is much more than I expected" (Nov. 10, 1785). Fifteen years later (and two before his death), on Apr. 20, 1800, he complained to Thomas Kerrich, the Cambridge University Librarian, of the small legacy he had received from Dr. Glynn (R. Smith's *Chattertoniana*).

As a pundit Catcott was completely discredited, if not before, at any rate since, his attack on the historian of English Poetry in the *Gentleman's Magazine*†; nor, in spite of the noble Lords Charlemont, Dacre, and Camden, had the priestly bard yielded a financial result commensurate with his importance. Burgum and Warton, Warton and Burgum, were the demons that beset his peace of mind; and though his correspondent ("an old doting physician and Chattertonian at Cambridge," as Horace Walpole styled him)‡ comforted him with phrases like "To state with accuracy or precision the respective infamy of each would be very difficult," and "Whatever share of glory be due

* Letter-book, p. 230.
† Aug., 1778.
‡ To the Countess of Upper Ossory, July 17, 1792.

to Rowlie, the next certainly is yours by most unquestionable right" (Dec. 29, 1782), he wrote, on Nov. 10, 1785, to that comforter, echoing the cadences of Wolsey's "Farewell," which he was so fond of reciting:

"I have frequently heard Chatterton say Rowley was his ruin; and no person in the world I think may more justly repeat it after him than myself; for I can truly say that had I taken half the pains to detect my late partner's villainy as in endeavouring to authenticate old MSS, my situation in life would have been very different from what it is at present or probably ever will; for let me ask, what emolument have I received from it; little besides an empty name, & what is that, why truly *vox & praeterea nihil.* Add to this my employers who know no pleasure but that of *getting* & *keeping* money very frequently tell me my head is fill'd with a parcel of damnd nonsense about Rowley and my thoughts never employ'd on my business."

A few days before, he had been told that, if he did not like his situation, he might leave it.

The recipient, Dr. Glynn (afterwards Clobery, 1719-1800), first appears in this connection in the pages of his fellow-Etonian Bryant, where his interviews, in 1778, with Messrs. Smith and Clayfield are given (pp. 527-534). He was introduced to Catcott by Dr. Woodward that year,* and was now to play a not unimportant part in Chatterton's story by stimulating Barrett effectively to the publication of his History of Bristol. In Bristol, at any rate, the appearance of this work was looked for as the final solution of the controversy.

Barrett's attitude to his history and to Rowley *after* Chatterton's death can be arrived at with some degree of certainty through his letters. He writes to Lort on Feb. 1, 1772: "As to Rowley's poetry, as I told you before, I will not vouch for y[e] authenticity of all; y[e] originals I will abide by; and y[e] minstrels songs; tho' y[e] originals are destroy[d], I really believe to be authentic: tho' Chatterton might have thrown y[e] Tragedy of Ella into its form, much of it I believe to be the genuine production of Rowley. . . . Mr. S. Johnson, I hear, has denied y[e] authenticity of 'the Song to Ella,' but y[e] assertion of no

* Letter-book, p. 385. Catcott's first letter to him is dated Apr. 10, 1778.

critic in ye language shall weigh with me against ye authentic MSS. in my possession, &c."*

On March 7 of the same year he writes to Dr. Ducarel that the history is the amusement of his vacant hours, that his business allows him little time to make quick progress in it, and that he advances, though leisurely, in the work. He does not (to the same, May 23) want to make a book either for the profit of himself or anyone else, but wholly to do justice to the history of the city; and on July 20 he sends his correspondent a plan of it.†

On May 14, 1777, when Tyrwhitt's edition was under discussion, he writes to Lort:

> "As to the originality and genuineness of Rowley's poems and ye volume now publish^d, I have not come to any certain conclusion in my own mind—there is a great deal to be said on both sides of ye question.—Y^e medium perhaps is ye truest—that they are not wholly genuine nor all forg'd—tho' some bear certainly ye marks of modernity—yet it is improbable & almost impossible that all that I have seen & have in my possession under that name should be forg'd. Further enquiry into ye affair may throw new light upon the subject & satisfy our doubts."

And (to the same) on May 2, 1778:

> "I shall scarce be [letter torn ? "persuaded"] to believe ye whole MSS I have to be equally a forgery as there are some historical passages I am convinc^d he could not have forg'd nor have known without some original account in his possession he must have copied from."‡

Lort writes to Richard Gough on Aug. 20, 1777, that there were only ten subscribers to William of Worcester's History at

* 11457. This was written before the two parchments were lost; the "destroyed originals" are parchments supposed to have been destroyed by Chatterton. From two allusions in Dr. Johnson's letters for 1776 (May 22, June 3) it would appear that Barrett had declared "against Chatterton's productions," i.e., against Rowley, and had convinced Catcott, who had "written his recantation to Tyrwhitt." If Catcott was ever convinced, it can hardly have been before Southey and Cottle's era. He was a Rowleian in 1792, three years after Barrett's death, when he published his Pen Park Hole pamphlet; see p. 25 of it.

† *Gentleman's Magazine*, June, 1786.

‡ 11457.

Bristol, and Barrett said he should wait for its publication before he sent his own history to the press: "I believe he is much puzzled as to what reliance he may place on or what use he may make of the old writings he had from Chatterton."* Catcott tells Dean Milles on New Year's day, 1778, that Barrett intends his history to go to the press immediately after Nasmith's publication; "but as he has for some years amused the world with the idea of an approaching Publication I will by no means be responsible for his veracity in fulfilling his engagements to the public."† On Jan. 15, 1779, to the same, Catcott wonders if Barrett will ever publish, and on June 27, 1780, in his annoyance about *Love and Madness*, he does not forget to wish that "some effectual method could be thought on to oblige Mr. Barrett to publish his history of Bristol." Seven years later he tells Dr. Glynn that Barrett is revising the history for the press, but is still incredulous of publication—"he is I believe afraid of drawing on himself the criticisms of the reviewers, &c., &c."‡

The surgeon-antiquary had retired to his estate at Wraxall (Wraxall Mill Farm), some six miles S.W. of Bristol—whither Catcott would sometimes ride over to see him—crippled with gout (he had gout in the hand in 1772),§ and, if we believe him, with every intention of allowing his history to be a posthumous affair. On Sept. 8, 1787, he made his will,|| desiring his son, the Rev. William Tandey Barrett, and son-in-law, the Rev. Edmund Capper, jointly to transcribe it for the press, "which

* At Bristol Library, presented by A. H. Russell, Esq. 11666.

† Letter-book, p. 327. James Nasmith's "*Itineraria Symonis Simeonis et Willelmi de Worcestre*" was published at Cambridge in 1778; Barrett, Bryant, G. Catcott, Ducarel, Glynn, Gough, Bristol Society Library, Lort, Milles, Tyrwhitt, H. Walpole, T. Warton and Fr. Woodward appear among the subscribers.

‡ June 15, 1787. Letter-book, p. 443.

§ Letter to Ducarel, Apr. 11, 1772, *ap. Gentleman's Magazine*, June, 1786.

|| P. C. C. Bishop 58. This document begins, not unlike the *History*, "In the name of God, Father, Son and Holy Spirit, one adorable Jehovah"; the sixth clause is "Lastly I desire that wherever I shall happen to die that my corps may be roll[d] up in an old Blanket and put in a common shell or coffin and that it be buried in any churchyard nearest and adjoining and carried to the grave by six of the poor men of the parish who shall receive five shillings each and a crape hatband each for their trouble and a large flat stone only put over y[e] grave inscrib'[d] with my name."

will be no difficult task as y[e] most difficult part is finished and y[e] Parochial history easily compleated inserting therein only y[e] principal monumental inscriptions omitting all common ones also in y[e] annals omitting all frivolous and unimportant matters in each Mayoralty." This would bring the work to a reasonable size, one large quarto. They were then to open subscriptions, or sell the copy and plates to Payne (the publisher of Tyrwhitt's *Rowley*) or any other for what they could get for it, the money arising from the sale to be divided equally between Barrett's surviving children.

Dr. Glynn, however, "added a spur" to his irresolution by telling him, in Latin, to keep mortality before his eyes,* and the work was resumed, the subscription list being opened in 1788. It was published next summer by W. Pyne of Bristol, and dedicated to Levi Ames the mayor, the aldermen and common council (Apr. 15, 1789); the price to subscribers was a guinea and a half, two guineas to the rest of the world. In the list, which includes William Pitt, Michael Lort, Robert Southey (father of the poet), and three friends of Chatterton, John Allen the organist, Matthew Mease, and John Rudhall, Dr. Glynn's name alone—Prince William's stands outside the alphabet—appears in capitals. He perhaps could be relied upon to push the work at Cambridge; to Oxford fifty copies were sent, and forty-nine returned.

To a couple of persons at least the contents came as a surprise: "I remember two years ago," Lort wrote to Walpole on Aug. 4, "Mr. T. Warton declared that Barrett did not intend to make use of any of the MSS. he had received from Chatterton, as materials for his History of Bristol†; but the very reverse now seems to be the case, as he appears to have adopted them all indiscriminately, and as the old saying is 'without fear or wit,' and thus has afforded the Anti-Rowleians ample range for extending their triumph."‡

One who had received no reward for his "indefatigable

* *History of Bristol*, Preface.

† Cf. the statement in the *Biographia Britannica* (1789, IV, p. 579): "It is now said Mr. Barrett does not mean to insert any of these pieces in his History."

‡ Nichols, *L. I.*, VII, p. 554.

services" in procuring 178 subscribers, delivering the books, and receiving the money in person, besides the trouble of transcribing several Latin and English epitaphs, tables of charities, &c., &c., from different churches, complained to Dr. Glynn on Nov. 6, 1789, that "the name of Catcott does not once appear throughout the whole."*

The History, a work indeed not without value, apart from its poetical increment, was hailed with derision; if anything could add to the absurdity of the Chattertonian contributions, it was Rowley's drawings:—

"At the same time" (writes Michael Lort, *loc. cit.*) "Rowley is exhibited in another character—that of a familiar letter-writer, in which modern words and phrases and turn of diction stand forth as conspicuous as in any of the spurious poems. Still another character—that of a drawer and designer of architecture—, a copy of this I had as a great favour from Mr. Barrett ten or twelve years ago, when the dispute was yet in its infancy; and I have kept it very choice ever since, presuming it would never appear to illustrate the History of Bristol or any other."

Alas for Barrett, he had endeavoured to guard himself by having facsimiles engraved, and, in the majority of places, qualifying Rowleian matter with the name of Rowley, besides the sentence in his preface; "As to those manuscripts of Rowley now first published; whatever judgment be formed about them, they are here faithfully transcribed, that by producing all the evidence the judicious reader may be enabled the better to form his opinion concerning that controversy."† Barrett, indeed, showed an odd fastidiousness, if we are to believe what George Catcott told Dr. Glynn on Nov. 6, 1789: he did not print Section I of "Turgot" because he never saw the "original" (and it is still to be read only in Add. MS. 24891), nor, it may be added, did he transcribe the first eighteen lines of the "Purple Roll," an "original" (5766A, f. 4), Rowley's "Explay-

* *Alexander* Catcott's name appears, as Vicar of Temple or Holy Cross, p. 546, with the complimentary addition "author of an ingenious treatise on the Deluge."

† Lort, as was his wont, discriminated: "Barrett seems little disposed to believe all Rowley's MSS. genuine," he wrote to Percy as soon as the book came to hand. July 11, 1789. Nichols, *L. I.*, VII, p. 502.

neals" of the "Yellow Roll"; but he printed the whole of *The Parlyamente of Sprytes* "*verbatim et literatim* from Chatterton's own writing."

He died, on or about Oct. 13, on a visit to his son, the rector of Higham,* without seeing the review in the *Gentleman's Magazine*; and his Chattertoniana passed to Dr. Glynn,† by the terms of whose will‡ they came to the British Museum. But for Glynn it is doubtful if he would have exposed himself in his lifetime; without Rowley his *History of Bristol* would have been remembered; but Rowley gave it the stamp of a curiosity.

Walpole's petty exultation is well known: "I am sorry, very sorry," he wrote to Hannah More on Nov. 4, "for what you tell me of poor Barrett's fate. Though he did write worse than Shakespeare, it is a great pity he was told so, as it killed him."

Of no personage in Chatterton's circle, at this distance of time, is it so hard to form a clear and dispassionate judgment as of William Barrett. Uncritical, blind, self-indulgent, lazy, callous, worldly, and knowing, he appears all these. Of one thing we may be sure, he lacked the rarer gift of sympathy. At that moment when, after the threat of suicide to Clayfield, the poet stood before him in tears, how much might have been done! It was then, not indeed later, that a life was his to save.

Besides the death of Henry Burgum, 1789 also saw the publication at five shillings, sewed, of the first full-dress life of

* "Oct. 17, Wm. Barrett. Dum hic valetudinis causâ commovebatur vitam podagra confectam exspiravit, aetate 62." Higham Register (Burials). Catcott tells Dr. Glynn (Nov. 6) that the history is "greatly disliked" by Barrett's Bristol friends and acquaintance, and that he has been "credibly informd the latter part of the worthy author's life was renderd very unhappy by the reception of many anonymous letters complaining (perhaps justly so) of the badness of the plates and inaccuracy of the language."

† Catcott, on Dec. 28, 1789, wrote indignantly to Barrett's son about the disposal of the "Rowleyan MSS.," as Messrs Eagles, Seyer and Milton flattered themselves that it was Barrett's intention to deposit them in the Bristol Library. W. T. Barrett replied on Jan. 11, 1790, that he collected from his sister Susan that it was his father's intention to send them to Dr. Glynn, "the History not being receiv'd in Bristol with that approbation which might have been expected," neither did he see any absolute promise in the preface of giving them to the Bristol Library. R. Smith's Chattertoniana.

‡ P. C. C. Adderley, 183.

Chatterton. It was to have been written for the third volume of the *Biographia Britannica* by Croft, who changed his mind.* Andrew Kippis, the editor, who for some reason declined writing it himself, gave the materials to Dr. George Gregory (1754-1808) "a city divine"; as some of these were Lort's, this brought on an interview between Gregory and Lort, some of whose proposed alterations were adopted, others not.† On Dec. 3, 1787, Gregory, who felt "the want of oral or written information about the young man," wrote to Lort for assistance; "when the life is finished," he added, "I shall beg the favour of you to cast your eye over it, if it will not be too much trouble"; he mentioned what books he had, and that William Seward had furnished him with some matter. On Dec. 27, Lort lent him a collection of Chatterton's publications in the *Town and Country* (28 sheets), Mr. Lambert's account, remarks on time taken up in writing—for the Rowleians were fond of arguing that Rowley could not have been composed in the time Chatterton had—and an interleaved copy of *Love and Madness.* On Sept. 5, 1788, the book was offered to Lort for correction, who added the notes signed "O," desiring that his name "was not introduced but to authorize some important facts."‡ This remark is largely the justification for the present writer's latterday (though, in a sense, pre-Gregorian) attempt, as many of Lort's memoranda were not used, if indeed they were seen, by the clerical biographer. As an eighteenth century unsentimental view of the poet, Gregory's *Life,* short and restricted as it is, must always command respect.

* Lort writes to Percy on June 6, 1783: "I am told Herbert Croft is going to publish Rowley's poems, clothed in a modern dress, and, having declined to write Chatterton's life for the Biographia Britannica, Kippis has himself undertaken it." On Feb. 24, 1784, he tells Percy, "Herbert Croft is preparing an edition of *all* Chatterton's works—all his political and obscene ribaldry"; and on July 27, "Herbert Croft had promised Kippis a life of him for the third volume of the Biographia, but altered his mind, and now means to make a volume of it." Nichols, *L. I.*, VII, pp. 459, 462, 465. For a protest against the fitness of inserting Chatterton in the *Biographia,* and answers thereto, see *Gentleman's Magazine,* Feb., March, 1783.

† Lort to Percy, June 14, 1789, *ibid.* p. 500.

‡ 11457. Portions of this collection, and 11063 (both in the Bristol Library) are doubtless the identical material submitted to Dr. Gregory. This library also possesses all or most of Lort's collection of books on the subject.

On Feb. 20, 1790, Mrs. Newton, happy to have it in her power "to oblige so sincere a friend," sent specimens of her parents' handwriting and some details concerning her father to Dr. Glynn, who had asked for them through Catcott: "I have been a widow," she wrote, "more than 4 years with one daughter. My mother has had a cancerous complaint in her breast, near 4 years, wch for these seven months has terminated in a running ulcer; this affliction obliged her to resign her school Decem[r] 21st 1788. She has lived with me 14 months, and remains in so weak a state, as not to have been out of the house many times this 9 months past, or to attend herself."*

According to one Molly Hayfield, a servant who lived eight years with Mrs. Newton, and three with Mrs. Chatterton while she kept her room, this affliction was caused by a throw from a chaise when a balloon was let off in Bristol, when her breast was bruised, of which she took little notice at the time; but three years later, "contrary to the advice of an eminent surgeon," went to an old woman who broke it. This informant said Mrs. Chatterton was "attery," or passionate.† Poor woman, she may well have been so then; a writer in the *Gentleman's Magazine* for Aug., 1790, draws a sad picture of the little household. The eminent surgeon does not seem to have been Barrett, who, Southey collected, only attended Mrs. Newton twice, and both times gratis, for breast trouble and a whitlow on her finger.‡

At the same time, granted that Barrett was no benefactor, the financial status of the two women is puzzling. In Catcott's letter book, after the transcription of an epistle to Dean Milles, there is this note§:

* 5342, f. 480.

† Cumberland MS. Wright's *Dialect Dictionary* glosses "attery" as "purulent," applied to a sore, and "irritable, fretful, grim," as applied to persons. The "throw" probably took place on Apr. 19, 1785, when the balloon was let off from a field in St. Philip's. Latimer, *Bristol in the Eighteenth Century*, p. 464.

‡ *Monthly Magazine*, Nov., 1799; and see *L. and M.*, p. 131.

§ 5342. f. 373.

" Benefactions to Mrs. Chatterton & Mrs. Newton

		£	s.	d.
From Dr. Glynn by Geo. Catcott		20	0	0
From Yourself [sc. Dean Milles] by M[r.] Blake		21	0	0
From Mr. Bryant by Do. to Mrs. C-n	21 . 0 . 0			
From Mr. Bryant by Do. to Mrs. Newton	21 : 0 . 0	42	0	0
* From George Catcott		6	6	0
From Mr. Willm. Seward by himself		2	2	0
From Mr. George Steevens by himself		1	1	0
From Mr. Herbert Croft by Mr. Rudhall		10	0	0
From Sundry Persons by Miss Hannah More		30	0	0
From Sundry Persons by George Catcott		6	6	0
		£138	15	0
To Mrs. Chatterton		117	15	0
To Mrs. Newton		21	15	0
		£138	15	0
From the Rowleyans		£127	14	0
From the Anti-Rowleyans		11	1	0
		£138	15	0

" N.B. The above Donations were all given prior to the Date of the preceding Letter Viz., April 8th, 1782. Probably they may have received other Donations which never came to my Knowledge."

No one ever seems to have seen the family other than poverty-stricken from the time of Chatterton's death to that of Southey and Cottle's edition, and it is difficult not to believe that secret hoarding was the cue all this while, under the appearance of distress. No doubt their circumstances were brightest in 1782, when the controversy was at its height ; but from the late autumn of 1785, when Mrs. Newton was robbed of a husband's support, there was but one extra person to provide for, and one benefactress at least on the scene.

* He gave £6 6s. out of what he received for the Rowley MSS. according to the *Gentleman's Magazine*, Feb., 1800, p. 100. Lort (note in B.11060) says he received sixty guineas. Yet the sum he gave, according to Mrs. Chatterton and Mary, would seem to have been five guineas ; see note at end of chapter, and *L. and M.*, p. 131.

On March 26, 1787, George Symes Catcott had sat down to the transcription of all the letters he had written and received about Rowley, arranged under the correspondents' names, his one service to students of English Poetry, and a task that occupied him till March 19, 1799, at least, when he had a return of his asthma: but just two months to the day after Mrs. Newton's unhappy letter to Dr. Glynn, his fortunes turned, and he was inducted sub-librarian at King Street with a yearly salary of £31 . 10, still poor enough for Dr. Glynn to defray his expenses for a journey to see the wonders of Cambridge in the summer of his rehabilitation. This post he held to his death (Nov. 19, 1802*), and here, say his nephews, he was much teased by some of the younger readers, who, while he dozed, once removed his spectacles from his pocket to between his neck and stock, which transmigration he ascribed to witchcraft, and penned a narrative thereof. While he was gone for books, too, the same "knot of wags" would pick his greatcoat (which he hung up as soon as he entered the library) of its case of pens, and split up the latter, much to his "sputtering and astonishment" when he came to enter the items for which they had pestered him.† Here, moreover, he had a passage of arms with the author of *Christabel*, whom, in May, 1797, he made pay five shillings for the postage of books to Bristol from Stowey:

"With respect to the Bruckers‡, altho' by accident they were register'd on the 23rd of March, yet they were not removed from the Library for a fortnight after: and when I received your first letter on this subject, I had had the two volumes *just three weeks.* Our learned & ingenious Committee may read thro' two quartos—i.e., *two thousand and four hundred pages of close printed Greek & Latin,* in three weeks, for aught I know to the contrary. I pretend to no such intenseness of application or rapidity of Genius . . . I subscribe to your Library, Mr. Catcott, not to read novels, or books of quick

* Buried, Nov. 24, in a brick grave in Temple Churchyard, not, however, before an intended slight on the name that had won him recognition and friends of influence; for on March 19, 1799 to Dr. Glynn, about Southey, he wrote, "whose poetical abilities are superior to the late unfortunate Thos. Chatterton."

† 5258, Bristol Library.

‡ i.e. *Historia Critica Philosophiæ*, Ed. Altera. Lipsiæ 1767, 6. 2 Tom. The books are in the Bristol Library, Coleridge's letter in the Bristol Museum.

reading & easy digestion—but to get books which I cannot get anywhere—books of massy knowledge."

With this triumph over the Arts we can leave him.

On February 6, 1791, Mrs. Chatterton wrote, from Cathay, in a firm hand to Francis Freeling (of Redcliff) who rose to be secretary to the Post Office, expressing her deep gratitude for several presents made to her on her son's account.* She died on Christmas Day, aged sixty-one, and her funeral, as that of the last of the Chattertons,† was largely attended. Probably at no period after 1770 had she been wholly neglected, and latterly Hannah More (who had come to live in Bristol as a child of eleven about four years after the poet's birth) and her sisters were kind to her. At Beilby Porteous's in April, 1782, Hannah More had sat next to Dr. Johnson, who "continued his jokes and lamented that I had not married Chatterton, that posterity might have seen a propagation of poets."‡

The *European Magazine* for Apr., 1792, informs its readers that the citizens of Bristol are about to erect a cenotaph to the memory of their extraordinary fellow citizen in Redcliff Church, by subscription; they should, however, build a spire: the papers announce Mr. [Thomas] Banks (1735-1805) of Newman Street, London, as the sculptor, who executed the Shakespeare at the Shakespeare Gallery, Pall Mall.§

* Sotheby's Sale Catalogue, Apr. 17, 1929, lot 640.

† Pryce, *Fact versus Fiction*, p. 98. "Dec. 28, 1791, Sarah Chatterton." *Redcliff Register* (Burials).

‡ Hannah More, *Memoirs* I, p. 25. So perfect a judge of the subject was Miss More that she wrote to Catcott (Mar. 14, 1777): "The authenticity of Rowley's poems is so clear from the *internal evidence alone* that it stands in need of no other proof"! Letter-book, p. 54.

§ Dr. Glynn refers to this, "the most fantastical Cenotaph that ever was to the fantastical merit of the greatest profligate that ever was," in a letter to Catcott of July 1, 1791, adding, "Why do they not do something for honest *George*?" In denying this rumour (July 18) Catcott candidly acknowledges "upon the authority of all his friends" that Chatterton was a most surprising genius, and goes on to quote phrases from Dean Milles's letter of Sept. 30, 1780, as if they were his own. He was finding the letter-book useful just then. On Jan. 10, 1792, he writes: "There really is a scheme on foot for erecting a *cenotaph* to the memory of the unfortunate *Chatterton*," proposed by Wm. Broderip, apothecary, intended to be in Redcliff Church, and to cost £200, design by John Bacon (1740-1799), inscription by Mason, subscription begun by Mr. Broderip with ten guineas. Catcott told Broderip that Glynn would disapprove; "the subscription fills very slowly, and unless he can raise at least £100, the design must drop." See Shiercliff's *Bristol Guide*, ed. 1793, p. 42, *n*.

The first Cambridge *Rowley* (Oxford did not publish till 1911), intended to be a cheap edition—5 /—appeared in 1794, edited by Lancelot Sharpe (1774-1851) an undergraduate of Pembroke.* The preface, that of a very young man indeed, states "that many years have elapsed since the controversy subsided, but "no decision, which can be regarded as final, has hitherto been given." The text is Tyrwhitt's, plus Milles's glossary, and an explanation or two of Mr. Sharpe's; Coleridge's *Monody*, unsigned, was prefixed by "the permission of an ingenious Friend." At this point, though Thomas Warton had declared for him sixteen years before, Chatterton passes from the antiquaries to the poets.

The large engraving by Edward Orme of Henry Singleton's (1766-1839) *Death of Chatterton* was published on May 1 of this year, a wretched picture—I have not seen the original, nor know where it is—but possibly the first really imaginative treatment of the poet by a painter; though J. T. Smith, in his *Remarks on Rural Scenery* (1797, p. 24), speaks in high terms of the "chilly coloring" of a picture of the same subject by John Cranch, a native of Kingsbridge in Devon (b. 1751), Fellow of the American Society of Arts, who taught himself oil-painting after the age of thirty-six; this was then in the possession of Sir James Winter Lake, Bt., at Edmonton. Under his engraving of Cranch (1795) Smith speaks of this picture as "unique."

In 1795 *The Revenge* was printed, at five shillings, but according to Joseph Haslewood, never regularly published.† There was an Edinburgh publication of *Rowley* and a selection from the *Miscellanies* (prefaced by a memoir drawn mainly from Croft and Gregory) by Mundell and Son in the same year, as part of Vol. XI of Robert Anderson's *British Poets*

After her mother's death, Mrs. Newton took over her school. She had experience in teaching, and about 1783 was governess in the family of Philip George‡ (thrice sheriff of Bristol) to whom she gave the MS. of her brother's lines on Horace Walpole,

* B.A., 1796; M.A., 1800; afterwards Rector of All Hallows Staining, London. See *Notes and Queries*, June 16th, 1888.

† *Works*, III, p. 537.

‡ W. R. Barker, *Catalogue of Chatterton MSS. &c., in Bristol Museum*, p. 43.

who, as Lord Orford, died in 1797. Let us, in justice, here remember that Chatterton could *never* have imposed on this man, for, in the event of *more* encouragement, if we are to believe the poet's own words to Barrett (who had no motive for perverting them), the fabricated " originals " would next have been sent to Arlington Street,* an action which would have wholly destroyed any chance of Walpole's realizing that his correspondent was an author.

To return to Mrs. Newton ; Southey mentioned as a fact that she was once confined in an asylum, and inferred therefrom that there was a taint of insanity in the family, which explained the eccentricities of her brother's life and " the deplorable rashness of his death."†

However that may be, on June 19, 1796, the year following the great rise in prices, on the advice of a gentleman to whom she had shown Croft's letters (Joseph Cottle, not impossibly), she wrote to Sir Herbert Croft, soliciting the aid he had promised eighteen years before—" Justice to my situation would long since have compelled me to address you, but have been, till a few days past, unacquainted with your residence." No answer was returned, and she wrote again on Aug. 4. However culpable, it was perhaps not unnatural in Croft, after such a gap of years, to suspect an imposition from this quarter. He replied brutally on Sept. 1 : " The sort of *threatening* letter which Mrs. Newton's is will never succeed with me ; but if the clergyman of the parish will do me the favour to write me word, through Mrs. Newton, what Chatterton's relations consist of and *what characters they bear*, I will try, by everything in my power, to serve them ; yet certainly not if any of them pretend to have the smallest *claim* on me."‡ Croft was imprisoned for debt in a year's time, and, his duty apart, was hard up.

But a new spirit was astir in Bristol, a zeal for poetry, confused, no doubt, with wild idealistic schemes, but disinterested. Southey had written to Cottle from Lisbon on Feb. 1,

* Barrett to Lort, Feb. 1, 1772. 11457.

† Letter to John Britton, Nov. 4, 1810, in Bristol Museum.

‡ *Monthly Magazine*, Nov., 1799, where both Mrs. Newton's letters and Croft's are given in full.

1796, possibly having in mind the *Bristol* (1794) of his short-lived friend Robert Lovell: " Bristol deserves panegyric instead of satire. I know of no mercantile place so literary."* Cottle, at all events, was soon at work, for Southey wrote to John May, on July 11, 1797: " The sister and niece of Chatterton are now wholly destitute. On this occasion I appear as editor of all his works for their relief; this is an heinous sin against the world's opinion, for a young lawyer, but it would have been a real crime to have refused it. We have a black scene to lay before the public. . . . Cottle has been with me a few days and we have arranged everything relative to this business."† In Sept., Coleridge wrote to Cottle, " Herbert Croft is in Exeter Gaol! This is unlucky. Poor devil! He must now be unpeppered."‡ But Coleridge was apprehensive of the venture, and had written at length to Southey in July, attempting to dissuade him, as follows:

" You are acting kindly in your exertions for Chatterton's sister; but I doubt the success. Chatterton's or Rowley's poems were never popular. The very circumstance which made them so much talked of, their *ancientness*, prevented them from being generally read, in the degree, I mean, that Goldsmith's poems or even Rogers' thing upon memory has been. The sale was *never* very great. Secondly, the London Edition and the Cambridge Edition, which are now both of them the property of London booksellers, are still in hand§, and these booksellers will " hardly exert their interest for a rival." *Thirdly, these are bad times.* Fourthly, all who are sincerely zealous for Chatterton, or whom from knowledge of her are interested in poor Mrs. Newton, will come forwards first, and if others should drop in but slowly, Mrs. Newton will either receive no benefit at all from these her friends, or one so long procrastinated, from the necessity of waiting for the complement of subscribers, that it may at last come too late. For these reasons I am almost inclined to think a *subscription* simply would be better. It is unpleasant to cast a damp on anything; but that benevolence alone is likely to be beneficent which *calculates*. If, however, you continue to entertain higher hopes than I, believe me, I will shake off my sloth, and use my best muscles in gaining subscribers.

* Cottle, *Early Recollections*, II, p. 6.

† Southey's Life and Correspondence, ed. by his son (1849), I, p. 319.

‡ *Early Recollections*, I, p. 253.

§ Copies of the Cambridge edition of 1794 with a fresh title page dated 1799, are sometimes met with.

I will certainly write a preliminary essay, and I will *attempt* to write a poem on the life and death of Chatterton, but the Monody *must not be reprinted.*"*

Truly a shrewd letter from a poet of twenty-five to one of twenty-three; but, alas, the writer was S.T.C., and neither essay nor poem made its appearance.

A complete edition of Chatterton's works had been desiderated by a correspondent signing himself "Juvenis" in the *Gentleman's Magazine* for Dec., 1787; and to an enterprising twenty-seven year old publisher—Cottle took no profits in this affair—with six years' experience of bookselling in Bristol, and some taste in literature imbibed from his tutor John Henderson, besides the knowledge that Anne Yearsley, the milk-woman (Hannah More's former protégée), had latterly usurped the city's laurels, the time might well seem ripe, in 1797, for a movement in favour of the Redcliff poet. Still, to induce an adequate subscription, public sympathy and imagination needed to be jogged. Mrs. Chatterton was no more, her widowed daughter's sight was failing, and *she* had a little girl. There was Croft, who had made money out of those letters, and turned his back on the survivors. Croft was the hors d'œuvre required, and by the autumn of 1799 the hour had come for repeppering. Accordingly Southey wrote to him, asking what steps he intended to take in the matter of Chatterton's sister, and then sent a letter to the *Monthly Magazine* (Nov. 1799) fully documented, detailing his offence, and a scheme for a two volume edition to be printed by Kearsley at sixteen shillings:—

"Mr. Croft has been privately addressed upon the subject without effect; his conduct is now made public in the hope that general liberality may be excited by general indignation."

Sir Herbert Croft's longwinded and evasive reply (*Gentleman's Magazine*, Feb., Mar., Apr., 1800) is the ultimate yelp of eighteenth century bravura against the young romantic idea. Most of it is levelled against Pantisocracy and *Joan of Arc*:

* *Letters*, ed. E. H. Coleridge, Vol. I, p. 221.

"He [Southey] writes prose somewhat like bad poetry and poetry somewhat like bad prose." Croft insists that he intended to have published Chatterton's works when he quitted the Bar for the Church in 1781, but Dr. Johnson decidedly thought it would not succeed, and Lowth (the Bishop of London) wrote a letter, "which I still have," giving the same opinion. Croft had ideas about an edition, and has MSS. of Chatterton, presented to him by Percy, "which I certainly shall not communicate to such an editor as Mr. Southey for the sake of Chatterton's reputation." But he admits taking the letters, and does not deny publishing them without the knowledge of the family, for his own emolument. These two points, it was thought, were all that was necessary, and Southey wrote quite shortly to the *Gentleman's Magazine* in March, restating them, and allowing the clerical baronet to have the last word. Croft survived his exposure and the 1803 edition, not dying till 1816, nine years after the main line of the Chattertons was extinct.

On Feb. 9, 1800, Southey had written to John May asking him to assist the subscription; 177 names have come in, mainly from Bristol and Cumberland, 20 or 30 more from Hampshire are expected; 750 copies would produce between four and five hundred pounds.* But the money did not come in, and at the end of two years, Southey says,† the subscription would not have defrayed the costs of publication.

Late in October, 1800, with a sad lack of fitness, Cottle invited W. H. Ireland, the Shakespeare forger, who happened to be in Bristol, to insert specimens of his ability at the end of one of the Burgum copy-books, then in Cottle's possession. Either on this or an earlier visit Ireland called on Mrs. Newton, who, according to his account, positively denied, with tears in her eyes, that her brother had been partial to the society of abandoned women, describing him as thin of body, but neatly made, not handsome, but of striking appearance, owing to his eyes—the left eye seemed to "flash fire"—, reserved, and fond of seclusion, so that they often missed him for half a day together. Once (I believe Ireland here) he was most severely

* Letter in Bristol Museum.

† *Gentleman's Magazine*, Aug. 1804.

chastised for a long absence, but did not shed a tear, but merely said, "It was hard indeed to be whipped for reading."* He was also told that the child was taught his letters from an old black-letter Bible, and would not take his lesson from any book of modern type, a variation perhaps of "always objected to read in a small book" in her long letter to Croft of 1778.*

The next step in the matter of publication was an arrangement with Messrs. Longman and Rees of Paternoster Row, who produced the work at their expense, allowing Mrs. Newton 350 copies gratis and a reversionary interest in any future edition; the price of the three volumes was £1 8s. to subscribers, to others a guinea and a half.

Mrs. Newton, though once confined in a mad-house,† did not mean to be a loser by local idealism. On March 25, 1802, she wrote to Cottle, in Crane Court, Fleet Street, where the *Works* were printed, approving of the publication and requesting the advance of a few pounds before the sum was settled in "annuitys"; she speaks of the trying times of the last two years, and placing her daughter to a mantua-maker.‡ On Jan. 22, 1803, she made her will (P.C.C. Heseltine 631), appointing Francis Freeling of the General Post Office, London, Esq. and Robert Lewis of the City of Bristol, Esq., trustees of all that she might be entitled unto at the time of her decease "from the sale of certain works the production of my late brother Thomas Chatterton deceased which are now in course of publication," and Hannah and Sarah More executrices of her residuary estate (to be laid out in the purchase of Government stock) and guardians of the person and fortune of her daughter Mary Ann Newton until her majority or marriage. In the event of her daughter's death under twenty-one and unmarried there were legacies of £100 to Henry Newton of

* W. H. Ireland, *Confessions* (1805), p. 12, *sqq*.

† "Chatterton *was* insane—better proof of this than the coroner's inquest is that there was insanity in his family. (His sister, Mrs. Newton, was for some period confined in a mad-house). His biographers were not informed of this important fact; and the editors of his collected works forbore to state it, because the collection was made for the benefit of his surviving relations, a sister and niece, in both of whom the disease had manifested tself." Southey, *ap. Chatterton's Poetical Works* (1842) p. 625, *n*.

‡ Letter in the Bristol Museum.

Lambeth Street, Goodman's Fields, London, cooper, £30 to his son Henry Newton, £10 apiece to his five remaining children, £10 to Hannah, wife of George Spurwey, baker, of Bristol, £10 to Mary Ithel of Westbury on Trym, widow, and £20 to the charity school for girls on Redcliff Hill. Oh Feb. 8, 1804, she added a codicil revoking the legacy to Hannah Spurwey, and making provisions in case of her daughter's marriage and coverture. On March 12, 1803, she had received £30 on account of her brother's remains.*

The *Works*, in no sense a critical edition (the only research seems to have been done by Cottle, apropos of the de Bergham pedigree†), appeared at, or just before, the beginning of 1803, with a preface stating the object, by Southey, and Dr. Gregory's *Life* reprinted as introduction; though the editors provided engravings of the Redcliff muniment room, exterior and interior, and of coats of arms, drawn by Chatterton, no portrait of him was forthcoming; and indeed Cottle, who owned portraits of Southey, Coleridge, Wordsworth, Lamb, and Henderson, often expressed his regret that the absence of any authentic portrait of Chatterton prevented the chance of including his amongst them.‡ True, the MSS. bequeathed to the British Museum by Dr. Glynn were consulted; but the three volumes are too patently a monument of charity rather than of intelligent respect; they evoked, however, an important review by Sir Walter Scott in the *Edinburgh* (Apr. 1804). Southey had no real interest in the author of Rowley, and not long afterwards placed the Nottingham poet Kirke White on an equality with his fellow townsman,§ whom he mentions in *A Vision of Judgement* (1821), with the parenthesis:

* Note by Cottle in Bristol Museum.

† The copy of Barrett's *History of Bristol* used by the editors is in the British Museum.

‡ *Notes and Queries*, July 11, 1857.

§ Letter, Feb. 3, 1807; *Correspondence*, Vol. III, p. 65. In *Specimens of the Later English Poets* (1807) Southey included four of the avowed poems only, with a flamboyant notice, starting "Chatterton's sad story is well known; his life the wonder, his death the disgrace of his country." Vol. II, pp. 420, 427. In the *Quarterly Review* for July, 1814, he fiercely inveighed against Alex. Chalmers's life of Chatterton, in Vol. XV of *English Poets*, on the ground of "pharisaic morality"; that life is probably the soundest piece of Chattertonian biography we have between 1789 and 1869.

For not to his affectionate spirit
Could the act of madness innate for guilt be accounted.

In the Bristol Museum is an illuminating letter (Feb. 22, 1804) from Cottle to his co-editor on Mrs. Newton's affairs. She worried him for money; nothing is so distressing to his mind as a behaviour which implies a suspicion; his mother has advised him to throw up the business. Mrs. Newton is a woman who knows nothing of the world, and seems to have wondered that the money for her copies should not have been paid almost as soon as the work was published. During last year she called on him several times, and once said Longman and Rees ought to give *her* a bond, for she had nothing. When she did not come herself, she sent people, among them a Mr. Lewis: "This man thought he must say something to me about Poetry, so he remarked that he thought Milton has borrowed from others almost all his *Paradise Lost*." They said Mrs. Newton was in a poor state of health, but did not then stand in need of any money. He went with another person and gave her £154.15s.* She was in bed, and said to her daughter, "Well, Mary, I have often had valuable papers in my hands, but I never had such a valuable paper as this before."

She died, apparently the day after Cottle's letter, aged fifty-five, and was buried on the 27th.† One can understand her anxiety to have the money in her grip; she must have died happy, for she certainly received £184. 15s. from her brother's works, and £96. 1s. was paid to her executors for her daughter's benefit.‡ Her will was proved at £300.§

Soon after Mrs. Newton's death, Hannah More invited the poet's orphan niece, Marianne, to spend a few weeks at Barley-

* The receipt, dated Feb. 7, 1804, is in the Bristol Museum. Cottle (*Early Recollections*, I, p. 271) gives the date Feb. 2; there he says she was paid more than £300 "either by ourselves or through the hands of others." The £154. 15s. was the last instalment. I have seen a note in Cottle's hand:

Copies				
142 Pd. Mrs. Newton	184	15	1	She received £30. Receipt given Mar. 12, 1803.
208 to receive for ..	319	12	0	
Profit to Mrs. N. ..	504	7	0	

† Family Tombstone, Redcliff Register.

‡ *Gentleman's Magazine*, Aug., 1804.

§ Probate Acts, 1804, Sept.

wood, Wrington, as an honoured visitor* ; but she did not long survive her good fortune, dying at the early age of twenty-four, on Sept. 7, 1807 ; she was buried in the family grave on the 14th. She had made her will (P.C.C. Lushington 911) on May 22, appointing William Newton of the Little Minories, London, trunk maker, her sole executor ; to him she left all interest arising from "the sale of certain works the production of Thomas Chatterton deceased," and, with certain exceptions, her furniture and personal effects.

He was instructed to pay the following legacies "now in the publick stocks three per cent. consolidate Bank annuities in the name of Francis Freeling . . . and Robert Lewis . . . as trust for the aforesaid Marianne Newton, and also the money in the name of Marianne Newton," namely, £100 to himself, the same to Elizabeth Newton, the same to her sister Ann Copeland, the same to Henry Newton, and the same to Benjamin Purnell. The last was her betrothed, not an attorney, as has been stated, but in business as a tobacco and snuff manufacturer and vinegar maker, at 119-120 Redcliff Street. He died at 13 South Parade, Clifton, Dec. 13, 1860, aged seventy-seven.† George Cumberland states that Miss Newton died at the house of Mr. Bampfylde, a cooper, opposite the Lamb Inn in West Street, and that she possessed none of her uncle's manuscripts.‡ Her personal bequests are her watch, silver cream jug, black silk gown, hair-chain and desk to Anne Garrett, spinster, of Bedminster, half her clothes to Jane Purnell, spinster, as a token of love for her kindness, the other half to Ann Webb, and a smelling bottle and case to Lucy Ann Howell, spinster, of Kingsdown. The will was proved at £800.§

By his premature self-murder the poet does not seem to have served his folk so badly, after all.

---

* Pryce, *Fact versus Fiction*, p. 98.

† Note by Geo. Pryce in a copy of *Fact versus Fiction* (p. 99) in Bristol Library.

‡ Cumberland MS.

§ Probate Acts, 1807. Nov.

NOTE: GEORGE STEEVENS'S LETTER TO THE "ST. JAMES'S CHRONICLE," MARCH 28, 1782

MR. BALDWIN,

Notwithstanding Dean Milles, in his preliminary Dissertation, p. 12, has observed, that Mrs. Mary Newton (Chatterton's sister) "like her brother, seems attached to the cause of truth," it appears to me that one part of this family was not less addicted to fable than the other. At the conclusion of Mr. Croft's letter to Mr. Steevens (published in Mr. Warton's *Enquiry, &c.*) we have the following assertion. "Chatterton's sister, when she thanks me in a letter dated April 20th, 1781, for what I had sent her mother, through Mr. Rudhall, says, that *the only benefits they have received from the labours of her dear brother, are what they have received from me.*"

To show what dependence can be safely placed in the narratives of Mr. Croft's fair correspondent, I shall present your readers, Mr. Baldwin, with the exact copy of an original letter now before me.* It was written by the same young woman to another gentleman. The date will prove its antecedency to her communication with Mr. Croft.

"Sir,

Your Favour of the 6th ult. with my brother's letters, I received by Mr. Catcott, together with the poems my brother copied from Rowley; for which I am greatly oblig^d.—Mr. Catcott, in pursuance to his promise to you, a few [days] after you left Bristol, *presented my mother with 5 guineas.* My mother is well, and joins with me in grateful acknowledgement of all favours; which concludes me, Sir, your very respectfull and oblig^d humble servant

MARY CHATTERTON.

Pile Street, Bristol, Feb. 19, 1777."

From this letter (the original of which is left in the hands of the printer) it is plain that Mr. Croft's ten pounds was *not the only benefit* the Chatterton family had reaped from the labours of the deceased.—I may add, from my own certain knowledge,

* The autograph is in the British Museum, bound in with C. 39, h. 20, Milles's *Rowley*; it is sealed, postmarked (Feb. 21), and addressed, "Mr. George Steevens, Hampstead-Heath, Middlesex." The words italicized are, of course, not underlined.

that they had received other pecuniary favours from other gentlemen on the score of our young poet, whose works have raised so much contention among the learned.

I should add, in justice to Mr. Catcott, that having been paid the sum of money he asked for his transcripts, &c., of the pretended Rowley, he voluntarily gave the five guineas mentioned in the letter, that the mother and sister of Chatterton might have some share in the profits arising from the sale of his poems.—If Dr. Glynn also, when he went to Bristol, did not reward the Chatterton family for their information, it is the first time he ever avoided an opportunity of being generous and charitable; for, to use the words of his friend Gray, a "liberal hand and open heart" have been the Doctor's invariable characteristicks.

I am, Sir,

Your very obedient servant, &c.

[" G. Steevens " and " 28 Mar. 1782 " added in Joseph Haslewood's hand at the foot of the newspaper cutting in C. 39 h. 20.]

Chapter XX

FAME

"Excellence," writes Thomas Warton, "must struggle into observation"; at last we begin to breathe "an ampler ether, a diviner air"; among the subscribers' names to the edition of 1803 are S. T. Coleridge and W. Wordsworth.

As we have seen, Chatterton was a subject of verse in the second month after his death; and well before half a century had passed he had been bewailed by a host, of whom Macaulay's phrase "the illustrious obscure," can without injustice be predicated, a host including Pye, Scott (the Muse of Amwell), Mrs. Cowley, Mrs. Robinson ("Too proud for pity and too poor for praise"), Helen Maria Williams, Ann Yearsley, William Headley (an ode in the metre of "Pyrrha" and Collins's *Evening*), John Rannie, Thomas Russell, W. H. Ireland (acrostic), Thomas Dermody, James Montgomery, Kirke White, and, of course, Hayley. By far the best tribute to him, in Coleridge's opinion,* was "Neglected Genius," by Edward Rushton, a blind sailor (1756-1814). Robert Southey's copy of *Poems* (1806), in which this occurs, is in the British Museum; one stanza runs:

Stung by the world's neglect and scorn,
 While conscious merit fir'd his mind,
Unfriended, foodless, and forlorn,
 With low'ring eye the bard reclin'd;
When lo! his mantle cover'd o'er
With streaming, and with clotted gore,
The offspring of despair and pride,
Came stalking in, fell Suicide;

* Cottle, *Early Recollections*, I, p. 35.

Wreaths of dark foxglove, hemlock green,
And poppy round his brows were seen,
And now his purpose dire, his blood-stain'd eyes,
And rugged front, were veil'd in soft compassion's guise.

The first draft of Coleridge's famous *Monody* was written at the age of sixteen, and copied at that of eighteen into Christ's Hospital Book (1790); the picture of youthful hope was in the original version of 90 lines:

Elate of Heart and confident of Fame,
From vales where Avon sports, the Minstrel came,
Gay as the Poet hastes along
He meditates the future song,
How Ælla battled with his country's foes,
And whilst Fancy in the air
Paints him many a vision fair
His eyes dance rapture and his bosom glows.

Coleridge told Cottle on May 27, 1814, that lines 1-4, as first printed in 1829,

O what a wonder seems the fear of death,
Seeing how gladly we all sink to sleep,
Babes, Children, Youths, and Men,
Night following night for threescore years and ten!

were written when he was "a mere boy"*; and again, on Apr. 22, 1819, he told William Worship that they were written "in his thirteenth year as a school exercise."†

The printed version of 1794 (107 lines) has a new beginning, and the final image

Anon upon some rough Rock's fearful Brow,
Would pause abrupt—and gaze upon the waves below.

is clearly coloured by one in Thomas Warton's ode *The Suicide* (of which Richard Mant expressly declared that Chatterton was not the subject, an opinion having prevailed that he was):

Oft was he wont, in hasty fit
Abrupt the social board to quit,
And gaze with eager glance upon the tumbling flood.

* *Reminiscences*, 1847, p. 348.
† *Coleridge's Poetical Works*, ed. E. H. Coleridge, I, p. 125, *n*.

Thirty-six lines were added in 1796, while Pantisocracy and Susquehannah filled S.T.C.'s vision, including the beautiful:

> O Chatterton! that thou wert yet alive!
> Sure thou would'st spread the canvass to the gale,
> And love with us the tinkling team to drive
> O'er peaceful Freedom's undivided dale;
> And we, at sober eve, would round thee throng,
> Hanging, enraptur'd, on thy stately song,*
> And greet with smiles the young-eyed Poesy
> All deftly mask'd as hoar antiquity!

No one has crystallized the elusive and capricious charm of Rowley so aptly as do the last two lines. Charles Lamb wrote to Coleridge on Dec. 2 of this year: "I want some loppings made in the 'Chatterton': it wants but a little to make it rank among the finest irregular lyrics I ever read. Have you time and inclination to go to work upon it?—or is it too late?—or do you think it needs none?"†

Coleridge's own view at this time was caustic: "But on a life and death so full of heart-going *realities* as poor Chatterton's, to find such shadowy nobodies as cherub-winged *Death*, Trees of *Hope*, bare-bosomed *Affection*, and simpering *Peace*, makes one's blood circulate like ipecacuanha." He excepted only the last eighteen lines from censure, with the wise remark: "But so it is. A young man by strong feelings is impelled to write on a certain subject, and this is all his feelings do for him. They set him upon the business and then they leave him."‡

He continued working on the *Monody* till the year of his death; it numbered 135 lines in 1797, 119 in 1803, 143 in 1828, 154 in 1829, and 165 in 1834, not being included in "Sibylline Leaves"

* John Davis, who produced a duodecimo popular life of Chatterton in 1806, quotes this passage with the observation that Coleridge, Southey, and Lovell "would, more probably, have damned his song with faint praise, or heard it with sad civility" (p. 130). Southey, who saw this book in MS., characterized it as "flimsy and worthless," adding, "I shall *not* advise Longman to print it, and shall *warn* the writer to expunge an insult to you and to myself, which is not to be paid for by his praise." Letter to Coleridge, March 14, 1804. Thomas Tegg published the little volume.

† *Letters of Charles Lamb*, ed. Ainger, I, p. 51. Lamb had written in June: "I rather wish you had left the monody on Chatterton concluding, as it did, abruptly. It had more of unity." *ibid.*, p. 9.

‡ To Southey, July, 1797.

(1817).* The *manus ultima* was to insert, with four variants, into the body of the poem (ll. 103-113) the eleven lines that formed the conclusion of the Christ's Hospital version, changing "storms" to "storm" in the last of them :

> And soar beyond the storm with upright eye elate !

where note the resemblance to

> Such is greete Canynge's mynde when payrd to God elate.

This, and this alone, is fame, to live continuously thus in the heart and thoughts of a great man. True, no mention of Chatterton in Coleridge's *Table Talk*, and the promises of 1797 were not kept to the letter, but how far more eloquent is the history of this poem than any more direct encomium !

On Wordsworth, born in the year of his death, Chatterton has exercised, in one poem, *Resolution and Independence* (1802), a singular power. The designation of him, in the same verse as Burns, as

> the marvellous Boy,
> The sleepless Soul that perished in his pride.

is familiar to thousands who never read a line of him, yet the masterpiece in which it occurs is written in the Miltonic measure of *Elinoure and Juga* and *The Balade of Charitie.* Not only so ; its burden is the same as the latter's. In either (the words in inverted commas are Wordsworth's in sending a copy of *Resolution and Independence* to a friend†) a man "is rescued from dejection and despair almost as an interposition of Providence" by another man. In Chatterton's poem, a pilgrim, after being denied by an abbot, receives material alms and a cloak from a licensed begging friar ; in Wordsworth's a young poet, "overwhelmed by the thoughts of the miserable reverses which have befallen the happiest of all men—viz., poets," receives spiritual comfort from the presence and words

* These statistics are E. H. Coleridge's ; Clarendon Press, *Coleridge's Poetical Works*, I, p. 126.

† Poems, ed. W. Knight, II, p. 322.

of the solitary leech-gatherer, and goes on his way strengthened and rejoicing.

Moreover, either poem starts with a description of a sunny day (the storm in Wordsworth's is outside the action), the stock-dove taking the place of the " peede chelandri " in the fifth line of the later one's first stanza, and ends with two lines of apostrophe to heaven on the poet's own part :

Vyrgynne and hallie Seyncte, who sytte yn gloure,
Or give the mittee will, or give the gode man power.

" God," said I, " be my help and stay secure,
I'll think of the leech-gatherer on the lonely moor ! "

Before 1802, the *Balade of Charitie* had been printed certainly five times, in Tyrwhitt's three editions, Dean Milles's, and the Cambridge edition, which contained the *Monody*.

Wordsworth's enthusiasm did not expire with the payment of his subscription, though he does not seem to have fulfilled the vow expressed in a letter to a correspondent unknown, of Apr. 21, 1819 :

" I would readily assist, according to my means, in erecting a monument to the memory of the Poet Chatterton, who, with transcendent genius, was cut off while he was yet a boy in years ; this, could he have anticipated the tribute, might have soothed his troubled spirit, as an expression of general belief in the existence of those powers which he was too impatient and too proud to develop. At all events, it might prove an awful and a profitable warning."*

On Jan. 16, 1842, Crabb Robinson was a guest at Rydal

* W. Knight, *Letters of the Wordsworth family*, III, p. 403. While the present work was in the printers' hands a curious proof of Chatterton's influence on the Lake group was afforded by a battered and imperfect copy of the *Miscellanies*, bearing the late eighteenth-century ticket of the Manchester Circulating Library and notes in de Quincey's autograph. This was knocked down to Mr. R. N. Green-Armytage of Bath at the Francis Fox sale of Bristoliana (Feb. 26, 1930), an occasion which seems to have found the dealers for once asleep, and (with a generosity rare among collectors) presented to me. Examination revealed that de Quincey was reading the Romantic poet about the time of his marriage to Margaret Simpson, the " estatesman's " daughter ; for he has written " M-t S-n " and " M-g-t S-mp-n " respectively at the top of two pages in " Adventures of a Star." He has also written " Thomas Chatterton Bristoliensis " at the end of the Phillips *Elegy*, and " Te veniente die, te decedente canebam " next to the words " unfortunate author " in the Preface (p. xxi), and filled up " J.B."[roughton], tbe editor's initials, so as to

Mount, and finding Dix's *Life of Chatterton* there, picked it up and read it without being hugely impressed with the poet's achievement; he entered in his diary the next day: "I asked Wordsworth this evening wherein Chatterton's excellence lay. He said his genius was universal; he excelled in every species of composition; so remarkable an instance of precocious talent was quite unexampled. His prose was excellent; and his power of picturesque description and satire great."†

The poet Crabbe perhaps did not read *Resolution and Independence*, which appeared in 1807, but in the fifth of his *Tales*, published in 1812, there is a collocation of Chatterton and Burns:

> "I much rejoice," he said, "such worth to find;
> To this the world must be no longer blind:
> His glory will descend from sire to son,
> The Burns of English verse—the happier Chatterton."

The tale in question, "The Patron," could hardly have been written without some allusion of this sort‡; but it is impossible to read the passage describing the return from disillusionment to sanity, without wishing that something analogous had happened in the Bristol poet's career:

> And he was cured; for quiet, love, and care,
> Strove with the gloom, and broke on the despair.

read "J. Booby." On the inside of the back cover he has entered a note on Kant, a list of letters to be written, including the names of Southey, Cottle, and Coleridge, a note of purchases, a corkscrew and *Christabel* among them, and a date, "Thursday June 19. 1817." This fixes his ownership of the volume to the Townend Grasmere period, of which he speaks in the *Opium-Eater* ("up to the middle of which latter year [1817] I judge myself to have been a happy man"), when drawing a sketch of "the interior of a scholar's library in a cottage among the mountains." See *Times Lit. Supp.*, May 8, 1930. De Quincey regarded Chatterton's impositions as "most venial," because he deceived "nobody but those who well deserved to be deceived, viz., shallow antiquaries." He felt "the profoundest pity" for him, "and even love, if it be possible to feel love for one who was in his unhonoured grave before I was born." See *The New Review*, Jan. 1891, pp. 36–40. *Ex inf.* the Rev. W. C. Hall.

† Diary ed. 1872, II, p. 230. Chatterton was on the tapis just then; Dix's *Life* had been published in 1837, and this year (1842) saw the two volume Cambridge edition, with illustrative notes, printed for W. P. Grant. It was the work of two undergraduates, C. B. Willcox, who had to decamp before it was completed, and one (?) McCall. Letter (Sept. 28, 1865), from Alex. Macmillan to Sir D. Wilson, *penes me*.

‡ Chatterton's "fate and disappointments" inspired "Modern Patronage, an Ode," in Charles James's *Poems* (1792). I owe this reference to Mr. Norman Ault.

Yet slow their progress, and, as vapours move
Dense and reluctant from the wintry grove;
All is confusion, till the morning light
Gives the dim scene obscurely to the sight;
More and yet more defined the trunks appear,
Till the wild prospect stands distinct and clear;
So the dark mind of our young poet grew
Clear and sedate; the dreadful mist withdrew;
And he resembled that bleak wintry scene,
Sad, though unclouded; dismal, though serene.

Lord Byron, who emulated Chatterton in reading voraciously as a child, has set him between Burns and Wordsworth in an odd paragraph embedded in the second letter to Bowles, when complaining that it is in their *finery* that "the new under school of poets" are *most* vulgar: "Burns," he writes, "is often coarse but never *vulgar*, Chatterton is never vulgar, nor Wordsworth."* The epithet "gore-faced" (*Goddwyn*, l. 210) will be found in *Childe Harold* (I. 48).

Sir Walter Scott, whose octosyllables were foreshadowed in *The Unknown Knyght*, lamented that the life and character of Chatterton had never been drawn by a master; he has left discerning remarks on them, and on the poet's motives: "It may be thought that Chatterton would better have consulted his own fame by avowing these beautiful poems; but the pride of everyone is not sustained by the same nutriment. He probably deprecated the doubtful fame of an ingenious but detected impostor, and preferred the internal consciousness that, by persisting in the deception he had commenced, future ages might venerate the poems of Chatterton under patronage of the fictitious Rowley."† This marks an advance, maybe, even on Thomas Warton's view, and is, in fact, a poet's reading of a poet's secret.‡

In passing to Keats, it is desperately easy to say too much, to read into a poet's rarefied vision of beauty and delight something more than:

* Ravenna, March 25, 1821; first published 1832 (*Works*, Vol. VI, p. 413).
† *Edinburgh Review*, April 1804.
‡ Many years before Lort had noted *Junius's* words of himself in this connection, "If I am a vain man, my gratification lies within a narrow circle. I am the sole repository of my own secret, and it shall perish with me," wittily adding, "Et fugit ad salices *nec* se cupit ante videri." 11457.

The grandeur of the dooms
We have imagined for the mighty dead;

It will be wise, therefore (with but one short excursion) to confine the enquiry to what is indisputable.

In 1814, at the age of nineteen, Keats addressed an indifferent sonnet, with a bad first line, to Chatterton (he wrote one to Byron at the same time):

How soon that voice, majestic and elate,
Melted in dying numbers! Oh! how nigh
Was night to thy fair morning. Thou didst die
A half-blown floweret which cold blasts amate.
But this is past: thou art among the stars
Of highest heaven.

This was not included in the *Poems* of 1817. "Elate" may be a memory of the *Monody* or *Onn oure Ladies Chyrche*; but the echo of Ælla's "Thou doest mie thoughtes of paying love amate," and Celmonde's "Ontylle thou doeste mie brendynge love amate," must be intentional. Keats had read of Chatterton as well as in him, since he speaks of

That eye
Whence Genius mildly flashed and high debate.

though one may quarrel with the qualification in "mildly." The "floweret," I think, derives less from

Thieselfe, a flowrette of a small accounte,
Wouldst harder felle the wynde, as hygher thee dydste mounte.*

than from Coleridge's "On observing a Blossom on the First of February, 1796," where the object is compared to

Bristowa's bard, the wondrous boy!
An amaranth, which earth scarce seem'd to own,
Till disappointment came, and pelting wrong
Beat it to earth?

In the *Epistle to George Felton Mathew* (1815) Keats writes:

* The early lines *To Hope* perhaps show that *Nygelle* has been read, by their refrain:

Sweet Hope, ethereal balm upon me shed,
And wave thy silver pinions o'er my head.

O Mathew lend thy aid
To find a place where I may greet the maid—
Where we may soft humanity put on,
And sit, and rhyme, and think on Chatterton;
And that warm-hearted Shakespeare sent to meet him
Four laurell'd spirits, heaven-ward to intreat him.

This is a flight in the manner of the *Monody*; "heaven-were," glossed "heavenward or Godward" (*Goddwyn*, l. 146), is used certainly thrice by Chatterton in a place where it would be remembered, at the end of the line—e.g. And puryfye them heavenwere (*The Parlyamente of Sprytes*, l. 88). Keats is indulging his fancy, and a prosaic reader may indulge his, perhaps; it would be in Chatterton's manner to send back the spirits with a message to Shakespeare to come himself, if he wanted him.

Endymion (1818) is next, "inscribed to the memory of Thomas Chatterton"; but the original dedication ran:

INSCRIBED,
WITH EVERY FEELING OF PRIDE AND REGRET
AND WITH "A BOWED MIND"
TO THE MEMORY OF
THE MOST ENGLISH OF POETS EXCEPT SHAKESPEARE,
THOMAS CHATTERTON*

and the close of the preface (Teignmouth, March 19), which was rejected upon the unfavourable verdict of Reynolds and others, was:

"One word more—for we cannot help seeing our own affairs in every point of view—should any one call my dedication to Chatterton affected I answer as followeth: Were I dead, sir, I should like a Book dedicated to me."

At the same time, from Teignmouth, he enclosed in a letter to Haydon the four verses beginning:

Where be ye going, you Devon maid?
And what have you there in the basket?

* Sotheby, *Sale Cat.*, July 1, 1907. Lot 93 (Stuart M. Samuel's library); and see Keats's letter to Reynolds of Apr. 9th, 1818.

of which rhyme and metre hark back to Syr Thybbot Gorges's song in *Ælla*; there is an embrace in the last stanza of either piece.

Ought we to read its dedication into *Endymion*, the subject of which, according to Professor Bradley,* is the Poet's striving for union with his Ideal, the Principle of Beauty? There is a temptation so to do. Keats, of course, must have known of the moon's effect on Chatterton, as on Milton; and in the third book, where the hero and Glaucus advance to their work of deliverance, more than one reader of both romantic poets may have detected allegory rather than myth, though such a conception is perhaps less in Keats's manner than in that of the Goethe who visualized Byron as Euphorion. At the same time, on any showing, the action, as between Endymion and Glaucus, is an excrescence on the classic legend of Glaucus and Scylla, and undoubtedly a romantic vagary of the poet's. The peculiar features are these: Immediately after Endymion's apostrophe to the moon:

> What is there in thee, Moon! that thou should'st move
> My heart so potently? When yet a child
> I oft have dried my tears when thou hast smil'd.
> Thou seem'dst my sister:

he sees the old man Glaucus sitting on a weeded rock, with a pearly wand beside him, and a book in his lap. Glaucus recognizes him at once as his redeemer, who will give him back his youth—"Thou art the man,"—and describes himself as "a friend to love, to loves of yore." Together they speed on their task:

> So saying, this young soul in age's mask
> Went forward with the Carian side by side.

(a phrase suspiciously like

> the young-eyed poesy
> All deftly masked as hoar Antiquity.)

Glaucus telling him of his love for Scylla and enchantment by Circe on the way. The task resolves itself as the raising up

* *Oxford Lectures on Poetry*, p. 187.

of dead lovers by scattering on them the " minced leaves " of Glaucus's scroll, which, together with the wand, was put into his by an old man's hand emerging from the sea, which had engulfed a ship and her crew: but, before this is done, " some fragments light " are scattered in Glaucus's face, and

> A youthful wight . . .
> Outsparkling sudden like an upturn'd gem
> Appear'd.

Endymion leaves him united with the revivified Scylla.

It may be prying too curiously to seek to establish the exact meaning of the Keatsian myth (which I may not have summarized accurately); Endymion may stand for Keats himself, Glaucus for Rowley-Chatterton, and their task for the deliverance of English Poetry from the death-like bondage of the eighteenth century. But, taken into connection with the dedication of *Endymion*, and the familiar image of the dead Chatterton with his manuscripts torn up " in pieces small " beside him, the episode surely has to be considered in any estimate of the latter's influence.*

In Sept., 1819, Chatterton was much in Keats's mind. In his letter to Reynolds of the 22nd—for Woodhouse, on the same day, he had copied out the *Ode to Autumn*—he writes: " I always somehow associate Chatterton with autumn. He is the purest writer in the English Language. He has no French idiom or particles, like Chaucer—'tis genuine English Idiom in English words. I have given up Hyperion—there were too many Miltonic inversions in it. English ought to be kept up."† During the same month, at Winchester, he copied *The Eve of St. Mark* into the journal-letter to his brother George; here, where the old English diction is employed, it can be by no mere accident that the name Bertha was chosen.

Lord Houghton says: " Chatterton, of whom he ever speaks with a sort of prescient sympathy "; in the class from which they

* This is no whimsy of mine: it was suggested to me by Mr. Matt. Richardson, of Bristol, who mentions particularly these lines in Book III, 292 sqq., 310, 372-392, 667-670 (the " scroll "), 711, 770 (" scatter the same around ").

† *The Letters of John Keats*, ed. H. Buxton Forman, p. 380.

sprang, no less than in their all-consuming ambition, the two poets were alike. It may be added that in Richard Woodhouse's list of Keats's library there is a copy of Bailey's Dictionary.*

It remained for Shelley, in *Adonais*, to add, by the proximity of Sir Philip Sidney's name, that touch of patriotism to the image of the poet which was lacking in Wordsworth's two lines :

> The inheritors of unfulfilled renown
> Rose from their thrones, built beyond mortal thought,
> Far in the Unapparent. Chatterton
> Rose pale,—his solemn agony had not
> Yet faded from him ; Sidney, as he fought
> And as he fell and as he lived and loved
> Sublimely mild, a Spirit without spot,
> Arose ; and Lucan, by his death approved :
> Oblivion as they rose shrank like a thing reproved.†

There is a poetic fitness in this collocation ; if the love passages in *Ælla* be compared with a poem like " My true love hath my heart, and I have his," it will be seen how, in his Saxon English, Chatterton has forsaken his century, reverting to pre-Shakespearean type.

Before Hazlitt is approached, the question obtrudes itself what it was in Chatterton's work that appealed to these poets just over one hundred years ago. I think a single line can explain, in part, his influence on them :

> With hys goulde honde guilteynge the falleynge lefe

Such writing is in direct contravention of eighteenth century mode ; the line does not divide into two precise halves, and the two present participles negate formal symmetry : but to the early nineteenth century Romantics, cradled in the *Faerie Queene*, and harking back to Nature and the Elizabethans, this word-painting, together with the autumnal cadence, was a

* Colvin, *Life of Keats*, p. 558.

† Helene Richter compares with the last line of the *Balade of Charitie*:

> The good want power, but to weep barren tears.
> The powerful goodness want : worse need for them.
> *Prometheus Unbound*, I, l. 625.

windfall; they could see and hear the parti-coloured leaf in its fluttering descent from the twig to the bare earth.

The Lectures on the English poets were delivered early in 1818, and Chatterton was dismissed shortly at the close of the sixth; after quoting the lines on him and Burns in *Resolution and Independence*, Hazlitt continued: "I am loth to put asunder what so great an authority has joined together; but I cannot find in Chatterton's works anything so extraordinary as the age at which they were written. They have a facility, vigour, and knowledge, which were prodigious in a boy of sixteen, but which would not have been so in a man of twenty. He did not show extraordinary powers of genius, but extraordinary precocity. Nor do I believe he would have written better had he lived. He knew this himself, or he would have lived. Great geniuses, like great kings" (Hazlitt was perhaps thinking of Napoleon), "have too much to think of to kill themselves."

This gave offence to some of the audience at the Surrey Institution, and the next lecture—on Burns, and the old English Ballads—was prefaced by a lengthy explanation, with citations from Warton, Malone, Croft, and Knox, and "O! synge untoe mie roundelaie" was quoted in full, as a sop. The only fresh point adduced is that Hazlitt never heard any one of Chatterton's works spoken of as if it were an old well-known favourite: "it is his name, his youth, and what he might have lived to have done that excite our wonder and admiration. He has the same sort of posthumous fame that an actor of the last age has*—an abstracted reputation which is independent of anything we know of his works."

Keats wrote to his brothers on Feb. 21, 1818: "I hear Hazlitt's lectures regularly. . . . I was very disappointed at his treatment of Chatterton."

In 1824 *Brystowe Tragedy* and the *Mynstrelles Songe* were printed in *Select British Poets*, where the editor's note is: "Chatterton's *Remains* show great premature power, but are

* There is a comparison between Chatterton and W. Betty, "the infant Roscius," in *The Saunterer* (Newcastle 1805) No. 39; *ex inf.* R. L Watson, Esq.

chiefly interesting from his fate. He discovered great boldness of spirit and versatility of talent; yet probably, if he had lived, would not have increased his reputation for genius."

He is a bold critic who would gainsay William Hazlitt; there is perhaps no answer to his judgment on Chatterton except that (1) some of the peaks of English poetry—e.g. Spenser's *Epithalamion*—are not spoken of as if they were old well-known favourites; and (2) Hazlitt was not an English poet.

Whether he be a bolder critic who would gainsay Thomas Carlyle, I do not know; here I will record a fact merely. In the summer of 1928, grubbing in the upper storey of an Exeter bookshop, I came upon a shabby bound octavo volume of letters written to Sir Daniel Wilson relative to his *Chatterton, a Biographical Study* (1869). Among them was the following, not, I think, printed before; it was obviously dictated (Carlyle's right hand became paralysed two years later), but the last four words, the sage's name, and his addressee's, are in his writing:

"5 Cheyne Row, Chelsea,
10 January, 1870.

Dear Sir,

Accept many thanks for your Volume on *Chatterton*; which I received two or three days after your Letter; and have read with unusual interest and attention.

The Narrative, in spite of its abstruse and much obscured subject, is at once clear and concise; and throws an unexpected illumination upon Chatterton. Indeed it is the first time I have fairly been able to understand what Chatterton and his affairs really were. To sympathetic minds, it is a deep and painful tragedy; and to all minds, it is a wonderful physiological prodigy,—in which latter sense at least it may long have its interest among mankind.

Beyond doubt you are abundantly sympathetic to the poor Boy: and his fate and history are indeed sad in the extreme. But I had here and there a feeling withal that perhaps he was incapable of being saved; that, besides these lamentable obstructions of his childhood, there was something wrong in the original conformation of him. Too much of vehemence and violence for any piety and loyalty he had;—clearly a considerable want of *reverence*, and an enormous overflow of mere ambition and egoism? —I remark, too, in his marvellously precious Poetry, far more of shining *colour* and grandiloquent *sound* than of any finer spiritual element:—in short, one has a feeling that perhaps his thrice-miserable death at that early stage may have been the *least* miserable ending for him. Poor Boy; poor, erring, struggling, vainly soaring brother mortal, what a dismal painful bit of Human History, however that may be!

I remember well your pleasant visit here, and also my reading of your former Book. With myself much is mournfully changed since then*; but not my goodwill towards you, and such as you. Believe me, dear Sir,

Yrs sincerely,

T. CARLYLE.

Professor D. Wilson, &c., &c.
Toronto."

The statement about "the *least* miserable ending" finds a curious echo from Chatterton's loudest-voiced enthusiast, D. G. Rossetti, who, in answer to a complaint of "want of sincerity," wrote: "As to what you say of Chatterton's want of political sincerity (for I cannot see to what other want you can allude), surely a boy up to eighteen may be pardoned for exercising his faculty if he happens to be the one among millions who can use grown men as his toys. He was an absolute and untarnished hero, but for that reckless defying vaunt. Certainly that most vigorous passage commencing—

Interest, thou universal God of men, &c.

reads startlingly, and comes in a questionable shape. What is the answer to its enigmatical aspect? Why, that he *meant* it, and that all would mean it at his age, who had his power, his daring, and his hunger. Still it does, perhaps, make one doubt whether his early death were well or ill for him."†

Rossetti's copy of the poet, Sir Hall Caine tells us, bore the date 1848, his twentieth year, but his zeal was revived, according to that biographer, by Theodore Watts, who contributed the notice in the third volume of Ward's *English Poets* (1880); to accompany this enlightened essay Rossetti wrote one of the finest sonnets in the language, which was considered too extravagant (though, in the eighteenth century, Shakespeare had been mentioned by Malone in relation to Chatterton) for

* Death of Mrs. Carlyle, and reading of her journal, no doubt, are indicated.

† Sir Hall Caine, *Recollections of D. G. Rossetti*, p. 189; the section on Chatterton is pp. 184-191.

insertion by the friend of Swinburne's latter years. Like Keats, Rossetti wrote another sonnet on a poet (Blake) at the same time. The sestet of that to Chatterton immortalizes the Bristol environment:

> Thy nested home-loves, noble Chatterton;
> The angel-trodden stair thy soul could trace
> Up Redcliffe's spire; and in the world's awed space
> Thy gallant sword-play:—these to many an one
> Are sweet for ever; as thy grave unknown
> And love-dream of thine unrecorded face.

Elsewhere he wrote:

> Keats withered, Coleridge pined, and Chatterton,
> Breadless, with poison froze the God-fir'd breath.

His sanest observation on the subject (following a remark that the Annians created a style in prose, and wrenched its characteristics to form their poetry) is: "Chatterton can only be underrated if we expect that he should have done by intuition all that was accomplished by gradual inheritance from *him* half a century later."* As a young man, his brother says, he had read the poems "with cursory glance and unexcited spirit"†; still, when one reads of him, at the British Museum, poring over romances of chivalry in the hope to "pitch upon stunning words for poetry,"‡ one cannot but think that Chatterton had already taught him something. At all events, if of late recrudescence, this zeal grew on Rossetti, and in the last two or three years of his life "abnormal" is the word his brother uses of it. To this period the Caine correspondence belongs, where are to be found such sentences as:

"He was as great as any English poet whatever, and might absolutely, had he lived, have proved the only man in England's theatre of imagination who could have bandied parts with Shakespeare."

"Not to know Chatterton is to be ignorant of the *true* day-spring of modern romantic poetry."

"The finest of the Rowley poems, Eclogues, Ballad of Charity, &c., rank absolutely with the first poetry in the language."

* *Works*, ed. 1911, p. 606. † *Ibid* p. xvi.

‡ J. Knight, *Life of Rossetti*, p. 28. Personally, I have not found traces of Chatterton in Rossetti's poems, but am far from denying that such exist.

Narva and Mored and its two companions are also mentioned as *poetry absolute.* At the same time, in reference to Skeat, " a thorough philologist," Rossetti admits that there are occasions when " substitution becomes unavoidable in the text."

" Perfect specimens " among the acknowledged poems are, he tells his young correspondent, *The Revenge,* " To use a worn-out simile," *Journal 6th, The Prophecy,* and the opening of *Interest.* More valuable perhaps are the statements that " strong derivative points are to be found in Keats and Coleridge from the study of Chatterton," and that the Bristol poet (who did not have the advantages of Oliver Madox Brown), " at sixteen or less," said,

> Flattery's a cloak, and I will put it on;

and Blake, " probably late in life," said,

> Innocence is a winter's gown.

There is little English appreciation of Chatterton in Victorian times beside this. Masson's brilliant biographical novelette appeared (reprinted from the *Dublin University Magazine* of 1851), with other essays, in 1856, and 1865 saw a selection of the poems with an introduction by Frederick Martin. Wilson, Skeat, and Buxton Forman's critique of Skeat take us into the '70's, and in 1872 the Hon. Roden Noel found that Chatterton was " far more a colourist and musician of poetry than a mere poetic thinker." Theodore Watts's prosodic aperçu of 1880 remained undeveloped till Professor Saintsbury's *History of English Prosody* (1906-1910). The mediævalism of William Morris was derived (with a difference) from Gower, Chaucer, Froissart and Monstrelet,* that of Swinburne (in *The Masque*

* Yet how much more *essentially* mediaeval is:

> Encreaseynge yn the yeares of mortal lyfe,
> And hasteynge to hys journie ynto Heaven,
> Hee thoughte ytt proper for to cheese a wyfe,
> And use the sexes for the purpose gevene.

than this sort of thing:

> My arms lay back behind my head,
> Over my raised-up knees were spread
> A samite cloth of white and red,
> A rose lay on my face.

of Queen Bersabe) from the Miracle Plays; the resemblances in *Harold* to *Goddwyn* and *The Tournament* may be accidental. Save in histories of literature—Courthope, incidentally, is far from adequate here—Chatterton's work has remained unexplored, but for a word of praise here and there, by later editors, critics, and poets; though Edward Bell's *Life* (1871) is not to be despised.

But, besides Masson's treatment of the subject (the most audaciously successful since *Love and Madness*), 1856 brought forth Henry Wallis's picture, "Chatterton," which, exhibited at the Royal Academy, and after belonging to Augustus Egg, R.A., was presented to the nation in 1900 by Charles G. Clement, and, hanging at Millbank, can bid fair to be the *ideal* representation of the poet to-day. Ruskin wrote of it thus: "Faultless and wonderful, a most noble example of the great school. Examine it well, inch by inch; it is one of the pictures which intend and accomplish the entire placing before your eyes of an actual fact and that a solemn one."*

The accessories are historically admirable, the composition probably without a flaw; but the dress of the subject, and his appearance after death, are in defiance of what is actually known.†

A macabre anecdote was given to the world in 1919 from the diaries of the poet W. S. Blunt, in the words of Mr. Wilfred Meynell, who told it to Blunt in August, 1907, when Francis Thompson (who died on Nov. 13) was on a visit to the other poet at Newbuildings Place, Sussex: "He [Thompson] used, before I knew him, to sleep at night under the Arches of Covent Garden, where every quarter of an hour he was liable to be kicked awake by the police and told to move on. It was in an empty space of ground behind the Market where the gardeners threw their rubbish, that, just before, he had resolved on suicide. He then spent all his remaining pence on laudanum,

* Percy Bate, *English Preraphaelite Painters*, p. 86.

† Other pictures are, one of Chatterton writing Rowley, by R. Jeffreys Lewis (1846) engraved by R. McInnes, which is probably one of the world's worst pictures; "Chatterton, 1765," by Mrs. E. M. Ward, (Royal Academy, 1873), now in Bristol Art Gallery; a small one by J. J. Barker, (c. 1820-1904), in the Bath Art Gallery; "Chatterton," by W. B. Morris, (Royal Academy, 1869), engraved by W. Ridgway.

one large dose, and he went there one night to take it. He had swallowed half when he felt an arm laid on his wrist, and looking up he saw Chatterton standing over him and forbidding him to drink the other half. I asked him when he told me of it how he had known that it was Chatterton. He said, 'I recognized him from the pictures of him—besides, I knew that it was he before I saw him—and I remembered at once the story of the money which arrived for Chatterton the day after his suicide.'* Just the same thing happened to Thompson, for a friend having seen the copy of 'Merrie England' told him about it the very next morning with the result I told you of."†

Squares in Bristol are called after Chatterton and Rowley respectively, and a street in North London bears his name.

It is thus hard exactly to define this poet's position in his native land; most have heard of him, few have read him, fewer loved him; but to him who loves him he becomes

Bone of hys bone, and chyld of hys desire.

In France the story of young neglected genius fired the romanticism of the '30's. Alfred de Vigny (1797-1863) dealt twice with him, in his novel *Stello* (1832. ch : xiv-xix) and the prose drama *Chatterton* (1835), performed on Feb. 12 of that year; in an appendix to which he printed with remarks portions of *Battle of Hastings*, *Englysh Metamorphosis*, and the whole of the *Balade of Charitie* with a prose translation. A mythical family called Bell is introduced into the play, also a Quaker, three English lords, and Lord Mayor Beckford (alive in August, 1770); but the description of the poet as "*sur le défensive avec tout le monde*" is just, and the work is clearly inspired by affection. It created a stir in French dramatic circles, but I am unable to say whether it has held the stage, though it is read in girls' schools. In 1839, as a result of the interest thus excited,‡ the *Works* of 1803 were translated into French prose by Javelin

* A confusion of the Hamilton story, and Dr. Fry.

† Wilfred Scawen Blunt, *My Diaries*, II, p. 191.

‡ After the performance Comte Maillé de Latour-Landry gave a sum to the Académie Française for distribution every two years to a strugglIng poet. *Notes and Queries*, Sept. 20, 1890.

Pagnon, preceded by a life by A. Callet, of which the note is "*Il fallait l'admirer, lui, et non le plaindre.*"

Germany followed suit in 1840 with a memoir, introduction, and translation of seven of the Rowley Poems by Hermann Püttmann; in 1887, Chatterton was the subject of a four act tragedy by Heinrich Blau; and quite recently a novel, *Der arme Chatterton*, by Ernst Penzoldt, was published at Leipzig. It should be mentioned, too, that "Chatterton," a play in one act, by the late Sir H. A. Jones and H. Herman, was produced at the Princess's Theatre, London, with Wilson Barrett in the title rôle, on May 24, 1884.*

De Vigny's piece excluded, perhaps, Chatterton seems (resembling Nelson in this respect) to be hardly a lucky subject for dramatic treatment, and still unluckier for musical. At the age of eighteen a composer left the Naples Conservatoire with the diploma of maestro, and set to work on an opera, the libretto being an adaptation of the French drama of 1835. At Bologna, whither he had gone to attend the lectures of the famous poet Carducci, he completed the opera, and arranged for its production; but at the last moment the impresario decamped, leaving him almost penniless: in despair he was compelled to undertake any work that would keep him from starvation. This was Ruggiero Leoncavallo (1858-1819),and *Chatterton* was produced at the Teatro Nazionale, Rome, on March 10, 1896, without success.†

The poet, who had been the occasion of a forgery in the *European Magazine* for Feb., 1804,‡ speedily became that of gossip. In the autumn of 1808, or thereabouts, George Cumberland, a credulous artistic Bristolian (better known as a friend of William Blake), made enquiries concerning a report of his reinterment in Redcliff Churchyard. This he traced to the wife of a basket-maker, a Mrs. Stockwell, who said she would swear it on oath, if another woman, a Mrs. Kirkland, could have

* For a list of plays about Chatterton, with their dates, see *The Stage Cyclopædia*, 1909; one in three acts was played at the theatre in King Street, Bristol, as late as the autumn of 1925.

† Grove. *Dictionary of Music and Musicians*, art. Leoncavallo.

‡ *Metrical Epistle from Chatterton, the Poet, to a Lady*, declared spurious in the July number.

been found to join her; he also interviewed relatives of Chatterton, the Phillipses, Molly Hayfield (a servant), and a Mrs. Edkins (née James), who claimed to be the poet's "foster mother"; from these no more on this score was to be obtained, but various *ana*. Some time between 1823 (water-mark) and 1837 (Dix's *Life*)—probably about 1827—he copied his researches into a quarto note-book, still extant*; and they were used, for the most part, by Dix, as an appendix to his *Life*, and have been incorporated in all later lives, except Ingram's, who was not aware of this MS. Shadowy and mainly unreliable, as regards Chatterton, they cannot fairly be neglected as regards his family.

It cannot be repeated too emphatically that there is no authentic portrait of Thomas Chatterton, another distinction he shares with Richard Savage. On May 24, 1797, Joseph Cooper Walker (1762?-1810), an Irish antiquary and littérateur, wrote thus to George Catcott: "Permit me to ask if there be any portrait of him extant. If not, should not some attempt be made to hand down to Posterity even an imperfect resemblance of him? You, Sir, and other of his friends who recollect his face, might assist some skilful pencil in delineating it. Something, too, of his features might be gathered from carefully studying Mrs. Newton, and the faces of her children. Almost every family has a set of features peculiar to it."† A reply was sent on June 24: "You seem to wish that a portrait from memory might be taken of Chatterton. I know no man more capable of this than my friend [Thomas] Eagles; who has a perfect recollection of his person, and is a draughtsman; but he declares tho' he can at any time recall a likeness of Chatterton to his mind's eye, yet he cannot transmit it to paper to his satisfaction. He is quite an *Anti-Chattertonian.*"‡

This very year, the draughtsman and antiquary, J. T. Smith, appointed Keeper of Prints and Drawings at the British

* *Penes* A. H. Russell, Esq., Secretary to the Bristol Chatterton Society; the handwriting of the MS. is undoubtedly George Cumberland's.

† A P.S. adds that one of the minstrels of Henry V was named Thomas Chatterton, and "we have in Ireland one family of the name of Chatterton: it is settled, I believe, in Cork." Letter-book, p. 510.

‡ *Ibid.* p. 511.

Museum in 1816, observed that the public had lately been imposed upon in a very unwarrantable and audacious manner, "by an ugly goggle-ey'd portrait," prefix'd to some periodical publication [*The Monthly Visitor*, Jan., 1797], and asserted to be a likeness of Chatterton by the very persons who had confessed it to be a mere fabrication, "and (for anything that is now known) destitute of any resemblance whatever."*

Nevertheless, "one particular type, which first found currency at the time of the publication of the life by Dix, persists as a popular representation of the poet."† The oil painting on which this (engraved by N. Branwhite as a frontispiece to Dix's *Life*, 1837) is based, now in the Bristol Art Gallery, presented by G. W. Braikenridge, is *not a portrait of Chatterton at all*, but was declared in 1838 to be the son of one Morris, a Bristol painter. The Rev. John Eagles (son of Catcott's friend), who said so, knew "the whole history of the person who put Chatterton's name on the back to sell it."‡ On March 25, 1762, the date it bears, Chatterton was at Colston's Hospital; his hair would have been closely cropped, not long, and his dress blue, not red; quite apart from the fact that oil paintings, even of this sort, were in the eighteenth century luxuries of the rich, a fact which negatives the legends of portraits of the poet by Gainsborough and Wheatley.

A *copy* of this picture, made surreptitiously in 1837, has had an undeserved history: it was sent to Southey by a "young friend" of Dix's in that year. Southey recognized in it a resemblance to Mrs. Newton, and wrote telling Dix and W. S. Landor so,§ and this has gone far to bolster up the imposition. On Southey's death it was purchased at the sale of his effects

* *Remarks on Rural Scenery* (1797), p. 25.

† The words in inverted commas are those of Mr. Hake, Keeper of the National Portrait Gallery, who has had the misfortune to pronounce on more alleged portraits of Chatterton than most of us.

‡ J. Eagles, letter to R. Smith (Feb. 15, 1838), R. Smith's *Chattertoniana*, p. 283, Bristol Museum, and see *Gentleman's Magazine*, Dec. 1838, p. 607.

§ Southey's letter to Dix (Jan. 7, 1837) is in the Bristol Library; his letter to Landor (Mar. 31, 1839) is printed in *Life and Correspondence*, VI, p. 384. There he says, "The portrait of Chatterton which Mr. Dix discovered, identifies itself if ever portrait did. It brought his sister, Mrs. Newton, strongly to my recollection. No family likeness could be more distinctly marked, considering the disparity of years."

by Miss Fenwick, who gave it to Wordsworth, with a reversion to Sir Henry Taylor. Seven years it was owned by Wordsworth, thirty-six by Sir Henry Taylor, on whose death, in 1886, it passed to his son, Harry Taylor, who lent it to the Guelph Exhibition in 1891. There was then some debate as to its authenticity, and Sir E. Maunde Thompson thought the "2" of the 1762 in the endorsement was an alteration. On its return the owner cut out the backing of the frame to ascertain the truth, and was rewarded by finding on the back of the canvas in ink:

H. S. Parkman
Bristol
1837.

This left no doubt in his mind that it was a copy of Mr. Braikenridge's picture, and he wrote to the *Athenæum* (Apr. 18, 1891) expressing his satisfaction at reducing the frauds by one, and regretting that he had not examined the canvas sooner. The curious may be referred to Sir George Scharf's conclusive letter in the *Athenæum* for Apr. 4 of that year.*

One of George Cumberland's informants speaks of seeing, at Richard Phillips's, a picture, not framed, of Chatterton in his blue coat, cap in hand, with his mother leading him towards a tomb; she thought it was drawn by Chatterton. This is no more grotesquely improbable than that the "picture" may have been copied by him from a book illustration, such as, it may be, the folding plate to Jeremy Taylor's *Holy Dying* (1651). A poet so much, and so prematurely, aware of his own existence may reasonably be supposed to have drawn himself in other than words. But at this distance of time, what means of detection have we, and in what better position are we than the editor of 1803, who, after producing his memorial volumes with no portrait, was so egregiously deceived?

The salient facts of the poet's appearance, however, are

* Rossetti was aware of this picture and one in the Salford Museum (now ascertained to be a self-portrait of Hogarth); in the Caine correspondence he writes: "I *suspect* there may be a sidelong genuineness in them," and suggests that they may have derived from some likeness (not *ad vivum*) by Alcock, the miniature painter, on whom Chatterton ("Asaphides") wrote a poem. Sir H. Caine, *op. cit.*, p. 190.

familiar: the grey eyes, one more brilliant and therefore appearing larger than the other.* George Catcott said he could never look at it long enough to see what sort of an eye it was, but it seemed to be a kind of hawk's eye, he thought: you could see his soul through it. Barrett never saw such eyes; one was still more remarkable than the other. You might see the fire roll at the bottom of them, as you sometimes do in a black eye, but never in grey ones, which his were. Barrett's remark that he would differ from him to make him earnest and see how wonderfully his eye would strike fire has been quoted in another connection.† By their evidence concerning this eye these two men stand self-condemned on the charge of which Horace Walpole, who never *saw* the poet, was innocent. Capel, the jeweller's apprentice, noted a light in Chatterton's eye "upon his being irritated or otherwise greatly affected"‡; and indeed the feature seems to have been observed sufficiently to be made use of in the worthless engraving denounced by J. T. Smith. "Who has a daring eye," writes Lavater, "tells downright truths and downright lies."§ The colour of his hair is not mentioned, save by one of Cumberland's informants, no earlier than 1808, as "flaxen," but even if this were accepted, children's hair often darkens. A face otherwise remarkable is not claimed for him, and a big mouth "like his father's" is an addition of the vapouring Mrs. Edkins. Croft's words,

* C. V. le Grice in *Gentleman's Magazine*, Aug. 1838. His informant used the word "glittering," and Sir Daniel Wilson (p. 315) finely alludes to the Ancient Mariner here. Mrs. Newton, le Grice says, had fine grey eyes, which an admirer would call blue." He adds that the peculiarity of one eye appearing, from its glittering, larger than the other, is also recorded of Byron.

† *L. and M.*, p. 241.

‡ Bryant, *Obs.*, p. 525. Mr. A. C. Hudson, the oculist, writes to me: "My opinion, for the little it is worth, is that the peculiarity of expression noted may have been due to a widening of the space between the eyelids in moments of excitement, so that the white of the eye became visible all round the circle of the iris. One sees this sometimes, and it was possibly a peculiarity of the monk Rasputin." Professor F. G. Parsons, an authority on the anatomy of expression, confirms this to some extent: "I have little doubt that Chatterton had unequal pupils, a condition which sometimes accompanies an unstable mental condition. With regard to the occasional brightening of his eyes, there is nothing in the eye itself which can make it brighten or 'flash fire,' or any of the other phenomena so loved of novelists. What happens is that during mental excitement the upper lid is raised a trifle, and this admits a high light on the eye which makes it appear brighter."

§ *Aphorisms on Man* (1788). No. 124, p. 47.

and the scraps from Michael Lort's notes, must be the authorities here, and most would prefer to dwell on the former's "all agree that he was a manly, good-looking boy—that there was something about him, which instantaneously prepossessed you in his favour," and retain that as a true portrait of Chatterton, when the melancholy or choleric fit was not on him: he was probably not boasting greatly when he wrote to his mother, "I contracted an immediate acquaintance, which you know is no hard task to me." (May 14, 1770.) The student and antiquary will, no doubt, prefer Lort's "He had a large quick grey eye; rather slovenly in his dress; not vain, but proud; something like his sister, who was of a sallow complexion" (11457).

The plan for a monument, mooted in 1792, was taken up in 1813,* when a meeting was held on Apr. 22, with John Evans in the chair: a circular was sent round on May 1, stating that subscriptions would be received "for the present" by Mr. John Fry, 1 St. John Street†; but nothing was done for twenty-four years.‡ Then one of the new projectors, Charles Bowles Fripp, wrote to the laureate for an inscription, mentioning Wordsworth also, and received the following reply:

"Keswick,
23 Feb., 1838.

DEAR SIR,

It so happens that many years ago when a monument was projected to the memory of Burns, Mr. Wordsworth and I had some conversation on the subject. We agreed in thinking that such monuments are fitting marks of respect for men whose public services ought to be held in remembrance in honour to themselves and as examples to others, soldiers and sailors, statesmen, discoverers in the sciences or useful arts, and persons who in any other way have been eminently useful to their fellow citizens, or their fellow creatures; but that of all men they are least required for authors, and of all authors least for poets, who have raised their own monument in their works.

* John Flaxman made "a slight sketch in terra cotta" for a memorial tablet; a facsimile of a pen and ink sketch sent in Nov. 1812 to John Britton will be found in the *Appendix to Britton's Autobiography*, (1850), p. 68.

† B.33. Bristol Library.

‡ *Athenæum*, Dec. 23, 1837. Dix's *Life* clearly inspired this revival of interest.

I have seen Mr. Wordsworth, since your second letter reached me, and he has authorized me to say that his views on the subject, like mine, have undergone no alteration. But tho' a tribute of this kind is by no means necessary for the honour of Chatterton, it would be highly becoming that the wealthier inhabitants of Bristol should erect one for the honour of the city.

With regard to an Inscription, there would be so much presumption in composing one for Chatterton's monument, that he must be a bold person who should attempt it. All circumstances considered, a plain sentence saying that the monument was erected by some of his townsmen to Thomas Chatterton would seem to be more suitable than the most elaborate epitaph. For these reasons, even if I had leisure, I should think it right to decline the task of furnishing one. But my time is fully occupied, and indeed my tribute to Chatterton's memory was paid when, with the assistance of my old friend, Mr. Cottle, I published the only collection of his works for the benefit of his sister and niece.

I remain, dear Sir,

Yours with sincere goodwill,

ROBERT SOUTHEY."*

Thereupon Mr. Fripp wrote to W. S. Landor, who replied (March 19):

"To be thought worthy of writing the epitaph of Chatterton for a public monument to be erected in his native city is indeed a high distinction, and I do not allow a single hour to pass away without acknowledging the honour you have thus conferred on me. But when I consider that the most illustrious writer in existence is your townsman, and that his zeal for Chatterton has been manifested long ago to the benefit of that unfortunate youth's family, and to the glory of his birthplace, I must entreat you to think again and again not only how greatly more able but also how greatly more proper is Southey's pen on this occasion."

Two days later Landor wrote again:

"The instant I had written my last letter to you I wrote one to Mr. Southey. I hope he may yet be induced to do what is so easy to him. In my opinion his inscriptions are incomparable, the most classical productions of our contemporaries." Of himself he said, "I could neither point a moral nor adorn a tale upon a tombstone, and neither the life nor the death of Chatterton affords the materials

* Autograph at Bristol Museum, in a black volume lettered "Chatterton's Monument." Printed in *Notes and Queries*, Oct. 24, 1857.

which I should be desirous of employing on such an occasion."*

One notability was still left, and from him Mr. Fripp, a year later, received this note :

"61 Lincoln's Inn Fields,
London, 11 April, 1839.

SIR,

I am exceedingly sorry to inform you that in consequence of my numerous occupations and indifferent health and eyesight I am totally unable to comply with the wishes of the Committee for the monument of Chatterton at Bristol. There is a poem on the subject of Chatterton by Coleridge, from which I think a suitable inscription for the monument might be extracted.

I have the honour to be, Sir,
Your obedt. servt.,
T. CAMPBELL."†

Campbell, it should be said, had included *Bristowe Tragedy* in *Specimens of the British Poets* (1819), and there written of its author : " His works had nothing of the definite neatness of that precocious talent which stops short in early maturity. . . . No English poet ever equalled him at the same age."

Meanwhile local and other literati, since the publication of Dix's *Life*, were busy flooding the press or Committee with suitable epitaphs or inscriptions ; one even came from John Galt, beginning :

Justice may linger, but it comes at last,
So do your best, and trust to fate and time.‡

By 1840, in spite of a protest from Bath that Chatterton did not write Rowley and was disreputable,§ the money, £100, was raised, the sonneteer W. L. Bowles contributing five pounds, Cottle, Richard Smith, and Dr. Symonds (whose son, John Addington Symonds, wrote three essays on Chatterton in 1861, *aet.* 21‖) a guinea apiece, and George Cumberland half a guinea.

* Autograph of both letters in " Chatterton's Monument " volume ; both printed in *Notes and Queries*, April, 1871.

† Autograph in " Chatterton's Monument " Volume.

‡ Dated 23 Nov., 1837. *Greenock Advertiser*.

§ E. M[angin], *Letter to the Admirers of Chatterton* (1838).

‖ H. F. Brown, *J. A. Symonds, A Biography*, 2nd ed., 1903, p. 86. J.A.S. reviewed Skeat's edition in the *Academy*, Dec. 15, 1871. There he says, " There is something that ' fascinates and is intolerable ' in the sphinx-like personality of a youth so utterly beyond the ordinary laws of life."

A pentagonal monument, thirty-one feet high, in three stages, crowned by a capped and standing figure of a bluecoat boy with a scroll inscribed " Ella, a tragedie," in his left hand, was set up, from a design by S. C. Fripp, cousin of the chief projector (a design by John Britton, the historian of St. Mary Redcliff, being rejected), at the north-west angle of the churchyard, between the tower and the famous porch, the "worthy vicar," the Rev. Martin Whish (d. 1852), having refused it entrance *within* the church, and acting as censor of inscriptions. The poet's own words in his " Will " : READER ! JUDGE NOT. IF THOU ART A CHRISTIAN, BELIEVE THAT HE SHALL BE JUDGED BY A SUPERIOR POWER—TO THAT POWER ALONE IS HE NOW ANSWERABLE*, eked out with a quotation from Young's *Night Thoughts* and six heroic couplets by a local clergyman, atoned, it was possibly thought, for the abstention of Messrs. Wordsworth, Southey, Landor, and Campbell.

The *Gentleman's Magazine* of July, not entering into the controversy on its " moral propriety," which had engaged the *Bristol Journal*, pronounced it disgraceful to Bristol, and preferred the new Martyrs' Memorial at Oxford. Six years later (Jan., 1846), just before the restoration of the church,† it was, by the vicar's order, removed to the crypt, where it remained for eleven years ; and on July 31, 1857, at the joint expense of Aldermen T. Proctor and Sholto V. Hare (who tended the grave of the Chattertons), it was re-erected in a more easterly position, the ground on which it had stood being required, ostensibly, for church purposes.‡

If any lesson can be drawn from the fate of Chatterton beyond the plain truths that honesty is the best policy and the

* Compare Manfred's words to the Abbot of St. Maurice :—

> I hear thee. This is my reply : whate'er
> I may have been, or am, doth rest between
> Heaven and myself. I shall not choose a mortal
> To be my mediator.

Byron, *Manfred* (1817), Act III. Sc. 1.

† Nichols and Taylor, *Bristol Past and Present*, III, p. 345.

‡ " As this site was objected to on account of it being consecrated ground, the monument was removed and laid in the crypt until the present situation was decided on, the spot on which it stands not being consecrated, but occupied a few years since, by some old houses forming part of Pyle Street."

G. Pryce, *History of Bristol* (1861), p. 365.

writing of Poetry, in most cases, its own reward, it would seem to be this: that the one laurel, which unencouraged genius, or talent, can wrest from contemporaries, is doggedly and humbly to have persisted in life, seeing that fame, the sure end of merit, is, of its very nature, a quiet and an immaterial thing. His career is rightly spoken of as a tragedy, and the epithet most commonly applied to him after his death, "unfortunate," is exact. The insipid and pretty antiquarianism, which the age immediately succeeding the appearance of the *Reliques* demanded and received, was scarcely for him. The Poems of Rowley could not compete with the first book of *The Minstrel, or The Progress of Genius** ; and had their creator lived, he might, and most probably would, never have known applause, or what the world calls fame, their antiquity once exploded (we can take Coleridge's word on that), but for his worst work, which is no charity.

His monument still stands, on unconsecrated ground, facing the Pile Street School; one side of that street has long been cleared of squalid dwellings, and the vista of the noble church, now spired, is all unbroken, as he may have seen it in his dreams. In consecrated ground, not far from the South Porch, lie his kinsfolk, and, a pace or two from them, an animal, the church cat, which died, according to its tombstone, in 1927. Though there be nothing so heedless or casual as mankind, the Muse of England is justified of her child:

"The gloomy mantle of the night,
Which on my sinking spirit steals,
Will vanish at the morning light,
Which God, my East, my Sun, reveals."

* Beattie says in his preface to *The Minstrel* (1771): "Antique expressions I have avoided; admitting, however, some old words where they seemed to suit the subject; but I hope none will be found that are now obsolete, or in any degree not intelligible to a reader of English poetry."

APPENDIX A

TABLE OF THE CHATTERTONS

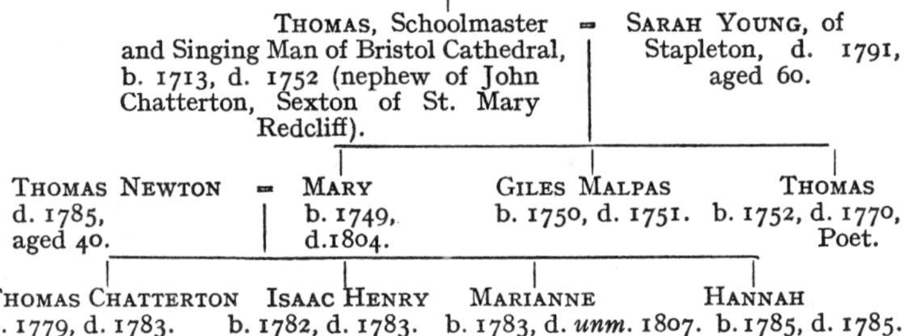
WILLIAM CHATTERTON
THOMAS, Schoolmaster and Singing Man of Bristol Cathedral, b. 1713, d. 1752 (nephew of John Chatterton, Sexton of St. Mary Redcliff).
=
SARAH YOUNG, of Stapleton, d. 1791, aged 60.
THOMAS NEWTON d. 1785, aged 40.
=
MARY b. 1749, d.1804.
GILES MALPAS b. 1750, d. 1751.
THOMAS b. 1752, d. 1770, Poet.
THOMAS CHATTERTON b. 1779, d. 1783.
ISAAC HENRY b. 1782, d. 1783.
MARIANNE b. 1783, d. unm. 1807.
HANNAH b. 1785, d. 1785.

APPENDIX B

CHATTERTON'S HOROSCOPE

(from Ebenezer Sibly's *A New and Complete Illustration of the Occult Sciences*, 1797, p. 807, sqq.)

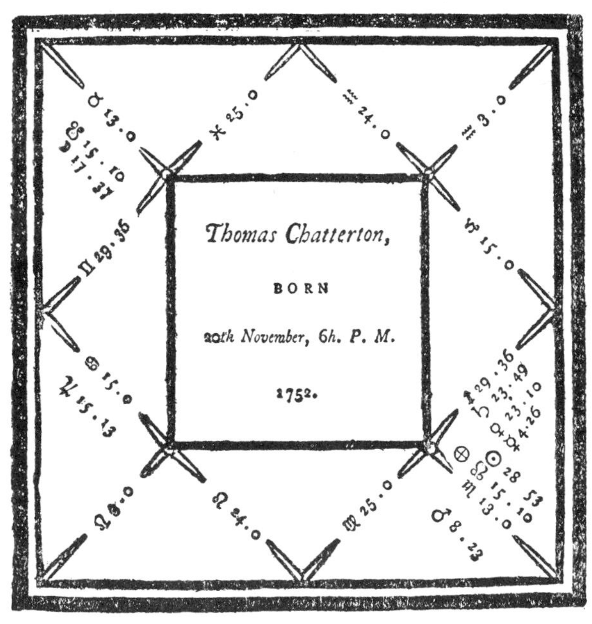

LATITUDE.

♄	0	58	N.
♃	0	1	S.
♂	0	26	N.
☉	0	0	
♀	1	8	S.
☿	1	0	S.
☽	0	3	S.

THIS gentleman was a native of Bristol, much celebrated for his literary productions, and for the originality of his ideas, which rose early in the horizon of his life, and set as prematurely upon its hemisphere, without even allowing him to attain its meridian altitude. In short, this is a very remarkable, at the same time that it is a most unfortunate, geniture. Upon the ascendant we find the sign Gemini, and Mercury lord thereof, which lays the foundation of a sharp wit, and an acute understanding. But then Mercury, his principal significator, is posited in the sixth house, in his detriment, and in combustion of the Sun ; an infallible argument of a wretched life and a fatal end.

This judgment is corroborated and confirmed in a most extraordinary manner, by the coalition of the Sun, Saturn, Venus, Mercury, and the Part of Fortune, in the sixth house, which presages every species of misfortune that can arise from poverty, and from the chicanery of prostituted women ; the immediate effect of the baleful rays of Saturn and Venus. This fatal conjunction, to which Mars is approaching with accumulated malevolence, hath designation of a thousand distressing occurrences, which occasionally torment, and alternately pervade, the native's mind.

We likewise find the Moon posited in the twelfth house, receding from a sextile with Jupiter, and forming an opposition with the Sun ; that is, departing from the early good and prolific temperature, to increase the virulence of the other malefic rays. The Moon is lady of the second house, and therefore in a more particular manner governs his substance ; and, by being in the twelfth house, the house of imprisonment and affliction, denotes a frequent want of present cash, and the dangers to which the native would be often exposed on that account ; which would have been dreadful indeed, and perhaps secured the native for a length of time within the iron gates of a prison, had not the more benevolent planet Jupiter been in his exaltation in the second house, which fortunate configuration lessens the foregoing baleful influences, and is the means of producing timely and unexpected relief, in pecuniary matters, to the native, when nothing but the most dull and barren prospects stood before him ; and but for which fortunate occurrence, he had certainly experienced the most abject penury and want. And here it is remarkable, that whatever blessing, or whatever abundance, should be thrown in his way by the genial influence of Jupiter, is either abused, or improvidently squandered away, under the opposition of the Sun and Moon ; and by the Moon's conjunction with her unfortunate node, we are more clearly convicted that the native will experience very embarrassed circumstances.

The Part of Fortune unluckily falls in conjunction with Saturn and Venus ; and, as Saturn is posited in a sign out of all his dignities, and is the lord also of the eighth house, his influence is implicative of certain ruin by means of wicked and debauched women, described by Venus, conjoined to the worst rays of Saturn. This construction is abundantly confirmed by the constitution of the hylegiacal and anaretical places of the figure, and the disposition of the significators by which they are respectively irradiated. The ascendant, in this horoscope, must be considered as hyleg, or giver of life, since neither the Sun, Moon, nor Part of Fortune, is so posited in the geniture, as to entitle either of them to the pre-eminence ; and it is the peculiar quality of the ascendant, occupied by Gemini, and governed by Mercury, to stamp upon the native so early and so extraordinary a turn for literary pursuits ; which are too well established to need any other proof, than that they were communicated to the intellectual faculty by this construction of the hyleg and circumambient matter at the time of birth.

We are here likewise to remark, that Saturn is the anareta, or destroyer of life, and is posited in the most noxious position that could have happened, and where he usually prenotes the fatal commission of suicide, without so much as one friendly ray to oppose his influence, or to render the shocking attempt partial, or less destructive than a cause that will certainly touch life. On the contrary, here is a concatenation of evil rays, which in a remarkable manner contribute to a premature death. The Sun and Moon are in opposition to houses that are under the influence of the worst causes of death ; and as Venus is in conjunction with Saturn, who rules these evils, and draws them as it were within the focus of her own orb, it is evident that his death would come by his own hand, under the pressure of despair, heightened by meagre want, through the perfidy of some abandoned female. . . .

If we consider the quality of the direction which produced his death, we shall find the manner of it most aptly described in his figure of birth. Saturn thus configurated with Venus, in that particular part of the heavens, and under such noxious irradiations, hath at all times, as well by Ptolemy as by every other respectable professor of this science, been found to occasion death by poison ; and so many concurrent testimonies in the house of sickness and disease bear the strictest affinity thereto ; and this fatal direction is much strengthened by coming up with the revolution of Saturn.

APPENDIX C

A POEM AND THREE FRAGMENTS

(A) Bristol MS. 11063, f. 109.

From Sarah Farley's Paper, Bristol Jan. 25, 1769.
On Mr Broderip's excellent Performance on the Organ.

Aid me, ye ever tuneful mine,
To sing in harmony divine
  Broderip's immortal touch;
Exert the mighty powers of song,
Be like his music sweet and strong,
  You cannot say too much.

Italia, boast thy sons no more,
They ope to latent vice, a door,
  And lull the soul to rest;
But Broderip's solemn melting strains,
Unbinds the soul from earthly chains,
  And wings her to the blest.

Say can the sprightly Lydian airs;
The fancied Music of the Spheres
  To Broderip's touch compare?
When from the lute his measures roll,
He wakes to love the softer soul,
  Such love as angels bear.

But when the trumpets lively sound,
Re-echoes through the sacred ground
  Joy fills the raptured mind:
Through diapason's solemn key
Sage melancholy does convey
  Her precepts to mankind.

Oh why ! ye sons of sea-girt isles,
Shall foreign nations gain your smiles,
  Whilst Britons court in vain ?
What Combes* shall set, let Broderip play,
And not the tuneful god of day
  Shall sound so sweet a strain.

Chatterton Asaphides.

These were communicated to Michael Lort as " Chatterton's verses on Broderip " by the Rev. D. Debat on July 6, 1778. 11457.

(B) The following fragment was printed in the *Bristol Times and Mirror* June 27, 1904 from a note-book in the possession of S. G. Percival Esq., which contained the first 168 lines of *Bristowe Tragedy*, the handwriting of which appeared, from the facsimile, to resemble Chatterton's.

p. 5. Where woodbines hang their dewy Heads
And fragrant sweets around disclose.

2

Old oozy Thames that flows fast
  Along the smiling valleys plays,
His glassy Surface cheers the Eye,
  While thro' the flow'ry mead he strays.
His fertile Banks with Herbage green
  His Vales with golden Plenty swell,
Where e'er his purer stream is seen
  The gods of health and pleasure dwell.

3

Let me thy clear, thy yealding Wave,
  With naked arm once more divide,
In thee my glowing bosom lave
  And Stem thy gently rolling tide
Lay me with Damask roses crown'd,
  Beneath some osier's dusky shade,
Where Water lilies paint the Ground,
  And bubling springs refresh the Glade.

4

Let chaste Clarinda too be there,
  In azure Mantle lightly dress'd,
Ye Nymphs bind up her silken Hair,
  Ye Zephirs fan her panting Breast.

* Organist at the Cathedral. [Note in MS.].

O haste away fair Maid and bring,
  The Muse the Kindly Friend to love,
To thee alone the Muse shall sing,
  And warble thro' the vocal grove.

(C) Copies of two fragments left at Lambert's Office; Paget papers, Bristol Museum.

(1) March, an Elegy—

Hark. 'tis his Knell—I tremble as I hear
How wells the chilling Current to my heart
Why weeps my Darla? Why the starting tear?
Ah! can I comfort unpossest impart.

Since Hardwicke's dead, the Lover the friend [" gone " scratched through]
Now Darla prove thy Excellence divine
[" Think with resignation " scratched through]
With resolution let thy Soul ascend,
Superior to the Sighs of Sorrow shine
[" Just " scratched through]
Tho' blooming in the Spring of youth he fell.

The allusion to the death of Lord Chancellor Hardwicke shows that this was written in 1770, doubtless a satirical elegy in the manner of *February*.

(2) He flamd

Eternal Vengeance flaming oer his head
[" the " scratched through]
He clashed the Clouds bade swelling Thunders sound
And rapid whirls the forky Lightnings round
A Triune Substance of etherial Smoke
[" refining " scratched through]
The godhead stood confest & thus he spoke.

Ingram plausibly suggests that this may have formed part of *Amphitryon.*

APPENDIX D

MAY

Sung by Master Cheney at Marybone Gardens

shepherds are forming a ring. To dance, to dance to the
honour of May, And welcome the pleasure of Spring. And
welcome the pleasure of Spring. The shepherdess labours a
Grace, And shines in her Sun-day ar - ray. And

bears in the bloom of her face,
The charms and the beauties of
May,
The charms and the beauties of
May.
1
2
May.

Away, to the Woodlands, away,
And join with the amorous train;
'Tis treason to labour today,
Now Cupid and Bacchus must reign.
With garlands of Primroses made,
And crown'd with the sweet blooming spray
Thro' woodland, and meadow, and shade
We'll dance to the honour of May.

APPENDIX E

CARY'S ELEGY

(from the *Town and Country Magazine*, Oct. 1770)

Elegy to the Memory of Mr. THOMAS CHATTERTON,
late of Bristol.

How shall my pen make known the sad event,
  How tell the loss, O earth ! by thee sustain'd ;
In what expressions give the tidings vent,
  Of which the thought, my soul, so oft has pain'd.

Why wilt thou torturing reflection mad
  Each fond idea of the blessings past ;
Blessings which only to thee anguish add ;
  O did their pleasing efficacy last !

Think of his tender op'ning unfledg'd years,
  Brought to a final crisis ere mature :
As fate had grudg'd the wonders nature rears,
  Bright genius in oblivion to immure.

Weep, nature, weep, the mighty loss bewail,
  The wonder of our drooping isle is dead ;
Oh could but tears or plaintive sighs avail,
  By night and day would I bedew my bed.

O give his mem'ry reverential due,
  His worth a tributary tear demands :
Still holds his many virtues in your view,
  Then must a free-will offering 'scape your hands.

Had but his tender budding genius thriv'd,
  Still blooming on, spite of the frosty blast ;
Till ripen'd into manhood still surviv'd,
  The fruits full ripe—how rich the sweet repast !

Ere vital utterance could scarce transpire,
His infant lips evinc'd a manly soul ;
Predicting that heroic mental fire,
Which reign'd supreme within the mighty whole.

Friendship cemented by the slightest ties,
Full hardly brooks the intervening cause
That separates the friend we lightly prize,
Bursting the bonds of friendship's sacred laws.

Then how can I but feel the dire effect,
Where infancy began the social tie,
Which still increas'd—(void of the least defect)
As each revolving year did multiply.

Tho' great the loss to me—heav'n knows how great !
Were it but individually known,
I would not vainly thus repine at fate,
But providential justice ever own.

No—that's not all—my country feels the stroke,
The public good was ever in his view,
His pen his lofty sentiments bespoke,
Nor fear'd he virtuous freedom to pursue.

Yes, Liberty ! thy fair, thy upright cause
He dar'd defend, spite of despotic force,
To crush his much-lov'd country's wholesome laws,
It's noble constitution's only source.

Ye muses ! leave your florid airy smiles,
And thou mercurial Euphrosyne,
Forget thy wanton cranks, and am'rous wiles,
To sympathize with sad Melpomene.

Your pride is fall'n—your chief, your great support,
Lies mould'ring to his own primæval dust :
To you while living ever was his court,
Dead—in return, let not his mem'ry rust.

What ease within his sweet'ned numbers flow'd,
What symmetry each well-pen'd line evinc'd ;
Such just connection on each verse bestow'd,
Ev'n Envy of his worth must stand convinc'd.

His lofty numbers, how sublimely great!
  Lifting the ravish'd sense to heights supreme,
Again with fancy-painted woes elate,
  He shews the passions of the tragic theme.

Sharp-visag'd satire own'd him as her lord,
  Exclusive of her hand-maid in her train,
Ill-nature—curst attendant of the board
  Of those who stigmatize mankind for gain.

Not so with him—he paints each reigning vice
  In strongest colours of their genuine hue;
Sweet'ning the bitter draught with sav'ry spice,
  The moral picture relishing the view.

O could my pen but catch his livid fire,
  Hear thou my invocation, mighty dead;
My infant muse with life mature inspire,
  Thy shade may dictate, tho' the substance's fled.

Antiquity! bewail his cruel fate,
  He paid thy hoary head the rev'rence due;
Thy valu'd acts reviving out of date,
  Recalling ages past to present view.

To truths long dead, he gave a second birth,
  Rescuing from oblivion occult stores;
Treasures within the bowels of the earth,
  Unheeded by the vulgar mind—explores.

Most strange! ideas of so vast extent
  Could e'er within his tender mind reside,
No art or science but some influence lent,
  His intellectual parts to make more wide.

Why fancy, wilt thou paint him to my eyes,
  Why form the fond idea in my mind;
O couldst thou but some plastic means devise
  The substance with the shadow still to find.

Bristol, October, 1770. T. C.

APPENDIX F

ÆLLA'S SPEECH TO HIS SOLDIERS

(*Ælla,* ll. 589-693)

ÆLLA, CELMONDE, and ARMIE near WATCHETTE

ÆLLA

Now havynge done oure mattynes and oure vowes,
Lette us for the intended fyghte be boune,[1]
And everyche champyone potte the joyous crowne
Of certane masterschyppe upon hys glestreynge browes.

As for mie harte, I owne ytte ys, as ere
Itte has beene ynne the sommer-sheene of fate,
Unknowen to the ugsomme gratche[2] of fere;
Mie blodde embollen,[3] wythe masterie elate,
Boyles ynne mie veynes, and rolles ynn rapyd state,
Impatyente forr to mete the persante[4] stele,
And telle the worlde, thatte Ælla dyed as greate
As anie knyghte who foughte for Englondes weale.
Friends, kynne, and soldyerres, ynne blacke armore drere,
Mie actyons ymytate, mie presente redynge[5] here.

There ys né house, athrow thys shap-scurged[6] isle,
Thatte has ne loste a kynne yn these fell fyghtes,
Fatte blodde has sorfeeted the hongerde soyle,
And townes enlowed[7] lemed[8] oppe the nyghtes.
Inne gyte[9] of fyre oure hallie[10] churche dheie dyghtes[11];
Oure sonnes lie storven[12] ynne theyre smethynge[13] gore;
Oppe bie the rootes our tree of lyfe dheie pyghtes,[14]
Vexynge our coaste, as byllowes doe the shore.
Yee menne, gyf ye are menne, displaie yor name,
Ybrende yer tropes,[15] alyche the roaryng tempest flame.

[1] Ready. [2] Hideous garb. [3] Swelling. [4] Piercing. [5] Advice. [6] Fate-scourged. [7] Fired. [8] Lighted. [9] Dress. [10] Holy. [11] Clothe. [12] Dead. [13] Smoking. [14] Pluck. [15] Burn their troops. (the " y " is the Anglo-Saxon thorn).

Ye Chrystyans, doe as wordhie of the name;
These roynerres[1] of our hallie houses slea;
Braste,[2] lyke a cloude, from whence doth come the flame,
Lyche torrentes, gushynge downe the mountaines, bee.
And whanne alonge the grene yer champyons flee,
Swefte as the rodde for-weltrynge[3] levyn-bronde,
Yatte hauntes the flyinge mortherer oere the lea,
Soe flie oponne these royners of the londe.
Lette those yatte are unto yer battayles[4] fledde,
Take slepe eterne uponne a feerie lowynge[5] bedde.

Let cowarde Londonne see herre towne onn fyre,
And strev[6] wythe goulde to staie the royners honde,
Ælla and Brystowe havethe thoughtes thattes hygher,
Wee fyghte notte forr ourselves, botte all the londe.
As Severnes hyger[7] lyghethe[8] banckes of sonde,
Pressynge ytte downe binethe the reynynge[9] streme,
Wythe dreerie dynn enswolters[10] the hyghe stronde,
Beerynge the rockes alonge ynn fhurye breme,[11]
So wylle wee beere the Dacyanne armie downe,
And throughe a storme of blodde wyll reache the champyon crowne.

[1] Ravagers. [2] Burst. [3] Blasting. [4] Ships. [5] Flaming. [6] Strive. [7] The bore of the Severn. [8] Lodgeth. [9] Running. [10] Sucks in. [11] Fierce.

Gyff ynn thys battelle locke[12] ne wayte oure gare,[13]
To Brystowe dheie wylle tourne yeyre fhuyrie dyre;
Brystowe, and alle her joies, wylle synke toe ayre,
Brendeynge perforce wythe unenhantende[14] fyre,
Thenne lette oure safetie doublie moove oure ire,
Lyche wolfyns, rovynge for the evnynge pre,[15]
See[ing] the lambe and shepsterr nere the brire,
Doth th'one forr safetie, th'one for hongre slea;
Thanne, whanne the ravenne crokes uponne the playne,
Oh! lett ytte bee the knelle to myghtie Dacyanns slayne.

Lyche a rodde gronfer,[16] shalle mie anlace[17] sheene,
Lyche a strynge lyoncelle[18] I'lle bee ynne fyghte,
Lyche fallynge leaves the Dacyannes shalle be sleene,
Lyche [a] loud dynnynge streeme scalle[19] be mie myghte.
Ye menne, who woulde deserve the name of knyghte,
Lette bloddie teares bie all your paves[20] be wepte;
To commynge tymes no poyntelle[21] shalle ywrite,
Whanne Englonde han her foemenn, Brystow slepte.
Yourselfes, youre chyldren, and youre fellowes crie,
Go, fyghte ynn rennomes[22] gare, be brave, and wynne or die.

[12] Luck. [13] Cause. [14] Unaccustomed. [15] Prey. [16] Fen meteor. [17] Sword. [18] Lion's whelp. [19] Shall. [20] Daggers. [21] Pen. [22] Reputation.

I saie ne moe ; youre spryte the reste wylle saie ;
Youre spryte wylle wrynne,[1] thatte Brystow ys yer place ;
To honoures house I nede notte marcke the waie ;
Inne youre owne hartes you maie the foote-pathe trace.
'Twexte shappe[2] and us there ys botte lyttelle space ;
The tyme ys nowe to proove yourselves bee menne ;
Drawe forthe the bornyshed bylle wythe fetyve[3] grace,
Rouze, lyche a wolfynne rouzing from hys denne.
Thus I enrone[4] mie anlace ; go thou shethe ;
I'lle potte ytt ne ynn place, tyll ytte ys sycke wythe deathe.

[1] Discover. [2] Fate. [3] Comely. [4] Unsheath.

SOLDYERS

Onn, Ælla, onn ; we longe for bloddie fraie ;
Wee longe to here the raven synge yn vayne ;
Onn, Ælla, onn ; we certys gayne the daie,
Whanne thou doste leade us to the leathal playne.

CELMONDE

Thie speche, O Loverde,[5] fyrethe the whole trayne ;
Theie pancte for war, as honted wolves for breathe ;
Go, and sytte crowned on corses of the slayne ;
Go, and ywielde the massie swerde of deathe.

[5] Lord.

SOLDYERRES

From thee, O Ælla, alle oure courage reygnes ;
Echone yn phantasie do lede the Danes ynne chaynes.

ÆLLA

Mie countrymenne, mie friendes, your noble sprytes
Speke yn youre eyne, and doe yer master telle.
Swefte as the rayne-storme toe the erthe alyghtes,
Soe wylle we fall upon these royners felle.
Oure mowynge swerdes shalle plonge hem downe to helle ;
Theyre throngynge corses shall onlyghte[6] the starres ;
The barrowes brastynge wythe the sleene schall swelle,
Brynnynge[7] to commynge tymes our famous warres ;
Inne everie eyne I kenne the lowe [8] of myghte,
Sheenynge abrode, alyche a hylle-fyre ynne the nyghte.

[6] Darken. [7] Declaring. [8] Flame.

Whanne poyntelles of our famous fyghte shall saie,
Echone wylle marvelle atte the dernie[9] dede,
Echone wylle wyssen[10] hee hanne seene the daie,
And bravelie holped to make the foemenn blede ;

[9] Valiant. [10] Wish.

Botte for yer holpe our battelle wylle notte nede;
Our force ys force enowe to staie theyre honde;
Wee wylle retourne unto thys grened mede,
Oer corses of the foemen of the londe.
Nowe to the warre lette all the slughornes sounde,
The Dacyanne troòpes appere on yinder rysynge grounde.

Chiefes, heade youre bandes, and leade.

LIST OF MSS.

THE Chatterton literature is large, and there are two sound bibliographies:—

1. F. A. Hyett and W. Bazeley, *Chattertoniana*, reprinted (with additions by F. A. H.) from the Bibliographer's manual of Gloucestershire literature. *Gloucester*, 1914.

2. E. R. Norris Matthews, *Thomas Chatterton, a bibliography*, being a section of *Bristol Bibliography*, a catalogue of matter relating to Bristol in the Bristol (Central) Reference Library, *Bristol*, 1916.

These being accessible, no less than the General Catalogue of printed books, in the Reading Room of the British Museum (where additions, or some of them, can be seen), I have confined myself here to MS. matter, the first section of which, Chatterton's *own* script, his future editors must surely make their prime concern. The list certainly does not pretend to be exhaustive; it is provisional, or tentative rather.

I. MSS. IN CHATTERTON'S HAND.

LONDON, BRITISH MUSEUM.

5766 A, B, C, Dr. Glynn's bequest.
A contains Rowley "originals," i.e. fabricated parchments.
B contains poems, prose writings, letters, drawings, coats of arms.
f. 50 is in Barrett's hand, endorsed in Chatterton's.
ff. 52-53 are not in Chatterton's hand, possibly in W. B. Smith's, who may have written these three poems.
f. 92 is in a female hand, endorsed in Chatterton's.
C. is "The Rolle of St. Bartholomeweis Priorie."

An abstract of these, inaccurate as regards the "Yellow Roll," is in Skeat, Vol. I, pp. 375-378.

12050. *The Revenge* (wanting ll. 25-52, and 445-497).

24890. Three *English Eclogues*, and *Goddwyn*.

24891. *A Discorse on Brystowe, by Thos Rowleie* (containing the first portion of *The merrie Tricks of Laymyngetowne*, and "Stay curyous Traveller.") The leaves in this MS. are misplaced, f. 3 should follow f. 7. A. Hooke's *A Dissertation on the Antiquity of Bristol* (1748) clearly inspired this essay.

BRISTOL, MUSEUM AND ART GALLERY.

The "Will."

"Antiquities Book 3rd," which includes *The Unknown Knyght* and 549 lines of *Battle of Hastings* (I).

"Account of the family of the De Berghams" in two copy-books; the first includes (at the other end) *The Tournament* and *The Gouler's Requiem*; the second *The Romaunte of the Cnyghte*, and its modernisation.

The merrie Tricks of Laymyngetowne, Discoorses II (from "Home newes well let alone"), and III (to l. 22).

The Revenge (a leaf, ll. 25-52).

Lines to Horace Walpole.

Kew Gardens (a leaf, numbered "29," ll. 1009-1092).

Letter to George Catcott, Aug. 12, 1770.

Letter "To Dr. Newton Bishop of Bristol."

Here also are the poet's pocket-book, apprenticeship indentures, &c.

BRISTOL, CENTRAL LIBRARY.

Letter to Mr. Stephens (July 20, 1769), and copy of Horace Walpole's letter (March 28, 1769) on the same sheet.

Bill (Rowley's Executors) to George Catcott [5375].

Here is Esther Saunders's letter, with Chatterton's remarks and endorsement.

BRISTOL, TEMPLE CHURCH.

Rowleian account of the Church [parchment "original" at British Museum, 5766A, f. 9].

OXFORD, BODLEIAN LIBRARY.

MS. Eng. poet. e. 6. Two printed works by the Rev. A. Catcott, containing MS. poems, i.e. *Epistle to the Rev^d Mr Catcott*, *Sentiment*, *The Methodist*, "If wishing for the mystic Joys of Love," *The Defence*, last six lines of *Heccar and Gaira.*

U.S.A. COLUMBIA UNIVERSITY.

Note-book (in the Phœnix collection), containing poems written in Autumn 1769; i.e. "Interest," *Elegy written at Stanton Drew*, "*Far from the reach of critics and reviews*," *Elegy on T. Phillips*, *Elegy, Oct.* 29, "Hervenis." [Not seen; described by T. O. Mabbott in *Modern Language Notes*, Apr. 4, 1924].

PRIVATE OWNERS.

Sir William Rose Smith, C.B., K.C.V.O., possesses the parchment "originals" of *Songe to Ælla* and *Yeloue Rolle.* [Text and facsimiles in Sir Ernest Clarke's *New Lights on Chatterton*, 1916.]

S. P. Perceval, Esq., possessed in 1904 a MS. of the first 168 lines of *Bristowe Tragedy* and a fragment (Appendix C.); the handwriting was pronounced Chatterton's by John Taylor, Bristol City Librarian, in 1885, and appears to resemble his from the facsimile in the *Bristol Times and Mirror*, June 27, 1904. I have not seen this MS.

According to *Catalogue of the Johnsonian Collection of R. B. Adam*, holograph MSS. of *Sly Dick*, *A Hymn for Christmas Day*, and Chatterton's letter to James Dodsley of Dec. 21, 1768, are in this library. I have not seen these.

II. OTHER MSS.

London, British Museum.

40015. f. 11. Letter of Horace Walpole to Thomas Chatterton. March 28, 1769.

35350. f. 41. Letter of 2nd Lord Hardwicke to Oliver Goldsmith, Apr. 24, 1771; *ibid.* f. 45. Letter of Michael Lort to 2nd Lord Hardwicke, May 11, 1773.

12527. Letters of Michael Lort to Horace Walpole. [Printed in Nichols *L. I.*, Vol VII.]

32329. f. 72. Letter of Thomas Percy to Lord Dacre, Sept. 6, 1773; *ibid.* ff. 76, 83, letters of Thomas Warton to Thomas Percy, July 29, 1774; Jan. 25, 1776.

5811. f. 58 b, *sqq.* Note of William Cole's conversation with Michael Lort on Sept. 18, 1773, with cross-reference to 5840, ff. 212-215.

39168. f. 81. Letter of George Catcott to Lord Charlemont, Oct. 30, 1774*; *ibid.* f. 83. George Catcott's "Appendix to my Introduction," &c., Jan. 1, 1776.

C. 39, h. 20 [Printed Books] contains letter of Mary Chatterton to George Steevens, Feb. 19, 1777.

N.B. A collection of Chattertoniana, with many valuable notes, and two volumes rich in magazine and newspaper extracts (11, 12) is numbered C. 39, f. 1-19.

Bristol, Museum and Art Gallery

Letter of George Catcott to Thomas Chatterton, Aug. 8, 1770.

Brystowe Tragedy, catalogued as in Chatterton's hand, but I doubt this; some of its readings are important; e.g., "earlier," l. 3, "place of cares and pain," l. 211, "tuned the Psaume bataunt," ll. 276, 292.

The Exhibition.

Letter of George Catcott to Joseph Cottle, March 18, 1802.

Letters of Mary Newton to Joseph Cottle, March 25, Oct. 17, 1802.

Letter of Robert Southey to John Britton, Nov. 4, 1810.

* In Catcott's Letter-book this letter is dated March 20, 1775.

Richard Smith's *Chattertoniana*. These include many letters received by George Catcott during the Rowleian controversy, and transcripts of Rowley MSS. by the same.

Correspondence relating to Chatterton's monument.

Arthur Paget's papers (valuable for Lambert).

Bristol, Central Library

11063. Collectanea of Michael Lort, including extracts from magazines.

11457. A miscellaneous bundle, including notes by Lort, and letters to and from him.

11666. Letter of Michael Lort to Richard Gough, Aug. 20, 1777.

5342. George Catcott's Letter-Book, an invaluable source. [For Catcott's transcripts of Chatterton's poems see *Bristol Bibliography*, art. Catcott (G. S.)]

6493. Thomas Fry's transcript of some of the Rowley Poems.

5199. Anonymous essay on the Rowley Controversy, dated March 30, 1783.

4533. ff. 117-121. Notes by Samuel Seyer "concerning Rowley and Chatterton."

Private Owners

A. H. Russell, Esq., possesses George Cumberland's "Circumstances relative to the life of Chatterton."

The present writer possesses an early transcript of *Elinoure and Juga*, reading "The minstrel Dame" (l. 23), letter of Horace Walpole to Thomas Percy, Jan. 11, 1779, and Sir Daniel Wilson's "Chattertonia" (1869).

LIST OF ILLUSTRATIONS

INDEX

B.

C.

D.

E.

G.

H.

I.

J.

K.

M.

N.

O.

P

Q.

R.

S.

T.

U.

Y.